D1626573

INTO THE JAWS OF DEATH

The sand of the desert is sodden red,
Red with the wreck of a square that broke,
The Gatling's jammed and the colonel dead,
And the regiment blind with dust and smoke.

Vitaï Lampada, Sir Henry Newbolt

INTO THE JAWS OF DEATH

British Military Blunders, 1879–1900

Lieutenant Colonel Mike Snook

Frontline Books, London
Naval Institute Press, Annapolis, Maryland

Into the Jaws of Death

British Military Blunders, 1879–1900

This edition published 2008 by Frontline Books, an imprint of Pen & Sword Books Limited, 47 Church Street, Barnsley, S. Yorkshire S70 2AS

Published and distributed in the United States of America and Canada by the Naval Institute Press, Beach Hall, 291 Wood Road, Annapolis, Maryland 21402-5034
www.navalinstitute.org

British Library Cataloguing in Publication Data
Snook, Mike
Into the jaws of death : epic fights of Victoria's army
1. Great Britain. Army – History – 19th century
2. Great Britain – History, Military – 19th century
I. Title

355'.02'0941'09034

Frontline edition
ISBN: 978-1-84415-706-8

NIP edition
ISBN: 978-1-59114-400-7

Library of Congress Catalog Card No. 2007933198

Maps drawn by Red Lion Prints

Printed and bound in the U.S.A.

This book is dedicated to the memory of

David Rattray

1958–2007

Historian, peerless raconteur, friend of the Zulu and a great South African.

Contents

Illustrations

Maps

Tables

PREFACE

It is not alone in the hour of success and in the triumph of victory that the qualities of true soldiers are displayed. They are called for no less when the tide of battle runs against them, in the stubborn resistance and perilous retreat; such occasions afford special opportunities for the display, not only of that valour and discipline which are common to all British troops, but also of the noble qualities of pity and self-sacrifice.

Lord Ripon, Viceroy of India, addressing the officers and men of E/B Battery, RHA[1]

That the British Regular Army has always enjoyed a formidable reputation and can take justifiable pride in an extraordinary fighting record is a contention that few military historians would take issue with. 'Tommy', it is clear, is hard to beat.[2] And yet, strangely, the British nation-state has never been institutionally or instinctively militaristic in outlook. On the contrary, whatever the standing Army has accomplished in the field over the course of a long and distinguished history dating back to the restoration of the Stuarts, it has generally had to pull off in the face of shortages occasioned by a broadly insensitive and invariably thrifty political establishment. It is a function of long-standing necessity, therefore, that the governing philosophy of the British military down through the ages has been a determination to 'improvise, adapt and overcome'. For the most part, the British fighting man has coped admirably with the seemingly endless succession of international crises in which, by virtue of his nation's global role, he has become embroiled.

Ironically, the greater the Army's success, the greater has been London's post-conflict enthusiasm for military retrenchment. Periodic downwards spirals in capacity are the inevitable consequence of such an approach, to the extent that they have long since become a national tradition. From time to time, though, too much has been asked of the Army – testing scenarios, characterized by a want of resource, which no amount of goodwill, ingenuity or improvisation can overcome – leading on occasion to military disaster. It is perhaps unsurprising that it takes a shocking failure for an all-professional Army deployed in far-flung corners of the world – out of sight and out of mind – to attract the attention of a busy, bustling citizenry perennially preoccupied with trade, commerce and prosperity. Only at times of crisis does the wider public begin to comprehend what extraordinary demands have been made on the military and what miracles are being worked in its name by tiny handfuls of soldiers. It is perhaps because military disaster is almost always traceable to the indifference of the political establishment or to the neglect of the high command – a stratum of society which the rest of us love to hate – coupled with the fact that extreme adversity seems to bring out the best in the ordinary British soldier, with whom by contrast we are inclined to empathize, that we take a peculiar pride in the Army's off-days. What the nation will not tolerate, however, as the Crimea, Gallipoli, Norway and Singapore showed, is systemic failure.

Now a venerable 347 years of age, the standing Army was but a child of four when it suffered its very first military disaster. Unsurprisingly it occurred in a colonial setting, when a host of Moorish cavalry severed the Earl of Teviot's line of retreat to the walls of Tangier. A bastion of the Christian west in the heart of Islamic North Africa, the troubled colony was the dowry-gift of a canny Portugal to an unsuspecting Charles II. Teviot and 400 red-coated infantrymen – the uniform colour of the fledgling army's fledgling regiments – clustered back to back beneath a blazing sun and made a determined stand atop a low desert hillock. Wielding weapons we associate with Marston Moor and Naseby, the 15-foot pike and the matchlock musket clubbed like a cudgel, they fought furiously, until at length they were overcome.

It is because 'Tommy' is not prone to run or surrender when the tide turns against him, but rather to brace himself for still more determined resistance, that we are disinclined in this country necessarily to equate military disaster with embarrassment, disgrace or national humiliation. Arnhem, for example, may safely be counted a disaster of the greatest magnitude – yet the heroic conduct of Roy Urquhart's 1st Airborne Division rightly remains a source of great national pride.

Occasional military disasters, then, were the inevitable consequence of a routinely chaotic or lackadaisical governmental approach to military affairs. Most commonly, like General Braddock's 1755 misadventure in the backwoods of Ohio, they were one-off fiascos, brought about by a unique combination of local circumstances, and tended not to bespeak wider or institutional failings. This book, however, concerns itself with military disaster in the high Victorian Age, and specifically the period 1879–1900, when disaster started to strike with unnerving frequency and began to hint at systemic failings in the Army.

In the wider context of the art of war, most of Queen Victoria's battles were fought during the important period of transition sandwiched between the close of the Crimean War, in effect the end of the horse-and-musket era, and the turn-of-the-century conflict with the Boer republics, which for the British represented the first painful glimpse through the looking glass at the nature of modern war. This span of less than five decades encompassed more substantive military innovation than had the preceding two centuries. Never before had weapons technology moved so fast, the first beginnings of an exponential rate of change in fields destined to transmute all too rapidly into sciences of mass destruction.

In the absence of any involvement in the major North American or European conflagrations of the era, the British Army was obliged to modernize itself against the background of the so-called 'small wars' of empire, conflicts waged principally in remote and inhospitable corners of Africa or in the northern swathe of the Indian sub-continent. At the time many eminent military men, Sir Garnet Wolseley amongst them, believed that Britain's imperial skirmishes were of great benefit to the Army. Other theorists, less intimately concerned in the active pursuit of glory, argued that small wars bore little or no relevance to the future European battlefield. In fact there was merit on both sides of the argument and the objective truth lay somewhere between the poles of opinion.

It is ironic that while the War Office was striving to come to terms with lessons arising from the American Civil War (1861–5), the Austro-Prussian War (1866) and the Franco-Prussian War (1870–1), British commanders in the field were often compelled to revert to the tactics of a bygone age. Following the battles of Isandlwana and Maiwand in which extended formations were comprehensively outflanked by a numerically superior foe, even the obsolescent 'receive cavalry' square would come back into its own. Now these densely packed battlefield hedgehogs were resurrected – no longer to keep French cuirassiers at bay – but to repel Zulu and Hadendawa warriors, whose heroic and lightning-quick charges demanded a comparable degree of circumspection. Conceptually such pragmatic tactical expedients were directly at odds with the rise of the breechloader and the coming of the machine gun. For the Indian Army the picture was rather more mixed. In Afghanistan there were occasional pitched battles cast from the same mould as the major engagements of the Zulu and Sudan campaigns, whereas inside the boundaries of North-West Frontier Province extended-order skirmish tactics were much more typically the norm.

Even if the resurrection of fighting formations such as the two-deep line and the four-deep square meant that some colonial engagements more closely resembled Napoleonic battles than modern ones, it was also true that senior British officers and their subordinates were learning sound practical lessons about campaign planning, coordinated staffwork and logistics, all of which had been sadly neglected arts up to this point. At the tail-end of the era those self-same subordinates, some of them now general officers themselves, came face-to-face with an entirely new enemy. Much to their surprise 'brother Boer' proved not to be the rag-tag farmer they had been led to expect, but an instinctive and proficient exponent of a new mode of warfare. Probably the most troublesome battlefield characteristic of an Afrikaner commando was its apparent invisibility, whilst at the operational level it set new standards in mobility and logistic self-sufficiency.

Into the Jaws of Death, then, traces the transition of the British Army from the old world to the new, and shows how a series of failures in the last two decades of the nineteenth century – which with the Empire at its zenith ought, in theory at least, to have been unthinkable – alerted the political and military establishment to the need for a thoroughgoing overhaul of the British military system. It deals in particular with the close military detail of salient campaigns and battles, and not with their political context which has been amply covered by other writers.

The battle narratives which are the mainstay of the book are underpinned by a rigorous examination of official reports, participant accounts and other primary source material, designed to establish what really happened and how the events of the day are interrelated in time and space. In other words one of my principal objectives in researching these battles was to comprehend them better, specifically as acts of war. In presenting my findings to the reader I have set out to omit nothing which in my judgement exerted a significant bearing on the conduct, course or outcome of the fight. I hope that the end result is a series of historically faithful and illuminating narrative accounts of some of the British Army's most celebrated if least successful fights.

Inevitably I have had to be selective in deciding which campaigns to include and which to exclude. Some episodes have been chosen because they incorporate inspirational examples of courage, self-sacrifice and fortitude, some because they are worthy of study as cautionary tales, others simply because they are compelling stories of men at war – that most extreme yet all too commonplace realm of human endeavour. Having subjected the Isandlwana disaster to detailed scrutiny in *How Can Man Die Better* (2005) and *Like Wolves on the Fold* (2006), I hope I may be forgiven for covering the battle here only by way of a scene-setter.

In tracing the causes of burgeoning systemic failure, I begin with a necessarily brief overview of the British Army in the second half of the nineteenth century. In many ways it was a quaintly old-fashioned and quirky organization, in which the regiment was everything and brigades and divisions were thrown together at the last moment. It was quite unlike any of the major continental armies, for its principal concern was the policing of empire, a task generally conducted by colonels and captains and, at moments of particular crisis, by generals behaving like colonels. By taking the end of the Crimean War as my start point, I exclude the first third of Queen Victoria's reign and with it such notable reverses as the Retreat from Kabul, the bloody repulse of the 24th Regiment at Chillianwallah and, of course, the Charge of the Light Brigade at Balaclava. In essence I have omitted the horse-and-musket era into which Victoria was born, in order to concentrate on British military operations in the ensuing age of transition. Included, then, are such notable actions as the Battle of Maiwand, Sir George Colley's defeats at Laing's Nek and Ingogo, the fiasco at Majuba Hill, the desert actions at Abu Klea and Abu Kru, and the costly attempts to force Louis Botha's defences at Colenso and Spion Kop. One chapter, 'White Pashas', does not directly concern the fighting record of the Regular Army, but instead looks at British officers in the contract employ of the Khedive of Egypt, as it would be quite impossible to reflect on the Gordon Relief Expedition without first setting the rise of fundamentalist Islam in the Sudan in context. Hence the Hicks disaster, First El Teb and the Siege of Khartoum, fascinating episodes in their own right, are also included.

While the British Army was preoccupied with imperial policing, the grand-strategic situation in Europe was being transformed by the rise of a new continental superpower. If, as a maritime trading nation, Britain had one timeless and overriding foreign policy objective, it was the maintenance of a balance of power in Europe. Just as the British had confronted Louis XIV and Bonaparte in their turn, from 1871 onwards it became increasingly apparent, year on year, that they would one day have to turn traditional enmities on their head and align themselves with the French, in order to contend effectively with a newly unified and increasingly militaristic Germany. It took two decades more for the old antagonists to appreciate that their strategic interests had slowly been converging. Even at the last gasp they almost turned on each other at the time of the Fashoda Incident. The crisis averted, it was clear that when the impending strategic imbalance finally arrived at its tipping point, war on an unprecedented scale must follow. The British Army of the late nineteenth century was hopelessly ill-prepared for such a conflict. It is a common misconception that it emerged from its Crimean nightmare as a markedly different organization. It did not. The Army of 1894 needed reform every bit as much as the Army of 1854. Above all else it needed to be shocked into grappling with professionalism, modernity and scale. This book describes how the colonial adversaries of the Queen Empress exposed Britain's military frailties on land. In the grand scheme of things it would prove to be no bad thing. Many of the lessons learned along the way have an eternal quality and are as relevant today as they were to officers of Kitchener's generation.

A number of people have been kind enough to assist with the preparation of the book in various ways. I am particularly indebted to: Ron Sheeley, who kindly provided a number of important contemporaneous photographs as illustrations; to Richard Stackpoole-Ryding and David Gore, both of whom provided access to primary source material relating to the Battle of Maiwand; to Clive Morris, the regimental curator of the Queen's Dragoon Guards, who provided source material concerning the role of the old KDG in the Transvaal Rebellion; and to the ever-helpful library staff at the Defence Academy who sought out many dusty and venerable tomes for me and forgave their invariably late return. I must of course express my gratitude to Michael Leventhal of Greenhill Books, for his friendship, guidance and encouragement, and similarly to Kate Baker, Donald Sommerville and Johnathan Young of Red Lion Mapping, all of whom played crucial roles in turning a humble typescript into so handsome a book. Last but not least I must also express my thanks to John Young who provided a rarely seen portrayal of my regiment at Isandlwana.

It is difficult now to think of that most haunting of African battlefields without reflecting on the vile and senseless killing in January this year of David Rattray, the best-known historian of the Anglo-Zulu War. Not only one of the world's most captivating raconteurs, David was also a philosopher, a fighter and a great South African. With his death his country has lost one of its greatest ambassadors and one of its most strident advocates of reconciliation, a loss it can assuredly ill afford. It is to David's immortal memory that I respectfully dedicate this book. None of us in the developed world should fight shy of visiting the battlefields of Zululand as a result of this lamentable incident, or from continuing to give all possible support and encouragement to a great African people.

Turning to historiography, it would be remiss of me not to single out Edward M. Spiers's *The Late Victorian Army 1868–1902* as the single most useful reference I encountered in seeking an understanding of the administrative and organizational dynamics of the Victorian military. Brian Bond's *The Victorian Army and the Staff College* is similarly invaluable in tracing the development of professionalism within the officer corps. The British cavalry arm of the period is nowhere better covered than in the Marquess of Anglesey's epic work *A History of the British Cavalry 1816–1919*. I have drawn much of the acute detail contained in my narrative accounts from the indispensable official histories of the era, such as Colonel H. E. Colvile's *History of the Sudan Campaign* and Major General Sir Frederick Maurice's *History of the War in South Africa 1899–1902*. The map packs carefully drawn in support of the official record by officers of the Royal Engineers have proved particularly useful in analyzing the battlefields they describe. The official history of the Second Afghan War was not published until 1908, but was based on a two-volume confidential report raised by Army Headquarters India more than 20 years earlier. The work is cited in both of its guises in the bibliography. Mindful of a number of significant flaws enshrined in the official *Narrative of Field Operations for the Zulu War*, I have treated the official histories with a certain amount of circumspection and have gone to pains to cross-check them, in the case of Abu Klea for example, with such invaluable primary sources as Sir Charles Wilson's *From Korti to Khartum*, Lieutenant Count Gleichen's *With the Camel Corps up the Nile*, Colonel Sir Percy Marling's *Rifleman and Hussar*, and Admiral Lord Charles Beresford's memoirs. I have been struck by how much of the official history pertaining to the period was written by members of the 'Wolseley Ring', but more of that later.

The tunnel vision of close combat is too well-known a factor to require any amplification here. Suffice it to say, that I was not surprised to uncover many interesting anomalies across all of the campaigns I have covered here. As a result I have often had to weight the sources at my own discretion, drawing largely on soldierly instinct in so doing. In essence I have set more store by the accounts of men who in my judgement were best placed to see a particular event with their own eyes, and have preferred accounts committed to paper whilst still fresh, ahead of memoirs penned in old age. Usefully the itinerant life of a soldier has taken me to South Africa, 'the land of misunderstandings' as Sir Evelyn Wood liked to call it, and to Afghanistan, enabling me to familiarize myself with all of the South African battlefields mentioned in the text, and with Kabul and its environs. I have not yet made it to the Sudan or to Maiwand, and in these two cases have had to derive a theoretical knowledge of the ground from key primary sources and the Victorian military mapping earlier alluded to.

The Earl of Cromer's (formerly Sir Evelyn Baring) *Modern Egypt* (1908) is essential reading for the strategic, political and diplomatic background to the Egyptian intervention and the Mahdist revolt. Fergus Nicoll's *The Sword of the Prophet* (2004) is particularly noteworthy for looking at the uprising from the Sudanese side of the fence. Dominic Green presents an engaging overview of events in Egypt and the Sudan in his newly published *Armies of God* (2007). A good deal of valuable source material relating to the Transvaal Rebellion, including many of Sir George Colley's official reports, is to be found in Charles Norris Newman's *With the Boers in Transvaal* (1882), though 'Noggs's' narrative should be treated with a degree of caution. Ian Hamilton's *Listening for the Drums* offers important insights into Majuba Hill. For wider examinations of the Second Anglo-Afghan War see Brian Robson's *The Road to Kabul* (1986) and Lord Roberts's all-important memoir, *Forty-One Years in India* (1905). It is impossible to write of Maiwand without drawing on Colonel Leigh Maxwell's *My God Maiwand* (1979), as he was able to explore the battlefield just before southern Afghanistan became a no-go area for the casual visitor. For shrewd analysis of the British Army on the eve of the Boer War and much interesting reflection on contemporaneous military thought, see Colonel G. F. R. Henderson's collected essays. Maurice's official history of the Boer War is occasionally inaccurate and sometimes shallow in outlining events at Colenso and Spion Kop, and was also sanitized for reasons of political sensitivity. By contrast Leo Amery's *The Times History of the War in South Africa* is overtly hostile to Sir Redvers Buller, not in my view entirely unreasonably. In the mid-1970s Norman Dixon famously, but perhaps rather unfairly, subjected a long-dead Buller to psychoanalysis in his *On the Psychology of Military Incompetence*. For a balanced counter-argument to Amery and a robust dismissal of Dixon's interpretation see Geoffrey Powell's 1994 biography of Buller. In the particular context of Buller, I am inclined to subscribe to Powell's disavowal of Dixon who, it seems to me, stretches his case too far in places. At the same time, like Dixon, I too am drawn inexorably towards the conclusion that Buller was temperamentally unsuited for the daunting task confronting him in Natal. In a wider context, anybody with a professional or academic interest in military affairs should find time to read Dixon's highly illuminating text.

The stories in these pages are stories of war and, as must inevitably be the case given a paucity of written sources from 'the other side of the hill', are recounted from a principally Anglocentric perspective. It is probably fair to say that I have not pulled any punches in describing the political leadership and governance of the old Boer republics. I need hardly add that in so doing I mean no offence to modern-day Afrikaners, amongst whom I have a good many friends and of whose future peace and prosperity I am strongly supportive. As this is a purely military history and not a history of empire, the constraints of space demand that I take the presence of the British in far-flung corners of the globe as read. I have avoided politically correct platitudes about the ethics of empire, as the subject merits only deep and objective contemplation and lies safely outside the scope of this book. For the twenty-first century's first eminent and balanced assessment of Britain's role as the first global superpower, see Professor Niall Ferguson's *Empire: How Britain made the Modern World* (2003).

Except in so far as they establish a basic background to conflict, the main narrative chapters do not set out to explain in any great depth why the protagonists were fighting, but rather how they went about it and what happened when they did. In passing they will demonstrate that any notion of a well-armed British military regularly gunning down feebly equipped 'native' enemies, a cliché much beloved by propagandists of the political left, is by no means an accurate reflection of any kind of historical norm. In truth battlefield mismatches in the high colonial era were few and far between. Much more typically Queen Victoria's Army had to live on its wits, against well-led, resourceful and numerically superior enemies, inclined to give battle on their own terms, in ground of their own choosing. It should be no surprise, therefore, that it did not invariably succeed.

Few books, even history books, can get by without heroes and villains. If this book can be said to have a hero, it is the ordinary fighting man – be he an ennobled Old Etonian in the Grenadier Guards, an ordinary 'Tommy' soldiering for two square meals a day in the ranks of the old 35th, a young Muslim sepoy in Jacob's Rifles, a wizened Sikh officer in the Corps of Guides, a Zulu warrior in the iNgobamakhosi, a Hadendawa 'fuzzy-wuzzy', or an Afrikaner farmer in the Potchefstroom Commando. All of them did their duty as they saw it and are therefore worthy of our respect. As to villains the reader is perfectly at liberty to choose his or her own. It will be as well to remember as we go that no war in history, not even the great wars of conscience, has been waged without wrongs being perpetrated by both sides. It is in the nature of war, the most terrible yet seemingly compulsive of mankind's besetting sins.

Mike Snook
London, 2007

Author's Note

Conventions Used in the Text

Ranks

In the Victorian Army officers' ranks were divided into the following categories: Regimental rank, Army rank, temporary rank, and honorary rank. *Regimental rank* was an officer's paid or substantive rank, held against a vacancy on the establishment of his regiment. Brevet promotions were awarded for distinguished service in the field, were unpaid, and would advance an officer in his *Army rank* but not his regimental rank. A captain breveted to major continued to be paid in his regimental rank, but would wear the higher rank. The *temporary rank* category was divided into 'acting' rank and 'local' rank. The former allowed for temporary paid tenure of a higher rank for a specific purpose limited by time, while the latter allowed for temporary unpaid tenure of a higher rank on the authority of the local commander. *Honorary rank* entailed a notional unpaid promotion by one rank, typically granted to officers on their retirement.

Except where relevant to the narrative, officers are referred to in the rank that they wore on their uniform at the point under discussion.

Rendering of Rank

The convention in Victorian times, (and down to the modern day) was that regardless of their formal rank in the Army List, all general officers (general, lieutenant general, major general and brigadier-general in descending order) would be referred to conversationally or informally simply as 'general'. Thus Major General Gordon was commonly called 'General Gordon', even though a 'full' general is two grades senior to a major general. Similarly, although a 'full' colonel is one grade senior to a lieutenant colonel, officers in the latter rank are also referred to informally as 'colonel'. Because repetitive use of formal ranks can become tiresome to the reader, I have resorted to informal renderings of rank at the second and all subsequent mentions of an officer's name. Hence 'Lieutenant Colonel Percy Barrow CB, CMG' becomes 'Colonel Barrow' – which is how the officers of the 19th Hussars would have referred to him.

Appointments

Although today we are used to referring to the senior officer of a battalion or regiment as its 'commanding officer' or CO, up until the 1890s 'officer commanding' was more usual. It should also be noted that 'brigade-major' is an appointment (today called a brigade chief of staff), not a rank, and might on occasion be held by a senior captain.

The Prophet Muhammad

It is now the convention in English to render the name of the Prophet as 'Muhammad'. In Victorian times there were as many as four or five anglicized spellings in use. In the interests of authenticity and for the avoidance of confusion I have rendered the names of historical characters in the anglicized forms most commonly found in contemporaneous English language sources. I have made an exception in the case of Muhammad Ahmad, who called himself the Mahdi, whose name tended to rendered as 'Mohamed Ahmed' in Victorian times.

CHRONOLOGY

Victorian Military Affairs

1837	**Canada**	Republican and French-Canadian Rebellions
1838	**South Africa**	Boer–Zulu War
16 Dec 1838		Battle of Blood River
1839–42	**Afghanistan**	**First Afghan War**
1839–42	**China**	**First China or 'Opium' War**
1839	**Afghanistan**	HEIC Army of the Indus takes Kandahar and Kabul
1841–2	**Afghanistan**	
Nov 1841		Murder of British envoy and uprising in Kabul
6–13 Jan 1842		Retreat from Kabul
Apr–Sep		March of HEIC's 'Army of Retribution'; Kabul recaptured
1842	**China**	
29 Aug 1842		Treaty of Nanking, Hong Kong ceded
1842–3	**Natal**	Anglo-Boer clash and annexation of Natal
1843	**India**	**Conquest of Sind**
17 Feb 1843		Battle of Meanee
1845–6	**Punjab**	**First Sikh War**
18 Dec 1845		Battle of Mudki
21–2 Dec 1845		Battle of Ferozeshah
28 Jan 1846		Battle of Aliwal
10 Feb		Battle of Sobraon
11 March		Treaty of Lahore; Punjab becomes a protectorate

1845–7	**New Zealand**	**First Maori War**
1846–7	**Cape Colony**	**War of the Axe** (Seventh Cape Frontier War)
29 Aug 1848	**South Africa**	Battle of Boomplaats
1848–9	**Punjab**	**Second Sikh War**
22 Nov 1848		Battle of Ramnagar
13 Jan 1849		Battle of Chillianwallah
21 Feb 1849		Battle of Gujerat; Punjab annexed
1850–3	**Cape Colony**	**Eighth Cape Frontier War**
1852–3	**Far East**	**Second Burma War**
	South Africa	**Basuto War**
1853	**Home Army**	Introduction of the Enfield Rifle
1854–6	**Crimean War**	
20 Sep 1854		Battle of the Alma
from early Oct 1854		Anglo-French investment of Sebastopol
25 Oct 1854		Battle of Balaclava
5 Nov 1854		Battle of Inkerman
1855	**Whitehall**	Office of Secretary at War abolished
1856	**Whitehall**	Duke of Cambridge becomes C-in-C
	South Africa	Zulu Civil War
1856–7	**Persian Gulf**	**Persian Campaign**
1856–60	**China**	**Second China War**
1857–8	**India**	**Indian Mutiny**
10 May 1857		Outbreak at Meerut; massacre of Europeans at Delhi
6–26 June 1857		Siege of Cawnpore
27 June 1857		Cawnpore Massacre
July 1857		Havelock's Battles of Fatehpur (12th), Aong (15th) and Cawnpore (16th)
25 Sep 1857		First relief of Lucknow
14–20 Sep 1857		Storming of Delhi
16 Nov 1857		Second relief of Lucknow
Jan–June 1858		Sir Hugh Rose's Central India campaign
19 June 1858		Battle of Gwalior; end of the Mutiny
1 Sep 1858		HEIC cedes governance to the Crown
1858	**Home Army**	Staff College founded, Camberley
1859–60	**China**	**Second China War**
25 June 1859		British attack on the Taku Forts
21 Aug 1860		Capture of the Taku Forts; advance on Peking

1860–72	**New Zealand**	**Second & Third Maori Wars**
1861	**India**	Merger of HEIC European regiments into British Army
1861–5	**Warfare**	**American Civil War**
1863	**Egypt**	Ismail Pasha becomes Khedive of Egypt
	China	Gordon assumes command of the 'Ever Victorious Army'
1866	**Warfare**	**Austro-Prussian War**
1867		**Abyssinian Campaign**
		Andaman Islands Incident
1868	**Whitehall**	HMG restricts flogging to active service
1869	**Home Army**	Wolseley publishes *A Soldier's Pocket Book for Field Service*
1870	**Whitehall**	War Office Act; Army Enlistment Bill (introduction of short service)
	Canada	**First Riel Rebellion; Red River Expedition**
24 Aug 1870		Wolseley recaptures Fort Garry
1870–1	**Warfare**	**Franco-Prussian War**
1871	**Whitehall**	Regulation of the Forces Bill (abolition of purchase); formal adoption of Martini-Henry rifle; Wolseley to Assistant AG
1871–2	**India**	**Looshai Expedition**
1872	**Whitehall**	Localisation Bill
1873–4	**West Africa**	**Second Ashanti War**
31 Jan 1874		Battle of Amoaful
Feb 1874		Wolseley takes Kumasi
1874	**India**	**Naga Hills Expedition**
	British Army	Short service extended to the cavalry; Martini-Henry on general issue
1875–6	**Malaysia**	**Perak Campaign**
12 April 1877	**South Africa**	Shepstone annexes the Transvaal
1877–8	**Warfare**	**Russo-Turkish War**
1877–8	**South Africa**	**Ninth Cape Frontier War**
13 Jan 1878		Battle of Nyumaga
7 Feb 1878		Battle of Centane
1878–80	**Afghanistan**	**Second Afghan War**
Nov 1878		British invasion of Afghanistan
2 Dec 1878		Roberts forces the Peiwar Kotal
11 Dec 1878		British ultimatum to King Cetshwayo

1879	**Natal**	**Zulu War**
22 Jan 1879		Battles of Isandlwana & Rorke's Drift
28 Jan–4 Apr 1879		Pearson's No 1 Column immobilized at Eshowe
28 March 1879		Battle of Hlobane; Buller wins VC
29 March 1879		Battle of Kambula
		Battle of iNtombi Drift
3 April 1879		Battle of Gingindhlovu
1 June 1879		Prince Imperial killed
4 July 1879		Battle of Ulundi
1879	**Transvaal**	Sekhukhune Campaign
1879	**Egypt**	
25 June 1879		Ismail Pasha deposed by the Sultan; Tewfik succeeds
1879–80	**India**	**Second Naga Hills Expedition**
1879–80	**Afghanistan**	
May 1879		Treaty of Gandamak
5 Sep 1879		Cavagnari Massacre in Kabul
6 Oct 1879		Battle of Charasiah
12 Oct 1879		Roberts takes Kabul
23 Dec 1879		Battle of Sherpur
19 April 1880		Battle of Ahmad Khel
27 July 1880		Battle of Maiwand
9 Aug 1880		Beginning of Roberts's march from Kabul to Kandahar
1 Sep 1880		Battle of Kandahar
1880	**Whitehall**	Wolseley to QMG
1880–1	**Basutoland**	**The Gun War**
1880–1	**South Africa**	**Transvaal Rebellion**
20 Dec 1880		Battle of Bronkhorstspruit
30 Dec 1880		Proclamation of ZAR
28 Jan 1881		Battle of Laing's Nek
8 Feb 1881		Battle of Ingogo (or Schuinshoogte)
27 Feb 1881		Battle of Majuba Hill, Colley killed
5 April 1881		Treaty of Pretoria
1881–5	**Sudan**	**Mahdist Rebellion**
11 Aug 1881		Battle of Aba Island
22 Sep 1881	**Afghanistan**	Abdur Rahman defeats Ayub Khan
1881	**Whitehall**	Abolition of flogging; Childers's amalgamations
1882	**Whitehall**	Wolseley to AG

1882	**Egypt**	**Nationalist revolt**
May–June 1882		Alexandria riots
11 July 1882		Bombardment of Alexandria
13 Sep 1882		Battle of Tel-el-Kebir
1882	**Sudan**	
May 1882		Battle of Massa; Yussuf Pasha defeated
8 Sep 1882		Battle of El Obeid
Sep 1882–Jan 1883		Siege of El Obeid
9 Dec 1882		Defeat of Rashid Bey near Jebel Gadir
6 Jan 1883		Fall of Bara
17 Jan 1883		Fall of El Obeid
4 March 1883		Hicks Pasha arrives in Khartoum
29 April 1883		Hicks wins a victory near Aba
July 1883		Hicks elevated to C-in-C Sudan *vice* Suleiman Pasha
9 Sep 1883		Kordofan expedition departs Khartoum for El Obeid
5 Nov 1883		Battle of Sheikan; Hicks Disaster
1883–4	**South Africa**	Zulu Civil War
1884–85	**Southern Africa**	**Bechuanaland Expedition**
1884	**Sudan**	
3 Feb 1884		First Battle of El Teb; Baker Disaster
Feb–April 1884		First Suakin Expedition
29 Feb 1884		Second Battle of El Teb
12 March 1884		Mahdi closes up to Khartoum; Gordon besieged
13 March 1884		Battle of Tamai
April 1884		Gladstone orders withdrawal from Suakin
28 May 1884		Fall of Berber
4/5 Sep 1884		Battle of El Eilafun; defeat of Mohamet Ali Pasha
10 Sep 1884		Stewart and Power leave Khartoum aboard *Abbas*
18 Sep 1884		Stewart's party massacred; Wolseley appointed to command relief expedition
Dec 1884		Desert Column advances into the Bayuda Desert
17 Jan 1885		Battle of Abu Klea,
19 Jan 1885		Battle of Abu Kru (or Gubat)

25/26 Jan 1885		Fall of Khartoum, Gordon killed
28 Jan 1885		Wilson reaches Khartoum
10 Feb 1885		Battle of Kirbekan
20 March 1885		Battle of Hashin
22 March 1885		Battle of Tokrek
21 June 1885		Death of Muhammad Ahmad
30 Dec 1885		Battle of Ginniss
Mar-May 1885	**Canada**	**Second Riel Rebellion**
12 May 1885		Battle of Batoche
1885–89	**Far East**	**Third Burma War**
1886	**Transvaal**	Gold strike on the Rand
1887	**Home Army**	Buller to QMG; adoption of the Lee-Metford rifle
1887	**India**	**Hazara Campaign**
1889	**Burma**	**Chin Field Force**
1890	**Home Army**	Buller to AG *vice* Wolseley; Wolseley to Ireland
1891	**India**	**Manipur Expedition**
1893	**Rhodesia**	**Matabele War**
1893	**India**	White to C-in-C India *vice* Roberts
1894–5	**India**	**Waziri Campaign**
1894	**Whitehall**	Wolseley to field marshal
1895–6	**West Africa**	**Third Ashanti War**
1895–8	**NW Frontier**	**Pathan Uprising**
4 Mar–20 Apr 1895		Siege of Chitral
1895	**Home Army**	Wolseley to C-in-C *vice* Duke of Cambridge; Roberts to field marshal and to Dublin *vice* Wolseley
1895–6	**Transvaal**	
29 Dec 1895		Jameson Raid begins
2 Jan 1896		Jameson surrenders at Doornkop; Kaiser's telegram; Rhodes resigns
1896	**Home Army**	HMG buys 40,000 acres on Salisbury Plain
1896–8	**Sudan**	**Reconquest of the Sudan**
1897	**NW Frontier**	**Malakand Field Force, Mohmand & Tochi Valley expeditions**
Oct-Nov 1897	**NW Frontier**	**Tirah Expedition**
18–20 Oct 1897		Battle of Dargai
1897	**Home Army**	Wood to AG *vice* Buller; Buller to GOC Aldershot

1897	**Rhodesia**	**Matabele Uprising**
1897	**East Africa**	**Bombardment of Zanzibar**
1897	**South Africa**	Sir Alfred Milner to the Cape as High Commissioner; Treaty of Mutual Assistance between Transvaal and OFS
1897–98	**West Africa**	**Benin Expedition**
1898	**Sudan**	
8 April 1898		Battle of Atbara
2 Sep 1898		Battle of Omdurman
July–Nov 1898	**Southern Sudan**	**The Fashoda Incident**
1898	**Home Army**	Resumption of large-scale summer manoeuvres, Salisbury Plain
1899–1902	**South Africa**	**Boer War**
May 1899		Bloemfontein Conference; Wolseley secures Buller's appointment to South African command
28 Sep 1899		Mobilization of 1st Army Corps; White to GOC Natal from QMG
9 Oct 1899		Kruger serves ultimatum on HMG
11 Oct 1899		HMG rejects ultimatum
20 Oct 1899		Battle of Talana Hill
21 Oct 1899		Battle of Elandslaagte
30 Oct 1899		Battle of Nicholson's Nek; siege of Ladysmith begins
23 Nov 1899		Battle of Belmont
25 Nov 1899		Battle of Graspan
28 Nov 1899		Battle of Modder River
6 Dec 1899		Buller assumes command on Ladysmith Front
10 Dec 1899		Battle of Stormberg Junction
10–11 Dec 1899		Battle of Magersfontein
15 Dec 1899		Battle of Colenso, last of three defeats of 'Black Week'
24 Jan 1900		Battle of Spion Kop
5 Feb 1900		Battle of Vaal Krantz
15 Feb 1900		Relief of Kimberley
18–27 Feb 1900		Battle of Paardeberg
28 Feb 1900		Relief of Ladysmith
13 March 1900		Fall of Bloemfontein
May 1900		Buller clears Northern Natal
17–18 May 1900		Relief of Mafeking

31 May 1900		Fall of Johannesburg
5 June 1900		Fall of Pretoria
Nov 1900		Boer 'bitter-enders' resort to guerrilla warfare
Dec 1900		Roberts hands over to Kitchener
1900	**China**	**Siege and relief of Peking legations**
1901	**Home Army**	Roberts to C-in-C *vice* Wolseley on retirement; death of the Queen Empress; accession of Edward VII
May 1902	**South Africa**	**Treaty of Vereeniging ends Boer War**
1904	**Home Army**	Roberts retires as C-in-C; post abolished

Prologue

ZULULAND

January 1879

In good fortune and in ill it is rare indeed that a British regiment does not hold together; and this indestructible cohesion, best of all the qualities that an armed body can possess, is based not merely on hereditary resolution, but on mutual confidence and respect. The man in the ranks has implicit faith in his officer, the officer an almost unbounded belief in the valour and discipline of his men.[1]

Colonel G. F. R. Henderson

Satisfied that his sights were aligned on the swathe of waist-high grass in which he had seen 50 or more warriors go to ground, Sergeant William Shaw braced himself for the bruising thump to come and squeezed the trigger. Now in his early thirties, he had been in the 2nd Battalion of his regiment for close to a decade and like the rest of his peers knew his business inside out. He had undergone his basic training with the .577-inch Snider-Enfield rifle, an economical but serviceable conversion of the muzzle-loading Enfield into a stopgap breech-loader. Now, on the afternoon of Wednesday 22 January 1879, Shaw was carrying the first purpose-built breech-loader to enter service with the British Army. Everybody in authority, it seemed, had readily accepted that the .450-inch Martini-Henry had revolutionized both the capability and the capacity of the infantry, though Shaw and his fellow sergeants knew that like all rifles it had its limitations and its foibles. Each had been obliged, for example, to sew a cowhide hand-guard around the barrel and fore-end to prevent burns to his hands. They had also learned for themselves that the rifle was not at its best in the dark, when severe muzzle flash tended to ruin the firer's night-vision. But it was not the sergeants who were running the show. Lieutenant General Lord Chelmsford, for one, took the view that, in terms of campaigning around Southern Africa, the Martini-Henry had made his redcoat infantry battalions all but invulnerable. The weapon was 50 inches long, weighed the best part of 9 pounds and, its peripheral defects aside, was a beautifully balanced, hard-hitting and accurate firearm. Compared to its predecessors it represented a quantum leap in small-arms design.

As Sergeant Shaw pulled down on the lever behind the trigger guard, a spent brass cartridge case came flying from the breech to fall tumbling to earth amongst the sandstone boulders at his feet. The rocky ridge was an unimpressive geographical feature, but stood just high enough above the general lie of the land to dominate the usually dry but deep-scored watercourse a few hundred yards to its front, and so to shape and define the British line of defence. Shaw squinted through a mostly transparent bank of gun smoke in search of a fresh target, as the billowing white cloud which accompanied the precise moment of discharge made it impossible to know whether his most recent shot had found its target or not. In one flowing movement of the right hand, he scooped a fresh round from the expense-pouch he wore suspended from the back of his waistbelt, thumbed it into the chamber, and snapped the lever home to close the breech and cock the weapon. Before he could even think about taking a fresh aim, he was obliged to drag a grubby scarlet sleeve across his forehead to prevent any more beads of perspiration trickling into his eyes from under the hat-band of his foreign-service helmet.

Although in the past year Sergeant Shaw had participated in low-key operations to flush Xhosa fighters from their remote forest hideouts in the Amatola Mountains, this was his first big fight. As was sometimes the way with such things, it had descended upon him like a bolt from the blue. Six companies of the 2nd/24th had left the camp at dawn, confident in the belief that they were on their way to bring the enemy main body to battle. Instead Ntshingwayo kaMahole, the Zulu army commander, had outmanoeuvred his hapless opposite number, so that instead of the battle being fought on the eastern side of the plain as his lordship had anticipated, the great enemy host had fallen upon the thinly defended camp in the west. Five companies of the 1st/24th under Lieutenant Colonel Henry Pulleine, and Lieutenant Charles Pope's G Company of the 2nd Battalion – not quite 600 officers and men in all – were now being asked to do the work of twice their number in defence of a badly over-extended perimeter. In addition to the 90 or so men of Pope's command, his battalion had left behind a miscellany of minor details which together amounted to another 80 potentially invaluable riflemen. One of the subalterns assisting Colonel Pulleine had come galloping back to the tents from the firing line to round up all the spare hands he could find. With the help of Sergeant Shaw and a few other NCOs, he soon located 50–60 men from the 2nd Battalion's rear details, organized them into a composite half-company, and doubled them down to the rocky ridge to take post on G Company's right. Their deployment extended

Pulleine's firing line a little further to the south, in the direction of Colonel Anthony Durnford and his black African troopers, who by now were fighting on foot from the lower reaches of the Nyogane Donga (*donga* – a watercourse or stream bed).

After a year's soldiering on the Cape Frontier and in Natal, William Shaw and the other 2nd Battalion sergeants thought they knew Africa reasonably well, though they willingly deferred to the expertise of their 1st Battalion comrades who had arrived in Cape Town over the Christmas and New Year of 1874–5 and had since scored some signal successes against the Xhosa. Both battalions had heard much about their new Zulu enemy and had been warned by just about every settler they encountered at their wayside halts that King Cetshwayo presided over a fiercely militaristic nation. But it had been evident from the contradictory nature of much that was said that not everybody was the expert he pretended to be. Prior to crossing the Buffalo River into Zululand on 11 January 1879, the sergeants had been left wondering what to believe and what not to believe. They had been wise enough to infer that a short-lived skirmish at Sihayo's Kraal the following day offered no compelling insights into the nature of the big fight to come. Since 8.00 a.m. that morning, however, when Colonel Pulleine had first assembled his force in front of the tents, the sergeants had been forming their own first impressions of Zulu military capacity. Now it was gone 1.00 p.m. and Colonels Pulleine and Durnford had played all the cards in the British hand. The battle was hanging in the balance and the sergeants had long since concluded that there could be no more formidable adversary in the whole of Africa than the Zulu.

Both sides, it turned out, had surprised the other. Sergeant Shaw had never seen so many black Africans in one place and had never imagined that any of the Bantu tribes could be capable of manoeuvring such a vast army with such evident tactical agility, such remarkable cohesion or so clear a sense of purpose. With an *impi* of some 24,000 warriors executing a 'horns of the buffalo' double envelopment across a frontage of more than five miles, the sense of impending encirclement was becoming palpable on some parts of the field. Sergeant Shaw was one of those who could sense trouble in the wind.

At the foot of the long slope, several hundred yards to his front, a young Zulu called Mehlokazulu kaSihayo was down on his belly, concealing himself as best he could in the lush long grass of summer. He was surrounded within a circumference of only a few yards by several dozen other 24-year-olds from the iNgobamakhosi, the 6,000-strong age-grouped regiment to which he owed his allegiance, not all of whom were still breathing. In many cases the soft-nosed .450-inch bullet fired by the Martini had inflicted grotesque injuries on the Zulu dead and wounded. Never before had the young men of the iNgobamakhosi heard a man-made sound as loud as the company volleys which had first deprived them of all forward momentum, and then driven them to ground along the general line of the donga. Now they were being held in check by means of alternating, more discriminating and less ammunition-intensive section volleys directed by the sergeants. In the space of the last 35 minutes, Mehlokazulu and his comrades had learned a healthy respect for the red soldiers' way of war. Though none of them would care to admit it, for the time being the iNgobamakhosi's will to win had succumbed to the murderous effects of modern firepower. Unless something gave soon the young warriors were going nowhere, except perhaps scuttling for home with their tails between their legs.

Away to the left, few of Sergeant Shaw's 1st Battalion counterparts were at all concerned with how the battle was going. They and their sections had the uNokhenke, umCijo and uMbonambi regiments pinned down in the Nyogane Donga at a safe distance, had plenty of ammunition left in their pouches, with more on the way, and believed the battalion's flanks to be secure – its left resting on the lower slopes of Isandlwana and its right on Mr Pope's reinforced G Company. It was a quirk of the ground that most 1st Battalion men could look over their right shoulders to see their 2nd Battalion comrades deployed along the line of the rocky ridge, periodically raising their rifles into the aim in the smooth and rhythmic fashion of well-drilled regular infantry, but could see nothing of the targets they were engaging, or of the great expanse of plain to the south. What they could not see and could not influence, the 1st Battalion men were not going to worry about and for the time being they were to be seen laughing and joking amongst themselves, confident in the knowledge that they were giving the enemy regiments to their front a hiding they would long remember.

Charlie Pope was not laughing or joking. His own right flank was not resting securely on anything. Instead there was an oblique gap of 600 yards from the south end of the rocky ridge to Colonel Durnford's more advanced position in the southern reaches of the donga. Pope had stretched the 2nd Battalion contingent as thin as he dared to minimize the gap but could do no more. Durnford commanded two 50-strong troops of mounted black irregulars, one of Basutos and one of mission Christians from Edendale near Pietermaritzburg. Additionally, following his ill-advised foray into the plain, Durnford had taken Lieutenant Durrant Scott and a score of Natal Carbineers under command. He had been further reinforced in the meantime by a 60-strong miscellany of colonial volunteers, mounted policemen and Regular Army mounted infantrymen under Captain Robert Bradstreet of the Newcastle Mounted Rifles. Because they had ridden down from the camp with full bandoliers of ammunition, the arrival of Bradstreet's men had enabled Durnford to hold his ground a little while longer. Problematically his fields of fire petered out at the top of the Nkengeni Ridge, 250 yards away at best, beyond which there was a sea of dead ground and a great many as yet uncommitted Zulus.

Charlie Pope had been looking to his right since the battle started and had already been forced to shift position twice, in order to prevent the iNgobamakhosi outflanking his company. The 23-year-old bucks of the uVe regiment were about to pull off what their 24-year-old elders and betters had been unable to achieve. Looking through his field glasses Pope was mortified to observe a thousand warriors or more, around a third of the uVe's total strength, spilling down the forward slope of the Nkengeni Ridge, half a mile south of Durnford's position. The game was up. Already the troopers in the donga were falling back on the horseholders arrayed behind them. Durnford was retreating and the British right would be left swinging in the air. For the hopelessly outnumbered infantrymen of the 2nd/24th, the only defence now was distance.

In next to no time Durnford's command had cleared out completely, galloping hard over the long uphill mile back to the tents, with only the courageous Scott and a handful of his carbineers riding in the very teeth of the enemy by way of a rearguard. The retreat left nothing between Pope's 150 redcoats and around 6,000 battle-crazed young Zulus. Not only were all 3,000 men of the uVe surging uphill into the vacuum to Pope's right, but the left wing of the iNgobamakhosi, another 3,000 men, Mehlokazulu amongst them, were also exploiting the yawning gap. Menacingly the iNgobamakhosi were not only gaining ground uphill, but were also right-wheeling to steer a collision course for the rocky ridge and any potential line of retreat to the tents. Pope scanned the intervening ground and grappled with estimates of time and space. Against such lightly equipped and athletic protagonists even a whole mile of space translated into a few short minutes of time. The companies had been deployed too far forward into the plain, his own furthest of all. As he could see no way out, he stood his ground, dashing up and down the line bellowing orders for the section commanders to maintain as hot a fire as possible.

The officers and NCOs of the 2nd Battalion cocked their ears between volleys to take in the sound of a bugle call. They identified it as the 'Retire' and sensed that it was coming from somewhere near Colonel Pulleine's position, not far from the brace of Royal Artillery 7-pounders. Soon the call had been picked up by the company buglers and was repeated up and down the line. Somebody on the rocky ridge deemed it prudent to raise the nerve-tingling cry to 'Fix bayonets!' and in a matter of moments that order too was racing back and forth. If he had paused long enough to think, William Shaw would have felt an adrenalin rush coursing through his body as he groped for the 1860 Pattern sword-bayonet slung from his waistbelt. Nearby a young C Company private called Private Thomas Jones 976, enlisted and trained at the regimental depot in Brecon only two years earlier, reached for the new 1876 Pattern 'lunger' bayonet with which everybody below the rank of sergeant was equipped. It was not long before Pope's relentless volleys had driven elements of the iNgobamakhosi back onto their bellies some way short of their objective – but 300 yards to the south there was next to no hope of preventing the line being rolled up from the right. Here the intervening distances were already too short, the men too thinly spread, and the defensive fire too diffuse to prevent the onset of a close-quarter brawl.

Aware that they were in dire trouble, and a mile or more from the nearest help, the men fighting on Pope's open flank were already edging nervously backwards, looking over their shoulders for potential rallying points. Private James White, another young C Company soldier in his early twenties, could see nothing but a bare downhill slope and, a few paces to his rear, the familiar features of Sergeant Shaw. Private Ben Latham, a 21-year-old who had enlisted at Newport in Monmouthshire, was also close at hand and like the other young men around him now knew in his heart of hearts that he was about to die. The temptation to break ranks and run was almost unbearable. Two things prevented his doing so. First, his instincts told him that soldiers of the 24th didn't do that sort of thing. Second, his common sense told him that any man who ran but did not die could expect to be shunned by his mates and flogged by his colonel. Neither *esprit de corps* nor iron discipline were lacking in the old 24th. They were attributes which in the right circumstances could turn the tide of battle; today was not going to be one of those days. It was as well that they could also help a man to die.

Suddenly the line came under direct assault and, lacking any weight or substance, immediately began to give way at all points. Away to the left where the iNgobamakhosi's right wing had yet to come to blows, Lieutenants Pope and Godwin-Austen were gathering their soldiers into a rallying-square, the drill-book name for an irregular cluster of men standing shoulder-to-shoulder and back-to-back, to present an impenetrable hedgehog of bayonets. Closer at hand other men were closing around Sub-Lieutenant Thomas Griffith, not because they believed for one moment that a callow youth of 21 could devise some miraculous means of salvation, but because that was what their training had taught them to do – in a crisis, fix bayonets, rally on the nearest officer and fight like fury until told to stop. Such was the ferocity of the iNgobamakhosi assault, and so easily was the thin red line breached, that for many men the lateral movement necessary to reach an officer proved quite impossible. Instead they were driven down the reverse slope of the rocky ridge, where they rallied to NCOs in twos and fours and sixes and made the best fight of it they could. Mehlokazulu was one of several Zulu participants who recounted how closely the red soldiers stuck together and how difficult it was to kill them. It is impossible to know precisely how it came to pass, but amidst all the confusion Privates Benjamin Latham, James White and Thomas Jones 976 rallied around Sergeant William Shaw to form a tiny red island in a raging sea of black.

Standing back-to-back with one last round in the breech and their bayonets braced, the quartet scorned any notion of flight and prepared to sell their lives as dearly as possible . . .

* * *

Corporal John Bassage of the 2nd/24th's C Company would have known William Shaw well, and the three young privates who died with him at least in passing. Quite how he was able to identify their mortal remains, when at last in June 1879, some five months after they fell, the 24th Regiment was able to return to the battlefield to bury its dead, is a detail he chose not to record in the fleeting entry he made in his pocketbook.[2] That it could not have been by means of their fresh-faced features is not in doubt. The precise 'British' loss that day will never be known, but counting all ethnicities, all troop types and an uncertain number of black civilian wagon workers, is believed to be around 1,420 human souls.[3] The Zulu fatal loss is conventionally placed at around the 1,500–2,000 mark, with an equal or marginally greater number of wounded. By the time Lieutenant Colonel Wilsone Black's burial parties had completed their grisly task, they had interred 16 officers and 396 other ranks of the 1st Battalion, and 5 officers and 171 other ranks of the 2nd Battalion. Notably, in the only instance of its kind in the long history of the British Infantry, not a single man of the six companies fighting on the firing line had survived the battle. In the context of battalion-sized actions, there are massacres and there is Isandlwana.

But it is also commonplace for the battle to be described variously as the worst military disaster 'of the Victorian age', or 'of the colonial era', or 'in the history of the British Empire', sometimes even 'in the history of the British Army'. Of course 'worst' is too loose an adjective and in truth none of these labels can be fairly applied to the events of 22 January 1879. It can be trumped under almost any set of criteria by such unhappy events as the Braddock disaster, the retreat from Kabul, the Saratoga and Yorktown campaigns, any number of failed Great War offensives, the surrender of Singapore, Arnhem, and, in the particular context of Southern Africa, by the Battle of Majuba Hill of which more later. It is undoubtedly true that Isandlwana was the *most unexpected* defeat of the Victorian era, if nothing else because nobody in London even knew that the country was at war with the Zulus. Because it came as such a bolt from the blue, it is also safe to regard it as the *most shocking* military disaster of the age. As we shall see the British Empire might have been at its zenith, but, for the Queen Empress and her subjects, Isandlwana would not be the last such shock.

Chapter 1

THE VICTORIAN ARMY IN AN AGE OF TRANSITION

The Challenge of Modernization, 1854–1899

If an officer was inclined to read, there was no one to whom he could apply for advice as to what to read; his education in the higher branches of military science was no one's business but his own. He was even told that a knowledge of strategy – and strategy is at least one half, and the more important half, of the art of war – was required from staff officers alone; and in consonance with this extraordinary doctrine, military history was taught officially nowhere but at the Staff College.

Colonel G. F. R. Henderson, February 1903,
Essay on the British Army before the Boer War

It was always said that the Queen Empress's German grandson had scornfully dismissed the British Expeditionary Force of 1914 as a 'contemptible little army'. It was a memorable phrase, even if in reality it cannot be convincingly demonstrated that the Kaiser ever uttered it. But as a once avid reader of the two-volume analysis of the Boer War compiled by the German General Staff, it was the sort of thing he might have said and, for bantering British 'Tommies' huddled around their campfires in Flanders, that was good enough. Perhaps because it seemed to fit such a posturing braggart so very, very well, its authenticity was never in doubt. To be fair to Wilhelm II, if in sharing his thoughts with his generals he did indeed pour scorn on the size of Sir John French's command, he was but making a perfectly sustainable point. By continental standards the BEF was a little army – British armies always were. But nothing about the Army of 1914 was contemptible, least of all the hard-case regulars in its ranks who, with the ironic sense of humour that has always characterized their kind, proudly labelled themselves 'the Old Contemptibles' and began heaping scorn upon their apparently ungracious royal detractor. The Tommies proceeded to make good their point by shooting a number of attacking German divisions to pieces, demonstrating such a remarkably high standard of musketry in the process that enemy intelligence officers convinced themselves that British battalions were equipped with many more machine guns than they actually possessed. Unusually for the British, even in retreat, in accordance with the operational-level demands of the Mons campaign, the BEF's logistic systems proved robust enough to meet a succession of demanding tactical crises. These days the received wisdom amongst military historians is that the BEF may well have been the *best* army ever to leave these shores.

The Make-Do-and-Mend Army

But how times had changed over the preceding 60 years. We would be deluding ourselves if we imagined for one moment that no 'contemptible' armies have ever marched to war beneath the Union Flag. All too often in the history of the British military, assembling a field force for war went little further than appointing its senior commanders and then earmarking a random selection of regiments, battalions and batteries to do the fighting. Brigades and divisions were *ad hoc* groupings thrown together in the field rather than the permanently established all-arms formations of today. The expedition to the Crimea provides an excellent example of the genre. When war broke out in 1854 the Army was 140,000 strong, about a third larger than it is today. It was presided over by a civil–military bureaucracy so inherently chaotic that even the most basic planning proved tortuous in the extreme. Assembling sufficient combat-ready regiments for an expedition of any size was invariably a struggle, as the majority of units were committed to the policing of India or to an increasingly fractious Ireland. Units of the home Army seldom attained full fighting strength as they were regularly required to provide drafts for units serving overseas and, in any case, were pegged-back by unreasonably tight peacetime establishments.[1] For fairly obvious reasons under-strength is virtually synonymous with poorly trained.

Whenever an unexpected crisis blew up, it was necessary to top up the deploying regiments to fighting strength with drafts from any number of similarly roled units, a convenient but ultimately harmful expedient, which when pursued as a norm guarantees a widespread lack of cohesion at precisely the least opportune moment. Expeditionary forces of greater than divisional strength ran the risk of leaving Britain all but denuded of regular troops. Assembling a balanced force for the Egyptian intervention of 1882 was no easier for Sir Garnet Wolseley than it had been for Lord Raglan almost 30 years earlier. It was not until 1888 that a workable plan for the generation of significant contingency forces was evolved. From that point on it was at least theoretically possible to mobilize two all-arms corps and an independent cavalry division.

The odds had long been stacked against Army reform. Although significant change in the governance of military affairs had been contemplated in the 1830s, the programme had faltered and had not in the end been seen through to a rational legislative conclusion. In the run-up to the Crimean War, therefore, the Army was directly answerable to two ministers, the 'Secretary at War', the more junior of the pair, and the 'Secretary of State for War and the Colonies', whose increasingly unmanageable portfolio at last provided the catalyst for change. In June 1854 the senior appointment was formally divided into its component parts, an arrangement which served only to accentuate the Army's problems by creating a second full-time minister for military affairs. In February 1855 the situation was rationalized with the abolition of the Secretary at War. Even with the war in full swing, the constituent parts of the War Office remained scattered through a number of government buildings in the environs of Pall Mall. In all around a dozen government departments had some sort of role in military administration. For all its outward professions of concern, and despite the presence in both Houses of a considerable number of ex-officers, Parliament was no friend of the soldier. Given the choice of an effective way of resourcing a military measure, or a cheap but less effective way, the Commons would usually identify an even cheaper and almost wholly ineffective third way.

Even with 'War' and 'the Colonies' separated, operational control of the overseas garrisons remained vested in the Colonial Office. There were other anomalies. While the Commander-in-Chief controlled the cavalry, the infantry and the Guards, he did not own either the Royal Artillery (RA) or the Royal Engineers (RE), both of which answered to the Master General of the Ordnance (MGO). Responsibility for commissariat and transport matters rested with the Treasury, and in consequence they were run on a shoestring. For the time being not only did most of the major departments of state have a finger in the military pie, but the reality was that the pie itself was divided into several distinctly separate slices – there were in fact no fewer than seven semi-autonomous British armies. Even the Regular Army, which ought to have been simple enough to administer, was divided between the home Army, a number of sizeable overseas garrisons, and the 'Army in India' – which was not the same thing as the 'Indian Army' – not that in reality there was any such thing as an Indian Army. Rather the expression was little more than a convenient descriptor for the armies of the Bombay, Madras and Bengal Presidencies, three quite separate military establishments which would not be merged into a single entity until as late as 1895. The sixth and seventh armies for prospective reformers to contemplate were the Militia and the Volunteers, both of which had stronger ties to the Home Office than to the War Office. Indeed control of the Militia rested with the lord lieutenants of the shires rather than the Secretary of State for War. The old Volunteer movement, once a bulwark against Revolutionary France but never a wholly credible military resource, had new life breathed into it in 1859 when a new cross-Channel invasion scare threatened. Many professional soldiers complained that the Volunteers consumed revenue but provided little meaningful military capacity in return. To a parsimonious House of Commons, which since Trafalgar had grown accustomed to playing fast and loose with the landward defence of the realm, large numbers of virtually untrained but sublimely inexpensive volunteers represented a grand return on a minimal investment.

The 'Army in India' was the informal name given to that slice of the Regular Army leased by the Crown into the service of the Honourable East India Company (HEIC). The 'Queen's' regiments concerned were so remote from the control of Army headquarters at Horse Guards that each became a private army in its own right, determined above all else to stand on its dignity and to assert its superiority over its Indian Army counterparts wherever and whenever the opportunity presented itself. It remained a long-standing bone of contention that the most junior Queen's officer counted as senior to any HEIC officer of equivalent rank. Since many of the Company officers were battle-hardened veterans, and many of the newly-arrived Queen's officers were both foppish and inexperienced, the convention was the cause of considerable rancour. Eventually there would be only one Commander-in-Chief India, but for the time being each of the three presidencies had its own. By virtue of his physical proximity to the governor-general (later the viceroy), C-in-C Bengal acted as the *de facto* chairman of the triumvirate. Throughout our period neither the Secretary of State for War nor Horse Guards was capable of exercising any meaningful central authority over Indian military affairs, as both the Army in India and the three presidency armies were funded by the Indian taxpayer and answered in the first instance to the viceroy and his council.

Up to and including the Crimean War precious little thought was ever given to the Army's administration in the field – to its resupply, its transport arrangements, its quartering, its nourishment, its foul-weather clothing, or its medical and veterinary support. Far easier to restrict one's objectives, utilize a small expeditionary force, stick close to the coast and rely on the infinitely better-organized Royal Navy for administrative support. Army logistic systems, such as they were, had to be improvised from scratch. For a long time British general officers had not only to master the art of war but, if they were to succeed beyond the limited environment of small-scale amphibious expeditions, had of necessity to be brilliant and instinctive logisticians too. Behind much of the battlefield success achieved by Marlborough and Wellington lay their talent for piecing together necessarily *ad hoc* but nonetheless sound logistic systems.

The two great dukes succeeded in war not merely because they were masters of the operational art, but because they recognized the crucial importance of administration and logistics, and were prepared to devote a significant proportion of their time to overseeing the relevant staff functions in person. His morning ride aside, Wellington worked every hour that God sent him, pretty much scorning leave of absence for the duration of the Peninsular War. They say that nobody is indispensable, but the Duke of Wellington was assuredly an exception to the rule. Great Britain had been fortunate in both the War of the Spanish Succession and the long conflict with Napoleonic France, to have two such *bona fide* military geniuses at its disposal. Indeed the good reputation enjoyed by the Army at the time of Victoria's accession was in large part attributable to the prodigious talent of the two dukes. In the absence of a contemporary military genius, the Crimea would expose the foundations of sand beneath the glittering façade of scarlet and gold.

Time and again the members of Lord Raglan's army demonstrated that man for man they were more formidable in the fray than their Russian counterparts. But there were too few of them to begin with, and it was not merely shot and shell that took so heavy a toll of their lives. They died in even greater numbers away from the battlefield. They died of cholera, of dysentery, of malnutrition, of infected wounds, of cold and of sheer despair. It was the Crimean army's clutch of dreadful senior officers, famously exemplified by the asinine brothers-in-law at the helm of the cavalry division, coupled with the absence of anything remotely resembling a credible logistic system, that rendered the Army of 1854 quite so contemptible. For all his close exposure to the 'Iron Duke', Lord Raglan seems not to have absorbed very much of the great man's military acumen. Tactically and conceptually the Army of 1854 had not moved on from Waterloo, but neither had the Russians moved on since Borodino, so that in the end no real harm came of its theoretical obsolescence. Logistically, however, the Crimea was little short of a disaster. The blatantly obvious suffering of the soldiery was morally indefensible, for this was a foreign war of choice and the undernourished frost-bitten wretches being stretchered out of the trenches by the thousand were faithful servants of by far the richest country in the world.

If the home Army's principal problem was the absence of sound organizational and administrative systems fit to bind a miscellaneous collection of regiments into an army of divisions, brigades and support services, there was not much wrong with the basic building block itself. British regiments, cavalry and infantry alike, could be stuffy, quirky, insular, claustrophobic and conservative, but each was unique and each had its own mystical formula for inspiring devotion amongst its officers and men – if mere devotion can ever be a strong enough word to describe the sentiment. Matchless *esprit de corps* was the principal hallmark of the British regimental system. And it worked; it won battles which the generals did not entirely deserve to win. In the two Sikh Wars of the 1840s, for example, General Sir Hugh Gough failed to exhibit any tactical finesse whatsoever. The all-out frontal attack became his hallmark, an approach which his all too expendable officers and soldiers came to parody as 'Tipperary tactics'. Direct assault had worked countless times before on the irresolute armies of the minor nawabs and princes, but the Sikhs were in a different league altogether – fearless, militaristic, dogged in defence and well-provided with modern artillery. The result was a succession of bloodbaths which, thanks to the heroic and seemingly unstoppable attacks of the British regiments, well supported by the Company's Indian units, passed in the end for victories. Remarkably, when the fighting was over, the Sikhs became staunch allies of the British and would provide some of the Indian Army's best and most faithful regiments.

No, the problem was seldom the regiments or the men. The officers and soldiers launched by Lord Raglan into a similar 'Tipperary' frontal attack on the formidably strong defensive position above the Alma performed a magnificent feat of arms in driving the Russians from the heights. By contrast their commander was so out of his depth that at one point in the battle, he led his entourage of mounted staff officers to a vantage point that placed them closer to the enemy than any of the assaulting regiments. There, but for the grace of God, the army commander could have been killed, like an over-animated subaltern, in the first hour of the first engagement of what was certain to be a very long war. Even more notoriously it was Raglan's poor eye for ground which lay behind the destruction of the Light Brigade in the next major action of the campaign.

From his commanding vantage point on the Sapouné Heights, Raglan seems to have been quite incapable of comprehending that the quarrelsome brothers-in-law, Lords Lucan and Cardigan, enjoyed only an indifferent view, and that precise, unambiguous orders would be required if they were to reflect his intent correctly. From the low ground the dreadful duo could see nothing much of the wider situation, and certainly not any enemy batteries they would ordinarily have considered attacking. 'Attack, sir!' bristled Lucan at Raglan's courier, after skimming through his lordship's all too sloppily expressed written order; 'Attack what? What guns?' In one of the iconic moments of British military history, Captain Louis Nolan replied with ill-disguised insolence, 'There, my Lord, are your guns!' In coupling his venom with a wild gesture in the direction of the North Valley, altogether the wrong objective, Nolan sealed the fate of Cardigan's brigade. Into the jaws of death rode the six hundred. As usual both the regiments and the men performed magnificently, as Private James Wightman recalled for *Nineteenth Century* magazine:

> For hell had opened on us from front and either flank, and it kept upon us during the minutes – they seemed like hours – which passed while

we traversed the mile and a quarter at the end of which was the enemy. The broken and fast thinning ranks raised rugged peals of wild fierce cheering that only swelled the louder as the shot and shell from the battery tore gaps through us, and the enfilading musketry fire from the infantry in both flanks brought down horses and men. Yet in this stress it was fine to see how strong was the bond of discipline and obedience. 'Close in! Close in!' was the constant command of the squadron and troop officers as the casualties made gaps in the ragged line, but the order was scarcely needed, for of their own instance and, as it seemed, mechanically men and horses alike sought to regain the touch.

We had not broken into the charging pace when poor old John Lee, my right hand man on the flank of the regiment, was all but smashed by a shell; he gave my arm a twitch, as with a strange smile on his worn old face he quietly said, 'Domino! Chum,' and fell out of the saddle. His old grey mare kept alongside me for some distance, treading on and tearing out her entrails as she galloped, till at length she dropped with a strange shriek. I have mentioned that my comrade, Peter Marsh, was my left hand man; next beyond him was Private Dudley. The explosion of a shell had swept down four or five men on Dudley's left, and I heard him ask Marsh if he had noticed 'what a hole that b—— shell had made' on his left front. 'Hold your foul-mouthed tongue,' answered Peter, 'swearing like a blackguard, when you may be knocked into eternity next minute!' Just then I got a musket-ball through my right knee, and another in the shin, and my horse had three bullet wounds in the neck. Man and horse were bleeding so fast that Marsh begged me to fall out; but I would not, pointing out that in a few minutes we must be into them, and so I sent my spurs well home, and faced it out with my comrades. It was about this time that Sergeant Talbot had his head carried clean off by a round shot, yet for about thirty yards further the headless body kept the saddle, the lance at the charge firmly gripped under the right arm . . .

Well, we were nearly out of it at last, and close on those cursed guns, Cardigan was still straight in front of me, steady as a church, but now his sword was in the air; he turned in his saddle for an instant, and shouted his final command, 'Steady! Steady! Close in!' Immediately afterwards there crashed into us a regular volley from the Russian cannon. I saw Captain White go down and Cardigan disappear into the smoke. A moment more and I was in it myself . . .[2]

The moment in time captured by the last few lines of Wightman's account, the point at which Cardigan disappeared into the gun smoke at the end of the North Valley, effectively sounded the death-knell of the gentlemen-first-soldiers-second approach which had prevailed in the British officer corps since the time of the Restoration. That the Crimea at least served as a turning point, and it was *only* a turning point, in terms of the wider professionalism of the British Army was in large part attributable to the debut of a new breed of journalist – the specialist war correspondent. With William Howard Russell of *The Times* to the fore, the pressmen ensured that the organizational and administrative failings of the Army were brought to the attention of Her Majesty's loyal opposition and the wider public:

> . . . you saw in one spot and in one instant a mass of accumulated woes that would serve you with nightmares for a lifetime. The dead, laid out as they died, were lying side by side with the living, and the latter presented a spectacle beyond all imagination. The commonest accessories of a hospital were wanting; there was not the least attention paid to decency or cleanliness – the stench was appalling – the foetid air could barely struggle out to taint the atmosphere, save through the chinks in the walls and roofs, and, for all I could observe, these men died without the least effort to save them. There they laid just as they were let gently down upon the ground by the poor fellows, their comrades, who brought them on their backs from the camp with the greatest tenderness, but who were not allowed to remain with them. The sick appeared to be attended by the sick, and the dying by the dying.

After that first dreadful Crimean winter of 1854–5, Russell observed that there seemed to be very few of the old familiar faces around. Small wonder he noticed the change; a Commons Select Committee would later report that the force suffered a 35 per cent mortality rate between the onset of winter and the coming of spring. A similarly sizeable proportion of Russell's other acquaintances would have been invalided home in the same period. Because the Army's failings were legion, military affairs quickly became a political hot potato which guaranteed at least the appearance of change, though it is instructive to note that the combined medical, transport and commissariat services remained a ludicrously small proportion of the Army's overall strength, and hence something of an Achilles heel, right to the end of our period.[3] At least the correspondents' colourful and enthusiastic descriptions of the heroic deeds of the war, coupled with their outspoken condemnation of the privations in the trenches and hospitals, brought about a fundamental change in how the public perceived the common soldiery. No longer to be regarded as a drunken beast best controlled with the lash, Thomas Atkins was transformed first into a martyr worthy of pity, and then, over the course of the next three decades, into a national hero. By the time of the Boer War, Tommy was teetering on the edge of respectability.

More often than not, we are told in history books that enlistment was regarded as the last resort of the desperate in the Victorian era, but this is a manifest over-simplification and the picture needs to be more subtly nuanced decade by decade. In reality both conditions of service and the Army's repute improved steadily in the aftermath of the Crimean War, so that there was a very pronounced difference between enlisting in 1845, when conditions genuinely were disgraceful, and joining up in 1875 when they were much improved. It is a military truism that the army reflects the society from which it is drawn. If the early Victorian Army was quartered in Dickensian conditions then this was merely a reflection of the condition of the urban working class at that time. As enlightenment and evangelism took hold of society and began to effect serious change for the better, so too the lot of the soldier improved.

In 1856 Sir Joseph Paxton rose to his feet in the Commons to point out that considerably more was spent on housing the average convict than the average soldier. With the post-Crimean furore at its height, Lord Ebrington, described by Sir John Fortescue as 'an enthusiast for sanitary science', toured most of the barracks and military hospitals in the land to inspect conditions. Having contracted an optical infection in one of the hospitals, Ebrington was blind in one eye by the time he made his damning report to the House of Commons. The military installations in and around London were singled out as being amongst the worst. Statistical analysis showed that where the annual mortality rate amongst men of military age in the civil population was between 7.5 and 9 in a thousand, it was 18 in the infantry, 11 in the cavalry and 20 in the Guards. In the specific case of deaths from consumption, the mortality rate in the Army was an extraordinary five times higher than amongst civilians.[4] Eventually even Her Majesty's Government could no longer deny that such statistical curiosities were a function of overcrowded barracks and poor sanitation. By 1860 mortality rates were beginning to show a downwards trend, though as usual there was a lack of governmental vigour in replacing crumbling barrack blocks with new ones.

If it were true that Queen Victoria's soldiers were enlisting only from desperation, then it would seem remarkable that an all-volunteer army was capable of fielding 225,000 men on the eve of the Cardwell reforms – not least because in a time of growing prosperity this reflected a proportionately huge increase of 85,000 men on its 1854 strength. Cardwell would reduce the size of the Army to around 185,000, but by the time of the Boer War it had crept back up to 233,560.[5] After the Mutiny, it was the norm for in excess of 70,000 members of the Regular Army to be stationed in India.

In reality men enlisted in the Victorian Army for much the same reasons they have always enlisted – some no doubt because they were desperate, some for comradeship, some to see India, some to test their mettle, some for a change, some because their fathers or brothers had gone before them, but most simply for a readily available job. Neither can such factors as patriotic duty or a sense of adventure be discounted: for example a remarkable 47,000 men enlisted in a 12-month period at the time of the Mutiny.[6] Regular soldiers were no better and no worse as men than the Victorian working class from which they were drawn. Of course there were bad pennies, but drunkenness in particular was nothing like as bad after the Crimea as it had been at the time of the Queen's accession. Boisterous when out on a spree for sure, by and large Victorian soldiers were a stolid, decent breed of men who lived their lives by a generally worthy honour code. It is a sad indictment of our time that the reputedly rough and ready Victorian soldiery abhorred the sort of foul language routinely used today by schoolchildren. As we have seen in James Wightman's account, even amidst the carnage of the most famous cavalry charge in history, with death and destruction raining in on all sides, the use of the word 'bloody' could elicit admonishment from one's peers.

If the social foppery of Regency England and the long peace after Waterloo had been generally detrimental to the relationship between officers and soldiers, the shared hardships of the Crimea, like those of the Peninsula, once again served to bridge the social divide and brought them much closer together. When it was over they did not again grow apart. Because regimental officers had been compelled to take on the wider system even to get rations or warm-weather clothing for their soldiers, the modern philosophy of benevolent paternalism towards the men in the ranks began to take a firm hold of the British officer corps.

The Cardwell Reforms, 1869–1872

As all of the campaigns covered in the book post-date the significant batch of reforms introduced between 1869 and 1872, it is appropriate to consider in some detail what Edward Cardwell was able to achieve and, just as importantly, to note what was left undone. His reforms were enshrined successively in the Army Enlistment Bill of 1870, the Regulation of the Forces Bill of 1871 and the Localisation Bill of 1872.[7] Born the son of a Liverpool merchant, Cardwell was the Secretary of State for War in a Liberal administration from 1868–74. Schooled at Winchester, he graduated from Balliol College Oxford, with a double first in classics and mathematics. After practising law for a few years, Cardwell became a Tory MP for one of the Oxford constituencies at the tender age of 29. By the 1850s he had found his way into government, serving successively as the Secretary of the Board of Trade, Secretary of State for Ireland, Chancellor of the Duchy of Lancaster and, 1864–6, Colonial Secretary. Along the way he had transferred his allegiance to the Liberal Party. Following the general election of 1868, Gladstone appointed him to the War Office. When it came to military affairs both Prime Minister and Secretary of State for War were interested first and foremost in financial retrenchment, though the stormy reception afforded to their Regulation of the Forces Bill would prove much more expensive than they bargained for.

There had been some fairly significant change at departmental level during and just after the Crimean War, but by and large it had been driven more by political expediency – the need to be seen to do something – than by *bona fide* expression of military necessity.[8] Cardwell took the view that it had all been conducted with indecent haste and little meaningful impact on War Office efficiency. At least the department now owned most of the essential administrative functions connected with the Army. Transport and supply had moved across from the Treasury in December 1854, and in May the following year the MGO finally ceded control of the gunners and sappers to Horse Guards. This was all well and good, except that Horse Guards itself showed little deference to the Secretary of State. When Cardwell came into office in 1868, the ancient constitutional haggle between Crown and Parliament for control of the Army had still not completely resolved itself.

The post of 'Officer Commanding-in-Chief'[9] had been occupied since 1856 by HRH the Duke of Cambridge, a first cousin of the Queen and a grandson of George III. The Duke had commanded the Guards Brigade at the Alma, and later at Inkerman where, it was whispered, he had been observed in a state of 'funk', a spiteful rumour which his detractors, Wolseley amongst them, would continue to propagate for decades. The C-in-C (let us call him) was responsible for command, discipline, training, promotions, appointments and readiness for war but did not give operational directives to commanders in the field, had no control over the Army's budget and, until Cardwell came on the scene, had never been explicitly subordinated to the Secretary of State. Rather he answered directly, where he was answerable at all, to the Queen, who like her late husband took a keen interest in Army affairs. The first of Cardwell's measures, the War Office Act of 1870, established a clear-cut constitutional arrangement which subordinated the C-in-C to the minister. As if to exert his new-found authority, Cardwell directed that the Duke move from Horse Guards to the new War Office in Pall Mall. The C-in-C insisted on having the last word by heading his stationery 'Horse Guards, Pall Mall'.[10]

The Army Enlistment Bill of 1870 was an important reform in that it aimed to attract a 'better class of recruit' and, for the first time, to generate a substantial and viable Army Reserve. It sought to achieve its goals by the simple expedient of curtailing the infantry soldier's engagement. Instead of committing to ten years' colour service with an option at that point to discharge or re-engage for a further 11 years, new recruits would now be required to complete six years' active duty with the colours and six years on the Reserve with a recall liability in time of war. Later this would be amended to a 7/5 split. Because men would come and go more often, a far greater throughput of recruits would be required. It also meant that within a few years the average age of the typical infantry battalion would start to come down. The Reserve would begin to swell with the first batch of six-year discharges in 1876. The eventual goal was a force of 80,000 men.

In practice, because soldiers were still permitted to re-engage at the six-year point, a step which some 25 per cent of infantrymen elected to take, the Reserve built up rather more slowly than had at first been anticipated. In 1874 short service was extended to the cavalry, where the deal was eight years' active duty and four on the reserve. In the Royal Artillery the incidence of re-engagement was about double that in the infantry. We may reasonably take such relatively high rates of re-engagement as a further indication that life in the late Victorian Army was nothing like as dreadful as some historians would have us believe. On the other hand, each year there were several thousand instances of desertion in the first few months of service. A not insignificant proportion of these were fraudulent enlistments, in which the 'recruit' intended only to pocket his enlistment bounty before absconding. Undoubtedly there were also many straightforward cases of disenchantment. Many formerly urban-dwelling recruits were undernourished or frail and suffered some form of physical breakdown leading to medical discharge. There was no real correlation then between the number of recruits gathered in and the number of trained soldiers emerging from basic training.

Cardwell reserved the right to reduce infantry colour service from a six-year engagement to a three-year one, but because this would have created an unrealistically high demand for recruits, he was never able to adopt the measure. Permissive three-year enlistments at reduced rates of pay were eventually introduced alongside the standard seven-year term in 1898 but, perhaps unsurprisingly, proved extremely unpopular. In failing to couple the introduction of short service with reform of the Army's antiquated pay system, Cardwell did nothing to assist the already hard-pressed recruiting sergeants. While the old style military 'lifer' had been prepared to tolerate the anachronistic system of stoppages from his pay on the basis that his employment was secure and he could look forward to a modest but worthwhile pension, the short-service soldier did not enjoy the same job security, did not qualify for a pension, yet could still expect to net only a few pennies from the headline 'shilling a day'. The failure to switch to a competitive flat rate of pay made it difficult for the Army to compete in the employment market and served to undermine one of the principal benefits of a short-service system.

The Duke of Cambridge was virulent in his opposition to short service, decrying the effect that a heavy preponderance of young soldiers would have on a battalion's 'steadiness' in action, but the rising stars of the Army, men such as Colonel Garnet Wolseley, fresh from the success of his Red River expedition, and Major George Colley, who from time to time had Cardwell's ear, backed the idea to the hilt. As if to vindicate the Duke's position some of the purportedly 'young' regiments sent to Zululand in the aftermath of Isandlwana proved decidedly 'windy', mostly as a function of the horror stories they were told about the slaughter of the 24th Regiment. At night-time they were inclined to take fright in their bivouacs and fire wildly into the shadows. As a result the incidence of flogging in the field, since 1868 the only environment in which it was still permitted, shot through the roof in the second half of the war.[11] If nothing else the alarming statistics from South Africa would help to precipitate the absolute prohibition of flogging by Gladstone's government in 1881, a measure enacted in the face of howls of protest from the Duke and other eminent military figures. Whilst in time the Army Reserve did indeed start to flourish, it was of little utility in fighting the small wars of empire which for the time being remained the Army's principal concern. Although there was a widespread call-up for the Boer War, the only other campaign in which limited recourse was made to the Reserve was the Egyptian intervention of 1882.

In accordance with the long-standing system known as 'purchase', officer vacancies in the Household Cavalry, the Brigade of Guards, the cavalry and the infantry counted as the incumbent's personal property and carried a cash value specified by Queen's Regulations. By way of example, the two majors in a line infantry battalion at the time of the Crimean War would be occupying vacancies with a capital value of £3,200 apiece. If the officer commanding was about to retire, the senior major would need to sell his vacancy to a captain and raise an additional £1,340 to acquire the vacant lieutenant colonelcy. To buy his majority the senior captain would have to round up £1,400 as his vacancy was worth only £1,800. For the senior lieutenant to become the junior captain required £1,100 on top of the £700 value of his vacancy. It was next to impossible to save such sums exclusively from Army pay. Even a lieutenant colonel drew less than a pound a day. For junior officers the combined cost of mess bills and uniforms invariably exceeded their salary. In most regiments a private income of several hundred pounds a year was an absolute necessity. It was society's way of ensuring that officers were also gentlemen. It was also true that, by the time of Victoria's accession, pomposity, snobbery and extravagance were completely out of control in the messes of the 'smarter' regiments, some of which drank fine clarets at breakfast.

Whilst the purchase system appears quite ridiculous to us today, it is important to bear in mind that the practice was of such long standing that it had originally served as a constitutional safeguard. After all, Cromwell's officers had been appointed purely on merit and they had turned from mere rebels into doctrinaire revolutionaries. But by the high Victorian age, times had moved on and both Crown and state had never been more secure. Purchase had long since become rotten to the core, with all sorts of highly irregular deals being struck. In his *History of the British Army*, Sir John Fortescue wrote, 'The system, being utterly illogical, iniquitous and indefensible, commended itself heartily to the British public.' Purchase was finally condemned as archaic by a royal commission convened in the immediate aftermath of the Crimean War. Even so it was not until Cardwell introduced the Regulation of the Forces Bill in 1871 that the prospect of abolition finally became a reality.

The purchase system allowed officers to buy promotions up to and including the rank of lieutenant colonel. Above that all promotion came by seniority. It was therefore in the interest of ambitious young officers to force their way to lieutenant colonel at the youngest possible age, so as to start their seniority clock running. Wellington for example had been able to obtain the lieutenant colonelcy of the 33rd Regiment in his late twenties. As a result he became a general officer while he was still in the prime of life. Because there were only a finite number of vacancies and it might be years before a vacancy in the next higher rank cropped up in one's own unit, well-to-do officers transferred freely between regiments in order to take full advantage of the system. Regardless of their ability, less prosperous officers might end up stagnating for many years in a relatively junior rank. Famously one of the great heroes of the Mutiny, Sir Henry Havelock, once remarked 'I was purchased over by three sots and two fools.' Although lieutenants in their late thirties were not uncommon, the social composition of the officer corps meant that the majority of officers could scrape together sufficient cash, when it came to their turn, generally by borrowing from their families.

Except in the case of a married officer killed in action, whose widow might benefit, a deceased officer's estate had no claim on his vacancy which passed as of right to the most senior officer in the next rank down. Thus when the subalterns of a regiment dined together, it was commonplace for them to raise their glasses with black humour to 'a bloody war and a pestilential season'. Surviving a costly action such as the January 1849 charge of the 24th Regiment at Chillianwallah, in which 22 officers were killed or wounded, might be a traumatic experience but, if one was lucky and the surgeons were as hopeless as usual, it was possible to retire to one's tent as a relatively junior lieutenant and wake up as the senior captain. If purchase had one thing to commend it, it was that it also doubled up as a pension system when an officer 'sold out' on retirement.

The artillery and the engineers did not practice purchase, but promoted on the basis of seniority alone. This amounted to a dead-man's-shoes system and made for a multitude of grey-haired RA and RE lieutenants. In a good many cases it took 25 years' service to attain the rank of captain. So aged were the RE colonels in the Crimea that without exception they broke down and had to be evacuated. As the abolition of purchase would reduce the infantry and cavalry to the same sorry state of affairs, it would be necessary to introduce terms and conditions of service incorporating a gratuity system as an inducement to premature retirement, rules for enforced retirement to make up any numerical shortfall, and a pension scheme for officers who had been retained over a full career. This work was undertaken in 1875 by a royal commission under the chairmanship of Lord Penzance.[12]

One of the problems for Cardwell in seeking to piece together a satisfactory compensation package was that of over-regulation payments. Although the practice was strictly speaking illegal, it had become commonplace for officers to pay additional cash sums to incumbents, above and beyond the regulation rate, often as an incentive to retire. The government could hardly be expected to compensate on such an irregular basis argued the ever thrifty Cardwell. Powerful vested interests in Parliament fought tooth and nail on the issue, however, arguing that, whilst the practice may not have been officially endorsed, the War Office had known full well what was going on. After a rocky ride through the Commons, the Regulation of the Forces Bill foundered in the Lords. Not to be so easily dissuaded, Cardwell had identified that the legal standing of purchase was enshrined not in an act of parliament but in a royal warrant. If the Queen could be prevailed upon to rescind the system by the same means, all might yet be well. As was her wont, Victoria made it icily clear to the Prime Minister that she did not much care for the idea, but ultimately had no choice but to agree. Outflanked by Cardwell's manoeuvre, the Lords relented and allowed the bill through. Purchase ended in November 1871 at the astronomical cost to the government of £6 million. Essentially the government had bought the Army's fighting regiments back from a stakeholder officer corps. The significance of the moment should not be underestimated; in effect the abolition of purchase marks the birth of the 'modern' British Army. The opportunity was also taken at this time to end the practice of 'double rank' in the Guards, under which a Grenadier captain, for example, automatically counted as a lieutenant colonel in the wider Army. The regulation bill also wrested control of the Militia from the lord lieutenants – an essential precursor to Cardwell's next major reform.

In February 1872 Cardwell introduced his Localisation Bill, one of the most significant moments in the long and distinguished history of the British infantry. This aimed to tie Regular battalions in pairs to specific county or regional recruiting areas, and to create an affiliation between the Regular units and two corresponding Militia battalions. There were to be 66 'brigade sub-districts' nationwide, each with its own depot, many of which would have to be built from scratch; hence today a good many of the old county towns are home to a red-brick barracks dating back to the 1870s. The most important operational aspect of the system was that the two regular battalions would be required to alternate between service at home and service overseas.[13] All newly trained recruits went to the home battalion in the first instance, which was chartered to provide annual drafts to its sister battalion overseas. It had long been government practice to save money by paring home establishments to the bone, so that apart from the handful of battalions which at any one time had been warned for a forthcoming tour of duty overseas, units on the home establishment were allowed only a little over 500 men. With officer's batmen, fatigues, guards and a myriad of other administrative details told off for the day, a company commander might be lucky to parade 40 men for drill or training – unless of course he happened to be riding to hounds, which many officers did twice a week. Tight establishments and the loss from the annual draft combined to make the home battalions all but operationally non-effective. In a memorable phrase Wolseley referred to them as 'squeezed lemons'.

At the time of Victoria's accession the infantry consisted of 109 battalions split between 3 Guards regiments, 99 line regiments and the Rifle Brigade. The Grenadier, Coldstream and Scots Fusilier Guards[14] each had 1st and 2nd Battalions, as did the 1st Regiment of Foot (The Royal Scots) and the 60th Rifles. The remaining 97 regiments of the line had only one battalion. The Rifle Brigade (formerly the 95th) had been taken out of the line after Waterloo, in recognition of its distinguished service in the battle, and also had two battalions. Just as the Grenadier Guards claimed the right of the line as a place of honour on parade, so the Rifle Brigade now claimed the left.

In the immediate aftermath of the Crimean War an extra 28 battalions were formed. First the 60th Rifles and the Rifle Brigade were authorized 3rd and 4th Battalions, and in 1858 the 2nd–25th Regiments of Foot were told to re-raise their old 2nd Battalions. In 1861 nine entirely new regiments came into being when, in the aftermath of the Mutiny, the old HEIC European battalions were transferred into the service of the Crown as the 101st to 109th Regiments. Made up of drifters, barflies, ex-seamen, time-expired Regulars and young Catholics recruited from a by now blighted rural Ireland, units such as the Madras Fusiliers were hard-fighting, hard-drinking outfits. Because the men in the ranks were not consulted over such a fundamental change to their terms and conditions of service, it proved to be a controversial transition and triggered the so-called 'White Mutiny', a mercifully bloodless but nonetheless serious outbreak of dissent. In the end it was resolved by giving the men the choice of transfer or discharge. In six cases the essentially Irish character of the new regiments would be reflected in their post-1881 titles. The HEIC gunners migrated contentedly enough into the Royal Artillery, happy no doubt to have somebody else to talk to, while three cavalry regiments also joined the Queen's service as the 19th, 20th and 21st Hussars.[15]

By the time of the Cardwell reforms the infantry consisted of 3 regiments of Foot Guards, 109 regiments of the line and the Rifle Brigade; 113 regiments in all, fielding 147 battalions between them. As the Guards were not routinely committed to duties overseas, Cardwell had only 110 regiments with which to police and safeguard the empire. Problematically only 27 of them had two or more battalions. In the 83 others the word 'regiment' was effectively synonymous with battalion. All told then, the Secretary for War had 141 battalions of line infantry and Rifles to incorporate into what would become known as the 'Cardwell System'. The two-battalion regiments presented no great difficulty, needing only to be localized. The single-battalion regiments on the other hand needed to be both localized and merged. The two four-battalion rifle regiments would not be localized, but would operate from a shared depot at Winchester. The Guards were unaffected by the changes. Neither they nor the Rifles had affiliated part-time units.

Instead of grasping the amalgamation nettle and upsetting too many vested interests at once, Cardwell settled for a twinning system in which two single-battalion regiments shared one of his brigade depots. Amalgamation into re-titled regiments of two battalions would have to wait until 1881, when the requisite mergers were finally enacted by the then Secretary for War, Hugh Childers. Although the much revered regimental numbers technically disappeared at this point, they continued to be used informally in the first 25 regiments of the line. The old Militia regiments were subsumed into the new localized regiments as their 3rd and 4th (Militia) Battalions. Inevitably it was a time of great turmoil and upset. The 26th Regiment (The Cameronians), for example, was merged with the 90th Light Infantry (Perthshire Volunteers), a change that was especially traumatic for the officers and men of the 90th who lost their name, their much treasured regimental number, and were required to become riflemen into the bargain. The two regiments became respectively the 1st and 2nd Battalions The Cameronians (The Scotch Rifles), though in December of the same year the Queen was pleased to approve the substitution of 'Scottish' for the out of vogue 'Scotch'. The new regiment's part-time 3rd and 4th Battalions were raised from what had formerly been the 2nd Royal Lanarkshire Militia, and were likewise required to become riflemen. Inevitably most serving soldiers were pierced to the heart by such wholesale change to the revered regimental system within which they had earned their spurs. But localization also brought significant benefits. The flow of men from the Militia units into their full-time sister battalions made an increasingly significant contribution to the never-ending quest for Regular Army recruits. Local civil–military relations also underwent a transformation; now whenever a home battalion departed for war or an overseas posting it was seen off from its home station by cheering crowds anxious to wish 'their' boys the best of luck. Both the 3rd (Militia) and 4th (Militia) Battalions of the Cameronians were amongst the part-time units mobilized for campaign service in the Boer War.

It is of note that throughout the late Victorian era the infantry made up more than 65 per cent of the Army's strength. The Cardwell system relied on the number of battalions serving overseas remaining at a constant 50 per cent or less. Since Waterloo, however, the old rule of thumb had been that a battalion could expect to spend only five of every 15 years at home; or to put it another way, it was a long-standing norm for two-thirds of the infantry to be serving in the colonies. In 1872, the year upon which Cardwell had based his planning assumptions, there was a perfect balance of 70 battalions at home and 71 overseas. The Ninth Cape Frontier War and the Zulu War provided the first major spanners in the works; by mid-1879 there were 82 battalions overseas and only 59 under-strength units at home.[16] The Cardwell System was fated never to recover its equilibrium. Once again Parliament had established an Army that was far too small to sustain its international ambitions.

While the infantry was undergoing these painful changes, a baffling series of reorganizations was taking place amongst the Army's cadre of professional logisticians. After the ill-considered disbandment of Wellington's Royal Waggon Train in the 1830s, the service had been without a logistic corps of any kind until January 1855, when desperate times in the Crimea led to the formation of the Land Transport Corps. This was disbanded after the war, to be replaced in 1856 by the Military Train, which at a strength of only 1,200 men was unfeasibly small. In 1869 the other ranks were moved into a new Army Service Corps (ASC), which was to be officered by members of the Control Department. In December 1875 the officers were renamed the Commissariat & Transport Department. In August 1881 the ASC was re-titled the Commissariat & Transport Corps, but the old name pretty much said it all, and in December 1888 officers and men alike were merged into a resurrected Army Service Corps.

Cardwell's reforms were undoubtedly important, but they were far from revolutionary and failed to address a number of key issues. Foremost amongst them was the Army's inability to deploy a significant expeditionary force without recourse to mobilization of the Reserve. A second serious defect was the continuing absence of a general staff. Although the formidable performance of the Prussian General Staff had caught the eyes of the world during the Franco-Prussian War, there would be no comparable British equivalent until 1906. Initially the very idea had been regarded with distrust by British parliamentarians, who feared that a general staff would act as a focus for creeping militarism. Only in the aftermath of the Boer War could the politicians be prevailed upon to modify their stance. It is perhaps not that widely appreciated that both the short-service system and the localization concept had been directly cribbed from Prussia, where a (conscripted) recruit served three years with his regiment, four years in the reserve, and was then transferred into the part-time Landwehr. Each of the provincial army HQs exercised peacetime authority over all the conscript and part-time units in its area, and on mobilization led them off to war as their corps headquarters.[17] The British version of localization was at best a pale imitation and had no comparable operational dimension.

The Changing Nature of War

The 60-year interval between the Crimea and Mons was time aplenty for serious reform programmes to make a real difference. Yet since Sir Redvers Buller also took a contemptible army into the field in South Africa in 1899, it must surely follow that three-quarters of the breathing space allowed to the Army between its major European embroilments was squandered; that serious modernization was squeezed into little more than a decade; and that so dramatic a transformation, in so short a time, can only have come at the price of great trauma. The trauma of course is readily identifiable: it came at the hands of the Boers whose field-craft and instincts for self-preservation led to the first genuine example of modern warfare, and subsequently, thanks to the stubbornness of the so-called 'bitter-enders', to the first recognizably modern guerrilla war.

The reality was not that Britain's general officers had conspired to squander 50 precious years, but rather that weapons technology had been continuously shifting under their feet. As a result none of the tactical norms they grew up with as regimental officers were still applicable by the time they became generals. For reasons largely beyond their control as individuals, the Army as a whole failed to adapt to change quickly enough. The failure occurred not in the physical or moral domains but in the conceptual. In the horse-and-musket era when time spent on the parade ground was virtually synonymous with training for war, the best-drilled troops on the battlefield usually won the day. The Queen's Birthday Parade still serves to demonstrate that there have never been better-drilled troops than British regulars, but as firepower improved and extended-order formations became the tactical norm, the importance of close-order drill as a battlefield skill went into terminal decline. Because nobody in the British Army had yet fought a modern European war, nobody knew except in the most superficial sense how to prepare for one. The enormous proportion of training time devoted to the attainment of drill-square perfection within the daily routine of the average battalion remained virtually unaltered but, from about 1860 onwards, this no longer constituted time well spent. That this was so dawned on most regimental officers in the 1870s, but it would take the passage of another two decades and many months of torture on the South African veldt for the Army to learn how it might better train itself in peacetime for the onset of modern war.

With the introduction of rifled barrelling as standard (greater accuracy to longer ranges), and the development of breech-loading designs (increased rates of fire), the reach and effect of the infantry battalion changed beyond all recognition in the second half of the century. In the British service the transformation began with the adoption of the 'Rifle Musket 1851', known colloquially as the Minié rifle, a weapon of .702-inch calibre which, although it was a muzzle-loader like the smoothbore muskets which preceded it, had a rifled barrel and was sighted to 900 yards. It was used in the Crimea by all but the 4th Division and gave the British infantry a formidable advantage over its smoothbore-armed adversaries. Even before the war was over the 'Enfield Rifle Musket 1853' had made its debut in the trenches. This was sighted to 1,000 yards, had a reduced calibre of .577-inch and was 54 inches long. Because its paper cartridge needed to be a particularly tight fit in the barrel, it was greased in animal fat for ease of ramming. The top of the cartridge had to be bitten off to access the usual measured charge of black powder, a practice which brought the rifleman's lips into contact with the animal fat. In India, of course, this would act as a catalyst to the growing disaffection of the HEIC sepoys. The Enfield rifle was in service 1853–65 and played a prominent part in the suppression of the mutiny it helped to ignite. In order to introduce a serviceable breech-loader quickly, the breech mechanism designed by Jacob Snider of New York was retro-fitted to the formerly muzzle-loading Enfield. The Snider-Enfield hybrid was enhanced by the adoption in 1867 of Colonel Edward Boxer's new centre-fire rolled-brass cartridge. The weapon saw service in Abyssinia and in Wolseley's Ashanti campaign but was only ever a stopgap design.

In 1871 the Martini-Henry was adopted. The Mark I version went on general issue in 1874, and with certain minor modifications was quickly upgraded to a Mark II pattern of 1876 and a Mark III of 1879. The rifle was sighted to 1,450 yards and against massed targets there was some merit in engaging with company volleys at 1,000 yards. It was more usual for company commanders to commence firing at 600–800 yards, whilst the effective battle range for aimed shots against point targets was 300–400 yards. It was crucial that company officers judged range accurately in giving their fire-control orders, and it was important that the appropriate adjustments were made on the rear sight as the range narrowed. The rifle enjoyed such great ease of operation that the firer could get off eight well-aimed shots a minute with time to spare, though such excessive rates of fire were never permitted in action. By the standards of the day it was a world-beater. As we saw in the prologue, it had its faults: in particular it did not much care for sand, whilst protracted firing quickly fouled the deep-cut grooves of the rifling, an effect which could cause shoulder-bruising recoil and, worse, a relatively high incidence of stoppages. The so-called 'lunger' bayonet was issued for the first time in 1876. Its blade was 22 inches long, triangular in profile and served to bring the overall length of Martini and bayonet to a formidable 6 feet. A short-barrelled carbine version of the Martini came into service with the cavalry in 1877, ending a period of turmoil in which a great many carbines had been trialled in quick succession.

Still weapons technology was moving on apace. In 1888 the .303-inch Lee-Metford was adopted. This was a magazine-fed, bolt-action weapon from which the legendary Short Magazine Lee-Enfield or SMLE would be derived. The first magazine for the Lee-Metford contained eight rounds, but a later mark was capable of housing ten. It was also possible to load the rifle round by round, thus preserving the contents of the magazine for any unexpected crisis in the battle. The much-reduced calibre enabled the soldier to carry many more cartridges than had been the case with the bulkier and heavier .450-inch Boxer, though the official increase in first-line scales from 70 rounds to 90 was not directly proportionate in terms of weight. Four years after the Lee-Metford was first introduced, an innovative cartridge incorporating cordite, Alfred Nobel's new smokeless propellant, dispensed with the characteristic bank of white smoke that up to that point had always shrouded the infantry firing line. Crucially, in terms of the art of war, the proliferation of smokeless powder meant that it was now becoming increasingly difficult to locate the enemy firer.

In concert with new-fangled multi-barrelled machine-guns, such as the Gatling and the Gardner, the breech-loading rifle began to stifle mass, shock-action and frontal assault. If the American Civil War suggested to the intelligent European observer that the old close-order formations were no longer tenable, the Austro-Prussian War of 1866 put the issue beyond doubt. Across Europe the tactical emphasis passed to open-order skirmish lines, coupled with more pragmatic use of ground and cover. Such drills demanded much greater initiative at lower levels of command than ever before. If anything, demonstrations of initiative below the level of regimental or battalion commander had been positively frowned upon up to this point. In part the British preoccupation with the drill square had been all about the suppression of individual initiative, for the best soldiers on the horse-and-musket battlefield were those who responded like automatons to the beat of the side-drum. Now subalterns, sergeants and even privates had to think for themselves – up to a point at least.

The shifting nature of warfare was far from imperceptible to British military theorists, who argued as eruditely back and forth as did their French and German counterparts. One of the most thoughtful and perceptive soldiers of the

Victorian age was Colonel G. F. R. (George) Henderson, a veteran of Tel-el-Kebir, whose observations on the art of war are quoted here at a number of chapter headings. Serious military thinkers of Henderson's ilk were far from numerous, but between them they were influential enough to ensure that Prussian 'swarm' tactics were not blindly emulated but rather improved on by the British infantry. The change resulted in battalions forming not in their traditional two-deep line of companies abreast, but in three separate groups of companies – the firing line, the supports and the main body, usually in a 2:2:4 configuration. The distance between the extended-order firing line and the supports depended on the ground but was typically 150–200 yards, while the main body was generally to be found some 200–300 yards behind the supports.[18] It would be quite wrong, as people are still sometimes wont to do, to imagine the British infantry moving about the battlefields of the Boer War in inflexible close-order formations, although on one notorious occasion at Magersfontein the Highland Brigade was caught flat-footed as it was emerging from a night approach march.

Organization of the Infantry

Throughout the period the full-strength infantry battalion was organized into a small headquarters staff, eight fighting companies, a band and a pioneer section. The all-powerful 'officer commanding' was usually a lieutenant colonel, though he might on the basis of promotion by seniority be raised to full colonel during the course of his command. It was not unusual up to the abolition of purchase for his tour of duty to span a decade, though thereafter five years became the norm. The senior non-commissioned man in the battalion was the sergeant-major. The eight companies were divided into two wings, each of four companies under the overall command of a major. Individual companies were commanded by captains and consisted of four sections. The company commanders were assisted by two subaltern officers who each led a half-company of two sections. Throughout the period senior subalterns were known as lieutenants, whilst junior subalterns went from being called ensigns, to sub-lieutenants and finally second lieutenants.

A section was commanded by a sergeant, assisted by a corporal and one or two lance corporals, and typically contained around 20–25 private soldiers. It would not be correct to think of the Victorian section as the equivalent of a latter-day platoon, as it contained no internal subdivisions. As the rank of Warrant Officer Class II had yet to be contrived, there was no such thing as a company sergeant-major. Instead the senior non-commissioned man in the company was its colour-sergeant whose duties stand fairly ready comparison to those of the latter-day CSM. There were also two drummers and one pioneer per company, though the pioneers, the regimental artisans, were usually pooled by the quartermaster and employed as an eight-man section under the pioneer corporal. The members of the band were musicians first and foremost, but doubled up in the field as stretcher bearers.

The battalion staff included the adjutant, the colonel's right-hand man, an appointment customarily held by the senior lieutenant, and the instructor of musketry, usually but not invariably the next senior subaltern.[19] Each battalion had its own medical officer attached from the Army Medical Department (AMD). The doctor generally held the rank of 'surgeon', the broad equivalent of a regimental captain, though might on occasion be a more experienced 'surgeon-major'. Other specialist officers included the paymaster and the quartermaster. Although the quartermaster enjoyed honorary status as an officer, he was usually a highly regarded ex-sergeant-major posted in from another regiment. He was assisted in administering the battalion by the quartermaster-sergeant, the next senior NCO after the sergeant-major.

While cavalry were seldom in short supply on the sub-continent, the same could not be said of Africa. From the mid-1870s onwards it became increasingly commonplace for infantry units serving in African campaigns to improvise an *ad hoc* mounted infantry (MI) section. The idea was formalized in 1888 with the formation of a number of mounted infantry schools. This enabled battalion commanders to maintain a cadre of around 30 soldiers trained in equitation, and gave the commander of a three-battalion brigade the option of grouping the sections as 'brigade troops' to form a MI company.

Cavalry and Artillery

If broadly speaking the infantry did its best to think for itself in reflecting the new realities of the age of the breech-loader, the cavalry and artillery were a little too inclined to copy the victors of 1870. The Prussians had concentrated their guns at the point of decision and fired over open sights at relatively short ranges. They also massed their cavalry and looked for things to charge, exactly as their Napoleonic predecessors had done, an obsolescent practice for which their British counterparts also retained a serious predilection. There was, it seemed, little to be learned from the unhappy French. Napoleon III's generals might have thought of themselves as cutting-edge practitioners of the military art, but the subsequent course of the war was ample testimony to their true worth. Not merely out-generalled at the strategic and operational levels, they also lost just about every tactical-level engagement along the way. However, just because Prussian artillery and cavalry tactics had undone the hapless French, it did not necessarily follow that they must perforce provide perfect tactical templates. Had the German Army fought the Boers, there is every likelihood that it would have fallen into precisely the same traps as the British. Almost certainly the Prussian inclination to bludgeon their way through a defensive position would have resulted in far heavier casualties. Where in this volume we speak of engagements in which a thousand men are lost as disasters, it will be as well to bear in mind the far heavier losses sustained on the North American and European battlefields of the era. In the meantime, however, many British officers noted and admired the Prussian way of war.

In fact the American Civil War would have provided a far better model for the modernization of the British cavalry than the war of 1870. The chances are that a cavalry genius like J. E. B. Stuart would have run rings round the Boers – it is easy to imagine him razing Bloemfontein to the ground in the first month of hostilities. Yet for some reason British cavalry experts chose to disparage American cavalrymen as mere mounted infantrymen. But that was precisely the point – the lance and sabre had had their day and the Americans had both realized it and then proved it, long before it dawned on their European counterparts.

The British cavalry consisted of three Household regiments – 1st and 2nd Life Guards, and the Royal Horse Guards (The Blues) – and 28 other regiments. By now the distinction between the light and heavy classes of cavalry no longer had any tactical significance, except in so far as a handful of regiments, such as the 17th and the 21st, were roled as lancers. The rest were either dragoon guards, dragoons or hussars who, whilst they all looked wildly different in their splendid dress uniforms, were indistinguishable from one another in the field. Originally a cavalry regiment contained no larger tactical sub-unit than the troop, but from the Cardwell era onwards it became the norm to group the eight 70-man troops by pairs to form four squadrons. Often only three of the squadrons proceeded on active service.

Previously Royal Artillery batteries were independent 6-gun units under the command of a major. Now they were being grouped in threes under a lieutenant colonel to form an artillery 'brigade' of 18 guns, later confusingly termed at the time of the Boer War a 'brigade-division'. In policing the Empire, however, the battery continued to be the Royal Artillery's tactical mainstay. Typically they paraded 150–180 all ranks. Internally the battery was divided into three divisions, each of two guns under the command of a lieutenant. A single gun, its limber and its accompanying ammunition wagon constituted a sub-division and was commanded by a sergeant. For the avoidance of confusion, in 1889 divisions and sub-divisions were re-designated as sections and sub-sections. The battery commander had a captain and a sergeant-major to assist him. Batteries of the Royal Horse Artillery or RHA were generally brigaded in support of the cavalry and utilised smaller-calibre guns than the conventional field battery, in effect trading off weight of fire in favour of superior mobility. For the officers and men of the RHA 'dash' was a byword, not that field batteries were not also capable of flying around the battlefield at the gallop when the situation demanded it. The really heavy ordnance was to be found in much more ponderous siege batteries and, save in early Victorian India (when there was still a multiplicity of hill-forts and fortress-towns to subjugate), was not customarily included in a mobile column or field force.

At first British designers had been at the cutting edge in the development of breech-loading field guns. The Armstrong 12-pounder RBL (rifled breech-loader) had seen active service in the 1860s in the Second China War and the Second Maori War, whilst both the Armstrong and the Whitworth were used extensively during the American Civil War. Towards the end of the decade the Royal Artillery decided to abandon breech-loaders and revert to muzzle-loaders, which it had concluded, in a not particularly prescient piece of thinking, were more reliable, simpler to operate, cheaper to manufacture and safer. From 1871 to 1885 the field artillery made use of a 13-pounder RML (rifled muzzle-loader) with a maximum range of 4,000 yards, while the horse artillery employed a 9-pounder RML of broadly comparable range. In the mid-1880s, with a number of technical difficulties having been overcome in the meantime, RMLs were at last replaced with breech-loaders, a 15-pounder and a 12-pounder respectively, both with a maximum range of 5,600 yards.

When it came to refining the tactical practices of the artillery, all that was required was a good dose of common sense. Once the world's infantry had been equipped with small-bore rifles sighted to 1,500 yards, it should have been a relatively short mental leap to the conclusion that bringing batteries into action at 1,000 yards was not on balance a particularly sound idea. Yet still Colonel Charles Long would behave as he did at Colenso – of which more later.

Deficiencies in Training

Two particular difficulties exerted a restraining influence on the modernization of the British Army. One was the preponderance of colonial small wars, each of them different in some way from the last, a fact of life which served to impede the development of standing tactical doctrines; and the other was the absence of adequate training facilities, a function as ever of governmental parsimony. With the exception of Aldershot, first acquired in 1853, and the Curragh in Ireland, both of them home to largely random agglomerations of units, there were no training areas capable of accommodating formation-level combined-arms training. It was not until 1898, two years after the government first acquired 40,000 acres of Salisbury Plain, that anything was done to remedy the situation. That summer large-scale annual manoeuvres were resumed for the first time since 1875, the year in which the government had cancelled them as a cost-cutting measure. Even now the Army undertook its field training in all the magnificence of its full-dress uniforms, hardly realistic preparation for the low cunning that would soon be required on the South African veldt.

But it was not merely space that the Army needed in order to train properly. Officer education was also in a dreadful state. Although the Duke of Cambridge had founded the Army Staff College at Camberley in 1858, its instructional staff was tiny (a colonel-commandant and eight others), and its output, based on completion of a two-year course of instruction, was a paltry 20 officers per annum, or 40 officers under instruction at any one time.[20] The size of the new intake was increased to 24 in 1870 and to 32 in 1886, still nothing like enough to meet the requirement, so that the majority of officers employed on the staff continued to be untrained for the role. At regimental level next to nothing was done to further the professionalism of the officer corps. Bored by Army bureaucracy and an interminable sequence of parades and inspections, many officers sought refuge in long leaves and vigorous field sports. It was not unusual for the colonel, the majors and the company commanders to be on leave for five months of the year, including an unbroken block of three months straddling the Christmas period.

If, like Lord Raglan's army, Sir Redvers Buller's 1st Army Corps of 1899 was also contemptible, then it was for a substantially different set of reasons. Shortages and crippling administrative inefficiency were no longer the issue. Buller's force was no less well drilled than Raglan's, but as we have seen this no longer meant that it was very well trained. The dramatic transformation in firepower meant that it was now vital that NCOs and soldiers be allowed, both as individuals and as small teams, to make the best possible use of ground and cover, and that they be permitted to fire their weapons at times and targets of their own choosing. But, while some commanders and regiments had accrued a good deal of operational experience in the small wars of empire, the Army as a whole shared no common doctrine, had not undergone any worthwhile combined-arms training, and was not yet ready to reach out and touch twentieth-century warfare. Its preoccupation with the moral effect of mass and with tightly controlled volley fire would continue to dog it well into the Boer War. Many regular soldiers were indifferent shots to begin with, while most of the mobilized reservists were hopelessly out of practice. Minor tactics were only part of the problem; higher tactics, staff work, communications, combined-arms co-operation and generalship all need to be practised in an annual round of formation exercises. Redvers Buller had never seen a khaki-clad army corps before attempting to command one in war. None of the lieutenant generals had been taught how to handle a division. Most of the brigade commanders had to introduce themselves to their battalion commanders in Natal. Many staff officers reported to their commander at the gangplank of a troopship.

One thing remained constant between 1854 and 1899 – the courage, resilience, selflessness and determination of the ordinary regimental officers and their men. By the time the war with the Boers came to its long-delayed end in 1902, the Army had changed forever. It was because the British were exposed in South Africa to an early glimpse of the future face of war, that they were able just over a decade later to field the fine fighting force that would be remembered in history as the Old Contemptibles. Time now then to consider the Army's progression from scarlet to khaki, from Snider to Lee-Enfield, from Gatling to Vickers, and, most importantly of all, from amateur to professional – a transformation which occurred in the school of hard knocks that was Queen Victoria's empire.

Chapter 2

'WOUNDED AND LEFT ON AFGHANISTAN'S PLAINS'

The Battle of Maiwand, 27 July 1880

One Jelaladin Ghilzai, who says he is in Sir Louis Cavagnari's secret service, has arrived in hot haste from Kabul, and solemnly states that yesterday morning the Residency was attacked by three regiments who had mutinied for their pay, they having guns, and being joined by a portion of six other regiments. The Embassy and escort were defending themselves when he left about noon yesterday.

Telegram delivered to General Roberts at Simla, 5 September 1879[1]

In 1876 a career diplomat and erstwhile poet called Robert Bulwer-Lytton took passage for India.[2] No ordinary traveller, the newly ennobled 1st Earl of Lytton would disembark as one of the most powerful men in the world. The new Viceroy was 47 years of age but, a great chest-length beard notwithstanding, looked much younger. Brilliant, resolute and occasionally mercurial, his critics whispered that his appointment owed much to his father's friendship with Prime Minister Disraeli.

Relations with Russia were no better now than they had been at the time of the Crimean War. When war broke out between the Tsar and the Ottoman Empire in 1877, it seemed highly likely that Britain would once again be drawn in. If it came to a fight it would take place in the Bosporus, a job for the Royal Navy, and, of more direct relevance to Lord Lytton, in southern Central Asia, where recent Russian encroachments posed a more immediate threat to Afghanistan, and hence to British India, than ever before.

Where previous viceroys had pursued a passive frontier policy, encapsulated by one of their number as 'masterly inactivity', Lytton arrived in India with a

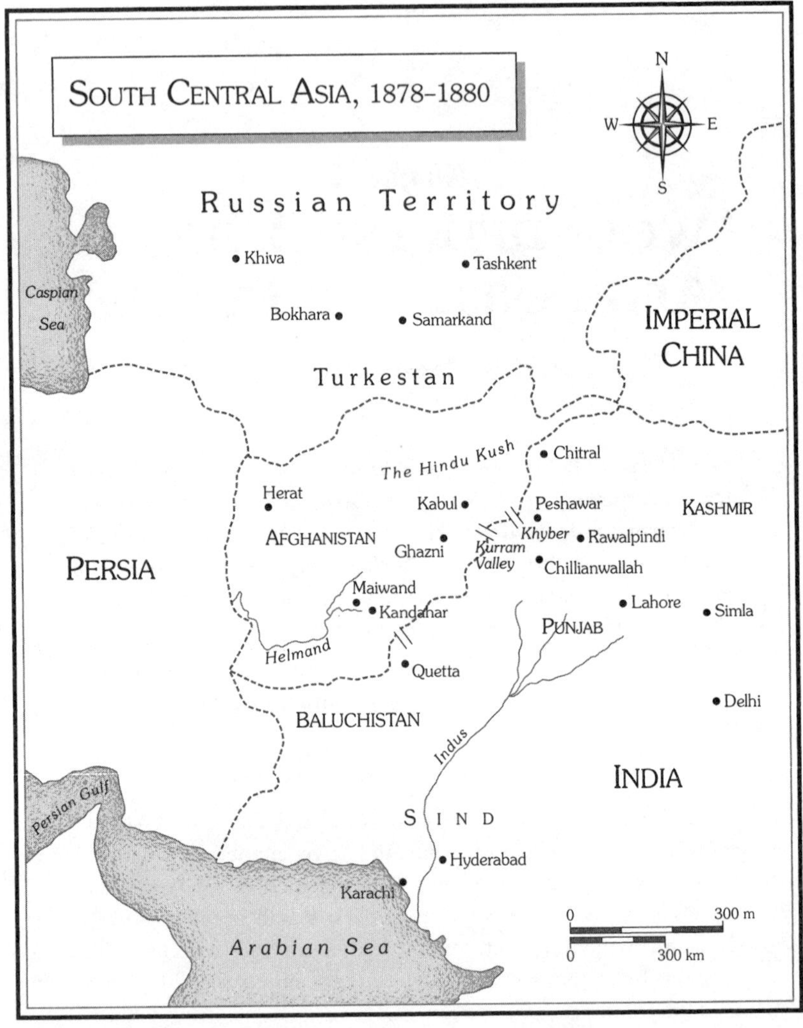

decidedly robust 'forward policy' in mind. The new strategy maintained that the sub-continent's defence should be delimited not by the arbitrary dotted lines to be found running through the tribal areas on the political maps of the day, but by the formidable natural barrier defined by the Hindu Kush. The British sphere of influence would be extended not by means of some vast and crude annexation of southern Afghanistan, but by the presence of an innocuous but strategically influential diplomatic mission in Kabul. One of Lytton's most important priorities on assuming his appointment, therefore, would be persuading Sher Ali, the *amir* (or prince) of Afghanistan, to welcome a British envoy.

Lytton was able to make little early progress with his initiative and in the event it was the Russians who secured the diplomatic advantage. In June 1878 General Stolietoff set off from Samarkand to lead a purportedly uninvited mission to Kabul. He was accompanied by 6 other officers, 22 cossacks and 15 naval ratings.[3] St Petersburg was to claim later that Stolietoff's embassy was a local initiative carried out without the sanction of national government, but as a result of some significant troop movements which took place at precisely this time, the contemporaneous British suspicion that Sher Ali was toying with the idea of a military adventure has never been convincingly disproved. Back in the diplomatic mainstream, the international climate was taking a turn for the better. The Russo-Turkish War having come to an end, the Bismarck-brokered Treaty of Berlin, signed in June 1878, was meant to herald a new and amicable relationship between the Queen Empress and the Tsar.

Not to be outdone by Stolietoff, Lytton hurriedly assembled a diplomatic mission of his own under the leadership of General Sir Neville Chamberlain, C-in-C of the Madras Presidency, and despatched it post-haste for the Khyber Pass. For the sake of form the expedition was preceded by a politely worded notification to Kabul that it was on the way.[4] Lytton's note arrived with Sher Ali on 19 August, a time of great trauma for the amir, whose favourite son and heir-apparent, the 15-year-old Abdullah Jan, died the same day. A week later the mischievous Stolietoff enquired of a grieving Sher Ali whether he intended to admit Chamberlain or not. In response the amir invited the general's advice. Tricky, said Stolietoff, with scant regard for the new Anglo-Russian rapprochement, to have embassies from two sworn enemies in one's capital at the same time.[5] And so the die was cast. Taking Stolietoff's words as representing some form of Russian military guarantee, Sher Ali gave orders that the British were to be rebuffed at the frontier. August had turned over to September by the time Chamberlain's mission reached the Khyber and the hilltop fort at Ali Masjid.

Try as he might Chamberlain's political adviser, Major P. L. N. Cavagnari, was unable to persuade the Afghan commander at Ali Masjid to allow the mission to pass. Faiz Mohamed was adamant that if the British tried to press on he would have no choice but to fire on them in accordance with his orders. As the negotiations wore on Chamberlain noticed that the mood in the Afghan entourage was turning ugly and wisely ordered a withdrawal. His report on the slight to British prestige was hastily conveyed to Lytton at Simla:

> Nothing could have been more distinct, nothing more humiliating to the dignity of the British Crown and nation; and I believe that but for the decision and tact of Cavagnari at one period of the interview, the lives of the British officers and the native following were in considerable danger.[6]

Having first secured an at best hesitant blessing from Whitehall, Lytton presented Kabul with an ultimatum on 2 November 1878. It was timed to expire not quite three weeks later and insisted that Sher Ali must apologize in writing for the slight to the dignity of the Queen Empress and admit a British envoy forthwith.

> Nevertheless you have now received a Russian Envoy at your capital at a time when a war was believed to be imminent in which England and Russia would have been arrayed on opposite sides . . . in consequence of this hostile action on your part, I have assembled Her Majesty's forces on your frontier. But I desire to give you a last opportunity of averting the calamities of war . . . Unless these conditions are accepted fully and plainly by you, and your acceptance received by me not later than the 20th of November, I shall be compelled to consider your intentions as hostile, and to treat you as a declared enemy of the British Government.[7]

As anticipated Lytton's ultimatum ran down without eliciting a suitably conciliatory response from Kabul, a final slight which the British had resolved to treat as an immediate trigger to hostilities. In the meantime there would be a vast amount of warlike preparation to be done.

The Afghan military could be expected to comprise three principal elements – uniformed and conventionally organized regular units of horse, foot and artillery, tribal fanatics from the hills, and looters and opportunists amongst the townsmen. Whilst they were not in general terms fit to match their Indian Army counterparts in a stand-up fight, Afghan regulars were only marginally less well-armed and equipped. The principal differences lay in their comparative indiscipline and the quality of their small arms. The Afghan infantry carried muzzle-loading Enfields, many of which had been provided by the Government of India in happier times. At two rounds a minute the Enfield could not begin to compare with the breech-loading Snider now in service with Indian regiments. Sher Ali had spent a good deal of Afghanistan's paltry governmental revenues on equipping his army and had provided it with a great walled barracks and arsenal on the outskirts of Kabul known as the Sherpur Cantonment.

Then as now, the rural areas of Afghanistan were infested with countless irregular militias which owed allegiance to their leaders on the basis of district, ethnic, tribal, clan or familial affiliations. Just about any combination of loyalties was possible whilst, for the average Afghan hill fighter, changing sides could be a seasonal occurrence and attracted no great stigma. Such militias were armed with a great variety of firearms ranging from local reproductions of the Enfield, to old style flintlocks like the India Pattern 'Brown Bess' or locally manufactured *jezails*. Afghan hillmen were notoriously cruel and it was not without good reason that to be taken alive was regarded, in the words of the cliché, as a fate worse than death. Most townspeople also kept a formidable array of firearms and knives under the bed, and in the right set of circumstances could be readily rabble-roused as 'the Kabul mob' or the 'Kandahar mob'. Finally an Afghan fighting force might contain many thousands of *ghazis*, religious fanatics whipped up by the mullahs to die as martyrs in the name of Islam. Often identifiable by their flowing white robes, their unsubtle political aspirations seldom extended much beyond the peremptory extermination of the faithless. The hills north and west of Kandahar contained large populations of the most fanatical strains of Islamist.

The Invasion of Afghanistan, 21 November 1878

The plan for the invasion involved some 36,000 British and Indian troops split between three strong columns operating largely independently of one another. The military objectives were limited to points south of the Hindu Kush and, for the time being at least, the capture of Kabul formed no part of the British plan. The northern column would be known as the Peshawar Valley Field Force and would advance from Peshawar to Jalalabad via Ali Masjid and the Khyber Pass. It would be commanded by the one-armed Lieutenant General Sir Sam Browne VC and would consist of 325 officers, 15,854 other ranks and 48 guns. In the centre the Kurram Valley Field Force would be led by the up-and-coming 46-year-old Major General (local rank) Frederick Roberts VC and would advance from a concentration area at Thal, through the Kurram Valley, and over the Peiwar Kotal (*kotal* meaning a mountain pass). Roberts had by far the smallest command with only 116 officers, 6,549 men and 18 guns. The southernmost column, the Kandahar Field Force, was almost twice as large with 265 officers, 12,599 men and 78 guns.[8] It was in the hands of the senior general officer of the trio, the 56-year-old Lieutenant General Sir Donald Stewart, and would launch from Quetta.

Sam Browne made hard work of an attack on Ali Masjid on 20 December, but nonetheless was able to make a successful entry into Jalalabad shortly afterwards. Stewart faced only negligible opposition on the southern front and within six weeks had crossed the great expanse of desert south of the Hindu Kush, to enter Kandahar on 8 January 1879. In the centre Roberts forced the Peiwar Kotal by means of a night march, a flanking manoeuvre and a stiff but victorious fight conducted over the first few days of December.

The Russians back Down

With the British advance achieving success on all fronts, Sher Ali appealed to the Russians for assistance. Stolietoff was quick to point out that the northern passes were already wintered in and that Afghanistan was completely cut off from

Tsarist Russia's sphere of influence. With barely a hint of irony he went on to point out that he and his associates could hardly prejudice improved Anglo-Russian relations with the ink on the Berlin Treaty barely dry. He had in fact received news of the treaty as early as 9 August, the day before his arrival in Kabul. In effect he had been leading the amir up the garden path ever since.[9] Now he announced that his party would withdraw to Mazar-i-Sharif to wait for the spring thaw, at which point it would tamely retire to Russian territory. Forced to recognize that his intrigues had pushed Lytton too far and that the Russians had sold him downriver, Sher Ali resolved to abandon his throne and flee north in company with Stolietoff. In the longer term he hoped to be able to make his way to St Petersburg, where he would lobby the great powers to press Disraeli for his restoration. With his preferred heir already dead, the amir had no choice but to turn to his estranged eldest son, the 30-year-old Mohammad Yakub Khan, who had been kept in arrest for the past few years but was now appointed regent.

On 21 February 1879, only weeks after quitting his throne, Sher Ali died in Mazar-i-Sharif. Realizing that the nation lacked the military wherewithal to resist a British advance on Kabul, the new amir decided to negotiate. The Treaty of Gandamak, signed after protracted talks on 26 May, brought a welcome end to hostilities. In return for an annual pension of £60,000 and unfettered control over Afghan internal affairs, Yakub Khan would be required to cede the Khyber Pass, the Kurram Valley and direct control of his foreign policy. This would become the business of a British resident quartered on Kabul. As a key player in the Gandamak talks, Major Cavagnari seemed to Lytton to be the obvious choice as envoy. In order to dignify him appropriately for the role, he was promoted lieutenant colonel and knighted as a KCB. The treaty further provided for a British military withdrawal by 1 September. Although the invasion had provoked an angry storm of protest from Gladstone and the Liberals, there was now a tangible feeling of relief that in the end it had all worked out for the best. The military men on the spot were less sanguine. Roberts recalled:

> My heart sank as I wished Cavagnari goodbye. When we had proceeded a few yards in our different directions, we both turned round, retraced our steps, shook hands once more and parted forever.[10]

The Cavagnari Mission

On 24 July Sir Louis Cavagnari rode into Kabul aboard one of the elephants Yakub Khan had sent to meet him on the road. Nine regiments of infantry were drawn up outside the city to welcome the envoy, with what passed for a military band murdering 'God Save the Queen' in the background. 'Embassy entered city and received most brilliant reception', Cavagnari telegraphed to Simla. He was accompanied by only three other Europeans, a political secretary from the Bengal Civil Service called William Jenkyns, an Irish surgeon, Dr Ambrose Kelly, and the 22-year-old commander of a token escort from the Corps of Guides, Lieutenant Walter Hamilton VC. Of the 77 Indian soldiers in the escort, 25 were *sowars* or mounted troopers, and 52 *sepoys* or infantrymen. After the majority Pathans, the next largest ethnic group in the escort were the Sikhs who included amongst their number one Jemadar Jewand Singh whose relatively junior rank was, as with most Indian officers, no measure of his age and experience.[11]

The British residency was established inside the Bala Hissar, the great bastioned citadel of old Kabul which, before it was reduced to a ring of shattered walls in the successive Afghan wars of the late twentieth century, used to dominate the eastern side of the city. It was based in two adjacent and commodious whitewashed houses, one of four storeys and the other of two, with wooden façades and shuttered windows. Considered to be amongst the best dwellings in the capital, the houses backed onto the bastioned wall of the citadel, beneath which there was a sheer drop to the Kabul River, an arrangement which rendered the residency impregnable save from *inside* the Bala Hissar, but also precluded any possibility of an evacuation into the open countryside. In front of the buildings was a spacious courtyard, bounded by a flimsy perimeter wall, which housed a stable block and a bath-house but was badly overlooked from nearby rooftops.[12]

On 3 September 1879 Sir Louis went for his morning ride as usual. All his diplomatic telegrams up to that point indicated that he felt no great anxiety. He had, however, been warned to be on his guard by an Indian Army risaldar-major called Nakshband Khan, who happened to be enjoying a spell of well-earned leave at a village on the outskirts of Kabul. The old soldier had been in the suburbs when half a dozen Herati infantry regiments marched in, and had witnessed them chanting anti-British slogans as they went. Cavagnari heard the old soldier out but went on to remark, 'Never fear . . . dogs that bark do not bite.'[13] Nakshband stood his ground and insisted that what he had seen was a pack of distinctly dangerous dogs.

Herat lay in the far west of the country on the ancient trade route between Persia and Central Asia and was governed by Ayub Khan, the amir's younger brother. He had sent a number of fresh regiments to Kabul in exchange for some of the units bested in the fighting with Roberts and Browne. For these as yet undefeated fighting men, brimming with the machismo of the Afghan warrior class, the presence of a foreign mission imposed by force was an unbearable national humiliation. Within days of their arrival they had grown accustomed to throwing their weight around and mocking those of their countrymen who had been involved in the brief and ineffectual resistance to the British.

Cavagnari returned from his ride safely at about 8.30 a.m., which he almost certainly would not have been able to do had there been a pre-meditated conspiracy afoot as was later suggested. Only a few streets away trouble was brewing at a long overdue pay parade for the Herati soldiery. Having been assured that their arrears would be settled in full, they paraded at the Bala Hissar as ordered, only to be insulted with part payment. The government paymasters were jostled but swore on their lives that they had no more money to give. Then somebody cried out that there was gold at the British residency, and in a matter of moments the soldiers were storming through the streets like a riotous mob.

Inside the compound there was a short-lived period of hesitancy which gave Cavagnari the opportunity to try and calm the rabble from a balcony. Nobody was much interested in what he had to say and quickly turned to looting the outbuildings. Some of the Heratis hurled stones at the stabled horses of the escort. In the circumstances the Guides had no choice but to open fire and clear the compound at the point of the bayonet. A brief lull ensued as the mutinous regiments broke away to collect their arms – perhaps the best pointer to a spontaneous rather than a pre-meditated eruption of violence. When the shooting started in earnest it quickly brought the Kabul mob onto the streets in search of plunder. Hamilton and the men of the Guides stood to their arms and fought from the buildings for the rest of the morning. Such was their fortitude that by midday Afghan casualties were already running into the hundreds. Some of the Heratis tried to break the deadlock by bringing two cannon to bear. In response the Guides made three successful bayonet charges to clear the enemy gunners from their pieces, but on each occasion heavy fire drove them back to cover long before they could manhandle the guns back to the buildings. Hamilton led all three sorties in person and each time was accompanied by one of the other Europeans – invariably with tragic consequences for his partner. Cavagnari himself was the first of the quartet to fall. Though his fate is far from certain, he seems to have been carried inside in a dangerously wounded condition. By mid-afternoon the two main buildings were ablaze, compelling their abandonment in favour of the bath-house. Hamilton was killed in a fourth and last sortie, fighting hard to cover the withdrawal of his men.

Realizing that all the British officers were now down, mullahs amongst the mob tried to lure the surviving Guides into surrendering. Jewand Singh was not about to be wooed by false promises and led the last dozen men into the open to fight to the death. An Afghan officer later bore witness that the jemadar killed eight men before he fell. Many members of the escort had fallen wounded in the fight, but by the time the mob had finished its barbaric knife-work, the slaughter appeared comprehensive. As shots were heard from the ruined residency the following morning, it is clear that a few well-concealed casualties survived the night, only to be discovered in daylight and promptly shot dead by looters. Only three sepoys, who had been outside the compound when the attack began, survived the massacre. Extraordinarily, a force of fewer than 80 men had held out for the best part of 12 hours and in the process inflicted more than 600 casualties on the enemy. It was a braver deed and a worse ordeal than even Rorke's Drift, but sadly is now all but forgotten.

Roberts Takes Kabul

Within 48 hours news of the massacre had been relayed to Lord Lytton at Simla, along with embarrassed and fervent telegrams from Yakub denying any personal culpability. Roberts happened to be in Simla as a member of a military commission and was instructed to hasten back to the old Kurram Valley Field Force, now re-designated the Kabul Field Force, tasked with forcing his way into the Afghan capital, exacting revenge and restoring British prestige. By the end of the month 'Bobs' had completed his preparations and was on the march at the head of two infantry brigades, a cavalry brigade, four batteries of artillery and two Gatling guns, a force of around 6,500 men in all.[14] Keenly aware that a campaign of national resistance must in the end prove futile, Yakub Khan decided instead to flee his capital and place himself under General Roberts's protection. Not all the amir's subjects followed his lead. By 5 October the British were within ten miles of Kabul with a strong rebel position to their front. The next day, in an action known as Charasiah, Roberts forced the Logar defile. Six days after the battle, he made a triumphal entry into a cowed and nervous Kabul.

Enquiries by British intelligence officers established that the city's governor had paraded Cavagnari's decapitated head through the streets in the aftermath of the massacre. He was one of about 80 people deemed to be ringleaders of the atrocity who were hanged by Roberts within days of the city's fall. The Kabul Field Force took up quarters in the Sherpur Cantonment and prudently set about repairing and enhancing its defences. Towards the end of the month Yakub Khan appeared in Roberts's tent to declare melodramatically that he would rather be a sweeper in the British camp than the ruler of Afghanistan. Even after he had thrown himself on the mercy of the British, he was strongly suspected of consorting with hostile elements in the environs of Kabul. On 28 October he abdicated and was ushered away into permanent exile in India.

Soon intelligence reports were indicating that a general uprising was being whipped up by a 90-year-old cleric called Mushk-i-Alam, and an artillery officer called Mohammed Jan. The outbreak came in mid-December when large numbers of tribesmen began gathering in the Chardeh Valley. At first Roberts tried to take the offensive, but, after a number of narrow scrapes against long numerical odds, he decided to fall back on Sherpur and invite attack. By 15 December the city and the Bala Hissar were in the hands of the insurgents. For the next week masses of tribal fighters continued to flock in from the hills. On the evening of 23 December 1879 the long awaited signal fire shot into the night sky. In his memoir *Forty-One Years in India* 'Bobs' was adamant that 100,000 men participated in the attack. It seems a vast number and may or may not be accurate, but by the time the Battle of Sherpur had drawn to a close something around 3,000 Afghans were lying dead on the field. Roberts had been presented with the decisive victory he knew would be an essential precursor to a meaningful negotiated peace. The search was now on for a successor to the feckless Yakub Khan, a head of state who could lead the country into a brave new future – a future which the Viceroy would insist was no business of the Tsar.

Having done his political homework amongst Kabul's dignitaries, Roberts telegraphed Lytton in support of the 35-year-old Abdur Rahman Khan, a son of the late Sher Ali's elder half-brother.[15] Shrewd, intelligent and ruthless, as any successful ruler of nineteenth-century Afghanistan would have to be, Abdur Rahman looked like a strong candidate. Problematically he had been living in exile in Russian Turkistan for the past 13 years, following an unsuccessful attempt to depose Sher Ali in favour of his father, and nobody in Kabul was quite sure how to get in touch with him. Eventually Sir Donald Stewart discovered that he was in correspondence with his mother in Kandahar and was able to open a channel of communication. Above all else, if a new amir was to outlast a British withdrawal and succeed in retaining the reins of power, he could not afford to be seen as a puppet of the Viceroy. In February 1880 Abdur Rahman travelled down from Samarkand to enter northern Afghanistan, but did not immediately move on to Kabul. Instead he entered into four months of political negotiations designed to emphasise his independence.

The Situation in Kandahar and the South

Although the occasional maddened *ghazi* was wont to hurl himself upon British servicemen in the backstreets of Kandahar, there had been no resistance to speak of in the south. In March 1880 the pro-British Sher Ali Khan Barakzai (not to be confused with the late amir) was appointed as the *Wali* or Governor of Kandahar. He was provided with 6,000 rifles and a battery of smoothbore cannon with which to re-equip the Kandahar-based units of the Afghan regular army. Because the south had been quite so quiet and Kabul quite so tempestuous, it was decided to move Sir Donald Stewart and a division of Bengali troops north to the capital. The Kandahar backwater would be left in the hands of a small Bombay division under the 60-year-old Major General J. M. Primrose.

Stewart and his men marched north on 27 March. Although it was hoped that the Afghan crisis was now winding down, not least because there was a general election looming at home which the political pundits reckoned would go badly for the Tories, the Second Anglo-Afghan War was still good for three major field actions. The first of them occurred on 19 April, when Stewart's division was attacked in transit at Ahmad Khel. For an awkward moment it looked like the British line would be outflanked by clouds of white-robed *ghazis*, but the British and Indian troops kept their nerve and calmly volleyed their way out of what might otherwise have been a tight corner. Stewart moved on to the capital as planned where, as the senior officer present, he took responsibility for politics and governance, leaving Roberts free to concentrate on the role of army commander.

In the meantime the political sands in London were shifting much as anticipated. On 28 April 1880 Disraeli's government fell and Gladstone took office. Lytton knew that the Liberals' vehement criticism of his forward policy meant the end and resigned as viceroy before he could be pushed. In due course the new government would nominate Lord Ripon as his replacement. One of Lytton's last moves in his quest for a political settlement in Afghanistan had entailed a partition scheme which would divide the country into three fiefdoms based on Kabul, Herat and Kandahar. The Shah of Persia was sensible enough to decline the suggestion that he should take responsibility for Herat, as the city was firmly held by Ayub Khan who might reasonably be expected to take a contrary view of the notion. Not only did Ayub rather enjoy the perquisites of the western governorship, he was now nurturing an altogether wider ambition, arguing not entirely unreasonably that his father's death and his brother's abdication made him the lawful amir.

The reason there had been no major resistance to the British around Kandahar was that many of the most militant leadership figures had fled west to join Ayub Khan's following at Herat. He could be sure of strong local support, the Kandahari exiles assured him, if he asserted his claim by first taking their home town and then using it as a stepping stone for an attempt on the capital. In the circumstances there was no shortage of intelligence on the situation at Kandahar. The most renowned British generals, Stewart and Roberts, were to be found in Kabul, along with the pick of the Anglo-Indian army, whilst at Kandahar there was only an old man called Primrose and a seriously weakened garrison. Nor it seemed could the Wali place much reliance on the 6,000

Afghans he had under arms. All in all there seemed to be reasonable grounds for optimism amongst the rebels.

Ayub Khan also had about 6,000 regulars immediately available, a combination of Herati and Kabuli regiments, but planned to drum up as much tribal support as possible during his long approach march. In detail the regular army contingent consisted of 9 infantry battalions, 3 cavalry regiments and 30 guns of various kinds, split between a mule-borne mountain battery and 4 well-drilled field batteries. Most of the guns were muzzle-loading 6-pounders but there were also half a dozen Armstrong RBLs. About half the regular infantry were armed with British-made Enfields and the rest with locally manufactured copies. Before it set off for Kandahar on or about 15 June 1880, the army's spirits received a lift when a mysterious Arab traveller presented Ayub Khan with a green Islamic banner given to him by a holy man in Baghdad, along with oddly prescient instructions to deliver it to the Governor of Herat to whom it would bring a great victory over the infidel.

The Opening of the Maiwand Campaign

Marching hard across more than 350 miles of inhospitable terrain, Ayub Khan was attracting a great many well-armed tribal supporters and *ghazis* as he went. The Wali of Kandahar decided to occupy a blocking position on the banks of the River Helmand near the village of Girishk. In stark contrast to his adversary's growing confidence, the Wali was rapidly losing faith in the loyalty of his troops. After a few days in the field he concluded that he would need British assistance if he was to contend with Ayub on equal terms. He duly wrote to Primrose asking that a brigade be despatched to his support. The request presented the general with a thorny problem: whilst the Wali had shown great spirit in taking the field, the British garrison at Kandahar would be reduced to dangerously weak levels if a brigade was to deploy for any length of time. Primrose tallied his command at 3,300 infantry, 1,100 cavalry and 400 gunners serving 16 guns[16] and concluded that on balance it was too small a force to accede to the Wali's request. Brevet Lieutenant Colonel Oliver St John RE of the political service disagreed, and thought that every effort should be made to support so valuable an ally. He worked on winning Primrose over, until at length the general telegraphed Simla to say that a brigade could go out if it was adjudged to be politically vital.

In Simla the political service backed St John's judgement, but the C-in-C, General Sir Frederick Haines, took a contrary view and ruled that the garrison was unable to spare a brigade. Eventually the Viceroy and his council were persuaded, but in view of the C-in-C's position took advantage of the burgeoning power of the telegraph to get the final decision referred to the

Secretary of State for India in London. Lord Hartington (who within a couple of years would be appointed Secretary for War and so become a key player in the Sudan Campaign) gave his approval on 1 July, though quite what qualified him to make such a judgement from a range of several thousand miles must forever remain a mystery.

The mainstay of the Girishk Column would be the 1st Infantry Brigade under the 53-year-old Brigadier-General George Burrows, until recently Quartermaster-General (QMG) of the Bombay Presidency. Burrows had been commissioned in 1844 and had last seen active service in 1857. Primrose decided to provide Burrows with two of the three regiments in Brigadier-General Thomas Nuttall's cavalry brigade. As Nuttall was the junior of the pair he would be expected to operate as Burrows's direct subordinate, though, in terms of command and control, fielding two brigadiers without a major general set over them constituted a far from ideal arrangement. Nuttall had served in Persia, in the Mutiny and on the transport staff in the Abyssinian Campaign of 1867. He was only marginally younger than Burrows, had spent a good deal of his Indian service in civil police appointments and, importantly, was not himself a cavalryman. Prior to going to Afghanistan he had been the Commandant of the Sind Frontier Force. The column departed Kandahar on 4 July 1880.

Even Wellington could find no way of campaigning around India without a vast baggage train in tow – a logistic tail running to many thousands of animals, accompanied by servants and camp followers of every description. Like any other nineteenth-century Anglo-Indian force, the Girishk Column would be slow-moving and difficult to protect in transit. In this instance there were more than 3,000 baggage animals, about two-thirds camels and one-third ponies and donkeys. It is remarkable, given that the column was departing Kandahar and must inevitably return there, that no limit was placed on the officers' baggage allowance. As a result all the major units took the field in style. The absence of restraint made for comfortable campaigning, but placed additional and unnecessary strains on a commissariat already struggling to move a month's worth of combat supplies into a blazing hot plain where water was certain to be in short supply. Bureaux, campaign chests, huge numbers of tents, camp-beds and cases of champagne lurched along beside boxes of rifle ammunition and water carts.

Left behind to hold the city was the 2nd/7th (Royal Fusiliers), a wing of the 19th Bombay Native Infantry (NI) and the Poona Horse. Arrangements had been made to push additional Indian battalions up the lines of communication. The 700-strong 4th Bombay NI would arrive at Kandahar on 23 July, to be followed five days later by the headquarters and three companies of the 28th Bombay NI.

Composition of the Girishk Column

The 1st Infantry Brigade consisted of one British battalion, two Indian battalions and a half company of Bombay Sappers & Miners. The British unit was the 66th (Berkshire) Regiment, a seasoned outfit which had been in India for a decade. It was commanded by Lieutenant Colonel James Galbraith, an officer of some 28 years' service, much of it in the sub-continent. Galbraith was of Anglo-Irish stock and had assumed command of his battalion as recently as November 1879. Whilst his service record did not include any significant field actions, Galbraith was a long-service regular and knew his business as well as the next man. He had marched his unit into Kandahar on 25 March 1880, at a strength of 19 officers and 679 other ranks. Before long, A and E Companies (4 and 140) had been detached to a garrison task at Khelat-i-Ghilzai, just to the north of Kandahar. A number of additional officers having come up in the interim, the six-company main body could still field 19 officers but now had a bayonet-strength of only 469 men. The battalion's two wing commanders were Majors John Ready and Charles Oliver. The 66th had exchanged their Sniders for Martini-Henrys in August 1877, but as it had been the practice since the Mutiny to keep sepoy units one mark of rifle behind their British counterparts, the two Indian battalions had not long since swapped Enfields for Sniders. The men of the 66th were clad in the standard lightweight foreign-service helmet, khaki tunics and trousers, black ammunition-boots and navy-blue puttees worn tight-wrapped to the knee. Their equipment was the standard white leather 1871 Pattern valise, which for some reason had been issued to the 66th with older pattern black leather ammunition pouches.

The sepoy battalions were also turned out in khaki, with the characteristically tall-fronted Indian Army turban as headdress The 1st Bombay Native Infantry (The Bombay Grenadiers) was the senior infantry regiment of the Presidency with a pedigree dating back to 1796. It was usual in Indian units for the colonel to be referred to as the 'commandant' rather than the 'officer commanding'. In the case of the Grenadiers this was Lieutenant Colonel Horace Anderson. With all eight of his companies in the field, Anderson was able to parade around 650 officers and men. He was supported by 22 other officers, 7 of them British, including Brevet Lieutenant Colonel C. M. Griffiths, his second-in-command, and Lieutenant C. W. Hinde, the regiment's 31-year-old adjutant. The junior unit in the brigade was the 30th Bombay Native Infantry (Jacob's Rifles) under Colonel William Mainwaring, a veteran of the Siege of Multan and the Battle of Gujerat. Mainwaring also had all eight of his companies available and a typical daily parade state of around 630 officers and men. The battalion contained a high proportion of younger, newly joined and only partially trained Muslim sepoys, some of whom were not fully conversant with their Sniders. In addition to the colonel-sahib there were 7 other European officers, including the second-in-command, Major James Iredell, and 14 Indian officers, presided over by Subadar-Major Haidar Khan. The final element of the brigade was a half-company of No. 2 Company, Bombay Sappers & Miners, commanded by a first-rate engineer subaltern called Lieutenant Thomas Henn. All told there were something around 1,700 bayonets in the brigade.

As was normal Brigadier-General Thomas Nuttall's cavalry brigade was substantially weaker than its infantry counterpart. It had been further weakened by Primrose's decision to retain the Poona Horse at Kandahar as the garrison's eyes and ears. Of the two remaining regiments one was significantly smaller than the other by dint of having detached a squadron to Khelat-i-Ghilzai.[17] Hence the 3rd Sind Horse under Colonel John Malcolmson CB could field only 5 British officers, 8 Indian officers and 247 sabres. Malcolmson's adjutant was Lieutenant E. V. P. (Edward) Monteith, seconded from the 2nd Sind Horse who, as was normal in an Indian cavalry regiment, also doubled up as a squadron commander. Monteith was one of three unrelated officers of that name in the force. Lieutenant A. M. (Arthur) Monteith was also a member of Malcolmson's regiment, while the third member of the clan, Lieutenant J. (John) Monteith, was serving on Nuttall's staff.

The 3rd Bombay Light Cavalry (Queen's Own) under Major Albert Currie was the stronger of Nuttall's units, with 6 British officers, 13 Indian officers and 297 sabres. The regiment's three squadrons were commanded by Captain Mosley Mayne, Lieutenant Thomas Geoghegan and Lieutenant & Adjutant William Owen. Amongst the regiment's Indian officers was Risaldar Dhokal Singh, whose claim to fame was that during the Mutiny he had saved the life of a subaltern called Evelyn Wood, now, as a result of his recent victory over the Zulus at Kambula, one of the most famous colonels in the Army. The cavalry regiments were armed with the .577-inch Snider carbine, a generally unsatisfactory weapon loathed by the sowars for its excessive recoil and tendency to jam after a dozen or so rounds.

The mainstay of Nuttall's firepower, however, was E Battery, B Brigade, RHA, commanded by the 42-year-old Major George Blackwood, a highly regarded officer who had last seen active service during the Mutiny. The battery was equipped with six 9-pounders and was not far short of full strength with 4 officers and 158 other ranks in the field. As was the norm in the horse artillery, everybody in E Battery whose duties did not entail driving the teams or riding an axle-seat was provided with a saddle horse. This gave Blackwood's command great mobility and dash. All it needed to show off in fine style was a glimpse of the enemy and some reasonably flat ground free of the muddy irrigation ditches that criss-crossed the inhabited parts of rural Afghanistan. The battery's three divisions were commanded by Lieutenants Hector Maclaine, Edmund Osborne and Newton Fowell. The job of ensuring that everything in E Battery was kept ship-shape fell to Battery Sergeant-Major Paton.

Treachery on the Helmand River

The 80-mile march to the Helmand took the British brigades a week, with the cavalry arriving at the river on 11 July and the infantry the following day. Both formations encamped on the east or home bank of the river opposite Girishk. For the present Sher Ali Khan was deployed on the opposite bank, some way south of his British allies, with his advanced elements thrown out 20 miles to the west attempting to acquire up-to-date intelligence on Ayub's advance. The British intelligence effort was led by Oliver St John, whose most recent assessment suggested that the enemy vanguard was still some 60 miles away.

With the enemy coming within striking distance at last, it became clear that the Wali's infantry could no longer be counted upon. Sher Ali Khan, Burrows and St John met on the afternoon of 13 July to discuss their options and concluded that they should try to force the issue one way or the other. They decided that first thing the following morning the Wali would bring his force across to the east bank, where his infantry would be formed up in front of the British and Indian troops and ordered to ground arms. In the event, while most of his 2,500 cavalry followed Sher Ali Khan over the river, the artillery and the infantry proved every bit as treacherous as expected and took off in quite the opposite direction. Though disinclined to mutiny, the cavalry had no such qualms about desertion and all but a few hundred of them abandoned their commander and rode away in the direction of Kandahar. Burrows and Nuttall were determined above all else that the six smoothbore guns gifted to their ally should not be allowed to remain in enemy hands.

Leaving most of the Indian infantry to guard his camp, Burrows gave chase with the cavalry brigade, four companies of the 66th and the Sappers & Miners. The 3rd Sind Horse was at the forefront of the pursuit. Having caught up with the smoothbores, Colonel Malcolmson mounted a text-book demonstration which denied the enemy gunners the opportunity to break clean. It was not long before Major Blackwood came galloping into action with the two leading divisions of his battery. At a range of about a mile the British gunners quickly drove their Afghan opposite numbers from their pieces. When the 66th came up and formed for an attack, the mutinous infantry showed a clean pair of heels. Mounting up on the unhitched teams and saddle horses of the battery, the Afghan gunners abandoned the smoothbores and fled west, with their infantry comrades straggling behind them. With the gifted guns back in the hands of the donors and the mutineers scattered all over the countryside, the GOC saw little point in pressing the pursuit any further.[18] Indeed he had

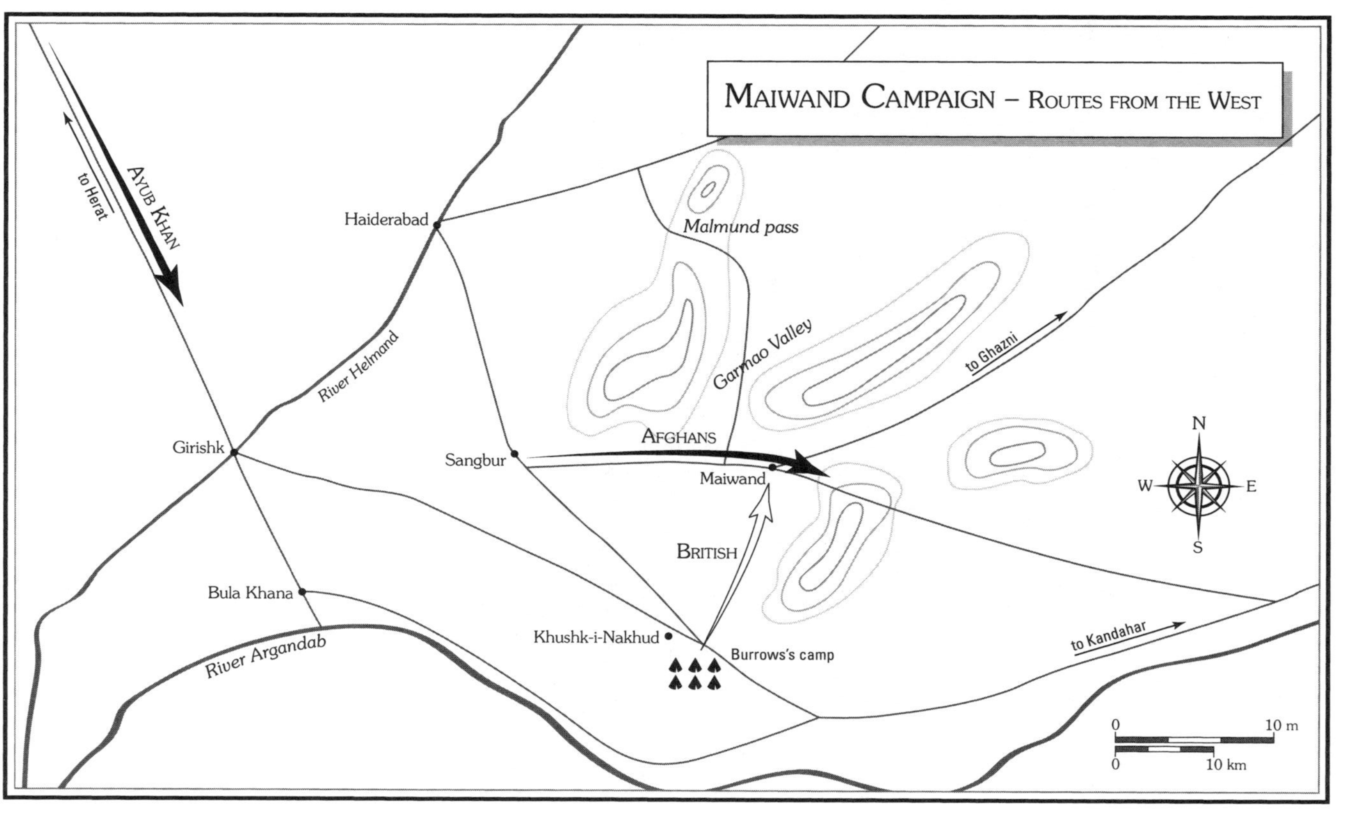

Maiwand Campaign – Routes from the West
Ayub Khan
to Herat
Haiderabad
Malmund pass
River Helmand
Garmao Valley
to Ghazni
Girishk
Sangbur
Afghans
Maiwand
British
Bula Khana
Khushk-i-Nakhud
Burrows's camp
River Argandab
to Kandahar
N
W
E
S
0
10 m
0
10 km

already infringed the strict letter of his orders by crossing the Helmand in the first place.

Burrows now decided to fall back about 35 miles to occupy a blocking position at the village of Khusk-i-Nakhud. Here he would be astride two of the five western approaches to Kandahar and would be relatively well poised to interdict the other three – one to the south along the River Argandab, and two to the north: the first via the village of Sangbur on the plain, and the other, the northernmost of the five options, through the Shah Maqsud Mountains via the Malmund Pass and the Garmao Valley.

By 19 July rumours had reached General Primrose that Ayub had no intention of attacking Kandahar, but would swing north to threaten the town of Ghazni, a move which would throw open the possibility of a direct advance on Kabul. Primrose telegraphed the intelligence to Simla where it caused considerable consternation. In fact Ayub was still bound for Kandahar but, as ever in the cauldron of active operations, the British could not be entirely sure.

On 19 July Burrows decided to supplement his artillery component by using the recovered guns to fit out an *ad hoc* 'smoothbore battery'. The general's orderly officer, Captain John Slade RHA, originally E/B Battery's second-in-command, was released from his duties on the staff in order to take command of the new unit. His guns, four 6-pounders and two 12-pounder howitzers, would be manned by 17 NCOs and gunners seconded from E Battery and 42 infantrymen detached from the 66th under Lieutenant Granville de la Motte Faunce. In addition to Faunce, two artillery subalterns were found to command the battery's other divisions: ordinarily Lieutenant T. F. T. Fowle was a member of 5/11 Heavy Battery back in Kandahar, while Lieutenant G. S. Jones was on the transport staff of the cavalry brigade. Unfortunately the mutinous Afghan gunners had retained sufficient presence of mind to sabotage the battery by running off most of the draught animals and cutting through the harness of the ammunition wagons. Because of a general shortage of horses Burrows directed that the three ammunition wagons should be destroyed and their contents thrown into deepwater pools in the Helmand. This left only the contents of the limbers, a little over 50 rounds per gun.

Meeting Engagement

The British remained encamped at Khusk-i-Nakhud for the best part of ten days. During that time Burrows received a copy of a telegram from the C-in-C at Simla to General Primrose at Kandahar:

> You [General Primrose] will understand that you have full liberty to attack Ayub, if you consider you are strong enough to do so. Government consider it the greatest political importance that his force

> be dispersed, and prevented by all possible means from passing on to Ghazni.

Although not addressed personally to Burrows, the message made it clear that he was now expected to attack Ayub on the line of march. On 23 July cavalry patrols made contact with elements of the enemy vanguard near the village of Sangbur, 14 miles to the north-west. From Sangbur the road ran due east to a critical road junction at the village of Maiwand, where it was possible to swing north via the Khakrez Valley towards Ghazni, or to move south-east through the hills towards Kandahar. Two days later a substantial body of Afghan cavalry was detected midway between Sangbur and Maiwand. These contacts, coupled with reports from St John's spies, amounted to a clear indication that Ayub Khan was in the process of bypassing the British to the north but, for reasons best known to themselves, the senior officers prevaricated, convinced that the enemy main body was still on the Helmand. As a result Burrows failed to act until the evening of 26 July, when additional intelligence reports and a sighting of 2,000 enemy cavalry finally convinced him to march hard for a blocking position to the north. As both of the northern routes converged just west of Maiwand, the village constituted a vital choke-point.

In a report written a month after the battle, designed to explain if not to excuse his defeat, Burrows gave what is a nonetheless broadly honest flavour of the problems he faced with his intelligence and surveillance effort:

> I have the honour to report, that, on the 26th ultimo, whilst encamped at Khusk-i-Nakhud, I received information that 2,000 of the enemy's cavalry and a large number of ghazis had arrived at Garmao and Maiwand, and that it was Ayub Khan's intention to follow with the main body of his army immediately. A sketch is attached to this report, showing the positions of Maiwand and Khusk-i-Nakhud, from which it will be seen that to carry into effect the instructions I had received, viz., to prevent Ayub Khan from passing on to Ghazni, it was incumbent on me to intercept him either at Maiwand or Khusk-i-Nakhud. Hitherto I found it impossible to obtain any reliable information regarding Ayub Khan's intended movements, for, although when the expedition set out, it was understood that we were to operate in a friendly country, and in concert with a loyal army, the actual circumstances were the reverse of this. The Wali's army had gone over to the enemy; the Wali himself was a refugee in my camp. Whatever little political influence there may have been in the country, was at an end, and every man's hand was against us.
>
> In the absence of intelligence beyond such as my cavalry patrols brought in, and from which I knew that the enemy's advanced post was at Sungboor [*sic*], twelve miles in my front, on the Khusk-i-Nakhud

> road, I considered it advisable to await events in the position I had taken up at the latter place. On learning, however, that the enemy was making for Maiwand I determined to move on that place at once. The force marched at 6.30 a.m. on the 27th July, encumbered by an enormous quantity of ordnance and commissariat stores and baggage.[19]

Burrows is seeking here to account for the lateness of his decision to relocate from Khusk-i-Nakhud, but fails to mention that it was not made until 10.30 p.m. the night before the battle, nor does he cover any of the consequences of its lateness for his soldiers. Captain Mosley Mayne remembered the practical implications much more directly:

> The orders for our move to intercept the enemy at Maiwand had been given the night before, much of which had been spent in packing up our camp at Khusk-i-Nakhud which was to be struck by 05.30 a.m. It was thus an already tired force that began marching north early that morning, the 27th July, few of whom had eaten since the previous evening.[20]

In addition to their other tribulations, hunger and fatigue amongst them, Jacob's Rifles also underwent a last-minute reorganization. A few days earlier an 80-man draft of recruits had come out from Kandahar with a supply convoy, to join their battalion for the first time. Once Colonel Mainwaring had detached one of his eight original companies to the baggage escort, supplemented them with a 40-man composite guard for the commissariat, and fallen out any untrained recruits to act as ammunition carrying-parties, he decided to redistribute the rest of his manpower into eight new sub-units of about 50 men apiece. It made for an unsettling start to the battalion's day.[21]

Maiwand was 13 miles from Khushk-i-Nakhud and about 16 miles from Sangbur. Ayub's main body had marched undetected into Sangbur late the previous afternoon, evidently not long after the daily British patrol had turned back to camp. On the morning of the battle, therefore, both armies were in effect marching up the sides of a triangle, with Sangbur and Khushk-i-Nakhud at opposite ends of the base line, and Maiwand at the apex. The chances are that at its height the temperature that day reached something in the order of 120 degrees Fahrenheit (50 degrees Celsius). Burrows threw a strong vanguard forward under Nuttall, consisting of all three squadrons of the 3rd Light Cavalry, one squadron of the 3rd Sind Horse and two of the three RHA divisions. In turn Nuttall threw out an advanced guard of 50 sabres under Lieutenant Geoghegan of the 3rd Light Cavalry, and deployed troops of the 3rd Sind Horse to the flanks, led by Lieutenant Arthur Monteith on the left, and Lieutenant Smith on the right. Moving behind the advanced guard in company with the horse artillery was Major Currie's regimental headquarters and two 3rd Light Cavalry squadrons under Captain Mayne and Lieutenant Owen. To the rear of the vanguard the main body was marching in five parallel columns – from left to right, the Bombay Grenadiers, the smoothbore battery, Jacob's Rifles, the Berkshires and, furthest from the direction of enemy threat, the straggling baggage train and its escort. Colonel Malcolmson brought up the rear with a 96-sabre squadron of the 3rd Sind Horse under Lieutenant Edward Monteith and a division of E Battery.

By 08.45 a.m. the British had covered about six miles, but the baggage column was straggling as usual and a 30-minute halt was necessary in order for it to close up. During the pause Burrows expressed displeasure at the numerical weakness of some of the cavalry squadrons. Major George Hogg of the Poona Horse, Nuttall's brigade-major, was called on to provide a parade state. It survives in Hogg's 'narrative account' (all surviving officers were required to submit such statements to the Intelligence Branch in Simla in the aftermath of the battle) and shows how quickly combat power can be dissipated by sickness, administrative tasks and, in the case of cavalry regiments, by lameness. All four troops of the 3rd Sind Horse were about 50 strong; 4 men were sick, 36 men had lame horses and were with the baggage train and 18 men were detached to a variety of administrative tasks. The three squadrons of Currie's regiment were 76, 72 and 74 strong respectively, which divided between the six largely notional troops meant that the stronger regiment had significantly weaker sub-units. The shortfall was accounted for by 12 sick, 13 men provided as orderlies/gallopers to the two general officers and the political officer, 26 men detached to the baggage guard, 11 men with lame horses and 16 detached to other administrative duties.[30]

Forty-five minutes after setting off again, the cavalry screen made contact. Captain Mayne recalled:

> About this time a note came back from Lieutenant Geoghegan . . . who was 5 to 600 yards ahead of us. I passed back the note by one of my men to General Nuttall. Soon after I saw larger bodies of cavalry to our left front moving obliquely in the direction of Maiwand, but the morning was peculiarly hazy . . . and it was impossible to see distinctly or to judge distance with any accuracy. At this time another note came back which I passed on as before. The halt then sounded and Generals Burrows and Nuttall and their staff rode up to the front. During this halt I rode up on to a small knoll and took a look round with powerful glasses. I saw several bodies of cavalry still moving towards Maiwand whilst smaller bodies came nearer and watched us. Beyond their cavalry and far away on the slopes beneath the high hills towards Garmao, I saw dark masses which I took at first for belts of jungle. This was Ayoub's [*sic*] army, as we ascertained afterwards, in column of route, marching from Sungbhur [*sic*] to Maiwand. I could see the trees and buildings of Maiwand about

> 3 or 4 miles ahead, and a village and enclosures about 1½ miles to our left front.[31]

Shielding their eyes from the glare and straining to penetrate the all-enveloping dust clouds on the plain, Burrows and his staff debated just what they were looking at. One thing was for sure: whatever the enemy's strength, advanced elements of Ayub's force were going to be at the mouth of the Khakrez Valley long before the British could cover the intervening distance. In effect this meant that the road to Ghazni was lying wide open. In order to prevent the enemy main body bustling through to Maiwand to link up with their advanced guard, Burrows concluded that he would have to drive hard into Ayub's right flank in order to arrest his further progress and force him to turn through 90 degrees to give battle.

About 2,500 yards in front of the British force were two typical Afghan villages, on the left Mahmudabad[32] and on the right Khig. Standing about 600 yards apart, the villages consisted of a few mud-grey dwellings, the odd walled compound or garden and a few outlying groves of fruit trees. Mahmudabad was small and compact, while Khig sprawled in a more linear fashion to the south. If Burrows could get forward to the villages and use one or the other to secure his baggage, he would then be able to rush his fighting units onto a line of battle on the plain beyond. With a dozen guns pouring shot and shell into his exposed flank, Ayub Khan would have no choice but to wheel right and accept the challenge. It was a bold plan. If the British cause was to prosper it would be necessary for Burrows and his subordinates to offset their numerical disadvantage by making the best possible use of ground to anchor their flanks securely. On the far side of the villages, running roughly north-east to south-west, was a deep sandy watercourse commonly referred to as the Mahmudabad Ravine. The ravine ran across the plain at an oblique angle to the villages, so that although Mahmudabad stood less than 200 yards from the south bank, the intervening distance had more than doubled in the vicinity of Khig. Between the two villages the ravine was 15–20 feet deep and around 35 yards wide. Although there were a few places along the bank where rainwater, subsidence or local pedestrian traffic had made it relatively easy to scramble across, getting formed bodies of troops from one side of the obstacle to the other would inevitably be an untidy and time-consuming process. Three smaller watercourses fed into the ravine from the north. The two westernmost of these *nullahs*, directly opposite Mahmudabad, were quite shallow, while the third, located about 1,000 yards beyond Khig, was deeper, wider and a good deal longer. Although there was a trickle of water in the bottom of the main ravine, all three of its tributaries were bone-dry.

Although he was still unclear on the precise size and composition of the enemy force, Burrows was content that he was sufficiently well-balanced to give

Table 1: The British Force at Maiwand

Unit	Commander	Officers		Other Ranks	
		British	*Indian*	*British*	*Indian*
1st Infantry Brigade	***Brig.-Gen. G. R. S. Burrows***				
Political Officer	*Lt. Col. O. B. C. St John*				
Brigade-Major	*Capt. P. C. Heath*				
DAAG	*Capt. T. Harris*				
Orderly Officer	*Maj. E. P. Leach*				
	Lt. G. Dobbs				
B, C, D, F, H Companies, 66th (Berkshire) Regt	*Lt. Col. J. Galbraith*	15[22]	–	364	–
7 companies, 1st Bombay NI (Grenadiers)	*Lt. Col. H. S. Anderson*	7[23]	12	–	457
8 companies, 30th Bombay NI (Jacob's Rifles)	*Col. W. G. Mainwaring*	7[24]	12	–	482
Half coy, No. 2 Company, Bombay Sappers & Miners	*Lt. T. R. Henn RE*	1	1	2	41
Smoothbore Battery (4 x 6-pdr, 2 x 12-pdr howitzer)	*Capt. J. R. Slade RHA*	4[25]	–	59	–
Cavalry Brigade	***Brig.-Gen. T. Nuttall***				
Brigade-Major	*Maj. G. C. Hogg*				
Orderly Officer	*Lt. J. Monteith*				
3 squadrons, 3rd Bombay Light Cavalry (Queen's Own)	*Maj. A. P. Currie*	6[26]	13	–	297
2 squadrons, 3rd Regiment Sind Horse	*Col. J. H. P. Malcolmson*	5[27]	8	–	247
E/B Battery RHA (6 x 9-pdr)	*Maj. G. F. Blackwood*	4[28]	–	141	–
Baggage Guard	*Maj. J. T. Ready, 66th Regt*				
G Company, 66th Regt	*Capt. J. Quarry*	3[29]	–	63	–
1 coy, 1st Bombay NI	*Lt. C. G. Whitby*	1	1	–	80
1 coy, 30th Bombay NI	*Lt. M. B. Salmon*	1	1	–	80
Detail, 1st Bombay NI – Ordnance Stores Guard		–	1	–	50
Detail, 1st Bombay NI – Treasury Guard		–	1	–	40
Detail, 30th Bombay NI – Commissariat Guard		–	1	–	40

(Plus miscellaneous details of sowars, included in the regimental strengths above.)

Total: 1,800 infantry, 560 cavalry, 150 gunners, 45 sappers, 12 guns

Including staff, orderlies and miscellaneous:

64 British officers, 51 Indian officers, 2,461 other ranks

battle. He sent orders to Nuttall directing him to throw elements of the vanguard into Mahmudabad, to ensure that it was clear of enemy patrols. Nuttall and his staff cantered forward in company with Major Currie and the two leading groupings of his regiment – Lieutenant Geoghegan's troop and Captain Mayne's No. 2 Squadron.[33] Operating in close support was Major Blackwood with Fowell's and Maclaine's divisions. The developing situation might have been tailor-made for RHA officers to give full vent to the 'dash' that so famously characterized their branch of the service. In preparation for driving hard into the enemy's flank, Blackwood called in his two subalterns and gave them their orders. Newton Fowell and his teams were to operate under the battery commander's immediate supervision near Mahmudabad, whilst the 29-year-old Hector Maclaine was to take his guns a few hundred yards to the left in search of a second crossing-point over the ravine. There would be a short delay while the infantry came up, at which point the horse artillery would effect simultaneous crossings and race forward into the plain to harry the Afghan columns on the line of march.

As he was trotting his division away to the south-west, Maclaine ran into Major Hogg who decided to attach Lieutenant Arthur Monteith's troop of the 3rd Sind Horse to the guns as their close escort. In the meantime Geoghegan and his sowars had begun clearing through Mahmudabad at Blackwood's request. Just behind the vanguard the infantry brigade was hastening forward in its parallel regimental columns. As usual the vexatious task of commanding the baggage train and its composite three-company escort had fallen to the field officer of the day – on this occasion Major John Ready of the 66th. The two Indian companies at Ready's disposal, commanded by Lieutenants Clement Whitby of the Bombay Grenadiers and Mordaunt Salmon of Jacob's Rifles, were both about 80 strong, while Captain John Quarry's G Company of the 66th was slightly weaker at 3 and 63. In addition to the formed companies of the escort, the baggage train was accompanied by a few dozen sowars detached from their regiments and three details of sepoys, specifically tasked under Indian officers to guard the treasury, the commissariat and the ordnance stores. Counting these additional assets Ready could dispose of 370–380 fighting men in all. He had not yet been left entirely to his own devices as Colonel Malcolmson was still hanging back with the rearguard squadron and Osborne's brace of 9-pounders.

The Horse Artillery Come into Action

As soon as the balance of the cavalry and the infantry battalions were within a reasonable supporting distance, Nuttall gave the signal for E Battery to begin crossing the ravine. Its great depth made it a testing obstacle and a good deal of heaving and cussing was necessary before Fowell's crews were able to gain the north bank. In order to protect the RHA as they worked, Captain Mayne and his sowars scrambled their ponies across and re-formed on the open plain beyond. For the time being Geoghegan's troop was to stay behind and secure Mahmudabad for the rest of the force. Several hundred yards to the south-west Hector Maclaine's division and Arthur Monteith's troop were executing an identical obstacle-crossing operation. When Blackwood could see that all four gun-teams were formed up on the flat of the plain, he instructed his trumpeter to sound the 'Advance'. The sight of a well-drilled RHA battery coming into action from the gallop was more than merely stirring. Invariably executed with a bustling sense of urgency, the drill demanded perfect unison of man and beast and seemed somehow to bespeak the military might of imperial India.

After a dash of only a few hundred yards Blackwood reined in, threw an arm in the air, and bellowed the all-important command 'Action Front!' This indicated to Fowell's two sergeants, the 'number-ones', that they should slow their teams to a halt, unlimber and load. In a matter of seconds the crews were down from their axle-seats and saddles, unhooking the guns amidst swirling clouds of dust and spinning them through 180 degrees to face the direction of enemy threat. As the gun-crews were racing through their loading drills, the drivers whipped their teams back into a trot and began wheeling wide to cover off behind the guns. As soon as Fowell had given an initial fire-control order, his 9-pounders served notice on Ayub Khan that he was under attack. Both Hogg and Mayne recorded that the first salvo was fired at 10.50 a.m.

Away to the left Maclaine was showing a little more dash with Nos. 5 and 6 Sub-Divisions than was altogether desirable. The battery's drills required that, having made the crossing, he should conform to Fowell's division and take post 50 yards to its left. Not only did Maclaine elect not to alter course and close in on the centre, he also failed to halt when he came up level with his battery commander. Instead he galloped a full 1,500 yards into the plain, dragging Monteith's troop after him. He was several hundred yards to the left of his comrades, and perhaps 800 yards in advance of them, before he finally reined in and brought his guns into action. His first target was a thin screen of enemy cavalry which he engaged at a range of about a mile. Both his battery commander and the GOC were unhappy with Maclaine's position. 'Those guns are going much too far to the left,' Blackwood observed, before despatching his trumpeter to recall them. Captain Thomas Harris of the 66th, serving with General Burrows's headquarters as the Deputy Assistant Adjutant-General (DAAG), was the first member of the staff to spot that Maclaine was out of position by a significant margin. Having had the faulty disposition of the guns pointed out to him, Burrows instructed another member of his staff, Lieutenant George Dobbs, to ride after them and bring them back towards the centre.

The opening salvoes from Fowell's Nos. 1 and 2 Sub-Divisions were fired at about 3,000 yards, but the heat haze was such that Blackwood had great difficulty in gauging fall of shot. Calling across to General Nuttall that he would have to get closer, he began barking orders to hook-in again. A few minutes later the guns, the cavalry brigade headquarters and Mayne's No. 2 Squadron, 3rd Light Cavalry, began trotting further into the plain. The range was down to about 2,500 yards when Blackwood signalled a halt and once again came into action against the dust clouds in the distance. This time the guns deployed behind the shallow upper reaches of the central nullah facing broadly east, with the mouth of the Garmao Valley to their half-left and the village of Maiwand, marked by a small fort and a domed mosque, more than three miles to their half-right.

Composition of the Afghan Force

As usual it is next to impossible to state the strength of a largely tribal force with any real certainty. Estimates of 30,000–35,000 have been bandied about, but such figures are hugely exaggerated. Writing a month after the battle Burrows said that, 'I believe I am within the mark when I set down his strength at 25,000 men.' That the regular army contingent, including mutineers from the Wali's force, came to about 7,000 men is reasonably certain,[34] so that an overall strength including tribal irregulars and *ghazis* of 15,000–18,000 would seem altogether more realistic. A suggested order of battle, based on the Official History, is given in Table 2.

The British Force Deploys

After observing fall of shot from Fowell's first salvo, Blackwood declared himself content with the new position and approached General Nuttall to ask that he press the force commander for the services of Captain Slade's smoothbores and the third division of his own battery. Nuttall agreed that the enemy could hardly ignore the flanking fire of a dozen guns and despatched Lieutenant John Monteith to relay the request to Burrows. Unsurprisingly, given that the shape and form of his battle was already in danger of slipping from his grasp, the GOC was hastening forward to examine the ground for himself and met Monteith coming the other way. Burrows approved the deployment of the artillery and continued on his way in search of Nuttall and Blackwood. Only a few hundred yards further south, Monteith happened upon Slade and his guns. Having passed on the order to deploy in support of E Battery, he rode on in search of Osborne's division.

Collocated with Nuttall and the horse artillery at last, Burrows raged about Maclaine for a moment or two and then got on with surveying the wider

***Table 2:* Ayub Khan's Army at Maiwand**

Regulars		
1st Infantry Brigade	*Taj Muhammad Khan*	
3 x Kabuli infantry regiments each of 500 men		1,500
2nd Infantry Brigade	*Saidal Khan*	
1 x Kandahari and 2 x Kabuli regiments each of 500 men		1,500
3rd Infantry Brigade	*Ghafur Khan*	
3 x Herati regiments each of 366 men		1,100
Kandahari mutineers from the Wali's army		1,500
Cavalry Brigade	*Abdul Rahman Khan*	
3 x Kabuli regular cavalry regiments each of 300 men		900
Artillery	*Ahmad Gul*	
Mountain Artillery:	1 x mule-borne battery of 6 guns	
Field Artillery:	4 x 6-gun batteries, including one of 3-inch Armstrong RBLs	500
	Total Regulars	7,000
Irregulars		
Herati light horse		1,500
Durani light horse		500
Tribal irregular infantry		1,000
Ghazis		5,000–8,000
	Total Irregulars	8,000–11,000
	Total Force	**15,000–18,000**

situation. It was now about 11.00 a.m. and the infantry battalions were coming up in the spit of land between the left-hand and central nullahs. In the south near Mahmudabad the two watercourses were only 150 yards apart but here, near the guns, the distance between them had widened to around 700 yards. In places the third or easternmost nullah lay a mere 300 yards from the barrels of the British guns,[35] but the rainy season had scored it deep into the plain making its existence far from obvious at anything much beyond a hundred yards. As it ran a lot further north into the plain than the other two tributaries, it offered the Afghan main body a ready-made infiltration route towards the British position. For the time being Ayub Khan's host was spread across a great arc from the foot of the mountains in the north, to Maiwand in the east. Several thousand *ghazi* infantry were leading the way, placing them due east of the British, while the three infantry brigades and the field artillery were to be found in a more northerly direction, ideally placed to make use of the prospective infiltration route.

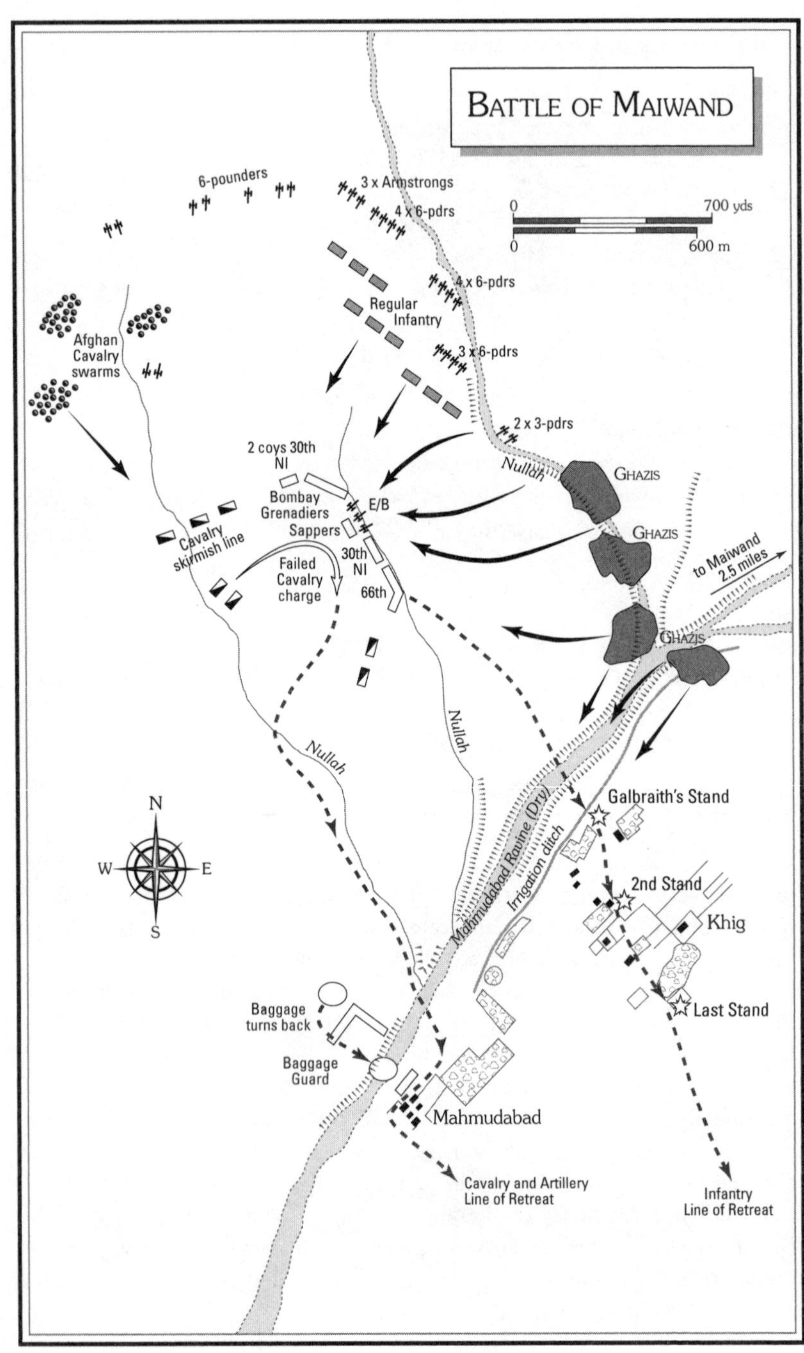

BATTLE OF MAIWAND
0
700 yds
0
600 m
6-pounders
3 x Armstrongs
4 x 6-pdrs
4 x 6-pdrs
Regular
Infantry
3 x 6-pdrs
2 x 3-pdrs
Afghan
Cavalry
swarms
2 coys 30th
NI
Bombay
Grenadiers
E/B
Sappers
30th
NI
66th
Cavalry
skirmish line
Failed
Cavalry
charge
Nullah
GHAZIS
GHAZIS
GHAZIS
to Maiwand
2.5 miles
Nullah
Nullah
Mahmudabad Ravine (Dry)
Irrigation ditch
Galbraith's Stand
2nd Stand
Khig
Last Stand
N
W
E
S
Baggage
turns back
Baggage
Guard
Mahmudabad
Cavalry and Artillery
Line of Retreat
Infantry
Line of Retreat

Slade's battery came up at a tolerably fast trot and was directed to take post 150 yards to the left of Fowell's division. Inexpert though Lieutenant Faunce's infantrymen were, with the help of their attached RHA 'number-ones' they succeeded in bringing their guns into action quickly enough. In contrast to the somewhat circumspect arrival of the smoothbores, Osborne's guns, Nos. 3 and 4 Sub-Divisions, came flying up from Mahmudabad at the gallop, to halt dutifully at the regulation interval on Fowell's right. In the meantime the three infantry battalions busied themselves with shaking out into line of battle. They were still 500 yards behind the gun line when they received orders to halt and lie down. Away to the left Hector Maclaine was receiving a dressing-down from Major Hogg: not only had he chosen to ignore the repeated calls of his battery commander's trumpeter, but he had also rudely dismissed Lieutenant Dobbs. There could be no ignoring the brigade-major. Even so, when a chastened Maclaine halted and came into action level with his colleagues, he was still four or five times the regulation distance to the left of Fowell's division. No doubt he was merely demonstrating to the rest of the world what he knew in his heart to be true – that Old Etonians can do no wrong.

It was naïve of Burrows to think that he could command the entire force effectively, whilst at the same time retaining personal command of the infantry brigade. Conventionally there was always the option of handing the brigade over to the senior battalion commander (Colonel Mainwaring), but the absence of their commandant could be unsettling to Indian battalions and on this occasion Burrows had chosen not to go down that road. It remained to be seen whether he would be able to manage the juggling act between the roles of GOC and brigade commander, an easy enough proposition in camp or on the line of march when time was seldom in short supply, but an altogether different proposition in the midst of a general engagement, when there was every danger of both posts simultaneously demanding his undivided attention. For now the immediate priority was to bring the infantry forward in support of the guns.

Colonel Anderson received orders to deploy the Bombay Grenadiers as the left-hand unit of the brigade and took post to the left of the guns facing north through north-east. To the right of the Grenadiers the half-company of Sappers & Miners was brought forward to support the gun line. Colonel Mainwaring of Jacob's Rifles was told to move a wing of his battalion up on the right of E Battery, but to keep his remaining four companies in hand as the brigade reserve. Mainwaring detailed his second-in-command, Major James Iredell, to take command of the left-wing companies and halt them a couple of hundred yards short of the guns. The colonel himself would take his right-wing companies forward and deploy a firing line running south from Osborne's guns. This left Mayne's squadron to Mainwaring's left rear. Finally Colonel James

Galbraith was instructed to deploy the British battalion on the right of the line to confront the *ghazi* swarms which, provoked by shell fire, appeared to be swinging back from the direction of Maiwand to attack from the east.

The 66th took post with B Company on the right and the other companies arrayed to the left in their lettered sequence – thus from right to left: B Company (Captain Francis Cullen), C Company (Captain Walter Roberts and Lieutenant William Lonergan), D Company (Captain William McMath and Lieutenant Hyacinth [*sic*] Lynch), F Company (Captain Ernest Garratt), H Company (Captain William Beresford-Peirse[36] and 2nd Lieutenant Harry Barr). Lieutenant Maurice Rayner, the adjutant, placed the colours behind D Company in the care of 2nd Lieutenants Walter Olivey (Queen's Colour) and Arthur Honywood (Regimental Colour). Although in theory each of the company commanders should have had two subaltern officers to assist him, none of them had more than one, whilst Captains Cullen and Garratt were the only officers in their companies. In part the shortfall was due to the temporary misemployment of Lieutenant Richard Chute and 2nd Lieutenant George Melliss, ordinarily company officers, now acting as the battalion's quartermaster and transport officer respectively. Including the doctor there were 15 officers and 364 other ranks on Galbraith's position.[37]

In the meantime General Nuttall and his brigade-major had been deploying cavalry assets to cover the flanks of the infantry as best they could. A 40-strong troop of the 3rd Bombay Light Cavalry under a native officer was sent to the right to cover the expanse of plain between the Mahmudabad Ravine and the 66th, where it was joined a short while later by Lieutenant Edward Smith's troop of the 3rd Sind Horse. The general himself rode out to the left with Lieutenant James Reid and a troop of the 3rd Light Cavalry. Several hundred yards to the left rear of the Bombay Grenadiers, they encountered several parties of Afghan irregular horse. Numerically too weak to clear the enemy with a charge, Nuttall ordered Reid to dismount and deploy a skirmish line along the general course of the westernmost nullah facing north through north-west

Perhaps because he was preoccupied with deploying his infantry, Burrows failed to send orders to Major Ready to halt the baggage train around Mahmudabad. Ignorant of any higher intention that they should take shelter in and around the enclosures and gardens of the village, the transport staff and the countless Indian civilians in their charge began pushing the ponderous procession of camels, donkeys, ponies and oxen across the ravine and into the open plain beyond. Fortunately General Nuttall spotted that things were going awry and sent Mr C. L. Griesbach, a civilian attached to his staff from the Geological Survey of India, galloping back to bring the situation under control. Aware at last that he was required to halt, Ready gave orders that the camp followers and baggage animals should be marshalled in the floor of the ravine, and that the three escorting companies should deploy just beyond the rim. In the meantime a fresh messenger had been sent dashing out to Hector Maclaine's guns to deliver an unequivocal instruction – Maclaine was to take post in accordance with the normal conventions of the RHA, 50 yards to the left of the battery's centre division or face the consequences. This time he obeyed. Once the guns were in position and no longer in need of an escort, Lieutenant Arthur Monteith was ordered to take his troop out to the left rear to marry up with General Nuttall.

Ayub Khan Changes Front

On the far side of the battlefield Ayub Khan had begun right-wheeling his columns to offer battle, exactly as the British commanders had hoped he would. Having despatched his cavalry to threaten the enemy's open left flank, his next task was to get his guns into action. It took time to manoeuvre them into position, but within 30 minutes of the British artillery opening up, the Afghan gunners had spread themselves out in a half-moon, a mile to the north, and fired their first return salvo. One of the first fatal casualties of their fire was Captain Hugh Smith, the adjutant of Jacob's Rifles. At first the prospect of a full-on artillery duel was greeted with relish by the supremely confident E Battery crews. Gunner Francis Naylor, a member of Sergeant Patrick Mullane's No. 2 Sub-Division, recalled that after three or four rounds of counter-battery fire Gunner Moorcroft remarked, 'We'll soon have 'em out of action!'[38] And so they might have done, if only it had been possible for Blackwood and his officers to gauge the range accurately. The evidence tends to suggest, however, that as a result of the heat haze, E Battery spent the afternoon overshooting. Outnumbered 5:2 by an enemy who did not seem to be experiencing the same difficulty in finding the range, the British gun-crews soon found themselves fighting at a significant disadvantage.

Before long the weight of enemy fire was such that the infantry colonels were obliged to order their men to lie down. The Indian cavalry and the gunners had no such option and soon began taking casualties. Gunner Naylor recalled the early death of one of his comrades:

> Almost at the outset, a shoeing-smith was ordered to fasten a shoe on the wheel-horse of the gun. He was a man who had been remarkable for his strength and freedom from sickness; but he was now ill, and, like most people of the sort, took his ailment very badly. He dismounted and as he began his work said, 'I hope the first shot they fire will blow me to bits.' Almost as soon as we got into action a shot came and killed him, as well as two or three natives.[39]

In the meantime the Afghan regular infantry had closed up between their supporting field batteries in preparation for an assault on the distant khaki line. To their left great crowds of *ghazi* fanatics, several thousand men in all, were closing fast on the British right flank. Most of them were advancing on the north side of the Mahmudabad Ravine towards the 66th Regiment and the two troops of cavalry echeloned to its right rear, but there were also a number of smaller parties pushing hard for Khig. Once they were into the village they would be well placed to menace both the right of the British line, and the baggage and its escort around Mahmudabad. Although there had been no heavy fighting up this point, both British flanks were already under pressure. The signs of impending danger should have been plain to see.

This was the time for Burrows to recognize that he had bitten off more than he could chew. If he was to fight an enemy force that was so clearly going to overlap his line at both extremities, it was essential that he fall back to some point on the ground where his flanks could be anchored, his infantry could find shelter from artillery fire and his baggage would be secure. Blackwood's gun-position had served its purpose – beyond forcing the enemy to deploy it had no wider tactical significance, and there was now far too great a distance between the fighting line and the baggage train, with its water carts, reserve ammunition and medical facilities. The Mahmudabad Ravine was the nearest natural source of water but lay a thousand yards to the south, leaving the regimental *bhistis*, or water carriers, terribly exposed as they dashed back and forth to replenish their skins. And by now it was more than merely hot. With the sun directly overhead in a cloudless bright blue sky, the plain was rapidly turning into a furnace. Except in the vicinity of the well-irrigated villages to the right rear of the British line, there was not a tree in sight and not a jot of shade to be had. It was not long before most of the soldiers' water bottles had been drained. The guns added to the discomfort by throwing up great clouds of dust, irritating the eyes, noses and throats of everybody in their vicinity.

Instead of giving ground and attempting to draw the enemy onto strongpoint positions in and around the villages, Burrows decided to stand fast on the open plain. It was probably already too late to make use of Khig as a defensive position, at least not without a stiff fight to clear it first. Encouraged by the approach of the *ghazis*, some of the villagers took up arms to engage the British from the flank.

At the left rear Lieutenants Reid and Monteith had spread their skirmish lines as far as they dared, but ultimately the enemy irregular horse had almost limitless room for manoeuvre. By keeping their distance the Afghan horsemen could slip past the carbine-armed sowars without significant loss. If the left was to be adequately protected, it was clear that it would need to be reinforced. Nuttall sent the hard-riding John Monteith to bring Lieutenant Edward Smith's troop across the battlefield from its flank-protection task on the right. When at length Monteith located the troop, Smith pointed out that he had a number of distant vedettes thrown out in the direction of Khig and would need a few minutes to concentrate his men. His immediate duty discharged, Monteith went on his way, never imagining for a moment that the general's order would be countermanded. Countermanded it was, however, when Colonel Malcolmson rode up to find out what was going on. Remarkably Malcolmson made no attempt to communicate to his brigade commander what he had done or why he had done it.

While the artillery duel had been raging in the centre, a few hundred Herati irregular horse had made their way back across the plain from the direction of Maiwand to join the thousands of *ghazis* massing in the easternmost nullah. Although the credit for the first attack is most often given by historians to the *ghazis*, Lieutenant Lynch's account shows that the first serious thrust of the day was made by the Herati cavalry. Lynch was on the D Company firing line alongside his company commander, Captain William McMath, a 35-year-old Irishman who until recently had been standing in as General Burrows's brigade-major. Captain Percy Heath, the full-time incumbent, had been struck down by illness just as the column was departing Kandahar, but had since recovered and had come into the field a few days earlier, freeing McMath to return to regimental duty. McMath typified the breed of fanatical sportsmen who populated the British officer corps in large numbers during the high Victorian era. Five years earlier he had survived a severe mauling at the hands of a wounded panther. Not only had he lived through a life-or-death tussle with the beast, but he also managed to add it to his bag in the process. Despite some dreadful injuries, he stubbornly refused to bleed to death whilst walking the six miles back to his camp. Skipping about the company position at her master's heels was McMath's pet dog 'Nellie'.[40] The centre sub-unit in a line of five, D Company was formed in a loose two-rank firing line, with its sections crouched low in the shallow cover of the nullah and the officers and sergeants arrayed a few paces to their rear:

> Early in the action I saw a lot of cavalry on our front, evidently preparing to charge us. This they did. McMath prepared for them and held his fire until they were quite near, within one hundred yards I should say. Then he let them have a volley. Several fell, horses and riders mixed up in great confusion. Many closed with us, but they had lost their formation and there was no shock. They came on, and when within striking distance the horses refused to face our bayonets and, turning to their left, rode along our front, pushing our bayonets to one side. The men on the knee and standing stuck men and horses as they brushed by. This was the only time during the fight I saw the enemy's

> cavalry actually close with us. When they passed away to the flank we opened fire on the riders and horses on the ground in front of us, and very soon disposed of them.[41]

Already Surgeon-Major Alexander Preston, the regimental medical officer (RMO) of the 66th, had been laid low. As he rushed onto the firing line to tend to the battalion's first casualty of the day, he was unfortunate enough to be hit by a stray round and thus became its second.[42]

The First Ghazi Attack

There was never any question that the repulse of the cavalry would deter the mass of *ghazis* north of the ravine. At some unknown signal dozens of flags inscribed with verses from the Qur'an were thrust skywards, the cue for a massed assault by perhaps 2,000–3,000 fanatics. Afghan folklore recounts that they were egged on by one of the women of Khig. Reciting traditional patriotic chants and flourishing a banner, the heroine Malala was at the forefront of the charge. By now the men of the 66th were lying down again to protect themselves from artillery fire, but as the *ghazis* broke from the cover of the deep nullah a cautionary word of command from their colonel, repeated up and down the line by his company officers, brought them up onto one knee to load. Realising that the enemy advance was in danger of lapping around his right, Galbraith instructed Captain Francis Cullen to wheel B Company back through 90 degrees so as to refuse the battalion's right flank.[43] In accordance with the colonel's most recent fire-control order, Cullen brought the men of B Company to their feet to loose the first in a sequence of hard-hitting company volleys. As the B Company soldiers dropped back onto their knees to eject their empty cases and reload, C Company was standing up to fire. So it continued, the deafening, thunderous broadsides rippling up and down the firing line, each of them momentarily immersing the company concerned in a billowing cloud of white smoke. Noting the devastating effect of one of his early salvoes, McMath was heard exhorting D Company with, 'That's right men, go on giving them volleys like that!'

A reconstruction compiled from survivor testimony by Lieutenant Manus O'Donel [*sic*] of the 66th, detached at the time of the battle to Khelat-i-Ghilzai, offers an interesting insight into the fighting techniques of the *ghazis*:

> Among the Ghazis nearly every man seemed to be carrying a standard of some description. At the beginning of their advance they made no rushes, but came on quietly a few paces at a time, then halting they would plant their flags in the ground, fire, and again move on. But when they got nearer and the volleys began to tell upon them, the slaughter

> of them was terrific: in some places they would be seen to fall three deep – and always as they went down those behind would quietly step over them and come on with their gleaming knives. All along our line a tremendous fire was kept up.[44]

Driven by regimental loyalty to keep a watchful eye over the 66th wherever he was able, Captain Thomas Harris of the staff suggested to Burrows that he redeploy one of Slade's divisions to assist Galbraith. With commendable speed Lieutenant Jones and his men brought their two 6-pounders out of action on the centre-left and back into action on the right, where they began belching case-shot into the leading wave of *ghazis*. In order to protect the artillery properly, Galbraith began shuffling his line to the right, until B Company had made sufficient ground to re-form on the far side of the guns.

In the face of such a storm of fire it was not long before the plain to the east was littered with hundreds of bloodied white-robed forms. To advance into the frontal arcs of five companies of British infantry over ground as flat as a billiard table was madness, and for all their fanaticism the surviving *ghazis* were quickly driven to ground along the general line of the nullah. One of the casualties on the British side of the battlefield was Captain Harris who had noticed from his elevated position on horseback that some of Galbraith's sections were firing low. Having dismounted to help with corrections, Harris was hit in the arm as he was climbing back into the saddle to rejoin the general.[45] By now 2nd Lieutenant Walter Olivey had also been hit and seriously wounded. He was observed with a handkerchief wrapped around a nasty head wound, but when somebody tried to relieve him of the Queen's Colour so that he could go to the rear he refused point-blank to leave his post.[46]

To the south of the 66th other uncommitted bands of *ghazis* and irregular horse were manoeuvring around the British right. Many of them took to the floor of the ravine, rendering themselves invulnerable to the heavy fire sweeping the field from the north. Scores of men armed with *jezails* and rifled muskets clambered up to the top of the bank and began a desultory fire-fight with Cullen's company. For the next 30 minutes dauntless bands of *ghazis* attempted further rushes against the 66th, only for each successive wave to be mown down in its turn. Other more prudent enemy groupings pushed on into Khig where they secured fire positions in some of the houses and gardens. This seemed to the British commanders in Mahmudabad to presage a heavy attack on the baggage train. It had been a struggle to get the leading pack animals back into the cover of the ravine, but somehow, urged on by the harassed commissariat and transport staffs, the camp followers had managed it. Now the baggage was crowded into a great anarchic huddle, a couple of hundred yards to the west of the village, where to some extent it was protected from the long-range fire from the gardens around Khig.

In order to cover the baggage train's chaotic about-turn and shield it from the irregular cavalry attempting to bypass General Nuttall's position, Major Ready had deployed his escort companies in a wedge-shaped firing line. G Company of the 66th took the left face and came into action periodically to keep the probing cavalry in check with long-range volleys. Lieutenant Whitby's company of Bombay Grenadiers occupied the apex of the wedge, with Salmon's company of Jacob's Rifles extended to their right. Geoghegan's troop of the 3rd Light Cavalry remained south of the ravine, covering Khig from the gardens and orchards on the eastern side of Mahmudabad. It was about now that Captain Quarry acquired an additional subaltern, when 2nd Lieutenant George Melliss left his duties with the baggage train and sought permission to join G Company as a company officer. Before long the pressure from the direction of Khig was such that Major Ready felt the need to deploy a Martini-armed G Company section to his right rear, where Geoghegan's sowars were struggling to hold their ground with their far less capable carbines. Quarry gave him 2nd Lieutenant Reginald Bray and 20 men. Ready dismounted, left his horse with G Company and took off on foot to direct Bray's deployment. After some preliminary skirmishing he positioned the section on the left bank of the ravine, where it was well-placed to counter attempts at infiltration.[47]

Despite the exposed nature of their position and the weight of artillery fire being brought to bear on them, the men of the Bombay Grenadiers appeared to be enduring the ordeal well. Away to the battalion's left loose swarms of irregular cavalry were now beginning to pressurize the firing line from the north. Somewhere behind the line the general was riding from unit to unit with his staff, pausing to confer with subordinate commanders where necessary and monitoring the effectiveness of their fire. In other words he was doing exactly what a good brigade commander should be doing – watching for enemy thrusts and deploying or concentrating assets to meet them. But the better he was doing his job as the infantry brigade commander, the more he was neglecting the role of GOC. There may have been some sensitivity about his issuing orders to units of the cavalry brigade without first going through Nuttall, as Mayne's squadron was still standing stock-still on the open plain, with troops deployed left- and right-rear of Osborne's guns. The two dozen or more horse carcasses scattered about the position indicated that the squadron was taking heavy punishment. Mayne wrote that there 'not a vestige of cover'. With the infantry already formed in close support of E Battery it should have been obvious that men and horses were dying to no good purpose, yet neither brigadier saw fit to move the squadron to a more sheltered position. Nor for a long time did Mayne seek permission to move on.

Worried by the continued cavalry probes between the Bombay Grenadiers and General Nuttall's skirmish line, Burrows ordered Colonel Anderson to refuse his left flank. Captain James Grant, commanding the battalion's left wing, immediately wheeled his two outermost companies back through 45 degrees. To protect the extremities of his battle-line further, the GOC decided to commit the Jacob's Rifles supports under Major Iredell – two companies to each flank. Iredell had only one other British officer with him, a newly joined 21-year-old called Duncan Cole. As the heaviest fighting to date had been on the right, Iredell decided to take that flank himself and to send his less-experienced subordinate out to the left. It was the work of only a few minutes to double the companies into place. Cole deployed his men to the left of Captain Grant, thereby further extending the refused left flank.

Mystified by the continuing absence of Smith's troop and concerned by the mounting pressure at the left rear, General Nuttall sent a message to the GOC asking for artillery support. Burrows responded by instructing Slade to send Lieutenant Trenchard Fowle and his howitzers to take post on the extreme left. The arrival of the guns came as a great comfort to Cole's nervous sepoys, who were already under heavy artillery fire and only too keenly aware of the yawning gap between themselves and the cavalry skirmish line. At least now the intervening ground would be covered by artillery fire.

Barely had Major Iredell settled into position on the right of the 66th, where for the last 15 minutes it had been relatively quiet, than he received orders to move back to the centre to join the rest of his battalion. The GOC's staff officers guided the jogging companies into the interval between the centre and right-hand divisions of E Battery. Working from right to left, then, the final configuration of the British line of battle was two troops of cavalry echeloned right rear of the 66th, B Company of the 66th, Lieutenant Jones with a pair of 6-pounders, C, D, F and H Companies of the 66th, 4 companies of Jacob's Rifles under Colonel Mainwaring, Osborne's division with No. 2 Squadron, 3rd Light Cavalry, echeloned to their rear, 2 companies of Jacob's Rifles under Major Iredell, Fowell's division, the Sappers & Miners, Maclaine's division, 7 companies of Bombay Grenadiers under Colonel Anderson, 2 companies of Jacob's Rifles under Cole, and finally Fowle with the two 12-pounder howitzers. Captain Slade, Lieutenant Faunce and the third pair of smoothbores were positioned slightly further back than the E Battery guns, firing through the interval between Maclaine's guns and the right-flank company of the Bombay Grenadiers. Several hundred yards to the west, Monteith's and Reid's troops were fighting an almost separate action at the left rear of the firing line.

The Afghan Infantry Attack the British Centre

Colonel Griffiths was on the right flank of the Bombay Grenadiers near Maclaine's guns when, at about 1.15 p.m., he observed:

> . . . the enemy bring up a battery of artillery and place them in a ravine about 500 yards [actually 300 yards] to my right front. With these guns were a regiment of regular infantry and numberless ghazis. I threw back the right company of my wing so as to bring a direct fire on the guns and infantry; but the cover they were under was so good that they did not sustain much loss, until some time after they made an advance and appeared in the open.[48]

The adjustment on the battalion's right flank was a minor one – a slight shift of position to engage fresh targets deploying along the lip of the nullah immediately in front of E Battery. A surprised Major Blackwood was heard to remark 'They have got a battery 500 yards right in my front.' Further up the nullah to the Afghan right, eight more 6-pounders were firing in enfilade on the left wing of the Grenadiers at ranges of 600–800 yards. The Afghan advance to which Griffiths refers occurred only about 15 minutes later.

For some little while beforehand it had been obvious to British commanders in the centre that Ayub Khan was about to launch a major attack with his infantry battalions. The 3rd Infantry Brigade was commanded by a Tajik officer called Ghafur Khan and consisted of about a thousand Heratis divided into three small battalions. At a given signal all three units broke cover and began closing on the ostensibly frail khaki line to their front. To the left of the Heratis, three Kabuli battalions from Taj Muhammad Khan's 1st Infantry Brigade were surging into a concurrent assault on the British centre. Facing them were the right-wing companies of the Grenadiers, the E Battery guns, the Sappers & Miners, and six companies of Jacob's Rifles. While the RHA 9-pounders exacted an early toll with common shell, the two infantry commandants waited patiently for the range to close. At length Anderson and Mainwaring began barking fire-control orders. Straining to hear the battalion commanders over the noise of the guns, the company officers brought their men to their feet and began firing a series of hammer-blow volleys which quickly blanketed the battlefield in smoke and inflicted ruinous casualties on the leading Afghan units. Colonel Griffiths recalled that 'at first volleys were fired by companies, but after a few rounds, such was the din that words of command could not be heard, and independent firing was carried on along the whole line.'[49] The foremost Herati battalion was hit particularly hard, not only by the infantry, but by murderous salvoes of case-shot from the artillery. In the face of such a barrage the Afghan regulars soon lost all forward momentum. Return fire took a toll of the now fully exposed British firing line; Captain James Grant was hit in the leg, but stayed on his feet and continued hobbling up and down behind his men. A few minutes more and it was clear that the first attack of the Afghan infantry was spent.

First Signs of Wavering

Burrows was still not content with the dispositions on the left, and rode over to Lieutenant Cole to instruct him to refuse his firing line still further. All that was required was a simple adjustment, a rearwards pivot through 20–30 yards in the left-hand company, and a correspondingly shorter distance in the right-hand one. But as soon as Cole gave the order to move, his men became seized with panic. Some even tried bolting for the rear. Cole and the staff berated the sepoys angrily and to the general's great relief succeeded in stopping the rot. Nonetheless it had been a deeply alarming incident which for a moment or two had seemed to threaten the wholesale collapse of the British left. Slowly but surely a series of adverse factors – thirst, hunger, fatigue, the exposed nature of the position and mounting casualties – were combining to overwhelm the fragile fighting spirit of the younger sepoys.

Amidst all the heavy fighting on the eastern side of Mahmudabad, Major Ready had resolved to try and restore the situation by taking the offensive. Leaving Quarry, Melliss and the balance of G Company to hold their ground in front of the village, Ready took Bray's section and elements of his two Indian companies away to the right to clear some of the orchards and gardens on the south side of the ravine. A good dose of bravado and a few minutes hard fighting soon brought the enclosures under his control. Encouraged by this early success he sent several parties of sepoys to clear along the floor of the ravine towards Khig. The *ghazis* and tribal irregulars between the two villages were giving ground before Ready's attack, when Colonel Malcolmson rode up to rein it in. It would not have pleased an experienced infantry field officer like John Ready, to be overruled by a colonel of Indian cavalry. Whether he was angry at the intervention or not, he had no choice but to obey and quickly fell back to the outskirts of Mahmudabad.

Lieutenant Salmon recorded some of the consequences of Malcolmson's over-caution:

> It is needless to observe that the enemy not only speedily reoccupied the gardens and enclosures, but emboldened by our retirement, came in greater numbers, and the fire we were obliged to sustain was proportionately greater; indeed it was almost a certainty of being hit if any one got up from the ground and moved from place to place. Seeing this the enemy became even bolder, and we were compelled to repel two very determined attacks which were made on the baggage later on.[50]

With the main force pinned down on the plain a mile away and the enemy pressing from all sides but one, the ever nervous baggage train was beginning to fragment. More and more camp followers, many of them Kandaharis of questionable loyalty to begin with, were concluding that their British masters were in trouble and that it might be prudent to slip away before it was too late. As for any disintegrating body of camp followers in any period of history, the secret was to get away with something valuable by way of compensation, be it an officer's portmanteau or a couple of camels laden with rifle ammunition. Not only were the least important civilians beginning to drift away, but the most important ones, the water *bhistis* and the *doolie* (stretcher) bearers, were refusing to go forward to the firing line, as the journey had become distinctly perilous.

Hard Pounding

By now Jones's and Fowle's divisions had been brought back from the flanks to rejoin Slade and Faunce on the smoothbore battery's original position, where it soon became clear that all six guns were down to their last few rounds. Some while earlier Slade had sent gallopers to scour the baggage train for more. Now in desperation he despatched his brace of RA subalterns. Without ammunition, there seemed little point in the battery continuing to hold its ground. Preoccupied with laying down a heavy weight of fire, the artillery officers had failed to appreciate that the departure of Fowle's howitzers had been every bit as distressing to Cole's sepoys as their arrival had been reassuring. Slade now compounded the effect by deciding to move the entire battery back to the baggage train to replenish. He might have been better advised to ask Lieutenant Faunce and his men to revert to their primary role as infantrymen, as the sudden withdrawal of the battery rattled the Indian troops so badly that many inferred a retreat had been ordered. With his guns trotting away towards Mahmudabad, Slade made his way over to the E Battery gun line to confer with Major Blackwood.

All the while the Afghan artillery had been maintaining its impressive performance. Not only were British casualties mounting, but the troops on the receiving end were beginning to feel the psychological and moral effects of a sustained pummelling. Captain Mayne's sowars had been cruelly exposed throughout: 'My squadron had by this time been standing passively for fully three hours under fire from artillery and now small arms, and I had lost more than a third of my horses and was at about only troop strength.' Having himself been twice wounded by shell splinters, Mayne at last sought permission to move the squadron to safer ground:

> I saw Captain Heath, General Burrow's [*sic*] Brigade Major, not far off, and rode and told him what I thought. He went and spoke to General Burrows and returning told me I could withdraw from where I was and go and watch at which ever flank I was most wanted.[51]

Mayne set off for the right but was advised on his arrival 'by some officer, I forget who' that the left flank was actually the harder pressed. He decided to turn about and marry up with General Nuttall and Major Currie. On his way across the battlefield he encountered some of the small groups of Afghan cavalry roving the plain between the infantry firing line and the baggage. At one point he was obliged to send eight sowars to the rescue of Surgeon Karoba Kirkitar, the Indian RMO of Jacob's Rifles, who in attempting to cross the plain on foot had been surrounded by a small group of enemy cavalrymen.

Eventually Mayne was able to dismount his battered squadron on General Nuttall's skirmish line, where he took up position to the right of Monteith and Reid. Pushing about half of his men forward into the cover of a shallow depression, he was able to get the better of a fire-fight with a body of *ghazis* about 300 yards in front of his position. With the enemy cavalry probing wider and wider, Nuttall had been forced to adjust and extend his skirmish line in conformity. For the time being, however, the arrival of Mayne's squadron had stabilised the situation on the left. Nuttall decided to leave Major Currie in charge and ride back across the battlefield with Major Hogg to check that all was well with the two troops on the right. It is possible that they undertook the journey in order to find out what had happened to Smith's troop, earlier retained by Malcolmson.

In the meantime Lieutenant Trenchard Fowle had located some ammunition and now tried to make his way back towards the firing line with his brace of howitzers. He was not able to get very far forward into the plain before the risk of interdiction by enemy horsemen became unacceptable. The division halted and came into action from an isolated position a few hundred yards south of the cavalry skirmish line. Viewed from the air, the British perimeter was beginning to look more and more like a horse-shoe.

Gunner Naylor's description of the action on the E Battery position captures something of the ferocity of the artillery duel.

> At Number 2 Gun . . . I fired no fewer than 105 rounds. That gun and the other guns became almost red hot, and some of the men had their hands burnt in handling them. It was while serving the gun that I lost my hand. I was taking a tube out of my pouch to fire another cartridge, when a six-pound shot ricocheted on the gun-wheel tyre, which is a broad iron band. The shot tore the tyre as if it had been India rubber, struck me on the left hand, and then broke one of the bones in one of our officers' arms.[52]

The officer in question was Lieutenant Newton Fowell, the divisional commander. While Naylor was being ushered away to a *doolie*, Fowell pulled himself together and tried to continue fighting his guns. Slade could see that he was far too badly injured and ordered that he be placed on his horse and led to the rear. For a while Slade commanded Nos. 1 and 2 Sub-Divisions himself, but when a few minutes later Major Blackwood was severely wounded in the thigh, he took over the battery. No longer able to ride, Blackwood tied up his leg with a handkerchief and was helped away in the direction of the 66th where, exhausted by the exertion, he sat himself down behind H Company to observe the fight. When he had gathered his breath, he made himself useful by assisting the company commander with his range estimates. The men were 'remarkably steady, only delivering their fire at the word of command', recalled Beresford-Peirse. When a fresh band of *ghazis* tried to mount an assault into the company's frontal arcs, a hard-hitting volley swept them away. Peering through the smoke Blackwood caught sight of a seemingly deserted plain and remarked to Beresford-Peirse 'By Jove! They are all gone!'[53]

By now most of the 66th had made serious inroads into the 70 cartridges with which they had started the fight and were replenishing their pouches from reserve stocks brought forward by Lieutenant Chute. Having shouted himself hoarse giving fire-control orders, Captain McMath was obliged to position himself just in front of D Company's right flank, where all his men could see him and a flourish of his sword could serve as the executive to fire.[54] A short while later he was wounded in the hand. Amongst the company's targets was the pair of 3-pounders, which it cleared of crewmen several times in succession. More testing were the mounted mullahs and other leaders, who from time to time rode into the open and wheeled their ponies back and forth in no-man's land, in an attempt to incite a renewed *ghazi* onslaught.

When Nuttall and his brigade-major reached the right flank, they noticed that a hundred or so *ghazis* had crept from the cover of the Mahmudabad Ravine onto the expanse of plain south of the 66th. The general decided to clear the infiltrators with a charge by the two troops echeloned to Galbraith's right rear. Major Hogg galloped over to Lieutenant Edward Smith to pass on the order and then turned away to rejoin his brigadier. When a few minutes later nothing much had happened, Hogg rode back again to find out why. 'He [Smith] said his men were out of hand, and asked me to help him. I observed that most of the men had carbines in their hands instead of drawn swords.' A few sharp words from the brigade-major did the trick. Just then Currie's adjutant, Lieutenant William Owen, rode up on some unknown errand, a fact which strongly suggests that the 3rd Light Cavalry Troop on the right was one of his. Hogg told him to take over from the troop's Indian officer, who like Smith appeared to have lost control of his men.

Following some animated words of encouragement from the British officers about the honour of their respective regiments, the delayed charge finally got under way. Both troops were well into their stride when Nuttall galloped up behind them and bellowed 'Halt!' The confused sowars wheeled left in disarray, a manoeuvre which attracted sarcastic jeering from the enemy. Owen and Smith set about re-forming their troops some distance behind the British centre. It transpired that Nuttall had stopped the charge out of concern that the nullah in front (the same one in which the 66th was positioned) might present a problem to riders. In fact it was nowhere near deep enough. After this first dismal performance by the cavalry, Nuttall and Hogg returned to the left rear with both troops in tow. For the time being the plain to the right of the 66th was devoid of friendly cavalry.

Behind the firing line the medical officers were doing their best for the men ferried back by stretcher parties. Surgeon Arthur Dane of the Bombay Grenadiers already had his hands full when the force chaplain, the Reverend A. G. Cane appeared at his aid post to advise that more than a score of casualties, a mixture of sepoys and gunners, were lying untended in a hollow 200 yards behind the guns.[55] In a manifestation of the age-old alliance between doctors and chaplains they dashed into the maelstrom with a handful of dauntless Indian stretcher bearers, to see what could be done for the stranded casualties.

By now Lieutenant Cole's companies had received a mauling from the Afghan artillery. The two company subadars were already down, leaving Cole and a lone jemadar as the only uninjured officers. To make matters worse the badly shaken sepoys had been rattling through their ammunition and now had very few rounds left in their pouches. Suddenly a roundshot came bouncing through the line to deposit young Cole's mangled remains several yards to the rear. Elsewhere Burrows and the staff were still ranging up and down the line, when the infantry brigade-major, Percy Heath, took a bullet in the head and fell dead at the general's side. All over the battlefield men were enjoying extraordinary good fortune or miserable bad luck according to their destiny. Lieutenant William Aslett of the Bombay Grenadiers was one of the lucky ones: first a bullet hit his helmet, spinning it around on his head; then a second near-miss ricocheted from the basket of his sword to kill one of the sepoys fighting beside him.[56] Captain James Grant had remained with his men despite his earlier injury, but was hit again, this time in the midriff. Fortunately the bullet was spent and though it dealt Grant a painful blow, it did no lasting harm. Further along the line, on Lieutenant Osborne's position, Gunner James Collis was forced to take command of No. 4 Sub-Division when Sergeant Wood became the fifth member of the crew to be killed by counter-battery fire. A short while later a roundshot ploughed into the limber-team, killing the wheel-horses and striking the limber-box. Remarkably the driver of the wheel-pair was left unhorsed but otherwise unharmed. By now the weight of enemy fire was such that some of the sepoys from Jacob's Rifles were crowding in on the guns and limbers in search of cover. Three of them even clambered under Collis's gun and were not easily driven from their place of refuge.

Back near Mahmudabad the adjutant of the 3rd Sind Horse had decided to use his initiative. In the absence of his colonel, Edward Monteith brought up the regiment's rearguard squadron and married up with Geoghegan, who so far had lost a dozen of his men defending the eastern side of the village. The pair agreed to cross the Mahmudabad Ravine together and make a charge aimed at clearing a number of enemy parties infiltrating between the baggage guard and the firing line. The combined command was poised with sabres drawn, just about ready for the off, when Malcolmson rode up to put a stop to the enterprise. Worried that the expanse of plain to the right of the 66th had been left unoccupied since the departure of Smith and Owen, he decided to allocate one of Monteith's troops to Geoghegan and send him across the ravine to protect the right of the firing line. Under orders to charge the *ghazi* infiltrators if they attempted to press any further forward, Geoghegan deployed his enlarged command to confront them from a distance of about 250–300 yards.[57]

The Break-In

It was about 2.15 p.m. when the Afghan guns suddenly fell silent. At first it seemed to the British that they had run out of ammunition. In reality thousands more *ghazis* had been working their way down the easternmost nullah and were now poised to mount a massed assault in the centre. Only moments after the guns ceased fire the *ghazis* came swarming from their cover, chanting prayers, shrieking their battle cries and brandishing keen-edged Khyber knives. Colonel Galbraith immediately brought his men to their feet and bellowed a fire-control order. The regiment's volleys were controlled with the customary rhythmic trio of executive commands. First Captain Francis Cullen's voice was raised above the din of battle: 'Ready . . . Present . . . Fire!' Treating B Company's 'present' as their cue, the men of C Company cocked an ear for the familiar tones of their own Captain Walter Roberts: 'Ready . . . Present . . . Fire!' With their C Company comrades shrouded in smoke, the D Company men came up to the present in their turn. Again and again the sequence of guttural commands echoed up and down the line. By the third or fourth time the men of the 66th had squeezed their triggers, the plain in front was strewn with scores more dead and dying *ghazis*, the heroine Malala amongst them. The noise, the smoke and the carnage was just enough if not to halt the fanatics in their tracks, at least to force them to fight shy of the formidable Martini-Henry. A largely instinctive veering movement drew yet more *ghazis* in the direction of the RHA guns. Colonel Anderson was quick to perceive the looming threat and immediately began refusing his right-wing companies. If the worst came to the worst he would now be able to bring enfilading fire to bear on the gun line. Notwithstanding the heavy punishment inflicted on their leading elements, the succeeding waves of *ghazis* succeeded in bursting into the E Battery position precisely as Anderson had anticipated.

Thousands more Afghans were assaulting from points further left. The men of the late Lieutenant Cole's command could take no more and cracked suddenly. Recoiling in panic and confusion from their position on the extreme left, the distraught sepoys began crowding in on the left wing and rear of the Bombay Grenadiers. With the *ghazis* charging home on all sides, Colonel Anderson and his officers realized instinctively that the time had come to form square. In a crisis the drill-book made provision for company rallying-squares, a formation which, because it required no interaction between sub-units, could be adopted at great speed. Unfortunately the adjutant seems to have raised the cry to form a battalion square, a much more complex drill movement requiring close coordination between companies.[58] There was neither the time nor the space for such a complicated manoeuvre to be effected smoothly. In a matter of moments the sepoys became bewildered and confused. Inevitably both wings of the battalion folded and gave ground before the furious onset of the enemy. As a result most of Anderson's soldiers ended up clustered into a solid wedge-shaped mass of humanity, frightened, shaken and unsure quite what to do next. They seem to have struggled even to fix bayonets or to defend themselves effectively in the crush. The *ghazis* were not slow to take advantage of the disarray and began butchering the disorientated sepoys by the dozen. Major Edward Leach VC, serving on the staff as Burrows's orderly officer, wrote that '. . . the indifference of the men to death was most extraordinary and numbers were cut down without a struggle.' In attempting to rally the sepoys into some semblance of order, General Burrows got caught up in the mêlée and was obliged to defend himself with his revolver. Colonel Mainwaring described how the panic appeared to him:

> The whole of the ground to the left of the 30th NI and between it and the Grenadiers was covered with swarms of ghazis and banner men. The ghazis were actually in the ranks of the Grenadiers, pulling the men out and hacking them down with their swords. I have not any idea how this state of affairs came about as the battery firing on my left prevented my seeing in that direction until it had moved away.[59]

Saving the Guns

Swept up in the sudden collapse of the Bombay Grenadiers, Captain Slade concluded that the time had come to get the E Battery guns away. He was with Lieutenant Fowell's now leaderless division at the centre of the RHA gun line when the crisis broke and was able to get Nos. 1 and 2 Sub-Divisions limbered up and clear of the fray without any resort to close-quarter fighting, though it was the closest of shaves. As No. 2 was about to pull clear, the young sergeant in charge, Patrick Mullane, saw one of his men go down. Disregarding his own best interests, Mullane dismounted and dashed to the rescue. Throwing the badly wounded Driver Istead over one shoulder, Mullane rushed back to the limber and heaved Istead aboard with seconds to spare. On the right of the E Battery position it was a similarly close-run thing. Lieutenant Edmund Osborne bought a few precious seconds of time by charging in amongst a group of *ghazis* wielding his sabre. They must have been scattered by Osborne's sudden onslaught, because a few moments later he was seen dismounted, heaving on the trail of one of his guns alongside his men. With Nos. 3 and 4 safely hooked in and trotting away to the south, Osborne turned back to his charger but was shot and killed before he could clamber into the saddle. That the bulk of the battery had been able to get clear was due at least in part to the quick thinking of Captain William Beresford-Peirse, who at the first sign of trouble turned the rear rank of his left half-company about and deployed them to fire into the throng around the guns.[60]

As usual Hector Maclaine thought he knew best and chose to ignore the order to limber up, in favour of firing one last salvo of case-shot. Writing some years later Gunner Collis recounted a hearsay story to the effect that Maclaine had heard Slade's trumpet call but called out to his men, 'Limber-up, be damned! Give them another round.'[61] No doubt it was a murderous salvo, but it was never going to stall the maddened rush completely. Maclaine's more experienced superior had given the order to retire at precisely the right moment. Now, having tarried even for a matter of seconds, it was far too late to get Nos. 5 and 6 Sub-Divisions clear without a close-quarter scrimmage, a mode of fighting for which RHA gunners were singularly ill-equipped. Scorning their sabres, a number of crewmen armed themselves with trail-spikes and stood at bay around the guns, doing their level best to brain the *ghazis* rampaging through the position. When one of the limbers was brought into the thick of the fray, the drivers were dragged from the saddle and done to death. In a matter of moments the guns became irretrievable. Slightly wounded and humbled by the loss of his guns, Hector Maclaine rode clear with a solitary limber, all that could be saved of his ill-fated division.

Within a few minutes the disorder on the left had spread to infect the two companies of Jacob's Rifles fighting in the centre under Major Iredell. Badly panicked by the deteriorating situation they ran to seek protection amongst the battalion's right-wing companies. In effect the British line was being rolled up from the left. Mainwaring described the collapse of his battalion thus: 'Immediately on seeing their left and rear were turned, the regiment got into confusion and crowded down towards the right, thus falling on the left and rear of the 66th.' With the exception of the British battalion all order had now been lost in 1st Infantry Brigade. Burrows rode clear to seek the assistance of Nuttall and the cavalry. Somewhere in the tumult, the colours of the Bombay Grenadiers were lying trampled in the dust.

The Cavalry Fail to Turn the Tide

As a result of the billowing smoke on the firing line, it was far from clear to distant observers just how serious the situation had now become. When Lieutenant Geoghegan looked over his shoulder and noticed the indecent haste with which the four remaining E Battery guns were moving back across the plain towards Mahmudabad, it was the first clear sign that things were going badly awry for the infantry brigade. Galloping to the rear of his sowars Geoghegan stopped a hard-riding E Battery trumpeter to find out what had happened. A few moments hater Colonel Malcolmson galloped up and ordered Geoghegan to move both of his troops into the centre to lend whatever assistance he could. Nor was this the only element of the cavalry brigade intent on bringing succour to the infantry. Alerted by Major Leach, General Nuttall now became aware of the chaos to his right rear. He responded by mounting the cavalry troops on the left and moving towards the clouds of dust and smoke hanging over the infantry battle. With the sepoy battalions shattered and the 66th beginning to come under serious pressure, a decisive intervention by the cavalry was the only hope of preventing wholesale disaster. Traditionally historians have portrayed the collapse of the Indian battalions as occurring in the blink of an eye. But in terms of the battle's time and space, it is important to note that the sepoys must have resisted to some effect at least, in order for the cavalry to be advised of the crisis, to contract their skirmish lines, mount up, and move back across the battlefield to intervene in the manner now described.

As they were redeploying to the support of the infantry, the cavalry officers could sense the gravity of the crisis for themselves. Suddenly the GOC appeared at the gallop and reined in beside their brigadier. 'Nuttall the infantry has given way,' Burrows gasped. 'Our only chance is a cavalry charge. Do you think you could get the cavalry to charge the line of *ghazis* in rear of the infantry, and they might then perhaps be induced to re-form?'[62] A little further forward General Nuttall gave the signal to halt and told his officers to 'Form a line here.' Mayne remembered it as the first order he had been given since the battle began. As the troops were wheeling into place, a shell exploded above them killing Lieutenant Owen instantly.

On the left of the first line was Mayne's squadron of the 3rd Light Cavalry, with Arthur Monteith's troop of the 3rd Sind Horse ranged to its right. In the second line were Lieutenant Smith's troop of the 3rd Sind Horse and Owen's squadron of the 3rd Light Cavalry, now under the command of Lieutenant Reid. An E Battery gunner called Smith, one of the few surviving members of Sergeant Wood's crew, decided to attach himself to the cavalry for the coming counter-attack and took post just behind the brigade commander.[63] As the *ghazis* and irregular horse earlier held in check by Nuttall's skirmish line were now closing on the cavalry from the rear, time was of the essence. The general had drawn his sabre and was about to sound the 'Charge' when Thomas Geoghegan and his troop arrived and began wheeling into line beside everybody else. Just as Geoghegan came level with the other officers, his horse lost its left foreleg to a roundshot and spilled him violently to the ground. By the time he picked himself up, everybody else had gone. He was lucky that William Owen's groom saw him fall and quickly brought up his late master's horse as a remount.

Quickly gathering pace the cavalry bore down on the swarm of *ghazis* locked in a hand-to-hand fight with the hard-pressed remnants of the sepoy infantry. On the left of the line Mayne's sowars kept station and charged boldly through the enemy, cutting a good many down as they passed. Their flashing sabres and the momentum of their charge bought a fleeting breathing space for the Bombay Grenadiers – time enough for Anderson and his officers to break clean and restore a modicum of order. In the centre, however, Thomas Nuttall, the inexperienced cavalryman, played a part in reducing the right-hand side of the charge to chaos. Having placed himself conspicuously at the head of the first line, he chose at the last moment not to carve his way through the enemy like a regimental commander, but to veer away to the right. Seeing the general apparently indicating a change of direction, Arthur Monteith's sowars followed his lead and likewise evaded contact. Major Hogg saw it differently: '. . . whilst personally engaged in combat with the enemy, I turned round to see if the men were following and found they had gone.'[64] Matters were not helped by the fact that Monteith was clinging to the pommel of his saddle, semi-conscious at best, following a blow to the head. Mosley Mayne recalled the failed charge in quite measured terms, but the truth was that a manoeuvre intended as a powerful counter-stroke had degenerated into a half-hearted gesture:

> A minute or two were spent in forming a sort of line but we were all mixed our men and Scinde horsemen. The word was given to 'charge' and we went off, heading to the best of my belief to about the point where the 66th had been before the break. We got among and cut up a group of ghazis who were closely pursuing the Grenadiers, then there was a general pressure from the left to the right and we retired into the large nullah in front of the village [Mahmudabad] and enclosures.[65]

Evidently fighting mad, Gunner Smith chose not to change direction with the brigadier, but to ride hard into the midst of the enemy where sadly he was quickly brought down and killed.

If Nuttall's charge achieved anything, it at least bought time for John Slade to rally E Battery on the north bank of the ravine, where he briefly brought the guns back into action. With his own guns in the hands of the enemy, a dejected Hector Maclaine assumed command of Osborne's division. Slade had fired only a few more rounds before Malcolmson rode up and ordered him to cross to the relative safety of the south bank. About this time Gunner James Collis saw General Nuttall 'crying from mortification'.

The Infantry Withdrawal

Up to the point at which the line collapsed, the 66th had been holding its own with relative ease. The shallow nullah in which Galbraith had positioned his men had provided them with reasonable cover, so that thus far the battalion had suffered less than a score of casualties. Now with the sepoys crowding in from the left rear, its tactical cohesion was beginning to fragment. Realizing that their companies were all but surrounded, Beresford-Peirse and Garratt had turned their rear ranks about and engaged the enemy front and rear.[66] Before long their rearwards fields of fire had been obstructed by panic-stricken sepoys. Somewhere on the field the 'Retire' was now drifting in the air. All over the plain the British were in headlong retreat, the whole force scattered into incoherent knots of men, some still fighting hard, others disheartened and running, the infantry mostly in the direction of Khig, and the artillery and the cavalry towards Mahmudabad. Alarm and hysteria spread through what was left of the baggage train like a brush-fire. A wave of frightened camp followers and skittish camels burst from the Mahmudabad Ravine intent only on stampeding in the direction of Kandahar. The injured Surgeon-Major Preston was amongst those swept up in the panic:

> After my wound had been attended to, I was lying quietly in my doolie, imagining that all was going well . . . when all of a sudden my bearers took up the doolie and commenced running off with me as fast they could go, shouting as they ran that the ghazis were on us. I raised the curtain of the doolie and looked out, and to my great surprise, saw a regular stampede, men and animals making off as hard as they could, all in utter confusion – no order of any kind, but everybody bent on doing the utmost to save his own life and get out of the way of danger as fast and as best he could. With this object all the loads had been thrown off from the baggage animals, which were at once appropriated for riding purposes. The ground all about was in consequence covered with camp equipage, boxes of ammunition and treasure, mess stores, wine etc. My

> doolie bearers had not carried me far before they deserted me to a man, and after two other modes of conveyance in which I had been placed that afternoon had failed, I was finally taken up by an artillery wagon.

Back on the forward position the surviving Bombay Grenadiers had done well to rally into a number of coherent fighting bodies centred on their surviving British officers. While Colonel Anderson stood fast with one such group to cover the retreat, his second-in-command, Colonel Charles Griffiths, fell back on Mahmudabad at the head of about 200 men. It was not long, however, before Anderson had been wounded – hit by half a dozen shell splinters just when his battalion needed him most. Within striking distance of a gang of *ghazi* cutthroats when he fell, he was sure his time had come, when a stretcher party of four sepoys led by Havildar Ganda Singh appeared from nowhere to spirit him away to safety.[67] William McMath had also been horribly wounded not long after the retreat began, when a roundshot came bouncing through his company and caught him a glancing blow which shattered his shoulder and left his arm 'hanging by a shred of flesh'.[68] McMath's faithful Indian servant Haider Beg came to his master's aid, put him on his horse and led him to the rear with the frightened 'Nellie' yapping alongside them.[69]

General Burrows galloped back from the forward area towards Mahmudabad, searching frantically for the senior cavalry officers as he went, still clinging to the forlorn hope that a whole-hearted charge might yet save the day. It was not long after 3.00 when Burrows happened upon Major Currie and a body of the 3rd Light Cavalry. According to the general's report, when he instructed Currie to organize a fresh charge, the major did not even do him the courtesy of responding. Later Currie would claim not to have heard the order, but it is unsurprising that in the aftermath of the battle Burrows took a dim view of his performance. Spotting General Nuttall at the head of some sowars of the Sind Horse, Burrows galloped over to join him. 'I went to him and called on him to charge and save the infantry. I added that it was our only hope. General Nuttall replied that he could not, [as] the men were out of hand.' All across the plain, bands of sowars were cantering hard for the ravine and the relative safety of the south bank. Angry and dismayed, Burrows gave up on the cavalry and rode back towards the infantry 'to see what might be done to save them from annihilation'. As he was in transit between the respective lines of retreat, he was unhorsed by a stray bullet. Fortunately a badly wounded sowar called Burmadeen happened by and nobly insisted that the general take his horse.[70]

Rearguard Actions

In so dire a situation the principal object of the infantry was to keep together, stay calm and lay down a heavy suppressive fire. At all costs the exultant enemy host had to be prevented from coming to close quarters. Earlier in the day the soldiers might have coped readily, but by now everybody on the battlefield was suffering from the physical effects of chronic dehydration and a mind-numbing tiredness brought on by hours of unrelenting exposure to the searing heat of the plain. In such a sorry physical state even fear, rage and adrenalin were stultified by exhaustion. Above the noise of battle an endless sequence of bellowed and frequently contradictory commands added to the confusion – a nearby sergeant saying one thing, the company commander something else. Once the dreaded *ghazis* were in amongst the companies in any strength, all would be lost. Much depended on the discipline, fortitude and fighting spirit of the 66th, and the ability of the officers in the broken Indian battalions to rally *ad hoc* groupings capable of supporting Galbraith's embattled companies.

It was 800 yards from Galbraith's position to the north bank of the ravine, 40 yards from one side of the obstacle to the other, and a further 300 yards after that to the first walled garden in Khig. Running along the edge of the village was an irrigation ditch which was sufficiently deep to shelter a kneeling man and so provide a potential rallying point.[71] Few details of the 66th Regiment's withdrawal have survived, but it is clear that the regiment was split into at least two large groups and that it was under severe pressure from the outset. In normal circumstances Galbraith would have attempted to withdraw by wings, making use of alternate fire and movement in accordance with the 1877 edition of *Field Exercise and Evolutions of Infantry*, but with the men of Jacob's Rifles running in amongst his left-wing companies, hotly pursued by *ghazis*, it would seem improbable that anything quite so ordered would have been possible. If all else failed there was the company rallying-square. It is likely that a recoiling 66th would have attempted to coalesce into such formations as it made ground to the south. If it succeeded in maintaining a hot enough fire, some broad semblance of a retirement by wings might have emerged from the early confusion. We are probably not too wide of the mark in imagining F and H Companies operating together on the left, with B, C and D Companies falling back some distance to their right. Beresford-Peirse, whose narrative account is frustratingly short of detail, wrote that '. . . as soon as the men perceived what was happening, they faced about and delivered their fire, (keeping the *ghazis* at about 25 yards distance) as they retreated to the gardens . . .'

The Afghan *ghazis* and regulars, now irretrievably mixed together, closed up and poured in a heavy return fire. The evidence of the British burials would suggest that it cost the lives of around 60 men as they stumbled away to the south. According to General Primrose's report of 1 October 1880, presumably compiled from survivor testimony, Captains Ernest Garratt and Francis Cullen were killed before they reached the ravine, '. . . up to the last moment commanding their companies and giving their orders with as much coolness as if on an ordinary regimental parade'. A private soldier in Garratt's company saw him fall. 'I stopped to see if I could render him any assistance. I then noticed that he had a bullet wound between the temple and the jaw-bone, and that his eyes were closed. I raised his arm and found that he was dead.'[72] There does not seem to have been any recourse to the bayonet in covering the first 800 yards, as doubtless most of the soldiers had at least some ammunition in hand and kept up a heavy rate of fire as they withdrew. It was to some extent inevitable that things would go wrong at the Mahmudabad Ravine. Considerable disarray set in as men scrambled pell-mell to cross the obstacle, so much so that McMath's colour-sergeant accidentally fell on his own bayonet and was killed.[73] It is clear that the wings lost touch with one another either just before or at this point. It is probable that enemy pressure forced the respective lines of retreat to diverge.

On the far side of the ravine a number of formed bodies were somehow held together to keep the enemy in check, while others made their escape. Although the Indian infantry have been accorded scant credit, there is some evidence – principally a witness statement by Charles Griffiths – to suggest that a hundred or more Bombay Grenadiers rallied back to back and fought desperately to reach the ravine. Although their own commandant appeared in testimony to contradict his second-in-command, in saying that he himself saw no such thing, it is clear that around 70 sepoys died in a cluster – a rallying-square in other words. As Anderson was being carried away in a stretcher at the time, it is not surprising that he saw nothing of what must have been his battalion's rearmost element. At the ravine Ganda Singh and his men handed their commandant over to Evelyn Wood's one-time saviour, Risaldar Dhokal Singh, who took Anderson up behind him and cantered away to the south. Some miles down the road the colonel would be placed aboard an E Battery limber for the rest of the journey to Kandahar.

It is often overlooked in accounts of the battle that Khig had been in the hands of the enemy for a considerable time and that the retreating infantry would have been obliged to fight their way through the village. Somewhere on its western outskirts the remnants of the 66th's left wing were rallying to Colonel Mainwaring, now frantically ushering anybody with a rifle into a walled garden to make a stand. Beresford-Peirse caught a glimpse of his own colonel shortly before entering the garden, but instead of seeking sanctuary with everybody else, it is clear that Galbraith made his way back into the thick of fight to see what had become of the rest of his men. Before long Mainwaring had gathered 150 men from all three battalions, more than half of them members of the 66th. Amongst the officers who can be shown to have been present in the garden were Major Oliver, Beresford-Peirse, who had just taken a round through his helmet, the wounded George Blackwood and Lieutenant William Aslett of the Bombay Grenadiers. In order to prevent desertions through a doorway at the back of the garden, Mainwaring sent a dazed Beresford-Peirse to stand guard over it with his revolver. Some of the dispirited sepoys he turned back into the garden merely crouched down against its back wall to await their deaths.[74]

In the meantime Mainwaring had been busy posting the men who still had some fight left in them around the mud walls of the garden. Believing the GOC to be dead, Mainwaring was more than a little surprised when Burrows came stumbling through the gateway. Although some of the men had been able to scoop a handful of muddy water out of the irrigation ditch as they passed, there was no more water to be had in the garden, nor was there a supply of reserve ammunition at hand. To compound the hopelessness of the situation, it was clear that the enclosure was slowly being surrounded and that the enemy were in the process of bringing up artillery. After resisting bravely for about 20 minutes, Burrows and Mainwaring concluded that the position was turning into a death-trap and that the time had come to break clean. Burrows located a bugler and ordered him to sound 'Retire'.[75] As the troops came pouring out of the back gate, Charles Oliver armed himself with a Martini and rallied a few members of his battalion into the semblance of a rearguard. A little further down the withdrawal route, General Burrows gave up his borrowed horse to the badly wounded Major Iredell.

Across on the British left, Captain Quarry and Lieutenant Salmon were directing determined stands just north of Mahmudabad. For a while their volleys succeeded in checking hovering bands of enemy cavalry. In spite of the smoke and confusion, 2nd Lieutenant Bray managed to reunite his section with the rest of G Company. It was not long, however, before a number of Afghan guns had been brought into action against the rearguard companies. The renewed bombardment forced Quarry and Salmon to fall back across the ravine. They came face-to-face with each other on the home bank. Quarry was exhausted and had decided that enough was enough. Declaring his intention to make a stand along the line of the irrigation ditch, he told Salmon, 'I shall not go a step further.' Somewhere nearby Subadar-Major Haidar Khan, a fearsome figure to the partially-trained young sepoys serving with Jacob's Rifles, was raging up and down Salmon's line ensuring that nobody else took the opportunity to slip away. Elsewhere on the field, Subadar-Major Bhoura Pallow of the Grenadiers had already fallen, no doubt playing a similarly inspirational role amongst the youngsters of his own battalion.

That Burrows, Mainwaring and the others had been able to hold their ground for as long as 20 minutes had much to do with the fact that they were not the rearmost element of the British force as they might at first have thought. Concurrent with their defence of the garden, a second significant stand had taken place under James Galbraith. When the remnants of B, C and D

Companies reached the irrigation ditch, they found their colonel waiting for them. Survivors of the retreat reported that he was down on one knee, holding the Queen's Colour aloft to mark his chosen rallying point.[76] Over the course of the next few minutes something like 190 officers and men of all units closed in on the colours and established a defensive position along the general line of the ditch. Haider Beg made it back to Galbraith's position with McMath, only for the captain-sahib to declare that he was in too much pain to go on. Nobly he insisted that his steadfast servant should leave him to his fate and make his way to safety. A series of volleys inflicted heavy punishment on the Afghans as they surged into a renewed assault. Laying down a heavy return fire, they began reaching out instinctively for Galbraith's flanks. His right must have been under heavy attack from the outset. During the course of the stand at the irrigation ditch something in the region of 60 men were killed or injured so badly that they would have to be left behind. Amongst those who lost their lives was the gallant Colonel Galbraith. Nothing is known of the manner of his death, but doubtless he was the epitome of defiance to the end.

It seems likely that the troops defending the ditch were ordered to fall back into the village by Captain Walter Roberts, almost certainly the senior surviving officer on that part of the field, when the 'Retire' came drifting across the battlefield from the direction of the defended garden. During the retreat the Queen's Colour passed into the care of 2nd Lieutenant Harry Barr of H Company, the 19-year-old son of an Indian Army lieutenant general. While some of the men maintained a bold front and laid down covering fire, others broke away to help the walking wounded to the rear. William McMath was just one of several badly injured men who had to be left behind. 'Nellie' remained faithful to the end and shared her master's fate when the *ghazis* finally overran the irrigation ditch. As he was making his way back through the village Lieutenant Lynch was shot in the leg, but managed to keep hobbling on until he was hauled up behind a well-mounted sowar and ridden clear of the chaos behind him.[77]

All the while G Company had been standing firm around Mahmudabad. Eventually Major Ready reined in beside Captain Quarry to point out that the 'Retire' had been sounded long ago. Due to the smoke, the dust and the intervening distance, Quarry had still not grasped the full extent of the disaster and enquired, 'Where is the regiment?' Pointing to the G Company firing line, Ready replied, '*There* is your regiment.'[78]

Last Stand

Two miles and more beyond Khig a straggling procession of frantic, harassed fugitives was making its way towards Kandahar, a long 45 miles distant, grateful that others were still fighting hard to deter a pursuit. General Burrows, Major

Oliver, Captain William Harrison of Jacob's Rifles and Lieutenant Lynch were amongst the last handful to catch up with the tail of the rout, all of them riding double behind selfless Indian rescuers from the cavalry regiments.[79]

Having bought precious time for others to make their escape, the survivors of Galbraith's stand, perhaps 130 men in all, fell back through the village fighting every inch of the way. Walter Roberts and the harassed remnants of the 66th were well supported by Lieutenant Henn and his Sappers & Miners, who had fought with distinction throughout the day, and by Lieutenant Charles Hinde, the adjutant of the Bombay Grenadiers, who had managed to rally about 30 sepoys around him. The colours of the 66th were drawing heavy fire wherever they went. 2nd Lieutenant Arthur Honywood of the 66th had been badly wounded in the legs but was still clinging bravely to the Regimental Colour. Realizing that he was at the end of his tether and would struggle to gain his feet again, the 19-year-old Honywood raised the colour aloft with a cry of 'Men! What shall we do to save this?'[80] A few defiant flourishes attracted the attention of dozens of nearby riflemen, one of whom shot Honywood dead. The colour was recovered from the dust by Lieutenant Maurice Rayner, the 23-year-old adjutant of the 66th, but only moments later he too was hit and fell badly wounded in the path of the enemy. Private Michael Darby, ordinarily the battalion's bass drummer, dashed to the adjutant's aid, while somebody else spirited the colour away. Despite being ordered to save himself, Darby stood by the popular young officer to the end. In the aftermath of the battle the bodies of the adjutant and the bass drummer, both in their way responsible for the standard of footdrill in the battalion, would be found lying side by side.

Captain Roberts and the handful of surviving officers ushered their men into an enclosed garden at the heart of the village and prepared to defend the walls. It is not entirely inconceivable that it was the same one earlier defended by Burrows and Mainwaring, though it might just as easily have been another. Thomas Henn had been wounded in the arm earlier but now lost his life to a headshot. Over the next few minutes, 16 of his men including both of his British NCOs, Sergeant Heaphy and Corporal Ashman, fell fighting around their officer's body. The other components of the rearguard also took heavy casualties in a resolute defence of the garden. More than 40 members of the 66th and a score of Bombay Grenadiers had been killed or badly wounded before a desperate remnant, perhaps 60 men in all, extricated themselves and fell back to the southernmost garden in the village. En route young Mister Barr and Sergeant-Major Cuppage also laid down their lives attempting to save the colours. When they reached the last garden the British stood their ground once more, blazing away with searing-hot rifles into the baying mob around them. Amongst others, the enemy return fire cut down Captain Walter Roberts and Major George Blackwood, the latter having clearly struggled to get clear of the village as a result of his leg wound. After another vicious bout of fighting against quite hopeless odds, a last handful of the 66th broke out of the garden to the south. They were quickly surrounded. Clustering back-to-back they stood at bay amidst a triumphant horde of *ghazis*. It is said that there were 11 of them and that they were accompanied by 'Bobbie', Lance-Sergeant Peter Kelly's little dog. Immortalized in history as 'the last eleven', they are customarily identified as Lieutenant Richard Chute, acting quartermaster of the Berkshires, Lieutenant Charles Hinde, adjutant of the Bombay Grenadiers, and nine unidentified soldiers of the 66th.

An Afghan artillery colonel, interviewed not long after the battle, described how the conduct of these men earned the admiration of the enemy. General Primrose encapsulated the broad gist of the colonel's account:

> They were surrounded by the whole Afghan army, and fought on till only eleven men were left, inflicting enormous loss upon the enemy. These eleven charged out of the garden and died with their faces to the foe, fighting to the death. Such was the nature of their charge, and the grandeur of their bearing, that although the whole of the ghazis were assembled around them, no one dared approach to cut them down. Thus standing in the open, back-to-back, firing steadily and truly, every shot telling, surrounded by thousands, these officers and men died and it was not until the last man was shot down that the ghazis dared advance upon them. The conduct of these men was the admiration of all that witnessed it . . . I think his Excellency will agree with me when I say that history does not afford a grander or finer instance of gallantry and devotion to Queen and country than that displayed by the 66th Regiment on 27 July 1880.

The only survivor of the final stand was 'Bobbie' who, despite being wounded, would escape not merely to Kandahar, where he was reunited with his injured master, but in time to England where the Queen Empress herself would decorate him with a campaign medal. The fall of the last eleven marked the end of the battle but not of the slaughter or the suffering. Somewhere along the trail of bloody khaki forms marking the regiment's line of retreat, the colours of the 66th had been trampled underfoot, fated never again to be gazed upon by British eyes. Some of the Afghan cavalry gave chase to the scattered British fugitives, but the pursuit was not hard pressed as the temptation to rob the dead and loot the baggage was far too great to resist.

In their various accounts of the battle, some of the cavalry and artillery officers would lay claim to having covered the retreat, but Captain John Quarry and the men of G Company were the last to leave the field and it was the steadiness of their musketry which kept the early pursuit in check. It was not until sunset that any of the rallied squadrons came far enough back along the straggling column to constitute a rearguard. On a number of occasions in the hours ahead, Burrows would be obliged to send messages ahead instructing the cavalry commandants to slow down. It is fair to say that neither Currie nor Malcolmson distinguished themselves during the retreat. Burrows took particular note that at no time did either of them join the rearguard in person.

The Retreat to Kandahar

The retreat covered inhospitable, waterless terrain and lasted all night and into the afternoon of the following day. Although Ayub Khan's force was less than relentless in hounding the British, the hostility of the tribesmen and villagers along the line of retreat more than made up for any want of energy on the part of the rebel army. For stragglers to fall behind meant certain death. Captain Slade left one of the most atmospheric accounts of the retreat. Here he describes the immediate aftermath of the battle:

> All over the wide expanse of desert are to be seen men in twos and threes retreating. Camels have thrown their loads; sick men, almost naked, are astride of donkeys, mules, ponies and camels; the bearers have thrown down their dhoolies and left the wounded to their fate. The guns and carriages are crowded with the helpless wounded officers and men suffering the tortures of the damned; horses are limping along with ugly wounds, and men are pressing eagerly to the rear in the hope of finding water. The distant booming of cannon is still heard; the hordes of irregular horsemen are to be seen amongst our baggage-animals relentlessly cutting one and all down, and looting. The survivors of the Battle of Maiwand owe their lives to the looting that took place in the retreat. A few alone remain with the General to try and turn the rout into an orderly retreat.

After his wounding on the gun line, Gunner Naylor had been placed aboard a doolie and moved back towards Mahmudabad and beyond. Some way down the road he had been thrown out of the litter when a gaggle of terrified camels jostled past. Fortunately E Battery's farrier-sergeant happened by with his horse-drawn forge and stopped to pick Naylor up. Gunner Collis got away on a limber seat but was wounded above the eye when a party of Afghan cavalrymen swept past flailing their *tulwars* (curved Indian swords).When one of them wheeled about to attack again, Collis let fly with his carbine, hitting his assailant in the chest. Later, while he was wandering about looking for water, Collis became separated from his immediate comrades and married up instead with No. 2 Sub-Division. Amongst the wounded men being carried aboard the axle-seats was a wounded colonel whom Collis did not know, who can only have been Horace Anderson.

Slade and the other artillery officers had managed to get ten of their 12 guns away from the battlefield, but the heat of the day and the absence of water had taken a terrible toll of the draught animals. One by one the horses collapsed with a shudder and lay panting helplessly on their sides until somebody stepped up to end their suffering. During the night Slade would be obliged to abandon five out of the six smoothbores in order to have enough horses left to keep the RHA 9-pounders on the move.

Major John Ready tried to bring some order to the confusion and panic, but was forced by the demoralization of the troops to content himself with the role of Good Samaritan:

> It was hopeless to enforce order on the march. All night I tried to get men to keep together in bodies, however small, but they were too done to care what they did. During the night I found a man of Quarry's – Black, Brook or some other name beginning with a 'B' – badly wounded in [the] right leg, put him on my horse and led him along some miles. He got off twice, and at last refused to try again. He could not sit up. I had to almost hold him on the horse poor fellow. He lay down at last and could not get up again.

Ironically it was the most fleet-footed of the sepoy fugitives who suffered the heaviest losses in the retreat. By the time they reached the vicinity of a village called Sinjiri, due west of Kandahar, night had fallen. Instead of crossing the River Argandab, the leaderless sepoys lost their way in the dark and pushed north-east in the direction of Mansurabad. They realised their error when the sun came up, laid low throughout daylight, and under the cover of darkness attempted to swing back south for Kandahar via the Baba Wali Pass. None of them made it; about a hundred men of Jacob's Rifles and fifty of the Bombay Grenadiers were cut down by hostile bands of tribesmen operating to the north of Kandahar.

It was broad daylight when Gunner Collis and No. 2 Sub-Division once again came under attack. Collis had wandered into a village to fetch water for the wounded and was 150 yards distant when he spotted a dozen enemy horsemen cantering to the attack. Instead of running off with everybody else, he lay down with a borrowed rifle and fought a one-man rearguard action, while the gun, the limber and the casualties cantered to safety. Firing around 35 rounds at a rapid rate, Collis convinced the hesitant enemy that he was not alone and succeeded in hitting one of the horses and two of the riders into the bargain. This caused the rest of the party to halt at a distance and exchange shots with him. Just then Nuttall arrived with a party of sowars and drove the enemy off with a charge. Reining in beside Collis the general remarked, 'You're a gallant young man,' and proceeded to note his name in his pocket-book.[81]

It was impossible to give any meaningful medical treatment to the wounded until they reached the sanctuary of distant Kandahar. Lieutenant Lynch's account of the retreat makes it clear that they suffered terribly, not merely from the pain and discomfort of their injuries, but from the anguish and frustration that comes with helplessness:

> To say that I suffered greatly from thirst is a mild way of expressing it. The gun I was on was so hot I could not touch it even with my boot. Slade caused several men to hold on to the limbers and walk. Many took advantage of this and were saved. The horses began to tire, and during the night one fell and appeared to have a fit. It had to be taken out and, I believe, was replaced by an officer's charger . . . Once during the night, during a brief halt, a man brought me some water in a tin. Just then we moved and I could not swallow the water, my tongue had become so swollen. We stopped and I heard a good deal of firing in front. One of my men (Burgess by name) took my sword and revolver off and said he would take them into Kandahar. The poor fellow must have been killed on the way, for I did not see him again. My sword was found six years later and sent to me. The wheel of the gun I was on had a bad dent in the iron tyre. This caused a constant jolting which gave me much pain. When near the villages outside Kandahar, I saw several of our men lying dead, having been shot by the villagers. The bodies in every case had been mutilated.

Inevitably the absence of water was a common refrain in all the survivors' accounts:

> And so it goes on for five or six miles, till the sun begins to sink serenely into the horizon; there is no change in the sunset from last night, it is the same glorious Indian setting. The cries for 'Water! Water!' become more frequent and louder. Men can hardly speak, the wounded open their mouths and show a dry parched tongue, and with a sad expression convey to your mind but a brief glimpse of their intense suffering. A cry now arises that there is water near at hand, and, after a long search in the dead of night, a deep well full of muddy water is found in the village of Hauz-i-Madat. There is just sufficient to satisfy the wounded and those who are fighting round the well for dear life, but none can be spared for the already worn out and exhausted horses. Once the column is in motion, plodding its weary way onwards, longing for the break of day which dawns as we enter the village of Ashu Khan which we found

> deserted, and where the water supply had been cut off. Every one's hand is against us. Heavy firing is heard in all directions . . . The march from Ashu Khan through Singiri to the river Argandab, a distance of about six miles, is a long and trying one under the circumstances. Villagers from all sides creep up behind the low mud walls and fire on us, and many a gallant fellow who had battled against the trials of the night fell a victim to the jezail.
>
> At last the river is reached; it is 11 a.m. and thirty-two miles from the battlefield. With what joy and delight do the unfortunate men and horses, who have not wetted their lips during the night, welcome the sight of it. A small relief force under General Brooke can now be seen advancing to our assistance from Kokeran . . . The rearguard ultimately reached Kandahar at 3 p.m. on the 28th July 1880, after thirty-three hours marching and fighting on practically empty stomachs, and with a scant supply of water.[82]

The impetuous Hector Maclaine wandered too far from the rest of the fugitives in search of water and fell into the hands of hostile tribesmen. He was held in tolerable conditions for the month it took Roberts to prepare and execute his famous 300-mile dash from Kabul to Kandahar. One of the most prominent units in the subsequent fighting was the 92nd (Gordon) Highlanders whom we shall shortly meet again in South Africa. In the aftermath of Roberts's victory, which effectively marked the end of the war, Maclaine's captors took their revenge by cutting his throat. It is believed a number of Indian prisoners shared the same fate.

Casualties

Some 1,500 Afghans were killed at the Battle of Maiwand, suggesting that as many as 2,000–3,000 more may have been wounded. There were roughly twice as many casualties amongst the *ghazis* and tribesmen as amongst the regulars. It was a grievous loss which caused many of the survivors to disperse for home in company with wounded comrades, but even so it fell some way short of the 44 per cent casualty rate suffered by General Burrows's command. Of 2,576 British and Indian soldiers who had gone into action, 962 were killed and 161 wounded. A significant proportion of the total number of fatalities expired during the retreat rather than the battle, some as a direct consequence of renewed enemy action, others from wounds received earlier in the day. Of the 20 officers and 469 other ranks in the 66th Regiment, 10 and 275 were killed, including the sergeant-major, four colour-sergeants and 14 sergeants or lance-sergeants. Three officers and 33 men were wounded. Around 240 members of the regiment lost their lives on the battlefield and 45 during the retreat.

Voortrekkers under attack by Zulus in 1838. The Great Trek helped shape the national psyche of the Transvaal Boers. Both the Zulus and the Boers in their different ways would humiliate the British military establishments later in the cenury.

'Forward the 42nd' by Robert Gibb, a depiction of the Black Watch at the Alma. The Crimean Army's mode of fighting was much closer to that of Waterloo, fought almost 40 years earlier, than to the Ashanti campaign of less than 20 years later.

The end of the 'horse-and-musket era'. Lord Cardigan leads the Light Brigade to destruction. Oil by Thomas Jones Barker.

A romanticized Victorian portrayal of the last stand of the 24th Regiment at Isandlwana.

'At Bay', an illustration from *The Graphic* depicting the final moments of the 24th Regiment at Isandlwana, 22 January 1879.

Rescuing the wounded in Afghanistan. Oil by Lady Elizabeth Butler.

The last stand of the 66th (Berkshire) Regiment at Maiwand, 27 July 1880. Clearly the artist had no knowledge of the terrain.

'Saving the Guns at Maiwand' by Richard Caton Woodville.

An Indian sowar. The 3rd Bombay Light Cavalry and the 3rd Sind Horse were badly mishandled by British commanders at Maiwand.

Transvaal Rebellion 1880–81. The 60th Regiment monument and cemetery at Ingogo, with Majuba Hill in the background.

Gordon Relief Expedition: the Heavy Camel Regiment defending the left-rear corner of the British square at Abu Klea. The battle saw one of the most vicious hand-to-hand fights of the era.

Famously it was said that the Mahdist onslaught broke the square. In truth, cavalry officers operating in the unaccustomed role of infantrymen ordered a naive manoeuvre which presented the enemy with a golden opportunity. Oil by W. B. Wollen.

Major General Andy Wauchope's Highland Brigade re-forming after their failed attack on the Magersfontein Koppies.

Where the 'small wars' of empire came to an end and the modern military era began: General Woodgate's marker at Spion Kop. Aloe Knoll and Twin Peaks are in the background. The whitewashed stones mark the left end of the trench now preserved as a war grave.

Above: Edward Cardwell, the reforming Secretary of State for War.

Above right: Lieutenant Charlie Pope, officer commanding G Company, 2nd/24th, at Isandlwana.

Below: Isandlwana, scene of the famous Zulu victory, where, despite valiant resistance, six companies of the 24th Regiment were massacred to a man. Later in the day, B Company of the 2nd/24th would fight tenaciously in defence of the mission station at Rorke's Drift.

Above: Sir Louis Cavagnari, British envoy to Kabul, killed during the course of the Second Anglo-Afghan War in 1879.

Above right: Lieutenant Walter Hamilton VC, commander of Cavagnari's escort.

Below: An accurate portrayal of the British Residency in Kabul. Hamilton's men inflicted over 600 casualties on the attackers before they were overwhelmed. A handful of wounded survivors were murdered the following morning.

Above: Major General Frederick Roberts VC.

Above right: Lieutenant Colonel James Galbraith, officer commanding the 66th (Berkshire) Regiment of Foot at Maiwand.

Below: Cavalry vedettes of the 3rd Sind Horse on the River Helmand, Maiwand campaign, southern Afghanistan, July 1880. Sketch by G. D. Giles.

Under heavy attack by hordes of *ghazi* fanatics, the 66th Regiment fights its way back to the village of Khig at the height of the Battle of Maiwand, 27 July 1880.

G. D. Giles's portrayal of E/B Battery RHA in action at Maiwand. Two of the battery's six 9-pounders fell into enemy hands.

Acting Major General Sir George Colley KCSI, CB, CMG. Memorably described by a junior officer as 'unfit for a corporal's guard', Colley was shot through the forehead on the summit of Majuba Hill on Sunday 27 February 1881.

Above left: Brigadier-General Sir Evelyn Wood VC, KCB. Well established as a 'fighting general' as a result of his exploits in the Zulu War, Wood returned to South Africa to act as Colley's second-in-command. Colley sidelined him before Majuba Hill in order that the credit for the coming victory would be his alone.

Above middle: Lieutenant Colonel Philip Anstruther, OC 94th Regiment. Shot five times in the legs at Bronkhorstspruit, he died on Boxing Day 1880.

Above right: Colonel Bonar Deane, killed in action at the head of the 58th Regiment at Laing's Nek.

Above left: 'Slim Piet' Joubert, Commandant-General of the Transvaal.

Above right: Nicholaas Smit, the victor of Ingogo and Majuba Hill.

Above left: Major William Brownlow KDG. After Laing's Nek, he refused to speak to the men of his squadron for several days.

Above right: Lieutenant Ian Hamilton, 92nd (Gordon) Highlanders. Seriously wounded in the rout at Majuba, he was located after the battle by his dog 'Patch'.

Below left: Lieutenant Robert Elwes, Grenadier Guards. Elwes died at Majuba with his old school motto on his lips.

Below right: Lieutenant Alan Hill, 58th Regiment, whose bravery at Laing's Nek would earn him the VC. He was wounded at Majuba.

'The Battle of Majuba Hill' by Richard Caton Woodville. Though small in scale, Majuba was Britain's greatest humiliation in South Africa. Colley is shown in his tennis shoes, with his back turned, on the centre-left.

Majuba Hill from the northern or Transvaal side, with Gordons' Knoll in the centre and Macdonald's Koppie on the right.

The hardest-hit unit in the force was the Bombay Grenadiers which from a start-state of 23 and 624, suffered 2 British and 8 Indian officers killed, 2 British and 2 Indian officers wounded, 347 other ranks killed and 55 wounded. Around a hundred of the sepoys who lost their lives fell in the course of the retreat, half of them in the slaughter in the Baba Wali Pass. The sources do not allow as complete a breakdown of the loss in Jacob's Rifles but in total the battalion lost 238 killed and 30 wounded out of 624. This was a loss of 43 per cent compared with the 66 per cent loss inflicted upon the Grenadiers, but as many as 150 of the regiment's dead fell during the retreat rather than the battle, two-thirds of them at Baba Wali. Across the force 11 Indian officers had been killed and 9 wounded. In detail, E Battery had lost 2 and 19 dead and 2 and 14 wounded, while of the battery's horses some 63 had been killed in the battle, with 46 more dying of exhaustion en route to Kandahar. The 3rd Light Cavalry lost 1 and 19 dead and 2 and 19 wounded, with 58 horses killed and 42 injured. The 3rd Sind Horse lost 14 sowars dead and 5 wounded, with 40 horses killed and 9 injured. The loss in No. 2 Company, Bombay Sappers & Miners, was 1 and 17 dead and 7 wounded. Something in excess of 450 camp followers were killed or reported as missing. The transport staff calculated the loss in baggage animals at 1,676 camels, 355 ponies, 24 mules, 79 bullocks and 291 donkeys.[83]

Aftermath

It was widely held that E Battery had played a sterling role in both the battle and the retreat. In his official report Burrows wrote:

> Of the conduct of the troops, generally, I have already spoken, but I wish to bring the artillery to special notice; their behaviour was admirable; exposed to a heavy fire they served their guns coolly and steadily as on parade, and when the guns were rushed they fought the ghazis with handspikes, sponge-rods etc.[84]

E Battery's conduct was recognized with a CB for Captain John Slade, eight DCMs, and VCs for Sergeant Patrick Mullane and Gunner James Collis. A few years later Collis would be convicted of bigamy and in accordance with regulations was stripped of his award. Under King Edward VII the nation became more ready to tolerate something short of perfection in its military heroes and Collis's VC was restored.

When the disaster at Maiwand came under the microscope, the Indian military establishment felt moved to focus its attention upon the conduct of the cavalry. Generals Burrows and Nuttall both complained that Colonel Malcolmson and Major Currie had failed to meet the exacting standards required of regimental commanders. Certainly neither covered themselves in glory during the retreat, a phase of war in which example is of paramount importance. They suffered the indignity of being court-martialled in Bombay in March 1881. Cowardice was just one of a number of accusations levelled against them, but both were acquitted with honour, a verdict which, given the gravity of the charges, made Burrows and Nuttall look foolish. In truth Nuttall was every bit as culpable as either of the regimental commanders for the woeful handling of the cavalry, whilst Burrows had failed to pay the scattered squadrons any attention until it was far too late. If Burrows had made fatal errors of judgement, he had at least shown conspicuous gallantry throughout the battle and the retreat. He was amongst the last to enter the gates of Kandahar. In the Victorian military, where courage was esteemed above all other qualities, it was enough to get him off the hook.

The gallantry of the officers and men of the old 66th, who in most cases gave their lives that others might live, is commemorated by the 'Maiwand Lion' in Forbury Gardens, Reading. Sadly 'Bobbie' was run over by a cab not long after his presentation to the Queen Empress but still to this day stands guard at the regimental museum beside Salisbury Cathedral.

Chapter 3

'FLOREAT ETONA'

The Battles of Laing's Nek and Ingogo, Transvaal Rebellion, 1880–1881

A field officer of the 58th, one of the defeated stormers, was brought in and placed beside me. He was shot through the chest and was dying; yet he was perfectly conscious. The doctor bent down and said sadly, 'I am very sorry, but I can do nothing more for you major.' 'No,' replied the Major, 'it is all over with me'. I turned round and looked at him with an awful fascination, and even then he asked huskily, with the kindness of a brave, unselfish gentleman, 'And where are you hit corporal?' I told him but he never answered, for even as I spoke he passed away.

Corporal Clark, King's Dragoon Guards, writing of the death of Major William Hingeston, OC 58th Regiment

For the most part their great-grandfathers would have thought of themselves as Dutch, French Huguenot or German, but by the dawn of the nineteenth century the settlers in the South African interior were known regardless of their origins as *boers* after the Dutch word for farmer. The Dutch colonial administration at the Cape had not been overly concerned with how its citizens scratched a living inland, nor had it been particularly interested in the probity of their relations with the indigenous population. When the British took possession of the colony in 1806 during the Napoleonic Wars their principal objective was to secure the sea lanes to India. With the discovery of diamonds and gold still some decades away, there was no particular governmental or mercantile drive to expand into the interior. The British might have continued the same *laissez-faire* approach as their predecessors were it not for their evolving national preoccupation with the philosophical and moral values of enlightenment.

The fledgling British community at Cape Town seemed to the Cape Dutch to be governed and preached at by high-minded men of principle – men whose leanings they regarded as altogether too enlightened, too liberal and too humanitarian for the rough and tumble of Africa. The clash of values with the deeply conservative *boer* communities of the hinterland was sure to be even more marked. Generations of isolation in widely dispersed farming communities had kept any hint of modernity at bay and slowly but surely turned the *boers* from a race of western Europeans into a fiercely competitive African tribe, a white tribe which in political and theological terms was not progressing but regressing.

When British legislators and administrators began 'meddling' in the private affairs of the *boers* – a practice known across the rest of the Empire as governance – whole families, clans and districts packed their farms into the back of their ox-wagons and trekked away from colonial jurisdiction. The nationalist propaganda of twentieth-century South Africa notwithstanding, the Great Trek was far from being a mass protest movement by an oppressed people; in truth a great many more *boers* knuckled down and remained contentedly within the borders of Cape Colony than felt the need to escape the British yoke by trekking. Between 1837 and 1845 perhaps 14,000 people migrated into the interior – a significant but far from crippling drain on the manpower resources of an expanding colony.

Pride and Prejudice

The principal catalyst for the Trek was not so much the abolition of slavery throughout the British Empire, as is often stated, but rather the outrage consequent upon the notion that British colonial courts would henceforth regard black and white as equal before the law. Coupled with this was British soft-peddling towards the Xhosa, both in terms of the government's sometimes inconsistent security policies and the allegedly subversive activities of Anglican missionary societies. Many frontier *boers* blamed the missionaries directly for the most recent Xhosa outbreak, the Sixth 'Kaffir' War of 1834–5. In fact the missionaries' 'crime' was the teaching of such radical concepts as equality before God, for their principal doctrinal handrail was that well known subversive text, the New Testament. The liberal-minded Anglican British, it would be fair to say, struggled to see things through Dutch-Calvinist eyes.

To the *boers* the British were powerful, a quality they admired, but patronising and meddlesome with it. In essence a deeply conservative and politically immature settler community had come into contact with cutting-edge liberalism on the brink of its golden age. If you could not beat them, and did not feel particularly inclined to join them, then trekking offered a way out.

Inevitably there were legal issues surrounding such a premise. Whether they liked it or not, in 1814 the *boers* had ceased to be nominally Dutch and became citizens of the British Empire. When at precisely the same point in the history of the United States, many thousands of Americans left the eastern seaboard to settle and exploit the North American interior, they did not cede their citizenship. Just as US jurisdiction advanced westwards by degrees to keep pace with the progress of the pioneers, so throughout the nineteenth century would successive colonial administrations feel forced to extend British jurisdiction northwards through Southern Africa. The essential difference between the two scenarios was that American pioneers expected civilizing influences and good governance to follow in their wake, whereas the *boers* expected to cast off all vestiges of citizenship the moment they set foot in independent black Africa – not of course that they intended the interior to remain either black or independent for very long. In the eyes of the British liberal elite such ambitions reduced the land-hungry trekkers to the legal standing of overland pirates.

Theological differences acted as a catalyst to the deepening cultural rift. Over the course of the Great Trek and subsequently, Afrikaner clergymen evolved ever more skewed variations on an originally Calvinist theme. It did not take them long to begin equating the *volk* with the chosen people of the Old Testament and black Africans with the cursed 'sons of Ham'. Nor was the notion peddled as a subtle analogy. Like all good propaganda lines it was hammered home repeatedly until it could pass unremarked for the truth. The meek and mild-mannered parables of the New Testament drew stifled yawns from a people who knew that the meek were not about to inherit the African interior. Nothing was better received by a *boer* congregation than tales of fire and brimstone in which the godless heathen were miraculously consumed. At the Battle of Blood River in 1838 the Lord accorded his favourites a miracle all of their own. Even Commandant-General Andries Pretorius was modest enough to acknowledge the part of the Almighty in his workmanlike victory over the Zulu.

The Rise and Fall of the South African Republic

The victory of 1838 had delivered a veritable land of milk and honey into the hands of the *boers*. Crucially, for a nation of stock farmers, it proved to be free of the tetse fly. Then, in 1842, the British military arrived in Natal and not without bloodshed annexed the promised land to the Crown. Most of the *volk* packed up in disgust and once again outran British jurisdiction by trekking north of the Vaal. The Sand River Convention of 1852 recognized the new *boer* sanctuary as the South African Republic or ZAR, which most people came to call the Transvaal, and which had its capital at a place the *boers* named Pretoria after the greatest of their commandant-generals. Arguably the convention was the most serious mistake the British made in the governance of nineteenth-century South Africa, legitimizing as it did the idea of Boers with a capital B – the concept not of a separate Afrikaner culture, but of an entirely new white African nationality. Over the years various postage-stamp republics came and went, but the Transvaal and the Orange Free State stayed the course and plodded doggedly on into the 1870s. Religion continued to play a dominant part in the life of the *volk* and under the tutelage of the likes of Stephanus Johannes Paulus Kruger, the language of fire and brimstone migrated freely across into politics and governance. As members of the *dopper* sect, Kruger and his closest confidants belonged to the most extreme and reactionary branch of Afrikaner Calvinism. To the secular, more liberal-minded British entrepreneurs and settlers who over the course of the century moved north to Pretoria, the Boers came across as a xenophobic and ignorant people.

In the modern world the pre-annexation Transvaal would be labelled a 'failed state'. Its citizens were fractious, un-taxable and next to ungovernable, whilst the Volksraad or parliament seemed unable to agree on anything of consequence. Lawless burghers stirred up their African neighbours by raiding their homesteads to press land claims, steal stock and abduct children to work as farm 'apprentices', a practice which the disapproving British rightly perceived as slave-raiding.[1] When such freebooter depredations triggered serious trouble with the indigenous population, the republican government found that it lacked the wherewithal to wage war effectively. The straw that broke the camel's back came in 1876 when the republic decided to make war on Sekhukhune, the paramount chief of the Pedi. With the majority of its citizens opting out of a war tax of £5, not it must be said for reasons of conscience, the government quickly found itself bankrupt and humiliated. President Thomas Burgers despaired of ever imposing order. Then, on a sunny afternoon in January 1877, Sir Theophilus Shepstone rode into Pretoria at the head of a small personal staff (including H. Rider Haggard), and an escort of precisely 25 mounted policemen. Shepstone had been appointed by Lord Carnarvon, the Colonial Secretary, as London's Special Commissioner to the Transvaal, under secret orders regardless of guarantees afforded by the Sand River Convention to further London's confederation strategy by annexing the ZAR to the Crown. After three months of negotiations Shepstone concluded that annexation would probably meet with tacit acceptance.

On 12 April 1877 Rider Haggard hoisted the Union Flag in Church Square, then a much dustier and more rustic place than it is today. Everybody in Pretoria held their breath but nobody, not even the fiercely nationalist Vice-President Paul Kruger, had the nerve to take the flag down again. That there was no resistance was partly a function of Shepstone's breathtaking daring, but mainly because after years of anarchy most people could see no other way out. The already sizeable *uitlander* population breathed a sigh of relief – thanks to the Special Commissioner they were British once more. Even a good many Boers had been persuaded by Shepstone's rhetoric. Perhaps life as a subject of the Queen Empress would not be so bad after all. Kruger of course tongue-lashed all such faint-hearts, drawing as ever on his skewed theological invective in so doing.

The Road to Rebellion

By 1880 the *volk* had recovered from their surprise, and simmering resentment at the British occupation had become widespread. Since annexation Kruger had twice led deputations to London to press a case for the restoration of independence, only to meet with rebuffs at the hands of Lord Carnarvon and, his successor as Colonial Secretary, Sir Michael Hicks-Beach. There had also been an embarrassing British military failure in a short-lived, under-resourced and half-hearted campaign against Sekhukhune. For a time the difficulties with the Pedi had been put into abeyance, as the main focus for the military lay further south with the terrifying warrior hosts of Zululand where, as it turned out, far worse humiliations lay ahead. Shepstone, whom most Boer leaders found not unreasonable, departed for Natal half-way through the Zulu War, leaving the administration of the Transvaal in the hands of Colonel Sir Owen Lanyon. Not only did the new Administrator make a poor fist of governance, thereby opening a window of opportunity for republican malcontents, he was also the subject of a vicious smear campaign. In the eyes of a deeply race-conscious society Lanyon was all too readily undermined by a dark complexion – in truth he was as British as roast beef, but Kruger's acolytes lost no opportunity to sneer behind the back of a 'mixed-race' administrator.

The combination of Lanyon's political mismanagement, his personal unpopularity and plain old-fashioned subversion quickly bred the antipathy to governance that is the first and most important pre-condition for revolution. For a short while the military might of the Zulus and the presence of the strong imperial army ranged against them made any Boer military challenge unthinkable. The republicans used the breathing space to persuade or intimidate those of their brethren who still appeared to be either pro-British or neutral. Citizens of the Orange Free State were also regularly harangued by deputations from the Transvaal, as were influential Cape Dutch pressmen who, their mother-tongue apart, had little in common with their rough-hewn kinsmen from the north.

By the close of 1879 not only had the Zulus been vanquished by Lord Chelmsford, albeit at an embarrassing second attempt, but Sekhukhune and the

Pedi had also been much more efficiently and ruthlessly crushed by Sir Garnet Wolseley. Most of the *rooinek* (Afrikaans 'red-neck') regiments now seemed to be on their way home. Then, having unnecessarily ruffled Boer feathers with a series of scathing, indiscreet and eminently quotable remarks on their national character, Wolseley too sailed for England. He had at least been wise enough to advise Whitehall that the Boers were quite irreconcilable to any political outcome short of independence – not that he had shown even momentary sympathy in the presence of their representatives. 'So long as the sun shines the Transvaal will remain British territory,' he had insisted. With Wolseley's departure the posts of High Commissioner for South-Eastern Africa, Governor of Natal, and GOC passed to the 45-year-old Major General Sir George Pomeroy Colley, a thoughtful, scholarly Anglo-Irish officer and a leading member of the 'Wolseley Ring', the circle of staff henchmen with whom the great man liked to surround himself. Colley was well known for having graduated from the Staff College more than a year early with the highest examination marks ever.

The new High Commissioner was no stranger to Southern Africa having served as a subaltern in the Cape in the late 1850s, as a staff colonel under Wolseley in 1875, and again as his chief of staff in the second half of 1879. Born on 1 November 1835, Colley was the youngest son of the Honourable George Francis Colley (formerly Pomeroy), a one-time naval lieutenant. Young George was commissioned into the 2nd (Queen's) Regiment of Foot at the age of 17, served as a captain in the Second China War of 1860, as the brigade-major of Western District in 1864–6 and in May 1871 was made a staff professor at Sandhurst. It was in the Ashanti War of 1873–4 that he first caught the eye of his great patron. Wolseley employed him as his director of transport and saw to it that his services were rewarded with a CB. In between his two tours of duty with Wolseley he had been employed in India on Lord Lytton's staff. Colley was 43 before he married and in Edith Althea Hamilton, the daughter of an Indian Army general, he acquired a wife some 15 years his junior. With a happy marriage and a shining career behind him, Colley came to think of himself as naturally lucky. He was intelligent, well-travelled, a sound administrator, a thorough staff organizer and a reliable number two, but crucially he had never commanded troops in the field at any remotely serious level, nor had he ever really been left to his own devices. Even so in April 1880 he found himself being recalled from his second stint with Lord Lytton to take over from Wolseley in South Africa. He was granted acting rank as a major general in order to do so, and would fulfil his various political and military functions from Pietermaritzburg, the by now anglicized capital of Natal.

For the Boer malcontents the last hope for a peaceful resolution to the annexation issue rested with a change of government in London. Kruger had at first been greatly heartened by Gladstone's denunciation of Tory foreign policy during his Midlothian election campaign, but the harsh realities of office soon brought about a change of heart in the new prime minister. Such is politics but to the Boers Gladstone's U-turn served only to confirm the perfidious character of the British. In fact it had been furious lobbying by London's powerful liberal–humanitarian elite that had swung the prime minister's decision – self-determination for a few thousand white Afrikaners is one thing Mr Gladstone, but what of the hundreds of thousands of black Africans who will be obliged to live under their yoke? So ran the argument and there was little a Liberal prime minister could say to counter it. In June 1880 Gladstone wrote to Kruger and his right-hand man, former ZAR vice-president Petrus ('Slim Piet') Joubert,[2] to advise them that for the sake of British Transvaalers[3] and the indigenous African population he did not now feel able to revoke the annexation. The Boer leaders took comfort from the notion that a man who changed his mind quite so readily might be 'persuaded' to change it back again. By the second half of 1880 the great imperial captains and the chastened African kings had departed. Political negotiations were at an impasse. Now from Wakkerstroom in the south to Marabastad in the far north, and Rustenburg in the west to Lydenburg in the east, the stores and trading posts seemed to be full of farmers buying cartridges for their favourite hunting rifles.

The fuse was lit in Potchefstroom in November 1880, when a local called Piet Bezuidenhout declined to pay the magistrate's court a disputed sum of tax arrears. Local republicans watched developments with interest – a namesake of the defendant had been hanged by the British in 1815 for an act of armed insurrection in the Cape. The case quickly became a *cause célèbre* and just as quickly ran out of control. The *landrost*, or magistrate, had Bezuidenhout's wagon seized in order to recover court costs. On the day it was to be auctioned off, a heavily armed republican posse stormed into town to remove it forcibly. In response Sir Owen Lanyon directed the military commander of the Transvaal, Colonel William Bellairs, to move two companies of the Royal Scots Fusiliers (RSF) down to Potchefstroom, one from Pretoria and the other from Rustenburg, to uphold the authority of the civil power. With British redcoats on the march, the republicans retaliated by bringing forward a mass rally originally scheduled for January.

Up to 5,000 burghers, comfortably more than half of the old republican electorate, met at a farm called Paardekraal near modern-day Krugersdorp. They were there for the best part of the week of 8–15 December, during which time they voted overwhelmingly to resurrect ZAR. They went on to elect a presiding triumvirate consisting of Paul Kruger, former president Marthinus Pretorius, son of Andries, and Piet Joubert. The 49-year-old Joubert was also appointed as the republic's commandant-general. The first shots of rebellion were fired at

Potchefstroom on 16 December, when a Boer commando galloped into town to seize the printing press with which they intended to promulgate the Paardekraal decisions and publicize their cause. It turned out to be a momentous day. By sunset the newly arrived British garrison had been bottled up inside an earthwork by a strong republican force, whilst at Heidelberg, now the rebels' provisional capital, the Triumvirate proclaimed independence.

The Military Situation in the Transvaal

Largely as a function of the disdain that Sir Garnet Wolseley felt for the Boers, the British military position in the Transvaal was fragile in the extreme. That said, in the absence of good hard intelligence that armed rebellion was imminent, it would have been difficult for anyone, even the great Wolseley, to have made a strong case for the retention of a much larger garrison. The demands of imperial policing were such that most of the military assets shipped to South Africa in response to the Isandlwana disaster had departed again within a few months of Lord Chelmsford's victory at Ulundi. In late 1880 only one battery of 9-pounders (N Battery, 5th Brigade, RA), and four infantry battalions, the 2nd/21st (Royal Scots Fusiliers), the 58th (Rutlandshire) Regiment, the 3rd/60th Rifles and the 94th Regiment were garrisoned within a practicable striking distance of likely Transvaal trouble-spots. As had been the case at the outset of the Zulu War, there were no regular cavalry assets to hand, though fortunately the depot troop of the 1st King's Dragoon Guards (KDG) was a few weeks behind the regimental main body and had yet to depart South Africa.

The Boer military system was not even remotely sophisticated, yet for all its commendable simplicity would prove itself capable of generating a 'burgher' citizen force which would perfectly reflect the changing nature of warfare. Even with the advantage of living amongst their erstwhile enemies, not a single British officer in the Transvaal had yet realized the Boers' true military potential. The commando system might best be summarized as a general levy of all able-bodied males from 16–60, turned out and commanded in the field by locally elected officers. Probably its greatest strength was that conventional military logistics did not really come into the equation. Every man was expected to ride in to the rendezvous with his own weapons, ammunition and remounts. Because he shot for the pot, liked stalking and might at any time be called upon to defend his homestead, the average burgher was very much at home with firearms and kept himself supplied with the most accurate and modern breech-loaders. For rations he relied on coffee, maize and biltong, strips of dried salted meat which no matter how hot the weather would keep for weeks. If a long campaign was in the offing men from half a dozen neighbouring households might club together to provide themselves with a wagon-load of creature comforts.

The commando system's greatest weakness was the absence of anything that a conventional military force would recognize as discipline. A burgher on campaign could pretty much come and go as he pleased. In perilous situations he often had to be dissuaded from flight and prevailed upon to resist. Offences which in the British Army could attract capital punishment might warrant a rebuke at worst. Even arrant cowardice in the face of the enemy might be overlooked as just one of those things. The commandants and their *veldtkornets*, the elected equivalents of lieutenant colonels and captains respectively, were obliged to discuss their plans with their men and canvas their approval, as

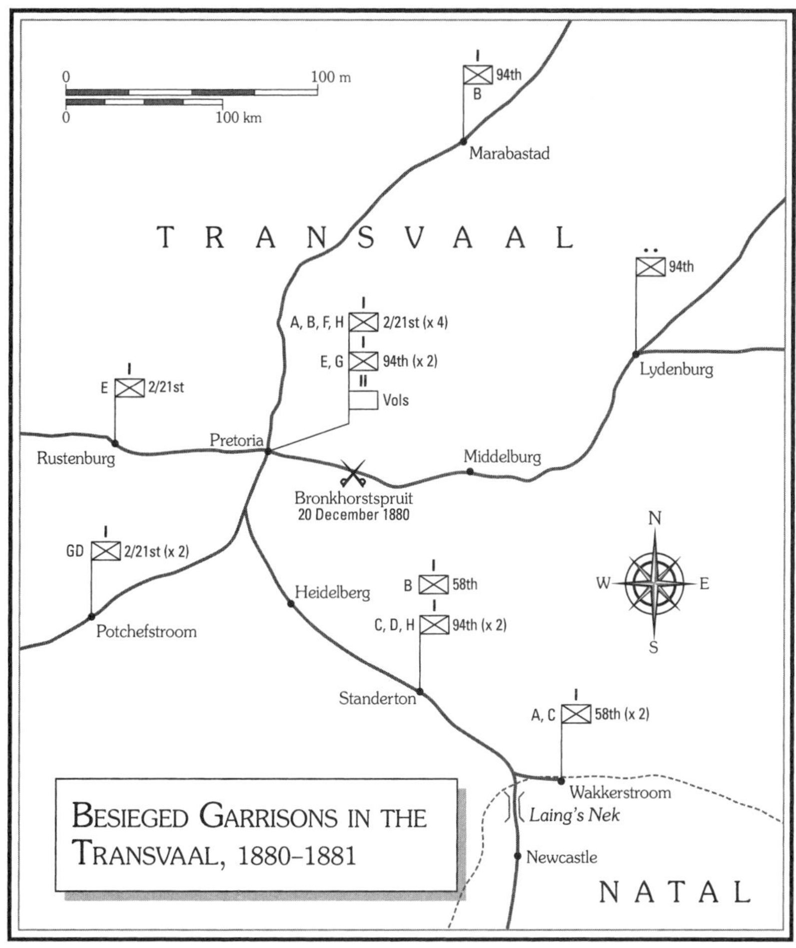

BESIEGED GARRISONS IN THE TRANSVAAL, 1880–1881

ultimately a commando had to be commanded by consent. One of the consequences of such institutionalized indiscipline was that it was next to impossible for a commando to mount a bold offensive operation in which heavy casualties seemed likely, such as an assault on a strongly held position.

To a marching infantryman the Transvaal is vast, whereas to a well-mounted horseman making 60 miles a day it is much less so. When the outbreak came, it could go only one way. Most of the principal towns had small British garrisons which, in the absence of artillery and barring a fluke, would be difficult for the ill-disciplined burghers to overrun. By the same token there was very little that a few ponderous companies of redcoats could do to oppose so mobile an enemy. Given the respective military limitations of the protagonists, the campaign was set to follow a predictable course. As the British units flying the flag in the Transvaal were going nowhere quickly, the rebellion would be focused in the

***Table 3:* Besieged Garrisons in the Transvaal**

	Commander	*Strength*	*Remarks*
Pretoria	*Col. William Bellairs*		
Regulars		650	
5 coys and ½ MI section, 2nd/21st Regt		(300 approx.)	HQ, A, B, F, H Companies
E & G Coys, 94th Regt		(150)	
2 x 9-pdr N/5 RA		(60)	
REs		(45)	
ASC & AHC details			
Volunteer Units		710	Original strength
D'Arcy's Horse		(120)	Increasing to 150
Pretoria Carbineers		(120)	Increasing to 150
Nourse's Horse		(70)	Increasing to 100
6 x companies, Pretoria Rifles		(400)	Increasing to 500
Volunteer artillery			4 x Krupp 4-pdr, 1 x Whitworth 3-pdr
Civilian Volunteers		650	Increasing to 750
Standerton	*Maj. William Montague*	405	
C, D & H Companies, 94th Regt		(257)	B Coy of the 58th and C & D Coys of the 94th left Wakkerstroom for Standerton on 17 Dec under the command of Capt. George Froom
B Coy, 58th Regt	*Lt. Thomas Compton*	(76)	
Volunteers		(70 approx.)	

first instance on the capital and the six other garrison towns. It remained to be seen which would hold out and which might fall. At some later point, once the British units in Natal had been formed into a relief column, the emphasis would shift to the strategically vital Laing's Nek, where the road from British South Africa climbed over the Drakensberg onto the republican high veldt. The rebellion was set to become a war of low-key sieges and one all-important blocking action.

In the last few days before the outbreak, Colonel Bellairs appealed for reinforcements from Natal. In the meantime he did his best to concentrate elements of his own command into a meaningful field force based on Pretoria. In particular he was keen to reassemble Lieutenant Colonel Philip Anstruther's widely dispersed 94th Regiment. Unfortunately Lanyon prevaricated and took a week to approve his military commander's proposals. Only one of the 94th's

	Commander	*Strength*	*Remarks*
Potchefstroom	*Maj. Charles Thornhill* RA	180	Lt. Col. R. Winsloe RSF from 12 Dec
C & D Companies, 2nd/21st Regt		(125)	D Coy came originally from Rustenburg; C Coy and MI det. were deployed from Pretoria
½ MI section, 2nd/21st Regt		(25)	
2 x 9-pdr N/5 RA			
Lydenburg	*2 Lt. Walter Young*	60	
Rear details 94th Regt			HQ, Band, A & F Coys 94th Regt left Lydenburg for Pretoria on 5 Dec. Intercepted at Bronkhorstspruit 20 Dec.
8 x REs			
Rustenburg	*Capt. Daniel Auchinleck*	62	
E Company, 2nd/21st Regt			
Marabastad	*Capt. Edmund Brook*	60	
B Company, 94th Regt			E & G Coys 94th Regt left Marabastad for Pretoria on 30 Nov, arriving on 10 Dec.
Wakkerstroom	*Capt. Harloven Saunders*	165	
A & C Companies, 58th Regt		(120)	Saunders and the two 58th coys left Newcastle for Wakkerstroom on 14 Dec.
Volunteers		(45 approx.)	

eight companies was already in place at the capital. The battalion headquarters, A and F Companies and the Band were stationed at the town of Lydenburg 190 miles to the east, while C and D Companies were at Wakkerstroom, H Company at Standerton, and the remaining two companies at Marabastad in the far north. Anstruther was to leave Lydenburg in the care of a small guard force and bring A and F Companies in to Pretoria. It was agreed with Sir George Colley that Captain Harloven Saunders of the 58th Regiment would march two companies of his regiment up from northern Natal to relieve the 94th companies quartered on Wakkerstroom. Their arrival would enable Captain George Froom to leave for Pretoria with C and D Companies of the 94th, accompanied initially by B Company of the 58th, the only company of the regiment already committed to the Transvaal. This last company would be dropped off at Standerton in lieu of the 94th's H Company, which would then continue on to Pretoria with C and D Companies. Only one of the two 94th companies in the north, B Company under Captain Edmund Brook, would remain in place at Marabastad. The second company and the regiment's mounted infantry section were also to come in to the capital. Once these preparatory moves were complete, Anstruther would have seven of his companies at Pretoria, which together with the four companies of Lieutenant Colonel George Gildea's 2nd/21st would give Bellairs a not inconsiderable task force with which to disperse rebel concentrations. It remained to be seen whether the new dispositions could be effected without interference from Kruger and the militants.

The Bronkhorstspruit Disaster, 20 December 1880

The 94th Regiment, it is clear, did not travel light. It took Colonel Anstruther more than a week to round up sufficient transport assets to meet his needs. When eventually he set out on 5 December 1880, there were as many as 30 ox-wagons to sustain a column of fewer than 270 officers and men. Evidently a lot of unnecessary paraphernalia which could and should have been left under guard at Lydenburg was packed instead for Pretoria. In addition to the heavy transport the column also included an ambulance, two mule-drawn wagons and a water cart. Not only had Anstruther been slow to get under way, but he covered an average of only nine miles a day when eventually he did. With only a modicum of urgency the 94th could have been safe in the capital long before the Triumvirate could have concentrated a commando against it. In the event Anstruther's dilatory approach to the move and his open contempt for the Boers was to cost the regiment dear. Nobody would pay a higher price than the colonel himself.

By the afternoon of Sunday 20 December 1880, the plodding column had been on the road for more than a fortnight but was still 40 miles short of

Pretoria. Three days earlier Anstruther had received a message from the capital warning him to be on his guard. The security of the column was badly hampered by a dearth of mounted men – there were only four mounted infantrymen who, for want of numbers, could not afford to stray too far from the main body. The colonel was riding at the head of the column in company with his adjutant, Lieutenant Herbert Harrison, his paymaster, Captain John Elliott, and Senior Conductor Ralph Egerton of the ASC, the last dressed in civilian clothes. Immediately behind the officer commanding and his entourage were the 40 men of the Band & Drums, who struck up from time to time with the customary mixture of rousing military marches and popular songs of the day. Behind the musicians came the two fighting companies, F followed by A, with a five-man colour party marching in the interval between them. Ordinarily the colours would have been in the care of subalterns, but for the want of young officers they were being carried on this occasion by Sergeant Maistré, the orderly room clerk, and Sergeant Pears, the master-tailor. In order to protect the expensively embroidered silks from wear and tear, the colours were carried furled inside their black leather cases. In addition to the stand-in ensigns, there were three more senior NCOs immediately behind the colours as their close escort. The two company main bodies contained only about half their respective strengths, as the balance of the men were marching in single file down the half-mile flanks of the convoy. At the tail of the column there was a rearguard of section strength. In between the rear of A Company and the first of the wagons marched a handful of regimental defaulters under the watchful eye of Sergeant Newton and the other provost NCOs. The two wagons immediately behind the prisoners were flying small red flags to denote that they were carrying ammunition.

All told the 94th fielded 6 officers and 246 other ranks. Somewhere back amongst the wagons were to be found 2 officers and 4 other ranks of the ASC, Surgeon Ward of the AMD and three Army Hospital Corps (AHC) medics. Also present were Mrs Fox, the wife of Anstruther's sergeant-major, Mrs Maistré, the widowed Mrs Smith and her daughter Jessie (the family of the recently deceased bandmaster), one other child and around 60 black drivers and *voorloopers* (drivers' assistants).

At about 1.20 p.m. the column was a mile and a half east of Bronkhorstspruit on a flat piece of veldt, which in the immediate vicinity of the road was devoid of ground cover. From a British perspective it was not the place to pick a fight. But it was not the men of the 94th who were intent on doing so. For most people in the column the first indication that something was amiss came when the tune being belted out by the Band & Drums, 'Kiss Me Mother, Kiss Your Darling', suddenly tailed away to nothing. The musicians had been thrown off their stride by the sight of dozens of armed Boers riding onto a low ridge 400 yards to the left of the road. At the foot of the ridge there was a belt of scrub which ran to within 150 yards of the column. Colonel Anstruther was not slow to sense the danger. He immediately cantered back to his fighting companies, halted them in the road and told them to prepare to defend themselves. A bugle sounded; the call was almost certainly the 'Alarm', the signal for the soldiers of the 94th to load. Often unfairly portrayed as an ambush, the Battle of Bronkhorstspruit was in fact nothing of the sort.

'I Go to Pretoria'

Looking up at the ridge Senior Conductor Egerton estimated the rebel strength at about 150. Still for the time being mounted on their ponies, they were deployed at intervals of roughly ten yards. Not all of them were yet in view, however, and in reality the commando was about twice as big as Egerton thought it was. Under the leadership of Commandant Frans Joubert (an uncle to 'Slim Piet') and Commandant Nicholaas Smit, it had been despatched from Heidelberg specifically to interdict the 94th on the road. Almost immediately a lone Boer emissary, one Paul de Beer, appeared from the scrub under the protection of a white flag.[4] Riding to within a hundred yards of the British, de Beer called out that he wished to speak to somebody in authority. In the temporary absence of the colonel and the adjutant, Egerton rode forward to begin the parley. De Beer said he had a note for the officer commanding. Egerton offered to lead de Beer to Anstruther, but he replied that he was under strict instructions not to get too close to the troops. Egerton turned his horse and went to fetch the colonel. According to de Beer, while he was waiting the British turned the first six wagons in the convoy into what he called a 'sort of camp', a reference presumably to some kind of rudimentary laager – though it is noteworthy that none of the principal British sources mentions this. Eventually a deputation of four, Anstruther, Harrison, Elliott and Egerton approached the emissary on foot. De Beer kicked up his pony and rode 50 yards to meet them. In his official report Anstruther wrote:

> The bearer handed me an English letter, signed by P. Joubert, and countersigned by other Boers, requesting me to wait at the spot where I then was until a reply had been received to an ultimatum that had been sent to Sir Owen Lanyon. I told the interpreter[5] I could not do so, as I had orders to proceed with all possible despatch to Pretoria, and that I had no wish to meet him hostilely. He said that he would take my message to the Kommandant-General, and I asked him to let me know the result, to which he nodded assent.

The actual text of the message was as follows:

To The Commander-in-Chief of Her Majesty's troops,
on the road between Lydenburg and Pretoria

Sir

We have the honour to inform you that the Government of the South African Republic have taken up their residence of Heidelberg.

That a Diplomatic Commissioner has been sent by them to His Excellency Sir Owen Lanyon.

That until the arrival of His Excellency's answer, we do not know whether we are in a state of war or not.

That consequently, we cannot allow any movement of troops from your side, and wish you to stop where you are.

We, not being at war with Her Majesty the Queen, nor with the people of England, who we are sure to be on our side if they were acquainted with the position, but only recovering the independence of our country, we do not wish to take up arms, and therefore inform you that any movement of troops from your side will be taken by us as a declaration of war, the responsibility whereof we put on your shoulders, as we know what we will have to do in self-defence. We are, Sir, your obedient servants,

S. J. P. Kruger
M. W. Pretorius
P. J. Joubert[6]

In de Beer's version of the encounter he claims to have told Anstruther that he had only five minutes to give his reply and then to have asked him three times, 'Do you mean peace or war?' On each occasion the colonel responded with, 'I go to Pretoria.' By now the bandsmen of the 94th had recovered their composure and struck up in the background with 'God Save the Queen'. The parley drew to an unceremonious close when an irritated Anstruther, who was quite prepared to defend himself but was not in the business of declaring war on anyone, told de Beer to go back to his commandant and tell him that the 94th had been ordered to Pretoria, and that to Pretoria it would go.

The moment de Beer was close enough to shake his head at the commandants, Nicholaas Smit waved his men onto the offensive. Urging their ponies downhill at the gallop, the Boers rode into the scrub to dismount and find fire positions. Anstruther dashed back to his men, bellowing orders for F and A Companies to deploy extended order skirmish lines. The bandsmen dropped their instruments and doubled back to the wagon with their rifles, whilst the provost detail and the prisoners dashed into the cover of the ammunition wagons and began breaking open boxes of cartridges, as for some reason the men were carrying only 30 rounds in their pouches, rather than the customary 70. At the rear of the column the black drivers and *voorloopers* dived beneath the wagons or took to their heels across the veldt as they each judged best. By the time the men of A and F Companies had deployed and were ready to open fire, the scrub was filled with gun smoke and the first dead redcoats were already sprawled in the grass.

The soldiers of the 94th loaded and fired into the scrub as fast as they could in a vain attempt to gain the upper hand, but in the heat of the moment many of the younger men failed to take account of the Boers' sudden advance and did not lower their sights. As we have seen it was standard practice at this time for company officers to observe fall of shot and give corrections for range, but A and F Companies could field only three officers between them where ordinarily there should have been six, and all three were hit in the first few minutes. As a result most of the British return fire sailed harmlessly over the scrub to land on the now deserted ridge beyond. The principal figures in the battalion headquarters fared no better than the company officers. Anstruther himself was badly wounded in the legs, the adjutant was shot through the head and killed at his side, while Sergeant-Major Fox was hit in the arm. Back amongst the wagons Mrs Fox was merely a human silhouette like any other and was also hit by an incoming round. Of the three company officers Captain Stanford Nairn was killed, Lieutenant John Hume severely wounded and Lieutenant James MacSwiney mortally wounded. Assistant-Commissary[7] Ernest Carter was hit three times and left dangerously wounded.

Early in the fight a large party of mounted Boers under the command of Veldtkornet D. J. Erasmus swept around the rear of the column, where they compelled the surrender of the rearguard and then dismounted to bring the rest of the 94th under fire from the right of the road. This manoeuvre denied the British the opportunity to find good cover behind the wagons. At the head of the column, where the troops had been caught in the open, there was a bloodbath. After a cruelly uneven fire-fight of about 20 minutes' duration, Anstruther realized that further resistance could only result in annihilation. By now he himself had been hit in the legs no fewer than five times. Many other men suffered multiple gunshot wounds, including Private Duffy shot a remarkable nine times.

Surrender and Aftermath

Anstruther had the word passed for the uninjured survivors to cease firing and wave their helmets in the air to betoken surrender. Somebody else climbed onto a wagon waving a white flag. When an uneasy silence had settled over the veldt, a motley crowd of long-bearded men in battered slouch hats and everyday clothes, draped in bandoliers and cartridge belts, emerged from the scrub to take control of the situation. In all the confusion the quick-thinking NCOs of the colour party tore the two silks from their pikestaffs and hurried them down the length of the convoy to where the unfortunate Mrs Fox was being tended to. Trusting that the Boers would not presume to disturb an injured female, they hid the colours beneath the folds of her dress. Some little while later two bandsmen smuggled them across to a tent which had been erected to shelter the wounded.

Afrikaner writers have often remarked that the Boers demonstrated great magnanimity to the British wounded in the aftermath of Bronkhorstspruit, glibly overlooking the fact that this is no more than civilized norms require. In fact there were far more sinister dimensions to the after-action conduct of the rebels. Decent treatment at the hands of a Boer commando was all too commonly conditional upon skin colour: one contemporary African source records that the Boers shot dead a number of wounded *voorloopers*. Certainly they did not hesitate to rob the British dead and wounded of money, pocket watches, rings and even items of clothing. One of the surviving bandsmen would record further abuse at the hands of Veldtkornet Solomon Prinsloo, a bullish republican whose farm had been used by the rebels as a rendezvous prior to the action.[8] Some days later, whilst moving some of the prisoners to Heidelberg, Prinsloo had 16 members of the 94th yoked to a wagon like draught animals and then whipped them across the veldt for an hour. In a separate atrocity a party of Boers meant to be escorting the paroled Captain Elliott across the border into the Orange Free State murdered him in cold blood instead.[9] Touching nationalist references to the provision of milk, eggs and fresh fruit for the British wounded pale into insignificance alongside such conduct.

The 94th lost 2 officers and 53 other ranks killed, and 3 officers and 88 other ranks wounded. Subsequently 2 of the wounded officers and 6 of the other ranks would die of their injuries. The ill-fated Captain John Elliott was the only officer left unharmed when the shooting stopped. The ASC lost Conductor Bancroft and two NCOs killed, with Assistant-Commissary Carter, Conductor Egerton and two NCOs wounded. Two of the AHC medics had been wounded, and although Surgeon Ward was wounded in the thigh he was well enough to work indefatigably for the next two days. Anstruther lived long enough to record in his official report, 'Ward's work can hardly be described. It was endless for 48 hours; until assistance arrived, he had not one moment for himself.' The colonel was well placed to comment on the untiring efforts of the doctor. He suffered in agony for the best part of a week, until eventually it was decided that one of his legs would have to come off. He lingered through Christmas, but on Boxing Day his strength finally failed him.

Poor Anstruther died with only one consolation – that of knowing that his colours had not fallen into enemy hands. In the immediate aftermath of the battle he had prevailed upon Frans Joubert to issue Conductor Egerton with a letter of safe conduct, so that he could push on to Pretoria to summon help for the wounded. It was agreed that Egerton would be accompanied by Sergeant Bradley, the officers' mess steward. For some reason Bradley, like Egerton, was dressed in civilian clothes, suggesting that Joubert failed to appreciate that they were soldiers. Given that they were about to undertake a mission of mercy, the Boers' insistence that they walk to the capital was churlish in the extreme. Before departing the scene of the defeat, the pair called at the hospital tent to wish the wounded well. The Boers failed to notice that Egerton put on a few pounds round the midriff during the course of his short visit. The colours of the 94th arrived safely in Pretoria at 4.00 a.m. the following day. It had taken Egerton and Bradley, anxious not to be stopped and searched, 11 hours to cover the distance. Egerton's reward would be a commission in the 94th, soon to become the 2nd Battalion The Connaught Rangers.

The Natal Field Force

Sir George Colley was celebrating Christmas Day when news of Bronkhorstspruit reached his ears. By the New Year he had all the military assets he could lay his hands on marching hard for the tiny border town of Newcastle, the northernmost settlement in Natal, and now the assembly area for a relief column to be known as the Natal Field Force. From Fort Amiel, the old Zulu War fortification overlooking the town, the road into the Transvaal ran out into an undulating plain, made its way over a low rocky plateau known as Schuinshoogte, descended to a double *drift* (a ford or other crossing point) over the Ingogo and Harte Rivers and then entered a wide steep-sided valley which both narrowed and climbed until it reached the all-important pass known as Laing's Nek – a journey of around 25 miles in all. Two dominating mountains overlooked the road from the western side of the valley. The more southerly feature, closer to Newcastle, was known as Nkwelo, and the more northerly as Amajuba, a Zulu name meaning 'hill of doves' – today far better known as Majuba Hill. At the top of the climb from the valley floor, the road ran through a bottleneck only a few hundred yards in width, with the lower slopes of Majuba on its left-hand side, and a flat-topped feature to the right which British scouts soon took to calling 'Table Hill'.

Because Colley was the overall military commander of both Natal and the Transvaal, he decided to entrust direct command of the force assembling at Newcastle to the 41-year-old Colonel Bonar Deane of the 19th Regiment, until recently a staff officer in Cape Town. As one of the two most senior political figures in Southern Africa, it was Colley's task to attend to the wider strategic situation, including the most pressing political imperative – that of keeping the Orange Free State out of the war. He had already exchanged diplomatic telegrams with President Brand, when on 30 December he followed up with a private letter:

> I wish also to write privately to tell you how deeply distressed I am at what has occurred in the Transvaal, and how grateful I shall be to you for any advice or assistance you can afford me in endeavouring to bring about a settlement . . . The sudden outbreak and attack on our troops has been a heavy blow to me, for our troops had strict orders to avoid bringing on a collision, and to act only on the defensive . . .
>
> How hopeless the contest the Boers are now entering on is, you must be well aware. There are now, I believe, two cavalry regiments two infantry regiments and two batteries of artillery on their way to reinforce me, and twice that number more would reach me here within a month if only I telegraph home the wish. What I most fear, and what I am striving most to check, is this extraordinary fever spreading beyond the Transvaal.

Although a few Free State hotheads crossed the border to fight alongside their kinsmen, on this occasion there was no wider drift towards a fully fledged Anglo-Boer War. Wisely, President Brand made himself useful to both sides, in the roles of go-between and honest broker. In the meantime Colley did his best to keep Pietermaritzburg calm by continuing the usual round of gubernatorial engagements right up to the last safe moment. Leaving Lady Edith in residence at Government House, he finally left for the front on 10 January, the same day that the Colonial Secretary, Lord Kimberley, established secret telegraphic contact with President Brand. Already Gladstone's government was toying with the idea of selling out its soldiers and representatives in the field. On the other side of the Drakensberg 'Slim Piet' had disposed his commandos with the dual objects in mind of keeping the British garrisons in the north safely bottled up, and holding Laing's Nek against the relief column he knew must attack from the south.

At dawn on 24 January 1881 the Natal Field Force set out from Fort Amiel, bound in the first instance for a holding position about 3½ miles short of the nek. As was usual for the time of year it had been raining heavily for days and the road was in poor condition. The logistic train consisted of 82 ox-wagons, 23 mule-wagons, 16 carts and 10 ambulances, drawn by 1,340 oxen and more than 400 horses and mules. It seemed to take forever for the ox-wagons to get across the Ingogo River, so that it was not until the afternoon of 26 January that the force encamped itself on a flat-topped ridge known as Mount Prospect. At a strength of something around 70 officers and 1,400 men, the Natal Field Force did not amount to much of an army.

Nor was quantity the only issue; unusually there were issues around quality too. The mounted squadron under Major William Brownlow KDG, for example, was a scratch force made up of 35 *bona fide* KDG cavalrymen, 25 men of No. 7 Company, ASC, who whilst they were routinely employed on mounted duties could not by any stretch of the imagination be categorized as cavalrymen, and the recently formed mounted infantry sections of the 58th and 3rd/60th. Also present was a small contingent of the Natal Mounted Police under their veteran commandant, Major John Dartnell, a leading player in the Isandlwana campaign. Unfortunately Colley was so anxious to avoid lasting difficulty between the civilian populations of Natal and the Transvaal, that he had determined to keep the police out of the fighting, a largely meaningless political gesture he could ill-afford. Later he would even go so far as to order the NMP back to Newcastle. Even the ordinarily stalwart infantry battalions available to Colley had cohesion, training and morale issues to worry about. Several hundred infantrymen, a significant proportion of the total, had only just arrived in Natal as new drafts. They were unacclimatized to African conditions, unassimilated into their companies and short on rifle practice. In the case of the older sweats there were morale issues arising from the long and tedious stints of garrison duty that had followed the Zulu War. All of the regiments had been troubled with significant desertion and drunkenness problems. If nothing else the prospect of active service had salved flagging spirits.

With three of its companies besieged upcountry the 58th (Rutlandshire) Regiment, a conventional scarlet-clad regiment of the line, its cuffs and collars faced in black, could parade only five sub-units under the command of its senior field officer, Major William Hingeston. The 3rd/60th, commanded by the splendidly bewhiskered Lieutenant Colonel Cromer Ashburnham, known affectionately to his men as 'Old Bristles', was a rifle regiment clad not in scarlet but in dark bottle-green, with black leather belts and pouches. Ashburnham had disbanded one of his companies in order to man his mounted infantry section and the improvised artillery division he had been asked to form around two spare 7-pounder mountain guns. Having been told to leave two of his companies to secure Newcastle, he too had been left with only five deployable sub-units. A new draft of 2 officers and 80 men bound for the 2nd/21st represented the only element of that battalion not trapped in the north. In its usual helpful way the Royal Navy had done its best to assist a short-handed Army by deploying a small naval brigade equipped with two Gatling guns and three 24-pounder rocket troughs.

Like the cavalry squadron, the artillery component was also a scratch organization. It was commanded by Captain Carlyle Greer RA, a veteran of the Second Maori War and the ill-fated attempt to storm the Gate Pah. The rough equivalent of a formed battery, Greer's command consisted of the two mule-

Table 4: **Composition of the Natal Field Force, January 1881**

Commanding Officer		***Col. Deane***	
CO & Staff			5 & 6
Naval Brigade	(2 x Gatling guns, 3 x 24-pdr rockets)		5 & 122
Bn HQ & 5 Coys, 58th (Rutlandshire) Regiment		*Maj. Hingeston*	15 & 487
Bn HQ & 5 Coys, 3rd/60th Rifles		*Lt. Col. Ashburnham*	17 & 411
Draft, 2nd/21st Regiment (Royal Scots Fusiliers)		*Capt. Whitton*	2 & 80
Mounted Squadron		*Maj. Brownlow*	6 & 124
1st King's Dragoon Guards			(approx. 35)
Section, No 7 Company ASC			(approx. 25)
MI Section, 58th Regiment			(approx. 30)
MI Section, 3rd/60th Rifles			(approx. 30)
Natal Mounted Police		*Maj. Dartnell*	3 & 70
Artillery		*Capt. Greer*	
Division, N/5 Battery RA	(2 x 9-pdr)	*Lt. Parsons*	4 & 75
Division, 10/7 Battery RA	(2 x 9-pdr)	*(Capt. Greer)*	
Division, 3rd/60th, RA NCOs	(2 x 7-pdr)		1 & 20
Royal Engineers			1 & 6
Logistic Details			8 & 37
Army Medical Department			5 doctors
Army Hospital Corps			0 & 22
Army Service Corps			3 & 11

drawn 7-pounders manned by the Rifles, Lieutenant Charles Parsons's division of N/5 Battery, properly equipped with two horse-drawn 9-pounder field guns, and finally an *ad hoc* division of 10/7 Battery equipped with a pair of 9-pounders drawn by trek-oxen. Ordinarily the men of 10/7 Battery were employed in the role of garrison artillery at Cape Town.

The Battle of Laing's Nek, 28 January 1881

Conscious that Potchefstroom in particular might not be very well provisioned, and estimating that reinforcements would take at least three weeks to reach him, Colley wasted no time in striking at the Boer force deployed to deny him entry to the Transvaal. In all Joubert had about 2,000 men occupying the nek, including something around 600 positioned on or near Table Hill under Commandants Greyling and Engelbrecht. The Boers administered themselves from three large wagon-laagers sited on the reverse slopes north of the nek.

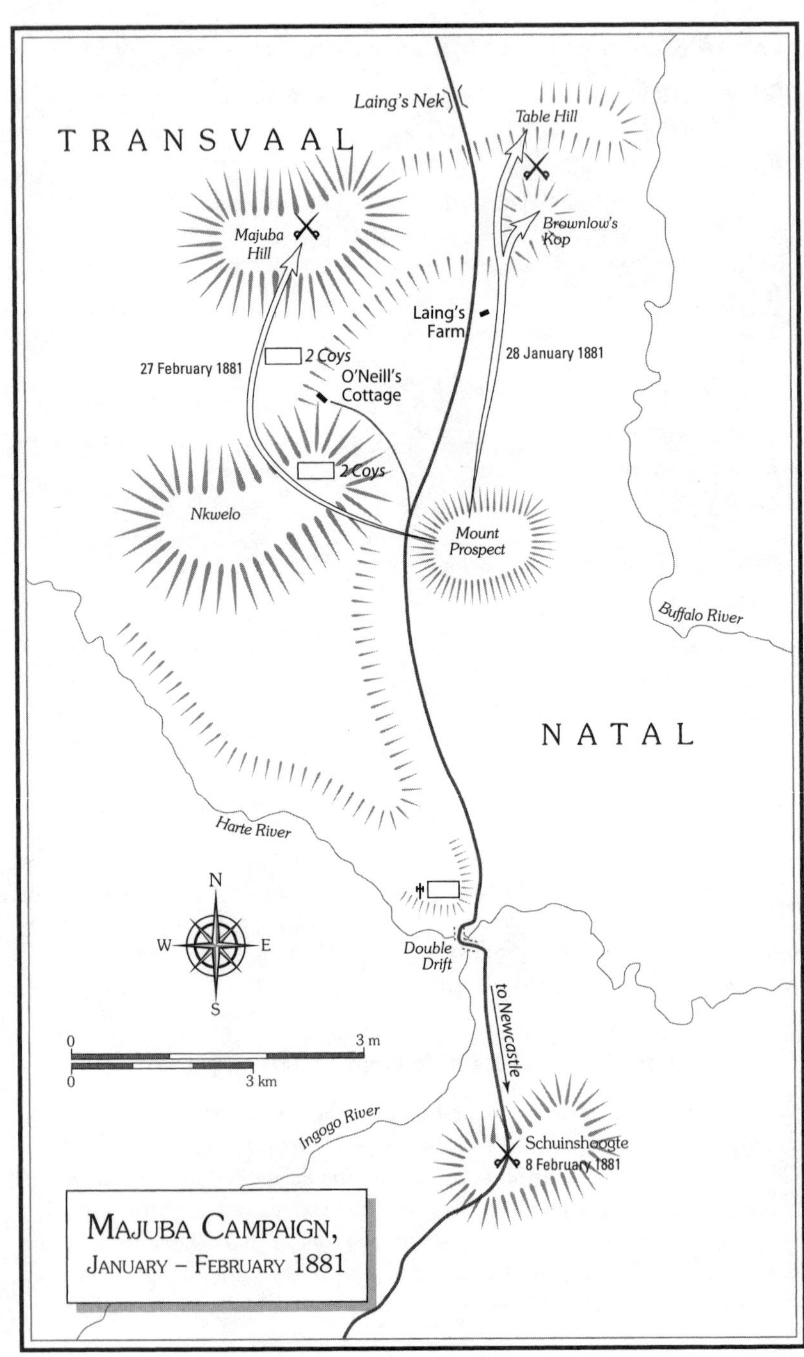

TRANSVAAL
Laing's Nek
Table Hill
Majuba Hill
Brownlow's Kop
Laing's Farm
27 February 1881
2 Coys
O'Neill's Cottage
28 January 1881
2 Coys
Nkwelo
Mount Prospect
Buffalo River
NATAL
Harte River
N
W
E
S
Double Drift
to Newcastle
0
3 m
0
3 km
Ingogo River
Schuinshoogte
8 February 1881
MAJUBA CAMPAIGN,
JANUARY – FEBRUARY 1881

Having spent Thursday 27 January in reconnoitring options for an assault, Colley decided to attack in daylight the following morning.

The general's orders required that the Natal Field Force operate in four main groupings, three of them committed to the attack and one to the security of Mount Prospect. The strengths shown below are the fighting strengths of the units on the day as listed by Colley in his official despatch. On the British left would be an all-arms grouping consisting of the mounted police (3 and 63), four companies of the 3rd/60th (13 and 321), most of the naval brigade (4 and 84), two of the rocket troughs and all six guns. This force would have the task of fixing the enemy from the area of Laing's Farm, and laying down suppressive fire. Major Brownlow's cavalry squadron (6 and 113) would be much further east securing the right flank, while in the centre would be the main strike force – D, E, F, G and H Companies of the 58th Regiment (15 and 479) under Major Hingeston. The camp would be left in the care of the 2nd/21st detachment, the fifth company of the 3rd/60th and the balance of the naval brigade with the two Gatlings. With logistic details the camp guard came to about 260 men in all and was placed under the command of Captain James Whitton RSF. Colley's plan of attack was simplicity itself. After a short preliminary bombardment from the guns and rockets, the 58th would force Table Hill at its eastern extremity. Having gained the summit the battalion would wheel left and clear along the line of Boer positions as far as the nek. And all bar the shouting that would be the end of the Transvaal Rebellion.

As if to signify his contempt for the rebels, Colley made no attempt whatsoever to achieve surprise. Instead the 1,200 soldiers involved in the operation moved out of Mount Prospect at about 6.15 a.m.,[10] by which time it was already broad daylight. It took the best part of three hours for the troops to position themselves for the assault, allowing every Boer for miles around all the time in the world to deploy to the series of *schanzes*, or rough stone breastworks, they had raised over the previous few days. As planned, the British left wing moved into the vicinity of Henry Laing's Farm, which lay just to the right of the road in the valley floor, some 1,200 yards short of the nek. The guns were unlimbered on a low rise near the farm buildings, from where the range to Table Hill was about 2,300 yards.[11] The main body of the Rifles took post just to the rear of the guns, with Lieutenant Dudley Ryder's company thrown forward as skirmishers. The naval brigade pushed to the left of Ryder's men in order to gain a field of fire for the rocket troughs. The rifle-armed sailors shook themselves out along the stone walls bounding Laing's spread and almost immediately came under fire from a nearby *kloof* or wooded ravine. Their well chosen cover stood the 'bluejackets' in good stead and they suffered very few casualties in consequence.

The general gave the order for the artillery to open fire at around 9.30 a.m. The guns and rockets provided a spectacular and heartening show for the watching infantrymen, and spread alarm and consternation amongst some of the Boers. Up in the nek a number of tethered saddle horses broke loose, but otherwise the bombardment did little harm to an enemy who was both well dispersed and hunkered low amongst the rocks and hollows. While the rockets engaged the nek, the guns concentrated on the eastern end of Table Hill. After only 15 minutes of preparatory bombardment, William Hingeston received the order to advance. Then, in a very strange move indeed, Colonel Deane and four mounted staff officers cantered to the head of the battalion to lead the attack, dislodging the officer commanding at an absolutely critical moment.

The 58th set off for the base of Table Hill in column of companies. This meant that each of the companies was formed in a two-rank line of roughly 40 files in width, officers to the front and sergeants to the rear, with all five companies moving one behind the other. When in due course Major Hingeston gave the order to extend into line, the rearmost companies would push up level with the leading company in turn, until all five sub-units were advancing abreast of one another in a two-rank fighting line of more than 200 files. The column formation would offer better cross-country manoeuvrability in the approach, whilst moving into line at the appropriate moment would maximize the battalion's firepower and serve to present a less dense target to the enemy. As ever the timing of the transition from one to the other would be crucial.

It was now, at a very early stage in the proceedings, that the Battle of Laing's Nek began to go wrong for the British. According to Brownlow, clear direction had been given that the 58th and the mounted squadron should attack the saddle between the eastern end of Table Hill and the conical *koppie* (small hill) about a thousand yards to the right.

> The other mistake was that Sir Gorge Colley gave distinct orders for the officer commanding the assaulting party to go up the connecting nek where I went . . . in place of which they actually did go half a mile to my left; if Colonel Deane had followed the directions he received, it would have been a far easier ascent for his troops and it would have made all the difference to me.[12]

Perhaps if the attack had been left to the regimental officers things would not have gone so badly awry, but with the staff taking a last-minute lead it was not to be. Instead of attacking in close concert with the mounted squadron, the infantry veered too far to the left so that the assault went in against a steep spur at the eastern end of Table Hill. Here the approach would be hindered by a severe gradient and long damp grass which the soldiers found extremely slippery underfoot.

It was a hot, still day and, clad as they were in scarlet serge tunics, the men of the 58th had worked up a good sweat long before they started scrambling up the spur, striving hard in spite of the slope to maintain their dressing. It was now that the toiling redcoats discovered that the Boer left flank was not in fact resting on the eastern extremity of Table Hill, as they might reasonably have expected, but rather on the conical koppie over their right shoulders. Soon to earn itself the sobriquet 'Brownlow's Kop', the feature was held by about 50 burghers under Commandant Engelbrecht. Fortunately, at 900 yards and more, the range was long. It was typical of Colley's unfailing courtesy and generosity of spirit that his official despatch omitted any mention of Deane's navigational error. He did publicly admit, however, that he wished he had cleared Brownlow's Kop before sending in the 58th against Table Hill. Although this remark has been allowed to pass largely unremarked by historians, it represents a damning admission and serves as a pointer to a poor eye for ground. But let it not be said that Colley had no plan for dealing with a threat to his right – he did – and Major Brownlow was now hurrying to put it into effect.

Brownlow claimed in 1882 that his orders were to 'charge the enemy no matter what their strength and to clear the rear and flanks of the 58th'. Whatever had been said to him, he was a free-thinking field officer and was at liberty to respond to an immediate tactical problem as he thought best. He decided to wheel his squadron right into line, with one troop echeloned behind the other, and to make a mounted charge up the side of the koppie. Such was the gradient and the poor quality of the squadron's horsemanship that it lost all momentum long before it came within striking distance of Engelbrecht and his men. At the top of the slope the Boers poured in a heavy fusillade which reduced the leading troop to chaos; a number of men were killed and wounded and more than 20 horses brought down. Brownlow and Lieutenant Henry Lermitte of the RSF were amongst those unhorsed in the first salvo, while Brownlow's batman, Private John Doogan, was amongst the wounded. The squadron's second wave, following up under Captain Cecil Hornby of the 58th, baulked at the apparent destruction of the leading troop and reined in half-way up the slope. Troop Sergeant-Major James Lunny of the KDG was the only man in the squadron to cause the enemy any real discomfiture. Armed only with a revolver, he rode in amongst Engelbrecht's men and shot two of them down before he was killed. Notwithstanding his injury Private Doogan rode to his master's aid and insisted that the major take his horse. All the while Brownlow was expecting his second troop to come surging through to exploit the momentary confusion caused by Lunny and others but, for an apparent want of fortitude, it was destined never to arrive. At some stage in the proceedings Doogan was hit again, but somehow both he and his master succeeded in scrambling away to safety. His courage and selflessness in rescuing the squadron commander would later be adjudged worthy of the VC. Brownlow felt so betrayed by the lack of determination shown by the men of Hornby's troop that he refused to speak to them for days afterwards. For the time being the squadron was scattered across the hillside, resoundingly defeated and making its way downhill in disarray.

The Playing Fields of Eton

The officers and men of the 58th had no choice but to press on with their attack, despite the resumption of the long-range fire from their right rear. A party of Boers also came scrambling down from the top of the spur to infiltrate in against the battalion's right flank, compelling the right-flank company commander to wheel back his outside half-company to return fire. By now the slope had become so steep that the breathless soldiers were hauling on tussocks of grass to heave themselves up. Eventually they struggled onto the less severe gradient near the top of the spur, where the order was given to extend into line. There were only some 80 burghers nestled amongst the man-made schanzes and the outcrops of rock directly in the path of the 58th. The battalion paused momentarily and opened fire at a range of about 150 yards, but for men heaving from physical exertion the half-hidden Boers were not the easiest of targets. It quickly became clear that the British were getting the worst of the exchange. After a couple of minutes Colonel Deane, who was in action for the first time, insisted on a charge. Major Hingeston and his officers raised the cry to fix bayonets and urged their men back to their feet. With only a half-hearted, breathless cheer, instead of the fierce roar that traditionally accompanies the British infantry into a close-quarter assault, the exhausted 58th plunged forward once more.

Foolishly Colonel Deane remained mounted at the head of the troops. This sort of bravado might have done in the Crimea, but this was the dawn of the modern military age and in the circumstances the lion-hearted colonel might as well have unholstered his revolver and shot himself through the brain. As soon as the advancing line broke cover he went reeling from the saddle. Clambering to his feet he cried out 'I am alright', but only moments later was hit again and killed. In declining to dismount Deane had obliged his staff entourage to follow suit. The slaughter spread quickly. First, Lieutenant the Honourable Richard Monck, the adjutant of the 58th, was unhorsed. Lieutenant Robert Elwes of the Grenadier Guards, Colley's ADC, was trotting past as Monck went sprawling. Both were Old Etonians and Elwes tried to encourage his friend back onto his feet with the old school motto, 'Come on Monck – Floreat Etona! We must be in the front rank!' Seconds later Elwes was shot dead. The same fate befell two of the three remaining staff officers. Major Ruscombe Poole RA was Colley's DAAG. A year or so earlier he had been appointed as the escorting officer to the deposed King Cetshwayo. A warm friendship had sprung up between gaoler and captive and it is said that when the king heard of Poole's death, he drew his blanket over his head and refused to eat or drink for two days. Deane's orderly officer, Lieutenant Edward Inman of the 60th Rifles, was also shot dead at about the same time.

The loss amongst the regimental officers was correspondingly heavy. When Major Hingeston was badly wounded, command of the battalion devolved upon the senior company commander, Captain Edward Lovegrove. Elsewhere Lieutenant Henry Dolphin was shot dead and Lieutenant Charles O'Donel was severely wounded. Nor was the carnage restricted to the officers; most of the company colour-sergeants and a good many of the section commanders also fell. Moments after taking command, Edward Lovegrove was seriously wounded, leaving Lieutenant Stephen Jopp in charge. But the senior officer left on the hillside was not Jopp but Major Edward Essex of the 75th Regiment, an Isandlwana survivor and now the only living member of Colonel Deane's staff. Essex had been unhorsed by the fusillade that had killed the rest of his colleagues. Staggering to his feet he could see dozens of broken scarlet forms strewn across the hillside and was quick to realise that the Boer fire was simply too heavy and too accurate for the 58th to charge home. Wisely he gave the order to fall back. Taking command of what was left of the two left-hand companies Essex posted his men along a rock ledge and gave covering fire to the withdrawal of the right wing.

For the third time in two years the presence of a set of colours on the battlefield had become problematic. The colours of the 58th had been carried into action by Lieutenant Walter Peel (Queen's Colour) and 2nd Lieutenant Launcelot Baillie (Regimental Colour). Since neither of them was hit until after the retreat began, it can safely be inferred that Hingeston had instructed the colour party to keep well back from the line during the assault. Now though, with the Boers following up the retreat, the ensigns were exposed to a plunging fire from the hillside above. Baillie was the first to be hit. Walter Peel tried to help him up but was rebuffed with, 'Never mind me, save the colours.' Peel did as he was told and struggled away with both pikestaffs. A little way down the slope he tripped and fell. Thinking that Peel had been shot, Sergeant Bridgestock scooped up the colours and carried on downhill. At the foot of the spur they were taken into the care of Lieutenant Robert Wallace, the quartermaster. It was a great relief to the remnants of the 58th when eventually the colours were brought safely out of action. Never again would British regiments carry their colours on a battlefield.

Despite the regiment's heavy casualties the men of the 58th kept their nerve and, with the aid of covering fire from the artillery and a brisk supporting action by two companies of the 60th Rifles, pulled off a well-ordered withdrawal. One of the last members of the 58th to be killed was the already twice-wounded Sergeant-Major Murray, who despite his injuries refused to be helped to the rear and stayed with the rearguard to the end. Elsewhere some of the wounded and dying officers were helped away by their men. Major Hingeston was helped downhill by Private Godfrey, while nearby Boy Martin of the Band tried to assist Captain Lovegrove.[13] Sadly, as described at the start of the chapter, Hingeston was dead by morning. Lieutenant Alan Hill distinguished himself with a number of courageous attempts to bring casualties back down the hillside. First he attempted to get 2nd Lieutenant Baillie away by heaving him into the saddle of a riderless horse. The animal proved too skittish, however, so Hill tried to carry his comrade away himself. Unfortunately Baillie was hit again, this time fatally. Undeterred by the failure of his first rescue attempt, Hill made two more, both of which proved successful. He returned to the aid of the wounded a fourth time, but stayed with them so long that he was captured by the Boers, though later in the day they would be generous enough to set him free. Hill's selflessness would be recognized with the award of the second VC of the battle. Sergeant-Major Murray, Sergeant Bridgestock and Private Godfrey would all receive the DCM.

By 4.00 p.m. a dejected and badly mauled Natal Field Force was back at Mount Prospect, licking its wounds and negotiating for the recovery of its wounded and the burial of its dead. Colley struggled with the causes and consequences of the defeat. To mitigate the scale of the disaster he fell back on flowery rhetoric, both in a personal address he made to the troops and in his written daily orders. During the course of his speech Colley took full responsibility for the defeat and went to great pains to exonerate the 58th of any share in the blame. Colley's long official despatch heaped praise on just about everybody, some of them still living but most now dead.

In a wider sense the British losses at Laing's Nek were insignificant, but in the particular context of south-eastern Africa in 1881, they were grave indeed. Seven officers and 77 other ranks had been killed, 3 officers and 110 other ranks wounded and 2 men captured. The prisoners were Private Joseph Venables of the KDG, unhorsed and captured in Brownlow's charge, and Sergeant Madden of the 58th, knocked unconscious and left behind on the spur. Seventy-four of the dead and 101 of the wounded were members of the 58th. Brownlow's share in the loss was 4 killed, 15 wounded and 1 man missing (Venables).[14] The squadron also lost 29 horses killed or missing, with 5 more wounded. The Boer loss was said to be 14 killed and 27 wounded.

The War Office Responds

Inevitably the news of the Bronkhorstspruit disaster had caused a stir at the War Office. With long experience of South Africa behind him, including his famous victory at Kambula, it was decided that Colonel Sir Evelyn Wood VC, KCB would make an ideal second-in-command to Colley. The theory was that military command should rest with Wood, an officer of proven tactical ability, leaving Colley free to concentrate on political affairs. Having first insisted on his promotion to brigadier-general, Wood sailed for South Africa on 14 January, but Colley's pride was so badly wounded by the rebuff at Laing's Nek a fortnight later, that any prospect of him ceding field command evaporated long before the hero of Kambula disembarked in Durban. A number of special service officers were despatched for Natal at the same time, including Lieutenant Colonel Herbert Stewart of the 3rd Dragoon Guards, destined in due course to become Colley's chief of staff.

Only three days before the Battle of Laing's Nek, HMS *Euphrates* arrived at Durban from India and landed the 2nd/60th Rifles, most of the 15th Hussars and F Battery, 3 Brigade, Royal Artillery. Two days later HMS *Crocodile* disembarked the 83rd Regiment and the 92nd (Gordon) Highlanders. As usual the British had started a small war badly but with high-grade reinforcements on their way upcountry, most of them veterans of the Afghan campaign, there was every reason to expect that the fortunes of war would quickly swing back in their favour. Until the new units came up from the coast, there was little Colley could do but improve the fortifications around Mount Prospect and hatch plans for how best to employ Evelyn Wood and the reinforcements. The one thing he could not afford to do in the meantime was to make a distinctly indifferent military situation worse by courting a second defeat.

Intercepting the Mail

Given the mobility of the Boers and the dearth of British mounted troops, a problem exacerbated by Colley's refusal to make use of the NMP, trouble on the Newcastle road was to be expected. The threat manifested itself on 7 February 1881, ten days after the Battle of Laing's Nek, when couriers bearing the morning mail and their mounted infantry escort, a corporal and five men, were fired on not long after crossing the Ingogo River, half-way between Mount Prospect and Newcastle. The party was forced to turn back to camp where they reported that they had been harried by a force of 50–100 Boers.[15] As there were two important logistic movements planned for the following day, Colley spent the afternoon worrying about the security of his lines of communication. A convoy of five mule-drawn ambulance wagons bearing about 20 of the wounded from the Laing's Nek fight was due to move south first thing in the morning. More significantly a slower-moving convoy of 40 ox-wagons bearing foodstuffs, ammunition and other military commodities would be departing Newcastle for the camp at roughly the same time.

By 'lights out' Colley had worked up a plan and given the orders to make it a reality. A strong column would push south of the Ingogo, rendezvous with the supply wagons somewhere north of Newcastle, and then turn about to see them safely in to Mount Prospect. The column's principal component would be the headquarters and 5 companies of the 3rd/60th Rifles under Colonel Ashburnham, a total of 15 officers[16] and 295 other ranks. Major Brownlow would act as the eyes and ears of the column with a 38-man detail from the mounted squadron, while Captain Greer would provide its fire support with four of the guns. Lieutenant Parsons' division of N/5 Battery (1 and 28) would provide the professional field gunnery, while the *ad hoc* artillery section drawn from the 3rd/60th (but commanded by Lieutenant William Young RSF), would do their best with the mountain guns. The only doctor warned-off for the operation was an Irish AMD surgeon called James McGann, who would be accompanied by an AHC orderly and a four-man stretcher party from the 2nd/21st. Apart from the N Battery limbers the only other wheeled transport was a mule-drawn ambulance and a wagon-load of reserve artillery ammunition. Together with the shells aboard his limbers, Parsons calculated that he would have a total of 234 rounds available for the 9-pounders. Surprisingly nobody thought to detail a water cart or a reserve of small-arms ammunition, thus badly undermining the column's self-sufficiency.

With fewer than 400 men committed to it, command of the operation was a job for a lieutenant colonel or a senior major. The 49-year-old Ashburnham was a veteran of the storming of Delhi, had not long since returned from serving under Roberts in Afghanistan and was an experienced battalion commander. In short he was the perfectly qualified candidate. Even so General Colley was unable to resist taking personal command of the foray. In fairness a serious fight was not anticipated – if Boer raiders were encountered, it was to be expected that they would avoid a general engagement with a relatively strong force well-provided with artillery.

The Battle of Ingogo (Schuinshoogte), 8 February 1881

The dawn revealed a clear blue African sky and gave the men of the 60th Rifles every reason to anticipate a typical Natal summer's day. Once the sun had warmed up the veldt, the morning would feel pleasantly warm. The middle part of the day would be too hot for comfort, especially if one was flogging back uphill as today seemed likely. Around tea-time there would be a fair chance of the sky filling with dark storm clouds, harbingers of one of the late afternoon downpours typical of the summer months. The orders of the previous evening had indicated that the general expected to be back at Mount Prospect by 3.30 p.m. – the time set for the returning troops' main meal of the day. With some half-decent luck on their side, the men of the Rifles would be home and dry well before the heavens opened.

The ambulance wagons set out not long after breakfast without the benefit of an armed escort but under the protection of the Red Cross. As there was no lawful reason for the Boers to interfere with the administrative movement of British casualties, it was not until 8.30 a.m. that the fighting troops left camp. Colley had made no allowance, though, for the opportunism of the average Boer rustic who, whilst he knew that the rules of war demanded he respect the non-combatant status of the enemy's wounded, was little inclined to pass up the opportunity to run off livestock. So it was that the ambulances were waylaid by Boer horsemen in the approach to the Ingogo, parted from their draught animals, and left stranded on the road.

From Mount Prospect the Newcastle road snaked its way downhill, beneath the spurs and lower slopes of Nkwelo Mountain. After about four miles it arrived at Fermiston's Inn and the T-shaped confluence of the Ingogo River with a mountain stream known to settlers as the Harte River and to Zulus as the Imbezane. Only a hundred yards separated the pair of river drifts which allowed the traveller bound for Newcastle first to cross the Harte from north to south, and then the Ingogo from west to east. Colley judged that it would be prudent to secure the double drift before pushing on to rendezvous with the convoy. Calling Ashburnham and Greer to his side, he ordered that Lieutenant Young's mountain guns and one of the infantry companies be detached to the task. As it was safely within small-arms range of the river crossings and would allow the gun-crews to make best use of the 3,660-yard maximum range of the 7-pounders, the prominent spur above the inn was chosen as the ideal position for the guard force. The job fell to Lieutenant Dudley Ryder's company. Before moving off the staff made arrangements for a company of the 58th to come down from Mount Prospect to take the task over from Ryder, who, as soon as his relief arrived, would be free to dash on after the rest of his battalion. In the meantime the main body of the 60th, C, G, H and I Companies, began wading the knee-deep water obstacles, cursing as infantrymen always have the prospect of a hard day's marching with wet feet. By the time everybody was across the second drift it was almost noon.

From the river crossings the road ran south for about 4,000 yards, climbing a gentle incline as it went, until at length it reached a low rocky plateau known as Schuinshoogte. Brownlow and some of his riders cantered on ahead to gain its highest point and so obtain a decent view in the direction of Newcastle. This was the very ground where the mail had been intercepted the day before, so as an added precaution the infantry companies were instructed to throw out flankers. In front of the leading company of the 60th and not far behind Brownlow, rode the general and his staff. Accompanying him on this occasion were 'Lucky' Essex, *de facto* chief of staff for the day, Captain John MacGregor RE, the general's assistant military secretary, the newly arrived Lieutenant Bruce Hamilton of the 15th Regiment (Lady Colley's brother),[17] the Reverend George Ritchie, chaplain to the force, and Mr Marthinus Stuart, ordinarily the resident magistrate of the Ixopo district of southern Natal, but now employed as the general's interpreter.

At this stage in the campaign, with the main Boer force committed to the positional defence of the nek, it was the hard-riding Commandant Nicholaas Smit who had once again become the principal thorn in the side of the British. For the past few days he had been roving northern Natal making a thoroughgoing nuisance of himself. It was Smit's men who had ambushed the mail the previous day, who had harried various other movements in and out of Newcastle, and who that very morning had profited from the immobilization of Colley's ambulances.

On reaching their chosen vantage point Brownlow and his horsemen made visual contact with around 100 of Smit's men, who were deployed in a mounted skirmish line in the low ground 600 yards to the front. Brownlow dismounted his men to secure the plateau and opened fire. At the sound of gunfire from ahead, Colley wasted no time in urging his main body forward. Greer and Parsons pulled the guns clear of the infantry and had the N Battery drivers whip their teams into a brisk trot for the top of the plateau. Behind the guns Colonel Ashburnham and his company commanders had broken their riflemen into the comfortable jog-run known to the infantry as the 'double'.

At the top of the slope the artillery drivers wheeled their guns into the fire positions pointed out to them, on the left by Captain Greer, and on the right by Lieutenant Parsons. The guns were separated by about 150 yards and as usual the crews vied with one another to come into action first. Although the Transvaalers had embarked on their rebellion in some dread of British artillery, a good deal of their anxiety had been allayed by the ineffectual bombardment of Laing's Nek less than a fortnight earlier. Even though Smit's men would not on this occasion enjoy the benefit of fighting from schanzes, they were able by means of dispersal, use of ground and the maintenance of a heavy return fire largely to neutralize the British artillery. They began by picking off the man doing all the shouting; Carlyle Greer was amongst the first to die.

A few moments after the 9-pounders had let fly for the first time, only to overshoot the low ridges and gullies where most of the Boers had dismounted in cover, the green-jacketed infantry came doubling up the road to be fed into the fight by half-companies. By the time a coherent extended-order firing line had been established around the edge of the plateau, Ashburnham had committed three of his companies, leaving only I Company under the 22-year-old Lieutenant John Garrett in reserve. The flat ground at the top of the plateau encompassed about four acres in all and was roughly triangular in shape, with western (right flank), southern (front) and eastern (left flank) rims. Initially the British line followed the southern and western rims of the feature, and continued a short distance beyond the corner at the south-east angle. The rest of the eastern rim did not appear to be threatened and for the time being was left undefended.

The first few casualties were down even before the perimeter had been established, some of them limp and lifeless, others writhing in pain and bemoaning their luck through gritted teeth. For the time being their mates paid them little heed, except to yell at them to keep still or risk being hit again. The air was thick with lead and the firing line far too exposed for many of the wounded to be stretchered away to the surgeon. Nor would the lone ambulance be able to come forward and help, as the Boers had shot Dr McGann's mules down in their traces, leaving the vehicle stranded on the road some way short of the plateau.[18]

All around the perimeter the soldiers of the 60th were doing their best to scan for targets, but all obvious movement was drawing heavy fire, forcing most of them to content themselves with loosing the odd un-aimed shot in the approximate direction of the enemy. For the time being Ashburnham kept his reserve company out of harm's way by sheltering it 200 yards behind the firing line, where a minor reverse slope sufficed to keep a prone human being out of the line of fire. It was quite impossible to keep the horses safe, however, and the plateau was soon strewn with carcasses. Mr Thomas Carter, representing the *Times of Natal* (who had decided to keep contemporaneous pencil notes throughout the action, making him an uncommonly valuable primary source), noted that his own horse was hit twice in the first ten minutes of the fight.[19]

The western rim of the plateau, occupied by Captain Charles Smith's C Company and half of Captain Ernest Thurlow's H Company, was defined by a linear jumble of granite boulders. There were very few places where the rocks stood four feet above ground level, and all such sanctuaries were quickly given over to the badly wounded and the handful of men who laid aside their rifles to attend to the stomach-churning task of patching up torn bodies. In most areas there was only about two feet of cover to be had. It wasn't much, but the Rifles kept low and the line of boulders just about sufficed to protect them from wholesale annihilation at the hands of Smit's well-concealed marksmen.

Ordeal by Fire

For 30 minutes Lieutenant Parsons dashed back and forth between his 9-pounders, watching for targets and directing their fire. It was testing work as the Boers were far too adept at field-craft and the tactics of dispersal ever to present a worthwhile artillery target. By contrast the toiling gunners were exposed to return fire at ranges of 500–600 yards – a distance which did not even require a particularly demanding shot. Already both guns were ringed with casualties. The scene around the limbers, where many horse carcasses lay intermingled with dead and dying members of N Battery, was no less harrowing. Colley could see that too much was being asked of the gunners and ordered Parsons to withdraw his guns from the rim of the plateau into the less-exposed centre. Whilst pulling back would deny the guns short-range targets immediately in front of the infantry, they would still be able to engage the more distant ridges and gullies around the British position, and the decision might just allow Parsons and the remnants of his division an outside chance of survival. Any more N Battery casualties and it would be necessary to call for volunteers to man the guns.

The Boers, meanwhile, were working hard at infiltrating around the flanks of the *rooineks*. Their move against the British right was much too obvious and was quickly identified by Colley and his staff, as they crouched amongst a cluster of boulders watching the battle unfold. Major Brownlow was called across to the general and told to take his horsemen down the western slope, to check the enemy's outflanking manoeuvre and secure the right of the line. It was a bad idea – even before the mounted infantry had clambered into the saddle they were drawing heavy fire. The panic amongst a number of wounded animals quickly communicated itself to the rest, making them next to unmanageable and further delaying the attack. Brownlow could see it was hopeless and bellowed the order to dismount and take cover on the right of the line. Now there seemed to be dead and dying horses everywhere. Some wild-eyed animals broke loose and caused great distress to the British casualties by galloping amongst them as they lay helpless on the ground.

The 3rd/60th had left camp with 70 cartridges apiece, the standard first-line ammunition scale of the day. As there had been no expectation of a major action, no provision had been made for reserve ammunition. Colonel Ashburnham was no spring chicken, but at considerable risk to life and limb had already dashed around the perimeter a couple of times to lend moral support to his men. Now he embarked on yet another tour, sprinting from cover to cover, seeking out his officers and sergeants to exhort strict fire-control. He would repeat the risky journey several times more before the day was out.

The sergeant-major of the 3rd/60th was also on the move, encouraging the men as he passed and lending a helping hand with his rifle wherever he could. Sergeant-Major Wilkins was a noted shot, perhaps the best in the battalion, and as such must have made one of the most effective contributions to the defence of the perimeter. Colley would later report in his formal despatch that the sergeant-major was generally to be seen wherever the incoming fire was heaviest. At one point Wilkins sought the general's leave to lead a bayonet charge, but was refused. A few moments later a Boer mounted on a white horse came into sight, way out beyond the British left flank. The man dismounted and tried a long-range shot in the direction of Colley and the staff. Like the rest of his officers the general was armed only with a revolver, capable of hitting targets at 25 yards at best. As they looked on, the Boer remounted, rode forward to close the range and dismounted again for what he hoped would be a more fruitful second shot. Colley gave vent to his annoyance, demanding angrily whether any of the men around him had a rifle. Fortunately Sergeant-Major Wilkins was still on hand and in response to the general's challenge dropped quickly into a fire position, adjusted his rear-sight, steadied his breathing and squeezed off a faultless shot. On the ridge opposite the impertinent Boer suddenly crumpled into the grass. It was a rare moment of triumph for the huddle of staff officers.

By 2.30 p.m. the action had been under way for more than two hours. There were several dozen casualties amongst the Rifles and most of Brownlow's men were permanently afoot. Thomas Carter recorded in his notebook that Charlie Parsons passed him at this point and in response to his questioning replied that only five gunners were still unharmed.[20] As he was not yet completely surrounded Colley took the opportunity to smuggle a courier out, with orders for two more companies of the 58th to move down from Mount Prospect to the river. The battle was turning into a trial of endurance. There was simply no option to withdraw in daylight, as the mobility of the enemy and the open nature of the ground between the plateau and the river would be bound to guarantee annihilation.

Over the next half hour the enemy's fire seemed to Thomas Carter to tail away somewhat. In part this was because the Boers had by now taken all the easy shots to be had. They had caused a good many casualties in the process and given the British an object lesson in the use of cover. The survivors were now hunkered down amongst the boulders presenting only poor targets. All the while the midday sun had been beating down remorselessly, causing the soldiers to slug heavily from their water bottles. Now there was virtually no water left. The shortage was particularly hard on the wounded, some of whom were suffering from multiple gunshot wounds. Second Lieutenant W. S. S. Haworth of G Company, for example, only recently joined from Sandhurst, had already been shot four times.[21] With everybody on the British side down on their bellies, it was difficult for the Boers to tell from afar which of the prostrate forms in their sights were casualties and which were still legitimate targets.

Committing the Reserve

At about 3.00 p.m. the situation took a turn for the worse when, having slowly and patiently infiltrated in through patches of long grass, a party of Boers came into action from beyond the south-east angle. From their new position in an outcrop of boulders they were able to engage the British sanctuaries on the gentle reverse slope. Colley sent his assistant military secretary, Captain John MacGregor, to bring up the reserve company so that a firing line could be extended to face the new threat. When MacGregor joined Ashburnham to advise him that the general wanted I Company brought forward, 'Old Bristles' baulked at the idea, concerned that the deployment would deprive the hard-pressed force of its last reserve. He queried whether a half-company might not suffice, but MacGregor could only repeat that the general had asked for the company. The colonel had no choice but to concede the point and resolved to reconstitute a small reserve by withdrawing a section from C Company on the right.

In an act of foolhardy bravado fit to match the example of the late Colonel Deane, John MacGregor mounted up to guide Lieutenant Garrett and his men into position. He was dead within minutes, but not before he had led the hapless I Company men much further down the slope than Colley had ever intended. They found themselves deployed in a place of particular exposure, where the Boer infiltrators were able to enfilade their line. Throwing themselves down, they began scanning for the puffs of smoke that would indicate the presence of a Boer sniper. There were no boulders or bushes on their position and the grass was no more than ankle high. Nor did the lie of the land offer much protection. Over the course of the next two hours the company was slowly shot to pieces. John Garrett himself was killed relatively early on, leaving the remnants of the company in the hands of 2nd Lieutenant Francis Beaumont. I Company held the left as instructed, but at a terrible price – only Beaumont and four of the men would come through the ordeal unscathed.[22] More than 50 others were killed or wounded. Elsewhere on the field the N Battery losses had now reached the point where it had indeed become necessary to call for volunteer crews.

Not long after I Company deployed, Lieutenant Maurice O'Connell of C Company received orders to extricate a section and fall back into dead ground as the new battalion reserve. The eldest son of an Anglo-Irish baronet from Killarney and still in his early twenties, young O'Connell was not the man to hang back from a fight. Having led the section into position as instructed, he left it in the care of an NCO and went to rejoin the rest of his company on the firing line. He was killed only minutes after making his way forward again.[23]

Touching Victory

Nicholaas Smit had started the action with approximately 200 men under his command, a significantly smaller force than the one he had run to ground on the plateau. Throughout the afternoon small parties of Boer reinforcements came riding down from Laing's Nek, bypassing the British positions above the double drift, until at length Smit's command had increased by half and achieved parity with the remnants of Colley's. It was obvious to the burghers that they had succeeded in inflicting a serious loss on the enemy, in return for only minimal casualties to their own side. The shape and form of their imminent victory was becoming apparent. They would keep the British pinned down until they ran out of water and ammunition, at which point the surviving *rooineks* would be forced into a humiliating surrender – a surrender which would encompass two modern field guns, with potentially dire consequences for the besieged garrisons of nearby Wakkerstroom and Standerton.

By the time Smit's reinforcements had tethered their ponies and infiltrated into fire positions facing the western rim of the plateau, the sky was growing dark, a stiff breeze had sprung up and there was grumbling thunder in the distance. The arrival of some much needed cloud cover and the prospect of rain cheered the sun-baked, thirsty soldiers no end. By now it was 4.00 p.m., the time at which Thomas Carter noted a renewed outbreak of heavy firing from the west. Notwithstanding the continuing slaughter of I Company on the left, and the renewed pressure on the right, the sorely tried remnants of the 3rd/60th somehow held their ground. After a while the weight of enemy fire eased off again. In the meantime the rumbling from the heavens had been growing louder and more persistent. Next came intermittent flashes of lightning, each more dramatic than the last, until at length a fierce electrical storm arrived directly overhead.

According to Carter the storm broke at 5.25 p.m. The rain fell in torrents, soaking everybody to the skin in moments. At least now there was something to drink. But after a day baking in the sun, suffering from shock, dehydration and blood loss, the last thing a badly wounded soldier needs is a chill. Before long Surgeon McGann noticed that many of his patients were shaking with cold. Based as it was on nothing more than a ring of dead horses, the makeshift aid post was scarcely worthy of the name. Even so, because there was always a chance that a trained surgeon could keep a man alive where lesser mortals might fail, it was desirable that as many of the wounded as possible were gathered in to be examined by McGann. Many of the men who had been brought in thus far owed their lives to a man called Allan McLean, a stray member of a volunteer outfit called the Transvaal Light Horse. McLean repeatedly caught Thomas Carter's eye as he lugged maimed and helpless men into the aid post from far-flung corners of the perimeter.

Down at the river some more ambulances had arrived from the camp. Lieutenant Ryder, earlier charged with securing the double drift, instructed the AHC medics to cross to the south bank and push on to join the general. The ambulances had not gone very far up the track before they were intercepted by Boer horsemen who refused them safe passage. Proceed and you will be fired on, the medics were told. They were left with no alternative but to turn back for the north bank. Sensibly, Ryder made no attempt to move his company across the river to the support of his comrades, as his position above the drift represented their only lifeline.

It had been pouring with rain for about 15 minutes when the men huddled on Schuinshoogte heard the 7-pounders at the river open up. Closer to home, many of the Boers were still sniping away at anything that made an injudicious move. On the British side Lieutenant Charlie Parsons was no less vigilant and spotted that a number of Boers had bunched in a clump of bushes to the right rear of the position. This may have been part of the more general drift in the direction of the river observed at about this time. The manoeuvre was aimed at keeping the British trapped south of the crossing and at preventing Colley's reinforcements fighting their way through to the plateau. Parsons quickly dashed across to the right-hand 9-pounder and brought it bear. Although they failed to score a direct hit, the crew did well enough to scatter the enemy party.

Not long afterwards a white flag was raised by the Boers fighting on the British left flank. Perhaps the men responsible for the gradual slaughter of I Company were anxious that their victims should receive succour. Having observed the company's annihilation from the far side of the plateau, the British commanders were no doubt just as anxious to give whatever help they could. Indeed Marthinus Stuart, the general's interpreter, had been killed only a short while earlier whilst attempting to lead a handful of black Africans acting as stretcher bearers to the aid of I Company. When Colley's attention was drawn to the white flag, he had the word passed to cease firing. After a 10-minute cessation on the part of the British, there was still no sign of the incoming fire from the western side of the perimeter abating, so the general gave permission to commence firing once more. It was about now that Charlie Parsons's luck finally ran out. He had fought his guns under a heavy fire for something close to six hours, without regard for his own safety, and had demonstrated formidable qualities of leadership into the bargain. Men have been awarded the Victoria Cross for less. With Parsons severely wounded, command of the guns now devolved upon his number two, Sergeant-Major O'Toole.

With Colley's blessing, Chaplain George Ritchie volunteered to go forward and make a fresh attempt to initiate a cease-fire. He went out to the left under a flag of truce, but there was still so much firing that Colley was quickly obliged to call him back to cover. At 6.40 p.m. Thomas Carter noted that the guns at the river had come into action again and that their shells were landing amongst the Boers on the right. The 58th companies ordered out by Colley earlier had arrived at the river, had forced a crossing and were now skirmishing on the south bank under the command of Captain Hornby.[24] Back on the plateau, Carter also observed that there were no longer any enemy riflemen operating on the left. They may have been driven under cover by the rain or may simply have quit the field, content after inflicting such devastation on I Company that they had done their bit for independence.

Before long the onset of darkness compelled Hornby's companies to break off and withdraw to the north bank. Back on the spur above the drifts, the men of the 58th sheltered themselves from the elements as best they could and settled down to await developments. Sir George Colley, meanwhile, was considering his options. All about him was a scene of bloody slaughter. His troops had done well to keep their nerve and hold their ground, but as near as anybody could tell had suffered around 150 casualties in the process, 70 of whom were beyond all help. There were no rations, precious little water, insufficient small-arms ammunition and no shelter. There could be no question of continuing the fight into a second day. It was clear that retreat was the only option but, as the old Africa hands were quick to point out, the rain had been so heavy that there was every danger of the rivers being in spate.

The best Colley could hope for was to extricate the remnants of the command back to Mount Prospect under the cover of darkness. Even if he took what was generally considered to be a measure of last resort and left the wounded to their fate, an unmistakeable and embarrassing admission of defeat, there could be no guarantee that a break-out attempt would succeed. For one thing the double drift might prove impassable; for another, the Boers might be waiting in ambush anywhere along the eminently predictable withdrawal route. Then there were the guns. Every schoolboy in England knew that the Duke of Wellington had never lost a gun. British generals did not lose guns. But how were Parsons's 9-pounders to be moved back across two fast-flowing water obstacles? Were there even enough horses left to get them down to the river? Of the 76 animals with which the British had started the engagement, around 40 were lying dead on the plateau. Others had broken free and run off into the countryside. Of those that were left, many were wounded, unfit even as saddle horses let alone as draught animals.

The Break-Out

Colley gave the order to prepare for a break-out attempt. Having manhandled the guns onto the road, Sergeant-Major O'Toole and his men fanned out in search of uninjured horses. Surgeon McGann, Padre Ritchie and Allan McLean volunteered to stay behind, to tend the wounded and treat with the enemy for their safe-keeping. All the blankets, groundsheets and greatcoats that had found their way out to Schuinshoogte were gathered in and distributed amongst the casualties. The general set the tone by giving his coat away. The surviving artillerymen found just enough uninjured horses to get the guns ready to move. The limbers, the ammunition wagon and the ambulance would have to be abandoned, as they would slow down a river crossing and ultimately it was only the guns that mattered. It was both a blessing and a curse that it was still raining hard. While the deluge served to conceal all the preparations for withdrawal from prying eyes, each passing minute was increasing the likelihood of flooding at the drifts. Ordinarily the early hours of the morning, when the enemy is at his drowsiest, are the best time for a surreptitious withdrawal, but the speed with which the rivers were rising dictated that Colley could not afford to wait that long. All the while the intermittent flashes overhead served for a second or two to turn dark night back into day.

The British need not have been quite so anxious, for the rebels had already been undone by the indiscipline of the commando system. Smit and his men had withdrawn to the cover of a farmhouse and its outbuildings, where they lit fires to dry themselves and brew piping-hot coffee. The commandant and his veldtkornets had little doubt that the wretched British would still be pinned to their rain-soaked hilltop when the sun came up in the morning. It was inconceivable that they would abandon their guns or their wounded – British officers, they knew, simply did not do that sort of thing. Apart from anything else horses would be needed to get the guns away, and the Boers had gained the impression that all the animals on the plateau had been killed. As insurance to his coming victory Smit ordered that the double drift be picketed, but it was still raining hard and, as was commonplace in a Boer commando, nobody was much interested in taking personal responsibility for a difficult or uncomfortable task which might just as readily have fallen to the next man. Roughnecks they may have been, but soldiers they were not. One by one the men posted at the river drifted away in search of cover from the rain, until at length the escape route lay wide open.

Colley led off for the river at 11.00 p.m. The Rifles were deployed in a loose square around the staff and the guns. Rather than follow the road, which might turn out to be picketed, Colley struck out on a cross-country right oblique. All the way down to the river the British had their hearts in their mouths, but for all their anxiety they arrived at the south bank without being fired on. The general's official report described some of the difficulties of the crossing:

> On approaching the double-drift the column halted, and a patrol was sent out to ascertain the drift was clear; and the column then filed across. A heavy thunderstorm had now come on the darkness was intense, and the river swollen by the rains, was deep and rapid. Some of the first men trying to cross were swept down, but saved by a projecting sandbank. The rest were got over in detachments, holding hands.[25]

Although Colley's report contains no direct reference to the fact, seven riflemen were swept away and drowned. Getting the guns across was a Herculean struggle which exhausted men and horses alike.

The four companies supporting the 7-pounders above the drift seem not to have posted a watch on the road, so that the general's column unknowingly slipped past in the dark without being seen. The road to Mount Prospect had been reduced to a quagmire and was so treacherous underfoot that the handful of exhausted horses could no longer cope. Ashburnham recalled the uphill leg:

> The night was black as ink, and we were all drenched to the skin; the road was so slippery that the horses could not stand . . . when near the top of the hill the guns stuck altogether. I was obliged to pull them up the rest of the way with my men (about 3 miles). When we arrived at camp at 5.30 a.m., it was quite daylight. Splendidly as the Battalion had behaved during the day, I think their conduct during this long and trying night march was even more creditable; the order, regularity and discipline maintained during the whole march was beyond all praise.

Even now there was one last tragedy still to come. Ashburnham's adjutant, Lieutenant Edward Wilkinson, had been fighting alongside his colonel all day and might reasonably have thrown himself down on his camp-bed, content with a harrowing day's work. But he had been so appalled by the condition of the wounded that, instead of resting, he collected a haversack of medical supplies from the hospital and set off once more for the battlefield. His body was found in the river ten days later, wedged in rocks several miles below the double drift.

Nicholaas Smit woke the next morning to find that his men had failed him utterly and that General Colley had escaped into the night. He absolutely refused to believe that the British had got their guns across the river and had search parties looking for them in the reeds for days afterwards. In the circumstances Colley had been more than merely lucky to get away. Although the battle had begun with the enemy's weight in the south, it is instructive to reflect that there may not actually have been a single Boer between Colley and Newcastle by nightfall. Although it would have required counter-intuitive thinking, the best course of action might in fact have been to break out to the south where there was no river, no enemy, no defile, no uphill leg and an infinitely greater choice of escape routes. Colley was right to count himself a lucky man.

It may in the wider scheme of things have been a small-scale affair, but the Battle of Ingogo had been a distinctly harrowing experience for its British participants. Having lost 2 officers and 56 other ranks killed, 3 and 60 wounded and 1 and 8 missing in action,[26] the 3rd/60th had been all but ruined as a fighting force. The Royal Artillery had lost Captain Greer and 3 men killed, and

Lieutenant Parsons and 10 men wounded. Brownlow's squadron lost only 3 men killed and 2 wounded, but 23 out of 38 horses. Once again Edward Essex's luck had held up. The Boer losses were 8 killed and 10 wounded, 2 of whom would die of their wounds.[27]

Colley was not an unpleasant man and the officers and men of the Natal Field Force had cheerfully put the defeat at Laing's Nek down to experience. When the traumatized remnants of Ashburnham's battalion came limping into Mount Prospect, however, the mood at the camp went into sharp decline. Another bout of flowery rhetoric from the general was unlikely to hold water, but he indulged in one all the same. Around the camp fires that night, all confidence in Sir George Colley evaporated.

Chapter 4
HILL OF DOVES
The Battle of Majuba Hill, Northern Natal, 27 February 1881

> ***But under fire which begins to kill at two thousand yards, not, as in the Brown Bess era, at two hundred, troops cannot march forward like a wall until they see the whites of the enemies' eyes, and combination and cohesion are only to be secured by the free exercise of trained intelligence, supported by individual discipline. Had the Boers possessed the last they would have been perfect skirmishers. As it was, their system of establishing a strong firing line by trickling forward a few men at a time, who crept on from boulder to boulder, from bush to bush, as at the Ingogo and Amajuba, and who were covered by the bullets of detachments posted behind convenient shelter in rear, was far less costly, and far better adapted to counteract the terrible power of the new armament, than the system which prevailed, not in the British Army alone, but in every continental army of the day.***
>
> **Colonel G. F. R. Henderson**[1]

Colley's only consolation in the aftermath of Ingogo was that the reinforcements despatched from India would soon be available for action. Although he turned his thoughts to the wider operational picture, he remained determined for the sake of his reputation to force Laing's Nek in person, and to be clearly identifiable in the eyes of the public as the man who had done so. The much stronger force now available would therefore operate in two columns, one under Colley's personal command operating as before against the nek from Mount Prospect, and a second under Wood which would move up on Colley's right and force the Wakkerstroom road. For Colley, the treacherous way in which war and rebellion had so suddenly descended upon this corner of Africa, coupled with the loss of so many members of his command, including virtually all of his staff officers, had given the conflict a very personal edge.

From the perspective of a twice-defeated general yearning for redemption, all was not necessarily well on the political front: Sir Hercules Robinson, the High Commissioner in the Cape, was already warning London of the dangers of a civil war between the Afrikaner and Anglo-Saxon populations; in the Free State, President Brand was having to contend with a domestic lobby anxious to drag his country to war in support of its sister-republic; while in London there seemed to be no good reason to risk the whole of Southern Africa for the sake of an impoverished and malcontent Transvaal. If one quietly overlooked the black Africans in the Transvaal, war seemed to be in nobody's best interest. Although the cabinet was split, the Prime Minister and the Colonial Secretary sided with those who argued for a swift negotiated solution. In Heidelberg, meanwhile, there was considerable consternation at the quantity of British reinforcements and the imminence of their arrival. Although Colley was thirsting for revenge, most of the other key players had come to the realization that things had already gone way too far. It was time to draw back from the brink. As ever a formula was required that would bring peace with honour. The stumbling block appeared to be that the Triumvirate wanted the British to revoke the annexation before they agreed to a ceasefire, while the British wanted these two key events sequenced the other way round.

On 8 February Lord Kimberley telegraphed Colley to say that Her Majesty's Government was prepared to negotiate if the Boers would desist from all armed opposition. Brand was also advised of London's position and relayed it to Heidelberg. Four days later the Triumvirate wrote to HMG through Colley to say that they were prepared to accept a royal commission on their future governance, which they were confident would recommend the restoration of their independence. If the annexation was not revoked, they warned, then they would be prepared to fight to the last man.

Wood led the hard-marching 'Indian Column' into Newcastle on 17 February. Tucked into his pocket was Lord Kimberley's response which he immediately shared with Colley, who had ridden down from Mount Prospect the previous night. The telegram stated that a royal commission would be acceptable to London and went on to state that Colley was free to conclude a ceasefire if the Boer leadership agreed to stand down the commandos in return. Kimberley's communication was meant to signify that the negotiations would be a formality, that the annexation would be revoked and the garrisons withdrawn, but that in return any transfer of sovereignty must be effected in a calm and dignified fashion, free of any hint of armed coercion. In effect the telegram meant the end of the war. In conversation Wood told Colley that he had met with the Colonial Secretary before leaving England, and that Kimberley had expressed an interest in the possibility of partitioning the Transvaal, in order that at least part of the black population could enjoy the benefits of liberal governance.

Wood had brought up two squadrons of the 15th Hussars (about 250 men), the 2nd/60th Rifles (720), the 92nd Gordon Highlanders (520) and a small contingent of additional naval personnel under Commander Francis Romilly of HMS *Boadicea*. Over the next couple of days the two generals busied themselves fleshing out the details of Colley's plan to operate in two columns. On the 18th Colley took time out from his military staffwork to fire off a telegram to Whitehall stating that he was dead set against any settlement entailing partition. Fight to win, or cede independence and have done with it, he argued. Meanwhile, in typically bustling style, Wood departed on the 19th with a squadron of hussars in tow, intent on a thorough reconnaissance of his axis.

With Wood away on a 60-mile patrol spread over two days, Colley took the opportunity to seek clarification of his most recent orders. 'Am I to leave Lang's Nek [*sic*], in Natal territory, in Boer occupation, and our garrisons isolated, and short of provisions, or occupy former and relieve latter?'[2] This sentence was meant to suggest that London's political direction was a public disgrace – that surely some mistake had been made. The Colonial Secretary replied in emphatic terms, which should at once have ruled out any thought of further military action.

> It will be essential that garrisons should be free to provision themselves and peaceful intercourse with them allowed, but we do not mean you should march to the relief of garrison or occupy Lang's Nek [*sic*], if arrangement proceeds. Fix reasonable time within which answer must be sent by Boers.[3]

When a furious Colley looked hard for any let-out clause, his eyes fell on 'if arrangement proceeds' and 'reasonable time'. In his heart of hearts he was sure that London was wrong.

Loose Cannon

It is difficult to say at precisely which point in time Colley made up his mind to disregard the political direction emanating from Whitehall, but there are two pieces of circumstantial evidence that suggest his disobedience was premeditated and more than a week in the planning. First, having given orders on the morning of Monday 21 February that the Indian Column would move out for Mount Prospect at dawn the following day, he told Sir Evelyn Wood he wanted him to go back to Pietermaritzburg to hurry up the rest of the reinforcements and 'expedite the transport of provisions'.[4] There is a strong probability that this was a contrivance: after all any reasonably competent staff officer could have attended to such matters. But if Colley was to play fast and loose with his orders, he could not afford to have another general officer observing his every move. And if as a result of his actions there was a redeeming victory, then it was only just, after what he had been through, that the credit for it should go to Sir George Colley and not to Sir Evelyn Wood. If Wood was absent at Pietermaritzburg, there could be absolutely no doubting whose victory it had been. Wood would be gone for seven days they agreed. Before going on his way he secured a promise that Colley would not undertake any major offensive movements in his absence.

Late that evening, when the rest of his work was done, Colley composed the note designed to convey HMG's terms to Paul Kruger. As directed it included a final clause allowing a 'reasonable time' for a response. The clause provides the second piece of circumstantial evidence to suggest that Colley was behaving deviously. Heidelberg was a hundred miles from Laing's Nek. The reasonable time Colley had allowed, however, was a mere 48 hours. Apart from the sheer practicalities of time and space, such a brisk timeline imparted the air of an ultimatum to the missive – a tone which the government had never intended it to have. 'I must add that if this proposal is accepted within 48 hours from and after the receipt of this letter, I have empowered a cessation of hostilities on our side', the letter closed. For the time being it went into his pocket.

Evelyn Wood left for Pietermaritzburg at 3.00 a.m. on Tuesday. Colley led out the Indian Column only an hour or so later. More than a hundred transport wagons accompanied the troops. After a difficult day on the rain-soaked road, the column overnighted on the banks of the Ingogo and arrived at Mount Prospect on Wednesday afternoon. One of the first things that Colley was briefed on by the staff was that the Boers had been observed digging trenches on the nek, where previously there had been only rock schanzes – in other words that the Boer defences were stronger than ever. Almost immediately the 2nd/60th and all but two troops of the 15th Hussars were turned about and sent back to Newcastle with a convoy of empty supply wagons. This meant that the only significant reinforcements staying on at Mount Prospect would be 120 hussars, 60 additional hands for the Naval Brigade, and the 17 officers and 501 other ranks of the Gordons – lean, bronzed, fresh from Afghanistan and clad for the first time in the history of the imperial garrison of South Africa in khaki. The Gordons had every reason to regard themselves as a fighting elite. In the past two years they had fought at the Battle of Charasiah, had played a leading role in the defence of the Sherpur Cantonment, had marched from Kabul to relieve General Primrose at Kandahar, and had rounded off the war by defeating Ayub Khan. It was a record to be proud of. The 92nd was under the command of its senior field officer, Major John 'Jock' Hay.

Amongst the telegrams the general sent during the course of the afternoon was one to the Secretary for War which assured him, 'I would not without strong reason undertake any operation likely to bring on another engagement.' Then he added innocently, 'I may have to seize some ground which has hitherto been practically unoccupied by either party, lying between the Nek and our camp.' To a cabinet minister in far away London, with no knowledge of the ground, Colley's remark sounded harmless enough. In reality it represents clear-cut evidence that Colley was plotting the seizure of Majuba at least as early as Wednesday 23 February, well in advance of his opening negotiations with the Boers. To be fair it does not necessarily follow that he was looking to pick a fight, in direct contravention of governmental intent, merely that he believed he could unhinge the Boer defences and so open up the nek by means of manoeuvre. But neither does it preclude the possibility.

First thing on Thursday morning, Colley sent the letter he had drafted a couple of days earlier up to Laing's Nek,[5] where it was delivered into the hands of Nicholaas Smit. As far as Colley was concerned, the clock was now running. Later in the day he departed Mount Prospect in company with his new chief of staff, Lieutenant Colonel Herbert Stewart, and rode into the valley to the west of Majuba on what was clearly a reconnaissance for the forthcoming operation. One of the matters requiring clarification was whether the Boer picket on top of Majuba was in place 24 hours a day, or whether it kept its ground in daylight only.

The next morning, Friday 25 February, Colley received notification that Kruger was at Heidelberg and that, although the letter had been sent on to him by galloper, obtaining a reply was bound to take at least four days. On Saturday the Boer command sent down news that Kruger had moved on to Rustenburg, double the distance again, and that there must perforce be a further unspecified delay. Although there had been no reply to either of their messages the Boers assumed, incorrectly as it turned out, that the British would extend the truce automatically and indefinitely. But Colley's original 48-hour deadline had expired that very morning. It was already too late: the planning of the Majuba operation was all but complete. For the time being its existence remained a closely guarded secret shared only by Colley, Stewart and, indirectly, by the Zulu scout they sent to the summit on Friday night to check that the Boer daytime picket did indeed, as they suspected, withdraw to the comfort of the laagers by night. Saturday 26 February was passed in quietly plotting the finer detail.

Colley Sets the Stage

There were two principal reasons for Sir George Colley to keep his men in the dark about the coming operation. First, he had to assume that his camp was under observation from distant vantage points and that any unusual rumpus, such as would inevitably be caused by half a dozen companies preparing for battle, would attract the enemy's attention. Second, he could not rule out the presence of enemy agents inside his camp. Not only was there a miscellany of white contractors coming and going from Newcastle, some of them of Afrikaner origin, but there were also a great many black African workers camped out beneath the commissariat wagons, any one of whom could have been in the pay of the commandants on the nek.

It was dark by 7.30 p.m. and 'lights-out' was sounded as usual about an hour later. The warning order for an impending night operation began to circulate almost immediately after that. The new OC of the 58th, Lieutenant Colonel William Bond, was to parade two of his companies, 'Old Bristles' two of his, Jock Hay three companies of the Gordons, and Commander Francis Romilly a 60-man party of the naval brigade – effectively the eighth and last sub-unit in a composite battalion. Counting the staff and a handful of medics, Colley's strike force would muster a total of 27 officers and 568 other ranks. Like the Schuinshoogte affair this was a lieutenant colonel's command, but both Bond and Ashburnham found themselves detailed to stay at the camp. Colley would come in for a good deal of retrospective criticism for not entrusting the Majuba operation in its entirety to Jock Hay and the veterans of the 92nd. There had been so little prior discussion of the operation that most of the general's reasoning would die with him, but his anxiety to keep Evelyn Wood out of the limelight is certainly indicative of a burning desire for redemption. It is probably fair to say that Colley took personal charge of the operation, not merely to command Laing's Nek, but also the newspaper headlines in London.

There were two further reasons for entrusting the operation to a composite force, though attempting to weigh their relative importance in Colley's mind must inevitably lead us into the realms of conjecture. It is distinctly possible that he wanted all the original units of the Natal Field Force to play a part in the operation, in order that they all gain a share in the victory; perhaps then the 58th and the 3rd/60th might feel that their cruel losses to date had not been in vain – that they had been a function of bad luck rather than incompetence. Then there was the Wolseley factor. As a mainstream member of the 'ring' Colley could hardly let his mentor down in the short-service/long-service debate. Circumstance and the geography of empire had conspired to preserve the 92nd as a living, breathing monument to the old system of enlistment. By contrast the 58th and the Rifles were very much modernized short-service battalions after the Wolseley-approved model. There was every danger if the veterans of the 92nd did well atop Majuba, that their success might throw the failures of the short-service men at Laing's Nek and Ingogo into sharp relief. If the press started that particular hare running again, as they had during the second invasion of Zululand, Wolseley's credibility as a reformer would be held up to ridicule.

However these factors played themselves out in Colley's mind, it was some combination of selfish, career-minded, and naïve reasoning that lay behind the militarily unsound decision to commit a composite force to a high-risk operation of war.

Night March

Even after the battalion commanders had detailed the participating companies, the only orders disseminated to the company officers were exclusively administrative in nature. The force formed up in ignorance of its destination, and without the vaguest knowledge of a battle plan. Nor had any contingency plans been laid to safeguard against the unforeseen. Operational security is one thing, but there comes a point when participating troops simply have to be fully briefed. This was assuredly it, but foolishly Colley let the opportunity slip through his fingers. In accordance with the little they had been told, the soldiers paraded with 70 rounds of ammunition, rolled greatcoats, groundsheets, full water bottles and three days' rations in their haversacks. Including their rifles the total load came to just under 60 pounds, a not insignificant burden on a mountainside, but a historically consistent average for operations of more than 24 hours' duration. A number of picks and shovels were also shared around the companies. Under the cover of darkness the colour-sergeants jostled their men into a long snaking column, the 58th in the van, followed by the Rifles, then the 92nd, with the naval brigade bringing up the rear. Two Zulu guides led the column off in the direction of the Laing's Nek road at around 10 p.m.[6] Riding just behind them came the general and three members of his reconstituted staff, Herbert Stewart, Major Thomas Fraser RE and Captain Alexander McGregor seconded from the Gordons. Also present in Colley's entourage was his chief clerk, the Rorke's Drift veteran Staff Sergeant George Mabin. For the sake of Lady Edith, Sir George made a point of leaving behind his brother-in-law, Bruce Hamilton, who had been unwell for the past few days and was already fast asleep in his tent. All the infantry detachments were in the hands of capable and experienced regimental officers – the 58th were led by Captains Augustus Morris and Cecil Hornby, and the 92nd by Majors John Hay and Loftus Singleton. Lieutenant Alan Hill, the hero of Laing's Nek, was amongst the other 58th officers, whilst the subalterns of the 92nd included a rough diamond called Hector Macdonald who, the story went, had been offered the choice of a VC or a commission by 'Bobs' himself, in recognition of numerous acts of gallantry as a company colour-sergeant with the Kabul Field Force.

The column crossed the road after about 15 minutes' march and began pushing uphill onto the lower slopes of Nkwelo. Some way up the hillside the guides turned to their right to gain the long saddle running north towards

Majuba. Here at the Nkwelo end of the saddle, Colley sent for the two Rifles company commanders. Captains Charles Smith and Robert Henley were told to peel off from the column and to establish an outpost on the north face of Nkwelo. They were to hold their ground until further notice, but they were not told why, nor were they told where the rest of the column was going in the meantime. It was around 11.00 p.m. when the Rifles fell out. Colley intended to deploy a second outpost half-way across the saddle, but not long after setting off again the head of the column became separated from the rear. An hour-long delay ensued while somebody went back to look for a missing company of Gordons and the Naval Brigade.

Once the two parts of the force had been reunited it was the turn of No. 5 Company of the Gordons to fall out. Captain Patrick Robertson was briefed by the general, and then led to a position about a hundred yards to the right of the track by Major Fraser. The direction given by Colley had been sketchy to say the least. Robertson was told to dig in once the rest of the column had passed, but was not advised that two companies of the Rifles had already fallen out and were fortifying a position on the other side of the saddle. Fraser told him that he could be expect to be reinforced first thing in the morning by an additional company from the camp and that in the meantime he should leave a detail of an NCO and four men on the track, so that the newcomers could not blunder past his position in the dark.

Even while the conversation between Fraser and Robertson was taking place, the additional company, from the 3rd/60th, was preparing to move out from Mount Prospect. It is not clear who briefed Captain Ernest Thurlow – it might have been Colonel Ashburnham or one of the staff officers who had been left behind. Either way something of the general's intent was lost in translation. Thurlow was told that he had been assigned to an escort task only – that once he had dropped off a dozen ammunition-mules with the company he would find on the saddle, he would be free to return to camp. The company paraded with 3 officers[7] and 77 other ranks and set out not long after midnight. Tagging along behind the ammunition mules was Surgeon-Major Henry Cornish and some AHC orderlies leading a few additional mules bearing medical supplies.

Back on the hillside the general and his staff officers were preparing for the ascent of Majuba. They would leave their horses with No. 5 Company. With the worst part of the route now looming ahead, Colley delved into his saddle bags for the white tennis shoes he intended to wear during the climb. The slope ahead was steep for most of its course, but over the final few hundred yards became almost precipitous. On the way up it was necessary to pause at frequent intervals so that the troops could gather their breath, but in between halts the column kept clambering inexorably upwards. In the later stages the soldiers had to haul themselves up by clawing onto handholds and tussocks of grass.

Occasionally one of them went sliding past his mates to end up in a bruised, grazed heap some way below. Fortunately nobody went over a precipice and no serious injuries were incurred. It was trying and exacting work, but in essence the occupation of Majuba went like clockwork.

Coup de Main

The Zulu guides at the head of the column reached the summit at about 03.40 a.m., having started the climb not long after midnight. As Colley and Stewart had anticipated, there was no picket *in situ*. It would take the best part of two hours, the second in broad daylight, for the men at the rear of the procession to reach the top. They were now 6,200 feet above sea level and about 2,000 feet above Laing's Nek. Having detached three of his companies during the approach, Colley had just over 400 men left with which to secure the summit – two companies of the 58th, two companies of Gordons, two sections of naval ratings and a medical section.

***Table 5:* The British Force on Majuba Hill**

Staff	3 & 1
Royal Navy	3 & 62
2nd/21st Regiment (Royal Scots Fusiliers)	0 & 6
58th (Rutlandshire) Regiment	7 & 164
92nd Regiment (Gordon Highlanders)	6 & 135
94th Regiment	2 & 2
Army Medical Department	2 & 0
Army Hospital Corps	0 & 12
Army Service Corps	0 & 1
Zulu guides	0 & 2
Total	23 & 385

Inevitably the companies had fallen into disarray during the ascent, so that it was necessary to feed composite details of men onto a temporary defensive perimeter until such time as the sun came up and they were able to muster under their own officers. The general was asked about digging in, but indicated that the troops were tired and should be allowed to snatch some sleep. In fact, whilst the climb was undeniably hard work, it takes much more than a two-hour approach march and a well-paced four-hour ascent to exhaust otherwise well-rested infantrymen. In his memoir *Listening for the Drums*, Lieutenant Ian Hamilton of the Gordons, later the British land commander at Gallipoli, firmly rebutted any notion that the troops were tired:

> Fresh from the victories of Afghanistan, every private in the 92nd Gordon Highlanders knew that whenever a detachment happened to hit on a weak spot in the enemy's line and made it good they built up a sangar or stonework defence as a matter of course – unless the ground happened to be stoneless when they had to dig themselves in. Apologists have since urged that upon this occasion the men were exhausted by their night-march and that the General had rightly refused, therefore, to set them to work with the heavy navvies' spades and pick axes they had so laboriously lugged up for that express purpose. This is just one of those exasperating little lies which buzz about the head of John Bull like flies whenever he is let down and hurt. Whatever General Colley himself may have felt, I have never felt less tired in my life than when I looked down at the Boer Army lying at our feet; and my men felt the same.[8]

Writing only a few months after the event, Herbert Stewart was equally dismissive. 'I utterly disagree with the view of the men being exhausted . . . the march was not rapid or over severe. Sir George was not a bit tired.' It is of course an immutable military principle that one should dig first and sleep later.

It was possible to discern the first hint of daylight at about 4.30 a.m. Over the next hour the troops began to unravel from their temporary groupings and to rally on their own company officers as properly constituted bodies of men. Hamilton described the daylight occupation of the perimeter under the direction of the staff.

> When my company fell in on the top dawn was just beginning to break, but it was still too dark to form much of an idea of the size of the place we were on. Captain MacGregor [*sic*] of my regiment who was acting as ADC to General Colley, took me and my company to the eastern [*sic* – more accurately north-eastern] side of the plateau and directed me to extend to my left until I touched the 58th. I first extended the men at six paces but finally had to increase the extension to twelve paces between each man to cover the ground. The men then by my orders collected stones so as to make some sort of cover for themselves. By the time this was done it was broad daylight and we could see the Boers streaming out of their trenches back to their laagers.[9]

In the low ground Captain Thurlow and his riflemen had come stumbling out of the dawn at No. 5 Company's position. Talking the situation through with Patrick Robertson, Thurlow learned that Fraser had intimated that the additional company would be staying put. In the circumstances he agreed to stay on. It is possible of course that it was not Thurlow who had been mis-briefed but Robertson – that it was Fraser who had the wrong end of the stick.

Comparing their respective seniorities, the two company commanders established that Robertson should exercise overall command. There was no immediate attempt to move reserve ammunition to the summit, nor any indication that they were required to do so. Thurlow's most pressing problem was that, unlike everybody else involved in the operation, his men had not been provided with haversack rations. Fortunately Commissary Jonathan Elmes,[10] who had gone at least part of the way to the summit with the main force, came past again at about 6.00 a.m., bound now for Mount Prospect, and agreed to sort out rations for Thurlow's men. Only a short while later a second logistician arrived. Conductor Field was leading a mule loaded with stores intended for the staff. There was some discussion as to whether it was advisable for him to push on alone, but he was adamant that he was duty-bound to do so and went gamely on his way. Now that it was daylight the two company commanders could make out a distant figure waving signal flags from the Nkwelo end of the saddle. 'Who are you?' signalled Robertson. 'Two companies 60th, left here all night,' came the response. 'What orders do you have?' queried Robertson. 'None', came the forthright reply.

The Summit in Daylight

Most people are surprised to learn that Majuba is an extinct volcano, though from certain vantage points to the south, such as the Schuinshoogte battlefield, the classic profile of a volcano is readily apparent. The summit covers about 4½ acres in all and, as a one-time volcanic crater, is lower-lying at the centre than at its edges. In places the difference between the rocky outer rim and the grassed-over crater is as much as 40 feet. Ankle-length grass aside there was next to no vegetation on the summit in 1881, or indeed on the lower slopes of the mountain, which were much more sparsely covered than they are today. As Natal is lower lying than the high veldt of the Transvaal, the climb to the summit from the south is much longer than the climb from the flat ground to the north of the nek, in 1881 the site of the rebel wagon-laagers.

The summit is broadly triangular in shape with north-western, eastern and south-western angles, and a circumference of roughly three-quarters of a mile. The British had ascended via the narrow ridge running down into Natal from the south-west angle. Just short of the summit there was a sheer-sided rocky outcrop which was occupied as a strongpoint and signalling station by members of the naval brigade. Today the feature is known as 'Sailors' Knoll'. At the north-western angle there was a similar rocky high-point, classically conical in shape, a little lower-lying than the summit, and separated from it by a narrow ridge of about 50 yards in length. In effect the ridge serves as a natural bridge between the rim of the mountain and the top of the knoll. As it lay on Ian Hamilton's

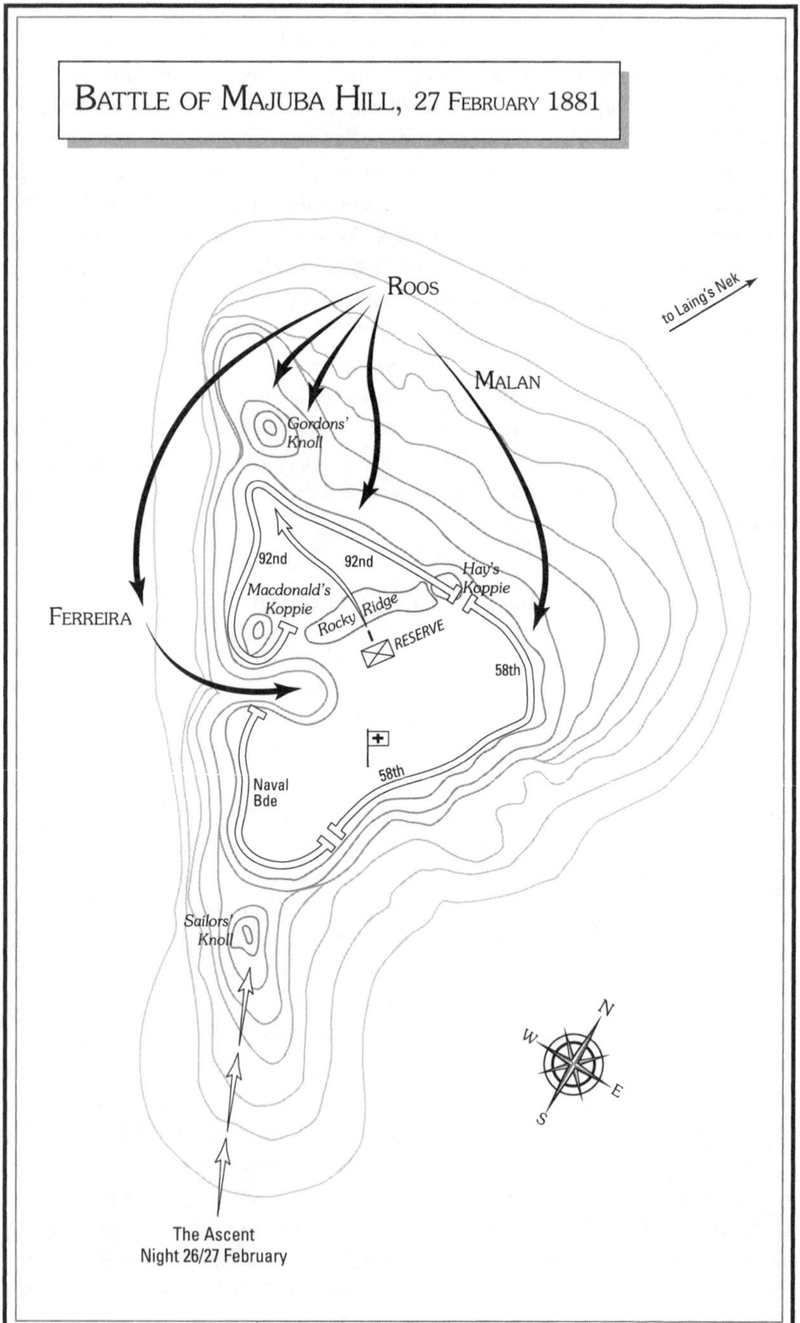

Battle of Majuba Hill, 27 February 1881

Roos
to Laing's Nek
Malan
Gordons' Knoll
92nd
92nd
Hay's Koppie
Macdonald's Koppie
Rocky Ridge
Ferreira
Reserve
58th
58th
Naval Bde
Sailors' Knoll
N
W
E
S
The Ascent
Night 26/27 February

sector, the feature would become known as Gordons' Knoll. Because it protrudes from the top of the mountain like a tower from a castle wall, the knoll offers enfilading fields of fire across the north-eastern face of Majuba and looks down on the wide grassy terrace half-way up the hill.

The highest point on the mountain was a rocky koppie on the western rim, half-way between Gordons' Knoll and Sailors' Knoll. There was a corresponding but much less significant high-point on the opposite rim, overlooking the nek. The two features were connected by a low rocky ridge which ran across the summit at roughly the mid-way point. The high point commanding the left end of the ridge is known today as Macdonald's Koppie, and the lower-lying one on the right as Hay's Koppie, both named of course after the officers assigned to defend them in 1881. The temporary perimeter hastily occupied in the pre-dawn had mistakenly followed the line of the rocky ridge, until at last the sun came up and it was realised that the north-eastern rim of the mountain was 150 yards further forwards.

Now that it was broad daylight, it was time to organize the perimeter properly. Commander Francis Romilly's two naval brigade sections would look after the south-west angle and the western rim as far as Macdonald's Koppie. From Lieutenant Macdonald's position on the battalion's left flank, the Gordons' line of defence ran up to the north-west angle, and then swung right through 45 degrees to follow the north-eastern rim all the way down to the eastern angle just beyond Hay's Koppie. The two 58th companies occupied the rest of the rim between Jock Hay's position and the south-west angle, at which point the right flank of the 58th met Commander Romilly's naval sections.

Continuing his predilection for composite tactical groupings, Colley assigned the task of force reserve not to a single formed company, but to an *ad hoc* grouping of 120 officers and men drawn from all the participating units. The reserve was posted in the shelter of the rocky ridge, in close proximity to the general's headquarters, where for the want of anything else to do the men threw themselves down to smoke, gossip and, in due course, fall fast asleep in the sun. The medical staff set up their aid post on the open ground in the lee of the rocky ridge. Two groups of soldiers from the reserve were set to digging wells and struck water, as the Zulu guides said they would, about three feet down.

What Next?

This was another appropriate juncture for the commander to call his officers together in order to outline his intent and explain exactly what was required of them. It would also have been an excellent opportunity to assemble the troops for a few words of praise and encouragement. Regrettably Sir George did neither of these things. His failure to do so reflects badly upon him, not only as a tactical commander, but also at the most basic of levels as a leader of men. The absence of clarity, even in respect of an important subject like rules of engagement, was amply demonstrated when the first target of the day presented itself.

> About this time the first shots were fired at a party of about thirty Boers who rode close under the hill, unconscious of our presence. Had a heavy fire been opened on them they must all have been killed, but some of the senior officers, not being sure if the general wished firing to begin, no orders having been given, made the men cease. The order was then given to fire if we had a good chance of doing damage, but by that time the Boers were well out of range.[11]

The 300 men lying on their sides around the perimeter could see very little of the low ground beneath them. They could improve their view by sitting up, crouching or standing but had not yet grasped just how badly this silhouetted them against a clear blue African sky. Something about Majuba's altitude mesmerized the British; looking down on the Boer laagers from such a lofty vantage point, they reasoned, simply had to give them an immense tactical advantage. In truth it did nothing of the sort. None of the officers in key positions of responsibility gave any serious thought to how they might defend the perimeter in the event of a counter-attack. If they had done so, the defenders would not have been spread out at intervals of several yards around the entire summit. Some stretches of the perimeter were so sheer-sided that it would be quite impossible for an attacker to scramble up at that point, or for soldiers posted there even to make use of their weapons. By contrast other sectors were easily accessible. Immediately south of Macdonald's Koppie for example, the elements had carved a wide gully into the mountain's western rim, and yet this significant and very obvious weak-spot was no more strongly defended than physically impassable sectors. The summit of Majuba was not indefensible, but like all complex tactical problems it cried out for a thoughtful command estimate aimed at identifying key defensive positions with the usual combination of cover, fields of fire and mutual support.

Quite what Colley intended to do next is open to debate – indeed he may not have intended to do anything. He cannot have known when he set out for the summit on Saturday evening that there would be a battle on Sunday morning. It can be argued that he might have been hoping for one, gambling that the seizure of Majuba must necessarily trigger a Boer counter-attack. But if that were so then he would undoubtedly have been better prepared for such an eventuality and would not have been so strangely uninterested in the proceedings of the morning. Furthermore, because a bold counter-attack was so completely out of character for the Boers, any hypothesis predicated on the expectation of one can be safely discounted. It seems much more likely that Colley was counting upon his *coup de main* seizure of Majuba to force Joubert to abandon the nek without a fight. But if that were indeed the case, then he had failed to realize that mere occupation of the summit would not in itself suffice. Without emplacing artillery, there was nothing the British could do from the top of Majuba which would compel an enemy 2,000 feet below to do anything. Though it had yet to dawn on him, all Colley had succeeded in doing was to poke his head into the lion's den, just as he had at Ingogo.

A number of events occurred during the course of Sunday morning, before any heavy fighting got under way, which indicate that the developing situation forced Colley to start thinking on his feet. First, we know that he announced his intention to return to Mount Prospect later in the day, leaving the force on Majuba under the command of the next senior officer, Commander Romilly. It is important to recognize that, by the time he made this intention known, the Boers were already firing on the rim of the mountain from its lower slopes. It is impossible to know with certainty, therefore, whether Colley's departure had always been on the cards, or whether it was a response to the full-scale resumption of hostilities unfolding around him. Second, he toured the summit just before 11.00 a.m. in company with Stewart and Romilly, to site the three small redoubts which he believed would be required as night-time strongpoints. Talking to a few of the men as he passed, he was heard to remark that he asked only that they hold the hill for three days. Third, we know that Colley signalled Mount Prospect at about 9.00 a.m. to say that the 15th Hussars and the 2nd/60th Rifles should be ordered up from Newcastle. Such a deployment would clear the way for some kind of twin-pronged operation against the nek, but because it had not been ordered as an overnight concurrent activity, meaning that there could be no attack before Monday morning at the earliest, we can deduce that this was a spur of the moment decision and not part of a pre-conceived plan. Whatever was going through Colley's mind, he failed to share his evolving plan with his second-in-command, his chief of staff or any of his principal subordinates. It was in any case about to be overtaken by events.

The case against Colley is complete. He intentionally sabotaged the political direction of the London government to move directly into a ceasefire. The fact that he took personal command of the Majuba operation when there were three battalion commanders on hand shows that there was some element of selfishness in play. Throughout the campaign he had been trying to achieve great things with insufficient resources. As a consequence he had been defeated twice, had been forced to bury most of his staff officers, and had subjected himself to enormous mental pressure. Even having gone to great pains to contrive an opportunity for redemption, he had come up with an unworkable tactical plan.

He had seized some apparently advantageous terrain, believing that the enemy must then follow a single pre-ordained course of action and withdraw from the nek. Only rarely in warfare will the enemy be so obliging. It is only fair to point out in mitigation that Colley had not set out to provoke a fight, and that he acted as he did because he genuinely believed that HMG had embarked on a disreputable course of action. He had made his bed and now he would have to lie in it. By mid-morning it had become abundantly clear that Joubert had no intention of abandoning the nek and that the London papers might not after all be singing the praises of Sir George Colley's brilliant *coup de main.* Instead he would have to use the 2nd/60th and the 15th Hussars to force Laing's Nek the hard way. Since no such plans had yet been laid, he himself would have to go down the mountain. The trouble was that, by the time he arrived at this conclusion, it was no longer possible to get down the mountain.

The Boer Response

It was the Sabbath, it was time for breakfast and, all things considered, all was well with Commandant-General Piet Joubert's world. The morning camp fires in the wagon laagers had not been ablaze for long when the first shots were fired from the summit of Majuba. It is said that 'Slim Piet' was told the news by his wife Hendrina, who like a number of other redoubtable Boer ladies had followed her husband to war and was outside rustling up breakfast when the shooting started. At first there seems to have been considerable dismay at the British seizure of Majuba. Many Boers expected to be brought under artillery fire at any moment and raced to inspan their trek oxen for a quick escape. When after 15 minutes nothing very much had happened, the occupants of the laagers began to calm down. Joubert and Smit were already conferring and quickly concluded that they needed to regain control of the mountain. The spirited Smit was the obvious choice to exercise tactical command of the counter-attack.

Dashing around the encampments in search of willing volunteers, Smit quickly fell in with Commandant Joachem Ferreira and Veldtkornet Stephanus Roos. By 6.00 a.m. the trio had cajoled around 300 burghers into taking part. The plan was simplicity itself. There would be two assault parties made up of younger, fitter men under Roos and Ferreira, and a covering party of veterans which would remain on the lower slopes sniping up at the rim of the mountain, to suppress the defenders with a long-range fire. Within a few minutes the inconspicuously clad Afrikaners had disappeared amongst the rocks and gullies. Nobody moved so suddenly that his movement betrayed his location, and longer approaches through good cover were invariably preferred to direct but more exposed ones. The slopes in front of the Boers were steep and in some places precipitous, but if one pushed left or right of the occasional perpendicular rock face, the north face of Majuba was far from being a difficult climb. For the time being the sound of the occasional rifle shot from the foot of the hill was the only indication that a counter-attack was under way.

In the meantime Piet Joubert had ridden across to stiffen the resolve of the burghers dug in on the nek. As it became increasingly obvious that the British had no subsidiary offensive manoeuvre unfolding, more and more Boers rode across to participate in the counter-attack. Smit was now able to start thinking on a grander scale. Not only did a third assault group start climbing the mountain under Veldtkornets Danie Malan and Stephanus Trichard, but Smit himself was able to set off at the head of around 150 mounted men, intent on manoeuvring around the blind side of the mountain, to harass the British left flank and rear.

The Battle of Majuba Hill

At 8.00 a.m. the headquarters signallers established communications with Mount Prospect and at the general's behest flashed a short message for onwards transmission to the Secretary of State for War: 'Occupied Majuba mountain last night. Immediately overlooking Boer position. Boers firing at us from below.' Ninety minutes later Stewart signalled the camp to report, 'All very comfortable. Boers wasting ammunition. One man wounded in foot.' If these two messages suggested that nothing very much had happened in the interim, it was because, to the officers sat idling amongst the boulders on the rocky ridge, that was just how it appeared. In reality Ferreira and Roos were now half-way up the north-west corner of the mountain, with Trichard and Malan echeloned not far to their left rear. From time to time members of the Gordons were kneeling or standing up in order to get off a decent shot, but they were having no real deterrent effect on the attack and were exposing themselves unnecessarily to the veteran marksmen below. Over the course of the next hour two more men were wounded and had to be carried away to the surgeons.

In response to the developing attack Colley conferred with Stewart and announced his intention to return to Mount Prospect. As chief of staff, Stewart would of course accompany his commander. Before leaving the summit the general would have to satisfy himself that everything was under control. It was now, at about 10.45 a.m., that he decided to order the construction of three improvised redoubts. He was standing with Stewart, Fraser and Romilly on the edge of the mountain, contemplating a potential site near the south-west angle, when Romilly looked down and observed that a Boer rifleman was aiming at them from below. Colley asked his colleagues what they thought the range might be. Lowering his binoculars, Stewart replied calmly that he thought it was about 900 yards. Just then Francis Romilly went reeling to the ground.

Surgeon Edward Mahon RN of HMS *Flora* had come across from the aid post to visit his brother naval officers, Lieutenant Trower and Sub-Lieutenant Scott:

> I had hardly been there three minutes when I heard a bullet explode close to us. I heard the general say 'Captain [*sic*] Romilly is hit,' and turning round saw General Colley kneeling by the side of the commander, who was lying on the ground about four yards from us. I sent for a stretcher, and proceeded to dress the wound, which I found to perforate the left side of the abdomen and coming out of the loins.[12]

Romilly was stretchered away to the aid post in a dangerously wounded condition. If nothing else, his demise made it abundantly clear that Colley no longer had an option to return to Mount Prospect. In fact, allowing not less than an hour to get down, his last safe opportunity to do so had been as early as 6.00: the solitary Conductor Field had been shot and captured along with his mule at around 7.00 a.m.

At 11.00 a.m., by which time the sporadic firing from the lower slopes had been under way for close to five hours, Colley signalled a new situation report to the camp, again intended in due course for the Secretary of State for War. This time he noted Romilly's injury and went on to remark that the Boers were 'still firing heavily on hill, but have broken up laager and begun to move away'. It was this assessment of the wider situation that lay at the heart of the general's continuing complacency; he was misinterpreting the scenes below to see only what he wanted to see. The wagons of a few faint-hearts might well have been on the move, but as often as not a burgher's wagon was moved around by his African servants, leaving him free to fight for days at a time from the contents of his saddlebags. For all their early morning jitters, the overwhelming majority of Joubert's men had, in the end, kept their nerve. In broad terms there were now 300 men clawing their way uphill, 150 sniping from the low ground and 150 roaming wide with Nicholaas Smit. The remainder were watching the nek as Joubert had instructed. Colley's 11.00 a.m. assessment was no more than wishful thinking.

Down in the low ground Captain Robertson's companies had completed a large rectangular redoubt, with earthen walls about four feet high and two feet thick and an entrance facing back towards Mount Prospect. Not long after 11.00 a.m., in fulfilment of Commissary Elmes's undertaking, Captain George Sulivan and a 50-strong troop of the 15th Hussars rode in with the extra rations for Thurlow's men. A veteran of the recent operations around Kandahar, Sulivan decided to stay out in support of the infantry and dismounted his men to the rear of the already crowded redoubt. It was about now that Robertson's command had its first sighting of Boer horsemen – once again Nicholaas Smit's raiders were infiltrating the British lines of communication.

Though it had yet to sink in, from mid-morning onwards Sir George Colley had in effect been invested on Majuba. It was no longer possible for the British to get up or down the mountain in daylight. Amongst many other defects in the plan, this meant that the reserve ammunition had been left in the wrong place.

The Break-In

The lie of the land on the north side of the mountain drew Ferreira and Roos inexorably towards Gordons' Knoll, at the foot of which there was an area of dead ground. In order to get safely into its cover it was necessary to leave the shelter of a nearby ravine and dash across 25 yards of open terrace. About 18 of Ian Hamilton's men were able to fire onto this area from the rim of the mountain. The Boer commanders overcame the problem by establishing a strong firing line along the lip of the ravine and laying down heavy suppressive fire each time a score of men had assembled to make the dash. To Hamilton it felt like there were 80 riflemen firing on his position at such times. However many firers there were in reality, the 18 Gordons were heavily outgunned and obliged to keep their heads down each time one of these heavy fusillades came pouring in. As no orders had been disseminated on the availability of reserve ammunition, the highlanders were further hampered by the necessity to conserve the rounds in their pouches. Having observed a number of successive enemy rushes into the dead ground, Hamilton slipped back to the rocky ridge to advise the general that around 100 Boers had installed themselves beneath his position. Colley thanked him for his report but took no action.

The build-up beneath the knoll was so worrying to Hamilton that at intervals of roughly 15 minutes he went back to the general to make a second and then a third report, indicating the presence of 200 and then 350 Boers. Whilst these were undoubtedly inflated estimates, Colley had no way of knowing this and, t. Tany vaguely competent battalion commander, Hamilton's anxiety would have been indicative of a burgeoning problem. At about midday he ran back to the rocky ridge for a fourth time, only to find that the general had decided to take a nap. It is unlikely that a good soldier like Herbert Stewart declined to wake his commander, so it is probably safe to assume that he was away from the headquarters at this time, the more so since Hamilton recounts that he felt moved in the end to deliver his fourth report to Jock Hay. Having done so, he dashed back to the threatened sector and threw himself down amongst his men.[13]

Veldtkornet Stephanus Roos was amongst the first, if not the very first, to pop his head over the edge of Gordons' Knoll. It was unoccupied but there was a thinly spread firing line of khaki-clad highlanders only 60 yards beyond. Roos was looking slightly uphill towards them. Their position was on a forward slope to the rest of the summit, leaving them out on a limb – none of the other

British positions were visible to Roos, nor were they able to provide Hamilton with fire support. Roos dropped back into cover and resorted to a stratagem to get his hesitant men into all-out offensive mode. There were only about 50–60 of them in his immediate vicinity, but that was enough to achieve a localized three-to-one advantage over the handful of Scots opposite. Waving his hat over his head, Roos cried out that the British were running. The burghers nearby were sufficiently heartened to throw themselves into fire positions on top of the knoll and commence a short-range fire-fight with Hamilton and his men.

> All of a sudden, about half past twelve o'clock, a tremendous fire was opened from this knoll on a part of my company immediately to my left. A space of ground sixty yards long and held by five or six of my men was covered with bullets. Two or three of the poor fellows were killed at once, one or two ran back. Where I and my men lay, seemed to be out of the direct line of fire.[14]

Rude Awakening

The sudden fusillade to the left front, far heavier than anything which had preceded it, woke up the men snoozing gently amongst the boulders on the rocky ridge, Sir George included. It was clear that some kind of crisis had indeed developed on the Gordons' sector. John Cameron, representing the *Evening Standard* and the *Illustrated London News*, described how Lieutenant Harry Wright of the 92nd came dashing back from the rim of the mountain shouting aloud for reinforcements. The general responded immediately by committing the reserve in support of Hamilton. While it is a common failing of generalship to refrain from committing the reserve until it is too late, it is also perfectly possible to mistime the decision by committing too soon. On this occasion Colley was probably around five or six minutes early.

Within a few seconds of their rude awakening, the mixed bag of soldiers and sailors comprising the reserve found themselves stumbling into a counter-attack. As soon as they left the cover of the dead ground and ran onto the forward slope behind Hamilton's hard-pressed firing line, they came under heavy fire. If the reserve task had been assigned to a single formed company and it had been kept poised, briefed and alert, then the chances are that the counter-attack would have had sufficient dash and momentum to throw the Boers back down the hillside at the point of the bayonet. In the event the reserve's lack of cohesion caused its members to react lamely. Instead of pressing the sort of bold attack that Roos and Ferreira simply could not have beaten back with single shot breech-loaders, they threw themselves down and opened fire in the general direction of Gordons' Knoll. Many of them could not see what they were shooting at, but in their anxiety to be seen doing something useful, loaded and fired anyway. Expecting a bayonet charge at any moment and only too keenly aware of the fragility of their toehold, the Boers dropped back into cover.

Observing that there were no longer any targets in sight, the officers of the reserve roared at their men to cease firing and conserve their ammunition. When, after a few minutes, no charge had materialized, the burghers began worming their way back to their fire positions. In next to no time the fire-fight began all over again, this time to much deadlier effect, the Boers emboldened by the all too obvious timidity of the British. Within a minute or two, 16 members of the reserve had been hit. In the face of such an intolerable fire, the survivors ran back into dead ground and, disregarding the angry rallying cries of their officers, began sprinting hard for the shelter of the rocky ridge. Deserted by their supports and hard-pressed by the enemy, Hamilton's men also fell back in disarray. Some were shot down as they ran.

Cross-Fire

Back in the relative safety of the ridge most of the troops rallied to the general and the officers of the staff. While Colley was attempting to regain control and establish a coherent line of defence amongst the boulders, many of Roos's men were busy occupying the north rim of the mountain, crawling their way into fire positions which would enable them to engage both the section of highlanders on Macdonald's Koppie and the mixture of men, perhaps 150 in all, deployed in the cover of the rocky ridge. John Cameron's account indicates that, for a while at least, the rallied troops were able to hold their own against the immediate threat from their front:

> Some of the Boers appeared, and the fire that was interchanged was something awful. Three times they showed themselves, and three times they as quickly withdrew [into cover], our men, when that occurred, at once stopping their fire. I could hear the soldiers ejaculate, 'We'll not budge from this. We'll give them the bayonet if they come closer,' and so on, but all the time dropping fast, for Boer marksmen had apparently got to work in secure positions, and every shot told, the men falling back hit, mostly through the head.
>
> It was a hot five minutes, but nevertheless I thought at the time we should hold our own. I expected every minute to hear the order given for a bayonet charge. That order unfortunately never came, although I am sure the men would have responded to it. But our flanks were exposed, and the enemy checked in front, were stealing round them.[15]

Beneath the abandoned edge of the mountain other Boer leaders were already leading strong parties of burghers around the British flanks. While Roos was forcing his break-in in the centre, Ferreira had been scrambling around the western face of the mountain for the wide gully south of Macdonald's Koppie. On the opposite flank Veldtkornet Danie Malan had wormed his way beneath Hay's Koppie, where he and his men were proving next to impossible to get at. More and more Boer fire positions were gradually being brought into play around the rim of the mountain. For the Afrikaners it was the best stalking they had ever known.

A runner despatched hot-foot by the naval officers drew the general's attention to the enemy infiltrators beginning to appear in the gully beneath Macdonald's position. Some of the officers, Stewart and Fraser amongst them, experienced great difficulty in getting even a few men to face in the direction of the developing threat. Some of the junior officers were anxious to try a bayonet charge. Hamilton for example gravitated towards the right of the line where he could see Major Hay and a cluster of Gordons. Having gathered a handful of stalwarts about him, Hamilton sought permission to charge. Hay thought them too few and turned the request down. In his inimitable way Hamilton worked his way down the line to try his luck with Colley; 'I do hope General, that you will let us have a charge, and that you will not think it presumption on my part to have come up and asked you.' By now Colley had drawn his .45-inch Holland & Holland revolver. 'No presumption Mr Hamilton,' he replied patiently, 'but we will wait until the Boers advance upon us, then give them a volley and charge.'[16] Yet again this was a tactical misjudgement – the Boers were never going to advance frontally on the rocky ridge like a conventional European enemy. Instead they were reaching out instinctively for the enemy's flanks and rear, intent on subjecting the British to a withering cross-fire. Before long a sense of encirclement was spreading down the line. The Boers continued coiling around Colley's embattled force like a constrictor, slowly crushing its ability to resist, even its very willingness to resist for very much longer. In desperation the staff officers finally gave the order to fix bayonets.

In the absence of clear direction and strong leadership, many young soldiers instinctively sought the close comradeship of their regimental mates. Before long a clustering effect had set in, making the unfortunate Tommies the easiest targets imaginable. Many of the 58th men holding the south-east rim became so alarmed by the heavy fighting to their rear that they abandoned their positions, turned about and advanced into the tumult on the rocky ridge. Amidst all the noise, confusion and lack of cohesion, few officers or sergeants were in a position to give fire-control orders to formed bodies of men. As a result many of the less experienced soldiers forgot to adjust their rear sights for range. After the battle the Boers noticed that many of the Martini-Henrys lying in the grass were still sighted at 400 or 500 yards. By contrast their own rifle fire was unfailingly accurate throughout. The combination of supremely skilful field-craft with deadly marksmanship, and the close integration of fire with movement, was simply too much for the bewildered and poorly led soldiers. Now Ferreira and his men were in the western gully enfilading the rocky ridge from the left, whilst Malan's were all over the south-eastern rim and Hay's Koppie, firing on the British from their right rear. The resultant cross-fire was both terrifying and deadly.

Hamilton was close to Colley as the situation reached crisis point:

> I was standing to the right of General Colley and ten paces from him, firing into the smoke, for I could not see anyone, with a rifle I had picked up. Sir George appeared quite cool, and was pacing up and down slowly with his revolver in his right hand, and looking on the ground. He said nothing. Towards the left I could see Major Fraser encouraging his men. On the extreme right Colonel [*sic*] Hay. Suddenly to my front, and not more than fifteen yards distant I saw a rifle barrel stuck up out of a tuft of grass, evidently to allow of a cartridge being put into the breech; looking more carefully I made out the head and shoulders of a Boer. I put up my rifle and covered him, but just as I began to press the trigger he sent a bullet through my left wrist causing my rifle to fall from hand unfired. I turned round in despair and saw that the whole line had given way. Sir George Colley had turned in the direction the troops were flying, and holding his revolver high over his head shouted out either – 'Retire and hold by the Ridge,' or 'Steady and hold by the Ridge.' I cannot be quite sure which it was, but it was something to the effect that we were to hold by the last ridge of the hill.[17]

Herbert Stewart, who was within a few yards of the general, heard him say no such thing. There are many inconsistencies between the evidence of the Gordons officers and the testimony of the staff, the former anxious to preserve the honour of their regiment, the latter to remain loyal to their general. One thing we can be sure of is that there was no shortage of ammunition as was erroneously reported at the time. Boer sources record emphatically that most British casualties still had 30–40 cartridges left in their pouches, a figure entirely consistent with the nature and duration of the fight.

Last Man Standing

All of a sudden everybody was running. Left with no other alternative, even officers of the calibre of Stewart and Hamilton were running. With Boers on three sides the only way out was south towards the original ascent route. There was a positive stampede across the plateau in the direction of the south-west angle. Many men were shot in the back as they ran. Only one British soldier was still standing fast at the end. Casting about himself, Sir George Colley realized that he was on his own. Captain Augustus Morris of the 58th had been badly wounded and later said that he saw Colley waving a white flag. One need only read Sir George's letter to Lady Edith, to be opened in the event of his death, to know that Morris was mistaken.[18] It seems likely that what he saw was the navy-blue uniform of a medical orderly, not the general in his patrol jacket. There are a dozen other contradictory accounts of the circumstances surrounding Colley's death, none of them more strongly corroborated than the others. For once we may safely indulge ourselves as historians by choosing our own ending from a range of possibilities. I am inclined when guiding battlefield tours on Majuba to end the story thus: knowing full well the consequences of his actions, the general cocked his revolver, raised it into the aim and advanced towards the enemy firing as he went.

We do know that Major General Sir George Colley was shot through the forehead from close range and that he must have died instantly. Some said that it was Roos who shot him, others that it was the 12-year-old Uys boy who participated in the battle. In an act of questionable taste Sir Evelyn Wood later forwarded Sir George's bullet-holed helmet to Lady Colley, to show that he died with his face to the foe. Lady Edith, nor anybody else who knew Sir George personally, had ever doubted it.

Lieutenant 'Fighting Mac' Macdonald had put up a brave fight against impossible odds from the top of the rocky koppie that today bears his name. Eight of his 20 men had been killed and all but two of the others wounded. Seeing the disaster unfolding below, Macdonald gave the word for those who were still capable of doing so to make a break for safety. Almost immediately 'Fighting Mac' ran into some Boers at the foot of the koppie. He briefly contemplated taking them on with his revolver, but they were generous enough to indicate that it would be wiser to drop the weapon instead. Macdonald heeded their advice.

As the Boers charged onto the summit firing mercilessly at the backs of the routed British, there was some difficulty in securing a ceasefire in the vicinity of the aid post. Surgeon Arthur Landon was shot in the spine as the Boers came storming onto the rocky ridge. Two of his medics also fell in the same fusillade. Lance Corporal Joseph Farmer of the AHC immediately stood up, waving a bandage overhead to signify capitulation. He was shot in his raised right hand. Most men would have buried their face in the grass at this juncture and hoped for the best. Instead Farmer picked up the bandage with his good hand and again began waving it back and forth above the wounded, only to be shot again, this time in the left elbow. Fortunately his brave efforts had caught the eye of some older Boers, who ordered the young men around them to stop firing in the direction of the aid post. Lance Corporal Farmer would be awarded the Victoria Cross, the only such award in an otherwise humiliating day.

The naval surgeon, Edward Mahon, and one of the medics working alongside him did their best to protect Commander Romilly, first by carrying him out of the line of fire on a stretcher, then by standing over him waving a white flag. There was no immediate reaction from the Boers: first the white flag was shot away, then Mahon's helper was hit twice in the helmet, miraculously without serious injury, and finally Romilly himself was hit again, further exacerbating his already critical condition. Eventually Mahon managed to obtain a local ceasefire by shouting to the approaching enemy that they were firing on doctors and casualties. Three young Boers came up and seeing the three rings of gold braid around Romilly's cuffs, the mark of a naval commander, convinced themselves that such an important personage simply had to be either Wood or Wolseley. With that they declared that it was their bounden duty to shoot 'the general' out of hand. Fortunately Ferreira came along and in response to Mahon's entreaties sent the bloodthirsty hotheads on their way.[19]

From the south-west angle the Boers continued to fire downhill at the backs of the routing *rooineks*. In their anxiety to get away some men fell over precipices to their deaths. Others suffered broken limbs or other serious injuries and were left stranded on the mountain. Major Thomas Fraser was lucky to survive a 300-foot tumble. A fortunate few were allowed to lay down their arms and surrender, while others tried to hide themselves in folds and gullies until the onset of darkness. Herbert Stewart had been wounded in the leg and was forced to secrete himself on the side of the mountain. He was captured the following day. Lieutenant Alan Hill had been badly wounded by a round which ripped his arm open from the elbow to the wrist and, like the correspondent Thomas Carter, was taken prisoner. The general's Zulu guides also fell into enemy hands but were categorized by Joubert as spies and separated from the British prisoners. They were never heard of again. It is not difficult to imagine what became of them.

Withdrawal of the Outposts

For most of the morning the officers at Mount Prospect and at the outposts on the saddle had been under the impression that their colleagues were meting out heavy punishment to the enemy. Then, in the early afternoon, the first of the stunned survivors came spilling downhill and the awful truth became apparent. Some of the 15th Hussars rode out to pick up wounded men. Robertson and Thurlow quickly came under pressure from the Boers who had come round the back of the mountain under Smit, and from a fresh party which descended from the nek under Commandant J. Uys. Although Robertson signalled Smith and

Henley for support, they seem to have left the forward companies to their own devices and to have made their way back to Mount Prospect independently. Robertson next signalled Colonel Bond, in command at the camp, for orders. He was told that, if he could get no instructions from the mountain-top, then he should fall back to Mount Prospect.

First Robertson got the reserve ammunition away, mule by mule, so as to avoid attracting too much attention with a single more obvious movement. Next he evacuated the wounded. Misfortune befell Surgeon-Major Cornish at this stage when, having stepped in to help out with a stretcher, he found himself challenged from close cover by Boers who saw only a British officer with a rifle slung across his back. According to the piper on the other end of the stretcher, the doctor answered the challenge with 'wounded men'.[20] Although Cornish had done no more than pick up the weapon in order to relieve a patient of an inconvenient load, it was enough to get him shot by men who, in all fairness, were probably oblivious to his non-combatant status.

After a brisk defence of their redoubt, the two company commanders in the saddle began to think about extricating their commands. It was arranged that Ernest Thurlow's riflemen would pull out first, with the Gordons covering them. A few hundred yards down the slope the Rifles would halt to cover the highlanders back. As the correspondent Charles 'Noggs' Norris-Newman heard it afterwards, Thurlow and his officers lost control of their men who bolted straight for the camp. The suggestion is firmly rebutted in General Sir Steuart Hare's *The Annals of the King's Royal Rifle Corps*, but as 'Noggs' heard it needless casualties occurred in Robertson's company, including the capture of Lieutenant George Staunton and the best part of a section.[21] Ten men of Thurlow's company were also captured. For all the difficulties that beset the operation, including the alleged misconduct of the Rifles, the majority were able to make it back across the Laing's Nek road to the sanctuary of the camp. That this was so was due in no small part to Robertson himself, who set an inspirational example to the men of the rearguard.

Flushed with unexpected success, the Boer commandants gave brief consideration to a full-scale assault on Mount Prospect. The British artillery and the sudden descent of heavy mist and rain quickly put paid to such ambitious plans. Later Captain Robertson would submit a blunt and angry report which pointed an accusing finger at the behaviour of the Rifles and at certain named officers. The report was entrusted to 'Lucky' Essex, who made an unsuccessful attempt to suppress it and would be chastised by Evelyn Wood for having done so. The inter-unit recriminations in the British camp that night were protracted and bitter. Everybody had their own pet theory on what had gone wrong. The only area of agreement amongst the participating regiments was quite how badly they had been failed by General Colley. One of the Rifles officers offered the cruel observation that he was 'unfit for a corporal's guard'. They failed to come to terms with the notion that it might not all have been Colley's fault or that they might perhaps not have done better themselves. Such was the agitation amongst the Gordons that eventually Sir Evelyn Wood had to investigate the conduct of the Rifles. Interestingly he found nothing wanting. If nothing else, it was at least a pragmatic finding.

Aftermath

When the fighting in the low ground had petered out, Piet Joubert made his way up to the summit of Majuba. As he wandered around amongst the British dead and wounded he could scarcely believe the scale of the victory. Boer losses had been astonishingly light. Only one man, Johannes Bekker of Middleburg, had been killed outright, and there were only six wounded, though Johannes Groenwald would die of his wounds a month or so later. Although the older Boers treated the British wounded kindly, there was also a great deal of shameless plundering of the dead. Many of the slain Gordons were stripped of their kilts and with them of all dignity in death. The prisoners could also expect to be robbed of both money and personal possessions. One Boer took a fancy to Hector Macdonald's sporran. The insolent burgher learned to his cost that 'Fighting Mac' was no mere idle sobriquet, when he was felled with a right hook. For a moment it looked like Macdonald would be shot out of hand, but he was spared to continue his famous rise from private soldier to general officer and, in the fullness of time, to sink into ignominy. But that is another story.

At the aid post Lance Corporal Farmer was in a great deal of pain. Nearby Arthur Landon was so badly injured as to be next to helpless, but when a Boer came within hailing distance he called him over, pointed out his instrument case and proceeded to instruct the man in how to administer pain suppressants. The Boer botched the task of injecting Farmer and succeeded only in causing him more pain. Frustrated by the ineptitude of his locum, Landon resolved to take the job over himself. 'You must lift me up, for my back is broken,' he explained quietly.[22] With his Boer helper holding him up in a sitting position, at the price no doubt of quite unimaginable pain, Landon proceeded to tend to Farmer. Not long afterwards Doctor Landon died.

Ian Hamilton spotted Joubert wandering over the field and approached the Commandant-General to see if he would help recover his claymore, a much treasured family heirloom once carried by his father. The conversation backfired and culminated in a heated exchange on the rights and wrongs of the war:

> He remarked, pointing to all the dead and the wounded lying about, 'This is a sad business.' I agreed with him. He continued, 'Why do you force it upon us?' 'We do not force it upon you,' I replied, 'you began it

> at Bronkhorstspruit and you will see England will go on to the end,' for I did not then know that the dead around me would not be avenged and I did not much care what I said, I was so sick at heart at all that had happened. 'Who told you that we began it?' I made the rather tame reply that I had read it in the newspapers. At his he seemed to quite lose his temper and stamped on the ground with his foot, saying, 'Those vile damned, accursed newspapers, they have made all this mischief and now you come here telling me of newspapers!' One or two of our wounded men were by, and were much alarmed, thinking he would order us all to be shot forthwith, but he grew cool again as quickly as he had got angry, and turned away to his work without troubling himself more about me.[23]

Hector Macdonald had rather more luck with his claymore. It had been presented to him by the officers of the 92nd to mark his commissioning and bore an engraved sentiment commending his valour in Afghanistan. This so moved Joubert that he was inspired to hand the weapon back to its owner with the words, 'A man who has won such a sword should not be separated from it.'[24]

Towards nightfall the walking wounded were set free and allowed to make their way back to Mount Prospect. Hamilton was in considerable distress from his wound and weakened by loss of blood. Although he made it down to the low ground, he eventually became disorientated and collapsed in a heap. The following morning he was woken by a strange sensation; he opened his eyes to find his fox-terrier 'Patch' licking his face and a British search party fast approaching. Thirty-six more seriously wounded had to spend the night on top

***Table 6:* British Casualties at Majuba**

Unit	*Killed*	*Wounded*	*Captured*
Staff	1 & 0	–	1[25] & 0
Royal Navy	1[26] & 16	1 & 15	0 & 3
15th Hussars	0 & 2	0 & 1	0 & 1
2nd/21st Regiment	0 & 2	–	–
58th Regiment	1 & 31	3 & 42	1 & 13
3rd/60th Rifles	–	0 & 1	0 & 11
92nd Regiment	0 & 34	3 & 63	4 & 21
94th Regiment[27]	0 & 1	1 & 1	1 & 0
Army Service Corps	–	0 & 1	–
Army Medical Department	2[28] & 0	–	–
Army Hospital Corps	–	0 & 2	–
Totals	**5 & 86**	**8 & 126**	**7 & 49**

of the mountain. Dr Mahon and the surviving medics did the best they could by draping their patients in the few greatcoats and groundsheets that had survived the burghers' pillaging of the battlefield, but the night was cold, there was heavy rain and, sad to say, men died for the want of succour.

The Peace

At the peace negotiations which followed the Majuba fiasco, Great Britain was represented by Major General Sir Evelyn Wood, who on the instructions of Her Majesty's Government was forced to suppress his soldierly instinct for revenge and to seek political rapprochement with the Triumvirate. The talks took place at R. C. O'Neill's cottage, just below Captain Robertson's old position on the spur. Today the cottage is much as it was in 1881 and is open to the public. Initially General Colley's body had been removed to the Boer camp, where it was laid out in a tent and left in the care of a Gordons honour guard under Hector Macdonald. On 1 March it was returned to the British and buried on the ridge at Mount Prospect. No volleys were fired over the grave. In a letter to his wife Wood wrote, 'Colley is gone: the best instructed soldier I ever met.'[29]

The Mount Prospect cemetery is the final resting place to more than 50 men, many of whom we have encountered in the course of this chapter: Colonel Deane, Commander Romilly, Majors Hingeston, Poole and Singleton, Doctors Cornish and Landon, Captain Greer, Lieutenants Elwes, Wilkinson, Garrett, O'Connell, Inman and Trower, 2nd Lieutenant Baillie and Marthinus Stuart to name but a few. The balance of the graves are occupied by lesser-known men. Whilst their deeds may have faded into the mists of time, their names have not – amongst their number are Privates D. Fitzharris and F. Taylor of the old 58th Regiment, F. McKenzie and J. Graham of the Gordons, P. Hurley and D. T. Tilbury of the 60th Rifles, and J. Loveless and H. Croft of the Royal Navy. Whilst most of the officers were recovered to Mount Prospect as corpses, it is sadder still to reflect that the soldiers who now lie alongside them are by and large men who died lingering deaths in the field hospital at Mount Prospect. At the right end of the rearmost row, overlooked by Majuba, rests poor Sir George Colley, who tried so hard and failed so miserably. It is at least a pretty spot.

Wood had concluded a truce by 1 March 1881 and followed it with a full-scale peace three weeks later. The Transvaal could be self-governing in all its internal affairs, but would have to commit to legal and humanitarian safeguards for the black population and defer to a British resident in respect of its foreign relations. Over the next few years the Pretoria government would renege on all the treaty provisions and wrest ostensibly untrammelled independence. The British had been caught off-guard and embarrassed by the rebellion, but had not been defeated at anything beyond a minor and localized level. There had been no defeat, because by Sunday 27 February 1881 they had not yet begun to fight. The Natal Field Force did not even begin to represent the military might of the British Empire. Ian Hamilton wrote, 'We accepted the defeat of 365 men as the defeat of the British Empire although we had 5,000 men under Evelyn Wood within two day's march.'[30] The post-Majuba peace was a tribute to British moderation, a characteristic which the rebel leaders had counted on in all their strategic thinking. But it was also an act of appeasement and, like all acts of appeasement, would lead in the long run to far greater loss of life. Rapprochement and comfortable coexistence between the white races of Southern Africa might have looked attainable from Whitehall, but everybody on the ground knew that Anglo-Saxon and Afrikaner-Dutch values were so radically different as to be irreconcilable. Majuba merely closed a chapter in a tense and difficult relationship – a relationship destined in the long term to get a whole lot worse.

In military terms Majuba was no more than a skirmish, a distinctly harrowing skirmish for the men who fought in it to be sure, but a skirmish for all that. Its significance lay not in any of its military dimensions, nor even in its much more dramatic political ramifications; rather its true significance was psychological. Majuba represented a new Blood River for a new generation, a new military triumph against the odds and a new affirmation of divine favour. The true significance of Majuba was that it bestowed hero status and two decades of incontestable political pre-eminence on a *dopper* arch-reactionary, a man who, with the twentieth century fast approaching, still subscribed to flat-earth theory.

Chapter 5

WHITE PASHAS

British Contract Officers and the Mahdist Revolt, Sudan, 1883–1884

I am writing this under circumstances which bring me almost as near to death as is possible without being under absolute sentence of execution or in the throes of some deadly malady. However, to die out here, with a lancehead as big as a shovel through me, will meet my views better than the gradual sinking into the grave which is the lot of so many. You must know that here we are fifteen hundred miles away south of Cairo, in the midst of a wild unexplored country. The Egyptian army with which I am here camped on the banks of the Nile, will have but one chance given them – one tremendous pitched battle. The enemy we have to meet are as courageous and fierce as the Zulus, and much better armed, and our army is that which ran away before a handful of British troops at Tel-el-Kebir.

Edmond O'Donovan of the *Daily News*,
from Hicks Pasha's camp, October 1883[1]

By 1870 the impoverished Sudan had been in the hands of Egyptian colonial administrators for the best part of half a century. If it was true that the ruling pashas had brought some of the more basic trappings of civilization south with them, it was also abundantly clear that they cared little for their monotonous surroundings and even less for the subjugated inhabitants of the region. Naked commercial exploitation of the African interior sat squarely at the top of the Egyptian agenda. Although the various provincial governors were answerable to the central authority of a governor-general in Khartoum, in practice the sheer vastness of the Sudan guaranteed them considerable latitude. While the pashas brought the semblance of law and order to the principal towns, it remained necessary, nonetheless, to maintain a score of substantial military garrisons and dozens of remote government outposts. Beyond the immediate environs of the garrison towns, the wider countryside remained largely unchanged and generally lawless. One field in which significant strides did occur was that of communications. The trappings of governance now included a regular steamer service on the Nile, an overland telegraph and a reasonably reliable postal system. Whilst a small and suitably appreciative merchant class reaped the benefits, the great majority of Sudanese came to regard the Egyptian regime as exploitative, inefficient and corrupt.

Like the Soviet Russians in Afghanistan a century later, the besetting sin of the Egyptians was that they were foreigners. In the eyes of Sudanese Arabs the worst of their crimes was that they had fallen under the liberalizing influence of the British and had become abolitionists. Not only had the Cairo government committed itself to the military suppression of slave raiding, it had also pledged that the existing slave class would be emancipated by 1888. But for a good many Sudanese the slave trade was so central to their way of life that operations to suppress the age-old institution quickly bred smouldering resentment. Worse still the pashas seemed to tax everything and everybody, and in cases of non-payment were quick to resort to harsh punitive measures.

The final nail in the Egyptian coffin would be religious dogma. In the farthest-flung corners of the Islamic world, local clerics have seldom fought shy of denouncing unpopular outsiders as unbelievers. Despite the Egyptians' manifest fealty to the teachings of the Prophet, government officers were slowly undermined by the ravings of extremists, who cited the slightest deviation from their own particular brand of Islam as proof-positive of the foreigners' apostasy.

If the Sudan fell prey to generally inept and despotic governance, it is also true that things were not much better for the Egyptian agricultural poor, the *fellah* class of the Nile Delta. In a society where corruption was merely a norm, the ruling khedive had so few honest and competent officials at his disposal that it proved difficult even to administer his capital with anything approaching probity. With the efficacy of outlying centres of government declining in proportion to their distance upriver from Cairo, there was but little hope for the Sudan. Sixteen hundred miles and more to the south, in Khartoum and its outposts, the regime was administered and policed by officials of the lowest calibre. For such men as these, life in the barren, unbearable Sudan brought only one consolation – the opportunity to abuse public office for personal gain.

As Egypt was still technically a province of the ailing Ottoman Empire, the khedive remained answerable to the sultan in Constantinople. In practice Ismail Pasha enjoyed considerable autonomy and was intent on edging the land of the pharaohs towards full independence. The Sudanese for their part drew no distinction between types of foreigner and continued to use the word 'Turk' as an all-embracing pejorative for Ottomans, Egyptians and Europeans alike. With the opening of the strategically vital Suez Canal in 1869, Egypt entered the global mainstream, and slowly but surely fell more and more under the sway of the two principal European powers. Keen to modernize the country and to make Cairo 'the Paris of the Orient', the Khedive embarked on an ambitious programme of public works. For a while British and French bankers fuelled his internationalist ambitions and fed his ostentatious tastes. But always there was the interest. By 1875 the well-meaning but profligate Ismail was in debt to the tune of more than £90 million, a truly colossal sum by the standards of the day. Eventually he was left with no alternative but to sell his shares in the Suez Canal Company. With his official exchequer unable to react in a timely enough fashion, Prime Minister Disraeli arranged a snap loan from the Rothschilds and was able at the drop of a hat to secure a controlling British interest for less than £4 million sterling.

Chinese Gordon

Under pressure from the great powers to implement a programme of public reform in the interests of good governance, Ismail took on more and more European advisers. One of his more notable employees was Colonel Charles Gordon CB, RE, already a living legend when he entered the service of the Khedive. Born in 1833, the fourth son of an artillery officer destined to rise to the rank of lieutenant general, Gordon was educated at Taunton and the Royal Military Academy Woolwich. As a young officer he served with distinction in the siege of Sebastopol. In the early 1860s he won great acclaim in the service of the Emperor of China, when at the head of the small but well-drilled 'Ever Victorious Army' he played a leading role in the suppression of the Taiping Rebellion. From 1874 'Chinese Gordon' served Ismail as the Governor of Equatorial Africa, the tropical southern swathe of Sudan, before being elevated in 1877 to the post of Governor-General.

The enigmatic colonel was hugely able, highly principled and zealous in all things. For all his undoubted talent, the best of his qualities seemed to be twinned with eccentricities. Sustained and driven, above all else, by a profound but highly personalized code of Christian convictions, he was also opinionated, mercurial, changeable and argumentative. In his often rambling correspondence he was wont to wish longingly for his own death, but the notion was closely bound up with his belief in a glorious after-life and, whilst it is true that he suffered from periodic bouts of depression, there seems to have been nothing overtly suicidal in his character. Gordon's unshakeable faith did mean, however, that he was all but incapable of feeling fear. In keeping with the spirit of the age and his own liberal–humanitarian values, the suppression of slavery was his topmost priority. Just as had been the case at home, where all sorts of waifs and strays had received charitable handouts at the colonel's house in Gravesend, Gordon was troubled by the wretched condition of the Sudanese poor and was quick to enact measures to relieve the worst of their suffering. There was an aura about Gordon and the way he did business that seemed somehow to inspire the best in lesser men. Some of his Egyptian subordinates were sufficiently inspired to clean up their act, whilst others chose to take their corruption underground in an attempt to evade the fearsome wrath of their incorruptible master. Some tried intriguing behind Gordon's back, but all complaints were brusquely dismissed by the Governor-General's leading admirer, the Khedive himself. Gordon stayed until 1879 but under his Egyptian successor, Raouf Pasha, the country and its government quickly sank back into the old ways. For all his force of personality, Gordon had exercised only a transitory influence over the Sudan, but his regime had been distinctly different and his memory lingered amongst the leading players in Sudanese public life. He left Khartoum without ever having heard the name Muhammad Ahmad. How different it would be five years later when he was prevailed upon to return.

The Nationalist Revolt in Egypt

Gordon's departure had been triggered by Constantinople's dismissal of the bankrupt and discredited Ismail, a measure enacted largely at the instigation of the great powers.[2] Ismail's eldest son, Tewfik, succeeded in his stead. In order to bring the country's finances back onto an even keel, the exchequer was placed in the hands of British and French administrators. Within two years the economy was beginning to prosper as never before. One of the unintended consequences of the new governmental arrangement, however, was the growth of nationalist sentiment amongst Egypt's evolving middle class. Resentment of European and Ottoman influence bubbled to the surface most readily amongst junior and middle-ranking army officers of the *fellah* class. Foremost amongst their grievances was the perception that foreign-born Circassians were appointed to all the best military sinecures. On the other hand, if there was dirty work to be done in the Sudan, it was generally the *fellah* officers who were sent to do it. In September 1881 one of the malcontents, Colonel Ahmed Arabi, marched on the Khedive's palace to press a number of political demands. Distinctly short of viable alternatives, Tewfik was forced to embark on a policy of appeasement. A series of political confrontations between the Khedive and the army dragged on into the New Year.

At first there was some sympathy with the nationalist cause amongst the British diplomatic staff in Cairo. Their early advice to Whitehall suggested that Arabi posed no direct threat to Britain's principal commercial and strategic interests – London's extensive capital investment in Egypt, and freedom of navigation through the canal and the Red Sea. The French position though was rather less measured. Terrified that Arab nationalism might prosper and spread to its North African empire, Paris pressed Gladstone to back them in bolstering the khedival regime against the nationalists. Unaccountably, given the non-interventionist tenor of his political principles, the Prime Minister elected to fall into line with the French and found himself drawn into gunboat diplomacy. A diplomatic note was sent to the Khedive assuring him that the powers regarded the maintenance of his regime as a key interest. The so-called Joint Note was published in Cairo on 8 January 1882. The robust Anglo-French stance served only to deepen the political crisis in Egypt by outraging popular opinion, unifying the country behind the nationalists and triggering the fall of the government. The new hardline administration forced on the Khedive was led by a prominent nationalist called Mahmoud Sami, and included Arabi Pasha in the all-important office of Minister for War. One of the first measures enacted by the new government was the arrest and trial of 50 Circassian officers on trumped-up charges. When the Khedive declined to confirm their sentences, Mahmoud Sami pressed the Council of Notables to indict the Khedive as a tyrant. The country quickly spiralled into a fully fledged constitutional crisis. The European community in Alexandria were quick to sense that the mood was turning ugly and that nationalist agitators were actively engaged in turning the people against them.

On 19 May a joint Anglo-French naval squadron of two ironclads and four gunboats anchored off Alexandria. The small size of the flotilla suggested a lack of resolve and if anything only worsened the crisis by provoking the nationalists, without at the same time exerting the cowing effect of more resolute gunboat diplomacy. Nonetheless, egged on by the consuls-general of the two powers, Tewfik dismissed Arabi from office. This served only to trigger the resignation of the rest of the government and to inflame nationalist sentiment on the streets of Cairo. In response military commanders assailed the Khedive with peremptory demands for their hero's reinstatement. As there was evidently no intention on the part of Britain and France to land troops, the powerless Khedive could see no alternative but to retract his dismissal of Arabi. Emboldened by the climb-down, the Minister for War began to construct new forts and shore batteries commanding Admiral Sir Beauchamp Seymour's anchorage. One of the characteristics of sea power is that it can be discreetly echeloned 'over the horizon' and Seymour now took the opportunity to call the rest of his fleet up from Suda Bay in Crete. By the end of the month the Royal Navy had deployed 8 powerful ironclads, 2 gun-vessels, 3 gunboats, a torpedo-vessel and and a despatch vessel.

The storm broke on Sunday 11 June 1882, when in a day of severe rioting the Muslim population of Alexandria took its frustrations out on the city's Christian communities. By nightfall hundreds of indigenous Christians and more than 50 Europeans had been murdered. Thousands fled the city to be rescued from the beaches by British sailors and marines. In London there was an immediate political furore. Why, demanded the Conservative opposition, had the Navy stood by and done nothing while British citizens were being murdered under the guns of the fleet? Four days after the riot Gladstone's cabinet met to discuss the crisis. The following day Sir Garnet Wolseley was told to begin contingency planning a full-scale military intervention.

Born the son of a Regular Army major at Golden Bridge in County Dublin on 4 June 1833, Britain's 'only general' was now 49 years of age and at the height of his powers. His first campaign service came quickly, in the Second Burma War of 1852–3. Determined in the interests of swift advancement to win a VC, it was always on the cards that he would get himself severely wounded and invalided home without one. Transferring from the 80th Regiment of Foot to the 90th Light Infantry he sailed for the Crimea just in time to celebrate Christmas 1854 in the field. Twice wounded, blinded in one eye, and twice mentioned in despatches during the siege operations around Sebastopol, Captain Wolseley served through to the close of the campaign and re-embarked with a brevet majority in the bag. Bound in 1857 for China aboard the troopship *Transit*, Wolseley and three companies of his regiment found themselves stranded in Singapore when their vessel foundered en route. By the time they were embarked aboard a replacement, they were no longer bound for the Far East but for the inferno now blazing its way through the HEIC's Indian possessions. Not yet out of his mid-twenties, Wolseley saw heavy fighting under Campbell and Outram during the second relief of Lucknow. He went on to serve under Sir Hope Grant in the mopping-up operations around central India, before shipping east for the Second China War of 1860 as a member of Grant's staff. By now a lieutenant colonel, Wolseley was present at the storming of the Taku Forts, the capture of Tientsin and the allied entry into Peking.

He spent the 1860s on the staff in Canada, where he was promoted to colonel and wrote *A Soldier's Pocket Book for Field Service*, first published in 1869. The following year he was appointed to command the Red River Expedition. In the event the campaign proved to be little more than a demonstration of imperial 'reach' into the heart of the Manitoba wilderness. For administrating his way to Fort Garry successfully Wolseley was knighted and awarded a CB. In 1871 he was appointed as the Assistant Adjutant-General at the War Office, where he became heavily involved in Cardwell's reform programme, serving amongst his other duties as a member of the Localisation Committee. In 1873 he was despatched to West Africa to take command of impending operations against the Ashanti. In a campaign notable for meticulous staff planning, proper concern for the health of the troops and a consequent bustling sense of urgency, Wolseley carved his way through the forest towards the Ashanti capital.

Following victories at Amoaful and Ordahsu, his troops razed Kumasi to the ground and turned again for the coast, leaving a chastised but brooding indigenous population to their rear. Showered with honours, a large cash gratuity which turned him into a wealthy man overnight, and the grateful thanks of both Houses of Parliament, Sir Garnet Wolseley had become a household name and a byword for military efficiency. Now, if everything was going well in military affairs, they were said to be 'all Sir Garnet'.

After a tour in South Africa as GOC Natal, he was promoted to lieutenant general and posted to Cyprus as high commissioner. In the aftermath of the Isandlwana disaster he was sent scurrying back to Natal to supersede the hapless Lord Chelmsford. Racing to catch up with the army and to add yet more laurels to his crown, he was thwarted by Chelmsford's timely and decisive victory at Ulundi. As the High Commissioner for South-Eastern Africa he busied himself with an ill-considered post-war settlement of Zulu affairs, the consolidation of British rule in the Transvaal and a swift military victory over the Pedi. In the summer of 1880 he returned to London as the Quartermaster-General. Within two years he had been appointed as the Adjutant-General, in effect the most important military figure in the land after the C-in-C. He was still relatively new in his appointment when Egyptian affairs started going badly awry.

Back in Alexandria things were coming to a head. By now something in the region of 180 guns, served by 2,000 gunners, had been mounted in the embrasures of Arabi's coastal defences. Admiral Seymour (known to his men as 'The Swell of the Ocean') attempted to negotiate a de-escalation of the crisis and secured an undertaking that work on the forts would stop. At the same time, like Her Majesty's Government and most other members of the Royal Navy, he had been deeply embarrassed by the political storm surrounding his alleged failure to protect the European community ashore. To some extent at least, the naval officers were now looking for an excuse to open fire. Despite the recent assurances to the contrary, the Egyptians played into the hands of the Royal Navy by continuing to improve their positions under the cover of darkness. A naval officer operating ashore was quick to detect that there was treachery afoot. For Seymour the threat to his ships had become intolerable. On 10 July he demanded the surrender of the forts within 24 hours. At the news of the British ultimatum, the French captains promptly put to sea and steamed for the sanctuary of Port Said. At first light the following morning HMS *Invincible* signalled her consorts to open fire.[3] The Egyptians stood to their guns and fought bravely but were outclassed by the formidable firepower of the Royal Navy. By the end of the day the forts had been pounded into submission, around 700 Egyptian soldiers and civilians had been killed, and Alexandria had again been given over to riot, looting and arson. The ammunition expended by the fleet included 3,198 shells, 16,233 rounds from Nordenfeldt machine guns,

7,100 from Gatlings and 10,160 rounds from Martini-Henrys. The loss aboard the ships ran to only 5 killed and 28 wounded, but, notwithstanding the disparity in the respective casualty rates, it had by no means been a one-sided exchange. HMS *Sultan* was hit no fewer than 27 times. Aboard HMS *Alexandra*, hit 24 times in all, Gunner Israel Harding distinguished himself by scooping a fizzing Egyptian shell from the deck and dropping it into a bucket of water, a deed which earned him the VC. Naval landing parties secured the burning city three days later. Prudently the Khedive had fled the capital and made his way to Alexandria to take refuge in his palace at Ramleh. Although he was soon safely under the protection of the Royal Navy, he was no longer in any practical sense the ruler of Egypt.

Exactly a month after the bombardment of Alexandria, Sir Garnet Wolseley stepped ashore on Egyptian soil. Another month after that, at dawn on 13 September 1882, he attacked Arabi's army in an entrenched position at Tel-el-Kebir. More than 2,000 Egyptians died in the battle, for a British loss of 57 killed and 380 wounded. Amongst Wolseley's battalion commanders was Colonel Cromer Ashburnham, elevated just before the battle to lead the brigade containing his reconstituted 3rd/60th Rifles.[4] No resistance was offered to the subsequent advance on Cairo. On 3 December an Egyptian court martial sentenced Arabi to death. By pre-arrangement with the British, Tewfik commuted the sentence to banishment for life. Arabi's exile in British Ceylon was both dignified and comfortable, but he would not be permitted to return home until 1901.

With Arabi's rebellion decisively crushed, it was Gladstone's view that the reconstitution of a viable and suitably acquiescent nation-state was a matter for the Khedive and his officials. But so long as Britain continued to have a vital strategic interest in Egypt, the weakened Tewfik could hardly be left to his own devices. The best way to guarantee the security of the short-cut to India was to get khedival Egypt back on its feet in a stable, economically liberalized and modernized form, for which British financial support and political advice would be essential. It would also be necessary to maintain a substantial British garrison until a reformed and loyal Egyptian Army could be pieced together. Major General Sir Evelyn Wood VC was appointed as its first Sirdar or C-in-C. The principal diplomatic figure, the Consul-General, would be Sir Evelyn Baring. Like it or not William Ewart Gladstone, the so-called 'grand old man' of British politics, was now more fully embroiled in Egyptian affairs than he cared to admit. Importantly he had yet to come to terms with one of the most essential regional facts of life – with Cairo, came Khartoum.

Even as Arabi was confronting Wolseley at Tel-el-Kebir trouble was brewing in the south. By the time Arabi stepped ashore in Ceylon, the Sudan had reached boiling-point.

'The Divinely Guided One'

Muhammad Ahmad ibn 'Abd Allah was born in 1844 near Dongola, on a small island in the Nile known as Labab. His father was a lowly boat-builder who, for all his outward humility, claimed ancient familial descent from Fatima, the daughter of the Prophet. While his brothers followed their father into the family business, Muhammad Ahmad devoted himself from the age of five to Islamic asceticism. He studied under the most prominent local scholars in his youth, became interested in Sufi teachings, joined the Sammaniyah order and by the age of 30 was held in some awe for his piety and fervour. Around 1870 his three brothers relocated their business to Aba, a wooded island on the White Nile about 160 miles south of Khartoum. While his kith and kin plied their trade, Muhammad Ahmad lived austerely with his wives, his children and but few worldly belongings. Periodically he travelled away from Aba to preach and by his mid-thirties had attracted a small following of disciples.

It was at Mesalamieh early in 1881 that one 'Abd Allah ibn Muhammad, the illiterate son of a Ta'a'ishah tribal soothsayer, first encountered the mysticism of Muhammad Ahmad. At the time 'Abd Allah happened to be engaged in an obsessive quest for *al Mahdi*, the Islamic messiah. It is said that on his deathbed 'Abd Allah's father had proclaimed the imminent arrival of the 'divinely guided one', but it is also true that there was a more general expectation of the Mahdi's coming abroad in the Sudan at this time. To the indigenous population it was not the 1880s *anno domini*, but rather the last fifth of the twelfth century and in Islamic terms there were ostensibly sound theological reasons to associate the age with the near approach of the 'end of times'. Although belief in the coming of a Mahdi was not directly enshrined in the Qur'an, it had nonetheless become an accepted tenet of Islamic theology on the back of references in the Hadith – the reported sayings of the Prophet. The role of the 'guided one' was therefore widely understood amongst the Sudanese tribes. He would be the divinely appointed successor to the Prophet. He would demand true adherence to the faith, unify Islam and restore justice to the people. In doing so he would vanquish the enemies of Allah, punish the apostasy of 'the Turks' and, his earthly mission accomplished, would then preside over the Day of Judgement.

The charismatic Muhammad Ahmad enthralled his newest admirer. While praying he often drifted into an impressive trance-like state. He shared what he claimed were the same physical distinguishing marks as the Prophet: between his front teeth a V-shaped gap; on his right cheek a mole or birthmark. For the captivated 'Abd Allah, his hero's ancestry eliminated any remaining doubt. His quest was over. In short order he became a particular favourite of the guided one and swiftly rose to pre-eminence amongst his entourage.

In some quarters it is suggested that it was 'Abd Allah who first proclaimed

Muhammad Ahmad. It seems more likely, however, that he was merely responding to Muhammad Ahmad's none too subtle hints, as it is clear that a considerable amount of subversive groundwork preceded the rebellion. In later life, as the successor *caliph* or *khalifa*, 'Abd Allah would write that he was the first man in whom his master had confided. Either way round Muhammad Ahmad was soon regaling his disciples with tales of visions in which the Prophet had appeared to him and endorsed his nomination as the guided one. He was instructed he said, first to conquer and then to pray at the mosques in Cairo, Jerusalem, Mecca and Constantinople. His followers were to be known as the *ansar* (literally 'helpers') just as the Prophet's had been. It all amounted to a heady, powerful concoction and on 29 June 1881 'the Mahdi' went public with an open proclamation of his divinity. He then despatched a series of letters to prominent tribal leaders in which he recounted his visions and went on to demand their allegiance. Before long compelling stories of the miracles of the Aba holy man were spreading like wildfire through southern Sudan. In Khartoum the 'infidel' government pricked up its ears.

The Mahdist Revolt

Raouf Pasha's first response was a measured and pragmatic one: he despatched a delegation of officials to Aba to meet and assess the Mahdi, and to open negotiations with him. No rapprochement proved possible. Instead the Governor-General's representatives were dismissed with a show of arrogant contempt. Sure enough, the forces of law and order responded to the slight. Abu Saud, an ADC to Raouf Pasha, landed from the steamer *Ismailia* at the head of a company of 200 Egyptian infantry,[5] just after sunrise on 11 August 1881. With only 300 poorly armed followers at his heels the Mahdi fell on the advancing Egyptian square. In what was set to become a familiar pattern of events, the troops panicked at the sudden onset of the faithful and allowed themselves to be broken up and scattered. Their timidity cost them more than 120 fatalities. Remarkably, although the Mahdi himself was slightly wounded in the shoulder, only a dozen of his followers lost their lives.

The next day, as the *Ismailia* was carrying the stunned survivors back downstream to Khartoum, the Mahdi proclaimed a jihad against Egyptian governance of the Sudan. With this he crossed with his followers to the west bank of the White Nile and, in a staged fulfilment of an old prophecy, spent the next 79 days marching south-west for the Nuba Mountains of southern Kordofan. After three weeks the Egyptian pursuit ran out of steam and turned for home. Heartened by this early success, new recruits flocked to the Mahdi's hideout at the foot of the Jebel Gadir. In an ill-conceived operation Rashid Bey, the Governor of Fashoda, led a force of 400 Egyptian infantry and 1,000 black

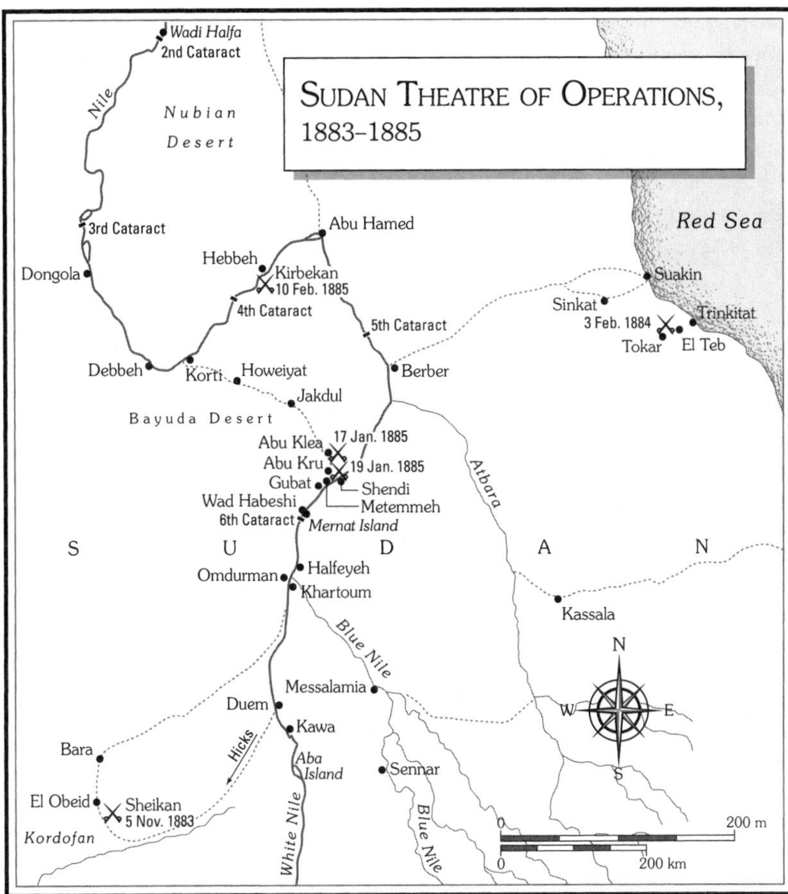

Shilluk tribal irregulars into the mountains. On the morning of 9 December Rashid Bey's parched troops came upon water at last and broke ranks to slake their thirst. Having fallen into disarray they were in no shape to resist a surprise attack.[6] What followed was little more than a bloody rout. Rashid's poor judgement cost him his life, while in Khartoum the fallout cost the Governor-General his job. Now whole clans of Kordofan desert-dwellers were throwing in their lot with the guided one. Gradually the rabble of *ansar* followers became an army of several thousand fighting men. Inevitably the menfolk came with a great host of non-combatant camp followers. In accordance with the strictures of Sharia law, the Mahdi began to govern the faithful with the firmest of hands.

With the rebellion assuming worrying proportions, the Egyptians began to concentrate a major military force which they were sure would put an end to the false prophet once and for all. In early May 1882 Yussuf Pasha, a Sudanese-born brigadier-general, entered the wooded Nuba foothills at the head of more than 4,000 men. For three weeks the army tramped fruitlessly over inhospitable and punishing terrain. On the night before the Battle of Massa it camped as usual inside the protection of a thorn-bush *zareba*, a traditional form of defence against human enemies and prowling animals. If Yussuf expected to fight a set-piece action in daylight, he was to be disappointed. Under the cover of darkness the *ansar* executed a silent approach march, which by daybreak had brought them within striking distance of a still slumbering bivouac. Surprise was total. Once again the Egyptian troops panicked and failed to mount a determined resistance. It is difficult to know how many men attacked the zareba that morning, but it was almost certainly in excess of 10,000 and may well have been half as many again. Two hundred of them lost their lives, but the Egyptian loss was virtually wholesale. Like Rashid Bey before him, Yussuf Pasha was cut down amidst the slaughter.

Over the course of the summer of 1882 the *ansar* roughly quadrupled in numbers, drawing in large part on the dreaded desert nomads of Kordofan, the Baggara,[7] until with the onset of autumn there were a number of separate Mahdist armies in the field. As it was now abundantly clear that the government's offensive capacity was spent, the time had come for the jihadists to seize the initiative. The remote and dismal garrison towns of El Obeid[8] and Bara would be their first major objectives. Far to the north Arabi Pasha had just been defeated at Tel-el-Kebir. With the Egyptian military in complete disarray, Khartoum's urgent pleas for reinforcement went unheeded.

The Siege of El Obeid

The garrison at El Obeid was under the command of the capable and determined General Mahmoud Said Pasha, the Governor of Western Sudan. Counting a strong contingent of loyalist irregulars under one Ahmad Bey Dafa 'alla, the governor had five guns and around 6,000 men at his disposal. Fortuitously a huge consignment of modern Remington rifles had arrived in June. The town stood on a barren scrub-covered plateau and was not at all well-protected. It was necessary for Mahmoud Said to improvise inner and outer rings of defence based on ditches and earthen ramparts sculpted from the excavated spoil. The barracks and other government buildings lay at the heart of the defences and offered a number of commanding rooftop fire positions. Despised by Sudanese townspeople as notoriously cruel and ruthless desert robbers, the Baggara (literally 'cattle people') were preceded by a less than flattering reputation. As Muhammad Ahmad's fundamentalist doctrines made no allowance for any concept of neutrality, the loyal and uncommitted alike either took refuge in crowded El Obeid or fled north for Khartoum. When the Mahdi's emissaries arrived to demand the surrender of the town, a resolute Mahmoud Said had them hanged from the nearest tree.

On 8 September the Mahdi ordered an all-out assault on the defences. Tens of thousands of men are said to have participated. Gravely hampered by their leader's naïve prohibition on the use of captured artillery pieces and firearms, the cowardly modern weapons of the godless, the *ansar* hurled themselves at the defences armed only with spears and swords. Despite the resultant carnage the Mahdists attacked again and again, clambering forward over great mounds of their dead and dying brethren. No great reliance can be placed on the rather excessive estimates of casualties, but it is certain that several thousand men were shot down around the perimeter. The garrison suffered around 290 casualties, indicating that there must have been serious hand-to-hand fighting at various points. The true significance of the Mahdist repulse lay not in the numerical slaughter, but in its moral effect on the faithful. Like all good cult leaders, Muhammad Ahmad had the answer. Had he not specifically told his commanders to attack from the east? And had they not failed so to do? He proceeded to berate them angrily for their poor sense of direction and arrant disobedience. On a more practical level, he now gave his assent to the use of captured weaponry. Despite the bloody reverse he had inflicted on the enemy, Mahmoud Said did not consider his force strong enough to launch a counter-attack. He did, however, mount a number of limited forays aimed at rounding up livestock. The Mahdi, for his part, determined to exercise more patience and starve El Obeid into submission. Sad to say, despite the garrison's protracted and heroic resistance, there was never any question of an enfeebled Khartoum despatching a relief column. As weeks grew into months, the daily ration grew ever smaller. By the New Year the siege was entering its fifth month and 30–40 defenders were dying of starvation each day.

There was, it seemed, some hope for Bara. Towards the end of September a relief column under Ali Bey Satfi, consisting of 850 mounted *bashi-bazouks* (irregular cavalry), two battalions of *fellaheen*[9] and a body of tribal irregulars, perhaps 3,000 men in all, set off from Duem to try and battle its way through to the town. The Mahdists had filled in all the wells on the road ahead, so that for seven consecutive days the force suffered great privation. The *ansar* finally fell upon the Egyptians near the village of El Kona. Ali Bey Satfi and most of his senior officers were killed in the early fighting, along with about a third of their men. It fell to a young captain to rally the survivors and beat back the attack. Although he led the battered remnants of the command safely into Bara, the enlarged garrison was forced to capitulate on 6 January 1883. The news came as a bitter blow to Mahmoud Said at El Obeid. Confronting starvation, desertions, crumbling morale and growing disloyalty amongst his hard-pressed troops, he was left with no alternative but to accept the ostensibly merciful terms proffered by the Mahdi. The surrender took place on 17 January. With this second capitulation 6,000 modern rifles and five more field guns fell into rebel hands. Some 3,500 members of the garrison had survived the siege and were duly assimilated into the rebel host. The Mahdi's mercy did not extend to Mahmoud Said himself, who was promptly beheaded. With his demise the whole of Kordofan fell under the sway of Muhammad Ahmad. In effect El Obeid was now the capital of a fundamentalist Islamic state – a state governed by an imam vested with absolute personal power, embracing both summary execution and mutilation.

Four weeks before the fall of El Obeid, Lieutenant Colonel J. D. H. Stewart CMG of the 11th Hussars arrived in Khartoum. His orders were to make an assessment of the military situation in the Sudan and report back to London. Needless to say he uncovered a less than rosy picture. The problem was no longer restricted solely to Kordofan: the southern provinces were now well and truly beyond the pale; Darfur in the west was in a state of anarchy; while on the coast a once prominent former slaver called Osman Digna was inciting jihad amongst the shock-haired Beja peoples of the region – the tribes soon to be immortalized by Kipling as the legendary 'fuzzy-wuzzies' of eastern Sudan.

Hicks Pasha

Although Tewfik was firmly back in control of Cairo he was no more able to support the hard-pressed Sudanese garrisons than the preoccupied Arabi had been. And yet he was anxious to defeat the Mahdi, if nothing else to bolster his own fragile domestic position. Prime Minister Gladstone was less than sympathetic to this particular khedival aspiration, insisting that the Sudan lay outside the British sphere of interest. If Tewfik was intent on victory in the Sudan, then it would have to be an Egyptian victory not a British one. But Egyptian military means were distinctly lacking: Arabi's rebellious regiments had been disbanded at London's insistence; Evelyn Wood's new model army was nowhere near ready to take the field; and the succession of disasters in Kordofan and Darfur had already cost the in-place garrisons more than 16,000 casualties.

If the Khedive could not secure the official services of the British Army, then he could at least hire in some of its expertise in the form of contract officers. Tewfik placed his trust in Colonel William Hicks,[10] a 53-year-old retired Indian Army man with a lingering aspiration for military greatness. A veteran of the Mutiny and of Napier's Abyssinian campaign, Hicks Pasha was immediately elevated to the rank of major general, and appointed chief of staff to General Suleiman Nyazi Pasha, his nominal superior as C-in-C Sudan. Hicks would be supported by a small team of British and European staff officers, who in the event proved to be of distinctly variable quality. Leaving his wife and children in Cairo, Hicks set off for Khartoum via Suakin on the Red Sea coast. In the meantime plans were laid for the Sudanese capital to be reinforced by 4,000 men conscripted from amongst the demoralized veterans of the old nationalist army. Few of Arabi's men went south willingly: significant numbers had to be kept shackled to prevent them deserting during the journey, whilst others resorted to acts of self-mutilation such as severing their trigger-fingers.

The new Governor-General, Ala el Din Pasha, welcomed Hicks and his officers to Khartoum on 4 March 1883. Having completed his assessment, Colonel Stewart was about to head north for Cairo, but tarried just long enough to share his gloomy prognostications with the newcomers. A major military expedition against El Obeid, he advised, could only end in disaster. It mattered not, as the Khedive had already set his heart on just such a course of action. History has been unkind to William Hicks, but to do justice to his memory it is important to acknowledge from the outset that he was no fool. Bennet Burleigh, an amiable Glaswegian Scot in his early forties, newly appointed to the staff of the *Daily Telegraph*, was no mean judge of a soldier:

> The acquaintanceship I formed at that time with him led me to conclude that no more gallant soldier or energetic officer could have been selected to send against the fanatics led by the False Prophet. He certainly did not underrate his enemy, nor the work before him; and it must have been because of some exceptional wrench of circumstances that any command under his leadership was forced to accept destruction at the hands of an uncivilized foe.[11]

With his scratch army in a generally parlous state, Hicks could not begin to think of mounting an offensive without first instigating some rigorous training. Over the ensuing four weeks his best efforts were hampered by the incompetence of his officers – including some of the Europeans – and by the constant interference of the ageing C-in-C. Despite these and countless other difficulties, Hicks took the field on 4 April with 200 Albanian *bashi-bazouks*, 3,200 *fellaheen*, 2 Nordenfeldt machine guns and a battery of 5 mule-drawn mountain guns.

The formal aim of the expedition was the dispersal of the Mahdist force threatening the town of Duem on the White Nile, but in truth the operation was as much a confidence-building jaunt as anything else. At Kawa, Hicks rendezvoused with 1,600 *fellaheen* under Brigadier-General Hussein Mazhar, before then pushing south to torch the old Mahdist dwellings on the island of Aba. The campaign reached its culminating point on 29 April, when around 5,000 *ansar* attacked Hicks at Marabieh. Forewarned of the coming assault by scouts and spies, he was given ample time to meet it in square. Armed with

Remington breech-loaders and clad in their loose white cotton summer uniforms and distinctive red *tarbooshes*, the six battalions of infantry did everything that had been asked of them. They kept their heads, fired low and, aided by the chattering Nordenfeldts, shot the charging *ansar* down in heaps. Hicks wrote, 'it is sickening to kill so many in such a one-sided affair, for we lost only seven, and five the day before, when they lost shoals.' Boosted by its workmanlike victory, the army marched back to Khartoum. In the light of subsequent events, it would seem likely that Hicks drew a number of false inferences from the ease of his victory.

Over the next ten weeks, when ideally Hicks should have been free to build on his early success, readying the army for greater challenges ahead, he was forced to contend instead with a string of counter-productive directives emanating from Suleiman Pasha and his aides. By July Hicks had become so disenchanted with the interference of his officious superior, that he telegraphed Cairo tendering his resignation. He allowed himself to be mollified by Suleiman's appointment as the Governor of Eastern Sudan, a measure which would remove him forthwith to Suakin, and by his own elevation to lieutenant general[12] and commander-in-chief – a promotion which attracted an additional £800 p.a., taking his salary to an impressive £2,000. Hicks might have done better to stick to his guns, but he was a man of honour and ultimately had no alternative but to confront his destiny on the road to El Obeid.

Disaster at Sheikan

On 9 September 1883 the Kordofan expedition left Khartoum, bound in the first instance for Duem, more than a hundred miles to the south. It took ten days to cover the distance. Such was the administrative disarray of the army that it was not until Hicks himself disembarked from a steamer, a full day after the arrival of the troops, that anybody thought of feeding and watering the baggage camels. The great size of the force, 10,000 fighting men in all, seemed hardly to matter for the regimental officers were manifestly incompetent and their men devoid of fighting spirit. From Hicks on down, not a single man amongst them expected their cause to prosper. The army was certain to be heavily outnumbered and now, with as many Remingtons in Mahdist hands as Egyptian ones, no longer possessed any sort of technological advantage. The 8,300 despondent conscript infantry made up the great bulk of the force, but there were also 100 chainmail-clad heavy cavalrymen, 400 *bashi-bazouks*, 800 Shaigiya tribesmen, 4 Krupp field pieces, 10 mountain guns and 6 Nordenfeldts. The ponderous baggage train consisted of 5,500 camels and more than 2,000 camp followers.[13] As four of his British officers had already been invalided back to Cairo, Hicks's staff consisted of just 8 combatant officers and 2 surgeons.[14] His chief of staff was Lieutenant Colonel Arthur Farquhar, late of the Grenadier Guards. There were also a number of European civilians present, including the well-known London correspondents Edmond O'Donovan and Frank Vizetelly, plus a handful of officers' servants.

Hicks's intent was to march on the great rebel encampment at El Obeid in search of a battle of decision. At least his plan had both simplicity and clarity of purpose to commend it, though quite what possessed him to imagine that he could ever win such a battle remains something of a mystery. The first major issue was the choice of route. Under orders from Cairo to accompany the army, Ala el Din Pasha had come up to Duem, and it was largely at his instigation that the most direct approach was shunned. Instead Hicks would strike south-west for Ageila and the Khor abu Habl, a swampy tributary of the White Nile which, it was argued, would be a much better-watered approach. From Ageila the army would march due west along the khor until it reached the villages of Rahad and Alluba. From Alluba it would swing north into the final leg. The route was almost twice as long as the more northerly alternative.

A second bone of contention was the security of the army's lines of communication. Hicks had intended to establish a series of fortified posts each protected by a detachment of 200 infantry, but Ala el Din advised him that the troops could not be relied upon to leave the sanctuary of their forts to escort supply convoys. Hicks convened a council of war to mull over the advice and found that the views of his senior officers largely coincided with those of the Governor-General. He was forced to abandon any idea of maintaining conventional lines of communication, and to advance instead with 50 days' rations carried aboard his carelessly tended baggage train. Hicks was not unaware of the risk he was taking:

> I am naturally very averse to this but if, as His Excellency assures me, it is a fact that the posts will not be supplied from the base at Duem, and supplies would not be forwarded through them, I should in garrisoning these posts only be weakening my force without gaining any advantage. I have therefore called a council, have had the matter explained, and requested the members to record their opinion.[15]

And so it was that Hicks's army disappeared into the wastes of Kordofan.

In the event the circuitous southern route proved to be not at all well-watered, the Khor abu Habl having all but dried up. For an agonizing month the column plodded on regardless, braving extremes of temperature and drinking only intermittently from desert wells and pools of rainwater. Mahdist scouts trailed its every move, while in an early example of psychological operations the route was littered with copies of an intimidating Mahdist proclamation:

> If your eyes are no longer blinded and you believe in God, the Prophet and the afterlife, then you will come and surrender to us. He who surrenders will be spared. But if you refuse to do so and cling to denial and reliance on your guns and powder, we have been assured by the Prophet himself that you will be killed just like those who came before you.[16]

Nor was this the only element in Muhammad Ahmad's cunning psychological campaign. A Mahdist deserter came in, spent the next few days with the army, and then disappeared into the night, only for the staff to discover subsequently that he had passed the time regaling the troops with tales of the Mahdi's miracles. The frequent rows between the patronizing know-all European officers and their apathetic Egyptian counterparts did little to enhance the fragile morale of the force. There was a string of desertions and intermittent harassment from the enemy. On 24 October the army struggled into Rahad, little more than a name on a map, where it encamped itself inside a thorn-bush zareba for the best part of a week. On Thursday 1 November the Mahdi brought his main force, a body of perhaps 50,000 men, within striking distance. For the next two days Hicks struggled on through difficult thorn country, his force deployed in a vast square, with the baggage and artillery sheltered in the centre. By day the army was harassed along its line of march, and by night its encampments were subjected to a galling rifle fire. With their constitutions failing them and their nerves in tatters, the ever fragile morale of the *fellah* infantry slumped to an all-time low.

By Sunday the cross-country going had become so difficult that movement in a single great square was no longer viable. From now on the troops marched in three smaller mutually supporting formations. On the morning of 5 November 1883,[17] Muhammad Ahmad finally unleashed his host. He had promised the *ansar* that 20,000 angels would lead them into battle, but it quickly became apparent that divine intervention would not be necessary. Faced with the usual heart-stopping Mahdist onslaught, the *fellaheen* deployed along the front face of the centre square were the first to lose their nerve. Similarly terrified and already responding badly to mounting pressure, the soldiers along the sides of the flanking squares began firing indiscriminately into the centre, hitting the enemy, their panic-stricken comrades and the baggage camels. It was not long before the other formations began fragmenting too. Within a matter of minutes the situation was worse than hopeless. With their stupefied infantry being butchered on all sides, Hicks Pasha and the other Europeans backed together to defend themselves with their swords and revolvers. Their resistance was spirited, heroic even, but they could no more turn back the tide than could Canute. The Battle of Sheikan,[18] in all its gory horror, lasted less than half an hour. The slaughter of course was wholly disproportionate – for the loss of only a few hundred men, the Mahdi had all but annihilated the Khedive's last army. It sometimes difficult to take in the awful violence of the Sheikan disaster, but cut away all but the essential details and we are left with a bloody massacre of close to 10,000 panic-stricken human souls, within half a square mile of ground, in safely less than 30 minutes.

For a time the road to Khartoum lay wide open but Muhammad Ahmad was nothing if not thorough in all his preparations, and felt no immediate compulsion to advance on the capital. Lieutenant Colonel Henry de Coetlogon, of whom Hicks had held a low opinion, had been left in command of the garrison. Having imposed a curfew on the jittery and heavily infiltrated civil populace, the colonel did his best to finish the city's landward defences, begun in June the previous year. It was fortunate that Khartoum's position at the confluence of the Blue and White Niles provided it with formidable natural moats on its other two sides. Although initially de Coetlogon had only 2,000 soldiers at his disposal, he was soon reinforced by the garrison of Fashoda and a number of other remote outposts, so that by January 1884 he could count on the services of more than 6,000 men.

Revolt in the East

Although it had taken place more than 500 miles from the Red Sea coast, the Battle of Sheikan gave the rebellion in the east all the encouragement Osman Digna could have hoped for. Open hostilities had begun three months earlier in August 1883, when Colonel Mohamed Tewfik Bey, the commander of the small Egyptian garrison at Sinkat, uncovered a proclamation calling the Beja tribes to arms. Confronted with such clear-cut proof of Osman's disloyalty, Tewfik Bey summoned him to Sinkat to explain himself. If the little town had any significance at all, it was as the 50-mile halt on the Suakin–Berber caravan-route, a journey of some 240 miles in all. If the garrison commander had expected a display of cringing humility from the self-confessed rebel leader, he could not have been caught more wrong-footed. Osman appeared with 1,500 well-armed Hadendawa at his heels and impertinently demanded the surrender of the town. Inevitably the parley swiftly turned to violence. The 100-man garrison raced to barricade their barracks and stood to their arms. Aided by a few dozen loyal citizens, the soldiers drove the enemy off with the loss of more than 60 lives, including two of Osman's nephews.[19] Osman himself was amongst the wounded and was forced to take to the hills.

A month later, having been reinforced in the interim, Tewfik Bey sallied forth in search of the rebels. On 9 September he was attacked whilst encamped near Handub, a small settlement located ten miles from the coast on the Suakin–Berber road.[20] The Egyptians stood their ground bravely, maintaining a heavy fire from the sanctuary of their zareba, until they had once again forced the withdrawal of the eastern rebels. For a while there was a stalemate, but Osman used the breathing space wisely to recruit amongst the Hadendawa and Amarar. At the end of October the new Governor of Suakin, the same General Suleiman Pasha who had driven Hicks to the brink of resignation, decided to reinforce Tewfik Bey with a further 160 men. Beyond Handub the road to Sinkat ran through a number of dangerous defiles in the hills, and it was in one of these predictable trouble-spots that the rebels sprang their ambush. The Beja spared the wailing widows and children of the slaughtered only in order to enslave them.

The other significant Egyptian outpost in the east was the penal settlement at Tokar. The town lay about 45 miles south-east of Suakin and around 20 miles from the coast, where it was serviced by a decidedly indifferent harbour known as Trinkitat. Osman was now strong enough to close up on Sinkat and Tokar and subject them both to a state of loose siege. In consultation with the military commander at Suakin, General Mahmud Tahir, and the British consul, a retired naval officer called Lynedoch Moncrieff, Suleiman Pasha decided to ship a force of 550 men down to Trinkitat under orders to effect the relief of Tokar. After a decade at sea from 1863–73, Moncrieff had gone on to serve with a unit of African levies in the Zulu War and had been slightly wounded at Ulundi. Indulging his highly developed sense of adventure once more, the British consul chose to accompany Mahmud Tahir and his men. The expedition came to grief on the morning of 4 November 1883, the day before Hicks Pasha met his end. The column was only 90 minutes' march out of Trinkitat and was approaching the wells at El Teb, when just a few hundred Beja warriors charged out of the scrub. The troops jostled into a jittery square and prepared to receive the customary onslaught. The front and right-face companies came into action promptly, shot straight, and at first succeeded in holding their own. On the left face, however, things quickly got out of hand. The catalyst was a rather improbable break-in by fewer than a dozen Hadendawa, who notwithstanding their pitifully small number wielded their swords to such terrible effect that all the *fellah* infantry in their vicinity immediately lost their nerve, threw down their weapons and ran hard for the coast. Whilst Mahmud Tahir was lucky enough to get away in the confusion, Moncrieff, 11 other officers and 142 other ranks were killed. Thereafter, boosted by their own local successes and heartened by the news from Sheikan, the rebels were sufficiently emboldened to raid the vicinity of Suakin on a nightly basis.

Once the Khedive and his advisers were over the shock of the Hicks disaster, their thoughts turned to the evacuation of Khartoum and the burgeoning problems in the east. There seemed to be much to commend a Suakin expedition. First, such an enterprise could secure the port and so safeguard Britain's strategic maritime interest in the Red Sea; second, it could attack and disperse the Beja rebels, thus checking the spread of insurrection; and third, with Osman Digna defeated, it would then be possible to open the Suakin–Berber road to government traffic and so permit the withdrawal of the Khartoum garrison to the coast. Just as there were three significant advantages inherent in the proposition, there were also three major stumbling blocks. First, water was often in extremely short supply on the Suakin–Berber caravan-route; second, the demoralized Egyptian military seemed to lack the capacity to disperse a crowd in the bazaar, let alone the warlike Beja; and third, the British would still not countenance the use of Evelyn Wood's new national army, which was less than a year old and earmarked for the maintenance of the khedival regime's domestic security.[21]

Baker Pasha

Once again the Egyptian authorities decided to meet their backyard colonial crisis by entrusting a scratch force to a contract officer. With the services of their own regular army denied them, they had no alternative but to turn to the gendarmerie. The chief of police was the controversial 'Major General' Valentine Baker, younger brother of the renowned explorer Sir Samuel. Val Baker's early career had showed signs of great promise. His first campaign service was with the 12th Lancers in South Africa, where he fought the Basutos at the Battle of Berea. Although he missed the better-known battles of the Crimean War, he was present at the cavalry action on the Tchernaya and at the fall of Sebastopol. In 1860, only a year after transferring into a major's vacancy in the 10th Hussars, Baker was promoted to lieutenant colonel and took command of the regiment. During the Franco-Prussian War of 1870, he accompanied the Prussians as a British military observer. He commanded his regiment for more than 13 years in all, during which time its reputation for efficiency was second to none. As a fashionable cavalry colonel Baker moved in the smartest social circles; the Prince of Wales was Colonel of the Regiment and became firm friends with its officer commanding. Then, on 17 June 1875, whilst serving as a staff colonel in Aldershot, Baker threw it all away in a moment of madness. His ruination could not have been more complete for not only was he dismissed Her Majesty's service, he was also detained at her pleasure.

The cause of the colonel's downfall was an alleged amorous advance in a first-class railway compartment. Baker's demeanour so startled the 22-year-old Miss Rebecca Dickinson that she threw open the door and, at great risk to life and limb, sought sanctuary on the top step outside – much to the consternation of a passing railwayman who ran to a nearby station and had the train stopped some little way down the line. Miss Dickinson's outraged family promptly pressed charges of indecent assault. Not unnaturally the country was scandalized and bayed for Baker's blood. He bore the disgrace manfully at least, electing at his trial not to utter a single word in his defence, and forbidding his lawyers even to cross-examine Miss Dickinson. Witnesses were few and far between, though two men in the next compartment testified that Baker's clothing had been dishevelled when the train came to a halt. Given that the victim had prevented herself from falling by clinging on to her 'assailant' through the open window, this was hardly surprising. In the event the prosecution managed to sustain two of the three offences of which Baker stood accused – those of common assault and indecent assault. Whatever the truth of the matter, it was to cost him a £500 fine, his commission, his future and 365 days of his life. His offer to resign his colonelcy was spurned on the specific say-so of the Queen, who insisted he be cashiered.

Baker fled into self-imposed exile on his release from prison and had been in the service of the Ottoman Empire ever since. In the Russo-Turkish war of 1877–8 he rose to command a division and distinguished himself by holding back the Russians in a brave rearguard action at the Battle of Tashkessan. After the war he was appointed to an administrative post in Armenia. In the aftermath of the Arabi rebellion he sought the Sultan's permission to go to Egypt to seek a role in reforming the Army. At first Baker had rather naively aspired to the post of Sirdar, but when, at the Queen's insistence, the War Office flatly refused to countenance the Khedive's British advisers serving under so notorious a figure, he was forced to content himself with command of the gendarmerie.

Whilst it was true that many former soldiers had joined the police and that the force was as well-armed and equipped as any Egyptian Army unit, it was not by any stretch of the imagination fit to undertake major military operations. Given that the Suakin expedition was to be entrusted to a third-rate force, the senior players in Cairo were forced to concede that their more ambitious strategic goals, such as opening the road to Berber, would almost certainly have to go onto the back-burner. For the time being Baker would have to content himself with keeping Suakin safe, a far from difficult task as the heart of the town was situated on an island in the harbour. Sir Evelyn Baring for one was in no doubt as to the fighting fettle of the gendarmerie. Furthermore he was only too keenly aware that Baker aspired to rehabilitation in the service of the Crown. For all that it amounted to little more than a pipe-dream, Baring sensed that Baker's thwarted ambition had the potential to make him dangerous:

> It was with the utmost hesitation that I consented to the despatch of General Baker's force to Suakin. I was under no delusion as to the quality of the troops which he would command. Moreover, I feared that Baker Pasha would be led into the committal of some rash act. He was a gallant officer, and it was certain that his military instincts would revolt at inaction, more especially when Sinkat and Tokar were being beleaguered

> in the immediate vicinity of Suakin. There were also special reasons which made me doubtful as to the wisdom of sending General Baker. He had been obliged to leave the British army [*sic*] under circumstances on which it is unnecessary to dwell. He was ardently attached to his profession, and it was well known that the main object of his life was to regain his position in the British army, which he hoped to do by distinguished service in the field. Before he left Cairo, I impressed upon him strongly that the necessity of avoiding any disaster must come before all other considerations, and that if he did not feel sufficient confidence in his troops to advance, he must remain and defend Suakin, however painful the consequences might be as regards the garrisons of Sinkat and Tokar. General Baker expressed to me his entire confidence in these views, and promised that he would act up to them.[22]

Although Baring had taken special steps to curtail Baker's exuberance, he had made no allowance for the offended sensitivities of the superseded Egyptian pashas. Such is human vanity that when Generals Suleiman Nyazi and Mahmud Tahir heard that Baker was under orders for Suakin, they decided to mount another sortie into the interior with the idea of redeeming the situation in advance of the Englishman's arrival. It was precisely the same manifestation of wounded military pride that had driven Sir George Colley to the summit of Majuba. The instrument of the pashas' redemption was to be the high-grade battalion of Sudanese blacks under Major Kassim Bey which had been hurriedly despatched to Suakin from Massawah further down the Red Sea coast. On the morning of 2 December 1883, with the advanced guard of Baker's force already at anchor in the harbour, Kassim Bey sallied south-west from Suakin to clear the Tamanib road with 500 Sudanese infantry, 200 *bashi-bazouks* and a mountain gun. At noon something around 3,000 Beja swarmed out of the heat haze to confront his column. Although the Sudanese infantry companies did their best to form up, they were thrown into confusion by the disorderly flight of the irregular horse. The resultant disarray gave the fearsome Beja the fleeting opportunity they needed. In a trice they were in amongst the infantry, carving men down with their swords. The ferocity of their onset broke up Kassim's battalion almost immediately. Only 2 officers and 33 men would survive the ensuing massacre to make it back to Suakin.[23]

After this latest disaster Baring and Wood decided it would be prudent to follow up Val Baker's oral instructions with a set of written orders from the Khedive himself. In a letter dated 17 December 1883, Tewfik wrote:

> The mission entrusted to you, having as its object the pacification of the regions designated in my above-mentioned order, and the maintenance, as far as possible, of communication between Berber and Suakin, I wish

> you to act with the greatest prudence on account of the insufficiency of the forces placed under your command . . .
>
> If, in the event of the situation improving, you should consider an action necessary, I rely on your prudence and ability not to engage the enemy except under the most favourable conditions . . . My confidence in your prudence enables me to count upon your conforming to these instructions.

Prudence, it seemed, was very definitely the order of the day. Baker landed at Suakin just in time for Christmas. On 11 January Sir Evelyn Wood wrote to him on behalf of the Khedive imposing even tighter constraints:

> 1. All that portion of your instructions which gives you discretion to open the Suakin–Berber route westward of Sinkat by force, if necessary, is cancelled.
> 2. If it is absolutely necessary to use force in order to extricate the garrisons of Sinkat and Tokar you can do so, provided you consider your forces sufficient and you may reasonably count on success. The enforced submission of the men who have been holding out at these two places would be very painful to His Highness the Khedive; but even such a sacrifice is better, in his opinion, than that you and your troops should attempt a task which you cannot fairly reckon to be within your power.
> 3. You are directed to continue to use every effort possible to open the route up to Berber by diplomatic means.[24]

As Baring had always suspected would be the case, the chief of police was not the man to disregard the increasingly desperate pleas from Sinkat and Tokar. Nor was Baker slow to spot the ambiguity of Wood's second paragraph and the freedom of action that ultimately it implied. The more he thought about it, the more he convinced himself that the evacuation of Tokar would be a relatively easy proposition. After all the town was less than 20 miles from the coast, and what was 20 miles but a day's march? In and out in 72 hours at worst – what could possibly go wrong?

On 28 January 1884 Baker's naval transports anchored at Trinkitat. A small flotilla of dhows, rafts and whalers began ferrying the troops to the shore, but it was a painfully slow process and disembarkation would take the best part of two days. The general began his campaign by securing Trinkitat with a hastily raised earthwork. In between the landing stage, on the seaboard side of a peninsula, and the mainland, was a salt lagoon of more than two miles in width. Flogging through the mud was a physically exacting journey at the best of times, but for heavily laden troops, manhandling artillery pieces and egging on overloaded baggage animals, it was distinctly punishing. In places the unwary could sink up to their chests, though generally the clinging morass was about a foot deep. It ended along the general line of a low ridge and it was here that a second redoubt known as Fort Baker was thrown up. By the time the fighting troops had assembled around the fort and gathered themselves for a further advance, it was 2 February. That afternoon Baker telegraphed Cairo to report that he intended to march to the relief of Tokar in the morning. He closed his message with the reassuring phrase 'There is every chance of success.'[25] No doubt he had been buoyed up by the presence of a few lion-hearts like Colonel Fred Burnaby of the Blues, but in reality there were no military factors in play to support such a wildly optimistic assessment.

Burnaby was one of the great heroic figures of a heroic age.[26] Now 42 years old and noted for his giant stature, his dash and his sense of adventure, he stood over six feet four inches tall and as a result of a predilection for boxing, weight training and sport of all kinds was as strong as an ox. On one occasion a horse dealer brought a pair of Shetland ponies to Windsor Castle for the Queen's approval. Bored as captain of the guard and fancying himself no mean judge of horseflesh, Burnaby had the ponies brought up to his quarters on the first floor. They seemed happy enough with the stairs on the way up but, when the inspection was over, steadfastly refused to go down again. Legend has it that Burnaby scooped an animal under each arm and carried them downstairs himself. In his thirties he had undertaken a series of daring escapades, including travelling the Sudan, where he met and interviewed Gordon, and, in the winter of 1875/6, making a solo foray into Central Asia. Because the journey was conducted in open defiance of Tsarist Russia, the then Captain Burnaby's account of his adventures, *A Ride to Khiva*, became a best seller and established him as a public figure. On another spell of long-leave he got himself involved in the Russo-Turkish War of 1877, ostensibly as the representative of a London-based humanitarian organization. This time he was accompanied by his trusty batman Radford, a man-mountain even bigger than his master. It was during the course of this campaign that he befriended Val Baker, by then a leading Turkish general. A close friend of Lord Randolph Churchill, Burnaby unsuccessfully contested a Birmingham constituency for the Conservatives in the general election of 1880 – the election that swept Gladstone back into power. The following year he took command of the Blues. It was hardly to be expected that the good colonel did anything too mundane with his spare time. Amongst his hobbies he counted long-distance ballooning. Famously he completed a successful solo crossing of the English Channel in March 1882.

All things considered, the ostentatious Burnaby was far from being the Duke of Cambridge's favourite cavalry colonel. Now, prompted by an anxious letter from Val Baker's wife Fanny, and without any form of official sanction from the War Office, Burnaby slipped away on yet another long-leave to join up with his old friend at Suakin. The trusty George Radford having died only two days after his master's return from the Russo-Turkish War, Burnaby's new travelling companion was a Private Henry Storey. Travelling across Europe by train, they took passage for Suez at Brindisi. Suakin was not entirely new to the colonel: during the course of his Sudanese adventure of 1874, he had travelled the overland caravan-route to Berber and thence by steamer to Khartoum. Dressed in a Norfolk-tweed jacket and equipped with an array of private firearms, including a double-barrelled shotgun, he would serve with Baker's cavalry in the technical capacity, if the War Office was to ask, of 'gentleman-volunteer'.

The First Battle of El Teb

The 'army' that took the field at 7.30 a.m. on the morning of 3 February 1884 consisted of 490 cavalry, around 3,000 infantry of various kinds, 2 Krupp field guns, 2 rocket troughs and 2 machine guns. Although the two battalions of black Sudanese were regarded as promising, the hard reality was that they were next to untrained and all but incapable of shooting straight. The jittery temperament of the gendarmerie battalions could be taken as read, and there was precious little evidence to suggest that the cavalry would be any more reliable. A strong body of black irregulars had mustered at Suakin at the behest of Zubeir Pasha,[27] an exiled slaver who had once been one of the most powerful figures in the Sudan. Despite a request from Sir Evelyn Baring that Zubeir be allowed to leave Cairo to participate in the expedition, London had vetoed the idea in order to avoid provoking the anti-slavery lobby. This was not the end of the Zubeir debate, but for the time being at least his services had been spurned. In the meantime the irregulars had been disheartened by the absence of the man they had agreed to serve.[28]

***Table 7:* Baker's Force at First El Teb**[29]

Mounted gendarmerie	300
Turkish bashi-bazouk cavalry	150
European mounted police	40
Alexandria gendarmerie battalion	560
Cairo gendarmerie battalion	500
Massowah Sudanese battalion	450
Senhit Sudanese battalion	421
Turkish infantry battalion	429
Zubeir's irregulars	678
Egyptian artillery	128
2 x Krupp field guns, 2 x Gatling guns, 2 x rocket troughs	

For the Sudan it was a far from typical morning. After Baker had been on the road for about an hour, it rained heavily for about 30 minutes. The column was moving across a relatively flat desert plain in the direction of the wells at El Teb, when the first signs of enemy activity were detected. Flat or not, there was a good deal of mimosa scrub along the axis, making the enemy's precise dispositions uncertain. The infantry and gendarmerie battalions were advancing in echelon, each of them deployed in column of companies, with parties of *bashi-bazouk* cavalry under Lieutenant Colonel Giles thrown out to the front and flanks. The guns, 300 baggage camels and an assortment of camp followers were trailing along at the rear. There had been daily drills at Suakin, during which the infantry had repeatedly rehearsed forming square. It may not have won the unreserved approbation of a British sergeant-major, but both the *fellaheen* and the Sudanese had learned to jostle themselves into roughly the right places, in something close to an acceptably quick time. Perhaps it was this rudimentary level of tactical proficiency that had inspired the reckless glimmer of hope in Baker's heart. The battle plan called for the infantry to form three squares in echelon – the gendarmerie units in the centre, the Turkish battalion to the left, and the two Sudanese battalions operating in concert on the right. Unfortunately, because most of the British officers were forward with the cavalry screen, the neglected infantry failed to keep station and soon blended into an amorphous mass of companies.

A line of flags and some long-range rifle fire from a low ridge in front served notice that a fight was in the offing. In response Baker promptly brought one of his Krupp field guns into action. Then a small party of Beja mounted on camels appeared from the scrub on the right. Baker ordered that a troop of the mounted gendarmerie be deployed to head them off, but such was the excitement amongst the Egyptians that the entire mounted regiment went charging off in hot pursuit. Fred Burnaby set off with one of Baker's aides, Major Harvey, to try and bring things under control, but it took a two-mile gallop just to catch up with them. As the regiment was making its way back towards the infantry, a mere trio of enemy horsemen charged over a nearby ridge to do battle. Instead of halting to face them, the Egyptians lost their nerve and rode off at the gallop. To Burnaby it seemed as if they were incapable of even putting up a fight:

> One of their Arab opponents rode deliberately into a squadron and I saw him cut down the officer in command, who made no attempt to defend himself though his sword was drawn. The Arab cut down two more men, who equally did not defend themselves and would doubtless have single-handed demolished the whole of the Egyptian cavalry if a pistol bullet had not stopped his work of destruction.[30]

With most of the mounted troops already seized by panic, there was nothing Burnaby or Harvey could do to prevent them galloping at full tilt towards the infantry.

To the left front Colonel Giles and the *bashi-bazouks* had also come unstuck. Having given chase to a party of enemy horsemen, they soon ran into a large body of Hadendawa, well concealed in dense scrub. A sudden ambush can shock and stupefy the best of troops but for the ill-disciplined Turkish irregulars, motivated largely by the prospect of booty, it was altogether too much. They were routed in moments and, like the cavalry on the right, fled back towards Baker's main body.

Already hundreds more Beja were bounding through the scrub in support of their brethren. It was time for the infantry to form square and come into action. The Turkish and Sudanese battalions had sufficient presence of mind to put into practice what they had learned at Suakin and to struggle into some semblance of order. Even so some of the men were already firing wildly, some of their ill-judged shots finding their mark amongst the routed cavalry on the right. In the centre, however, things were going badly awry for the police; in the military vernacular of the day the Alexandria men were seen to be in a state of 'funk'. John Cameron, the correspondent of the *Evening Standard*, reported that:

> . . . three sides were formed after a fashion, but on the fourth side two companies of the Alexandria Regiment, seeing the enemy coming on leaping and brandishing their spears, stood like a panic-stricken flock of sheep, and nothing could get them to move into their place.

The native drivers with the baggage train contributed to the confusion by trying to usher their camels through the disordered rear face of the police square. With the enemy closing fast, many of the frightened cavalrymen also began jostling their horses through the ranks of the harassed infantry to seek what they imagined would be the sanctuary of a rock-steady fighting square.

If a square was to hold its own, all its business had to be transacted in an atmosphere of calm resolve. It was already far too late for that. Most of the gendarmes were hysterical with a combination of panic, fear and confusion. Their rifle fire was almost wholly ineffective and did nothing to keep the Beja in check. Cameron observed that many of them fired into the air. The Krupp and Gatling guns were in the centre of the front face under the command of a British captain called Walker, but such was the disarray that neither the guns nor the machine guns seem to have fired a single shot.[31] In next to no time the fearsome desert fighters had come to close quarters, hacking about them with such fury that the terrified police battalions folded in seconds. Some men were cut down instantly, others dropped to their knees and begged forlornly for mercy; but most just turned and ran – some towards the nearest cover, some for the coast, but many towards the Turks and the Sudanese, whose squares were promptly disordered unto destruction. With the exception of the European police and the handful of British contract officers, including Captain Walker and the principal medical officer, Dr Armand Leslie, who rallied around one of the guns, Baker's force was no longer even defending itself. The collapse of the infantry was so sudden that few of the British officers had extricated themselves from the forward area by the time it took place.

Riding back towards the dust and chaos that had once been an infantry brigade, Burnaby could barely believe his eyes: 'The sight was one never to be forgotten some four thousand men running pell-mell for their lives with a few hundred Arabs behind them spearing everyone within reach.' He was able to bypass the massacre, outstrip the pursuit and make his way safely to Trinkitat. Just ahead of him was Private Storey, who had been thrown from the saddle, but somehow clung to the neck and collar-chain of his terrified horse to be dragged clear of the massacre. Storey was so exhausted that, when Burnaby finally caught up with him, he had to be physically heaved into the saddle. Baker and his staff drew their revolvers and reined in on the edge of the scrimmage as mere onlookers. The white summer uniforms of the gendarmerie served only to accentuate the bloody horror unfolding before their eyes. Major Harvey managed to save his wounded European servant by dismounting, throwing the man across the back of his horse, and then running alongside himself. Burnaby's Nubian cook saved himself by clinging to a horse's tail. Of 3,650 officers and men who had set out for Tokar, a total of 112 officers, including 16 Europeans, and 2,250 other ranks were cut down and killed.[32] Given the scale of the loss it is astonishing to reflect that only 1,200 Beja are thought to have participated in the battle.

Baker and his surviving staff officers married up with the handful of *bashi-bazouks* who had stood by Colonel Giles and cut their way out. Back at Trinkitat there was chaos on the beach as terrified survivors scrambled to board the handful of boats that happened to be inshore. Burnaby wrote that they were fired on by some of the Egyptian sailors. In the absence of a hard-pressed pursuit, Baker and the other British officers succeeded in restoring a modicum of order, only it must be said at gunpoint. They spent the rest of the day trying to re-embark as much military materiel as possible. The next day Baker drafted the telegram to Cairo that he knew would mark the end of his second and last military career.

> I marched yesterday morning with 3500 men towards Tokar; we met the enemy, after two hours march, in small numbers, and drove them back about two miles nearer the wells of Teb [*sic*]. On the square being only threatened by a small force of the enemy, certainly less than 1000 strong, the Egyptian troops threw down their arms and ran, carrying away the

> black troops with them, and allowing themselves to be killed without the slightest resistance. More than 2000 were killed. They fled to Trinkitat. Unfortunately the Europeans who stood suffered terribly. The troops are utterly untrustworthy except for the defence of earthworks.[33]

The news of the El Teb disaster caused a public furore in London. Gladstone's political opponents asserted that he bore direct responsibility for the massacre. The Prime Minister's cause was not aided by a number of careless public references to the Mahdist uprising in which he all but recognized it as a heroic liberation struggle. It was hardly a measured viewpoint for a Liberal premier and served only to demonstrate just how little Gladstone understood of Islamist dogmas. Those who better understood the orient tried to explain just how repressive a Mahdist regime would be: one of the first consequences would be the restoration of the slave trade; arbitrary killing would occur as a matter of course; and in next to no time personal liberty and freedom of thought, conscience and expression would become irrelevances. Egyptian governance of the Sudan might not be up to much, said the experts, but a theocratic regime with a self-anointed Mahdi at its head would be infinitely worse. For the time being Gladstone remained unconvinced, but even he could not shirk the overriding strategic importance of the short-cut to India. If the Red Sea was to be kept secure, then the British military would after all have to play a direct role at Suakin. As ever the first resort was the Royal Navy. Admiral Sir James Hewett's warships and marines moved to protect the port, until Major General Sir Gerald Graham VC could deploy at the head of two infantry brigades and two cavalry regiments. To all intents and purposes the sacrifice of Val Baker's gendarmerie had been entirely unnecessary. In the meantime the British political establishment did its best to divest itself of all blame, as exemplified in a speech made by Lord Derby:

> We may have known – we did know – that the composition of General Baker's force was not very good, but I venture to affirm that nobody supposed that a body of men calling itself a regular army would run away, almost without a shot fired, from half its own number, or less than half, of savages under no discipline whatever. It is a thing I should imagine, new in war. It is a misfortune, but it is a misfortune for which we, sitting in London, can hardly hold ourselves responsible.[34]

Five days after the Baker disaster, Colonel Mohamed Tewfik Bey decided to abandon Sinkat and cut his way out across the desert. At dawn on 8 February he spiked his guns, set fire to his reserve ammunition and formed his 400 soldiers into a fighting square, with the women and children of the garrison sheltered inside. Next to nothing is known of the ensuing action, except that Tewfik Bey put up a brave fight but did not get more than a mile and a half from the town.

Only 30 non-combatants and six of the soldiers survived. The garrison of Tokar capitulated a fortnight later, unaware that by the end of the month Sir Gerald Graham would have several thousand British regulars ashore at Trinkitat.

Gordon Pasha Returns

In response to the Hicks disaster of almost three months earlier, and a few days before Valentine Baker marched for Tokar, General Gordon arrived in Cairo, cast already in the roles of Governor-General of the Sudan, hero of the hour and miracle-worker. He was certainly the man of the moment. In early January, little suspecting that brother Val was about to hit the newspapers in dramatic style once again, Sir Samuel Baker had written to *The Times* to urge that Gordon be sent to Khartoum. Following an interview with Gordon himself (in which he seriously underestimated the true extent of the Mahdist threat), the *Pall Mall Gazette* picked up the refrain. Before long the clamour in the national press was all but universal. Send Gordon.

The general was seen off from Charing Cross by the Duke of Cambridge and Lieutenant General Lord Wolseley, now the Adjutant-General. It was late in the day and as usual Gordon was travelling light. Legend has it that Wolseley was obliged to scramble around a number of the smarter London clubs borrowing sovereigns from members, so that Gordon and his chief of staff could depart with £300 in gold to cover their expenses. The general's travelling companion was none other than Colonel J. D. H. Stewart, whose doom-laden but realistic reports had offered little hope for a revival of Egyptian authority in the Sudan. Gordon had planned to travel direct to Khartoum via Suakin but was intercepted en route at Port Said by Sir Evelyn Wood, who advised him that he was required (not unnaturally) to report to Cairo first. It was the first time Wood and Gordon had seen each other since the Crimea.[35] In the capital Gordon was received in turn by the Khedive, Prime Minister Nubar Pasha and Sir Evelyn Baring. Embarrassingly, Gordon had to begin his khedival audience with an apology for a recent public insult.

Gordon knew only too well that from Whitehall's perspective his mission was a gesture, a political expedient to get Gladstone off the Sudanese hook. Publicly he was once again Governor-General of the Sudan, the regional supremo, but in private he had been charged by Tewfik with evacuating the Egyptian regime and installing credible Sudanese self-government in its stead. Gordon concluded that he would need a local strong-man in his pocket, a Muslim authority figure fit to contend with Muhammad Ahmad. Surely, he reasoned, the exiled slaver Zubeir Pasha, to whom many of the rebels had once owed their allegiance, would give the Mahdi a run for his money. Although Zubeir agreed to meet with the new Governor-General, it quickly became obvious that he attributed the blame for the judicial execution of his son to Gordon personally and that he was in no mood to let bygones be bygones. Aware on the basis of his recent discussions with London that the involvement of a notorious figure like Zubeir would provoke a political storm amongst the British liberal elite, Baring was forced to veto the proposal, much to Gordon's ire. That evening when he learned that Wood had sided with the doubters, Gordon shunned the Sirdar's hospitality like a spoilt child: 'You were one of those who voted against Zubair [*sic*]; I won't sit down to table with you. I'll have a plate of soup in my rooms.'[36] Gordon and Stewart left Cairo on the evening of 26 January 1884, by which time the El Teb disaster was only just over a week away. In the meantime the general remained convinced in his own mind that the Zubeir option was the only game in town.

Still struggling for tenable strategies when he arrived at Berber, Gordon resolved to put Muhammad Ahmad's mettle to the test. In a long flattering letter accompanied by gifts, he offered a pathetic political compromise. Gordon harboured no hostile intent and hoped that they could meet in friendship so that he could appoint Muhammad Ahmad as the sultan of Kordofan – so ran the ill-judged letter. More than anything else it betrayed just how little Gordon yet understood of his protagonist. A reply would doubtless take some weeks. In the meantime the Governor-General would work on winning the neutral population over to the idea of a self-governing Sudanese state – a state he still intended to hand over to Zubeir. It was now that Gordon decided to expose the contents of his second and secret khedival *firman* (decree), the order instructing him to withdraw the Egyptian regime. On the morning of 12 February, having pondered the matter all night, he woke his chief of staff at 5.00 a.m. to tell him what he intended to do. At 2.00 p.m. he read his orders to an audience of government officials and tribal elders. Subsequently he would also have the *firman* read aloud as a public proclamation in Metemmeh. These were serious misjudgements and before the day was out Stewart at least had recognized it. The following day he wrote to Baring, 'Gordon has taken his leap in the dark and shown his secret firman. How it will act, and what will be the result, goodness only knows.'[37] Whilst there were still plenty of Sudanese who regarded Muhammad Ahmad as a false prophet, there could be no denying his burgeoning military might. If the government was not going to dig in and defend the principal towns on the Nile, what point could there be in remaining loyal? Gordon was all but burning his bridges behind him. When the news reached the *ansar* they were ecstatic – the 'Turks' intended to cut and run. And so Muhammad Ahmad's standing soared still higher – everything he had promised was coming true.

Gordon was not yet done with disseminating 'good news' to the citizens of Berber. He next proceeded to announce that he was rescinding the 1877 undertaking to emancipate the slaves by not later than 1888. But if the Sudan was to be self-governing, what did a dated Egyptian proclamation matter anyway? Without British or Egyptian involvement in the country there would be no question of emancipation and, as Gordon had only just announced, the 'Turks' were going home. It was a foolish and unnecessary thing to say. So far removed was it from his widely known personal values that it served only to accentuate the government's growing desperation. Worse, when the news reached London, Gordon's strongest supporters became enemies overnight, and the one thing he needed most was the undivided support of the British public. If there had been serious military disasters aplenty, events at Berber quickly turned into a political disaster fit to match any of them.

Gordon left Berber aboard the steamer *Tewfikieh* and disembarked in Khartoum amidst scenes of great rejoicing on 18 February 1884. Within days Henry de Coetlogon had gone, leaving Gordon, Stewart and Frank Power, the acting British consul, as the only Englishmen in Khartoum. It did not take the trio long to assess that an evacuation of up to 15,000 soldiers, officials and camp followers by steamer and *nuggar* (Nile sailing boat) would take not weeks, but more than six months. Even this extended timeline was predicated on the boats disgorging their passengers only as far north as Berber. The Nile was almost certain to be severed as a viable line of retreat long before such a protracted operation could be completed. And how was Khartoum to be kept from the enemy, if week by week its garrison was getting smaller? Retreat, it turned out, had never been an option. If only London and Cairo had bothered to do the logistic mathematics. Although Baring had done his best to persuade Whitehall that the Zubeir option should be adopted, it had now been definitively ruled out. On 12 March 1884 the Mahdist advanced guard arrived before the city walls and encamped itself to the south. Four days later Gordon's Egyptian commanders attacked the rebels, but were defeated with heavy casualties and the loss of a gun.

Sir Gerald Graham's intervention in the eastern Sudan was the last real card in Gordon's hand. British troops engaged Osman Digna and the Beja at the Second Battle of El Teb on 29 February 1884, and again on 13 March at the Battle of Tamai, both actions resulting in hard-won British victories. Amongst the officers killed at El Teb was Quartermaster Wilkins of the 60th Rifles, last encountered at Ingogo as a sharp-shooting sergeant-major, whilst amongst the wounded were Val Baker and Fred Burnaby. Graham and Gordon were both of the view that the Suakin expedition should be used to open the overland line of communication from the coast to Berber. Berber was only four or five days from Khartoum by steamer, and the early presence of British troops on the Nile was sure to undermine the rebel cause and encourage the loyalists. But with the Beja checked and Suakin safe, Gladstone was having none of it. Gordon had his orders

– evacuate. On the instructions of Her Majesty's Government, Graham and his troops sailed from Suakin in the first week of April. With the fall of Berber on 28 May, Khartoum was effectively cut off from the outside world. Gordon dug in with a garrison of 1,400 Egyptian infantry, 3,100 black Sudanese infantry, 1,900 Cairo *bashi-bazouks*, 2,330 Shaigiya tribal irregulars of questionable loyalty, and some 700 volunteers drawn from amongst the 34,000 townspeople.[38] Although many of the steamers mounted small brass guns in pairs, either fore-and-aft or amidships, this left only a dozen other pieces, a mixture of 2.5-inch screw-guns and Krupp field guns, for the city's fixed defences.

Khartoum lay on the south bank of the Blue Nile, directly opposite the inhabited island of Tuti, and about a mile and a half east of the White Nile. Tuti was more than three miles in length and roughly triangular in shape. For most of its length it was about a mile wide, but at its easternmost tip it tapered to a narrow headland where the Blue Nile branched down its long sides. The White Nile ran south-west to north-east across the two-mile base of the Tuti river triangle. Whilst some form of amphibious assault on Khartoum could not be entirely ruled out, the flotilla of 15 armed steamers provided a powerful deterrent to any such operation, and in any case the confluence of the two rivers north-west of Khartoum meant that the city was inherently more vulnerable from the south. Gordon turned his mind to improving the landward defences, the so-called South Front, which ran between the east bank of the White Nile and the south bank of the Blue Nile. The arcing line of defence lay about a mile from the suburbs and consisted of a deep ditch and an earthen rampart raised from the excavated spoil. There were four protruding bastions, which permitted guns to be mounted in defilade to the walls, and three gates, two to the south and one to the east.

The city was protected by five key outworks. The fort at Omdurman was located across the river, three miles west of the city. It was garrisoned by around 250 men and commanded the White Nile. Fort Mukran and Fort Buri[39] were both located on the south bank of the Blue Nile, west and east of the city limits respectively. The garrison of Fort Mukran was able to command Tuti Island, lend long-range artillery support to Omdurman, and shield the western suburbs. Fort Buri commanded the Blue Nile and served to anchor the left flank of the South Front. The North Fort, typically garrisoned by 700 men,[40] lay directly across the Blue Nile from the city, where it commanded the fork in the river and denied the north bank to enemy batteries. The White Nile was subject to significant seasonal variation which meant that in the summer Fort Mukran would sit squarely beside the confluence of the swollen rivers, whilst in the winter the point of confluence might occur anything up to two miles north-west of the fort. This meant that the low-water weak point would be on the extreme right flank of the South Front. The garrison's last bastion would be the

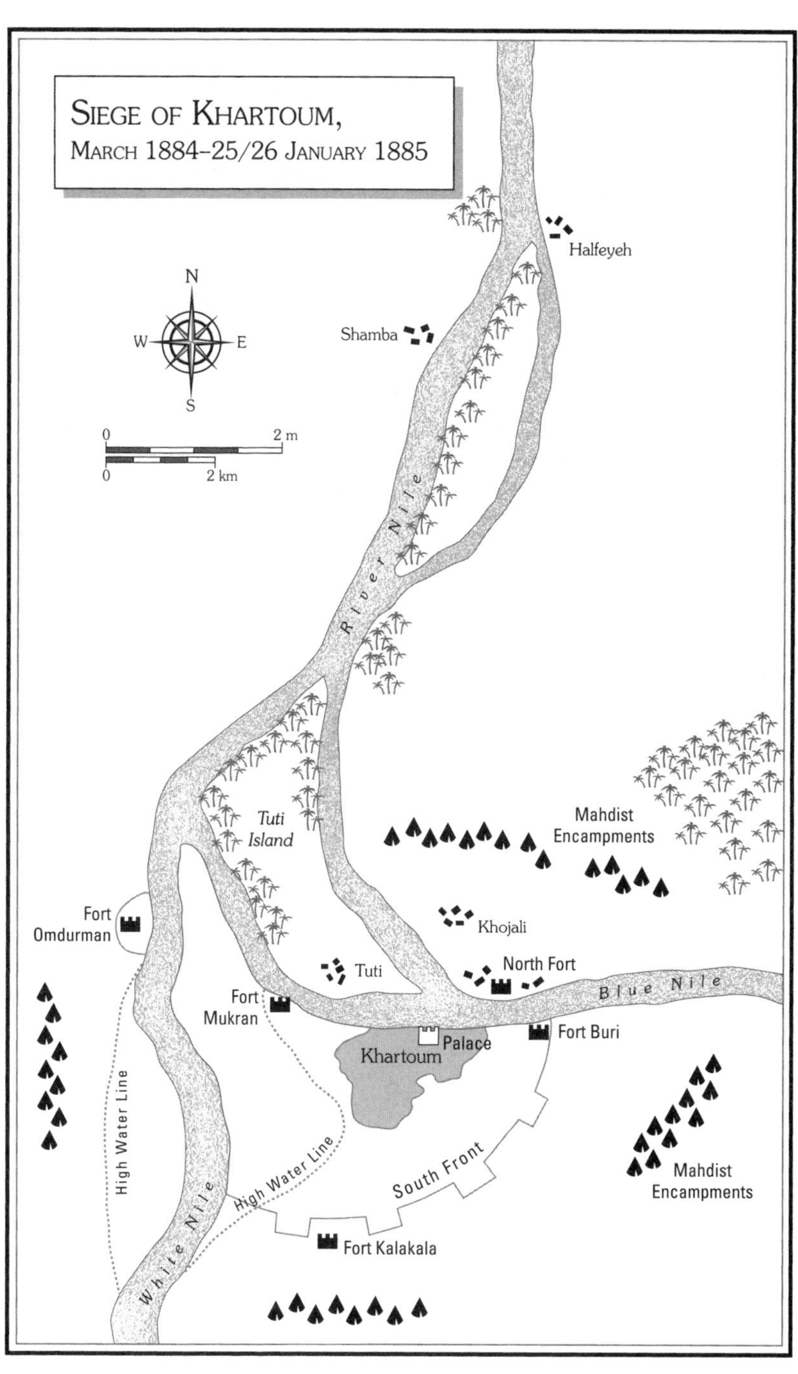
SIEGE OF KHARTOUM,
MARCH 1884–25/26 JANUARY 1885
N
W
E
S
0
2 m
0
2 km
Halfeyeh
Shamba
River Nile
Tuti
Island
Mahdist
Encampments
Khojali
Fort
Omdurman
Tuti
North Fort
Blue Nile
Fort
Mukran
Palace
Khartoum
Fort Buri
High Water Line
High Water Line
South Front
Mahdist
Encampments
White Nile
Fort Kalakala

governor's palace, a two-storey whitewashed building facing the river, set in its own walled compound. Other key points included the barracks and arsenal, both of which lay to the east between the suburbs and Fort Buri, and the Roman Catholic church, in the centre of the city, requisitioned as the garrison's magazine. Finally, eight miles north of Tuti Island, on the east bank of the merged Nile, the village of Halfeyeh was also in the hands of the Khartoum garrison. For most of the siege it was held by Shaigiya irregulars.

In addition to implementing many physical enhancements to the defences, such as mining and wiring the South Front, Gordon breathed life back into a flagging garrison. The black Sudanese were the pick of his troops and together with his little flotilla of steamers constituted the mainstay of the defence. There was no immediate shortage of mountain-gun ammunition (20,000 shells) or small-arms ammunition (5.5 million rounds). Stocks of the latter could be kept topped up by the Khartoum arsenal which was capable of manufacturing 50,000 cartridges a week.[41] Krupp ammunition (2,200 shells) was in much less plentiful supply. Water of course would not be an issue, but with more than 40,000 hungry mouths to feed, quality foodstuffs were certain to become a precious commodity. For a while successful amphibious raids up and down the river brought in additional quantities of grain and livestock, but as the siege tightened and the Mahdists emplaced more guns on the banks of the Nile, such expeditions became increasingly risky. Even so Gordon was optimistic. In a letter of 26 August he wrote:

> There is a bond of union between us and our troops – they know if the town is taken they will be sold as slaves, and we [the Europeans] must deny our Lord if we would save our lives . . . *D.V.* [Latin: God willing] we will defeat them without any help from outside.

The Mahdi led his main force out of his temporary capital at El Obeid in the third week of August. There may have been as many as 60,000 fighting men marching beneath his banners, while the vast columns of camp followers could be quantified only in miles. If Gordon had at first underestimated the Mahdist threat, the great tented towns he could see springing up, from his usual vantage point on the roof of the palace, left no room for further complacency. As Gladstone was repeatedly to point out, Gordon could have left Khartoum aboard a steamer at any point, but such an act would have amounted to a base betrayal of the loyalist populace and was quite beyond a man of principle. If the garrison and the townspeople were hemmed in, then the legendary Gordon would stand beside them as a willing hostage to fortune. Sooner or later, he reasoned, British public opinion would march to Khartoum's rescue; in the meantime Gordon's personal salvation was a matter for the Lord God Almighty, not the likes of William Ewart Gladstone.

In early September the situation took a decided turn for the worse. Gordon's most valued senior officers after Colonel Stewart were the Egyptian Mohamet Ali Pasha, and a prominent local Sudanese called Khashm el Mus. Mohamet Ali in particular had played a leading role in the daring raids of August. The arrival of the Mahdist main force had made riverine operations in the immediate vicinity of Khartoum altogether more difficult, but the successes of the previous month had been so encouraging that Gordon was now seriously contemplating an expedition much further afield. The loss of Berber had severed Khartoum's lifeline. There could be no better way of restoring the situation than by recapturing the town and reopening the Nile. Stewart would command the expedition and would have up to 2,000 men at his disposal. As a military plan, it certainly had boldness to commend it.

In the meantime there was intelligence to indicate that Sheikh el-Obeid, a famously devout rebel leader, was raising a strong force near the town of El Eilafun some 25 miles up the Blue Nile. Mohamet Ali Pasha suggested to Gordon that, before sending a quarter of the garrison away to the north under Stewart, it would be wise to disperse this new enemy concentration first. Gordon agreed the proposition and assigned a thousand of his best Sudanese infantry to the task. The operation was scheduled for 4 September 1884. The intelligence underpinning it proved to be sound; Mohamet Ali was able to disembark his force in safety and catch the rebels at El Eilafun off-guard. During the mopping-up operation, freshly gathered intelligence suggested that Sheikh el-Obeid had taken refuge at the village of Um Dibban. Mohamet Ali decided to chance his arm by staying out overnight and undertaking a 20-mile march into the desert the following morning. As nobody knew the route and there was plenty of thick ground cover, a number of local men were taken on as guides. Somewhere along the trail the column blundered into an ambush. Few details of the fight survive, but all of a sudden the undergrowth came alive with *ansar*. The Sudanese infantry were hemmed in from the outset and were quickly overpowered. Something in excess of 800 of Gordon's best fighting men were cut down or captured.

The disaster came as a crushing blow to the Governor-General; all traces of optimism disappear from his journal from this point on. There were no further references to restoring the military situation unaided. Instead, on 19 September, in stark contrast to his letter of 26 August, he poured scorn on the fighting qualities of the *fellaheen*.

> I think of all the pusillanimous businesses which happened in 1882, the flight of the Europeans from Alexandria before these wretched fellaheen troops, was the worst. Why, had they barricaded their streets, they would have held Alexandria against 50,000 of these poor things (like Abbot did his hotel and the Egyptian bank their offices). A more contemptible

> soldier than the Egyptian never existed. Here we never count on them; they are held in supreme contempt poor creatures. They would never go out to fight; it would be perfectly iniquitous to make them. We tried it once and they refused point-blank to leave the steamers. We are keeping them in cotton wool . . .

One of the immediate consequences of the grave loss incurred in Mohamet Ali's defeat was that the proposed attack on Berber had to be dropped. Instead, Stewart was to break out by steamer, fight his way past Berber and cruise on to Dongola and safety. He was to brief the authorities on the prevailing military situation and the implications of the recent disaster. Stewart was a far from willing volunteer and had to be ordered to go, not from any want of courage but because he was reluctant to leave his chief in the lurch. Gordon readily assented to the departure of Frank Power and the French consul Henri Herbin, both of whom were keen to leave. Power's significance lay not so much in his temporary diplomatic status, as in the fact that he was also *The Times* correspondent. Together the *Times*-man and the general plotted the press coverage that would bring a British expedition down the Nile. Gordon calculated that Power's telegrams would be published in London on 23 September. 'It makes me laugh to think of the flutter in the dovecot which will follow,' he confided to his journal. In fact both the national press and the Army had already been mobilized. Gordon would receive his first confirmation that a British relief column was coming around a fortnight after Stewart left Khartoum. But in the meantime the months had ticked by, the seasons had turned and the Nile was now falling.

Amongst the other souls on board the *Abbas* when she sailed on 10 September were 19 well-armed Greek merchants, 5 Egyptian artillerymen, 7 native crew-members, 4 Arab women, 4 slave women and a handful of male slaves.[42] Since there was every possibility that the *Abbas* might be damaged or sunk in running the gauntlet, it was decided that she should be escorted as far as Berber by *Safieh* and *Mansoura*. Stewart fortified the three vessels as best he could and stockpiled firewood aboard them in order to avoid too many risky landings in search of fuel. Three nuggars were towed behind the *Abbas* bearing an assortment of Greek, Syrian and Jewish refugees who had accepted passage on the strict understanding that Stewart might have to cut them adrift at any point.

The three steamers enjoyed a relatively trouble-free break-out from the immediate environs of Khartoum, though for mechanical reasons they had to overnight at the Halfeyeh outpost. Though they could expect to be subjected to pot-shots from either bank at just about any point in the journey, it was emplaced artillery batteries that posed by far the greatest danger. The next real troublespot, therefore, was likely to be Berber itself. The transit downriver passed off uneventfully and, although the little flotilla approached the town in a state of considerable anxiety, all three steamers were able to force a passage with relative ease. The following day *El Fasher*, a Mahdist-crewed steamer captured in the fall of Berber, gave chase, obliging Stewart to cut the nuggars free. *Safieh* and *Mansoura* were sent back to lend whatever assistance they could, whilst the *Abbas* picked up speed and dashed on.[43] Theoretically she had now passed beyond enemy territory and had only a safe home-run ahead. At 9.00 a.m. on 18 September, however, she struck rocks and began sinking by the stern, until only her bows and foredeck remained above water. Stewart's party took to a nearby island. Later in the day the colonel and the two consuls made their way to the village of Hebbeh on the west bank, where they intended to negotiate with local elders for the hire of a few camels. The meeting had been pre-arranged by Stewart's interpreter and the party was offered hospitality at the house of one Atman Fakri. Having failed to realise that they were walking into a trap, Stewart and his companions were overpowered and treacherously done to death on the orders of Sheikh Suleiman Wad Gamr of the Monasir tribe.

Before they left Khartoum both Stewart and Power had been quartered at the palace and had dined with the Governor-General as a matter of course. Now Gordon's only company of an evening was his African manservant, his Bible and a female mouse which was wont to climb boldly onto the table to eat from his discarded dinner plate.[44] Each night after scanning the northern horizon with his telescope, he would take brief consolation in his customary indulgences: a frugal supper, a box of Turkish cigarettes and the occasional large brandy and soda. For the rest of the evening, he kept his journal, read the gospels and prayed. As well he might.

'All Sir Garnet'

Throughout the summer months of 1884 the clamour for a relief expedition mounted, until at length the British premier found himself in a minority of one. The Queen Empress was for it, Baring was for it, the now ennobled Lord Wolseley was writing staff papers on how it could be done, and the press was baying for it. In the end it took a threat of resignation from the Secretary of State for War, Lord Hartington, to force the Prime Minister's hand. Wolseley's draft plan advocated a 1,650-mile river-borne advance along the Nile. It bore a strong resemblance to the Red River expedition and was not at all well received by the men on the spot. Both the Sirdar, Sir Evelyn Wood, and Lieutenant General Sir Frederick Stephenson, GOC Cairo, advised that the Red Sea route from Suakin to Berber would prove a much better bet. Even the fact that the Royal Navy assessed the river route as impracticable failed to dissuade Wolseley.[45] Command of the expedition was to have gone to Stephenson, but

Wolseley was able to exploit his reservations about the Nile route to his own personal advantage. Sure enough Hartington turned away from the apparently half-hearted Stephenson, in favour of the altogether more enthusiastic Adjutant-General.

The ministerial decision to mount an expedition came in August, but there would be a great deal of time-consuming preparatory work to be done before any fighting troops could arrive in the Sudan. Even at this late stage in the proceedings the government had sanctioned an advance only as far as Dongola. At least the presence of a substantial British garrison in Cairo meant that Wolseley would not be faced with a standing start. Even so it was clear that Stephenson's existing force levels would need supplementing from home and from the geographically convenient Mediterranean stations. But Wolseley would never be content with a simple measure like the despatch of a few extra battalions, if an innovative alternative fit to grandstand his originality presented itself. During the long months of waiting he had often pored over his maps at the War Office. Irritatingly, south of Wadi Halfa, the course of the Nile described a vast question-mark shaped bend, before straightening southwards again in the vicinity of Shendi and Metemmeh. The diversion would add weeks to the journey time to Khartoum. But, the great man noted, there was an overland short-cut, a 180-mile caravan-route between the towns of Korti and Metemmeh, which might shave weeks off the journey time. And so the idea of a Camel Corps was born.

In the meantime some of the battalions in Cairo could begin shipping themselves down the Nile. The job of moving troops as far as Wolseley's start point at Wadi Halfa was contracted out to Thomas Cook & Sons which even then operated a flotilla of Nile steamers for the benefit of tourists. Thereafter the fighting troops would have to row themselves upriver aboard a fleet of 800 specially commissioned whalers. These were 30 feet in length, came with both oars and sails and were designed to carry ten soldiers and two crewmen.[46] The watermanship required to get them through the Nile cataracts would be provided by a contingent of Canadian *voyageurs*, the backwoods river-men who had been instrumental in the success of Wolseley's expedition of 1870. What they knew about the safe navigation of the Nile could have been written on the back of a postage-stamp. Nor were the 1884 *voyageurs* even the same breed of hardy pioneers that had worked the Red River 14 years earlier. With the entire resources of the Royal Navy at the expedition's disposal it was a vacuous idea, but it was Garnet Wolseley's idea and went ahead regardless. A corps of 380 men including 93 French-Canadians and 77 Caughnawaga Indians was enlisted in Canada in September 1884 and was working the Nile by the end of October. It was always inevitable that staff sycophants would subsequently report on the corps of *voyageurs* as a great success.[47] Undoubtedly the Canadians toiled stoically and patriotically, even if their less than deferential manner was irksome to some British officers. But the original plan for their employment, which required that they stay with the boats, had to be changed so as to encamp them permanently in detachments, each beside its own allotted cataract, so that the men could become accustomed to its vagaries. Ultimately the *voyageurs* did nothing that the Royal Navy could not also have done. But the naval staff planners had contradicted the great man and if you weren't for Garnet Wolseley then you were against him and should expect at some point to pay the reckoning.

The transit of the Nile was a painstaking, monotonous process and one which tested the transport and commissariat staffs to the limit. In due course political clearance to push on to Khartoum came through. Wolseley chose Korti as his forward concentration area, but by the time his fighting units had assembled there it was already December. It was at Korti that he made the final division of his troops into a four-battalion River Column under Major General William Earle CB, a veteran of the Alma and Inkerman, and a Desert Column under the younger Brigadier-General Sir Herbert Stewart KCB, whom we last encountered as Sir George Colley's chief of staff. It would fall to Stewart to facilitate a symbolic early dash into Khartoum. The Desert Column would save precious time by crossing the Bayuda Desert between Korti and Metemmeh, thus short-cutting the great bend in the Nile. At Metemmeh, just under a hundred miles from Khartoum, the column would rendezvous with Gordon's steamers. Next a small detachment of British regulars would embark and push south to Khartoum as a tangible sign that help was at hand. It was anticipated that their arrival would inspire the loyal citizenry and dishearten the enemy, even to the extent that the Mahdi might raise the siege and retreat back into Kordofan. The Desert Column would garrison Metemmeh and build up a forward logistic stockpile there, pending the arrival of General Earle and the River Column. Khartoum would finally be relieved by the combined Desert and River Columns under Wolseley's personal command. The advance of Sir Herbert Stewart's Desert Column and Sir Charles Wilson's subsequent river dash were set to become two of the most dramatic military episodes of the high Victorian era.

Chapter 6

DESERT COLUMN

The Dash for Khartoum, Sudan, 1884–1885

Now mark this, if the expeditionary force, and I ask for no more than 200 men, does not come in ten days, the town may fall; and I have done the best for the honour of my country. Goodbye.

Gordon's Journal, 14 December 1884

The men of the Desert Column could not have wished for a more experienced or able commander. Now 42 years of age, Sir Herbert Stewart had been on virtually continuous campaign service for the past five years, having fought in Zululand, in the Sekhukhune campaign, at Majuba, at Tel-el-Kebir and most recently as Sir Gerald Graham's cavalry commander at Suakin. Wolseley thought particularly highly of him as a soldier and also counted him a close personal friend. A decent, even-tempered man whom most people warmed to readily, Stewart was a graduate of the Staff College, a sound tactician and an inspiring leader. If the camel-borne column was to reach the Nile in good time, in the face of determined resistance and logistic overstretch, then it would need to demonstrate resolve, courage and dash. These were qualities its commander possessed in abundance.

The mainstay of Stewart's force would be the highly innovative Camel Corps, first proposed by Wolseley to London as late as 11 September. It consisted of four composite regiments, two from the infantry and two from the cavalry, which together amounted to 94 officers and 1,600 men. The organizational arrangements reflected Wolseley's predilection for hand-picked troops. More than a decade earlier he had proposed using composite regiments for the Ashanti campaign, but the proposal had been blocked by Secretary of State Cardwell. As usual Wolseley's ideas rattled the Duke of Cambridge who heartily disapproved of any measure which undermined traditional regimental integrity. Conventionally lambasted by historians as an unthinking arch-reactionary, on this issue at least the Duke was right. Even so he chose on this occasion not to overrule the Adjutant-General, whose position as the leading British military thinker of the age was by now unassailable.

Whilst the Mounted Infantry Camel Regiment (MICR) had been formed from battalions already on garrison duty in Egypt, the other three units had been hastily despatched from home. As these regiments were drawn exclusively from the Guards and the Cavalry, the 'smartest' regiments in the land, Stewart's force would contain an unusually high preponderance of London society's best-heeled sons. Each of the home-based contributing units had been instructed to find a high-grade detachment of two officers, two sergeants, two corporals, a bugler or trumpeter and 38 privates. At Wolseley's insistence all were to be qualified marksmen and nobody was to be under the age of 22. The Light Camel Regiment (LCR) consisted of contingents from nine hussar regiments – the 3rd, 4th, 7th, 10th, 11th, 15th, 18th, 20th and 21st.[1] It was commanded by Colonel Stanley Clarke, an officer with no previous campaign experience, appointed at the instigation of the Prince of Wales. The highly judgemental Wolseley held the Prince and his set in such contempt that he brought his scathing condescension to bear upon the fashionable but untalented equerry as a matter of course. As a direct consequence of the general's hostility to their commander, the light cavalry detachments would find themselves consigned to escort tasks and would play no role in the fighting in the Bayuda Desert. For all the personal vindictiveness underlying LCR's treatment, it is probably fair to say that the other three regiments were much better led.

The Guards Camel Regiment (GCR) under Lieutenant Colonel the Honourable Edward Boscawen, Coldstream Guards, contained seven detachments of Foot Guards, drawn from 1st, 2nd and 3rd Grenadier Guards, 1st and 2nd Coldstream Guards and 1st and 2nd Scots Guards. Contingents of the same regiment were grouped together to form GCR's first three companies. Its fourth company was found by a detachment of four officers and 86 other ranks from the Royal Marine Light Infantry (RMLI) under Major William Poe, not long since recovered from a wound received at El Teb.[2] GCR companies were numbered 1 to 4 according to their seniority, but were more commonly referred to by their regimental names. Amongst a mere 300 guardsmen there were no fewer than seven lieutenant colonels, a seemingly top-heavy command structure. In fact the three Guards company commanders and the signals officer had been around long enough to pre-date the abolition of the double-rank system by which a captain of Guards took precedence in the wider army as a lieutenant colonel.

The Heavy Camel Regiment (HCR), commanded by Lieutenant Colonel the Honourable Reginald Talbot of the 1st Life Guards, was formed from ten cavalry regiments – 1st Life Guards, 2nd Life Guards, Royal Horse Guards

(Blues), 2nd Dragoon Guards (Queen's Bays), 4th (Royal Irish) Dragoon Guards, 5th (Princess Charlotte of Wales's) Dragoon Guards, 1st (Royal) Dragoons, 2nd Dragoons (Royal Scots Greys), 5th (Royal Irish) Lancers, and 16th (The Queen's) Lancers. HCR formed its five numbered companies by pairing regimental contingents in the order above, an arrangement which again reflected the respective seniorities of the contributing regiments. There was only one officer in HCR who was not either a peer of the realm or the son of one.

MICR was commanded by Major the Honourable George Gough and consisted of contingents from 12 infantry battalions. These were organized into four companies lettered A to D, each of them four sections strong in keeping with the conventional organization of an infantry company. Each section contained a subaltern officer, five NCOs and 25 privates. A Company consisted of sections from the South Staffords, Black Watch, Gordons, and King's Royal Rifle Corps; B Company of West Kents, Sussex, Essex, and Duke of Cornwall's Light Infantry; C (Rifles) Company of a further two sections of the KRRC and two of the Rifle Brigade; and D Company of Somerset Light Infantry, Connaught Rangers, Royal Scots Fusiliers and a second section of West Kents.

Even with LCR (21 officers and 380 other ranks) detached to escort duties, the Camel Corps was still almost 1,200 strong. HCR was the strongest of the main-body regiments with 24 officers and 376 other ranks, while MICR fielded 24 and 366, and GCR 19 and 365. As it was important that the Desert Column's lines of communication could be secured without prejudice to the fighting power of the Camel Corps, the 1st Battalion, The Royal Sussex Regiment (16 and 401) and a company of The Essex Regiment (3 and 55) were also placed under Stewart's command. The infantry companies were provided with camels only three days before the departure of the column and thus were far less expert than the men of the composite regiments. There were only enough riding camels for about half of the infantry to have one permanently assigned. The rest would have to be moved out to the desert wells under some kind of shuttle arrangement.

Reconnaissance would be in the hands of a two-troop squadron of horsed cavalry, eight officers and 127 men from the 19th Hussars under the command of Lieutenant Colonel Percy Barrow CB, CMG, ably assisted by Major John French. No doubt the high esteem in which Stewart held the squadron was due in no small part to the quality of its leadership; not only was Barrow a highly capable veteran of the Zulu War, the Transvaal Rebellion and the recent Suakin Campaign, but this was the same John French who would go on to relieve Kimberley and rise to command the BEF in 1914. The men of the 19th Hussars were mounted on hardy grey stallions imported by Egypt from Syria and were fresh from their service under Stewart at Suakin. Barrow himself had come perilously close to losing his life at Second El Teb where, wounded, unhorsed and surrounded, he had been snatched to safety in a VC-winning act by Quartermaster-Sergeant William Marshall. That the squadron did as well as it did in the coming campaign owed much to Barrow's skilful horse management. The Syrian ponies were ridden only when strictly necessary and their physical well-being was further conserved by the colonel's insistence that his troops stay line abreast at all times – a measure which avoided the animals breathing the clouds of dust invariably thrown up in column of route.[3]

Because his plan called for elements of Stewart's force to push south from Metemmeh aboard Gordon's steamers, Wolseley decided to reinforce the column with the grandly named First Division of the Naval Brigade, a detachment of 5 officers and 53 other ranks under Captain Lord Charles Beresford RN, a younger son of the 4th Marquess of Waterford.[4] Born into the comfortable lifestyle of the Anglo-Irish aristocracy, the 39-year-old Beresford was nonetheless a serious career officer and had commanded the gun-vessel *Condor* at Alexandria where he had displayed great daring during the bombardment of the forts. His standing as a naval captain made him the third most senior officer with the column. There were two principal tasks for Beresford's men: first they would carry out some long overdue maintenance on Gordon's flotilla of steamers, and then they would crew the vessels for the river dash to Khartoum. In the meantime Beresford planned to entertain himself on the overland leg of the journey with a five-barrelled Gardner machine gun of which he was inordinately proud. He chose not to mount himself on a camel like the rest of the naval brigade, but on a white donkey which he named 'County Waterford'. In addition to their sometimes temperamental Gardner, the sailors came armed with Martini-Henry rifles and naval cutlasses designed to double up as sword-bayonets. Contemporaneous sketches show them clad in white, with a blue pugaree wrapped around their foreign service helmets.

The final fighting element of Stewart's command was a half-battery of screw-guns under Captain Gilbert Norton RA.[5] Norton's three 2.5-inch mountain guns were served by 4 officers and 39 other ranks of 1st Battery, 1st Brigade, Southern Division, Royal Artillery, and were supported by 8 Egyptian artillerymen including an officer. Each gun was carried disassembled aboard three baggage camels, its wheels and trail on one, the barrel on another and the breech mechanism on a third.

The column's fighting components were accompanied by a number of smaller but no less important administrative details. Major James Dorward RE commanded a party of 2 officers and 25 men from 26 Company Royal Engineers, specially kitted out with water-pumping equipment for use at the various desert wells. The Principal Medical Officer (PMO) was Surgeon-Major Austin Ferguson, whose assets consisted of a field hospital section under Surgeon William Briggs, and two sections of a bearer company under Surgeon

Arthur Harding. The field hospital section amounted to 2 medical officers, 20 other ranks of the Medical Staff Corps and a dozen native drivers. The job of Harding's bearer sections was to carry any casualties the column might incur in crossing the Bayuda on to Metemmeh using litters and cacolets (a pair of counterbalancing canvas seats suspended from the flanks of a baggage camel). The combined strength of the bearer sections came to 2 medical officers, 40 medics and 57 native labourers and drivers. In addition to the doctors with the medical sections, each of the four major units had its own RMO. Finally, the transport and logistic details consisted of 7 officers, 33 other ranks and some 200 native camel drivers – the only men in the column obliged to travel on foot. Some of the locally employed civilians were Egyptians and some Sudanese but, thanks to General Stephenson's foresight, the majority had been shipped in from Aden and were demonstrably the better workers. In order that in the heat of battle the Arab labour force could be identified as friendlies, they were kitted out with blue tunics and red turbans. All told there were 160 horses and 3,028 camels assigned to the column, of which only 800 camels were permanently available as baggage animals.

Dress and Equipment

In keeping with their elite status the composite camel regiments cut a dash in a specially designed desert uniform. Their single-breasted grey tunics buttoned to the throat like the scarlet home-service equivalent, but were cut from a lightweight cloth instead of the usual heavy serge. In place of the grey trousers worn by the infantry battalions of the River Column, the Camel Corps wore yellow-ochre Bedford-cord riding breeches, with knee-length navy-blue puttees and brown leather ammunition-boots. The standard cork foreign-service helmet was light, comfortable and provided a good degree of protection from the sun for the head and neck; as an affectation some detachments adorned them with puggarees of regimental pattern. The Duke of Cambridge would have been pleased to know that Wolseley's 'chosen men' still preferred their parent affiliations ahead of any loyalty to mere composite units. Many of the regimental contingents cut distinguishing marks from red cloth and sewed them onto the right sleeves of their tunics just below the shoulder; '1GG' for 1st Grenadier Guards, 'RHG' for the Blues, '5L' for the 5th Lancers and so on.[6] As was the norm on active service the foreign-service helmet was stained with mud and boiled tree-bark, to turn it from pristine blancoed white to a dirty yellow-brown. As a defence against the desert glare and sandstorms the troops were issued with shaded goggles, which they generally wore perched on the front of their helmets. Personal equipment consisted of a brown leather waistbelt and ammunition pouch (containing 20 rounds), with a white canvas haversack and the 'Oliver' pattern water bottle slung over opposite shoulders. Fifty more cartridges were carried in a brown leather bandolier worn over the left shoulder.[7] With a heavy cartridge like the .450-inch Boxer, this was a far from ideal method of carriage: Private William Burge of the GCR wrote that the bandolier 'became a positive vice around your chest and shoulder in the course of a long hot march – and all the desert marches were like that'.[8] A further 100 cartridges, for a total first-line scale of 170 rounds per man, were carried in the men's saddle-bags.

The service rifle was still the Martini-Henry but instead of the usual 'lunger' bayonet, the Camel Corps was issued with the older 22-inch 1860 Pattern[9] sword-bayonet, ordinarily the preserve of rifle regiments and senior NCOs. The officers were dressed in a broadly similar way to their men, but were readily identifiable by the riding boots they wore in preference to puttees, and by their Sam Browne belts, swords and revolvers. Most company officers prudently supplemented their privately owned side-arms with the hard-hitting service rifle. Barrow's squadron was armed with the carbine variant of the Martini but did not carry a bayonet and in a hand-to-hand fight would have to rely on the 1882 Pattern sabre. Importantly the recent experience of Stewart and Barrow had demonstrated that horsed charges against an unbroken Mahdist host could safely be regarded as a bad idea.

Tactical Employment of the Camel Corps

Wolseley's tactical concept for the Camel Corps required that it should do battle on foot in accordance with the standard infantry drills of the day. On the march the column would move 40-abreast, with the camel regiments split front and rear of the baggage camels. Even with so wide a frontage, the column would still tail back for more than a mile. The 19th Hussars would be thrown out to the front and flanks as a wide-roaming reconnaissance and early-warning screen. If the initiative rested with the British, the camel regiments would leave their animals under guard and advance to battle on foot. If, however, they were attacked on the line of march, the camels were to be gathered in a great central mass and made to kneel down, while the troops formed two squares at diagonally opposite corners of the mass of animals. After a few brigade field days this rather novel formation could be achieved in truly impressive times of less than two minutes.[10] As the prospect of a panic amongst the camels was a great worry to some officers, the animals were put to the test on one of the Korti field days; the 19th Hussars charged a body of several hundred kneeling camels, whooping like fiends incarnate and firing blanks from their carbines. The only perceptible effect was that one camel stood up, looked around for a moment and then knelt back down.[11] As a result of the experiment the doubting-thomases were forced to concede that the camels' steadiness in action would be the least of their worries.

There were perhaps two serious flaws with the Camel Corps, one conceptual and one practical. The conceptual stumbling block was that HCR and LCR were made up entirely of cavalrymen, but would be required to operate as small infantry battalions. Crucially, in the context of the coming campaign, infantrymen were taught to believe in the impregnability of the defensive square, provided always that every man within it kept his nerve and remained rock-steady. Conversely, cavalrymen received no such training and all had their own pet theories on how to break a square. But the 'receive cavalry' square could only work if the men constituting its human walls felt able to trust each other implicitly and shared an absolute faith in their collective invulnerability. The second significant flaw was profound ignorance of camel management. The officers of the Camel Corps were to learn to their cost that their animals did not possess the mythical qualities of endurance popularly attributed to them. Although there was plentiful grazing in the Bayuda, it was almost invariably the practice to knee-lash the animals at long halts, so that they were seldom able to derive any benefit from it. As a result they soon became undernourished. Additionally, albeit with the best of intentions, the men of the camel regiments had rather spoiled their animals by watering them on a daily basis at Korti, a luxury they quickly grew accustomed to. By contrast the natives of the region tended to water their camels every two to three days, a regime to which the animals could also become accustomed and one which fostered much greater resilience. Remarkably somebody in the chain of command had given orders that riding camels were to be groomed daily.

Logistics

The logistic difficulties facing Stewart were formidable. He did not have anything like sufficient camels to meet his needs and would be totally dependent for his water on the string of desert wells along his axis of advance – Howeiyat, Jakdul and Abu Klea. To overcome the crippling shortage of baggage animals and secure his water supply, it would be necessary to use 600 riding camels to ferry a proportion of his stores as far as Jakdul Wells, a hundred miles into the Bayuda, before then returning the animals to their riders at Korti in time for the advance of the main body. One of the inevitable consequences of such tight logistic margins was that less than ideal quantities of ammunition could be carried. The fighting troops would all begin the march with 170 rounds of Martini ammunition, but as .450-inch cartridges came in boxes of 600 weighing in at over 80 pounds, only a small reserve could be taken along. Weighty artillery ammunition would be a particular problem. It was decided that the gunners would have to make do with only 100 rounds per gun, whilst Lord Beresford would have only 1,000 rounds for his beloved Gardner, sufficient for barely 10 minutes sustained firing.[12]

Not unnaturally, given the scale of the logistic undertaking, the officers and men of the Camel Corps had been exhorted to travel light, but even so the riding camels had to bear a significant burden. The nature of their load and its distribution was described by Lieutenant Count Edward Gleichen of GCR:

> Over the framework [of the saddle] are hung the girths, stirrups, and a pair of saddle-bags or 'zuleetahs,' of canvas and red leather, which amply contain all your kit; on the near side is strapped a rolled blanket and waterproof sheet, on the off a tente d'abri to every two men. The Namaqua rifle-bucket is attached to the off rear side of the framework, and secured by passing the long strap under the belly of the animal, over the two girths, and buckling it on the near side to a buckle nailed on for the purpose. On the after pommel is hung the leather water-skin or 'gerbah' . . . and the Egyptian water-bottle or 'mussek', a long stiff leather bottle, which unless it lets it all leak out in half an hour, makes the water beautifully cool. On the fore pommel hangs the camel's rations for three days, thirty pounds of corn. Over the saddle-bags are placed the second blanket, and over everything comes a padded red leather saddle cover, on top of which the rider is perched.[13]

Gleichen estimated the total weight of the burden, including the average rider and his ammunition, at about 340 pounds. He named his own mount 'Potiphar':

> I cherished a great affection for my own camel . . . a great upstanding white beast of some 22 hands, who reciprocated it by bellowing every time I came near, and making playful rushes at me. I really think I succeeded in making him know and care for me after a time, for he ceased his attacks, and reduced his bellow to a grumble; but he got no further in his love than that. His pace was usually very slow, and required continual whacking, but when excited he walked away from the others; his trot was not one of his good points – in fact, his chief talent lay in doing more work and breaking down less than any of the others.[14]

The Shuttle to Jakdul Wells

On 30 December Stewart set out for Jakdul with GCR, MICR, a troop of the 19th Hussars and the sappers. There were 1,400 camels carrying stores and baggage, including most of the HCR and LCR riding camels. Everything went well in this first phase of operations. Spirits were certainly high – the column was on the move as midnight approached on New Year's Eve, and as they plodded into 1885 the troops broke into a tuneful rendering of 'Auld Lang Syne'. After that they sang song after song, long into the night. Scouting the route ahead was Major Herbert Kitchener of the intelligence staff, disguised as usual as a desert Arab, and riding at the head of a handful of native friendlies familiar with the overland route to Metemmeh. En route a colourful desert freebooter called Ali Loda was captured and press-ganged into service as a guide. To say that he travelled light would be an understatement; everything he owned was carried aboard a single camel, including his wife and child who clung precariously to his saddle and seemed largely untroubled by their conscription into the British Army.

It took the column 63 hours and 45 minutes to reach Jakdul, about half of which was actually spent on the move. It arrived an hour before dawn on the morning of Friday 2 January. Having dumped his stores, Stewart wasted no time in turning back for Korti and was on the march again by 8.00 p.m. the same day. For the return journey the men of MICR rode their own camels and led two others. The dismounted Guards and Royal Engineers, some 420 men in all, were left behind at Jakdul under the command of Colonel Boscawen and Major Dorward respectively, the former to secure the area and the latter to get their pumping gear into order. The wells were located just over two miles to the north of the Korti–Metemmeh caravan route. There were three deep pools of about 20 feet in diameter,[15] one above another, in an otherwise dry watercourse draining down from a natural amphitheatre in the high ground. On closer inspection Dorward decided that the bottom pool was suitable only for animals and washing, but that there was good clean drinking water in the other two. He estimated the capacity of the upper pools at 120,000 gallons and that of the bottom pool at 420,000 gallons.[16] To protect this most vital of all commodities, the Guards constructed three stone redoubts including Fort Stewart covering the mouth of the gorge, Fort Boscawen on the ridge above the uppermost pool, and Fort Flagstaff on a third commanding vantage point.[17]

Kitchener and his scouts also stayed behind at Jakdul. Having set themselves up in a small cave, they spent the next few days riding around the Bayuda rounding up any stray locals they could find. All Kitchener's attempts to ascertain the situation at Metemmeh and Khartoum were hampered as usual by the timeless but ultimately unhelpful local habit of confiding to an inquisitor only what it was thought he wanted to hear. Kitchener's eventual assessment was that there was unlikely to be serious fighting during the crossing of the Bayuda, but that the situation in Khartoum was now very grave indeed. Only the second of these judgements was to prove correct.

By midday on 5 January, Stewart was back at Korti. Of the 2,195 camels which had set out on the shuttle run, 31 had died along the way. Whilst this was not a significant proportion of the total, it was nonetheless an unsatisfactory loss which tended to point to serious difficulties ahead. Much more alarming was the number of animals already suffering from sores. Beasts of burden they may have been, but it was essential that their loads were both manageable and evenly distributed. As any desert-dweller knew, the loading of a baggage camel was not a matter to be unduly rushed – under no circumstances could protruding edges or corners be ignored. Problematically, a busy military column racing against the clock was unlikely ever to find time for packing up properly.

Towards sundown on Wednesday 7 January, Colonel Stanley Clarke set off for Jakdul with a further thousand-camel convoy of stores. In his campaign journal, Wolseley reflected on Clarke's departure in his usual spiteful tone:

> Nothing could be worse managed: he had had the advantage of being with the previous convoy and seeing what a well-conducted convoy should be like and how it should be managed, but it was of no use to him. His heart was in Marlborough House or some Court circle. Any old woman who shines in such society would have done quite as well as he did. This is the first and shall be the last time that he followed [*sic*] my fortunes. Yet I have no doubt he writes to the Prince of Wales and tells him that everything here is badly managed. It is just such fellows as these who always find fault the most.[18]

Wolseley continued to harbour a nagging doubt about the senior command level. Despite the abundance of lieutenant colonels, there was a shortage of experienced 'fighting officers' at the next level up – Stewart might prove irreplaceable. Wolseley reflected in his journal that he lived in dread of 'some stray bullet going through him', but did nothing much about it. The Desert Column had no formally nominated second-in-command, and the next senior officers were Colonel Sir Charles Wilson of the Intelligence Department and Captain Lord Beresford, neither of them ideally qualified for a combat command of this sort.

The departure of LCR was followed a day later by that of Stewart and the main body: Barrow's squadron, five companies of the HCR, four companies of MICR, seven companies of the Royal Sussex, a company of the Essex Regiment, the naval brigade, the three medical sections and the screw-guns. It is important in the context of the shortage of camels to note that about half of the infantry companies were mounted aboard the temporarily spare GCR and RE riding camels. The troops passed in review before Wolseley as they left the camp at Korti. The gently swaying column must have made a remarkable and impressive sight. Some men were surprised by just how silently such a vast number of camels could move across the ground.

Stewart's written orders from Wolseley ran as follows:

> After such rest as your animals require [at Jakdul], you will proceed to Metemmeh . . . On reaching Abu Klea you will establish a post there garrisoned by from 50 to 100 men, Sussex Regiment, as the nature of the ground may require, 300 rounds per man, and 3,000 rations. You will then advance on Metemmeh, which you will attack and occupy . . . Having occupied Metemmeh, you will leave there the Guards Camel Regiment, the detachment Sussex Regiment, the Naval Brigade, detachment Royal Engineers, and three guns Royal Artillery, 25,000 rations, and 300 rounds small-arm ammunition per rifle; and return with the convoy to Jakdul . . . You will be particular to use every endeavour to keep me as well and as quickly informed of your movements as possible . . . On your return to Jakdul you will continue to forward stores by convoy to Metemmeh.[19]

In essence Stewart's job was to seize Metemmeh and begin building up a logistic stockpile there, pending the arrival of the River Column. As we have seen it would fall to Sir Charles Wilson, not to relieve Khartoum, but to open communications with Gordon. Wilson received his own written orders, which he was instructed to share with Stewart, and which threw rather more light on the fine detail of Wolseley's plan:

> 1. You will accompany the column under the command of Brigadier-General Sir Herbert Stewart, K.C.B., which will leave Korti tomorrow for Matammeh [*sic*]. Your intimate knowledge of Soudan [*sic*] affairs will enable you to be of great use to him during his operations away from these headquarters.
> 2. You will endeavour to enter into friendly relations with the Hassaniyeh tribe, and to induce them if possible to carry supplies for us across the desert, and to sell us sheep, cattle, etc.
> 3. As soon as Matammeh is in our occupation, Sir H. Stewart will dispatch a messenger to Korti with an account of his march, etc; and you will be good enough to send me by same opportunity all political information you may have obtained, all news of General Gordon, the so-called Mahdi, etc.
> 4. I am sending Captain Lord Charles Beresford R.N., with a small party of seamen, to accompany Sir H. Stewart to Matammeh, where, if there are any steamers, Lord Charles Beresford will take possession of one or two of them, as he may think best . . .
> 5. As soon as Lord Charles Beresford reports that he is ready to proceed with one or more steamers to Khartum [*sic*], you will go to that place with him, and deliver the enclosed letter to General Gordon. I leave it open so you may read it.

6. Orders have been given to Sir H. Stewart to send a small detachment of infantry with you to Khartum. If you like, you can, upon arriving there, march these soldiers through the city, to show the people that British troops are near at hand. If there is any epidemic in the town you will not do this. I do not wish them to sleep in the city. They must return with you to Matammeh. You will only stay in Khartum long enough to confer fully with General Gordon. Having done so you will return with Lord Charles Beresford in steamers to Matammeh.
7. My letter to General Gordon will explain to you the object of your mission. You will confer with him both upon the military and upon the political position. You are aware of the great difficulty of feeding this army at such a great distance from the sea. You know how we are off in the matter of supplies, the condition and distribution of the troops under my command . . .
8. I am sending with you the three officers named in the margin[20] who will accompany you to Khartum, and remain there to assist General Gordon until I am able to relieve that place.
9. It is always possible that when Mohamed Ahmed [*sic*] fully realises that an English army is approaching Khartum he will retreat and thus raise the siege. Khartum would, under such circumstances, continue to be the political centre of our operations, but Berber would become our military objective. No British troops would be sent to Khartum beyond a few red coats in steamers for the purpose of impressing on the inhabitants the fact that it was to the presence of our army they owed their safety . . .
10 . . . Upon your return to Matammeh you will rejoin my Headquarters at your earliest possible convenience.[21]

The Desert Column plodded across the Bayuda without incident until, on the morning of 10 January, it reached Howeiyat Wells, where Captain William Carter's company of the Essex Regiment was dropped off to secure the first important water source on the lines of communication. Following the passage of Stanley Clarke's convoy, the wells were already alarmingly low. Successive night marches brought Stewart to Jakdul Wells on Monday 12 January, where it took the rest of the day just to water the camels. The following day would be used for final administrative preparations, including the detailed organization of the baggage train by the commissariat staff. The administrative pause would bring the added benefit of a few hours' decent grazing for the camels.

Given the concern over the lack of a suitably qualified second-in-command, it seemed a particular stroke of luck when Fred Burnaby rode into Jakdul at the head of a small convoy of baggage camels on Tuesday morning. As a conspicuous and ardent Tory, Burnaby knew the War Office was in the hands of his avowed political enemies, so in order to throw the authorities off the scent he had indicated that he would spend his winter leave in South Africa. Since setting out surreptitiously for the Sudan he had been careful to avoid all the communication hubs where a telegraphed recall might be awaiting him. Knowing that he would need the force commander to turn a blind eye to his presence, and that Wolseley could be counted amongst his admirers, Burnaby telegraphed the great man to advise him that he was on his way. He was readily taken onto the staff, but even Wolseley dare not appoint him to a senior command in open defiance of the politicians.[22] The officers and men of the Blues greeted the arrival of their legendary colonel with a cheer. 'Am I in time for the fighting?' he enquired anxiously. As Sir Charles Wilson was Burnaby's senior in the Army List, Stewart was unable to nominate him formally as his second-in-command. Instead he was appointed commandant-designate of Metemmeh. In the meantime the column could console itself with the thought that at least there would now be a real 'fighting-man' on hand to guide and advise the scholarly Wilson, should any mishap befall Stewart.

Since we last met him, soldiering alongside Val Baker, Burnaby had found his way into the newspapers once more. At the Second Battle of El Teb, he was forward with the cavalry screen when his horse was killed under him. Disregarding his tumble, he went on to fight in the thick of the fray with the infantry. He was reputed to have killed no fewer than 13 Beja with a shotgun, before being wounded in the arm. In the comfort of London clubs and drawing rooms the use of heavy-gauge buckshot on human targets was seen as not altogether respectable and triggered a mischievous, politically motivated furore in the newspapers. For all that his reputation as a dashing hero preceded him wherever he went, Burnaby's private life was far from being a bed of roses. Six years earlier, at the age of 36, he had married the 18-year-old Elizabeth Hawkins-Whitshed, an Anglo-Irish heiress from County Wicklow who, it is said, became keen to meet the famous hero after reading *A Ride to Khiva*. Two years after they married Lizzie gave birth to a son called Harry, but she suffered from an inherited lung complaint and before long had moved to Switzerland for the sake of her health. Fred wrote to her dutifully and lovingly but they were fated to see little more of one another. For some time Fred himself had been suffering from a heart condition and periodic bouts of excruciating pain caused by a serious liver ailment. Inevitably the 'black dog' of depression settled over him from time to time. Probably as a function of his ill-health, he seems to have been past caring whether he survived the Sudan or not. Certainly there are stories that, just before setting out, he gave open indications to his friends and servants that he would not be coming back. Before sailing he asked Val Baker to act as young Harry's guardian in his absence.

Sir George Colley fights it out on top of Majuba Hill, 27 February 1881.

Above left: Muhammad Ahmad, the self-anointed Mahdi.

Above right: Hicks Pasha.

Below left: Lieutenant Colonel J. D. H. Stewart, 11th Hussars. Stewart was Gordon's chief of staff in Khartoum.

Below right: Lieutenant Colonel Arthur Farquhar, late of the Grenadier Guards. Farquhar was Hicks's chief of staff and was killed at his side during the Sheikan disaster.

Hicks Pasha's Kordofan Expedition marches towards disaster at Sheikan in November 1883.

Sudanese infantry in the employ of the Egyptians face the Mahdist onslaught.

Above left: 'General'Valentine Baker Pasha. Cashiered as a British cavalry colonel for an 'indiscretion' on a train, Val Baker entered the Ottoman service, and in 1884 led the Egyptian gendarmerie to disaster in the First Battle of El Teb.

Above Right: 'Major General Sir Gerald Graham VC. Graham was able to defeat Osman Digna's force at the Second Battle of El Teb.

Below: The Egyptian square collapses at the First Battle of El Teb.

Above: Major General Charles Gordon – 'Gordon Pasha'.

Right: George William Joy's famous portrayal of the death of General Gordon on the night of 25/26 January 1885. Although popular legend has it that he made no attempt to defend himself at the end, this is at odds with several contemporary sources, including the account of an Egyptian officer who saw him fighting in defence of the palace compound.

Above: A view of Khartoum at the time of the siege. The Governor-General's Palace is in the centre foreground with a flag flying from the roof; the 'South Front' defences are at the left rear; and the fort at Omdurman is in the far distance across the White Nile.

Below left: Bennet Burleigh of the *Daily Telegraph*, one of several prominent war correspondents who accompanied the Gordon Relief Expedition.

Below right: Major General 'Andy' Wauchope, late of the Black Watch. Severely wounded at Kirbekan whilst serving with Wolseley's River Column, he would be killed in action 14 years later at Magersfontein.

Brigadier-General Sir Herbert Stewart KCB. Stewart was chief of staff to Colley at Majuba and subsequently commanded the Desert Column during the Gordon Relief Expedition. Captured by the Boers in February 1881, he was mortally wounded at the Battle of Abu Kru on 19 January 1885. Extremely highly regarded by Wolseley, had he recovered from his injury he would undoubtedly have gone on to command at the highest levels.

One of the great heroes of a heroic age, Colonel Fred Burnaby of the Blues. Soldier, explorer, adventurer, parliamentary candidate, best-selling author and long-distance balloonist, Burnaby was killed in action at Abu Klea.

The Camel Corps fighting in square at the Battle of Abu Kru, the second action fought in the Bayuda Desert in January 1885. Harassed by heavy rifle fire throughout their advance, the men in the square raised a cheer when at last the enemy made their charge.

Above left: The armed steamer *Safieh* runs the gauntlet on the Nile to effect a rescue of Sir Charles Wilson.

Above right: Captain Lord Charles Beresford RN.

Dr Jameson and his raiders are run to ground at Doornkop, a portrayal by Richard Caton Woodville.

Above: The War Office, Pall Mall, 1885.

Below left: HRH The Duke of Cambridge, C-in-C of the British Army for most of the high Victorian era. Renowned as an arch-reactionary, he was constantly at odds with Wolseley and other reformers.

Below right: Sir Garnet (later Viscount) Wolseley, talented field commander, army reformer and thoroughgoing egotist. He would succeed the Duke of Cambridge as C-in-C in 1895 but by then was well past his prime.

Above left: Paul Kruger, President of the Transvaal.

Above right: Sir Alfred Milner, High Commissioner for Southern Africa.

Below left: Dr L. S. Jameson, leader of the infamous 'Jameson Raid' of 1896.

Below right: Lord Lansdowne, Secretary of State for War at the time of the Anglo-Boer War.

Above, both: General Sir Redvers Buller VC. Buller's physical decline between 1885 and 1899, a function of a healthy appetite, physical inactivity over a decade spent at the War Office and a great fondness for food and champagne, is only too apparent. Brave as a lion and hugely experienced, his return to active command in South Africa was to cost him his hard-won reputation.

Below left: Lieutenant General Sir George White VC, commander of the Ladysmith garrison.

Below right: General Louis Botha (*centre*), the Boer commander on the Ladysmith front.

F.A. Stewa

Attempting to save the guns at Colenso.

Colenso Railway Bridge from the south bank of the Tugela. The koppie in the background is Fort Wylie.

Above left: Lieutenant General Sir Charles Warren, overall commander of the Spion Kop operation.

Above right: Major General Edward Woodgate, mortally wounded at Spion Kop, 24 January 1900.

Below left: Major General Fitzroy 'No Bobs' Hart, commander 5th (Irish) Infantry Brigade at Colenso.

Below right: Lieutenant the Honourable Freddie Roberts VC, KRRC.

Lieutenant Colonel Blomfield and the officers of the 2nd Lancashire Fusiliers.

A gruesome and iconic image of the scene on Spion Kop the day after the battle. The British dead are in the trench that would serve as their grave.

Stewart Marches for Metemmeh

Stewart wrote a progress report to Wolseley on Wednesday morning and started the column for Metemmeh at 2.00 p.m. that afternoon. Lieutenant Colonel John Vandeleur, the officer commanding the Royal Sussex, was left behind to secure Jakdul with three of his companies, around 150 men in all. His remaining four companies would push on under the command of the regiment's next senior field officer, Major Marsden Sunderland. Clarke's LCR set out at the same time as the main force but, much to their dismay, in quite the opposite direction, bound once again for Korti. Accompanying them was a fuming Major Kitchener who had received word that his services were urgently required at Wolseley's headquarters. The final fighting configuration of the Desert Column is given below.

In total some 1,800 Britons and 300 native workers started from Jakdul for Metemmeh. With the exception of Barrow's hussars and Stewart's staff, who rode horses and ponies, and the native drivers who walked, the rest of the force was camel-borne.

Table 8: The Desert Column

Force Marching to Metemmeh	***Brig.-Gen. Stewart***	
Headquarters Staff		
5 companies, Heavy Camel Regt	*Lt. Col. Talbot*	24 & 376
4 companies, Guards Camel Regt	*Lt. Col. Boscawen*	19 & 365
4 companies, Mounted Infantry Camel Regt	*Maj. Gough*	24 & 366
4 companies, 1st Bn, Royal Sussex Regt	*Maj. Sunderland*	12 & 250
1 squadron, 19th Hussars	*Lt. Col. Barrow*	8 & 127
Detachment, 26 Company RE	*Maj. Dorward*	2 & 25
Half-battery, 1/1 Southern Division RA	*Capt. Norton*	4 & 39 (+ 1 & 7 Egyptians)
Naval Brigade	*Capt. Lord Beresford*	5 & 53
1 section Field Hospital	*Surg. Briggs*	2 & 20 (+ 12 native drivers)
2 sections Medical Bearer Company	*Surg. Harding*	2 & 40 (+ 57 native drivers)
Commissariat & Transport Details	*Comm. Nugent*	7 & 33 (+ 200 native drivers)
Detached to Lines of Communication		
1 company, Essex Regiment	*Capt. Carter*	3 & 55 (Howeiyat Wells)
3 companies, 1st Bn, Royal Sussex Regt	*Lt. Col. Vandeleur*	7 & 150 (Jakdul Wells)
4 companies, Light Camel Regt	*Col. Clarke*	21 & 380 (Korti)

Two days' march brought the Desert Column within striking distance of the all-important wells at Abu Klea. On the morning of 16 January the force set off at daybreak and made its way over a gravel plain where expanses of sand alternated with stretches of flat black rock. At 11.00 a.m., with the column about five miles short of its objective, Stewart called a halt for a belated breakfast. Throughout the morning the line of march had been bounded on both sides by low ranges of hills, generally at distances of about a mile, but now the high ground had converged into a narrow, shallow valley. Some way ahead the track climbed up a low ridge, commanded on both sides by higher ground. The rudimentary maps at the disposal of the staff indicated that the wells lay about 3½ miles further on. As soon as the hussars had snatched a bite to eat, Stewart sent them on ahead to secure the wells and water their desperately thirsty ponies. Long before the camel regiments were ready for the off, Major French was back to report that the ridge ahead was in the hands of the enemy.

Stewart and his staff reconnoitred forward in company with Barrow, French and their troopers, and quickly concluded that it would be folly to push straight up the track. Through binoculars it was possible to make out a line of stone sangars running across the front of the position. Also visible was a long line of flags and a single conspicuous Arab tent. As a good light cavalry squadron should, the 19th Hussars were already probing the ground ahead in order to ascertain the enemy's strength and dispositions. At one point Lieutenant Edward Craven and three or four of his men had a narrow scrape when, on giving chase to some enemy scouts, they ran into a large body of spearmen concealed in long grass. No sooner had Craven clapped a hand on one of the fleeing scouts, than he was forced to abandon his prisoner and ride for his life.[23]

The British commanders concluded that there were at least 2,000 Mahdists deployed ahead of them. In fact the main enemy force was still out of sight and was far stronger than Stewart and the officers of the 19th Hussars imagined. Unsurprisingly the shuttle to and from Jakdul had been detected by desert-dwellers loyal to the Mahdi. This compromised Wolseley's intent so far in advance that Muhammad Ahmad had been given plenty of time to organize a strong defence of the Bayuda. In the wider context of the campaign, the compromise was to prove decisive.

At around 1.00 p.m. Stewart decided to push closer to the enemy position in the hope that the *ansar* would descend from the high ground and attack him in the open. Essentially he was counting on the enemy's indiscipline to draw them into an impulsive tactical error, but was also keenly aware that time was not on his side. He had to seize the wells at all costs and push on to the Nile. If an attack did not materialize that afternoon, he would be left with no alternative but to assault the enemy position the following morning. The British force crawled forward cautiously, moving down the right side of the valley in parallel regimental columns, the Guards on the right, the Heavies in the centre and the Mounted Infantry on the left. The baggage train followed up behind the camel regiments, with the Royal Sussex bringing up the rear. There was no immediate indication that an aggressive response was to be expected. Soon it was 2.00 in the afternoon, too late in the day in Stewart's view to mount a major offensive operation. Now there was no alternative but to dig in for the night and tough out the hours of darkness.

Eve of Battle

The column began to establish itself on a flattish piece of ground near the head of a dry, wide khor which ran south-east down the valley in the direction of the wells. The main enemy position lay about 2,500 yards distant. While the camels were being knee-haltered in a great square mass, two companies were thrown forward as a skirmish line to keep enemy riflemen in check. On the right there was a rocky peak and a number of smaller hills, but at 2,000 yards these features were too far away for small-arms fire to pose a significant threat. On the other side of the valley there was a lower-lying range of hills. As they were only about 1,200 yards away, Stewart decided it would be necessary to deny them to the enemy and detached a half-company of MICR and the Naval Brigade to occupy them. Beresford was instructed to construct a biscuit-box redoubt on a high-point and cover the valley floor with the Gardner. On the main position officers and men alike laboured hard to construct a low rock wall along the front of the perimeter. The best that could be done before sunset was to raise it two feet high, just enough to protect the men in a prone fire position and to keep them safe as they slept. As the wall did not run all the way round the perimeter, it was necessary to protect the flanks and rear with a thorn-bush zareba. Fortunately the rear half of the position was located on slightly lower-lying ground and was to some extent protected from direct fire. A second biscuit-box redoubt was constructed to serve as Stewart's headquarters.

With the light fading fast, parties of enemy riflemen were sufficiently emboldened to advance down the valley and take possession of a low spur about 1,200 yards from the British perimeter. From here they opened a long-range fire to which Captain Norton's gunners replied gamely, but with seemingly little effect. At sunset the guns ceased fire. While the exchange was in progress, the Heavies, Guards and Royal Sussex were deployed around the perimeter in a two-deep line and instructed to lie down. For the rest of the night it was foolhardy even to sit upright. If the men kept low, the enemy's harassing fire could be largely neutralised; Gleichen recorded that only one hussar and a native camel driver were wounded by it. Enemy drums beat throughout the evening, mostly from afar, but from time to time seemed to come much closer, creating the impression that an attack was imminent. Private Harry Etherington was a member of a Royal Sussex picket deployed a hundred yards beyond the perimeter. He remembered Burnaby visiting the position and saying 'Don't strike a light and don't fire on any account, or you will show the enemy where you are; wait till you see the whites of their eyes and then bayonet them.' Inevitably there were two false alarms during the hours of darkness, but both were quickly calmed and most men were able to snatch a few hours' sleep.

In their isolated redoubt Beresford and his sailors passed an altogether less comfortable night:

> As the darkness thickened, there arose that maddening noise of tom-toms, whose hollow and menacing beat endlessly and pitilessly repeated, haunts those who have heard it to the last day of their lives. Swelling and falling, it sounds now hard at hand, and again far away. That night we lay behind the breastwork, sleepless and very cold, and the deadly throbbing of the drums filled the air, mingled with the murmur of many voices and the rustle as of many feet, and punctuated with the sullen crack of rifles, now fired singly, now in a volley, and the whine of bullets. At intervals thinking the enemy were upon us we stood to arms.[24]

The Battle of Abu Klea, 17 January 1885

With the coming of the dawn the men in the outpost withdrew to the main position. Before long the enemy had closed up on the zareba and subjected it to a galling fire. The troops were forced to breakfast lying on their sides, on the hard-tack biscuits in their haversacks. For a while Stewart hung on, hoping, as he described in his official report, that the enemy would attack:

> In our front the manoeuvring of their troops in line and in column was apparent, and everything pointed to the probability of an attack upon our position being made. Under these circumstances no particular hurry to advance was made, in the hope that our apparent dilatoriness might induce the enemy to push home.

In the meantime he gathered his staff and began contingency planning an advance in square. As usual the officers showed scant respect for enemy fire, and as usual some of them paid the price: Major John Dickson of the Royals, serving on the intelligence staff as one of the three officers meant to accompany Wilson upriver to Khartoum, was hit just below the knee; Lieutenant Charles Lyall RA took a round in the back and lungs; and Major George Gough, commanding MICR, was 'knocked senseless'[25] by a spent round which penetrated his helmet with a sickening crack heard all around the position.

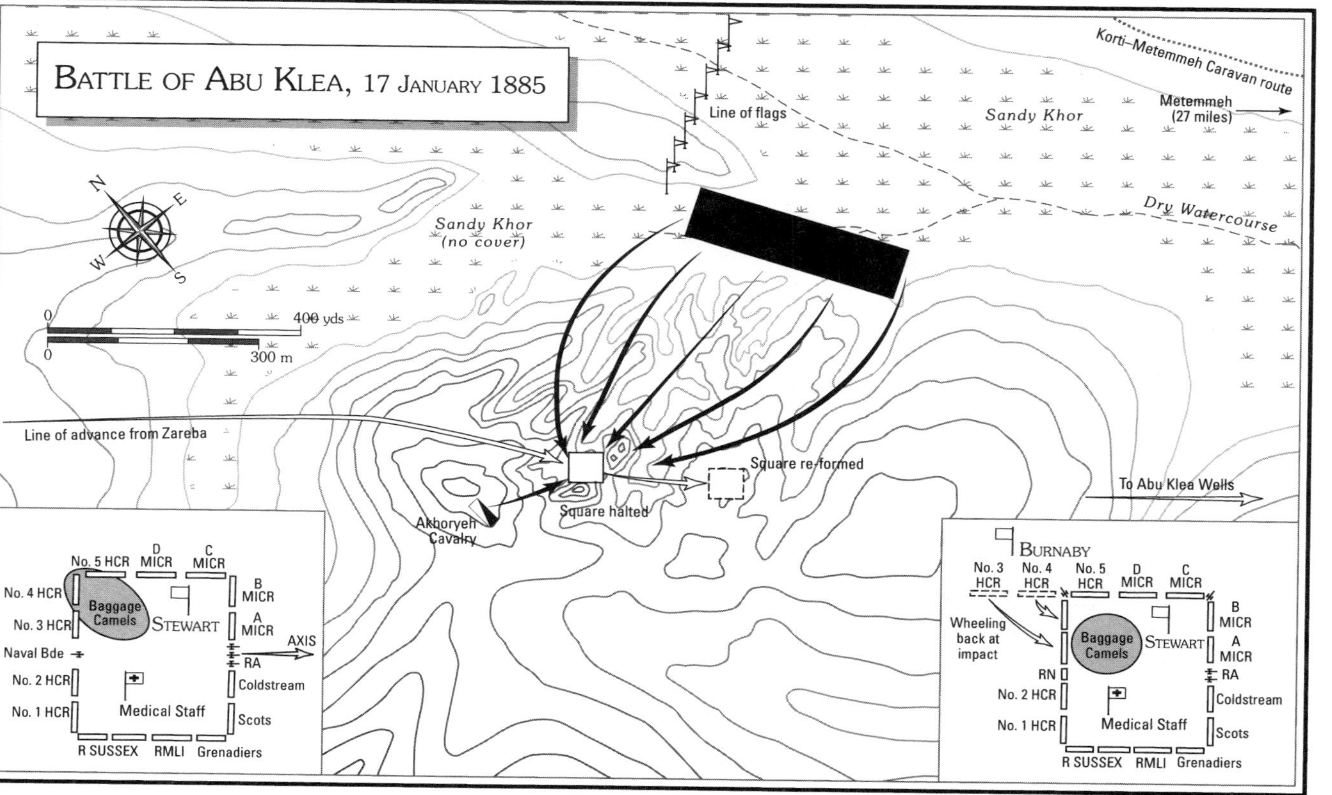

BATTLE OF ABU KLEA, 17 JANUARY 1885
Line of flags
Sandy Khor
Korti–Metemmeh Caravan route
Metemmeh
(27 miles)
Dry Watercourse
Sandy Khor
(no cover)
N
E
W
S
0
400 yds
0
300 m
Line of advance from Zareba
Square re-formed
To Abu Klea Wells
Akhoryeh Cavalry
Square halted
No. 5 HCR
D MICR
C MICR
No. 4 HCR
Baggage Camels
B MICR
No. 3 HCR
STEWART
A MICR
AXIS
Naval Bde
RA
No. 2 HCR
Coldstream
No. 1 HCR
Medical Staff
Scots
R SUSSEX
RMLI
Grenadiers
BURNABY
No. 3 HCR
No. 4 HCR
No. 5 HCR
D MICR
C MICR
B MICR
Wheeling back at impact
Baggage Camels
STEWART
A MICR
RN
RA
No. 2 HCR
Coldstream
No. 1 HCR
Medical Staff
Scots
R SUSSEX
RMLI
Grenadiers

Command of the regiment devolved upon Major Charles Barrow, Percy's younger brother.

Remarkably and rather foolishly, Stewart and Burnaby insisted on riding about on their horses. At one point Beresford dashed across to them and implored them to get down, but to no avail. Eventually Stewart's bugler was shot out of the saddle. A few minutes later Burnaby himself was unhorsed when his pony took a round through the fetlock. As Beresford helped him to his feet, he joked 'I'm not in luck today Charlie!' He was able to scrounge a fresh mount, a pony called 'Moses', from a 23-year-old subaltern in A Company MICR, who despite his tender age was already in his third campaign and had a VC to show for it. Lieutenant Percy Marling of the KRRC had fought in defence of the double drift at Ingogo and had won the revered bronze cross at Tamai.

The Mahdists made three significant demonstrations in strength during the first half of the morning – the manoeuvres that led Stewart to believe he might be attacked. One enemy group, about 200 strong, was driven off by a mounted sortie made by a troop of the 19th Hussars. Not long afterwards some 500 spearmen, supported by a few Baggara horsemen, swept down from the right as if to attack, but fell back when a 7-pound shell exploded above their heads killing three or four of their number. Later a much larger body of 3,000–4,000 men deployed on the high ground to the left of the British position. As they showed no sign of coming on, Stewart instructed the younger Barrow to send out a detail of skirmishers to try and lure them down by means of a feigned withdrawal. The ruse was tried twice, without success, and it fell to Captain Norton's guns to drive the enemy back into cover.[26] All the while the casualties from incoming rifle fire had been mounting. By 9.00 a.m., the time at which Stewart finally took the decision to advance, 14 men had been killed and 20 wounded.

The casualties, the sick, most of the medics, the logisticians, the native workers and the camels would be left at the zareba in the care of two companies of the Royal Sussex[27] under Major Arthur Gern and a 40-strong half-company from B Company MICR. The rest of the force quickly moved into the open, formed square and prepared to advance. In order to maximize the square's firepower and present a less densely packed target, the 14½ companies concerned formed up in two ranks, instead of the four conventionally adopted by the infantry to 'receive cavalry'. Along the front face from left to right were the second half of B Company MICR, A Company MICR, Norton's screw-guns, the Coldstreamers and the Scots Guards. Down the right face from front to rear were the Grenadiers, the RMLI, and two companies of the Royal Sussex, fielding between them about 125 men under Major Sunderland. The rear face was manned from the right-rear corner to the left by Nos. 1 and 2 Companies HCR, the Gardner and around 40 members of the Naval Brigade, then Nos. 3 and 4 Companies HCR. Finally the left face, from rear to front, was occupied by: No. 5 Company HCR, D Company MICR; and C (Rifles) Company MICR. In the centre were the general and his staff, some doctors and medics, a handful of sappers and around 100 baggage camels, half of them given over to water and reserve ammunition, and the rest to litters and cacolets intended for casualties.[28] Stewart was accompanied by his brigade-major, Captain the Earl of Airlie of the 10th Hussars, his DAA & QMG, Major Frederick Wardrop, a fellow member of the 3rd Dragoon Guards, and by his ADC, Captain Frank Rhodes of the Royals, elder brother to the legendary Cecil. All told there were roughly 1,400 combatants in the square, with 300–350 bayonets on each of the faces. By one account executive command of the formation rested with Burnaby, though Bennet Burleigh, the *Daily Telegraph* correspondent, who had a long talk with him the previous evening, recalled how he expressed delight at having been given command of the left face and rear on the morrow.[29] The contradiction tends to suggest that the command and control arrangements made the previous evening were changed during the course of the morning. Judging the principal threat to be on the left, Barrow led 90 of his men off in that direction, leaving the remaining 30 members of his squadron to cover the right.

Static defensive squares like the ones so famously employed at Waterloo were a simple enough proposition, but Stewart's battle square would have to advance across broken ground and maintain its dressing with a significant number of obstinate and moody camels in the centre. Veterans of the Suakin campaign knew that the maintenance of cohesion would be all-important. The rate of advance would necessarily be slow and there would have to be frequent halts to prevent the formation falling into disorder. The advance finally got under way at about 9.45 a.m.[30] The Royal Artillery began the march with their guns disassembled aboard baggage camels but, with a good many long-range targets in view on the high ground to the right, Captain Norton soon received orders to come into action. Thereafter the 7-pounders had to be manhandled forward by their hard-toiling crews. The even more cumbersome Gardner was drawn from the outset by sailors hauling on tow ropes.

Although there were no longer any substantial enemy bodies in sight, there were literally hundreds of riflemen infesting the scrub and the high ground, keeping pace with the British advance and maintaining a heavy fire. Frequent halts had to be made to place casualties aboard cacolets and litters, the adjutant of the Heavies, Captain Lord St Vincent, amongst them.[31] To everybody's regret logic dictated that, for the time being at least, the dead would have to be left where they fell. The 19th Hussars were meant to be protecting the square from enemy riflemen, but Barrow's main body quickly became embroiled in a skirmish on the left, where a force of around 200 horse and 300 foot were trying to infiltrate towards the zareba. Barrow dismounted to engage the enemy with carbine fire, but due to the broken nature of the ground the encounter developed into a protracted fire-fight destined to keep the hussars gainfully occupied for the rest of the battle. As there could be no question of waiting for Barrow, Stewart decided to protect the square by throwing out skirmishers. Each of the camel regiments was ordered to send out a section. Within MICR a section from Captain Thomas Phipps's C (Rifles) Company was the obvious choice for the task. Phipps took a KRRC section forward under Lieutenant Johnny Campbell and fanned them out across the left front of the square. On the opposite flank the Scots Guards pushed Lieutenant Frederick Romilly's section forward. At the rear Colonel Reggy Talbot of HCR assigned the job to his No. 1 Company, under Major the Honourable Charles Byng of the Life Guards. For some reason Byng, like Phipps, felt the need to take personal command of his skirmishers, more properly a job for a subaltern. Towards the left-rear corner of the square a number of temperamental baggage camels were already playing up and inflicting periodic bouts of disarray on the HCR companies in their vicinity.

The main caravan track to Metemmeh ran parallel to a wide khor, not far from its left bank. Initially the square moved along the right bank, but as time wore on Stewart had the formation steered up the gentle slopes on the right until the khor lay about 600 yards downhill from the left face. Although they can have numbered only about 60 men in all, the GCR and MICR skirmishers enjoyed considerable success in driving back the enemy in front, and suppressing if not entirely neutralizing their fire. The right flank, though, continued to be troublesome. It took the best part of a harrowing hour to outflank the main Mahdist position. Now that their original line of defence was unhinged, Mahdist resistance was becoming stiffer by the minute. The GCR medical officer, Surgeon James Magill, was shot in the leg after being called forward to tend to a casualty on Romilly's skirmish line, and was only brought in 'with some difficulty'.[32] From time to time large clusters of white-robed *ansar* could be discerned forming up in the scrub on the right, creating the impression that the long-awaited assault was imminent. Bennet Burleigh estimated one such group at 1,500 strong. Where such tempting targets presented themselves, Colonel Boscawen secured permission to halt the square and engage them with volleys from the Grenadier, RMLI and Royal Sussex companies. Each time the *ansar* reacted by falling back to dead ground.

Because the right-face companies were coming into action most often, Stewart and his officers continued to infer that the enemy's weight was concentrated in that direction. Around 10.45 a.m., however, a number of green Islamic banners were sighted on a low ridge about a mile to the left front, just above the lip of the khor. There was some speculation amongst the Guards officers that they marked either a burial-ground or the enemy's camp, but Captain Norton could make out human forms amongst them and called for a halt so as to bring the guns to bear. As soon as his shells began exploding on the ridge, several hundred *ansar* leapt to their feet and dashed back into dead ground. Some officers concluded that this short bombardment had cleared the left flank. Lieutenant Douglas Dawson of the Coldstream Guards (whose brother Vesey was in the same company) heard Stewart indicate a change of axis to Burnaby with, 'Move a little more to the left; I want that green flag.'[33] In the meantime the volume of fire from the right had become so heavy that the native drivers with the baggage camels had begun edging away from it. In so doing they caused further problems for the HCR companies struggling to keep station at the left-rear corner of the square.

Charge of the Ansar

Stewart and his staff remained largely oblivious to the difficulties at the rear and pressed on down the valley until the line of flags and banners was some 700–800 yards to the left of the square. Observing the progress of the skirmishers with his field glasses the general was heard to remark 'There's old Phippy; he'll have some of those flags in a minute.'[34] Then, as if from nowhere, a hundred or more additional flags and banners suddenly appeared, betraying at once that this was no mere graveyard. A minute or two more and something in the region of 5,000 *ansar* had broken cover. A massed attack was precisely what Stewart and his officers had been hoping for, but it was a daunting sight nonetheless. To Wilson the enemy appeared to be formed in three wedge-shaped phalanxes, each led by a mounted emir carrying a banner.[35] Although at first they were in plain view from the front and left faces of the square, at about 500–600 yards the centre and right-hand phalanxes disappeared into dead ground at the foot of the slope. By the time they came back into view, they were more squarely aligned with the British left. Wheeling smartly into a crescent-shaped formation all three phalanxes began a blood-curdling charge for the square. Spearheading the assault were hardy desert-dwellers from the Duguaim, Kenana and Hamr tribes.

As he stood beside Stewart waiting for the company commanders to commence what he knew would be a murderous fire, Sir Charles Wilson could not help feeling a mixture of pity and admiration for the enemy. Somewhere beyond the advancing host was a large reserve of Ja'aliyin tribesmen, and separate bodies of townsmen from Berber and Metemmeh. On the other three sides of the square thousands more *ansar* were skulking through the brush at relatively safe distances, in groups of anything between 50 and a few hundred. Also prowling the field were parties of horsemen from the Akhoryeh tribe. In overall command was one Abd-el-Majidel-Kalik of Berber. All told there may have been 12,000 *ansar* on the field. Mostly they were hardy Baggara peasant stock, dressed in white skull caps and dirty white or buff-coloured wraparound garments, many of them naked to the waist, others with their robes thrown over one shoulder like highland plaid. By contrast the men sent down from Khartoum were generally clad in turbans and knee-length white *jibbehs* adorned with patches of coloured cloth, a costume recently adopted as the hallmark of the Mahdist faithful. The predominant close-quarter weapons were broad-bladed stabbing spears and straight cross-hilted swords best suited to a hacking stroke. After the battle it was noted that no shields had been carried.[36] This transpired to be at the specific injunction of the Mahdi, who did not want his followers unnecessarily encumbered in what after all was a divinely assured victory.

Even though the square was at a halt, the Mahdist attack had caught it at a particularly inopportune moment. Just in front of the leading companies was a shallow depression with a low knoll just beyond. Burnaby yelled at the officers of the front face companies to push their men forward, so as to gain the rise and maximize their fields of fire.[37] In effect the move amounted to a sudden 30-yard lurch. Inevitably it sent waves of disarray rippling down the sides of the square. At the rear it created something close to disorder. To make matters worse a number of exhausted camels chose precisely this moment to drop to their knees, amongst them one carrying the injured Lord St Vincent. The sudden lurching movement left the recalcitrant camels stranded to the rear of the struggling HCR companies. A number of terrified native drivers abandoned their animals, casualties and all, and fled for the sanctuary of the square. A Life Guards officer and two or three HCR privates ran out to effect a rescue and somehow succeeded in harrying most of the animals back onto their feet and in through the rear ranks of the square in the very nick of time.

Not unnaturally the MICR and GCR skirmishers had taken to their heels and were now sprinting back to safety. The KRRC section had a 200-yard head start on the *ansar* at best. Some historians have observed that a general raised in the infantry would not have encumbered a fighting square with skirmishers but, to be fair to Stewart, up to this point they had played a pivotal role in keeping the enemy's fire in check. Moreover such critics have failed to do their homework, for Stewart transferred into the 3rd Dragoon Guards only in 1873 and had been a regimental officer in the infantry for far longer than he had spent with the cavalry. That said, there can be no denying that the skirmishers were now well and truly in the way. Already the enemy were safely inside the optimal 400-yard killing range of the Martini-Henry; if the onslaught was to be stopped dead in its tracks the company commanders needed to open fire now. Somebody raised the cry for the skirmishers to lie down so that the front-face companies could volley over their heads, but Johnny Campbell was having none of it and yelled

'No! No! Run like hell.'[38] An officer's batman, probably Campbell's own, was too slow across the ground and was caught and killed by fleet-footed *ansar*.[39] Major Byng's HCR skirmishers were to cause a particular problem. Because they were preoccupied with a fire-fight at the rear, they did not immediately notice the charge of the *ansar* and were slower off the mark than Campbell's men.[40] In the meantime, the range had closed to a nerve-tingling 150–200 yards.

As the last of the KRRC men scrambled to safety, the front face and front-left corner of the square seemed to the charging *ansar* to explode. Six thunderous company volleys from the Coldstreamers, the Scots Guards and the MICR companies sent clouds of dense white smoke racing in all directions, making it well nigh impossible for most British riflemen to observe the effect of their fire. In the six or seven seconds it took to eject their spent cases, thumb home a fresh cartridge and ready themselves for the next 'present', the smoke had billowed above head height to reveal something of the carnage to their front. Burleigh was one of the few who did see the effect of the first volley; 'A hundred or more Arabs dropped, and for a moment I saw their force waver and halt, as a man stops to gasp for breath at any sudden surprise.' As the range shortened still further, Lieutenant Douglas Dawson of GCR noticed that, 'all the flags coming on, high up in the air were being riddled with bullets.' Little wonder then that in his account of the battle Private Burge recollected his company officers bellowing 'Aim lower men, aim lower!'[41]

Number 5 Company HCR (5th and 16th Lancers), the left-hand company of three on the left face, should also have been in action alongside the Mounted Infantry and the left wing of GCR, but was forced to hold its fire as Charles Byng and others were still inside its fields of fire. In the meantime the Guards and MICR company commanders volleyed again and again, each in their turn, until their every sense cried out that somewhere beyond the gun smoke the dead lay in heaps. For all the fanatical ardour of the *ansar*, this was the sort of murderous fire that inevitably brought the human instinct for self-preservation racing to the fore. To make matters worse the infantry volleys were supplemented by man-shredding salvoes of case-shot from Norton's 7-pounders, two of them positioned a few yards in advance of the front face, and the third at the front-left corner. With the leading wave of brave-hearts mown down, the weight of the Mahdist assault shifted more to its right, making ground with astonishing rapidity to threaten the left-rear corner of the square. On the right face where the enemy were maintaining a safe distance, the Grenadier, RMLI and Royal Sussex companies had no significant targets to volley at. For the time being at least, the action would be restricted to the British left.

Eager to bring the Gardner into action, Charlie Beresford had the gun manhandled out through the left-rear corner of the square, where Major Byng and the last of the HCR skirmishers were only now scrambling to safety – not everybody made it. Now that their fields of fire were clear, the officers of No. 5 Company were at last able to bring their men into action and quickly joined with the MICR companies to their right in volleying hard into the assault. But the damage had already been done – Byng and his men had cost the lancers the crucial three or four medium-range volleys that might have made all the difference. Instead the delay allowed the *ansar* to race within striking distance of the British line and to probe the all too obvious confusion at the left rear.

Just around the corner from the lancers, Major Wilfred Gough's[42] No. 4 Company (Royals and Scots Greys) was still struggling as a result of the last-minute lurch by the front face to close up and take station. Important primary sources such as Stewart's official report and Beresford's memoirs do not specifically record how it came about but instead of racing to take up their appointed places in the rear face, Gough's troopers ran to the left of the Gardner, deployed into line and opened fire. In doing so they extended the left face of the square in the principal direction of threat, but left a gaping hole at its left-rear corner. Such an improbable movement is unlikely to have occurred spontaneously and must logically have been directed by the company officers. No doubt in the heat of the moment it seemed to Gough to be the thing to do, but in reality it amounted to a terrible tactical misjudgement – a decision that no infantry officer would even have contemplated.

To Break a British Square

Abu Klea is always cited as one of the rare instances when a British square was broken, but in reality the square was no longer intact. Perhaps because it was to cost Wilfred Gough his life, his error was tactfully glossed over in Stewart's report. But the major was not entirely alone in underestimating two critical tactical factors – the vital importance of a square's integrity, and the astonishing mobility of unencumbered *ansar* fighters. Instead of riding over to recall No. 4 Company, Fred Burnaby compounded the problem by wheeling Major Walter Atherton's No. 3 Company (4th and 5th Dragoon Guards) out from the rear face and extending it on Gough's left.[43] In essence the three-company left face of the square had now become a five-company firing line with an open left flank, whilst the four-company rear face had been reduced to a two-company firing line with an exposed right. It is possible that Burnaby sensed No. 4 Company's vulnerability to an outflanking move and was seeking to protect its left flank. It is more probable, however, that like Gough he thought he was doing the right thing by bringing more rifles to bear. Either way, the ill-conceived manoeuvre was a recipe for disaster. Of course their decisions were made in the blink of an eye, in the midst of a highly charged situation, and in that context are at least understandable – but it is for the avoidance of unsound snap decisions that armies evolve standing battle drills, and the first commandment of fighting in square was 'thou shalt not break ranks'.

Charlie Beresford was unable to resist firing the Gardner in person:

> They were tearing down upon us with a roar like the roar of the sea, an immense surging wave of white-slashed black forms brandishing bright spears and long flashing swords; and all were chanting as they leaped and ran, the war song of their faith 'La ilaha ill Allah Mohamedu rasul Allah'; and the terrible rain of bullets poured into them by the Mounted Infantry and the Guards stayed them not . . . I laid the Gardner gun myself to make sure. As I fired, I saw the enemy mown down in rows, dropping like ninepins; but as the men killed were in rear of the front rank, after firing about forty rounds (eight turns of the lever), I lowered the elevation. I was putting in most effective work on the leading ranks and had fired about thirty rounds [more] when the gun jammed. The extraction had pulled the head from a discharged cartridge, leaving the empty cylinder in the barrel. William Rhodes, chief boatswain's mate, and myself immediately set to work to clear the barrel or to take out its lock.[44]

Despite the heavy fire from the Gardner and the companies of the left face, the *ansar* assault continued to make ground in the direction of the glaringly obvious British weak-spot. With the fast-moving surge for the open flank gathering both speed and momentum, Burnaby suddenly realised his mistake. Pushing his horse through the ranks of the Heavies, he began bellowing orders for the two misaligned companies to wheel rearwards, pivoting by the right so as to close the yawning gap in the rear face. On a parade ground a well drilled Guards battalion might have executed the manoeuvre with seconds to spare but this was Abu Klea, an undulating piece of desert, not Horse Guards Parade, and the troops at issue were not guardsmen but dismounted heavy cavalrymen. Furthermore there was a deafening noise, a fanatical enemy host closing fast and confusion in the air.

Just at this point an isolated body of Akhoryeh mounted on black horses appeared from the brush and made a brave attack on the right-rear corner of the square. Their sense of timing was impeccable, but nonetheless they met with a bloody repulse at the hands of No.1 Company HCR (1st and 2nd Life Guards) and the Royal Sussex companies, who like good infantrymen thought nothing of aiming for the enemy's horses. Over 30 ponies were shot down in the charge, to say nothing of the subsequent loss amongst the unseated riders.[45]

In the few short minutes before impact, Fred Burnaby had given all the direction a senior officer could give, not all of it tactically sound, but with the inevitable collision only seconds away it had become abundantly clear that the battle would be won or lost not by colonels, but by the tenacity of subalterns, NCOs and private soldiers. All that a colonel of the sovereign's bodyguard could do now was to wield his sabre like a common trooper. Spurring 'Moses' forward, Burnaby set his sights on a mounted emir. The *Daily Telegraph* correspondent was nearby:

> Ere the Arab closed with him a bullet from someone in our ranks, and not Burnaby's sword thrust, brought the sheikh to the ground. The enemy's spearmen were close behind, and one of them dashed suddenly at the colonel, pointing the long blade of his spear at his throat. Checking his horse and slowly pulling it backward, Burnaby leaned forward in his saddle and parried the Moslem's rapid and ferocious thrusts; but the length of the man's weapon – eight feet – put it out of his power to return with interest the Arab's murderous intent. Once or twice, I think the colonel touched his man, only to make him more wary and eager. The affray was the work of three or four seconds only, for the savage horde of swarthy negroes from Kordofan, and the straight-haired, tawny complexioned Arabs of the Bayuda steppe, were fast closing in on our square.
>
> Burnaby fenced smartly, just as if he were playing in an assault-at-arms, and there was a smile on his features as he drove off the man's awkward thrusts. The scene was taken in at a glance – with that lightning instinct which I have seen the desert warriors before now display in battle while coming to one another's aid – by an Arab who, pursuing a soldier, had passed five paces to Burnaby's right and rear. Turning with a sudden spring this second Arab ran his spear-point into the colonel's right shoulder. It was but a slight wound – enough, though, to cause Burnaby to twist round in his saddle to defend himself from this unexpected attack. Before the savage could repeat his unlooked for blow – so near the ranks of the square was the scene now being enacted – a soldier ran out and drove his sword-bayonet through the second assailant. [This was Corporal Mackintosh of HCR who was killed a few moments later.] As the Englishman withdrew the steel the ferocious Arab wriggled round and sought to reach him. The effort was too much however even for his delirium of hatred against the Christian, and the rebel reeled and fell. Brief as was Burnaby's glance backward at this fatal episode, it was long enough to enable the first Arab to deliver his spear point full in the brave officer's throat. The blow drove Burnaby out of the saddle, but it required a second one before he let go his grip of the reins and tumbled upon the ground. Half-a-dozen Arabs were now about him. With the blood gushing in streams from his gashed

> throat, the dauntless Guardsman leaped to his feet, sword in hand, and slashed at the ferocious group. They were the wild strokes of a proud, brave man, dying hard. Private Wood of the Grenadier Guards sprang to his rescue, but it was too late, for the colonel was overborne and fell to the ground.[46]

The crew of the jammed Gardner were also amongst the first to come to blows with the enemy. Charlie Beresford saw two of his men, Chief Boatswain's Mate William Rhodes and Armourer Walter Miller, speared to death either side of him. A huge able seaman nicknamed 'Jumbo' was also cut down beside the gun. Beresford himself was more than merely lucky. First he was knocked off the trail of the gun with an axe-handle rather than the blade; next he was able to catch a spear thrust with one hand; then, on scrambling to his feet, he was carried backwards in the crush into the reeling but as yet unbroken ranks of the Greys and the Royals. The other naval officers were less fortunate: Commander Alfred Pigott[47] and Lieutenant Rudolph De Lisle both lost their lives within 20 yards of the Gardner. Observing to their front and taking the odd pot-shot at the *ansar* riflemen still infesting the scrub, the men of the Guards, RMLI and Royal Sussex companies were oblivious to the looming crisis behind them. All of a sudden a terrific jolt was felt down all four sides of the square, as the leading wave of *ansar* made contact with the left face and left-rear corner. To many men the shockwave came like a bolt from the blue. Where moments before the officers of the front and right-face companies had been pacing calmly back and forth behind their men, watching for targets, they were now obliged to turn about with drawn swords and cocked revolvers at the ready. When Douglas Dawson realised that the enemy were inside the square, he felt compelled to step across to his brother and shake hands.

At the immediate points of impact the mêlée was bloody in the extreme, as Burleigh reported:

> Then the great onrush came, and with spear poised and sword uplifted straight into our left face, rear corner, the Arab horde struck us like a tempest. The Heavies were thrown into confusion, for the enemy were right amongst them, killing and wounding with demoniacal fury. Backward from the left face the square fell, staggering and irregular . . . Confusion for the instant reigned supreme.

The men of the three original left-face companies were forced slowly back in a heaving, struggling human swarm, through what had once been the centre of the square, until they were jammed against the baggage camels and the front-face companies beyond.

As this savage brawl was developing, hundreds more *ansar* continued to gain ground to their right, racing instinctively for the gap created by Burnaby's error of judgement, a gap which the HCR officers and sergeants were now striving desperately to close. In a few short seconds they were through, led by a mounted emir called Musa, the sheikh of the Duguaim tribe. The old man caught Sir Charles Wilson's eye:

> I had noticed him in the advance with his banner in one hand and a book of prayers in the other and never saw anything finer. The old man never swerved to the right or the left, and never ceased chanting his prayers until he had planted his banner in our square. If any man deserved a place in the Muslim paradise, he did. When I saw the old sheikh in the square, and heard the wild uproar behind the camels, I drew my revolver; for directly he fell, the Arabs began running in under the camels to the front part of the square.[48]

The onslaught swamped Nos. 3 and 4 Companies from both front and rear inflicting heavy casualties in the process, but mercifully lost much of its momentum amongst the baggage camels. Many of the wounded in the cacolets and litters were brutally hacked to death by frenzied, merciless assailants. When the camel carrying Lord St Vincent was cut down, it fell on top of him, trapping him beneath its flank. It might not have felt like it at the time but it was actually a stroke of luck; the soldier on the animal's other flank was left exposed to the enemy and was quickly done to death.[49] Lance Corporal Chowler and Private Hyam of the 5th Dragoon Guards sprang forward to defend St Vincent and were obliged to stand their ground in front of the recoiling British line. Somehow they survived the swirling mêlée. Their courage would be rewarded with DCMs.[50] Nearby Surgeon William Briggs was wielding a sword in the thick of the fight. His helmet knocked from his head, he was observed bellowing like a combatant officer for the men to rally around him.

Saving the Day

The HCR and Naval Brigade survivors fell back resolutely until they were packed together at the foot of the knoll occupied by the front face companies. While the men at the front of the scrum fought back with bayonet and rifle butt, the men behind them loaded and fired as fast as they could, shooting into the throng over the shoulders of their comrades at point-blank range. A number of rifles jammed inopportunely and cost men their lives. Bennet Burleigh also experienced a stoppage but was lucky enough to escape with his life. Having snatched up a Martini-Henry, he was able to fire only three rounds before it jammed. Hurling the rifle down in disgust he was obliged to defend himself with his revolver which, with its poor stopping power, was far from being a weapon of first choice in a close-quarter fight with maddened fanatics. Worse even than the many instances of jamming, a significant number of sword-bayonets proved to have been poorly tempered in manufacture and bent double in the fray. The frenzied *ansar* ran in all directions, shrieking wildly and flailing swords, clubs and spears. For all the terrifying savagery of their onslaught, the British knew they were fighting for their lives and were not to be easily outdone in a nose-to-nose killing match. Somehow a hedge of bayonets was quickly contrived at the foot of the knoll, some men safe within it, others fighting for their lives outside. At the top of the slope the officers of the front-face companies ordered their rear ranks to turn about and fire over the heads of the Heavies and the sailors into the scrimmage beyond. Officers fighting in the thick of the mêlée were convinced that the square shifted its ground to the right front, but the sensation was an illusion – the accounts of GCR officers make it clear that their companies stood rooted to the spot.

A significant number of British casualties were undoubtedly caused by friendly fire. According to Wilson both Major Wilfred Gough of No. 4 Company and Major Ludovick Carmichael of No. 5 Company were accidentally shot and killed by their own side.[51] Charlie Beresford had yet another close scrape when he took a round through his helmet, whilst Gleichen, Marling and Wilson all felt bullets passing uncomfortably close. But for all the deaths and near-deaths there can be no doubt that such desperate times fully warranted correspondingly desperate measures. Mahdists fell by the dozen to the plunging short-range fire. In his 1886 account of the battle for *Nineteenth Century* magazine, Colonel Reggy Talbot singled out the mounted infantry as the saviours of the day – amidst all the panic and confusion, the MICR men kept their heads and made every round count.

Somewhere near the front-left corner, the staff came under attack. Lord Airlie, the brigade-major, received two glancing spear wounds in the struggle. Sir Herbert drew his sabre and spurred his horse at the nearest assailant but was unseated almost immediately. Wilson thought his horse was brought down by a stray round from the mounted infantry, though Douglas Dawson wrote that it was 'by sheer weight . . . knocked off his legs and speared'. Three maddened desert warriors rushed forward to finish the general as he lay sprawled in the dust. Fortunately Sir Charles Wilson and some nearby MICR officers were able to shoot them down with their revolvers before they could do any serious harm. Stewart was quickly dragged to his feet and ushered to safety by his staff officers.

Nearby there was hand-to-hand fighting around the 7-pounder positioned at the front-left corner. Lieutenant James Guthrie RA was so intent on fighting his gun that when he came under attack he had still not drawn his sword or revolver. The 24-year-old Gunner Albert Smith raced to his rescue wielding only a trail-spike. He parried one blow from Guthrie's assailant, gaining the vital second the lieutenant needed to draw his sword and run his attacker through.

As the dying Arab sank to his knees, he lashed out wildly with a long knife wounding Guthrie severely. Smith promptly brained the man with his trail-spike and stood at bay to defend his prostrate officer against all comers. His selfless stand would earn him the VC.

Notwithstanding the earlier press furore centred on Burnaby, Captain Charlie 'Bloody-Minded' Pigott, commanding D Company MICR, was using a double-barrelled shotgun to deadly effect. With tribesmen weaving in and out of the heaving mass of camels, and even ducking beneath their bellies to get at the British, some of the naval ratings were giving Pigott target-indications. Beresford saw him riddle the shaven head of one man in response to a cry of 'Here's another joker, sir!'[52] A veteran of the Zulu War, Laing's Nek (where he was unhorsed in Brownlow's charge), Ingogo, Majuba (as a subaltern in the 3rd/60th company accused by the Gordons of misbehaviour), the Egyptian campaign, El Teb and Tamai, Pigott was in the process of transferring to the 21st Hussars. Evidently a sporting man, he had brought along not only his favourite game-gun, but his favourite gun-dog too. The animal seems to have shared its master's aversion to Mahdists as, at the climax of the battle, it had dashed out from the sanctuary of the square to bark at the charging enemy, before prudently bounding back to safety with the MICR skirmishers.

In a few short minutes the bare patch of desert which had once marked the centre of the square had been transformed into a scene of bloody carnage. In addition to the hundreds of dead and maimed human forms strewn across the desert, about 50 baggage camels had also been brought down. Despite the heavy British loss it was becoming clear that the hard-hitting Martini-Henry would prevail. Fighting to front and rear, with their left flank refused, MICR's C and D Companies had done terrible execution; while their rear rank men were snap-shooting into the crush around the baggage camels, the steady volleys of the front rank had prevented any significant reinforcement of the break-in. Before long almost all of the *ansar* who had come to close quarters had been shot down. A last handful broke away from the fight and ran back towards the khor to rejoin the thousands of men who had been first checked and then repelled by the fire of the mounted infantry. The retreat of this last remnant was the cue for a general withdrawal. Soon large parties of Mahdists could be seen jogging sullenly towards the hills on the far side of the valley. Others loitered at a distance causing Sir Charles Wilson to worry that they might come again while the troops were still badly disordered and 'wild with excitement'. A few shells from the 7-pounders and a last few volleys into the scrub hurried them on their way. All told the artillery had fired 38 rounds of shrapnel, 19 of common shell and 6 of case-shot.[53]

The Battle of Abu Klea was over. Breathless and incredulous, the wild-eyed British survivors raised a series of resounding cheers. Some of the enemy looked round at the sound and shook their fists angrily. If nothing else the wild men of the desert had earned the respect of Private Burge and his mates:

> I for one was glad that they went away unmolested. Of their kind they were the bravest of the brave. They did not know the meaning of fear. I was glad and relieved, too, and I do not think that there was either officer or man in the broken square who had not a feeling of thankfulness to see the backs and not the faces of them.[54]

Not more than about 20 minutes had elapsed since the enemy host sprang to their feet.

Having fought for their lives alongside everybody else, the doctors and medics were now able to throw down their weapons and begin tending to the most dangerously wounded. There were so many of them that the less severely hurt and the scores of men with cuts, bruises, gashes and grazes would not be seen to for hours.

The intensity of the fighting was reflected in the sheer number of men killed or wounded in so short a time. Perhaps 1,100 Sudanese Arabs lay dead or dying inside the square or in front of its left face. Hundreds more had been wounded and helped from the field. On the British side 9 officers[55] and 65 other ranks had lost their lives and a further 9[56] and 85 had been wounded. Inevitably it was the Heavies who suffered the heaviest loss with 6 and 48 killed and a further 28 men wounded. The 40-strong naval detachment had lost 2 and 6 killed, with another 7 men wounded, while the Royal Sussex had 5 killed and 25 wounded.

The Blues thought immediately of their gallant colonel and spread out in search of him. Lieutenant Lord George Binning, a young veteran of Kassassin and Tel-el-Kebir, was amongst the first on the scene:

> I made my way as best I could to the spot where I had last seen him, foreboding in my heart. But I was not the first to find him. A young private in the Bays, a mere lad, was already beside him trying to support his head on his knee; the lad's genuine grief, with tears running down his face, was touching as were his simple words: 'Oh sir, here is the bravest man in England, dying, and no one to help him.' It was too true, a glance showed that he was past help. A spear had inflicted a terrible wound on the right side of his neck and throat, and his skull had been cleft by a blow from a two-handed sword – probably as he fell forward on his pony's neck. Either wound would have proved mortal. The marvel was that he was still alive. As I took his hand, a feeble pressure and a faint look of recognition in his eyes, told me he still breathed, but life was ebbing fast, and it was only a matter of a few moments before he was gone. Amid the slain Arabs he lay there, a veritable Colossus, and alone of the dead his face wore the composed and placid smile of one

> who had been suddenly carried away in the midst of a congenial and favourite occupation.[57]

Some of the Blues were so distraught at the death of their colonel that they sat down and cried.

Bloody Aftermath

The battle was over by midday but, as was always the way in the Sudan, the killing went on for a while longer. Stewart immediately re-formed his square and pushed forward 150 yards so that the troops could recuperate away from the deeply unpleasant scenes of slaughter. The Guards officers gathered to talk and marvelled that, their doctor aside, not one of their number had been hurt. Work parties were sent back to pick up the wounded and bury the dead. From time to time they were attacked by warriors who had feigned death amongst the slain. Some of the enemy wounded clambered to their feet and made suicide charges, including a boy of about 12 who had already taken a round through the stomach. Another man ran at an officer with a spear, only for the officer to sidestep, grab the weapon with his left hand, and run his assailant through with his sword. The man remained upright writhing on the point of the sword, until a private soldier ran up and shot him dead at point-blank range.[58] Most of the enemy wounded refused all succour and lashed out with their weapons at passers-by. Charlie Beresford saw an Arab who had been shot in both legs, sit up and throw a spear at a soldier. All such cases attracted lethal retaliation. Beresford himself shot dead one enemy casualty who, having been placed aboard a cacolet, chose to scorn the magnanimity of his rescuers by trying to bite off the thumb of the wounded naval rating beside him.

So many baggage camels had been killed or harmed in the mêlée that some of the stores had to be burned. The exercise was badly handled and the flames spread to the pack-saddles of some of the dead and injured camels, the smell of burning flesh 'adding to the horrors of the day'. A great pile of enemy weapons and banners was made, and the Martinis of the dead and seriously injured were smashed at the stock before being abandoned in the desert. A burial party covered Burnaby's grave with rocks to protect his mortal remains from predators, but a constant stream of soldiers came wandering by to add a stone until at length the covering of rocks had grown into a cairn. Marling was amongst those who wandered across the field taking in the gruesome scene. Although he was uninjured his left sleeve was drenched in blood from the shoulder to the wrist. The fighting had been so intense that he hadn't the first idea whose blood it might be. Near Burnaby's grave he found the carcass of 'Moses' and cut a length of hair from the pony's tail as a memento. All the while the handful of doctors, Ferguson, Parke, Briggs, Dick and Maconachie, had been performing sterling work amongst the wounded. 'Jumbo' was amongst the many men who had good cause to be grateful to them – much to Beresford's surprise he had been found alive near the Gardner with no fewer than 17 stab wounds. Rudolph De Lisle's body had more than 50.

Despite his victory Stewart found himself in a more difficult position than ever. So far from a firm home base, his casualties were bound to prove a significant hindrance. Although he gave brief consideration to waiting for reinforcements, he concluded that Gordon's reportedly desperate position gave him no option but to push on for the Nile, now about 23 miles distant. The first objective, though, would be the all-important wells only three miles ahead. As usual the 19th Hussars trotted off ahead of everybody else. Not long afterwards the square set off. The wounded bore their suffering resolutely, as they bounced along on the flanks of the remaining baggage camels. By 5.00 p.m. the wells were in British hands and Barrow's men were at last able to give their tough little stallions a long-delayed drink. After everybody had drunk their fill the square was moved onto a nearby high-point for the night. Wilson busied himself with translating some letters found on a dead emir and with interrogating a number of prisoners rounded up by the hussars.

Despite the tiredness settling over the troops, the immediate priority was the reunification of the column. Three hundred volunteers were called for to march back to the zareba under the command of Captain Phipps and bring up the rear details. For the men left behind at the wells, the great majority, an intensely cold night was made worse by the mental and physical after-effects of so hard-fought an action. Nobody had thought to bring any blankets for the wounded, who could not be made comfortable as a consequence and suffered a night of abject misery. It was not until 7.00 a.m. that Phipps returned with Major Gern and his command. They brought four Sudanese blacks with them who had surrendered at the zareba the previous day, all of whom had been captured in the Hicks disaster and forced to change sides. As the great majority of the troops had not eaten since snatching a biscuit or two for breakfast the previous day, the next priority was a decent meal and a catnap. Sir Herbert gave orders that the column was to be prepared to press on by 4.00 p.m. The wounded, some stores and two companies of the Royal Sussex would be left behind at a new zareba to be constructed beside the wells. While the work was getting under way, the general settled down to write his official despatch to Wolseley.

Night March

Everything was ready by the appointed hour and the column marched as planned. The general intimation had been that it would cover as much ground as possible before halting for the night. But Stewart had already decided to try and reach the Nile by dawn and no halt was ever called. Ali Loda had advised that a few miles short of the river they would hit a wide belt of acacia trees which would prove difficult to traverse by night. Wilson spoke to Stewart confidentially, pointing out that the troops had not slept for the past two nights and questioning whether a night march was really necessary, but the general was adamant that they must push on. Undoubtedly his aim was to achieve surprise and so avoid a second engagement in the desert. More than anything it was Wilson's own interrogation of the prisoners that had shaped Stewart's thinking; the captives had indicated that another large Mahdist force was on its way up the west bank of the Nile from Omdurman.

The short evening march sailed by. Thereafter no lights were permitted and strict noise discipline was enforced. Without the benefit of moonlight, the column repeatedly fell into disarray. Everybody was exhausted and men fell asleep in the saddle by the score. As a result straggling became a problem, units ran into one another, loads slipped, and on a number of occasions the guides became hopelessly lost. At one point the column went round in a circle and the advanced guard came up behind the rear guard. It was a trying, vexatious and ill-tempered night for all concerned. Two hapless soldiers and a few of the native employees strayed from the column in the dark, while around a hundred baggage camels were lost. Private Dodd of 2nd Coldstream found his way back to the wells, but the other soldier and the natives were never seen again, though by one account it was later established that they wandered towards Metemmeh and were killed.[59] By the time the sun came up on the morning of Monday 19 January, the column had been marching for 14 hours but had gained only 18 miles.[60]

At about 7.30 a.m. the head of the column climbed a rise from which it was possible to see Metemmeh and the Nile. The river was still five miles away when the 19th Hussars came galloping in to report that the scrub ahead concealed a large number of enemy riflemen. If there was to be a second major engagement after all, Stewart knew he had to feed and rest his exhausted command, at least fleetingly, before fighting it. Having pushed on to within 6,000 yards of the river, the head of the column came to a small knoll in a clearing in the scrub. 'This position will do for me,' Stewart announced to the staff. 'Tell the officers and men we will have breakfast first and then go out and fight.'

'Terrible Interval'

The camels were knee-lashed in a compact central mass as usual, with the companies arrayed around them in a rough square, but long before breakfast could be completed in peace parties of enemy riflemen closed up and brought the position under fire. The troops were ordered to construct a breastwork of stores and camel saddles. The perimeter was barely 300 yards in diameter and with so many men and animals packed inside made for the easiest of targets. Around 10.15 a.m. disaster struck when Stewart, who had been standing on a biscuit box surveying the situation through his field glasses, slumped to the ground, shot through the groin.[61] He was quickly stretchered away to the surgeons who took next to no time in pronouncing his injuries mortal. The staff did their best to keep the seriousness of the general's condition from the troops, but inevitably word got out and spread like wildfire. Command of the Desert Column devolved upon the next senior officer, Colonel Sir Charles Wilson, head of intelligence, a man who had never before held a field command.

> After a short talk with Boscawen, who was next senior officer, we went together to Stewart, and found him very cool and collected, and apparently not in great pain; but on my saying I hoped he would soon be well, he at once replied that he was certain the wound was fatal, and that his soldiering days were over. I said what I could to cheer him; but as time was passing, and as I did not wish to disturb him more than was necessary, I asked him what he had intended doing if he had not been hit. He said the best thing to be done was to go straight at Matemmeh [*sic*] or to repeat the Abu Klea plan of going out to fight for the water, and then returning to the zeribah [*sic*] to carry the wounded and stores etc down to the Nile.[62]

Wilson decided on the second option, a re-run of Abu Klea, with part of the force advancing to the Nile and the remainder staying put for the moment, but knew that the current defensive position would have to be strengthened first. Before long the incoming fire had become intolerable. To counteract the worst of its effects the Guards and the Mounted Infantry each threw out a company-strength skirmish line. Seventy yards to the right front there was a small knoll which could not be allowed to fall into enemy hands and would necessitate the building of a small defensive outwork. The job of constructing it was assigned to a party of 2nd Life Guards under Captain Lord Douglas Cochrane[63] and some of the Scots Greys. Bennet Burleigh had fought for the Confederacy in the American Civil War and was no stranger to danger. Now, despite his civilian status and a heavy cross-fire, he lent a hand in carrying biscuit boxes and saddles out from the zareba, an act for which he would be mentioned in despatches, the first time such an honour was conferred upon a correspondent.

Inside the zareba the war correspondents attracted more than their fair share of incoming fire. The vastly experienced John Cameron of the *Standard* had been with Colley at Laing's Nek, Ingogo and Majuba, aboard Admiral Seymour's flagship at Alexandria, with Baker at El Teb, and with Graham at Tamai and Second El Teb. He was sitting near his camel when his servant proffered a tin of sardines for his lunch. As he stretched out his hand, Cameron was hit in the back and killed.[64] The no-less-experienced St Leger Herbert of the *Morning Post*, known to his friends as 'Sankey', was on his way back from visiting Stewart, a personal friend, when a round hit him squarely in the throat killing him instantly. Herbert had been a civil secretary to Wolseley in South Africa, had accompanied him in the Sekhukhune campaign, had fought as a volunteer at Tel-el-Kebir and had been severely wounded at Tamai. Melton Prior, the well-known war artist, was struck by spent rounds on no fewer than three occasions. Burleigh suffered a fright when he was hit in the throat by a ricochet which, although it caused severe swelling under his ear, did him no lasting harm.

Major Dorward of the engineer detachment supervised the raising of a second redoubt around the doctors and the wounded. Its capacity had been exceeded long before it was finished. Burleigh described the scene around the makeshift hospital:

> As stretcher after stretcher with its gory load was taken to the hospital, the little place was found too little, and the wounded had to be laid outside. Surgeon Major Ferguson and Doctor Briggs and their colleagues had their skill and time taxed to the utmost. Want of water hampered their operations; doctors and patients were alike exposed to the enemy's fire. More harrowing battle scenes in the course of a long experience I never saw.[65]

Count Gleichen was amongst the 40 or so men who in the course of those harrowing few hours were carried back to the hospital. He was forward on the Grenadier Guards skirmish line when, on kneeling up to use his binoculars, he was hit painfully in the midriff. He was carried to the rear by two of his men, but soon realized that a spent round had struck one of his buttons without doing any real harm. As soon as he had recovered his breath, Gleichen returned to duty on the skirmish line. According to Wilson, James Dorward managed to get Lieutenant Charles Crutchley (Adjutant GCR) shot by insisting that he sign a receipt for some entrenching tools – a somewhat officious act in the presence of the enemy to say the least. Unlike the night before Abu Klea, where they had been largely protected by the lie of the land, this time the camels were terribly exposed; dozens of them were shot during the course of the morning. A sense of frustration at the apparent inactivity of their commanders settled over many soldiers. Beresford encapsulated something of the mood in his memoirs:

> Then followed a terrible interval which lasted for hours. Under that pitiless fire, exposed to an invisible enemy, men and camels were being hit every minute. All this time the heat was intense. There we lay in the blazing sun, helpless, the rattle of rifles all around, the note of the bullets

> singing overhead, or ending with a thud close at hand, men crying out suddenly, or groaning, camels lying motionless and silent, blood trickling from their wounds and no one seemed to know what we were going to do.

During the course of the afternoon Marling, Burleigh and two soldiers scraped a hole in the sand to bury Sankey Herbert. Burleigh, whose boots had given out, spotted that Herbert had on a brand-new pair and remarked to Marling that it would be a sin to waste them on a dead man. 'I, being young and more squeamish in those days, protested and said, "Damn it Burleigh, you can't take the boots off poor old Sankey."' Leaving it at that, Marling made his way back to A Company in preparation for the coming fight.

The zareba would be left in the charge of Colonel Percy Barrow though, as a naval captain, Lord Beresford would technically be the senior man present. Barrow's guard force would consist of half of the HCR under Major Thomas Davison of the 16th Lancers, most of his own 19th Hussars, whose ponies were by now quite played out, the Royal Artillery detachment, half of the Royal Engineers under Dorward, the much depleted Naval Brigade and the usual medical and administrative details.

At about 2.30 p.m. the square formed up outside the rear face of the zareba where the enemy fire was marginally less severe. Even so the troops were made to lie down as they arrived to take post. Something around 900 men in all would have to fight their way to the Nile. Sir Charles Wilson would accompany the square but given his background would entrust executive command of the formation to Colonel Edward Boscawen. The next senior Guards officer, Captain & Lieutenant Colonel (Army rank) Mildmay Willson of the Scots Guards, took command of GCR in Boscawen's stead. The Guards companies would man the front face and extend half-way down the right flank. The second half of HCR under Talbot would provide the rest of the right face and the first third of the rear face. In the centre of the rear face were the two Royal Sussex companies under Major Sunderland. The Mounted Infantry under the younger Barrow would man the left face and the remaining third of the rear face. A number of important lessons had been learned at Abu Klea. As they tended to hinder mobility but provided only marginally more firepower, neither the guns nor the disgraced Gardner were taken along. In order to prevent any repetition of the difficulties at the corners of the square, a small reserve was posted at each of them. These reserve details were found by the other half of the sappers under Lieutenant Henry Lawson and parties of dismounted 19th Hussars under Lieutenant Craven. Despite the problems they had caused at Abu Klea, a number of baggage camels would have to be taken along to carry casualties.

The Battle of Abu Kru (Gubat), 19 January 1885

Given that a much stronger square had been penetrated only two days earlier, the sortie had the air of a desperate venture. Wilson noted that only one of the surviving war correspondents, Frederic Villiers of *The Graphic*, chose to accompany the square. Again the enemy in front numbered more than 10,000 men. The coming action would be christened the Battle of Abu Kru, though it is sometimes referred to as Gubat after the small village on the Nile that lay directly ahead. In a less than encouraging start, a number of men were shot as the order to stand up was given. They were left where they fell, to be recovered by carrying parties from the zareba. The square proceeded slowly and was subjected to the same sort of harassing fire that had dogged the advance at Abu Klea. As a result of the loud condemnation of Stewart's use of skirmishers by some of the infantry officers, none were employed on this occasion. From the zareba Beresford was able to rehabilitate the Gardner by breaking up a concentration of Baggara cavalry at long range. The gunners also did good service in support of the men in the square, by indicating to them with shell fire the presence of a number of as yet unseen enemy concentrations, until at length the little formation moved out of range.

Though Wilson and Boscawen steered a course designed to avoid the worst of the scrub, it was necessary from time to time to halt and fire volleys into it. At one point they were forced to backtrack, to get out of a particularly thick belt of ground cover. On occasion, when the enemy fire grew particularly heavy, the men in the square were ordered to halt, lie down and return fire from the prone position. For two dreadful hours the painstaking advance continued. The cacolets on the baggage camels had long since been filled with wounded, amongst them Wilson's interpreter Muhammed Effendi Ibrahim, a one-time member of the Egyptian secret police and friend to Arabi Pasha, who, his new employer noted, took advantage of the elevated view to enjoy a relaxing cigarette. Seven men fell dead in the two or three minutes preceding the battle's climax, including a marine who reeled from the rear rank of Major Poe's company into the arms of Sir Charles Wilson. It came as a great relief when the enemy were observed to be concentrating along the general line of a low gravel ridge 800 yards to the front. Suddenly the ridge came to life, as thousands of *ansar* leapt to their feet and streamed down the forward slope. The sight was so welcome to the sorely tried British Tommies that they raised a spontaneous cheer in response.

This time the square was perfectly formed and the attack was falling directly upon the Mounted Infantry and the Guards, the steadiest and best-drilled troops in the force. There was no last-minute lurch, nor were there any skirmishers obstructing the fields of fire. The first volleys were fired by the front-face

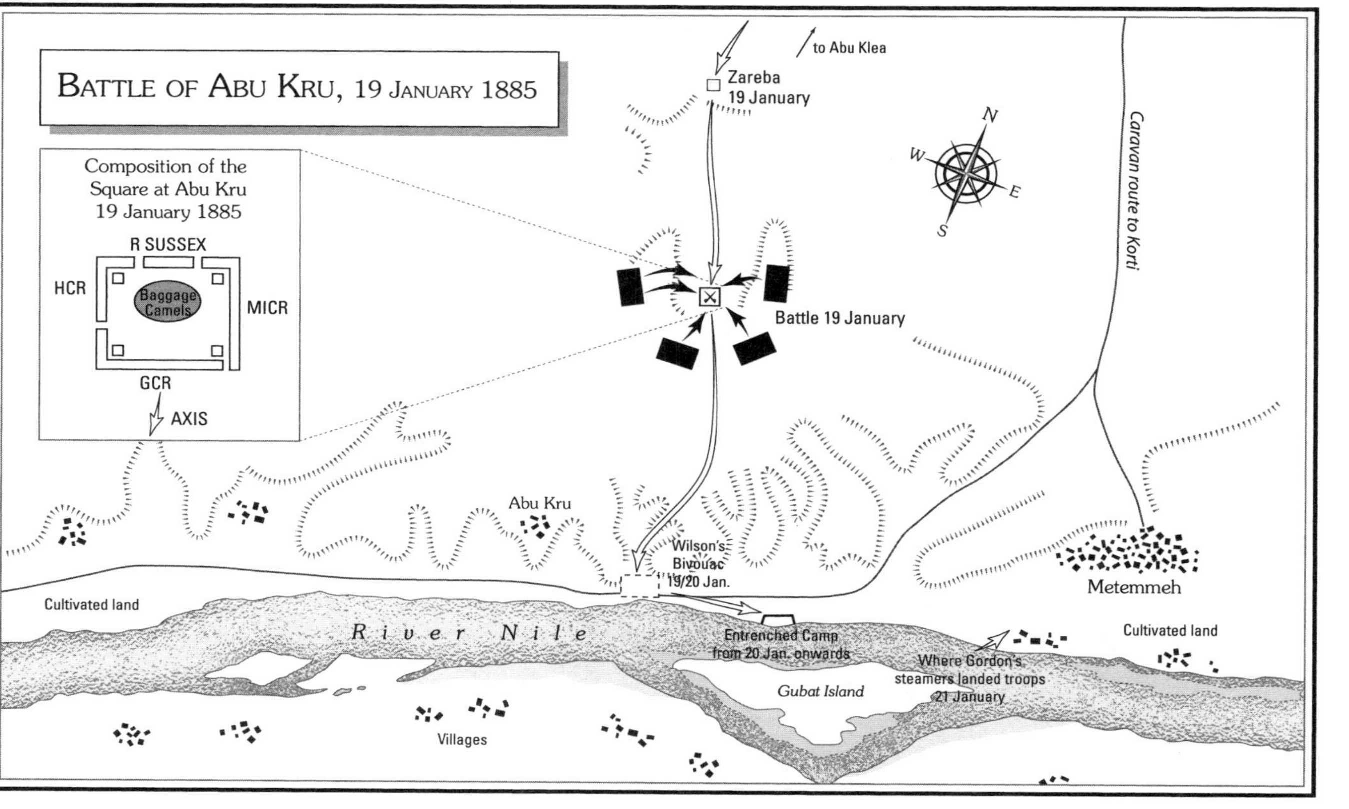

BATTLE OF ABU KRU, 19 JANUARY 1885
Composition of the Square at Abu Kru 19 January 1885
R SUSSEX
HCR
Baggage Camels
MICR
GCR
AXIS
to Abu Klea
Zareba 19 January
N
W
E
S
Caravan route to Korti
Battle 19 January
Abu Kru
Wilson's Bivouac 19/20 Jan.
Metemmeh
Cultivated land
River Nile
Entrenched Camp from 20 Jan. onwards
Where Gordon's steamers landed troops 21 January
Cultivated land
Gubat Island
Villages

companies at a range of 600 yards. Wilson and Boscawen observed that they had but little effect. In their eagerness to exact some measure of revenge for the preceding two hours, the troops had become over animated and seemed to be firing wildly. Boscawen decided to calm the excited soldiers by ordering his bugler to sound 'Cease Firing'. Much to Wilson's surprise there was a flawless response to the call. Now there was no other sound but the chanting of the enemy.[66]

Extolling the praises of Allah, the Prophet and the Mahdi, the great host charged on to destruction. The momentary breathing space served its purpose admirably by giving the subalterns and sergeants time to compose their men. When the range had closed to 300 yards, Boscawen had 'Commence Firing' sounded. The first GCR company to fire bowled over a score of *ansar*. The second, third and subsequent volleys were even more deadly and quickly forced the attack to ground. In a few short moments the first onset of the enemy crumbled. On its flanks the attack had sufficient momentum to reach down the sides of the smoke-wreathed square, allowing three of the four mounted infantry companies and the balance of the Guards to come into action. The volleys from the left and right faces were every bit as punishing as the hammer-blows from the front face, so that the Mahdist wings were also soon stopped dead. A minute or two later a few *ansar* brave-hearts leapt to their feet and tried again. Inspired by their example, hundreds more men surged forward until a renewed charge was rippling forward across a wide front. But the British continued to volley calmly and relentlessly until the *ansar* were once more driven to ground. A third charge met with a similar mauling. In the event not a single man made it to within 80 yards of the square. It took less than 10 minutes to break the back of the assault.

Once again the *ansar* streamed to the rear with British cheers resounding in their ears. This time they left only a few hundred men sprawled in the dust. Proportionately the British loss was the more grievous. Since the night march, 2 officers, 2 correspondents and 22 men had been killed, and 8 officers and 92 men wounded. But now, at least, the Bayuda was behind them, and the great river within striking distance.

The Nile at Last

Dog-tired but elated by their victory, the men in the square reached the river just as night was falling. With perfect discipline they waited their turn to drink, keeping three faces of the square formed up at all times. Once a series of strong pickets had been posted, they threw themselves down to sleep. They were woken, half-frozen with cold, at 5.00 a.m. and stood to their arms in the pre-dawn as usual. Wilson's immediate priority in daylight was to re-unite the two halves of his command by bringing up the men at the zareba. First he occupied the abandoned village of Gubat, which stood only a short distance from the river, about two miles upstream of Metemmeh. A hasty defensive position was improvised around a cluster of huts, where the wounded would be left in the care of the surgeons and 100 Heavies under Major Lord Arthur Somerset of the Blues, who had been slightly wounded the previous day but passed himself fit for duty.[67] Major Sunderland deployed his two Royal Sussex companies in the direction of Metemmeh as an outlying guard.

The Guards and Mounted Infantry formed regimental squares for the march back to the zareba, and were relieved to find their comrades much as they had left them. Although the position had been under fire throughout the afternoon, the night had passed off quietly. So quietly, in fact, that some of the medics had been at the medicinal brandy. Wilson found one still dead drunk and unfit for duty with wounded men on all sides. Lamenting the abolition of flogging four years earlier, Wilson had the wretch tied to a tree in the hot sun. Inevitably Barrow's force was still in a state of disarray. Almost all the baggage had been incorporated into the breastworks and barricades and there were at least a hundred dead camels sprawled around the position. It was the work of some hours to prepare the force for the forward move to Gubat. During the delay Marling wandered past Sankey Herbert's grave. 'There were his poor old feet in a pair of Tommy's grey socks sticking out of the sand.' There was a brief pause in the administrative preparation at about midday while Lord Beresford read over the graves of the fallen. When eventually the column moved off for the river, Bennet Burleigh and Melton Prior were amongst the men lugging casualties along on stretchers. Percy Marling could not help noticing that the *Telegraph* man had on a brand new pair of field boots, so ill-fitting that they had been nicked open at the back to accommodate his calves. Four years later when Melton Prior was covering the Burma campaign, a soldier tipped his hat to him and introduced himself as the man on the stretcher. The sun had set before the column struggled into Gubat.

As Wilson reviewed his position that night, he realised that the command was in serious difficulty. His men had been fighting or marching continuously for four days and were now utterly exhausted. Over 15 per cent of the force had been killed or wounded. Transport problems had been exacerbated by the heavy loss in camels. The remaining animals, including Barrow's ponies, were both fatigued and undernourished. Nevertheless, in accordance with Wolseley's instructions to Stewart, Wilson made preparations to advance on Metemmeh at 4.30 the following morning – Wednesday 21 January.

Clearly there had been a good deal of debate around Wilson's command post. Marling lamented in his journal:

> He [Stewart] is a fearful loss, as now he is wounded and Burnaby killed we have no real boss, although Boscawen is a right gallant fellow and did

> A1 yesterday in a very difficult position. We are now run by a committee – Wilson, Boscawen, two Barrows, Charlie Beresford, and David Airlie.[68]

It may not have been an altogether fair observation.

The Walls of Metemmeh

The three camel regiments, the naval brigade, the guns and a handful of sappers, around 1,000 men in all, set off downriver in two columns not long after sun-up. In the centre were a number of baggage camels carrying the Gardner, the 7-pounders, a quantity of reserve ammunition and some cacolets. Barrow and his hussars screened the outside flank and almost immediately made contact with about 50 enemy horsemen. A few dismounted volleys soon dispersed them. Wilson rode over to see Barrow and identify a position from which the guns could shell the town. In his absence Boscawen moved the main force to the south, as a Mahdist force had been sighted making its way along the river in the direction of Gubat. By the time Wilson had caught up with Boscawen, the enemy had disappeared into dead ground, but their presence compelled him to operate on the southern side of the town contrary to his original intent. The force formed square in case a rush was mounted from some as yet unseen hiding place. A long-range harassing fire was opened from the walls of the town, prompting Wilson to deploy skirmishers to answer it. The screw-guns also came into action but there was little prospect of such light guns causing significant damage, even to a mud-walled town. The strength of the enemy position and the evident futility of the current operation were becoming plain to see. Even if he could effect a breach, Wilson could not afford to get bogged down in street fighting. The town might well fall to a spirited British assault, but the resultant heavy casualties were certain to cripple the force and invite subsequent disaster. Just as spirits were beginning to flag, four of Gordon's steamers, *Bordein*, *Talahawiyeh*, *Safieh* and *Tewfikiyeh*, came into sight. As the square moved down to the river to effect a rendezvous, a Krupp field gun opened up from an advanced post in front of the town. Its fire was largely ineffective but Wilson noticed that a piece of shrapnel had carried away the lower jaw of one of the Royal Artillery baggage camels. The 'poor brute' carried its load faithfully to the end of the day.

Wilson hurried to meet the Egyptian commanders, who in effect had been been living as river pirates since early October, when Gordon sent them downriver to wait in the vicinity of Metemmeh for the relief column. The commander of the flotilla was an officer called Nushi Pasha, who hastily deployed 250 Sudanese troops and four of his six brass muzzle-loaders ashore. These returned the fire of the Krupp gun and shelled the town from the west, but with next to no effect on its loop-holed mud walls. Metemmeh would be important only when General Earle's ponderous River Column came up, but in the meantime the town's strategic significance was lost on Wilson. He decided to break off, withdraw to Gubat and leave Metemmeh in the hands of the enemy.

Given the already heavy loss in field officers, it was doubly regrettable that Major Poe was needlessly wounded only minutes before the withdrawal. Skirmishing in support of the guns, the RMLI were within 500 yards of the town. With plenty of Remington rifle fire cracking overhead it made good sense for the marines to ply their skill at arms from the prone position. Poe, however, chose to walk up and down the firing line As if that were not dangerous enough, he was clad as usual in his scarlet home-service tunic, the only man in the force so conspicuously attired. He paid the price of the typically rash bravado of the Victorian officer corps when a slug ripped through his thigh inflicting an ugly wound. Back at Gubat the surgeons would be obliged to amputate the injured limb just below the groin.[69] Despite their having been under fire for about five hours in all, there had been only one fatal casualty, although about a dozen other men had been wounded.

Sir Charles cut a sorry heroic figure and had few admirers amongst the more dare-devil officers of the Camel Corps. That night the young lions were loud in their camp-fire condemnation of the way things had gone before the walls of Metemmeh. No doubt the deference afforded them by Victorian society made them a cocksure bunch, but in asserting that they had come all that way expressly to capture Metemmeh, they were assuredly missing the point. Harsh reality bore no resemblance to the benign scenario envisaged by Wolseley when he issued his orders. As befitted a man of superior intellect, Wilson had worked out that what actually mattered most was not possession of Metemmeh *per se*, but possession of a defensible foothold on the Nile, and in Gubat he already had exactly that. For the time being Metemmeh could wait. Much of the subsequent rubbishing of Wilson's reputation originated with the camp-fire critiques of 21 January, but the decision not to press an attack was unquestionably the right one.

The thoughtful Wilson pondered his next move. Whilst he now knew that Gordon was still alive and well, the steamer captains had brought news of the fall of Omdurman, one of the most vital outworks in Khartoum's ring of defence. There were also intelligence indications that two large enemy forces were converging on Gubat, one from Berber to the north, and the other from the Mahdi's main field army at Khartoum. As a result Wilson decided to spend Thursday 22 January in reconnaissance. Barrow was sent upriver with a cavalry patrol, whilst Wilson himself embarked aboard one of the steamers and cruised past Shendi in the direction of Berber. Both parties returned to Gubat in the late afternoon without having uncovered any sign of major enemy movements.

That night Wilson gave orders that the two best armoured steamers, *Bordein* under Khashm el Mus, and *Talahawiyeh* under Abu ul Hamid, would leave for Khartoum the following day. As Wolseley's orders to Stewart included a clause instructing him to send back his baggage camels once he was safely established at Metemmeh, the colonel made arrangements for a convoy of 400 animals to leave for Jakdul at sunset on Friday. The 300-man escort would be a composite party from all three camel regiments.

In the event Wilson was still at Gubat to see the convoy off. The overhauling of the steamers and other preparations had taken all day – so long that it would not now be possible to depart until Saturday morning. Fate had intervened to lay low the man most qualified to supervise the work: Charlie Beresford had developed a boil on his backside that was so painful he was barely able to walk. All the other naval officers and petty officers had been killed or wounded at Abu Klea. With the Navy's principal representative awaiting surgery, it fell to Army officers to struggle through the preparation of the steamers as best they could.

The River Dash

Wilson finally steamed away from Gubat aboard the *Bordein* at 8.00 a.m. on Saturday. There were 110 Sudanese infantry on board plus, below decks, a strange assortment of civilian refugees, including wives and children of some of the soldiers. In accordance with Wolseley's orders a detachment of 20 scarlet-clad marksmen from the Royal Sussex was also taken along. Captain Lionel Trafford split his men evenly between the two steamers. As they had not brought their home-service tunics in their baggage, the handpicked score had been forced to scrounge substitute tunics from the Heavies. Trafford himself travelled aboard the *Talahawiyeh*, with 10 of his own men and 80 Sudanese riflemen. A further 40–50 Sudanese soldiers were towed behind the steamer in a nuggar.

The first day went well, with occasional sorties ashore to take on wood and question friendly locals. Sunday also passed largely uneventfully until, towards late afternoon, the steamers began the approach to the Shabluka or Sixth Cataract. Against the advice of the steamer captains, Wilson insisted on trying to clear the rapids before mooring for the night. By sunset they were just about through, when at the last moment *Bordein* stuck on a rock. *Talahawiyeh* was already through and cruised another 600 yards upstream to moor at Hassan Island. All attempts to re-float the stranded vessel having proved fruitless, she spent the night stuck fast. In daylight the hold cargo was shifted around and towing parties landed on a nearby sandbank. This combination of measures did the trick and *Bordein* freed herself at about 9.00 a.m. She steamed on past Hassan Island, but to everybody's disgust quickly ran aground again. She was freed in daylight but not without a great deal of time-consuming effort, so that

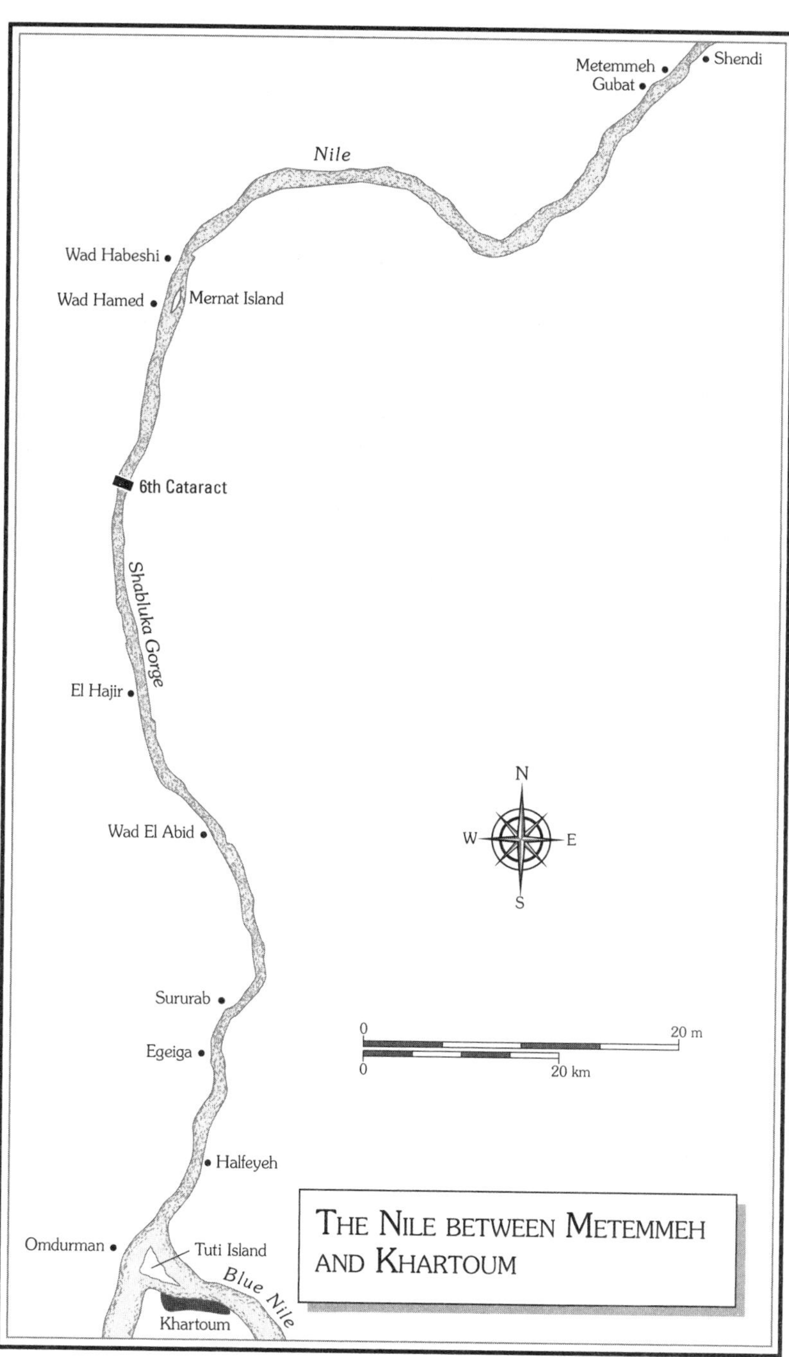

THE NILE BETWEEN METEMMEH AND KHARTOUM

Monday's progress upstream was limited to a miserable three miles. That night the captains warned Wilson that in the morning the Nile would enter a gorge of almost three miles in length. Riflemen on the high ground would be able to see everything on deck, regardless of the improvised defences.

In the event the dreaded gorge was cleared without a shot being fired. Wilson could barely believe his luck. Steaming on, he next put in at a small village on the west bank called Gos Nefia, to tear down some huts for firewood. During the afternoon a friendly local ashore called out that Khartoum had fallen. When Khashm el Mus remarked that such reports had been an everyday occurrence for the past few weeks, Wilson felt able to discount it.[70] From time to time the steamers came under harassing fire from small parties of Mahdists but nevertheless continued to make good progress. They were able to moor for the night on the west bank, with a protective screen of pickets deployed ashore. Wilson spent the evening mulling over what he would say to Gordon the following day.

As soon as it was light the steamers set off on the final leg. After about an hour and a half they could make out Tuti Island at the confluence of the Blue and the White Niles, and beyond, the outline of the city. Before long they met heavy resistance from both banks of the river. Captain Trafford's men, crack-shots all, combined with the rather less well-trained Sudanese to lay down a furious return fire. Fore and aft, the brass 4-pounders roared defiance from the shelter of their improvised 'turrets', in reality nothing more than flimsy barricades built from railway sleepers.[71] When they were abreast of Halfeyeh, once Gordon's northernmost outpost, four enemy guns opened up, but they proved to be poorly served and their shells ripped harmlessly overhead or threw up great plumes of water in the river. Both vessels were able to run the gauntlet without suffering a direct hit. South of Halfeyeh the river divided around a large island. Wilson took the western fork but again came under artillery fire, this time from the village of Shamba. Soon they were approaching Tuti. So many shots from the island landed amongst the enemy on the west bank, that at first Wilson was deceived into thinking it was still in the hands of the garrison, but the effect was only a by-product of careless Mahdist musketry. Between Tuti Island and the fort at Omdurman, the incoming fire became prodigious. Up to seven artillery pieces and a machine gun were firing from the west bank, the island and now – quite unmistakeably – from the city itself. When it was pointed out that the Egyptian flag which Gordon customarily flew from the roof of the palace was nowhere to be seen, Wilson's heart sank. Khartoum had fallen by storm, he would learn later, on the bloody night of 25/26 January. At the precise moment that Gordon fell, the *Bordein* had been stuck on a rock at the Shabluka Cataract. The Sudanese stokers and soldiers whose homes and families had been in Khartoum were beside themselves with grief.

Wilson quickly ordered the steamers put about, to run for home. By the time they were clear of the Mahdi's river defences they had been under heavy fire for more than four hours. Disaster struck the following morning when *Talahawiyeh* struck a rock so hard that she began to sink. Fortunately everybody on board was saved and brought aboard the already overcrowded *Bordein*. Two days later, on 31 January, *Bordein* too ran out of luck and was badly holed 40 miles from Gubat, not far upstream from an enemy battery at Wad Habeshi. Wilson took his ramshackle force ashore and into hiding on the island of Mernat. One of his subordinates on the intelligence staff, Lieutenant Edward Stuart Wortley KRRC, put a party of four Englishmen and eight Sudanese aboard a rowing-boat and set off for Gubat to raise the alarm. Fortunately for the stranded expedition a convoy was even now arriving at Gubat from Jakdul with another three screw-guns, a second Gardner and, crucially, the Second Division of the Naval Brigade. This would give Charlie Beresford, now recovered from his earlier discomfort, sufficient naval hands to crew a steamer as originally planned. When, on 1 February, a bedraggled Stuart Wortley arrived at Gubat, Beresford immediately threw his men aboard the *Safieh* and steamed to the rescue.[72] Both Gardners were mounted amidships to supplement the 4-pounders fore and aft. In addition to the naval stokers and machine gunners there were 20 KRRC riflemen under Lieutenant Bower aboard. Elevated from her formerly lowly station into the service of the Admiralty, *Safieh* now proudly flew the White Ensign from her stern.

On the third day out Beresford ran the gauntlet at Wad Habeshi. The enemy earthworks were on the west bank. Blazing at the embrasures with every weapon she had, *Safieh* was compelled by sandbanks to sail within 80 yards of four enemy guns and literally hundreds of riflemen. Bower and his men did so good a job in suppressing the Mahdist gunners that this most dangerous stretch of river was negotiated without serious mishap. Then, at the last gasp, a lucky shot from one of the enemy guns struck *Safieh* in the stern, holing her boiler. To the dismay of everybody on board, she lost steam and shuddered dead in the water. Beresford was forced to drop anchor, assess the damage and begin repairs. Fortunately for the British only one of the enemy embrasures faced upstream and this was quickly suppressed by the KRRC riflemen. Below decks Chief Engineer Benbow began his work.

In response to the firing in the north, Sir Charles Wilson moved his party from Mernat to the east bank and marched downriver until he was directly opposite Wad Habeshi. Here he deployed his troops and joined in the fight. Towards last light Beresford signalled that Wilson should move north and be ready to be picked up in the morning. Wilson sent his main body on ahead under Captain Trafford and Khashm el Mus, and stayed behind with 30 men to continue the fire-fight until nightfall. Beresford meanwhile was preparing a clever ruse. While there was still enough light for the enemy to see what he was up to, he had his small boats lowered as if to suggest that he intended to abandon ship under the cover of darkness. As night fell he darkened ship and prohibited any further firing. Benbow and his stokers worked all night.

When the sun came up the following morning *Safieh* appeared to be deserted. The Mahdist artillerymen relaxed beside their guns. After ten hours of hard toil, Benbow lit his fires at about 5.00 a.m. About 50 minutes later the boiler betrayed Beresford's secret by belching a cloud of smoke and ash from the funnel. Enraged by their own gullibility the enemy gunners raced back to their posts to renew the fight, but within 20 minutes Beresford had steamed safely out of sight. The exhausted Arab gunners dropped to the ground, bitterly disappointed that the British had hoodwinked them. Before they knew it Beresford was back, having executed a sharp turn some little distance upriver. Belching fire, smoke, 4-pound shells and five-round volleys from the Gardners, *Safieh* steamed bravely downstream. The disheartened Mahdist gunners could but duck below their embrasures and allow the Royal Navy to pass. A short distance downriver Beresford stopped to pick up Wilson. The rest of the journey home was mercifully uneventful.

Aftermath

The attempt to save Gordon had failed but it was assuredly no fault of the officers and men of the Desert Column who had given their all. The Nile campaign was quickly wound down, with no attempt to recapture Khartoum. At home most people viewed the failure to avenge Gordon as a national humiliation. Wolseley sent Sir Redvers Buller, up till now his chief of staff, forward to Gubat to superintend the withdrawal. For the most part the men of the Camel Corps walked back across the Bayuda; HCR returned with precisely 22 camels, MICR with 95. On 15 February 1885 Sir Herbert Stewart finally expired whilst travelling back across the Bayuda with a convoy of wounded. He was buried near Jakdul Wells. Writing to Lady Stewart, Wolseley consoled her with the thought, 'I would rather be his widow than the wife of most men I know.' To his own wife he wrote:

> After dinner a letter reached me from Reggy Talbot announcing the death of poor Stewart. I feel as if I have lost my right arm in this business, and I cannot hope to see his like again. He was out and out the best man I had about me, and to all his military achievements and qualities he added the rare advantage of being a universal favourite and of being the very pleasantest officer to do business with . . . this valuable life is an addition to the holocaust offered on the altar of Mr Gladstone's self-opinionated ignorance.

Sir Charles Wilson soldiered on and rose to major general. Wolseley detested him for ever more and was amongst the many military men who unfairly blamed him for the failure of the expedition. Wolseley demanded that he explain the two-day delay at Gubat and forwarded his written explanation to the Secretary for War under an icily disdainful covering letter. It was a monstrously hypocritical stance. Making progress south down the Nile had been Wilson's responsibility for precisely four days; prior to that it had rested with Wolseley for months. Wilson had taken entirely rational military decisions. More than anything else the short delay at Gubat was due to intelligence indications that the already badly mauled Desert Column was about to be attacked in strength by converging Mahdist forces. Such reports could not be disregarded. In truth it was the lack of security surrounding the advance across the Bayuda that had been the principal cause of the column's tribulations, and this had its origins in poor logistic staff-work at the army level. In other words the fault was ultimately the army commander's own. In essence Khartoum was lost for the want of a thousand camels. Wolseley shifted the blame for this particular problem in Buller's direction. Had there been sufficient baggage camels to permit a single transit of the Bayuda, the Desert Column could have reached Metemmeh unopposed and intact by 6 January, almost three weeks before Gordon died. In such a scenario Stewart could have thrown several hundred well-armed British troops aboard the steamers and into the city with a fortnight to spare. Egyptian entrepreneurs joked that there were still plenty of good camels available as the British had bought up all the bad ones. Interestingly Sir Charles Wilson remarked in his account of the expedition that it would have been perfectly possible at that time of year for the infantry to have marched across the Bayuda on foot. There is nothing about the time and space of the campaign to suggest otherwise. Wilson termed his observation a 'heresy' but may well have had a point. Had Wolseley's grand scheme for a Camel Corps been nothing more than a wasteful red herring after all?

Regardless of its mode of transport, Wolseley's concept for the Desert Column was not to get a portion of his force through to Khartoum by the fastest possible means; rather its operations were merely a logistic enabler to the advance of the Red River re-enactors of the ponderous River Column. The idea was that Lord Wolseley would exercise personal command of the unified force in some great battle of decision outside the city, and then march in to shake a suitably grateful Gordon by the hand. It was to be another great moment in his lordship's career and the credit was to be his alone. The choice of the Nile route ahead of the much shorter Suakin–Berber axis was Wolseley's own. His campaign plan would not have effected the relief of Khartoum until March at the earliest and the city fell in late January. The idea that the arrival of Wilson and 20 men in red coats could have prevented or affected the outcome of the

25 January assault is plainly ludicrous. If, in the eyes of the public, 'our only general' could do no wrong, the fault had to lie elsewhere. Overnight, Gladstone G.O.M., the 'Grand Old Man', was lampooned as Gladstone M.O.G., 'Murderer of Gordon'.

Muhammad Ahmad, it turned out in the end, was a phenomenon not a prophet; a conjuror not a miracle-worker; was self-anointed not divinely chosen. He died of typhus in a disorderly disease-ridden Khartoum only six months after General Gordon. He was 42. His right-hand man, the Khalifa 'Abd Allah ibn Muhammad, presided over a fundamentalist Islamic state until, some 13 years later, Major Kitchener returned, no longer disguised as a desert nomad, but in the uniform of the Sirdar.

Chapter 7

'Sold by a Damned Gunner'

Sir Redvers Buller and the Battle of Colenso, Natal, 15 December 1899

If the senior officers are never tested in time of peace, it is always possible that a man may be appointed to an important command in the field who has lost his nerve, whose brain is rusty, whose knowledge is out of date, who is unacquainted with the tactics of the latest text-books, or whose claims to high preferment rest upon a brilliant reputation, won perhaps in a less responsible rank, and on an easier field. Manoeuvres are the best means of making certain that the superior officers of an army do not grow stupid.

Colonel G. F. R. Henderson

George Henderson, known affectionately to his students at the Staff College as 'Henders', served at the express invitation of Field Marshal Lord Roberts as the Army's chief of intelligence in South Africa. When Henderson penned the lines quoted above he was in ill-health and writing of recent events with the benefit of hindsight. He was too polite to name the dunce under the cap, but there is little doubt to whom he was referring. Sir Redvers Buller had indeed grown a little stupid – and he was not the only one. A glance at the accompanying portraits will show the reason why. Phenomenally successful as a fit, fearless, hard-riding, hard-fighting field officer, Buller had the heart of a lion and sported a VC to prove it. But as a general officer he was fated to spend far too much time in the comfortable environs of the War Office where, feted and flattered as one of the great military figures of the Victorian age, he went to seed.

'All Sir Garnet': Military Power-Play in the High Victorian Age

General Sir Redvers Buller VC, KCB, KCMG, had risen to the top of his profession as one of the principal stars of the 'Wolseley Ring' the hand-picked cabal of ostensibly talented officers on whose services Wolseley was apt to call whenever there was some serious soldiering to be done. As the name suggests, admittance to the elite lay in the personal gift of its vainglorious leader. Acceptance was dependent upon fulfilling a number of criteria. First one had to be judged as professionally competent, so as to underwrite the operational success of the master. Second, one had to be socially acceptable, for raging snobbery was amongst the least attractive of Wolseley's flaws. Third, it helped to be utterly fearless, for courage was a quality the great man admired above all others. Fourth, one had to be a sycophant – for there was Wolseley's way and no other. Fifth, an active dislike of the Duke of Cambridge, the Prince of Wales and that 'scheming little Indian' Roberts would also go a long way. It is an unflattering picture but, as we have seen in some of the earlier chapters, for all his talent Wolseley was undeniably a nasty piece of work.

Ironically he has tainted his own place in history with his prolific private correspondence and journals – had he not been quite so inclined to commit his innermost thoughts to paper, only his reputation as a soldier and nothing much of the inner man would now survive. As it is, his egotism, arrogance and vindictiveness are firmly enshrined in the historical record. Wellington too had been an egotist and a snob, but perhaps because he was a *bona fide* military genius his flaws do not seem to grate nearly as much. Although Wolseley liked to trumpet his own achievements as if they were in the same league as the Duke's, in fact they were mostly pretty marginal and certainly do not allow of his inclusion amongst the 'great captains' of history. The Red River for example was no sort of a challenge, whilst with a few steady battalions at his disposal almost any remotely competent general officer could have bludgeoned his way into the Ashanti capital at Kumasi. Wolseley's great campaign in Egypt, culminating in the Battle of Tel-el-Kebir, was a victory over precisely the same fighting stock that was to perform so miserably in the Sudan. It is probably fair to say that a crushing British victory was inevitable from the outset. When faced with a genuine military challenge – that of getting to Khartoum in time – he failed; an outcome in which his ego played a not insignificant part. Perhaps his least endearing characteristic was his sheer spitefulness. When eventually 'Bobs' came home after 'Forty-One Years in India' and the two field marshals finally came face-to-face in Ireland, Wolseley wrote of Lady Roberts; 'My eyes what a woman! I have never seen a more hideous animal in my life.' This then, was the man who at one time had been lauded in the London press as 'our only general', a sobriquet repeated *ad nauseam* ever since. One need only think of Fred Roberts, his arch-rival and direct contemporary, to recognize the expression as mere journalistic hyperbole. Perhaps the most significant elements in Wolseley's legacy are to be found in his strident advocacy of promotion and appointment on merit, the creation of an Army Reserve and the infinitely more professional approach he brought to campaign planning.

Members of the 'ring' always did well as majors and later as colonels on the staff, for at that stage in their careers their master was usually to be found at the tiller. Eventually, though, some of them would become generals in their own right and would have to start thinking for themselves. Sir George Colley was a member of the ring, Sir Redvers Buller another, Sir William Butler, whom we shall meet shortly, a third. Between them these three came within a hair's breadth of losing South Africa. The ring, it turned out in the end, was not all it had been cracked up to be. One beneficial side-effect of Wolseley's preferment for graduates of the Staff College was that the credibility and popularity of the Camberley course increased steadily throughout the era. Wolseley's acolytes saw themselves as the cream of the home Army, the War Office professionals, an attitude of mind which made them strongly inclined to look down their noses at those who had made their way in India – people like Sir George White and Colonel Ian Hamilton, both late of the Gordons. The notion of a competing 'Roberts Ring' is not altogether valid, for while Roberts undoubtedly gave preferment to those who had served him well in the past, a practice followed by most Victorian general officers, he was less strongly inclined than Wolseley to gather his favourites around him in times of trouble and, as a consequence, to squeeze out officers with whom he was not personally acquainted. Even so, by the 1890s, the great men of the Army were firmly divided into a 'Wolseleyite' faction and an 'Indian' faction.

The Rise of Sir Redvers Buller

Buller joined the 60th Rifles in 1858, fought in the Second China War of 1860 and first caught Wolseley's eye a decade later as a company commander on the Red River, mainly because he always seemed to be mucking in and carrying heavy loads – which was what the much-vaunted Red River expedition was mostly all about. Much to the chagrin of the men who had travelled half-way across Canada to fight him, Louis Riel slipped across the US border at the last moment so that never a shot was fired in anger. This did not prevent the then Colonel Wolseley presenting his 'campaign' as a triumph. Three years later he chose Buller as his chief of intelligence for the Ashanti War, a selection he was to repeat for the Egyptian intervention. In between his 'intelligence' appointments – and Army intelligence in the imperial age was mostly about scouting and reconnaissance – Buller fought with distinction in the Zulu War, the campaign in which he first came to the attention of the general public. Whilst commanding the irregular horse in Evelyn Wood's No. 4 Column, he won the VC for rescuing wounded or unhorsed men during the fraught retreat from Hlobane Mountain. Stories of him riding in relentless pursuit of routed Zulu impis with a revolver in one hand, a knobkerrie in the other and his reins clenched between his teeth, made him into a national hero. In 1884 he commanded one of Sir Gerald Graham's brigades in the fighting around Suakin, and was subsequently appointed as Wolseley's chief of staff on the Nile. By any standard a service record which included Ashanti, China, the Ninth Cape Frontier War, Hlobane, Kambula, Ulundi, Tel-el-Kebir, Second El Teb and Tamai was more than merely impressive.

Flushed with the success of his early career, Buller became conceited and decadent. Moving in the smartest social circles, he began to overeat and to drink champagne to excess, habits which he would continue to indulge in his headquarters on the Tugela River. It had been no different 14 years earlier at Korti in the Sudan where, on 5 January 1885, Lieutenant Marling recorded in his diary, 'Lord Frederick Fitzgerald came to ask me to dine with Buller. Had a good tub and such a feed. Fizz *ad lib* and about seven courses.' Amongst the common soldiers and at home on his Devon estate, Buller was a different and happier man: liberal, paternalistic, popular and much-admired, perhaps even much-loved. After a tour of duty as the Quartermaster-General (1887–90), during which he sensibly merged commissariat and transport matters with the foundation of the Army Service Corps, he succeeded Viscount Wolseley as Adjutant-General, an appointment which in effect made him chief of staff to the ageing Duke of Cambridge. With his master tucked away in Dublin waiting for the Duke to retire, Buller substituted for Wolseley as the most powerful military figure in London. With staff officers and civil servants he proved to be bullish, autocratic and far too blunt to be well thought of. But he pleased the Queen Empress and by virtue of his hero status remained popular with the wider Army and the general public. It was 1895 before the Queen was finally persuaded to press cousin George to retire. Keen that another royal should succeed him as C-in-C, she agitated for the appointment of her third son, Arthur Duke of Connaught, even going so far as to convince her grandson Willy in Berlin that the rival candidate, Wolseley, would make an ideal ambassador to his court. But the politicians were having none of it. It had taken them decades to rid themselves of one royal duke and they were not about to saddle themselves with another.

Wolseley handed over the Irish command to Roberts who, since retiring as C-in-C India in 1893, had been raised to field marshal. Wolseley in turn moved back to London to become the new professional head of the Army. Wolseley and Buller worked together for two years, before the time came for Buller to hand over as Adjutant-General to Sir Evelyn Wood and assume a more active appointment as GOC Aldershot. In the resurrected summer manoeuvres of 1898, a major British military development, Buller commanded one side and the Duke of Connaught the other. Having led the Guards Brigade at Tel-el-Kebir the prince was no slouch as a soldier, and most impartial observers agreed that his performance far surpassed Buller's. After a typically acerbic debrief from the C-in-C, Buller was heard to remark 'I have been making a fool of myself all day'. For those with the eyes to see, all the signs were there – Buller was far from being the ideal candidate to command a real army in a modern war. Wracked with self-doubt, he was in many ways his own worst enemy.

The President's Gold

For a few years after the death of Sir George Colley, the Transvaal had muddled along in the same old chaotic way. Just as the Khedive of Egypt had imported Englishmen in an attempt to bring good governance to his country, Kruger tried importing 'Hollander' advisers from Europe. In a sign of changing times there was great concern in London and Cape Town that the Germans would soon have a foot in the door. Unfortunately the cabal of sophisticated Dutch advisers tended to look down their noses at ill-educated and uncouth Afrikaners in much the same way as Wolseley and Sir Owen Lanyon had done. It was not long before they had made themselves every bit as unpopular. Piet Joubert knew what Kruger was up to and heartily disapproved of the provocative presence of European advisers. Then, in 1886, everything changed. It was on the Witwatersrand, 'the ridge of white water', or the 'rand' for short, that South Africa's gold was discovered. It was far from being an everyday get-rich-quick gold strike. The deposits were the largest yet discovered, but they were deep underground and extracting them would require heavy capital investment. Problematically for Kruger and his henchmen, the ZAR electorate included stockmen in abundance, but few competent financiers or mining engineers.

Suddenly where once there had been open veldt, there was Johannesburg. A mere 30 miles south of Kruger's prim and proper capital at Pretoria, bustling, exciting, drunken Johannesburg appalled most Afrikaner elders. *Uitlanders* flooded in at a rate which terrified the wily old president. Taken literally the word translated innocuously enough as 'outsiders', but in reality it bore distinctly pejorative overtones. The newcomers were at best a self-centred, vociferous and obsessive bunch. While the European contingents were generally well enough behaved, the assertive British, Anglo-South African and American contingents all harboured inflated notions of their worth to the republic. As far as Kruger and his cronies were concerned the Transvaal was

God's gift to the old trekker families. The *uitlanders* were mere interlopers and represented a serious threat to the ascendancy of the *volk*. Within a decade the population of Johannesburg had risen to 100,000 souls, half white and half black, but a mere 6 per cent Afrikaner.

It did not take long for major capitalist concerns, the majority of them London or Cape Town based, to arrive at mutually beneficial arrangements with the government. In return for the healthy tax revenues they contributed to his fiefdom, Kruger gave the capitalists their head. Curiously, most of the republic's major political figures, including many of Kruger's best friends and relations, became wealthy men overnight. But citizenship, public probity, equality before the law and political rights were all major stumbling blocks. It was not long before the most self-important *uitlander* cliques, the British to the forefront, had taken vehement exception to being treated, as Sir Alfred Milner was later to put it, like a 'helot' underclass. They looked at the Boers with all their flaws and resented them. Public office of any kind, from president to police constable, was the exclusive preserve of Afrikaner burghers, all of whom had to be bought off if a foreign-owned commercial enterprise was to prosper. Government-chartered monopolies on such essential mining commodities as dynamite proved particularly irksome. It did not take long for the *uitlanders* and their capitalist backers to agree that they ought to have a proper say in running the country. But when it came down to it, the reformers divided into competing camps – the British and South Africans on one side, most of whom secretly aspired to see the Union Flag flying over a unified South Africa, and the Irish, Germans and Americans, prepared for any eventuality but that. The *uitlanders* could agree on only one thing – they must be granted citizenship and thus become enfranchised. Before long elements of the Anglo-South African faction had begun plotting and conspiring in dark corners. Their public face was the Johannesburg Reform Committee, which included the Abu Klea veteran Colonel Frank Rhodes amongst its most prominent members.

The Polarization of South Africa: Doctor Jameson and Kaiser Bill

The outcome was the ill-fated private-enterprise *coup d'état* known as the Jameson Raid, which in the weeks before it was launched may well have qualified as the worst-kept secret in Southern Africa. The stream of vacuous 'veiled speech' telegrams bouncing back and forth between Cape Town and Johannesburg would not have taxed the wit of the average telegraph clerk for long, let alone that of a government intelligence agent. The driving force behind the plot was, of course, the formidable Cecil Rhodes, founder of Rhodesia, one of the richest men in the world and, since 1890, Prime Minister of the Cape. The instrument of Kruger's downfall was to be a miscellany of well-armed Rhodesian policemen and volunteers under the command of Rhodes's right-hand man, Dr Leander Starr Jameson. Word of the conspiracy even reached London and the ears of Joe Chamberlain, the Colonial Secretary in Lord Salisbury's Conservative government, though whether he was an active participant or a passive observer has never been convincingly resolved.[1] At the last gasp the courage and commitment of the Johannesburg Reform Committee wavered. Sensing a strong likelihood of failure, Rhodes wired Jameson to call off the madcap adventure. The good doctor was far too animated by the excitement of it all and took the foolhardy decision to ignore Rhodes and press on regardless. He crossed the border on 29 December 1895 with about 460 men, a pair of 7-pounders and eight Maxim machine guns. By forcing the hand of the Johannesburg plotters, Jameson caused the rising to go off at half-cock. For a while the town was theirs, but they proved incapable of anything beyond arming and enacting a few local defence measures. In the absence of more proactive steps, the raiders were doomed to fail. The hapless Dr Jameson surrendered his harassed, exhausted and surrounded command to General Piet Cronje at Doornkop near Krugersdorp on 2 January 1896. Frank Rhodes and his co-conspirators were duly arrested, tried for treason and sentenced to death. Later Kruger would commute their sentences to 15 years' imprisonment. In due course they would be repatriated on payment of substantial fines.

In Europe, meanwhile, the Imperial Germany Navy had been busily laying the plans which would one day enable it to challenge the maritime supremacy of Her Britannic Majesty's Royal Navy. Grandson of the Queen or not, a new enemy for the new century was slowly but surely showing his hand. In the immediate aftermath of the raid, the Kaiser let the cat out of the bag with an open telegram to Kruger:

> I sincerely congratulate you that without appealing for the help of friendly powers, you with your people, by your own energy against the armed hordes which as disturbers of the peace broke into your country, have succeeded in re-establishing peace and maintaining the independence of your country from without.

Neither the British public nor Her Britannic Majesty cared much for the Kaiser's tone. The strutting emperor withered like a scolded child before the old lady's reproach and quickly despatched a grovelling letter of apology. It might have been amusing had not the German Navy approached the colonial authorities in Portuguese Mozambique for permission to move a detachment of marines through their territory to Pretoria.

The raid and the ill-considered intervention of the Kaiser polarized British and Afrikaner public opinion. Its repercussions were felt throughout Southern

Africa. In the Cape, Cecil Rhodes was obliged to resign the premiership, whilst the formerly contented Cape Afrikaner population became sullen and resentful overnight. Previously on relatively cordial terms with the British, the Free Staters were similarly outraged by such chicanery and left their president in no doubt where their sympathies would lie in a conflict. In Pretoria and the wider Transvaal, where Kruger's popularity had been in sharp decline in favour of 'Slim' Piet Joubert's progressive party,[2] the *volk* now rallied behind their dinosaur president. And in London where the chattering classes had been generally uninterested in distant South Africa, the public now found itself distinctly affronted by a combination of Afrikaner arrogance and German hostility. It was not long before the memory of Majuba had started playing up like an old war-wound on a chill winter morning. With all roads leading to London and the Queen's diamond jubilee fast approaching, it was not the best of times for tin-pot republics to be affronting the dignity of the Crown or, perish the thought, trampling an Englishman's rights underfoot. Just as in the 1830s the Boers had convinced themselves that they had been divinely 'chosen', so by 1896 loyal subjects of the Queen Empress had arrived at the inescapable conclusion that God simply had to be an Englishman. Kruger was too stubborn and turn-of-the-century Britain too haughty for compromise to prosper.

Irresistible Force and Immoveable Object: Milner and Kruger

When, in 1897, Sir Alfred Milner arrived in Cape Town as the new High Commissioner he was quick to realise just how tenuous the British grasp on Southern Africa really was. There seemed to be more Englishmen in the Transvaal than in the Cape, more Afrikaners in the Cape than in the Transvaal, and many more Afrikaners than Englishmen in Southern Africa as a whole. Ironically it was all held together with British capital. Worse than any numerical imbalance in the white population, it was clear in the aftermath of the Jameson Raid that the Transvaal was arming rapidly against the eventuality of war. Shipments included significant numbers of the latest German Krupp and French Creusot 75-mm quick-firers (QF) and more than 30,000 Mauser bolt-action rifles. The possession of such modern armaments by a numerically much stronger citizen-army suddenly gave rise to a regional military imbalance. With a strength of only 9,940 men (2 cavalry regiments, 6 batteries and 6½ battalions) the standing British garrison was just about capable of holding a decent military tattoo in Pietermaritzburg. Threatening the independence of the Boer republics, on the other hand, was quite beyond it. By contrast the commando system was capable of generating 40,000 hard-riding burghers in a matter of days.

Kruger's armament programme and his 1897 treaty of mutual assistance with the Orange Free State left the British squarely on the strategic back foot. All Milner could see was a dangerous and unenlightened aggressor, impertinently engaging in an arms race with the British Empire. Something would have to give. It was not going to be Kruger any more than it was going to be Milner. An ardent believer in the imperial system of governance, the High Commissioner had concluded that a stable self-governing dominion could only come about at the expense of the overtly corrupt oligarchy in Pretoria. In military terms the Empire was at a distinct local disadvantage, a situation the senior military man in the Cape seemed disinclined to remedy. The GOC was Lieutenant General Sir William Butler, husband of the well-known artist Lady Elizabeth. Sir William was an Irish Catholic who, for all his distinguished service, often found himself seriously out of step with government policy. He was also a dyed in the wool anti-Semite and regarded the Johannesburg Reform movement as a Jewish conspiracy. In practice he was determinedly pro-Boer and disinclined to make any meaningful military preparations in Natal or the Cape.

The prospect of an Anglo-Boer War shifted from a possibility to an inevitability at the Bloemfontein Conference of May 1899. Until 1882, four years before the gold was discovered, it had been possible to qualify for citizenship of the Transvaal in a year. Thereafter the qualification period had been successively hiked by the Volksraad, first to five and then to a nakedly protectionist 14 years. Face to face over the table at last, the polished, intellectual High Commissioner and the gnarled backwoods President went through the motions in the presence of the conciliatory President Marthinus Steyn of the Orange Free State. Return the period of qualification to five years, demanded the High Commissioner on behalf of the downtrodden 'helots'. Kruger made repeated attempts to deflect the negotiations onto other sources of Anglo-Boer friction. Milner knew an old fox when he saw one and in accordance with his instructions from Whitehall returned repeatedly to the question of the franchise. Eventually an offer of a seven-year period of qualification was extracted. Take seven, Steyn urged Milner, knowing that if it came to it he would be compelled to fight alongside his Afrikaner kith and kin. Five insisted the High Commissioner. War then it would have to be.

Reporting the unhappy outcome at Bloemfontein, Milner also took the opportunity to press the Colonial Office for the 'too awful' Butler's recall. In the event the GOC cooked his own goose by openly expressing his strongly held and supremely contrary convictions in his War Office correspondence. The Secretary of State for War, Lord Lansdowne, despatched a stinging rebuke, reminding his truculent subordinate that politicians not soldiers make government policy. Butler resigned to be replaced by Lieutenant General Sir Frederick Forestier-Walker. In the meantime Jan Smuts, ZAR's smart young

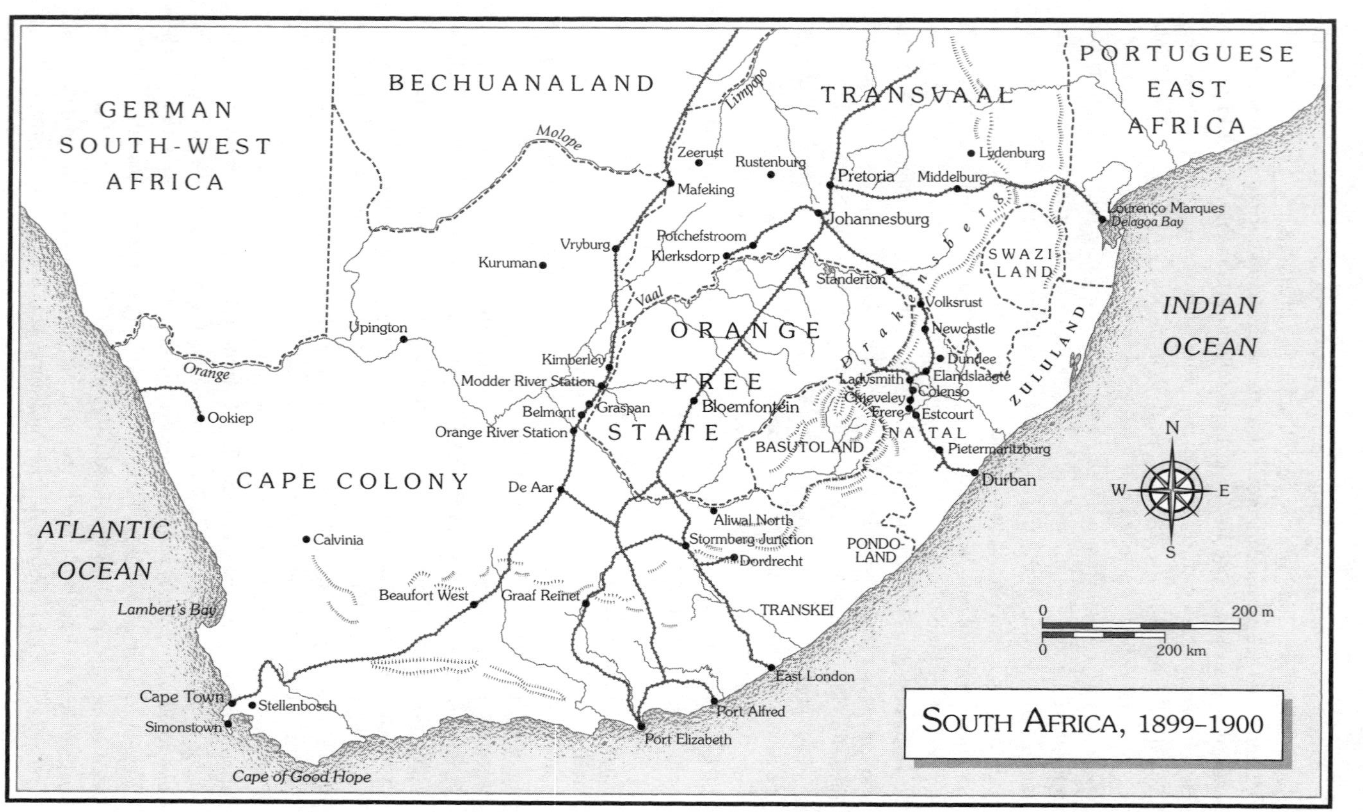

SOUTH AFRICA, 1899–1900
GERMAN SOUTH-WEST AFRICA
BECHUANALAND
TRANSVAAL
PORTUGUESE EAST AFRICA
ORANGE FREE STATE
CAPE COLONY
BASUTOLAND
NATAL
SWAZI LAND
ZULULAND
PONDO-LAND
TRANSKEI
ATLANTIC OCEAN
INDIAN OCEAN
Drakensberg
Limpopo
Molope
Vaal
Orange
Zeerust
Rustenburg
Pretoria
Middelburg
Lydenburg
Lourenço Marques
Delagoa Bay
Mafeking
Johannesburg
Potchefstroom
Klerksdorp
Vryburg
Kuruman
Standerton
Volksrust
Newcastle
Dundee
Elandslaagte
Ladysmith
Colenso
Chieveley
Frere
Estcourt
Pietermaritzburg
Durban
Upington
Kimberley
Modder River Station
Graspan
Belmont
Orange River Station
Bloemfontein
Ookiep
De Aar
Aliwal North
Stormberg Junction
Dordrecht
Calvinia
Beaufort West
Graaf Reinet
East London
Port Alfred
Port Elizabeth
Cape Town
Stellenbosch
Simonstown
Lambert's Bay
Cape of Good Hope
N
S
E
W
0
200 m
200 km

attorney-general, had initiated a fresh round of negotiations, but by now the Boers were merely playing for time, waiting for the seasons to change, so that when war came there would be good grass on the veldt for their ponies.

At the War Office, Wolseley pressed Lord Lansdowne to order the mobilization of an army corps of 30,000 men on Salisbury Plain – a useful rehearsal for the real thing and an unmistakeable warning shot across Kruger's bows. Anxious not to appear as the aggressors, the Prime Minister and the Secretary of State for War declined the C-in-C's advice, though they recognized the clear and urgent necessity to reinforce the outnumbered South African garrison. In September 1899 orders went out in the same old depressingly familiar Crimean vein for a miscellany of unconnected regiments to embark for Durban from India and the Mediterranean stations. Together they came to around 10,000 men – sufficient to reduce the Boer advantage from 4:1 to 2:1. Although a new GOC Natal was already *in situ*, the enlarged size of the command demanded the despatch of a lieutenant general from home. Major General Sir Penn Symons, late of the South Wales Borderers, who knew the colony well from his regimental service in the Zulu War, was to hold the ring north of the Tugela until the arrival of Lieutenant General Sir George White VC, GCB, GCSI, GCIE. Now 64 years of age, White was an old Gordons officer and had won his VC in Afghanistan. He had succeeded Roberts as C-in-C India in 1893, and had only recently arrived at the War Office as Quartermaster-General. Both White and Symons had acquired plenty of solid, successful command experience on the North-West Frontier, though unlike Symons, White had never before served in South Africa. Like many officers who thought they knew the Boers well, Symons was openly contemptuous of their military capacity and confidently expected to be able to hold northern Natal with a strong brigade, until such time as reinforcements came up from Durban.

Wolseley was certain that the services of the 1st Army Corps would be required eventually, and just as sure that the contemptible Boers would be soundly trounced by it. Day and night he fretted over the possibility that the South African command might go to Roberts. If that happened, the 'scheming little Indian' would go on to eclipse him as the greatest of Queen Victoria's generals. Distinctly spare in his Dublin backwater, Roberts was by far the best and most logical choice for the job. That he was not selected is a damning indictment of Wolseley's character and, ultimately, of his professionalism, the very attribute he had urged so vehemently on the rest of the Army. Instead, enter brave Sir Redvers. Remarkably neither Wolseley nor Buller, both of whom knew South Africa well, had given any serious thought to contingency planning for a war there. Even after he had been appointed as army commander designate, Buller sat back and waited to be told what to do. Placed in the same situation, the more dynamic Roberts would have bounced around the War

Office until a workable war plan had been hammered out and all the requisite resources had been secured. Buller, though, stayed distant, grand and aloof, as if the waging of war could only be contemplated upon its declaration. To be fair he agitated from time to time to be included in the relevant War Office cabals, but ultimately pressed his case with insufficient vigour and was left on the outside looking in. Extraordinary as it may seem, White left for South Africa without receiving any formal direction from either Wolseley or Buller. The received wisdom amongst the old South Africa hands was that attacking across the Drakensberg from Natal into southern Transvaal, as Colley had tried to do, would be fraught with difficulty. By far the better option would be to concentrate in the Northern Cape and attack across the Orange River towards Bloemfontein. This would convey the advantages of knocking the less hardline Free State out of the war early on, of bypassing the Drakensberg, and of opening up an altogether easier high veldt approach to Pretoria.

Natal was always going to be problematic for the British. A few miles north of Sir George Colley's grave, the colony abutted the Transvaal across the Laing's Nek pass. Unlike in the earlier conflict, however, the British garrison of October 1899 would also have to contend with Free State commandos operating along the colony's exposed western flank. Because the military initiative was bound at first to rest with the Boers, all the towns north of the Tugela, Newcastle, Dundee and Ladysmith included, would be located in a strategically vulnerable salient. The likely shape of the war was not difficult to guess at. In the opening phase Sir George White and the in-place force would have to block a Boer invasion of Natal along the line of the Tugela, thus shielding Pietermaritzburg, Durban and points further south. On the other side of the Drakensberg, the balance of the standing garrison would defend the Northern Cape and protect the diamond fields at Kimberley. This would mean that the war must inevitably be waged on a western or Kimberley Front, and an eastern or Ladysmith Front. In the second phase the army corps would concentrate along the Orange River in the west and, when Buller was good and ready, would advance to deliver a knock-out blow to Bloemfontein. This would oblige the Transvaal Boers on the eastern front to fall back to protect their own capital and so clear the way for White to cross the Drakensberg. Buller and White would then be free to advance to the capture of Pretoria in a third culminating phase. The one thing White could not afford to do in the meantime was to get the reinforced garrison of Natal, the equivalent of a strong division, trapped on the wrong side of the Tugela. To be fair to Buller, this was something he had both appreciated and intimated to White.

Naturally the Boers did not intend to sit idly by and allow the British to unfold their plan of campaign at their leisure. Instead they intended to fight an offensive war designed to force Milner to negotiate or face being driven into the sea. Opinion was divided as to which of these was the more credible war aim, but there were strong grounds for hoping that the Cape Dutch would rise against the British if the commandos could muscle their way far enough south. The immediate objective on the Natal front would be the defeat of Penn Symons at Dundee. Thereafter Joubert's commandos would capture Ladysmith, cross the Tugela and drive hard for strategically important Durban. There was a strong but unrealistic belief that possession of a sea port might just encourage friendly European powers to intervene on their side.

The Declaration of War

In Britain the order to mobilize an army corps of three infantry divisions and a cavalry division was given on 28 September. Kruger immediately responded in kind to the news, by ordering the commandos to muster, a lead followed by President Steyn four days later. On 9 October, with his citizen-army mustering and training, Kruger served an ultimatum on Her Majesty's Government which demanded that all troops landed after 1 June should leave South Africa, and all those still at sea should at once put about. He demanded a response by 5.00 p.m. on 11 October and received precisely the answer he expected:

> Her Majesty's Agency
> Pretoria
> October 11 1899
>
> Sir,
>
> I am instructed by the High Commissioner to state to you that Her Majesty's Government have received with great regret the peremptory demands of the South African Republic conveyed to me in your note of the 9th instant, and I am to inform you in reply that the conditions dictated by the Government of the South African Republic are such as Her Majesty's Government deem it impossible to discuss.
>
> I have the honour to be,
> Sir,
> your obedient servant
> *Conyngham Greene*

That ZAR had summonsed the British in so peremptory a fashion was of course tantamount to a declaration of war. Piet Joubert, still at the age of 68 the republic's Commandant-General, ordered the invasion of British South Africa to begin the following day.

The mobilization of the army corps went as smoothly as Wolseley had hoped and planned for, and provided a fitting climax to his career as an Army reformer. All told, Buller's force came to 47,081 men, including more than 30,000 infantry and 6,000 cavalry. An unprecedented 20,589 of the soldiers would be reservists. With the in-place garrison of Natal being considered as its 4th Division, the balance of the 1st Army Corps was organized into 1st, 2nd and 3rd Divisions, comprising a total of 8 regiments of cavalry, 4 batteries of horse artillery, 13 of field artillery, 3 of howitzers and 35 battalions of infantry. Almost all of the reservists recalled to the colours paraded as ordered. In many battalions they provided around 50 per cent of the unit's effective strength. On 14 October cheering crowds gave Buller and his staff a patriotic send-off from Waterloo Station. The Prince of Wales, the Secretary of State for War, the C-in-C and the Adjutant-General all turned up to see the general safely aboard his train.[3] That evening he embarked aboard the RMS *Dunottar Castle* at Southampton for a 16-day voyage to Cape Town. On the fifteenth day the ship crossed with a homeward-bound White Star steamer called *Australasian*. Hung over her side was a chalk-board which read 'Three Battles. Boers Defeated. Symons killed.' An agonizing 24 hours ensued before Buller could begin fleshing out the details.

The Invasion of Natal

It is often said that it was Sir Walter Hely-Hutchinson, the Lieutenant-Governor of Natal, who pressurized Sir George White not to cede any part of the colony to the enemy. In fact a young journalist called Winston Churchill established in an interview with White that Hely-Hutchinson expressed an opinion on the subject only when pressed to do so. His views were enough to tip the balance of White's decision on the distribution of his forces, but in no sense represented uninvited political dabbling in the military plan.[4] White decided to allow the supremely confident Symons to defend the colony's northern extremities from his forward position at Dundee. On the night of 19/20 October a Boer force under General Lucas Meyer seized the commanding high ground east of the town. At first light Meyer dropped a few shells into the British encampment from guns emplaced on Talana Hill. Ever anxious to caricature the Victorian military, some twentieth-century historians have portrayed a hapless Symons being woken from his bed by the dawn bombardment. In truth his outposts had engaged the approaching enemy during the course of the night and the day began precisely as the British had anticipated. Across on towering Impati Mountain an even more sizeable Boer force under General 'Maroola' Erasmus sat idly by, shrouded from the action below by a heavy morning mist.

Brimming with faith in the fighting qualities of his infantry, Symons put in a brisk frontal attack on Talana with Brigadier-General Yule's 1st KRRC, 1st Royal Irish Fusiliers and 2nd Royal Dublin Fusiliers. After some heavy

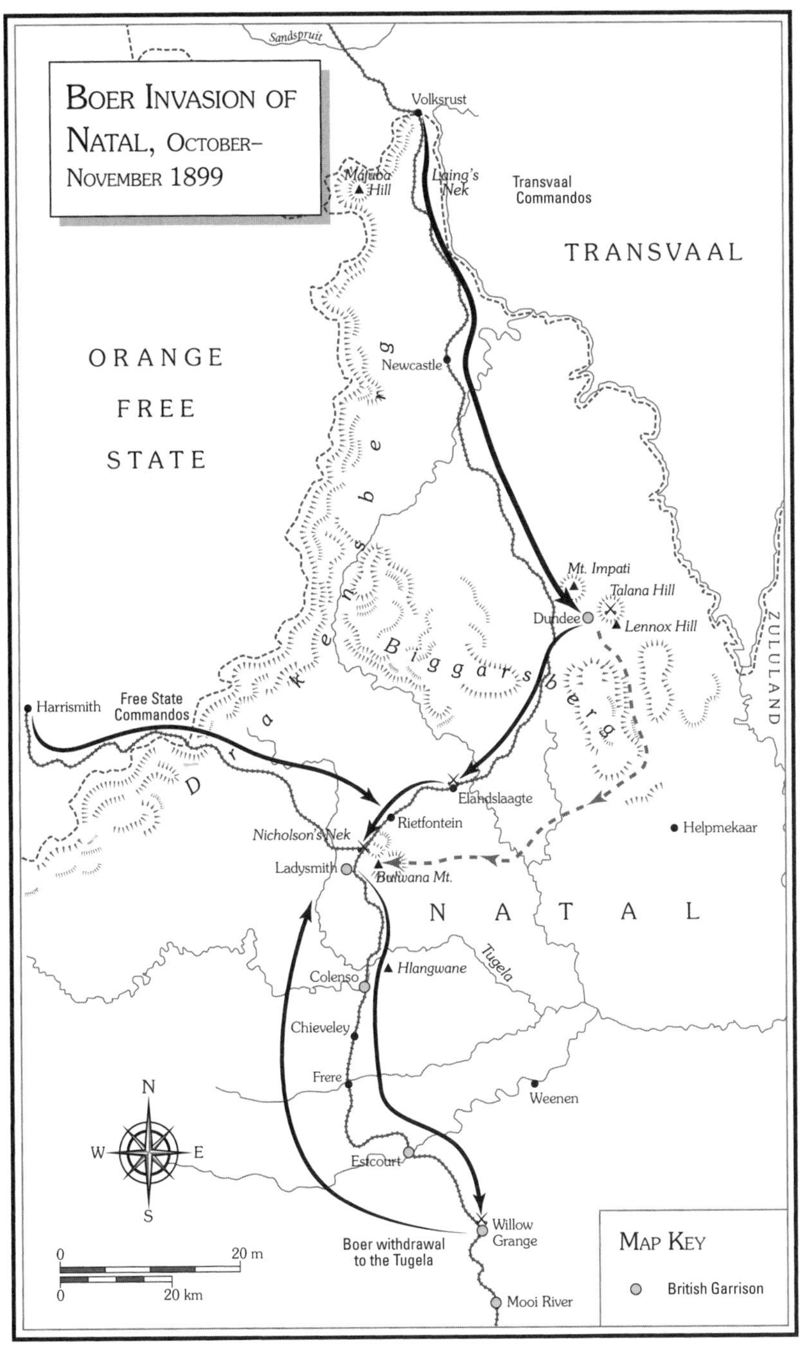
Boer Invasion of Natal, October–November 1899
Sandspruit
Volksrust
Majuba Hill
Laing's Nek
Transvaal Commandos
TRANSVAAL
ORANGE FREE STATE
Newcastle
Drakensberg
Biggarsberg
Mt. Impati
Talana Hill
Dundee
Lennox Hill
ZULULAND
Harrismith
Free State Commandos
Elandslaagte
Rietfontein
Nicholson's Nek
Helpmekaar
Ladysmith
Bulwana Mt.
NATAL
Tugela
Hlangwane
Colenso
Chieveley
Frere
Weenen
N
W
E
S
Estcourt
Willow Grange
Boer withdrawal to the Tugela
0
20 m
0
20 km
Mooi River
Map Key
British Garrison

fighting on the lower slopes, the three bloodied battalions finally succeeded in driving the Boers from the high ground. Fearless to the last, Penn Symons had been badly wounded egging his infantry on and was fated to die a lingering death back in the town. The already costly British victory was rendered Pyrrhic when Lieutenant Colonel Bernhard Möller of the 18th Hussars succeeded in getting the larger part of his regiment isolated in depth and was obliged to surrender.[5] Although the advanced brigade had successfully repelled Meyer's commando, its inherently exposed position in the north Natal salient compelled Yule to abandon Dundee and Glencoe and fall back on the main force at Ladysmith. Instead of following the direct route to the south, Yule diverted along the Helpmekaar road and, despite being hindered by driving rain and mired roads, was able to complete the 60-mile retreat without interference.

Amongst White's principal subordinates in Ladysmith was John French, whom we last met commanding a squadron of the 19th Hussars in the Bayuda Desert. Now a major general, French had been appointed to command Buller's cavalry division and had already arrived upcountry well in advance of his troops. Also present, with the one good arm left to him after Majuba, was Colonel Ian Hamilton, back on his old Natal stamping ground and thirsting for revenge. Unlike many of his colleagues Hamilton knew only too well that there were sound military reasons for treating a Boer commando with respect.

While Meyer and Erasmus were engaged around Dundee, General J. M. Kock pushed south down the railway at the head of the Johannesburg Commando. Unwisely he over-reached himself, isolating his command ahead of the other commandos just long enough for French and Hamilton to wreck it utterly with a set-piece demonstration of combined-arms tactics. The day after Talana Hill, Hamilton entrained the 1st Devons, 1st Manchesters and 2nd Gordons at Ladysmith and steamed in the direction of the railway halt at Elandslaagte. The infantry rendezvoused short of the objective with General French, two batteries of field artillery and single squadrons of the 5th Lancers and 5th Dragoon Guards. Kock had acted injudiciously in surging too far ahead of the rest of the invasion force and, after looting the railway station and drinking the hotel dry, had taken up a defensive position on three nearby koppies. The ensuing British attack was perceived to be such a model of all-arms interaction that it was used as a case-study by the German General Staff for a number of years afterwards. Once the infantry had fought their way over the koppies, the battle reached its bloody climax with a hard-hitting cavalry charge into the left flank and rear of the routing Afrikaners. Old General Kock himself was gravely wounded in a last-ditch defence of the koppies, living just long enough to die as a prisoner of war.[6]

For White it was a case of so far so good, but his base of operations at Ladysmith, stuffed to the rafters with military materiel, was located north of the

Tugela. On 30 October, as the enemy commandos circled round the town in their final approach, the third of the string of battles notified by the *Australasian* was fought. This time it ended in disaster for the British. White's plan included concurrent night marches by a number of columns, but was over-complicated and called for a standard of training and staff-work quite beyond the competency of a command not long since thrown together. A total of 37 officers and 917 men of the 1st Royal Irish Fusiliers and the 1st Gloucesters under Colonel Robert Carleton were compelled to surrender after becoming isolated at Nicholson's Nek. Casualties across the whole force came to 6 and 63 killed and 10 and 239 wounded. The scene in Murchison Street on 'Mournful Monday', as the various components of White's command came streaming back into town (the subject of a famous photograph), was one of alarm and confusion. As a result of this serious failure White lost all confidence, took to his headquarters and pretty much stayed there for the duration of the coming siege. The Boers closed round the town, severed the railway to the south and began emplacing their guns on the surrounding hills.

Instead of destroying his stores, retaining his mobility and falling back a mere 15 miles to the south side of the Tugela, where he would have been better able to protect the rest of Natal, White succeeded in getting the best part of 13,000 men bottled up in Ladysmith. Fortunately for the British cause, he sent John French out by the last train, though he rather unnecessarily retained three cavalry regiments which would have been invaluable to Buller. With only 24,000 Boers on the Ladysmith Front, there was little or no danger of the town falling by storm, except in so far as the strength of the garrison was dissipated by the length of the 14-mile perimeter. One of White's principal problems was that the Boer 155-mm 'Long Toms' on the hills outranged any of his guns. Fortunately for most members of the garrison the sporadic enemy bombardment only ever amounted to an irritating nuisance. In addition to his troops White had to worry about feeding almost 8,000 civilians, amongst them Dr Jameson and Colonel Frank Rhodes, now a *Times* correspondent.[7]

Although there were insufficient units south of the Tugela to prevent a determined Boer drive on Durban, what few there were managed to block Joubert at Willow Grange.[8] Joubert fell back to the north at the end of November, content merely to invest Ladysmith and to dig in along the general line of the Tugela. In doing so he threw up the republics' only real chance of winning the war. Some raiding to the south was permitted, leading on 15 November to the ambush of an armoured train by the Krugersdorp and Wakkerstroom commandos, and the capture of the courageous correspondent of the *Morning Post*. The remarkable Mr Winston Churchill would escape from Pretoria to Portuguese Mozambique and be back in Natal in time for Christmas.[9]

On the other side of the Drakensberg the much smaller garrisons of Kimberley (2,600 men) and Mafeking (1,200 men) commanded by Colonels Kekewich and Baden-Powell respectively, had also been encircled and besieged. As if the close attention of the enemy was not enough, poor Kekewich counted the irascible Cecil Rhodes amongst his more troublesome civilian charges.

Fighting on Two Fronts

Of the three short sentences displayed by the *Australasian*, Buller soon discovered that only the first and last were true. The second sentence, 'Boers defeated', was true of Elandslaagte and half-true of Talana Hill, but in the round amounted to a gross misrepresentation of the wider situation. At least major components of the 1st Army Corps were now being disembarked and despatched upcountry by rail with commendable efficiency. Once he had been fully apprised of the operational situation, Buller was forced to abandon any notion of concentrating his entire corps against Bloemfontein. With White bottled up in Ladysmith and the Tugela crossings in the hands of the enemy, southern Natal had been left all but defenceless. The 1st Army Corps would have to be split between the two major fronts, with a smaller third force, under Lieutenant General Sir William Gatacre KCB (General 'Backacher' to veterans of the Omdurman campaign), operating between them so as to cover the Northern Cape. The relief of Ladysmith would fall to Lieutenant General Sir Francis Clery KCB, and the salvation of Kimberley to Lieutenant General Lord Methuen CB, CMG. After three weeks in Cape Town, Buller moved on to Natal. Although Clery would remain the nominal commander of the eastern theatre of operations, in practice responsibility for the relief of Ladysmith would now rest with Buller himself.[10]

On the western front Paul Sanford, Lord Methuen, quickly got into his stride. Traditionally portrayed as a stiff-necked Guardsman, in that respect at least historians have done him a great disservice. Commissioned into the Scots Fusilier Guards in 1864, Methuen was a veteran of the Ashanti and Egyptian campaigns and had commanded a regiment of irregular horse in Sir Charles Warren's bloodless Bechuanaland Expedition of 1884–5. Now, at the age of 54, he was the youngest lieutenant general in the Army and was as serious a student of military affairs as could be found anywhere in the service. The first thing he dispensed with was the obsessive spit and polish of the Guards Brigade. This was war and this was the South African veldt not Horse Guards Parade, he reminded its battalion commanders. Having successfully completed his concentration around Orange River Station, Methuen began the 75-mile advance on Kimberley with a force of 10,000 men, based principally on the 1st (Guards) and 9th Brigades.[11] As was also the case on the Ladysmith front, Methuen's freedom

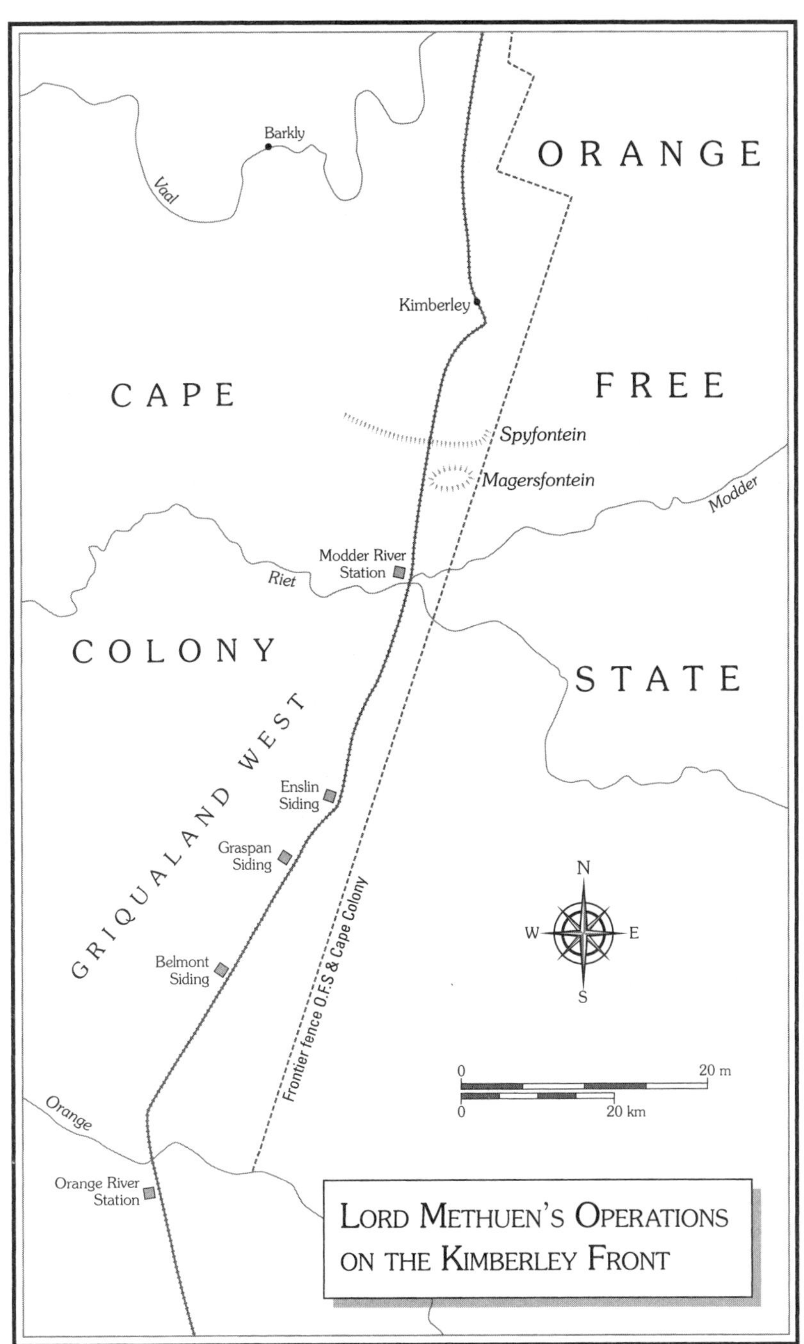

LORD METHUEN'S OPERATIONS ON THE KIMBERLEY FRONT

of action was hamstrung by dependence on a single railway line. Even more problematically he had only 900 mounted troops with which to scout his axis and protect his lines of communication. On 23 November he met the Free State commandos under Commandant Jacobus Prinsloo for the first time. The Battle of Belmont[12] resulted in a workmanlike victory for the British but, like most of their Boer War victories, was not accomplished without significant loss. The outcome was marred most of all by the cavalry's failure to inflict any serious damage on a retreating enemy.

Before the Battle of Graspan[13] was fought, two days after Belmont and about 10 miles further up the railway line, the badly shaken Free Staters had been bolstered by the arrival of around 700 Transvaalers under the famously devout General Koos De la Rey. De la Rey had been opposed to the war all along and had traded insults on the subject with Kruger in the Volksraad but, now that it had been forced upon him, had resolved to fight for the republic as ardently as the next man. Indeed he had told the president in no uncertain terms that he would still be fighting long after Kruger had fled to seek sanctuary in a foreign land – a pledge he would more than live up to. Despite the presence of the Transvaalers, the commandos were once more driven from their ground, this time by the sailors and marines of Methuen's naval brigade. Yet again they were able to get clean away. His patience stretched to breaking point, Methuen sacked his cavalry commander on the spot.

Anxious to retain the upper hand on both fronts, Kruger wired General Piet Cronje at Mafeking with orders to ride to the assistance of the Free Staters with every man who could be spared from the siege-lines. Cronje set off at the head of 1,200 men from the Klerksdorp and Potchefstroom Commandos, with two 75-mm Krupp QFs and three Maxim-Nordenfeldt 'pom-poms' – wheeled heavy-calibre (37-mm) belt-fed automatics. In the immediate aftermath of Graspan, Methuen quickly exploited as far as the Modder, the only major river line between his latest encampment and the outskirts of Kimberley. By the time he was ready to force a crossing on 28 November 1899, Cronje had successfully married up with Prinsloo and De la Rey. Cronje was famous as the commandant of the Potchefstroom Commando during the Transvaal Rebellion, and more recently as the man who had run Dr Jameson to ground, but beyond that his reputation as a military man was largely founded on brutalising hapless black Africans. The Battle of Modder River[14] was Lord Methuen's third general action in six days. He was hampered as usual by poor mapping and clumsy reconnaissance and, in ignorance of the enemy's great strength, blundered into a frontal attack around the river bridges. Worst of all, he finalised his plan only at the last minute and failed to allow his subordinate commanders time to reconnoitre their tasks, a mistake which would shortly be repeated on the Ladysmith front.

For a long while Methuen's infantry brigades were pinned down in the open with casualties mounting and defeat beckoning, but eventually the Loyal North Lancashire Regiment and the Argyll and Sutherland Highlanders worked their way across the river and established themselves in the hamlet of Rosmead. By nightfall the Boer position had been unhinged. De la Rey was left with no alternative but to break clean under the cover of darkness, furious that Cronje had done nothing to restore the situation with a counter-attack, and equally furious at another precipitate withdrawal by the seemingly half-hearted Free Staters. With 4 and 67 dead and 19 and 370 wounded, amongst them Lord Methuen himself, the British had paid a stiff price for crossing the Modder, but the loss was far from crippling and now only the Magersfontein koppies, some six miles to the north, and the Spyfontein high ground three miles beyond that, stood between Colonel Kekewich and salvation.

Methuen needed to recover from the bullet hole in his thigh and to reconstitute his supplies before pushing on into the open veldt. On the night of 4 December Kekewich's signallers flashed through that the town could hold out for another 40 days. On top of this welcome news, one of the most celebrated soldiers of the age, Major General Andy Wauchope, came marching in with the balance of his lion-hearted Highland Brigade. Wauchope was not long back from Kitchener's triumph in the Sudan, and was renowned for running Gladstone a close second in his home constituency during the general election of 1892. He had fought with the Black Watch in Ashantiland, at El Teb and with Earle's River Column on the Nile, but he was not a lucky man and had been badly wounded on each occasion. He had been left with such limited movement in his right shoulder since Kirbekan, that he been forced to seek a special dispensation from saluting on parade.[15] With the arrival of some of Scotland's finest warriors, it began to look as if the relief of Kimberley was in the bag. Such was the situation in the west when, on 6 December 1899, Sir Redvers Buller arrived on the Ladysmith front to assume control of operations in Natal.

The South Natal Field Force

The forward concentration area for Sir Francis Clery's force was centred on the otherwise insignificant railway halt at Frere, some 12 miles south of the major road and railway crossings over the Tugela at Colenso. The river itself was wide, meandering and fast-flowing, with few natural drifts. With the successful concentration of the equivalent of two infantry divisions and a strong cavalry brigade, the immediate threat to southern Natal had passed. All that remained to be done was to complete the logistic build-up and wait for Sir Redvers to select his point of attack. Again the railway would be all-important. Away from

Table 9: The South Natal Field Force, 15 December 1899

General Commanding-in-Chief	***Gen. Sir Redvers Buller***
Force Commander	***Lt. Gen. Sir Francis Clery***

2nd Brigade *Maj. Gen. H. J. T. Hildyard*	5th (Irish) Brigade *Maj. Gen. A. F. Hart*
2nd Bn Queen's (Royal West Surrey Regt)	1st Bn Border Regiment
2nd Bn East Surrey Regiment	1st Bn Connaught Rangers
2nd Bn Devonshire Regiment	2nd Bn Royal Dublin Fusiliers
2nd Bn West Yorkshire Regiment	1st Bn Royal Inniskilling Fusiliers
Supply Column – No. 16 Company ASC	Supply Column – No. 4 Company ASC
Bearer Company – No. 2 Company RAMC	Bearer Company – No. 16 Company RAMC
Field Hospital – Depot Companies RAMC	Field Hospital – No. 10 Company RAMC
4th Brigade *Maj. Gen. Hon. N. G. Lyttelton*	6th (Fusilier) Brigade *Maj. Gen. G. Barton*
2nd Bn Cameronians (Scottish Rifles)	2nd Bn Royal Fusiliers
3rd Bn King's Royal Rifle Corps	2nd Bn Royal Scots Fusiliers
1st Bn Durham Light Infantry	1st Bn Royal Welsh Fusiliers
1st Bn Rifle Brigade	2nd Bn Royal Irish Fusiliers
Supply Column – No. 14 Company ASC	Supply Column – No. 24 Company ASC
Bearer Company – No. 14 Company RAMC	Bearer Company – No. 17 Company RAMC
Field Hospital – also No. 14 Company RAMC	Field Hospital – No. 11 Company RAMC
Cavalry Brigade *Brig.-Gen. Lord Dundonald*	Artillery *Col. C. J. Long*
1st Royal Dragoons	14th Field Battery RA
13th Hussars	63rd Field Battery RA
Imperial Light Horse	64th Field Battery RA
Thorneycroft's Mounted Infantry	66th Field Battery RA
South African Light Horse	Royal Navy (12 x 12-pdr QF, 2 x 4.7-inch)
1 Composite Regiment*	7th Field Battery RA (Cav Bde)

* *inc. Bethune's MI, Natal Carbineers and Regular MI*

Infantry	416 & 13,521	**Cavalry**	126 & 1,251
Royal Artillery	39 & 1,074	**Royal Engineers**	14 & 419
Royal Navy	31 & 279	**Army Service Corps**	16 & 217
Royal Army Medical Corps	30 & 464		

Total strength: 706 officers, 18,672 other ranks and 44 guns

the tracks British lateral mobility and logistic self-sufficiency would be wholly dependent on an insufficient quantity of ox-drawn transport wagons. In the circumstances it would take weeks to build up meaningful logistic stockpiles at any distance from Frere or nearby Chieveley – the last stop before Colenso. Thus any flanking move to the west, where Potgieter's and Trichardt's Drifts provided tempting alternate crossing-points, would have to be limited in both scale and duration.

The worst aspect of the situation confronting Buller was that the north bank of the river was commanded by a long, jumbled range of hills and koppies which offered the Boers uninterrupted fields of view and any number of ready-made blocking positions. By contrast the rolling veldt to the south would offer the British next to no cover in their approach. Only to the right front of Colenso, where there was a prominent hill called Hlangwane, was it possible to command a crossing point from the south bank. By now Slim Piet Joubert had been taken ill, ostensibly with shell-shock, and had been evacuated to Pretoria.[16] This left the Tugela line in the hands of a vigorous and intelligent 37-year-old called Louis Botha. General Botha had 5,000–6,000 men deployed to defend the river, the majority of them centred on the most obvious river crossings around Colenso, though all the other drifts within striking distance were kept under surveillance. As he enjoyed the twin advantages of interior lines and superior mobility, it would be quite impossible for the British to concentrate in force and seize a bridgehead, either upstream or downstream of Colenso, without Botha being able to get his reserves into blocking positions with more than enough time to spare. It was a taxing tactical conundrum and, like all such problems, would demand an imaginative solution. The one thing that could be guaranteed not to work was the sledgehammer approach.

When Buller rode within sight of Colenso and scanned the ground across the river, he knowingly declared the position to be impregnable. As usual the staff nodded in sage agreement with their master. The great man was right as usual; only a madman would attack at Colenso. Buller concluded that, regardless of logistic constraints, he would have to move to the west, attack across Potgieter's Drift, seize the Ntabmnyama high ground beyond, and then break out to the north-east along the Acton Homes road. The force available for the coming operation is listed in Table 9. Barton's 6th (Fusilier) Brigade would be left south of Chieveley to entertain the enemy with a demonstration intended to suggest an impending attack at Colenso. To add to the deception some of the naval artillery would bombard the Boer positions throughout daylight on the 13th.

Botha felt sure that the British could not afford to roam too far from the railway and that, sooner or later, they would make a frontal attack at Colenso. The railway bridge had already been blown by the time he took command, but the iron road bridge just to the west was still intact. Botha ordered that it be mined for demolition but left standing. Rather than holding the British infantry south of the river, he planned instead to allow them into a metaphorical goldfish bowl on the north bank, to bring the bridge down behind them, and to destroy everything trapped inside the lodgement with a maelstrom of rifle and artillery

Table 10: The Boer Force on the Colenso–Tugela Line

Commander	***Gen. Louis Botha***	
Right Flank Protection		
Middleburg Commando		
Free State Commando	*Gen. A. P. Cronje*	
Johannesburg Commando	*Gen. Fourie*	
Right Flank		
Ermelo Commando	*Comdt. J. N. H. Grobler*	covering the bridle drift
Soutpansberg Commando	*Comdt. H. C. J. Van Rensburg*	on a low ridge overlooking the pont drift
Swaziland Police Commando	*Comdt. C. Botha*	river bank commanding the pont drift
Centre		
Heidelberg Commando	*Comdt. Buys*	river bank commanding the iron road bridge
Vryheid Commando & ZARPs[17]		in reserve on Colenso koppies
Krugersdorp Commando	*Comdt. Oosthuysen*	Fort Wylie commanding the railway bridge
Left Flank		
Standerton Commando	*Comdt. Muller*	Hlangwane
Wakkerstroom Commando	*Comdt. J. A. Joubert*	Hlangwane
Members of other commandos drawn by lot		
Artillery	*Lt. Col. S. P. E. Trichardt*	
1 x 120-mm Krupp howitzer		Colenso koppies
2 x 75-mm Creusot QF		right-flank high ground commanding the pont drift
1 x 75-mm Krupp QF		Colenso koppies
1 x 37-mm Maxim-Nordenfeldt		Colenso koppies
Total strength:	approx. 5,000–6,000 men and 5 guns (more 75-mm guns by some accounts)	

fire. The force at his disposal is listed in Table 10. All his units were under strict orders not to betray their positions by replying to British fire until he gave the signal, though in practice this was always going to be a tall order. There was only one thing wrong with the plan: nobody would be stupid enough to put his head into the noose, least of all the legendary Buller, the man who fought with a pistol in one hand and a knobkerrie in the other.

Change of Plan

On Monday 11 December Buller was rattled by news of a serious reverse suffered by General Gatacre at Stormberg Junction.[18] Wolseley's successful night approach march at Tel-el-Kebir seems to have started a fashion for such operations in the high Victorian Army, a fashion which the commanders in South Africa seemed hell-bent on emulating. Consistent success in night operations can only be achieved with practice, teamwork and rehearsal – and collective training was something the British Army had been studiously mishandling for decades. As at Nicholson's Nek, the approach to Stormberg Junction had gone horribly wrong. With 135 casualties and 13 officers and 548 men captured, Gatacre's command was reduced to helplessness. The following day Lord Methuen's despatches reported a second disastrous repulse, this time at the foot of the Magersfontein koppies.[19] Wauchope, it transpired, had also botched a night approach march – not this time by getting lost, but by failing to extend into open order in good time. The highlanders were caught flat-footed in the dawn and spent the best part of the day pinned down on the veldt. Eventually nightfall would have come to their salvation – but in the late afternoon a collective madness had swept through the brigade, inspired in part by the twin tortures of raging thirst and a blazing sun so hot that it blistered the backs of the highlander's knees. First one man got up and bolted for the rear, then another, until finally the contagion had infected hundreds. The resultant turkey-shoot was bloody in the extreme. Mercifully, gallant, unlucky Andy Wauchope had not lived long enough to see his beloved highlanders run,[20] but worse, much worse, than the loss of one celebrated major general, 21 other officers and 188 other ranks had been killed, 46 officers and 629 men had been wounded and 1 officer and 62 men were listed as missing. Instead of relieving Kimberley, it was clear that Methuen would now be struggling even to hold open his lines of communication. In the space of a few short days the war had been thrown into strategic reverse.

If Colonel Buller had been full of dash, General Buller was an altogether different man. He had been comfortable at the War Office, where if things were going to go wrong they generally took years to do so and there was little prospect of any mud sticking to the powerful military offices he held there. In the even more exalted position he now occupied, the very existence of British South Africa could be placed in jeopardy overnight and there would be no opportunity to shirk the blame. Tortured as he was by self-doubt, it was a level of responsibility he struggled to come to terms with. For reasons best known to himself he now decided not to outflank the Colenso defences via Potgieter's Drift as planned, but to batter his way through in the centre, a quite extraordinary U-turn. He justified his change of heart with the argument that, if the move to the west went wrong, he might be left stranded at some distance from the railway and would again have left southern Natal open to invasion. The argument assumed that the Boers were waiting like a coiled spring for the opportunity to bypass Buller and race for Durban, but any such aspiration had long since passed and, in any case, the Boers need only leap on their ponies to bypass Buller wherever and whenever they pleased. On Thursday morning Buller joined Barton's brigade beyond Chieveley to have another good look at the ground ahead.

In the meantime Botha's defence plan had been dealt a serious blow. As part of the original British deception plan, the naval artillery had been harassing the enemy's main defensive position throughout daylight on Wednesday 13 December. The primary tactical consideration of a Boer commando was always the security of its line of retreat but, positioned as they were on the same side of the river as the British, the 800 burghers on Hlangwane felt especially vulnerable. The incoming shell fire seemed to suggest that an attack on their position was imminent. The Wakkerstroom and Standerton Commandos bolted back to their ponies, fled to the north bank and declined, even in the absence of a British follow-up, to go back. Such an incident would have been unthinkable in a disciplined force, but this was a citizen-army commanded by consent and Botha had no recourse but to persuasion.

Hlangwane represented what would now be termed 'key terrain' to the Boers, though as yet Buller had failed to appreciate its potential. Its significance lay in the great northwards meander in the Tugela, which at first ran parallel to the Hlangwane high ground and then swung north-east behind it. Four much lower-lying koppies commanded the major crossings at Colenso and were vital to Botha's plan of defence. Hlangwane overlooked the koppies from across the river at a range of a little over a mile. If British guns could be emplaced there, the enemy positions above the bridges would quickly become untenable. The Boers rowed amongst themselves for a day, until in desperation Botha telegraphed his president for some statesmanlike expression of support. Kruger's reply was read to the truculent commandos; fired up by his old-world *dopper* rhetoric, they agreed to draw lots to see who should go back. Luck often rears its head in war and did so now – Hlangwane was reoccupied only hours before Buller's attack went in.

Act in Haste, Repent at Leisure

The most inexcusable aspect of Buller's change of heart was the indecent haste with which he proceeded to order and execute a frontal attack. As he sat looking through his telescope late on Thursday morning, there was not a single factor in play dictating that he must attack at dawn the next day – or the day after that – or at any point in the next fortnight for that matter. A commander obliged by circumstance, or the absence of alternatives, to order a frontal attack on a strong defensive position has a moral obligation to his soldiers to take every conceivable opportunity to maximize their chance of success. But in an act of outright military incompetence, Buller sent for his principal subordinates that very afternoon and proceeded to outline how he intended to attack Colenso at first light. In all the excitement he failed to notify White of his intention (they communicated by coded searchlight messages at night), thereby precluding the possibility of harassing operations against the Boer rear. The last message White had received was, 'Actual date of attack depends on difficulties met with; probably 17th December',[21] but it was now going in on Friday the 15th. The process by which an army moves from loafing around its camp fires into a deliberate operation of war is called 'battle procedure'. By definition it is a time-consuming activity. All sorts of administrative preparations have to be made and subordinate commanders, from brigade commander to section commander, all have to be briefed in sequence, so that by the end of the process everybody comprehends their part in the plan. Most importantly of all, provision has to be made for timely reconnaissance. Few operations are as inherently risky as an opposed river crossing. To advance against a defended river line without knowing exactly where the crossing-points are, or even whether they are passable, is tantamount to insanity and yet, under Sir Redvers Buller's leadership, that is precisely what happened at Colenso.

The British maps were poor. The iron road-bridge was still intact – why? It must have reeked of entrapment and yet still Major General Henry Hildyard was ordered to force a crossing there with his 2nd Brigade. There was also a wagon drift just downstream of the road bridge and a native drift to the right of the railway bridge, though whether Hildyard knew of their existence is doubtful; certainly they were not mentioned in his written orders. Four miles further west, stiff-necked, fearless, old-school Fitzroy Hart was to cross by a bridle drift with the Irish Brigade. And where, precisely, on the ground, sir, is the bridle drift – Hart simply has to have asked the question. Don't worry – Buller must have said with a vague waft of the telescope – I will give you an African guide who lives near there and knows the way. Will we be able to ford it when we get there – Hart must have enquired. Nobody knew for sure, but nobody was prepared to say so. Oh yes, the water is usually chest deep at this time of year – somebody must have piped up. And so the mad-cap orders group played itself out.

Neville Lyttelton was to move his 4th Brigade up in echelon, between Hart and Hildyard, and be prepared to exploit the success of either leading brigade. Geoffrey Barton was to move his fusilier brigade up on the right of Hildyard to protect his flank and support Dundonald's mounted brigade around Hlangwane. Brigadier-General the Earl of Dundonald, late of the 2nd Life Guards, was to demonstrate around the vital hilltop – not to capture it – but to protect the right of the main attack and to distract the Boers on the summit. He would have around 1,000 troopers and a field battery under his command. The rest of the cavalry would be dispersed to the flanks – 300 men in the west, and 500 in the east. Colonel Charles Long, the artillery commander, was to advance in the centre with a dozen 15-pounders from 14th and 66th Batteries RFA and six ox-drawn naval 12-pounders, his task to pummel the Colenso koppies in advance of Hildyard's attack. Don't get too close, Buller cautioned, indicating on his imprecise map, precisely where the all too dashing Long should go.

The British commanders went on their way, aware that they could expect to receive their written orders during the course of the night, and that they would need to have their brigades on the move before dawn. None of them were fools and they were far from inexperienced, yet not one of them seems to have raised a serious objection to the rushed nature of the attack, or to the absence of any worthwhile intelligence on enemy strengths and dispositions. Clery had been a key staff officer in the Zulu War and had been on Sir Gerald Graham's staff at Second El Teb and Tamai; all four of the infantry brigadiers had been at Tel-el-Kebir; Lyttelton, like Wauchope, had just come from commanding a brigade at Omdurman; Hildyard had taken over from Clery as Commandant of the Staff College; Hart and Hildyard had commanded Aldershot brigades under Buller; Dundonald had commanded the 2nd Life Guards contingent at Abu Klea;[22] while Charlie Long had served in the Second Afghan War and had only recently secured his place in history as Kitchener's artillery commander at Omdurman. Between them this cabal of senior officers counted a great deal of operational experience. It has to be supposed that at this early stage in the campaign, with Buller's reputation still intact, overawed subordinate commanders simply assumed that their legendary leader must know best. So complete was the failure to carry out battle procedure that not a single man in the 5th (Irish) Brigade, from the brigade commander to his batman, actually knew for sure where their crossing point was. The written orders were signed off in Clery's name at 10.00 p.m. and reached the major generals at about midnight.[23] It has to be doubtful if the battalion commanders knew much more than their ready-to-move time and their place in the order of march. Breakfast was at 2.00 a.m. It is often mockingly pointed out by historians that Hart put the Irish Brigade through half an hour's drill before setting off on his approach march, but it is unlikely to have been foot-drill – much more probably it was brigade drill conducted by way of rehearsal.

The Battle of Colenso, 15 December 1899

Botha had positioned his command post on the Colenso koppies, next to the Krupp howitzer with which he intended to give the signal to open fire. The sun

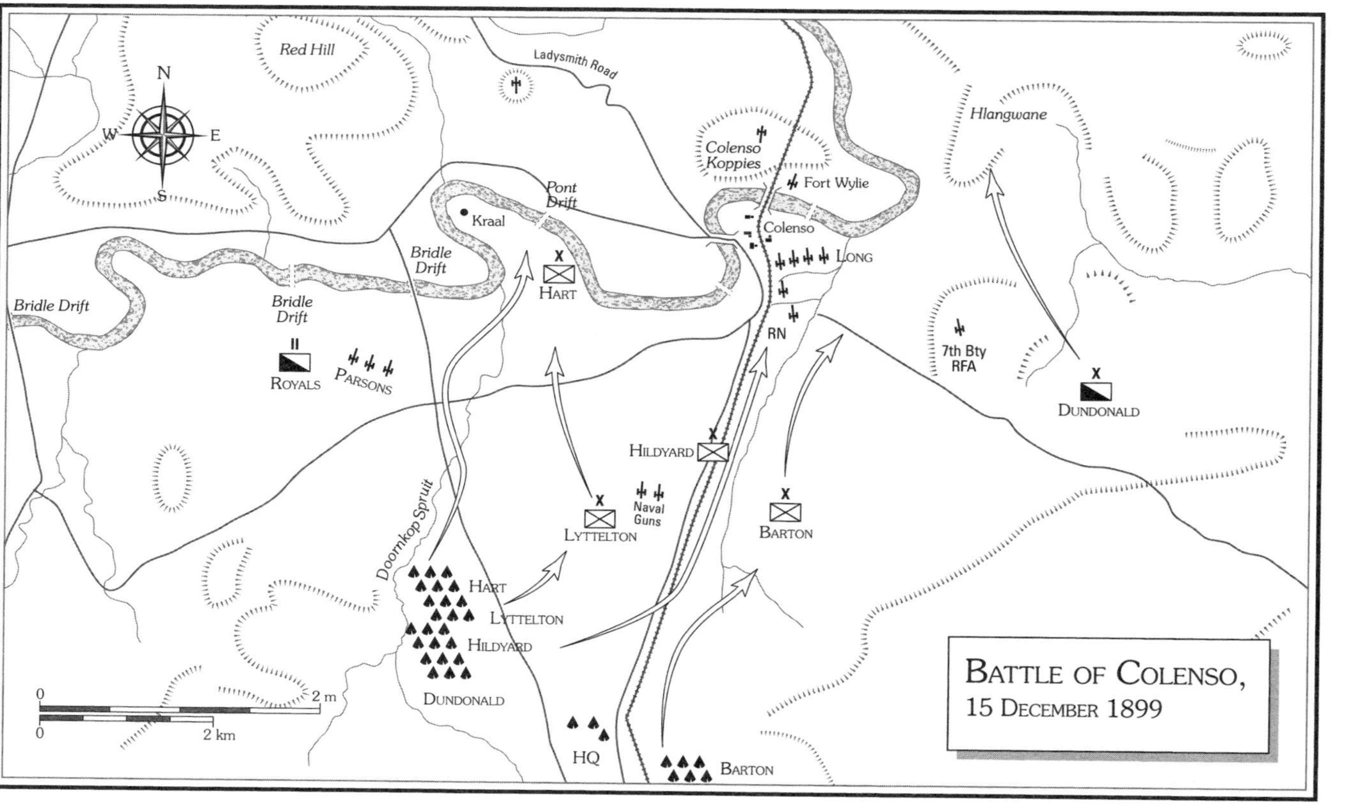

Battle of Colenso,
15 December 1899
Red Hill
Ladysmith Road
N
S
E
W
Colenso Koppies
Fort Wylie
Colenso
Long
RN
Hlangwane
7th Bty RFA
Dundonald
Pont Drift
Kraal
Bridle Drift
Bridle Drift
Bridle Drift
Hart
Royals
Parsons
Hildyard
Naval Guns
Lyttelton
Barton
Doornkop Spruit
Hart
Lyttelton
Hildyard
Dundonald
HQ
Barton
0
2 m
0
2 km

was up at the beginning of what was set to be a still and sweltering day. The only clouds to be seen were the kicked-up clouds of dust shrouding the British battalions and batteries on the long forward slope down to the river. It was painfully obvious to the waiting Boers that the *rooineks* were coming in force. The Naval Brigade had opened fire bright and early, engaging the Colenso koppies from Naval Gun Hill with six 12-pounders at around 4.45 a.m. At 5.20 a.m. the two 4.7-inch guns joined in the barrage. During the course of the day the two heavy guns would fire 80 rounds each, and the 'long twelves' about 600 rounds between them. Just as Botha had anticipated, there were plentiful signs of movement in the direction of the still intact iron bridge. It looked like the British were going to walk straight into his trap after all.

Over on the British left, General 'No-bobs' Hart was pushing further west than the African guide at his side seemed entirely happy with. In fact Hart was following a faint track in the grass that pointed to the banks of the Tugela – what better indication of the existence of a ford could there be? Speaking through Mr Norgate, the general's civilian interpreter, the guide indicated that the drift lay half-right of the brigade's line of march. As the man had been provided by the intelligence staff, Hart concluded that he must know what he was talking about and, disregarding the evidence of his own eyes, diverged from the track as suggested. Unfortunately the African was either eminently unqualified to guide anybody anywhere, or had been confused by the staff officers who briefed him. There was indeed a drift in the direction he was now leading, but it was not the fordable bridle drift that Hart was looking for. Instead the brigade was advancing directly into one of the great serpentine bends in the Tugela, at the head of which there was a pont drift, no longer operating, where in more peaceable times it had been possible to get a wagon towed across the river on a hawser-operated raft.

The Loop

Though nobody in the Irish Brigade yet knew it, 'the loop' was most certainly not the place for 3,200 infantrymen to try wading the Tugela – the water seems to have been 7–10 feet deep on the day. Worse the 'crossing' was located at the head of a natural salient, and by definition a body of troops advancing into a defended salient can expect to be swept by a murderous cross-fire. On marched the Irish, with only their leading battalion, 2nd Royal Dublin Fusiliers under Colonel Charles Cooper, extended in open order.[24] The remainder were in quarter column of companies, one battalion behind the other. In other words the main body of the brigade was one company wide, with an interval of only six paces between companies. Further west Lieutenant Colonel John Burn-Murdoch, who like Dundonald had served in the Heavy Camel Regiment in the Bayuda, was protecting the left flank with his 1st (Royal) Dragoons. Through his field glasses he could make out hundreds of Boers waiting patiently in their trenches for the report of Botha's howitzer. He sent a galloper to warn Hart what he was getting himself into, but before anything could be done to unpick the situation, all hell had been let loose.

It began not with Botha's howitzer, but with a shell fired from the commanding high ground astride the Ladysmith road. Hundreds of riflemen dug in near the river bank quickly joined in. The third shell to land took down nine men in the Connaught Rangers. Like the Guards at Modder River and the highlanders at Magersfontein, the Irish threw themselves down in the grass to find what cover they could. Remarkably Hart himself was still striding about, living up to his nickname by disdaining to 'bob' as he urged his men on towards the river. Eventually a few sections gathered their courage and began pushing forward in short bounds for the head of the loop. With four battalions trying to squeeze into a frontage of little more than a thousand yards, organizational cohesion was soon lost. The 1st Royal Inniskilling Fusiliers (Lieutenant Colonel Thomas Thackeray), 1st Connaught Rangers (Lieutenant Colonel Lionel Brooke) and the English interlopers from the 1st Border Regiment (Lieutenant Colonel John Hinde) all crowded in, behind and amongst the Dublin Fusiliers. At the head of the loop was an abandoned kraal where some of the Connaught Rangers were able to find some cover. A 14-year-old boy-bugler with the Dublins called John Dunn, who had disobeyed his captain's order to stay out of the fight, kept sounding the 'Advance' until at length he was wounded in the chest and arm.[25] Within minutes there were dozens of prostrate khaki figures strewn across the veldt behind the attacking battalions. Although some of the Dublins were brave enough to wade into the river they were either shot, swept away by the current or captured on the far bank. The Irish Brigade, it was clear, was going nowhere and settled down to a protracted fire-fight, though in the new age of smokeless powder they had very little idea where to aim. It was now about 7.00 a.m.

The Action in the Centre

Colonel Charlie Long's advance in the centre occurred concurrently with that of the Irish Brigade on the left. A firm believer in blazing away at what Prussian artillery theorists liked to call 'decisive' ranges, the colonel was excited by the prospect of clearing the way for Hildyard's brigade and pushed ahead eagerly at the head of 14th and 66th Batteries. The six ox-drawn naval guns under Lieutenant F. C. A. Ogilvy RN were much slower-moving and were quickly left behind. Long was also outstripping Barton's brigade, with which he was meant to make his approach, and moreover appears to have done so wilfully – it is clear that he disregarded a number of messages from Barton instructing him to slow down. At about 5.30 a.m. Barton reached the point on the ground where Buller's orders required him to halt. As the artillery clearly intended to plough on regardless, he detached two RSF companies from his brigade and sent them hurrying after the guns as their close escort. In company with Lieutenant Colonel Henry Hunt, commanding the 1st Brigade-Division RFA[26] to which the two field batteries belonged, Long led the guns and limbers across a large donga and continued towards the river. Four hundred yards further on they crossed a smaller donga. They were 75 yards beyond this second watercourse, with the railway station 450 yards to their left, before Long finally called a halt. It can be difficult to imagine the ground these days as much of it has been built on and a power station obscures the old fields of fire, but contemporary photographs show that in 1899 there was nothing but flat, open veldt between the gun line and the river. Squarely in the colonel's sights was the koppie overlooking the wrecked railway bridge, known to the British as 'Fort Wylie' after a minor defence work constructed there earlier in the war.

From his vantage point beside the big Krupp, Louis Botha could hardly believe his eyes. In contravention of all tactical norms, the British were leading with artillery. Everybody else was watching the spectacle too and, as most burghers lived in mortal dread of sustained artillery bombardment, several impassioned pleas to open fire soon came in from the veldtkornets. Long claimed later that he had intended to come into action at a range of something between 2,000 and 2,500 yards, but was already much further forward than he thought, barely 1,000 yards, in fact, from the nearest Boer trenches.[27] The subsequent fire orders to engage Fort Wylie would specify a range of 1,200 yards. Noting that the British guns were halting at last and would come no closer, Botha turned to catch the eye of the Staatsartillerie gunner nervously holding the lanyard of the big Krupp. With the report of the gun still ringing in their ears, the men of the Krugersdorp and Heidelberg Commandos sprang into action. The British gunners did what they knew best and returned fire as fast as they could load and lay. Nor were their efforts in vain. Fort Wylie was soon shrouded in pall of its own brick-red dust. Majors Arthur Bailward (14th) and William Foster (66th) commanded proficient well-drilled batteries. Their men served their guns bravely and well, showing scant regard for the hundreds of Mausers now playing on them.

Whilst a proportion of each gun's first-line ammunition was carried aboard its limber, there was also an accompanying ammunition wagon (in appearance much like a limber) per gun. Because they were expecting to lay down a heavy weight of fire from the outset, the battery commanders had given orders that the guns should be served directly from their ammunition wagons, each of which carried 104 rounds. This would enable the limbers to move back into the cover of the large donga and preserve the 'ready-to-use' ammunition for later. These were all routine tactical options for the artillery and, in accordance with well-rehearsed drills, the two battery sergeant-majors each brought up four of their six ammunition wagons. Enemy rifle fire took so heavy a toll of the horses on the gun line, that when the time came for the 14th Battery limbers to pull clear and be replaced by ammunition wagons, two of them had to be left where they were.

About 400 yards to the rear of the 15-pounders, the naval 12-pounders had come under fire from previously unidentified gun positions atop the Colenso Koppies. The 37-mm 'pom-pom' Botha had sited there proved particularly bothersome. All but one of the Navy's ox-teams were promptly deserted by their *voorloopers*, but Lieutenant Ogilvy and his ratings brought the guns up all the same. Robbed of the expertise of their African helpers, they managed to get the third and fourth guns snarled up in the large donga. Ogilvy brought his remaining four guns into action where they stood, the leading pair from the far bank and the rearmost pair from the home bank. Eventually the tangled guns were manhandled free and joined in the bombardment from the home bank. Ogilvy's guns would fire an average of 50 rounds apiece over the next hour or so. The chaos at the donga worsened when ten of the RFA limbers came trotting back to cover. Both battery captains, Adrian Goldie (killed) and Frederick Elton (wounded), fell while attempting to sort out the confusion.

Back on the forward gun line, the two colonels had also become early casualties; while Long had taken some shrapnel in the arm, liver and kidneys, Hunt had been shot through both legs.[28] Along with the rest of the wounded they were carried back to the right rear of the guns and placed in the shelter of the small donga. The early demise of his superiors left Arthur Bailward as the senior battery commander in overall command. Firing at a rapid rate for close to an hour, the two field batteries achieved a good deal of success in suppressing the enemy immediately to their front. By 7.00 a.m. though, most of the ammunition on the position, about 930 rounds in all, had been expended, with no sign of any more coming forward. Considering that Hart and the Irish Brigade had also been in action for close to an hour, it is astonishing that Hildyard's brigade had not yet passed through to begin its assault on the iron bridge. Either Hildyard was late or the gunners had started their bombardment too early. Either way round there had clearly been a dismal failure of command and control. Knowing that the enemy would soon gain the upper hand, and having first obtained Colonel Long's blessing, Major Bailward withdrew his harassed crews to the cover of the small donga at about 7.15 a.m.[29] When Hildyard was up and more ammunition had been brought forward, the gunners would return to their pieces to renew the fight. In the meantime the close escort to the guns, A and B Companies 2nd Royal Scots Fusiliers under Captain Dighton Dick, had come up and extended a firing line between the left of the gun line and the railway. Not long after this a wing of the Royal Irish Fusiliers under Major Claude Rogers also came forward to support the guns. Rogers sent one of his companies away to the left to take up position behind Captain Dick's companies, placed another in the large donga in support of the naval guns, and pushed the other two out to the right, where they lay down about 300 yards to the right rear of Bailward's guns.

Buller Intervenes

Buller had positioned himself on a rise just west of the railway line, from where the 4.7-inch guns were shelling the Colenso Koppies. He was a long way from the action and it was difficult to read the battle through the smoke, dust and heat haze, but he could see that the Irish Brigade was not where he intended it to be and could hear an ominous cacophony of small-arms fire. If Clery really was in charge, Buller should have been sat in a distant command post awaiting the tactical commander's battle reports, but it was all a façade of course and Buller and his staff now proceeded to ride around the battlefield with Clery and his aides in tow, amongst them Lieutenant Freddie Roberts KRRC, only son of Field Marshal Lord Roberts. On his way across to Hart's brigade, Buller suddenly became aware just how close to the river 14th and 66th Batteries were and sent an aide to see what Long thought he was playing at. The officer returned to report that the guns were under fire but seemed alright. Buller continued on his way to the left flank, where he was dismayed to find just how much trouble Hart and his Irishmen were in. He seems to have lost heart almost immediately and to have decided, as if in a fit of pique, to call off the entire battle there and then. Spurring across to Lyttelton's holding position, he told him 'Hart has got into a devil of a mess down there. Get him out of it as best you can.' Fortunately Lieutenant Colonel Lawrence Parsons, commanding the 2nd Brigade-Division RFA, was deployed on the far left and was busily pounding the north bank with his 63rd and 64th Batteries. Their fire brought some welcome succour to the Irish by silencing the two 75s emplaced on the high ground near the Ladysmith road. Lyttelton moved the 1st Rifle Brigade and 1st Durham Light Infantry down towards the loop, extended a six-company firing line across the mouth of the salient, and waited for Hart and his men to come trickling back. The rearmost elements of the brigade began coming through at about 7.30 a.m., but the order to withdraw would not reach the companies pinned down near the river bank until well after 10.00. Some groups were quite unable to extricate themselves and would eventually be taken prisoner. All the while the British guns in the centre had been keeping up a tremendous fire but, despite the staff officer's earlier assurance, now suddenly fell inexplicably and ominously silent. Across on the right Dundonald and elements of the cavalry brigade were starting to probe the lower slopes of Hlangwane.

As far as Buller was concerned, Hart had botched his carefully planned (!) attack and the whole thing was now off. The decision to cry off was made at about 8.00 a.m. Having made some basic provision for the extrication of the Irish Brigade and instructed Lyttelton not to become decisively engaged, Buller would now need to get across to the centre to prevent Hildyard and Barton going in. After that he would have to get over to the right to recall Dundonald – though why he felt the need to do all this in person is a mystery. It meant that the brigades would be reined in sequentially rather than concurrently, and must as a consequence have resulted in men dying unnecessarily. The reason for Hildyard's absence in the centre was that he had halted his brigade just in front of Naval Gun Hill to await the completion of the artillery preparation. As Buller approached the centre he was alarmed to see the twelve 15-pounders standing in the open, seemingly abandoned. He was now far too close to the action, in grave danger of behaving like an over-excited battery commander. His every thought concentrated on breaking off the action, Buller halted the ammunition resupply for Bailward's guns in its tracks[30] and then sent a staff officer to tell Hildyard to push some of his infantry into Colenso to secure the ground to the left of the gun line.

Over the course of the next 45 minutes 2nd Brigade pressed a well-dispersed and orderly advance with 2nd Queen's left forward, nearest the river, and 2nd Devons right forward, east of the railway line. The 2nd East Surreys were in echelon behind the leading battalions, with 2nd West Yorkshire held back in brigade reserve. The forward battalions were able to establish themselves around the town and its environs with relative ease and few casualties. Major William Burrell occupied Colenso with five companies of 2nd Queen's, while on the right Lieutenant Colonel George Bullock of the Devons managed to infiltrate two sections from his C and G Companies into the small donga alongside Bailward's gun-crews and wounded. Not long afterwards E and F Companies of the Devons occupied some farm buildings just west of the railway, where they were mixed up amongst the Queen's Regiment companies. The bulk of the Devons were deployed some little way to the rear of their commanding officer's position in the donga. At General Barton's order, Major William Young also pushed forward with E and F Companies of 2nd RSF and took up position in support of Captain Dick's A and B Companies. In the immediate vicinity of Long's guns, therefore, were five companies of the Queens, four of Scots Fusiliers, four of Irish Fusiliers and a whole battalion of Devons. The guns then were in no danger whatsoever. Enter Sir Redvers.

'A Perfect Storm of Shot and Shell'

Kicking up his horse the general led the accompanying gaggle of staff officers towards the large donga, a mere 475 yards from the line of 15-pounders and about a mile from the enemy. While they were waiting for the last of Hildyard's infantry to wriggle into their covering positions, a shell exploded in the donga killing Buller's staff surgeon, Captain M. E. Hughes RAMC. Though he gave no outward sign, the general himself also received a sharp blow in the ribs from a piece of ricocheting shrapnel. Brushing the injury aside, his next move was to order the immediate withdrawal of the naval 12-pounders. This was an act of crass stupidity as he was about to launch an attempt to extricate the 15-pounders, and Lieutenant Ogilvy's guns were ideally placed to lend fire support to the enterprise. It became necessary to use some of the RFA limbers to tow the 'long-twelves' clear, as many of the Navy's trek oxen had been killed and the rest had been spooked by the noise and gore. By turning around Major Bailward's ammunition and sending the naval gunners to the rear, Buller denied his field gunners any opportunity to reassert their earlier advantage. With nothing to keep the enemy's heads down, it was little wonder that the sound of Mauser rounds cracking overhead had become just about incessant.

Captain Henry Schofield, serving on the army staff as Buller's ADC, was an RHA officer and to Sir Redvers the obvious choice to lead a rescue attempt. A call for volunteers produced Corporal George Nurse and six other stalwarts from 66th Battery – Drivers Lucas, Petts, Rockall, Taylor, Williams and Young. Judging that the staff should set the example, Buller turned to his entourage and said 'Some of you go and help.' Captain Walter Congreve of the Rifle Brigade stepped forward, as did Clery's ADC, Lieutenant the Honourable F. S. Roberts. The three officers took off at the gallop, followed by Corporal Nurse and two limber teams. Of the officers, only Schofield made it to the guns. Congreve's horse was killed a hundred yards short and then, much to Buller's dismay, Freddie Roberts went reeling from the saddle just a little further on. Corporal Nurse remembered the dash as follows:

> As soon as I got them mounted I started off at a gallop for the guns, half a mile away [in reality it was less far]. The enemy were following with a perfect storm of shot and shell, one of which burst overhead just before we mounted and took the off-centre's eye clean out . . . When we got to the guns I went to the left hand one, and tried to pull it up to the limber, but it was stuck in the stones. I ran across to the others, some 20 yards away, and helped the staff officer [Schofield] to limber-up. I then ran back to the other one and managed to get it on the hook. The bullets were pattering around us like hail. One went through my haversack, piercing a hand-glass and piece of bread I had in it, hit my

> revolver pouch and splintered one of the fingers of my right hand in two places.

Private George Ravenhill of RSF was the only man to dash from the cover of the small donga to assist with hooking-in. Walter Congreve was back on his feet after his bone-jarring fall and limped away to the cover of the nearby watercourse, where Colonel Bullock of the Devons was the senior uninjured officer present. In the floor of the donga Colonel Long and the other casualties were at last receiving some basic medical attention from Surgeon-Major William Babtie RAMC who, on hearing of the high-drama on the gun line, had made his way forward to do whatever he could. While Schofield, Nurse and the drivers were hooking-in the guns and drawing most of the enemy's fire, Dr Babtie, Major Foster and Captain Congreve dashed out to Freddie Roberts, by now wounded in three places, and carried him back to the cover of the donga. Despite the hundreds of rounds cracking about them, Corporal Nurse's limber-teams somehow made it to safety with a pair of 15-pounders in tow, the maimed off-centre doing its duty as bravely and faithfully as any gunner. Encouraged by Nurse's success a third limber driven by Bombardier Knight and two others, dashed forward under the command of a pair of RFA subalterns. The attempt foundered almost immediately when a number of horses were brought down. Lieutenant C. B. Schreiber was killed and Lieutenant J. B. Grylls badly wounded.

The third battery of the 1st Brigade-Division, Major Clinton Henshaw's 7th Battery, was operating independently of the others in support of Dundonald's demonstration against Hlangwane. Observing the desperate plight of 14th and 66th Batteries, the second-in-command, Captain Hamilton Reed, decided to take three of his own limbers to the rescue. The ground was too open and the enemy's fire too heavy for the attempt to prosper. Long before they were half-way to the gun line, 13 out of 21 horses had been hit. Of the 13 artillerymen concerned, 1 was killed and 6, including Reed, were wounded.

Disengagement

Enough was enough. Unable to see any means of getting the guns away without further loss of life, the great man cracked and made a peremptory decision to abandon them on the veldt. Everybody was hustled away from the large donga for the rear. The men in the small donga were left to their fate. Lieutenant Colonel Edward Hamilton[31] commanding 2nd Queen's, at least spared them a second thought. Having received orders from Hildyard to fall back, he quickly scratched out a pencil-note to alert the men in the donga to their predicament: 'To OC RA or any other officer. I am ordered to retire; fear that you cannot get away.'[32] For some unknown reason the note never reached its intended destination. Major Burrell of 2nd Queen's appealed to his CO to be allowed to hold his ground in and around Colenso until nightfall so that the guns could be extricated in the dark but, having received clear-cut orders to withdraw, Hamilton was obliged to turn the request down. He had been told to pass on the order to the Devons, but even though the message made it across to the major commanding the supports, it failed to get all the way forward to George Bullock in the donga. The 2nd Queen's and the Devons fell back through a wing of the East Surreys under the command of Major Hugh Pearse at about 2.30 p.m. Although Pearse and his men held on for another hour in the hope that more stragglers would come through, their vigil was to prove fruitless. Worried that he was now far too isolated, Pearse was obliged to break clean and hurry after everybody else.

Having initiated a withdrawal in the centre, Buller had ridden on for the right so that Dundonald too could be recalled – from what might in fact have been a promising lodgement on Hlangwane. By 1.00 p.m. most of the battered and bruised British units were tramping disconsolately back across the veldt for Chieveley and Frere. From beginning to end, Buller's reading and handling of the situation had been appalling. The ill-conceived attempt to bring the guns away in daylight had been made entirely at his personal instigation. How much more sensible it would have been to have emplaced the naval guns in the large donga, to have supported them with infantry, and to have waited for darkness, before attempting to get the 15-pounders away.

Having heard nothing of a withdrawal, George Bullock assumed he was meant to protect the guns and the wounded crewmen until nightfall. At about 4.30 p.m., long after the British main bodies had quit the field, parties of Boers started filtering across the river to secure the abandoned guns. It was a blistering hot afternoon and with all the excitement having died down in the meantime, most of the soldiers in the bottom of the watercourse were drowsy or fast asleep. Eventually somebody peered over the lip and saw Boers moving around amongst the guns. Bullock immediately opened fire and drove the enemy back into cover. For a while the dauntless colonel covered the guns with rifle fire. Eventually the Boers showed a white flag and came forward to parley. There was a suggestion that Bullock would be allowed to evacuate the wounded, but not for the first or last time in the war the Transvaalers were using the white flag as a subterfuge. Around a hundred of them had stalked forward and quietly surrounded the donga. Suddenly the parley became a demand for unconditional surrender. Bullock snarled that he had no intention of surrendering and reached for his revolver, but one of the Boers leapt into the donga and felled him with a vicious blow in the face from his rifle-butt. There was no fight left in anybody else. About 40 Devons, 35 Scots Fusiliers and 50 gunners were taken prisoner.

The Battle of Colenso had cost the South Natal Field Force 74 officers and 1,065 other ranks killed, injured or missing. Seven officers and 136 other ranks lost their lives, 47 and 709 had been wounded, while 20 and 220 had been made prisoner or were otherwise missing.[33] The Irish Brigade's share in the slaughter was a total of 523 casualties – of which some 216 fell upon the 2nd Royal Dublin Fusiliers alone. Between them the hapless 14th and 16th Batteries lost 2 and 7 killed, 6 and 20 wounded, and 5 and 44 missing.[34] Three days after the battle Buller wrote to his wife,

> I had to have a play at Colenso, but I did not think I could get in . . . I think between you and me that I was lucky in not getting in as I should not have known what next to do . . . had I been well served I ought I think to have got in. Kismet. Better luck next time.[35]

In due course Captains Walter Congreve, Henry Schofield and Hamilton Reed, Lieutenant Freddie Roberts, Corporal George Nurse, Private George Ravenhill and Dr William Babtie would all be awarded the VC for their parts in the action. The addition of Freddie Roberts to the VC roll would produce an extremely rare father and son combination. Perhaps the most staggering thing about the Battle of Colenso is that the British had lost more 15-pounder field guns than they had killed Boers: the enemy loss was a paltry 8 dead and 30 wounded. The London newspapers would encapsulate the recent disastrous string of failures, Stormberg Junction, Magersfontein and now Colenso, as 'Black Week'. If it looked to the editors as if British generalship had sunk to an all-time low, they did not yet know the half of it.

Chapter 8

'THAT COMPLETE SHAMBLES'

The Battle of Spion Kop, Natal, 24 January 1900

> ***In the shallow trenches where they had fought the soldiers lay dead in swathes, and in places they were piled three deep. The Boer guns in particular had wrought terrible havoc and some of the bodies were shockingly mutilated . . . there cannot have been many battlefields where there was such an accumulation of horrors within so small a compass . . .***
>
> **Colonel Deneys Reitz**

By the time he got back to his quarters on the evening of 15 December 1899, Sir Redvers Buller was in severe pain and broken in spirit. The enormity of his mistakes was growing on him by the minute. Perhaps a hearty supper, washed down as usual with a bottle of good champagne, would help to push his troubles to the back of his mind. He must have called for a second bottle before finally adjourning to his desk to compose cipher telegram No. 87. The Secretary of State for War was the recipient:

> My failure today raises a serious question. I do not think I am now strong enough to relieve White. Colenso is a fortress . . . My view is that I ought to let Ladysmith go, and occupy good positions for the defence of South Natal and let time help us. But that is a step on which I ought to consult you. I consider we were in the face of 20,000 men today. They had the advantage both in arms and position. They admit they suffered heavily, but my men have not seen a dead Boer, and that dispirits them. My losses have been very heavy. I could have made them much heavier, but the result would have been the same. The moment I failed to get in with a rush, I was beat. I now feel that I cannot relieve Ladysmith with my available force, and the best thing I can suggest is

> that I should occupy defensive positions and fight it out in country better suited to our tactics.[1]

The telegram reeked of defeatism. Not only did it propound a strategically disastrous course of action, it also contained three falsehoods. Buller was notoriously prone to inflating estimates of enemy strength: later in the campaign London would be obliged to point out that some of his estimates exceeded the entire male population of the Transvaal. On this occasion he had magnified the enemy's strength at least fourfold; indeed it is doubtful if more than 2,500 Boers were in a position to fire their weapons that day. Neither did the enemy have any advantage in armament: the British had eight guns to every one of Botha's. Finally there had not been the merest hint of heavy enemy losses. Buller had merely fallen into the trap of assuming that a sustained bombardment simply had to have been effective. When Lansdowne's eyes fell on 'I ought to let Ladysmith go' he was horrified. The retention of Ladysmith was in fact the best guarantee the British had against invasion of southern Natal.[2]

More contemptible even than cipher telegram No. 87 was Buller's message to Sir George White:

> I tried Colenso yesterday but failed. The enemy is too strong for my force, except with siege operations, which will take one full month to prepare. Can you last so long? If not how many days can you give me to take up defensive position, after which I suggest your firing away as much ammunition as you can and making the best terms you can. I can remain here if you have alternate suggestions, but unaided cannot break in . . . [and in a later addendum] . . . Whatever happens recollect to burn your cipher and decipher and code books and any deciphered messages.

This was such a craven text that at first White refused to believe it had originated with a British officer and took it for an enemy subterfuge.

Lansdowne's response to cipher No. 87 arrived at Buller's headquarters hard on the heels of an equally robust reply from Ladysmith. The War Office's cipher No. 53 ran:

> HMG considers abandonment and consequent loss of White's force as a national disaster of the greatest magnitude. We should urge you to devise another attempt to relieve it, not necessarily by way of Colenso, making use if you think well, of additional troops now arriving in South Africa.[3]

Lansdowne had always been an admirer of Roberts, but despite being constantly at odds with Wolseley had nonetheless deferred to him when he recommended Buller for the South African command. The abject failures of 'Black Week' had been the Secretary of State's reward. Within 24 hours he had secured cabinet approval to Roberts's appointment as the new South African supremo. Wolseley was allowed no part in the decision and was only notified of it a full 24 hours after the fact. Although the office of C-in-C would not be abolished until 1904, (by which time Roberts was the incumbent), it was at the Defence Committee meeting of 16 December 1899 that its death knell was sounded. Even now, partly to appease the Queen, Lansdowne showed mercy – Buller could retain tactical command of the South Natal Field Force, with Roberts in charge at theatre level. A seething Wolseley predicted that Buller would never wear the insult and would resign. Unfortunately for Major General Sir Edward Woodgate and the men of the Lancashire Brigade, he chose instead to swallow his pride. Doubtless he considered it his duty to do so. In the meantime Lansdowne was obliged to engage with Roberts on a much more intimate level – young Freddie had died of his wounds in the field hospital at Chieveley and it fell to the Secretary of State to notify his father.

Sir Charles Warren

Amongst the reinforcements referred to by Lansdowne in Cipher 53 was the 5th Division under Lieutenant General Sir Charles Warren KCB. The War Office proposed that the division should be deployed to the Kimberley Front and that its GOC should supersede the defeated Lord Methuen. Buller was not prepared to countenance his dismissal and fired a reproving broadside at London:

> Commander-in-Chief, comfortable at home, has no idea of difficulties here. It would, I think, be fatal policy to supersede every General who failed to succeed in every fight, but I may say that, as I myself have since failed, I offer no objection in my own case, if thought desirable.

With Buller's recent humiliation at the back of his mind, Lansdowne conceded the point and had new orders sent instructing Warren to subordinate himself to Methuen. Warren and his staff were 500 miles upcountry, bound for Modder River Station, when Forestier-Walker, now GOC Lines of Communication, sent a peremptory message recalling them to Cape Town. Buller, it transpired, wanted the 5th Division in Natal. He may have been concerned that the notoriously 'difficult' Warren would prove unmanageable in the west – after all Methuen had been Warren's subordinate in Bechuanaland. An intelligent man certainly, GOC 5th Division could also be irascible and high-handed. Worse he was more than a little out of practice when it came to field soldiering. While he enjoyed the advantage of knowing Southern Africa well, he had spent the last few years dabbling in politics and freemasonry. He had even spent the period 1886–9 pursuing an alternative career as the Commissioner of

Metropolitan Police. Warren's tenure at Scotland Yard is chiefly remembered for three things: first, that he was inclined to issue his orders in rhyming couplets; second, for the original 'Bloody Sunday' in which he called in the Guards to disperse a socialist demonstration; and third, for his failure to catch Jack the Ripper – though to be fair the Yard's detective branch enjoyed a great deal of autonomy at this time. Warren resigned with the arch-fiend still at large in the backstreets of Whitechapel. Returning to military duty, he was appointed first as a staff colonel and later the GOC at the Straits Settlements, modern-day Malaysia, where he came into almost constant conflict with the governor, Sir Cecil Smith. Buller's dislike of Warren dated from this time, when as Adjutant-General he had been bombarded with letters of complaint about Smith. Driven to his wit's end by Warren's whining, Buller had eventually written back instructing him in no uncertain terms not to pester the War Office on the subject any further.

Warren had retired from the Army in 1898 and owed his recall as GOC 5th Division to Wolseley. In reflection of the C-in-C's failing powers of judgment, it was to prove another ill-founded selection. Because Warren was senior to the other lieutenant generals in South Africa, Wolseley had prevailed upon Lansdowne to entrust him with the so-called 'dormant commission', a secret arrangement which provided for his succession to supreme command in the event of any misfortune befalling Buller. Known only to the Secretary of State, the C-in-C, and Buller and Warren themselves, the arrangement was overtaken by events, in the aftermath of Colenso, with the appointment of Lord Roberts. Nonetheless, until such time as 'Bobs' arrived at Cape Town, Warren would be Buller's *de facto* second-in-command.

At Colenso the heavy responsibilities vested in him had caused Buller to fold like a house of cards. Now the War Office was pressuring him to make a renewed attempt to force the Tugela, a task, he had convinced himself, that bordered on the unachievable. As London's chosen man, Warren quickly succeeded in irritating his resentful superior by proffering a series of naïve and unrealistic suggestions. Wracked with self-doubt, sensitive to criticism, but still bristling with self-importance, Sir Redvers was anxious to step back from the tactical level of command. For a supreme commander, this would have been a perfectly proper course of action but now that he was only days away from becoming the designated commander of the South Natal Field Force, any attempt to shuffle off the tactical level of responsibility would represent an act of moral cowardice. There was heavy fighting around the Ladysmith perimeter on 6 January, including the Battle of Wagon Hill, where a gallant counter-attack by 1st Devons helped save the day. Even so it left Buller duty-bound to redouble his efforts to break through to the town. Compelled to do something – anything – he chose to resurrect the plan to manoeuvre west for Potgieter's Drift.

Lost Opportunities

On 10 January 1900 25,000 men set off upriver with around 650 transport wagons in tow. At so great a distance from the railhead, whatever needed to be done would have to be done quickly, or the logistic effort was sure to collapse in on itself. The shift to the west was so obvious a movement that at first Botha took it for a feint. A lodgement at Potgieter's Drift was duly secured by Dundonald and the cavalry, but the heights beyond were forbidding and more and more Boers were arriving there by the hour. Buller's head soon filled with thoughts of another Colenso. By 15 December he had decided to split his force and shift the responsibility for achieving a breakthrough onto Warren:

> The enemy's position in front of Potgieter's Drift seems to me to be too strong to be taken by direct attack.
>
> I intend to try and turn it by sending a force across the Tugela from near Trichard's [*sic*] Drift and up to the west of Spion Kop. You will have command of that force which will consist of the 11th Brigade of your Division, your brigade division Royal Field Artillery, and General Clery's Division complete, and all the mounted troops, except 400.
>
> You will of course act as circumstances require, but my idea is that you should continue throughout refusing your right and throwing your left forward till you gain the open plain north of Spion Kop. Once there you will command the rear of the position facing Potgieter's Drift, and I think render it untenable . . .[4]

In essence then, while Buller remained in a fixing position around Mount Alice with about 10,000 men, Warren was to push on to Trichardt's Drift at the head of Dundonald's cavalry, six field batteries and the 2nd, 5th and 11th Brigades under Hildyard, Hart and Woodgate respectively. All told he would have 529 officers, 14,853 other ranks and 36 guns at his disposal. Once he had forced the line of hills beyond the river, he was to sweep back eastwards to facilitate a break-out from the lodgement at Potgieter's by the 4th and 10th Brigades under Lyttelton and Coke. The reunited command would then drive hard for the open veldt and Ladysmith.

On the night of 16/17 January Warren was presented with a golden opportunity to turn the tide of the war. Having carried through an elaborate daytime deception plan, the British strike force pushed west under the cover of darkness. The regimental officers urged their hard-marching men on in hushed tones until, in the early hours of the morning, they were safely ensconced above Trichardt's Drift. On the other side of the river was a long steep-sided plateau called Ntabmnyama, which at this stage in the proceedings was picketed by the Boers but not defended in strength. To the right of Ntabmnyama, midway between the two principal drifts, was a commanding hill feature called Spion Kop, renowned as the vantage point from which the *voortrekkers* had first looked down into Natal. When the sun came up on the morning of the 17th there may have been as few as 500 Boers deployed in the west. Instead of acting boldly by throwing his cavalry across the drift at the earliest opportunity, and consolidating by moving the infantry over at first light (by means of wading with rope handrails), Warren took to his comfort zone and spent the next two days personally supervising the erection of a pair of pontoon bridges.

Needless to say, by the time Sir Charles got round to contemplating an attack on Ntabmnyama, Botha was ready for him, with a force which had quadrupled in the interim. Most regimental officers were incensed by such glaring ineptitude. Lord Dundonald at least was pressing ahead with vigour and quickly succeeded in securing the Acton Homes road. Now there was nothing between the cavalry vanguard and the outer defences of Ladysmith. Instead of reinforcing Dundonald's success, Warren first asset-stripped his cavalry commander, then denied him supplies, and finally recalled him. When Dundonald rode back to plead for the general's support, he found him personally supervising wagon drivers across an obstacle. Warren remained unshakeable and merely repeated what he had written to Dundonald at 7.00 a.m. on 18 January:

> Our objective is not Ladysmith. Our objective is to effect a junction with Sir Redvers Buller's force and then to receive orders from him. By detaching your cavalry from me you are hampering all my movements and forcing me to alter my plans.[5]

The accusation was wholly unwarranted and deeply unfair – in truth no other general officer was doing more to facilitate a successful outcome. Moreover Dundonald was doing precisely what Buller had intended.

The laggardly Warren finally got round to attacking Ntabmnyama on the morning of Saturday 19 January. Twenty-four hours later all that had been achieved was several hundred more British casualties. Buller visited on Monday morning and found that in contravention of the scheme of manoeuvre outlined in his letter of 15 January, Warren's right was in advance of his left, that all six of his artillery batteries were crowded together in an unsuitable position on his right, and that 'he had divided his fighting line into three independent commands, independent of each other, and apparently independent of him as he told me he could not move any batteries without General Clery's consent.'[6] Buller arrived for his second visit on the morning of Tuesday 22 January. Having expressed dissatisfaction at Warren's dilatory approach the day before, he was now roused to fury to encounter almost complete inaction. Warren blustered through his excuses, but Sir Redvers was having none of it. Attack at once or retreat he insisted. Implicit in the second option of course was Warren's dismissal. When they tried to agree a way ahead, Warren observed that it would be impossible to break out without first securing Spion Kop, to which Buller replied, perhaps a little too assertively, 'Of course you must take Spion Kop.'

Taking the Kop

It had been a difficult exchange. Once Buller had gone on his way, Warren and his staff began hatching the outlines of a plan to seize the kop that very night. There was nothing like enough time left to prepare such a major undertaking. Though nobody could say it aloud, the harsh reality was that Sir Charles had been panicked by his frustrated superior. When, at around midday, Major General Talbot Coke and the 10th Brigade arrived at Trichardt's Drift, virtually the entire South Natal Field Force was at Warren's beck and call. Wise enough to know that the expanded command would need to be reorganized so as to place an intermediate level of command between himself and the contact battle, Warren called Clery, Hildyard, Woodgate and Coke into conclave. It was decided that the infantry brigades and the artillery should be divided into two divisional-sized organizations. To avoid confusion with the original divisions, the two commands were designated 'Left Attack' and 'Right Attack' under Clery and Coke respectively. The orders to set the new arrangements in hand were issued at 1.20 p.m.[7]

The task of seizing Spion Kop would fall to GOC Right Attack, Talbot Coke, temporarily elevated from the command of his 10th Brigade, which would be commanded in his absence by its senior battalion commander, Lieutenant Colonel Augustus Hill of 2nd Middlesex. Faced with the unwelcome prospect of rushing into a major offensive operation, Coke very properly insisted that the seizure of the kop could not possibly be undertaken until the following night. For once sense prevailed. This did not prevent a furious Buller coming back on Wednesday morning demanding to know why no attack had yet been made. Eventually he was placated and accepted the logic of the case. After the plan had been outlined, he raised an objection to Coke commanding on the kop, on the grounds that he was still recovering from a broken leg and would struggle to cope with the physical demands inherent in such an operation. Buller suggested that Major General Sir Edward Woodgate of the 11th (Lancashire) Brigade would be a better candidate – Woodgate had been on the staff in the Ashanti War and had fought alongside Buller at Kambula and Ulundi. Warren had little choice but to agree the nomination.

The resonance with Sir George Colley's Majuba operation was pronounced. Once again a plan had been hatched to seize a commanding hill feature, and once again nobody had given any thought to what was to be done with it afterwards. Given the precedent of 1881 it is extraordinary that no follow-up plan was laid, either by Warren or by Buller. It is such a fundamental omission that it is difficult to avoid the conclusion that we are dealing with men who, while they enjoyed the pay and laurels of general officers, possessed few of the requisite attributes. After all one of the principal duties of a general officer is to think not merely of today, but of tomorrow and the day after.

The assault force would consist of roughly 1,700 men as shown in Table 11. Included amongst the major units was the 2nd Battalion of Woodgate's old regiment, the Royal Lancasters,[8] and a body of 200 *uitlander* refugees, men who, having fled the Transvaal on the outbreak of hostilities, had enlisted in a volunteer unit called Thorneycroft's Mounted Infantry (TMI). Their Regular Army CO was Lieutenant Colonel (local rank) Alex Thorneycroft of RSF, a veteran of the Zulu War and the 1881 siege of Pretoria. Thorneycroft was 6 feet 2 inches tall, broad-shouldered, formidably brave and devoted to the well-being of his men. Amongst the company commanders in the 2nd Lancashire Fusiliers was the 38-year-old Captain Charles Hicks, son and heir of the late Hicks Pasha. All the participating units were instructed to parade with 150 rounds a man and a day's rations.

***Table 11:* The British Force at Spion Kop**

GOC	***Lt. Gen. Sir Charles Warren***	
GOC Right Attack	*Maj. Gen. Talbot Coke*	
Assault Force	*Maj. Gen. Woodgate*	
2nd Bn Lancashire Fusiliers		*Lt. Col. Charles Blomfield*
6 coys, 2nd Bn King's Own (Royal Lancaster Regt)		*Lt. Col. Malby Crofton*
2 coys, 1st Bn South Lancashire Regt (att. to Crofton's bn)		
Half company, No. 17 Company RE		*Maj. Hugh Massy*
200 men, Thorneycroft's Mounted Infantry		*Lt. Col. Alex Thorneycroft*
Supports		
The Imperial Light Infantry		
2nd Bn Middlesex Regt		*Lt. Col. Augustus Hill*
2nd Bn Dorsetshire Regt (kept in reserve)		
3rd Bn King's Royal Rifle Corps (Twin Peaks sector)		*Lt. Col. Robert Buchanan-Riddell*
2nd Bn Cameronians (Scottish Rifles)		*Lt. Col. Ernest Cooke*
2 squadrons, Bethune's Mounted Infantry		*Lt. Col. Edward Bethune*

The one thing that people did recollect about Majuba was Colley's failure to dig in. Twenty years earlier the Boers had been mere rebel farmers. Now there were well-equipped, German-trained professional gunners amongst their number, and it would be essential to counter them by entrenching. There was to be no shortage of tools and a half-company from Major Hugh Massy's No. 17 Company RE would provide the force with the requisite expertise.

Woodgate ordered his force to assemble 'at White's Farm about half mile north-west of Pontoon Bridge by 7.00 p.m.'[9] In a less than encouraging start, this was not the same rendezvous specified by Coke in his orders, and some confusion ensued before all the participating units could be assembled behind the gun positions on Three Tree Hill.[10] After some discussion amongst the senior officers it was decided that Alex Thorneycroft should lead the way, as he alone had made good use of daylight by noting identifiable landmarks along the approach route. The column formed up in the half light of evening and duly marched off into a dark and overcast night at about 9.00 p.m. There was intermittent drizzle, though from time to time the clouds parted just enough for the stars to provide a faint glow. For two and a half hours the long snake of silent soldiers edged its way through the gloom in column of fours, until at last it arrived at the foot of the formidably steep spur by which the ascent would be made. It soon came to a physically exacting scramble in single file. Eventually somebody noticed the spaniel that had been trailing the column all night, tied a lanyard around its neck, and detailed a private soldier to lead it back to camp. Inevitably the climb was conducted in a highly charged atmosphere – nobody could quite believe that the enemy picket on the summit was unable to hear the seemingly deafening cacophony made by 3,000 hob-nailed ammunition-boots. Fortunately the evening breeze was in their favour and carried the most untoward sounds away from 14 drowsy members of the Vryheid Commando on night picket duty. Yard by yard the hard-breathing Tommies clambered within striking distance of the summit. It took most of the night.

Thorneycroft reached the south-west rim of the flat-topped summit after about four hours, where his soldiers began shaking out left and right of him. Behind the *uitlanders*, the Lancashire Fusiliers were deploying into four lines, each of two companies abreast. When Thorneycroft was sure he had enough men in hand, he advanced onto the summit. Suddenly an inquisitive '*Werda?*' came from the gloom. Thorneycroft's men threw themselves to the ground as their colonel had instructed and waited for the inevitable fusillade to go sailing overhead. Still not quite sure, the Boer sentry repeated his challenge, this time much more assertively. Moments later the shooting began. In addition to the forward picket, there were another 60 or so Boers sleeping on the north side of the plateau. Snapped awake in the midst of a fire-fight, they were thrown into such a panic that their only thought was to scramble away to safety. As a result the forward picket was left to shift for itself. When a momentary break in the firing indicated that the Boers had emptied their magazines, Thorneycroft launched his men into a fast-moving bayonet charge. One of the burghers was foolish enough to stand his ground and was skewered by Lieutenant Henry

Awdry of the Lancashire Fusiliers. His less resolute comrades took to their heels and gladly ceded the summit to the dreaded British bayonet. Thorneycroft's brilliant *coup de main* had not been accomplished entirely without loss. He reported later that 'about 10 men' had been wounded, though a note from Woodgate to Warren written only an hour after the fact mentioned only three casualties.

The Battle of Spion Kop, 24 January 1900

With no further need for silence and dawn not far away, the company commanders left trailing back down the spur urged their men to make all possible haste for the summit, so that a strong defensive perimeter could be consolidated. Woodgate called for three rousing cheers to let Warren know that the kop was in British hands. In turn Sir Charles had one of his batteries fire starshell to signal success to Buller at Mount Alice. Even though dawn was now breaking, visibility and communications were badly hampered by a dense morning mist. Taking Major Massy with him, Woodgate strode into the murk looking for the north face of the kop. When they reached the point on the ground where the gradient began sloping away from them, Massy called his men forward and set them to digging a 300-yard shelter trench. At both extremities short stretches of trench were refused through a 45-degree angle to cover the flanks. Unable to see five yards in front of their faces, Woodgate and Massy were not in fact on the north rim of the kop as they believed. Instead the slope in front of the trench continued downhill for another 150 yards, where it met the true rim of the plateau. This meant that riflemen lying prone in the trench would have highly limited fields of fire and would be quite unable to cover the low-ground approaches from the north. Worse the undefended rim to their front would make a gift of hard cover to any counter-attacking force. Not only had the trench been poorly sited, but the toiling soldiers hit solid rock only two feet down. They did their best to improvise a protective rampart by piling up excavated spoil and incorporating a few of the more manageable boulders lying around on the surface, but were able to manage only a very rudimentary defence work.

Still obscured in the mist was a narrow spur running from the eastern edge of the summit to a nearby conical high-point covered in aloes. Although the western or left half of the British postion was slightly higher than 'Aloe Knoll' and therefore in dead ground to it, on the east there was a downhill gradient to the connecting spur. This meant that the right-hand side of Massy's trench was exposed to Aloe Knoll in defilade at ranges of only 250–300 yards.

In the low ground behind the kop there had been a re-run of the events of February 1881. At first the British attack had spread alarm and despondency

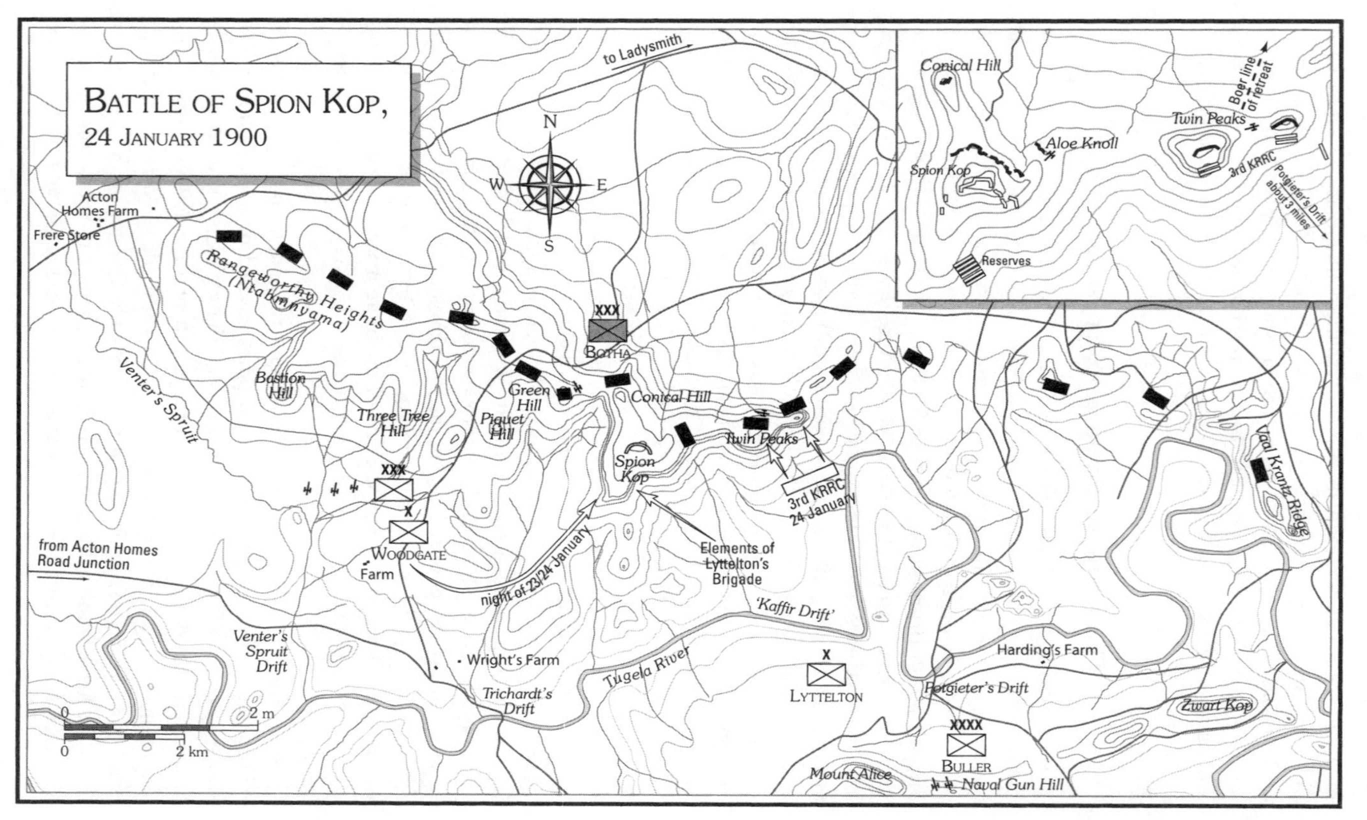

BATTLE OF SPION KOP,
24 JANUARY 1900
to Ladysmith
N
S
E
W
Acton
Homes Farm
Frere Store
Rangeworthy Heights
(Ntabamnyama)
XXX
BOTHA
Venter's Spruit
Bastion
Hill
Three Tree
Hill
Green
Hill
Piquet
Hill
Conical Hill
Twin Peaks
Spion
Kop
3rd KRRC
24 January
XXX
X
WOODGATE
Farm
from Acton Homes
Road Junction
night of 23/24 January
Elements of
Lyttelton's
Brigade
'Kaffir Drift'
Venter's
Spruit
Drift
Wright's Farm
Trichardt's
Drift
Tugela River
X
LYTTELTON
Harding's Farm
Potgieter's Drift
Zwart Kop
Vaal Krantz Ridge
XXXX
BULLER
Mount Alice
Naval Gun Hill
0
2 m
0
2 km
Conical Hill
Aloe Knoll
Spion Kop
Twin Peaks
Boer line
of retreat
3rd KRRC
Potgieter's Drift
about 3 miles
Reserves

through the Boer wagon laagers. Once again some kind of aggressive follow-up was anticipated, and once again it quickly became apparent that the *rooineks* had failed to plan for success. There was no follow-up. The British had possession of the high ground, and for the leaden-footed generals running the war in Natal that, it seemed, was enough. Once more the commandants rallied their men and called for volunteers prepared to participate in a counter-attack. The indomitable Louis Botha met a stream of men riding away from the heights and with threats, exhortations and pleas somehow turned most of them back for the kop.

Recognizing that most of his countrymen would think twice about coming to close quarters with a strong British force, Botha was quick to realise the crucial importance of his artillery assets. He began his day's work by siting two 75s on the reverse slope of Green Hill, a high point at the eastern end of Ntabmnyama which looked directly across a deep re-entrant to the summit of Spion Kop, from a distance of about 1,000 yards. The guns were emplaced in defilade to Woodgate's position, but were also carefully sited so as to be screened from British counter-battery fire. There was a third 75 and a pom-pom elsewhere on Ntabmnyama, both of which also had Spion Kop in range. On the other side of the kop, way out beyond Aloe Knoll, a knife-edge of high ground ran across to a pair of adjacent rocky outcrops known as Twin Peaks. From here a fourth Krupp was able to engage the summit. Finally, much closer in on the British right, on the spur just below Aloe Knoll, there was a particularly well-sited pom-pom. By electing to fight on the northern side of a range of hills, with all their guns deployed in low-lying ground to the south, the British generals had succeeded in neutralizing their artillery arm. Where previously it was the Boers who had lived in dread of bombardment, the Battle of Spion Kop would be fought with the shoe squarely on the other foot.

The Nightmare Begins

The engineers were making a largely futile attempt to dig new positions on the northern rim, when, at around 7.30 a.m., the mist began to clear. The first shots of the day were exchanged between parties of stalking burghers and infantry pickets posted amongst the rocks to protect the sappers as they worked. As it was impossible for them to continue, the engineers were withdrawn from the forward area and sent back down the mountain to do what they could to improve access to the summit. Now that visibility was improving, it was that clear that there was a second previously unidentified conical high point immediately in front of the British position. Like Aloe Knoll on the right, this newly unmasked feature also constituted 'key terrain' – defined today as a ground feature the possession of which will offer a marked advantage to one side or the other. 'Conical Hill' stood at the north end of a wide, flat-topped spur and served to screen another perfect avenue of approach for the Boers. Because Major Massy's trench was sited on a forward slope, it was exposed to firers on the lower-lying Conical Hill. This was also an ideal position from which to engage the rocky rim of the summit and, with visibility improving by the minute, it was to the rim that a number of British sections were now deploying. Whilst there were plenty of large boulders strewn about, providing a certain amount of low cover for the Lancastrians, genuinely well-protected positions were few and far between. On the main position Woodgate had assigned the right-hand side of the trench to four companies of the Lancashire Fusiliers, the centre to the 18 officers and 180 men of Thorneycroft's Mounted Infantry, and the left-hand side to the six companies of the Royal Lancaster Regiment. Some way beyond the left end of the trench, the two South Lancashire companies had raised a low rock sangar which faced north-west towards Green Hill. The remaining four companies of the Lancashire Fusiliers were committed to the corresponding position on the far right and likewise sought to protect themselves with a sangar.

First into action on the Boer side were 80 men of the Carolina Commando under the 38-year-old Commandant Hendrik Prinsloo, but it was not long before Botha had several hundred more burghers stalking uphill to their support. Minute by minute the volume of fire pouring into the British position seemed to increase. Aloe Knoll, Conical Hill and Green Hill all became key Boer fire positions. It was even possible to engage the area of the trench with Mauser fire, albeit at extreme range, from the area of Twin Peaks. By 8.00 a.m. the sun had burned off most of the mist. One by one the Boer guns came into action and began pounding away at the kop. At Mount Alice, Winston Churchill took out his watch and counted shells exploding within Woodgate's perimeter at an average rate of seven rounds a minute, and this made no allowance for the fire of the pom-poms whose fall of shot would not have been perceptible at any great distance.[11]

At various points around the rim of the plateau, a number of furious fire-fights were soon under way. From the outset the British right was the most hard-pressed sector. After about half an hour's heavy firing, Lieutenant Colonel Charles Blomfield of the Lancashire Fusiliers made his way back to Woodgate's position, to report that he could see a large party of Boers making their way uphill along a rough path. The general decided to go forward with Blomfield to see for himself, accompanied by his brigade-major, Captain Naunton Vertue of the Buffs. Woodgate was only a few yards behind the main trench, far too intimately concerned in the close battle, when a piece of shrapnel ripped into his head just above the right eye. He was carried into the cover of some nearby rocks, but it was clear that he was very badly hurt and that the wound might well prove mortal. Within minutes Vertue had also been gravely wounded. Aware that Lieutenant Colonel Malby Crofton, the CO of the 2nd Royal Lancasters, was his senior, Blomfield dashed across to notify him that Woodgate was down and that he should now assume command.

Before long the Pretoria Commando under Commandant 'Red Daniel' Opperman had joined with the Carolina men in attempting to force their way through the British forward positions at the edge of the summit. Despite mounting casualties the hard-pressed Lancastrians held their own. Although much of the fighting took place at frighteningly short ranges, it is unlikely that there were very many instances of hand-to-hand combat. Whilst this was the hardest-pressed offensive action ever fought by the Boers, it was simply not the burgher way to grapple at close quarters, a mode of combat for which they were untrained, ill-equipped and customarily fought shy of. With shells continuing to rain in and fighting raging back and forth round his perimeter, Colonel Crofton decided to advise Warren of Woodgate's demise and ask for reinforcements. After the battle Crofton insisted that he told Lieutenant Aylmer Martin, his signals officer, to send 'General Woodgate dead; reinforcements urgently required.' Called on a week later, when internecine recriminations were beginning to bite, to verify the colonel's version of events, Martin wrote:

> Sir,
>
> On 24th instant, soon after firing began, I was looking for some signallers, you met me, and said, 'I must have a signaller.' I said, 'I am looking for them.' You replied 'Get them at once and send a message to Sir Charles Warren and say General Woodgate is dead and ask for reinforcements at once.'
>
> I called for signallers, and two men of 2nd Lancashire Fusiliers ran up. We went to a spot that I selected, and found that there was already a signaller there, Private Goodyear of the West Yorkshire Regiment (he was with Lieutenant Doomer RA, observing the effect of artillery fire).
>
> I said to Private Goodyear, 'You might send a message for me while the helio is being set up.' I told him to call up 'G.O.C.' the station I wished to communicate with, and to say, 'General Woodgate is killed; send reinforcements at once.' I did not write the message down, as I had no paper.[12]

In the event the message received by Warren at 9.50 a.m. was altogether more emotive and caused an immediate stir: 'Reinforce at once or all is lost. General dead.'

Unknown to Crofton, Warren had already started two additional battalions for the summit in the past half hour; an *uitlander* unit called the Imperial Light

Infantry (ILI) at 9.25 a.m., followed by 2nd Middlesex about 15 minutes later. Alarmed by the tone of the recent message, Warren immediately signalled Lyttelton at Potgieter's:

> 9.53 a.m. Give every assistance you can on your side. This side is clear, but the enemy are too strong on your side, and Crofton telegraphs that if assistance is not given at once all is lost. I am sending up two battalions, but they will take some time to get up.[13]

With Woodgate down and Crofton apparently wobbling, Warren decided to send General Coke to take command on the summit. To stiffen Crofton's resolve until the arrival of the ILI and the Middlesex, Warren signalled the kop with '10.05 a.m. You must hold on to the last. No surrender.' As he was quite unaware that the expression 'all is lost' had been attributed to him, Crofton was bemused, alarmed and irritated that anybody would find it necessary to send him such a message.[14] At 10.15 a.m. the signallers at Lyttelton's headquarters jotted down a second message from the kop: 'We occupy all the crest on top of hill. Being heavily attacked from your side. Help us. Spion Kop.'[15] Neither the originator of this message nor his signaller were ever traced.

In response to Warren's signal of 9.53 a.m. Lyttelton ordered two dismounted squadrons of Bethune's Mounted Infantry and the 2nd Scottish Rifles to cross the Tugela at the so-called 'kaffir drift', just above Potgieter's, and make their way to the top of the kop. Bethune's would make the crossing at 11.45 a.m. and the Scottish Rifles at 12.30 p.m.

British command and control would be dogged throughout the battle by poor communications. Although it would have been relatively easy to run a telegraph cable up the spur, nobody thought to do so. Instead messages had to be laboriously spelt out by heliograph or flags, or after dark with signalling lamps. At first the mist had interfered with the work of the signallers. Once it had cleared they were hampered by incoming fire. There was a period of several hours when Warren was unable to get a response from the summit, though strangely there seems to have been little difficultly in flashing heliograph signals from the kop to Mount Alice. From there messages could be relayed back across the river to Warren's signallers on Three Tree Hill. This meant that for some considerable time the operational level commander, Buller, was getting first sight of signals intended for the tactical commander. It is clear that a coherent communications plan was sadly lacking. One of the most glaring errors in terms of command and control was Warren's failure to move his headquarters close to the foot of the kop. As a result it took runners from the summit the best part of three hours to reach him. He did move his headquarters at one point, but only across a distance of 200 yards to gain better cover – just far enough to make the new location difficult to find.

The terrible effects of the Boer bombardment were encapsulated in Colonel Blomfield's account of the battle:

> I well remember one shell that hit some men lying in a row behind some rocks that afforded protection to their front only. Two shells passed through the thighs of one man, and on through the legs of the man next to him, leaving only the trunk of the first and carrying away one leg of the second man. A sergeant of the RE was lying on the near side of the two men killed and I noticed that his canteen was glittering in the sun, and possibly drawing fire. I told him to turn it round out of sight. The sergeant looked at me, but never spoke or moved, merely turning his eyes towards me, and I learned afterwards that this unfortunate NCO had also been hit by this shell, which had touched his spine and completely paralyzed him.

At about 10.30 a.m. Blomfield decided to make his way across to the sector of trench occupied by his C Company. He was still 30 yards short of the position when he was bowled over with a round through the right shoulder. Major Edward Tidswell and Sergeant Lightfoot saw their CO go down and immediately left cover to dash to his assistance. Despite a storm of rifle fire they managed to drag him to the shelter of the trench where, like dozens of other casualties, he would lay untended for the rest of the day.

By 11.00 a.m. the British were losing control of the rim and were being driven back on the trench, though out on the far left the South Lancashires succeeded in holding their sangar. On the right, where a murderous fire was pouring in from Aloe Knoll, the living were crawling around amongst the dead and maimed. From time to time the British hold on the trench had to be restored by feeding fresh sections into the forward area. The first four companies of the ILI arrived on the summit at about noon and were immediately committed to the fighting on the left. At one point Thorneycroft led a counter-attack against the rim, but it was driven to ground some way short of the objective with considerable loss. Thorneycroft himself sprained his ankle in a fall, but managed to hobble back to cover without being hit.

Too Many Chiefs

Spion Kop so dominated the landscape that for miles around many thousands of people, Britons, burghers and black Africans alike, were able to see something of the high drama being played out on the summit. With the aid of a powerful telescope Redvers Buller could see more than most. The most worrying aspect of the spectacle was the sheer frequency with which plumes of white smoke were being thrown skywards. At 11.40 a.m. he signalled Warren with 'Unless you put some really good hard fighting man in command on the top you will lose the hill. I suggest Thorneycroft.'[16] Warren was in enough trouble with Buller as it was and in no position to spurn his latest 'suggestion'. He immediately signalled through to Crofton's command post that Thorneycroft was to take command and was promoted with immediate effect to local brigadier-general. It was a highly irregular arrangement to say the least. Ordinarily command would devolve upon the next senior officer, which in this case was Malby Crofton. Thorneycroft on the other hand was not even a substantive lieutenant colonel. Crofton, we know, took grave offence at being sidelined in such a way. For the time being the lion-hearted Thorneycroft was fighting from the cover of the trench and nobody with Crofton was quite sure where to find him. A messenger was sent to look for him but never arrived. Having already despatched Coke for the summit, Warren made no attempt to notify him that Thorneycroft was now in charge there. Something like half an hour elapsed before a subaltern called Rose, who had overheard some of the chatter at Crofton's headquarters, crawled into the trench next to Thorneycroft and congratulated him on his promotion. For the time being the Army's newest brigadier was too intimately involved in the close battle even to think straight.

All the while shells were hammering into the overcrowded British perimeter without let-up. Everybody found his own little bit of cover where he hoped somehow to be safe from the searching fire of the Mausers and the razor-edged shrapnel flying about the summit. The enemy's fire was so heavy and decent places of concealment so hard to find, that it was largely a matter of luck whether a man lived or died. If it was impossible for sane men to help the wounded, there was no shortage of madmen prepared to try. Many of these heroic Good Samaritans slumped dead over the men they had been trying to help.

By Boer standards the losses amongst the assaulting burghers had also been extremely heavy. In January 1900 Colonel Deneys Reitz, the author of the classic war memoir *Commando*, was a teenaged citizen-soldier in the Pretoria Commando. In his early thirties he would fight under Smuts and Botha once again, no longer as a Boer nationalist but as a South African Unionist. Once Imperial Germany had been relieved of its African possessions Reitz moved on to Europe, where he served in the trenches as a lieutenant colonel in the RSF. Despite being twice wounded he survived the war, returned home and went into politics. In late middle age, with a new German war under way and South African troops fighting alongside their British comrades in defence of the free world, Reitz returned to London as the South African High Commissioner. Four decades before he took up residence at South Africa House, however, the then 17-year-old Deneys and some of the other Pretoria men arrived on the north side of Spion Kop too late to join the first wave of attack. Quickly tethering their ponies, they set off on foot to catch up with their comrades:

> Dead and dying men lay all along the way, and there was proof that the Pretoria men had gone by for I soon came on the body of Johan Malherbe, our corporal's brother, with a bullet between his eyes; a few paces further lay two more dead men of our commando. Further on I found my tent-mate, poor Robert Reinecke, shot through the head, and not far off L. de Villiers of our corporalship lay dead. Yet higher up was Krige, another of Isaac's men, with a bullet through both lungs, still alive, and beyond him Walter de Vos of my tent shot through the chest, but smiling cheerfully as we passed. Apart from the Pretoria men there were many other dead and wounded, mostly Carolina burghers from the eastern Transvaal . . .

For the burghers fighting their way up the north slope of the kop that morning, the extent of their own loss was only too apparent. Ironically they had no idea of the carnage on the other side of the hill.

Crisis on the Right

So severe was the fighting on the extreme right that a few faint-hearts amongst the Lancashire Fusiliers felt moved to raise a white flag. A small party of Boers came forward to usher their prisoners away and, with very few of Colonel Blomfield's officers still uninjured, the capitulation began to spread down the trench like a contagion. Around 130 men had given themselves up and been ushered away before Thorneycroft realized what was going on. In an instant he was up on his feet and sprinting hard for the scene. Spotting that some of the Boers were beckoning the battalion's supports forward to join in the surrender, Thorneycroft interposed himself and roared at a nearby veldtkornet, 'I'm commandant here. Take your men back to hell, sir.' Snapping the men about him from their stupor, Thorneycroft quickly initiated a renewed fire-fight, while the Boers fell back to the captured stretch of trench and tried to consolidate their foothold.

Never has there been a more timely reinforcement than the arrival of Lieutenant Colonel Augustus Hill's 2nd Middlesex. One of the companies came charging past Thorneycroft to scatter the enemy and reoccupy the trench. Hill brought up the rest of his leading half-battalion and extended it in what little cover there was to the right-hand side of the trench. Together with elements of the ILI, the Middlesex had to fight hard to hold a Boer flanking move mounted from Aloe Knoll. Without the benefit of a trench or a parapet, Hill's soldiers were obliged to find cover amongst the rocks or in shallow folds in the ground.

At 2.30 p.m. Thorneycroft finally found the time to write a situation report to Warren:

> Hung on till last extremity with old force. Some of Middlesex here now and I hear Dorsets coming up, but force really inadequate to hold such a large perimeter. The enemy's guns on north-west sweep the whole of the top of the hill. They also have guns east; cannot you bring artillery fire to bear on north-west guns? What reinforcements can you send to hold the hill tonight? We are badly in need of water. There are many killed and wounded. If you wish to really make a certainty of hill for night, you must send more infantry and attack enemy's guns.[17]

The note was sent away in the hands of a runner and on its way downhill found its way into the hands of Talbot Coke. The general read through Thorneycroft's text, and then added at the bottom:

> 3.00 p.m. I have seen the above and have ordered the Scottish Rifles and King's Royal Rifles to reinforce. The Middlesex Regiment, Dorsetshire Regiment and Imperial Light Infantry have also gone up. Bethune's mounted infantry (120 strong) also reinforce. We appear to be holding our own at present.[18]

Read carefully, Thorneycroft's message might have conveyed a number of serious concerns. With the addition of Coke's last sentence the tone became altogether more ambiguous.

The tenor of the British situation reports can create the impression that Spion Kop was a one-sided affair, but one of the interesting features of the battle is just how little awareness there was, on either side, of quite how much damage was being done to the enemy. Deneys Reitz makes it clear that it was far from being a one-sided fight and that, as the afternoon wore on, most of the Boers lost heart:

> The sun became hotter and hotter, and we had neither food nor water. Around us lay scores of dead and wounded men, a depressing sight, and by midday a feeling of discouragement had gained ground that was only kept in check by Commandant Opperman's forceful personality and vigorous language to any man who seemed to be wavering. Had it not been for him the majority would have gone sooner than they did, for the belief spread that we were being left in the lurch. We could see large numbers of horsemen collecting in the laagers on the plain behind, but no reinforcements reached us throughout the day. I repeatedly heard Red Daniel assure the men that help would be forthcoming, but from the way he kept scanning the country below I could see that he was getting uneasy himself.

The Boer counter-attack had been a one-shot option. Their best men, those who were prepared to participate in such a dangerous operation of war, had come at Botha's first call to arms. But once the life-blood of the lion-hearts had been expended against the British defences, there was nobody else left – no supports, nobody in reserve, no fresh momentum. Up and down the Tugela a good many burghers were shirking amongst the rocks on an inactive sector, talking amongst themselves, drinking coffee and listening to the distant sound of battle. It was the commando way of war: soldiering by consent; operation by operation; fight one day, opt out the next – farm and family first. Hard-pressed assault was simply not part of the Boer repertoire.

By about 3.30 p.m. 2nd Middlesex had been forced through want of cover and mounting casualties to cede some ground on the British right. As Coke had decided to retain Bethune's Mounted Infantry and the Dorsets in reserve, the task of restoring the situation fell to Lieutenant Colonel Ernest Cooke's 2nd Scottish Rifles. Cooke fed his companies forward wherever he could see a gap, until he was satisfied the forward positions were as secure as they could be. In particular his riflemen showed great dash on the extreme right, where they succeeded in driving back a party of burghers who had been harassing 2nd Middlesex for the best part of two hours. One of Cooke's company commanders, Captain Fergus Murray was wounded no fewer than four times during the battalion's various counter-attacks. Incredibly he was still fighting at the head of his men when finally his luck ran out and he was shot dead. Chased off the south-eastern corner of the kop by such unrelenting bravery, the burghers fell back to Aloe Knoll and stayed there. Cooke's counter-attacks took the last remaining steam out of the Boer offensive. By 4.30 p.m. they had given up any idea of bludgeoning their way onto the hilltop as their fathers had done at Majuba. The job of containing the British would be left to snipers, pom-poms and 75s. Thus, although many Boers began making their way downhill to their ponies, there was still no respite for the hapless Tommies.

Major General Lyttelton resolved to relieve the pressure on the kop by pressing the enemy elsewhere, something both Warren and Buller should have been striving to achieve all day. Having already committed elements of his brigade to the kop, he now decided to feed 3rd KRRC into the fray a mile to the right. The battalion's objective would be the Twin Peaks. Lieutenant Colonel Robert Buchanan-Riddell led his men off for the river at about 1.00 p.m. Lyttelton saw him off in person, emphasizing that he would have to act at his own discretion, but should proceed with caution and keep a strong reserve. It was certain to be late afternoon before the battalion could get close enough to influence the fight on the kop.

Talbot Coke spent the early afternoon ensconced on a shelf below the summit, convinced that he was in command of the close battle. It was 4.00 p.m. before he finally decided to limp up to the summit. Oblivious to Thorneycroft's field-promotion, he consulted with Augustus Hill, the temporary commander of 10th Brigade. At about the same time the insatiably curious Winston Churchill arrived on the summit, accompanied by his friend Captain Ronald Brooke DSO of the 7th Hussars:

> Streams of wounded men met us and obstructed our path. Men were staggering along alone, or supported by comrades, or crawling on hands and knees, or carried in stretchers. Corpses lay here and there. Many of the wounds were of a horrible nature. The splinters and fragments of the shell had torn and mutilated in the most ghastly manner. I passed about two hundred while I was climbing up. There was, moreover, a small but steady leakage of unwounded men of all corps. Some of these cursed and swore. Others were utterly exhausted and fell on the hillside in stupor. Others again seemed drunk, though they had had no liquor. Scores were sleeping heavily. Fighting was still proceeding, and stray bullets struck all over the ground, while the Maxim shell guns scourged the flanks of the hill and the sheltering infantry at regular intervals of a minute.[19]

Shocked at the even more hellish scenes they encountered on the summit, Churchill and Brooke decided to go back down and brief Warren face-to-face on what they had seen.

Having likewise seen something of the conditions on top of the kop, General Coke decided to return to the signal station he had sited on the south-west spur, so as to report his reading of the situation to Warren. Before going down he told Colonel Hill that he would now be in overall command of the forward battle. Still oblivious to Buller's earlier intervention, he naturally thought he had every right to make such an appointment. Down at his signal station he composed his report and passed it across to his signallers for transmission. After several fruitless attempts had gone unacknowledged, he entrusted a written report to a staff sightseer called Colonel Morris.

Alone among the battalion commanders, Cooke of the Scottish Rifles had spoken to both Hill and Thorneycroft and had realized that both believed themselves to be in command. He tried to persuade Hill to make his way forward to speak to Thorneycroft, but for the time being there was more than enough coordinating work to detain to him at his command post. Some considerable time elapsed before Hill undertook the journey. The idea of a forward tactical headquarters and a rear link headquarters was no means a bad one, but the arrangement had emerged by accident not design, and in order for it to work well it would be necessary for Hill and Thorneycroft to reconcile their respective roles. For a good while they failed to do so and must at various points have given contradictory orders. If tactical command and control had fallen into a state of disarray, at the operational level it was characterized by inexcusable inertia.

Twin Peaks

It was already late in the day by the time 3rd KRRC was able to establish itself beneath Twin Peaks, but Robert Buchanan-Riddell was determined to do everything possible to support the men on the kop. Dividing his unit by half-battalions he mounted simultaneous assaults on the rocky crags above. The naval guns at Mount Alice chimed in with fire support. It was a long-drawn-out and breathtaking scramble, but the very steepness of the grade provided the Rifles with a good deal of protection and by 5.15 p.m. they had gained their objectives with minimal loss. John Atkins, the correspondent of the *Manchester Guardian* wrote of the attack 'I did not see it, and I am told that I missed the most splendid thing that day.' In gaining the heights the Rifles succeeded in driving away a Krupp 75, a pom-pom and elements of the Rustenburg and Heidelberg Commandos. Many burghers were seized by a panic which carried them eight miles from the scene of the action, spreading alarm and despondency as they went. If only Warren had attacked Green Hill with the sort of vigour shown by the Rifles, there can be little doubt that the entire Boer line would have crumbled. Back on the Twin Peaks the KRRC consolidated their perimeter and began digging themselves in as best they could.

Buller held out little hope of the KRRC making a worthwhile contribution to the battle in such difficult terrain, and during the course of the afternoon sent several orders via Lyttelton insisting that Buchanan-Riddell withdraw. Amply possessed of moral courage, the colonel chose to ignore his orders and press on with his attack. Keenly aware that his battalion had played a vital role in alleviating the pressure on the kop, he could now see no good reason to disengage. Sadly he was shot through the head and killed whilst reading through yet another order to withdraw. Major Robert Bewicke-Copley, the battalion's senior major, was advised by the signallers that they had received three such messages already, all of which had been tucked away safely in the colonel's pocket. Eventually Berwicke-Copley secured permission to hold on until nightfall, on the grounds that withdrawing down such a severe grade in daylight would be to court disaster. It says much about the standard of British generalship in this battle that a battalion commander should have to point this out.

The Onset of Doubt

At around 6.30 p.m. Thorneycroft at last extricated himself from the fighting in the trench and wrote a second situation report for Warren which again he despatched by hand:

> The troops which marched up here last night are quite done up . . . They have had no water and ammunition is running short. I consider that even

> with reinforcements which have arrived, it is impossible to permanently hold this place, so long as the enemy's guns can play on this hill. They have one long range gun, three of shorter range, and one Maxim-Nordenfeldt, which have swept the whole of the plateau since 8.00 a.m. I have not been able to ascertain the casualties, but they have been very heavy especially in the regiments which came up last night. I request instructions as to what course I am to adopt. The enemy at 6.30 p.m. are firing heavily from both flanks with rifle, shell and Nordenfeldt, while a heavy rifle-fire is kept up in front. It is all I can do to hold my own. If casualties go on occurring at present rate, I shall barely hold out the night. A large number of stretcher bearers should be sent up, and also all water possible. The situation is critical. Alex Thorneycroft, Lt. Col.[20]

For some unknown reason the message did not reach Warren until daylight the following morning.

About the only practical step Warren and Buller had taken all day was to order two naval 12-pounders and No. 4 Mountain Battery around to the foot of the kop, with the intention of moving them up to the summit under the cover of darkness. Not that these measures were enacted in anything like a timely enough fashion. Getting the mule-borne mountain guns up would have been difficult enough, but the naval guns would almost certainly have proved impossible. Churchill certainly thought so, though he found it refreshing that the naval gunners were at least prepared to try. A Royal Artillery officer who had been to the summit reported that it would not be possible to get guns up before sunrise, and that to entrench them properly would be out of the question due to the rocky nature of the ground. In the meantime Buller had again been busy-bodying. Because nobody on the staff had thought to arrange a preliminary move by No. 4 Battery, it had been forced-marching from Frere for most of the day. It was 5.00 p.m. before it arrived at Trichardt's Drift and Buller was adamant that the battery should be rested before making an ascent. But this was not an exercise – men were dying on top of Spion Kop in large numbers. Better that the unfortunate mules should have been pushed uphill until they dropped down dead, and that carrying parties should then have heaved their loads upwards, but once again Warren fell tamely into line with Buller's direction. It would be 9.00 p.m. before one of the naval guns and four of the mountain guns were given an executive order to begin the climb.

Darkness

Much to the relief of the shattered and bloodied men on the kop, the enemy's guns fell silent at around 7.00 p.m. when it started to get dark. The daylight defence of the kop had been a waking nightmare but now that it was over, the

British were still in possession of the summit. Surely they had won. Ten long hours of darkness lay ahead: a whole night in which to fortify the kop with well-sited trenches and sangars; all night to bring up guns; all night to fill sandbags; all night to raid the Boer gun positions; all night to break the Boer line with a night attack; all night to prepare a dawn break-out.

But Alex Thorneycroft was a broken man. The carnage in the main trench had been atrocious. He himself had been lucky to survive unscathed. Now he could get no indication from below that there was any fresh thinking afoot. Rather it looked as if dawn would merely bring a renewal of the slaughter, an action replay of the horrors he and his men had endured all day. He conferred with Malby Crofton of 2nd Royal Lancaster and Ernest Cooke of 2nd Scottish Rifles and found that they agreed with his dismal reading of the situation. It was not that they were short of men: the Dorsets were still intact in a reserve position on the spur. Psychologically isolated by their great height above sea level, and no doubt angry at the apparent inactivity of the brigades on Ntabmnyama, it seemed to the trio of colonels that their superiors had abandoned them to their fate. There did not seem to be enough water; there were too few doctors and medics for the great number of wounded; and there were no orders – no hint of what was expected of them. If, as the absence of orders seemed to suggest, they were required merely to hold on blindly, then their lords and masters were asking way too much.

Across on Three Tree Hill, Churchill had briefed Warren who listened 'with great patience and attention', although another version of the encounter suggests a heated dismissal of an over-animated Churchill. Either way Winston was asked by a member of the staff to go back up the kop with a note for Thorneycroft: 'The General Officer Commanding Force would be glad to have your views of the situation and measures to be adopted, by Lieutenant Winston Churchill, who takes this note.'[21] The message was timed at 8.20 p.m. It would take Churchill, a fit and vigorous young man, two hours and ten minutes to deliver it. Unbeknownst to the British, the Boers too were utterly broken in spirit. Dismayed by their atypically heavy casualties and their failure to pull off a second Majuba, most abandoned their positions at dusk. The slightest pressure that night would have achieved a major breakthrough, though through a lack of vigour the British remained ignorant of the enemy's disarray. It was in the first hour of darkness that 3rd KKRC finally broke clean from Three Peaks and began scrambling downhill for Potgieter's Drift.

Enough Is Enough

At 8.15 p.m. Thorneycroft took the decision to pull out. It was about now that Colonel Hill finally bumped into him. He argued against withdrawal, but

Thorneycroft was so inwardly angry at the failings of his superiors that he brushed all objections aside. There was much organizing to be done if the retreat was to be executed in an orderly fashion, and there was no immediate rearward move by the formed units. Even so it is clear that the withdrawal was a lot less orderly than some participant accounts pretend.

Because at this stage General Coke was still at the signalling station on the spur, all might yet have been well had not Warren made another extraordinary misjudgement. Despite his headquarters being located two miles or more from the scene of the action, he signalled Coke at about 9.00 p.m. to come down and report in person. Coke knew that the combination of his injury, a perilous gradient and a pitch-black night meant that it would take him three or four hours to get down safely, and even longer to get back up. He could not possibly be back on the kop before dawn. He wanted to dispute the order but his signallers had run out of oil for their lamps. In the circumstances he felt he had no choice but to obey. Leaving his headquarters in the hands of his DAAG, Captain Henry Phillips of the Welch Regiment, Coke set off into the gloom. Had he left even 20 minutes later he would have seen or heard Thorneycroft's command coming down the spur. As it was, the general would be moving ahead of the retreat for the best part of three hours. Grateful for the opportunity to snatch an hour's rest, Harry Phillips lay down in the grass and closed his eyes.

By now Churchill had reached the summit for the second time that day and went scurrying around the darks knots of figures assembling at the top of the spur, enquiring after Thorneycroft. Eventually he was pointed in the right direction. Exhausted, dehydrated, betrayed and almost certainly by now in a clinical state of shock, Thorneycroft could think of nothing else but evacuating his men to safety. His plans were laid and there would be no going back. The Scottish Rifles, the last battalion up, would provide the rearguard and be last down. 'Better six battalions safely down the hill than a bloody mop-up in the morning' he remarked to Churchill.[22] His reply to the note from Warren's staff was short and to the point:

> Regret to report that I have been obliged to abandon Spion Kop, as the position became untenable. I have withdrawn the troops in regular order, and will come to report as soon as possible.
>
> *Alex Thorneycroft. Lt-Col.*

The descent got under way at about 10.00 p.m. Now the 300 men who had lost their lives holding the kop would be going to the grave in vain. Their sacrifice was a strong argument against retreat, but to a shell-shocked Thorneycroft it would not suffice. Why should even one more life be sacrificed to the kop, if the great men below had no better plan than to wait like

Micawber for something to turn up. There is a limit to human endurance for even the bravest of men and Alex Thorneycroft had long since reached it. He led the long column of down-hearted troops into the night and began the descent. Inevitably there was considerable disarray and a good deal of straggling. As he was to put it in his formal report of two days later, he 'was obliged, owing to want of bearers, to leave a large number of wounded on the field'.

At about 11.30 p.m. Captain Harry Phillips woke with a start to find a seemingly endless string of men jostling past his position in the dark. Bellowing an order for the troops to stand still he rushed uphill in search of the battalion commanders. He found Cooke of the Scottish Rifles and remonstrated with him in General Coke's name, insisting that no retreat had been ordered and that the battalion commanders were acting without authority. To reinforce his case he wrote out a note to that effect. One of the fundamentals of a military staff system is that a trusted staff officer acting in accordance with his commander's intent does so with the full authority of the general he serves. The power of the scrap of paper that Phillips had now produced lay in the fact that it constituted written orders from a higher headquarters and would serve as incontrovertible evidence of wilful disobedience in any subsequent investigation.

> To Officers Commanding, Dorsetshire and Middlesex Regiments, Scottish Rifles and Imperial Light Horse, [*sic*]
>
> This withdrawal is absolutely without the authority of either Major General Coke or Sir Charles Warren. The former was called away by the latter a little before 10 p.m. When General Coke left the front about 6 p.m. our men were holding their own, and he left the situation as such, and reported that he could hold on.
>
> Someone, without authority, has given orders to withdraw, and has incurred a grave responsibility. Were the General here, he would order an instant reoccupation of the heights.
>
> *H. E. Phillips*
> *DAAG*

By waving his note under the noses of several senior officers, Phillips succeeded in halting the descent of the Scottish Rifles, the Dorsets and Bethune's Mounted Infantry.

Deneys Reitz was experiencing similar confusion on the other side of the kop:

> At last Opperman decided to retreat, and we descended the hill by the way which he had climbed up sixteen hours before, our feet striking sickeningly at times against the dead bodies in our path . . . The first thing to do was to quench our raging thirst and that of our horses at a spring nearby. We then consulted as to our next move. Most of the

> wounded had been taken off during the course of the day, but we found a few serious cases that would not bear transport collected in charge of an old man, who by the dim light of a lantern, was attending to their wants. We could get no coherent information and stood discussing what to do next, for we did not know that the English had also been fought to a standstill, and that they in turn were at that very moment retreating down their own side of Spion Kop. We fully believed that the morning would see them streaming through the breach to the relief of Ladysmith and the rolling up of our Tugela line.

Thorneycroft had taken a dreadful responsibility upon his shoulders and knew he must at once make his way to Warren's headquarters to explain himself. Near the foot of the spur, at around midnight, he encountered the mountain guns and an accompanying work party of sappers. Lieutenant Colonel George Sim RE was carrying a note from Warren containing a direct order for Thorneycroft to hold his ground. Thorneycroft read it, disregarded its contents and told Sim to turn his men about and start them downhill.

It was 2.00 a.m. before Thorneycroft arrived at Warren's command post. He arrived at precisely the same time as poor Coke, who had been stumbling around in the dark for some time, trying to find the general's new location. Warren was asleep and it was Churchill who politely shook him awake. All things considered, he took the news well. Eventually even the resolute Harry Phillips gave up the ghost. Somewhere nearby Mohandas K. Gandhi was amongst the corps of Indian stretcher bearers struggling manfully to ferry the wounded to the surgeons.

The Battle of Spion Kop was over. Buller arrived at sun-up by which time Botha and a last handful of stalwart Boers were already moving around on top of the kop amongst the British doctors and medics. The main trench served as a mass grave for the men killed defending it, and is still to this day preserved as a war grave by the Republic of South Africa. It is amongst the most poignant sights to be found on any of the world's battlefields.

Within 24 hours Buller's army was in full retreat for Chieveley and Frere, with more than a thousand wounded piled pitifully aboard the jolting ox-wagons of the commissariat. Every cloud, they say, has a silver lining: for Buller it was the complete humiliation of his second-in-command and erstwhile successor – a demonstration to those fools in London that forcing the Tugela was not nearly as simple as they seemed to think.

Official returns show that in the fighting conducted across Ntabmnyama and Spion Kop during the period 17–24 January 1900, the South Natal Field Force suffered a total loss of 1,733 officers and men. The officer casualties amounted to 42 dead, 65 wounded and 2 missing in action. The loss in soldiers was 370 dead, 969 wounded and 285 missing. The losses of the units intimately concerned in the fighting on the kop are summarized in Table 12. Amongst the 18 officer casualties in the 2nd Lancashire Fusiliers was Charles Hicks, killed in action like his father before him. For once the Boer loss had also been relatively heavy; the assault on the kop had cost the commandos 58 dead and 140 wounded.

***Table 12:* Losses of the Major Units at Spion Kop**[23]

Unit	*Killed*	*Wounded*	*Missing*
2nd Royal Lancaster Regiment	3 & 69	4 & 98	1 & 31
2nd Lancashire Fusiliers	5 & 83	13 & 169	1 & 137
2nd Cameronians	4 & 35	6 & 45	0 & 1
1st South Lancashire Regiment	2 & 6	0 & 33	0 & 13
2nd Middlesex Regiment	4 & 38	4 & 49	0 & 7
Imperial Light Infantry	2 & 30	3 & 28	0 & 64
Thorneycroft's Mounted Infantry	7 & 21	5 & 43	0 & 20
3rd KRRC *(Twin Peaks)*	3 & 21	5 & 73	0 & 0
Totals:	30 & 303	40 & 538	2 & 273

More battles remained to be fought, and many more lives would be lost before Louis Botha's line was finally breached and Ladysmith relieved. To Redvers Buller the unhappy events of December and January were everybody's fault but his own – Sir George White's fault, Fitzroy Hart's fault, Charlie Long's, Sir Charles Warren's. To his wife Buller wrote '. . . old Warren is a duffer and lost me a good chance' – as if somebody else had put a 'duffer' in charge of the greater part of the army. In his official report to the Secretary of State dated 30 January, Buller slated Warren and implied that London must also bear a share of the blame:

> We had really lost our chance by Sir C. Warren's slowness. He seems to me a man who can do well what he can do himself, but who cannot command, as he can use neither his staff nor subordinates. I can never employ him again on an independent command . . . On the 19th I ought to have assumed command myself; I saw that things were not going well – indeed, everyone saw that. I blame myself for not having done so. I did not because I thought that if I did so I should discredit General Warren in the estimation of the troops; and that if I were shot [a dig in respect of the dormant commission], and he had to withdraw across the Tugela, and they had lost confidence in him, the consequences might be very serious.[24]

Of Colonel Charlie Long's performance at Colenso, Buller commented privately that he had been 'sold by a damned gunner'. In the event the War

Office, the press, the public and, finally, even the previously devoted men in the ranks, did not quite see it like that. Neither did the German General Staff – their analysis of Colenso included the observation 'It was the general and not his gallant force that was defeated.' J. B. Atkins, the correspondent of the *Manchester Guardian*, had it right when he described Spion Kop as 'that acre of massacre, that complete shambles'.[25] Some people began to sneer at Sir 'Reverse' Buller, others to refer to him as 'the Tugela Ferryman'. His evasions and obfuscations regarding Colenso and Spion Kop, when after the war he was called to testify before a royal commission convened to investigate its conduct, were little short of disgraceful. He had an answer for everything and they all involved the failings of others. In truth his testimony amounted to a dishonest representation of what actually occurred on the Ladysmith Front. Perhaps by then Sir Redvers had unknowingly re-written the history of the war in the darkest recesses of a troubled mind. A well-lubricated after dinner speech, in which he was unreasonably critical of the government, finally brought Buller's long military career to an undignified end.

In the aftermath of Spion Kop it was Wolseley who telegraphed that perhaps Ladysmith should be given up. It was necessary to suppress this defeatist document, just as earlier it had been necessary to suppress Buller's telegrams of 15/16 December. But the truth will out. The 'Wolseley Ring' had had its day. Now the defeat of the Boers would fall to the 'scheming little Indian' and his newly appointed chief of staff – the one time blue-eyed Baggara spy, back from the Sudan at last, as Major General Lord Kitchener of Khartoum. Well might the Boer republics have shuddered at the news.

Epilogue

SCHOOL OF HARD KNOCKS

Defeat in the Colonies, 1879–1900

I need not say that no cross or stone marks the graves of the fallen; above them the Lion Kop, the majestic monument of Isandlwana, holds guard and forever tells that 800 sons of England lie beneath.

Lt. Col. Wilsone Black, 24th Regiment, July 1879

The Wisdom of Hindsight

Military disaster can exert a particular fascination. What went wrong? How could it have happened? Who is to blame? If the butcher's bill has been particularly heavy, there may even be unanswered questions about the precise nature of events and their sequencing. This is certainly the case with Isandlwana and the final stages of the Battle of Maiwand, for example. An anthology of disaster runs the risk of suggesting that the army at issue was inherently inept; but is this true of the high-Victorian Army?

The preface predicted that the hero of this book would prove to be the ordinary fighting man. Having read the various narrative chapters, the reader will now have a clear view of why this should be so. In none of the episodes we have examined was the ordinary British soldier to blame for the disaster at issue. That in itself constitutes a remarkable testament. It is probably fair to say that the British have always been their own harshest critics. The royal commission convened to investigate the conduct of the Boer War criticized just about every aspect of military affairs, but interestingly also took evidence from a number of witnesses who were disparaging about the quality of the men in the ranks. There is every likelihood, however, that this represents unjust and pompous testimony proffered by misguided representatives of a military establishment struggling to come to terms with its own inadequacies. Nowhere have I found evidence to substantiate such a claim. Staring out from an album, now in my possession, of numerous unit photographs taken on the cusp of 1st Army Corps' embarkation for South Africa, almost without exception, are mature, alert and physically well developed human specimens – everything one would expect of regular soldiers. The contrast between these Victorian 'team photographs' and those of the rapidly mobilized volunteer army of 1916–18, where a great many physically under-developed urban youths are usually readily identifiable, is pronounced. Fifteen years after Abu Klea, a battle which in itself speaks volumes for the quality of the Victorian professional soldier, our old friend Bennet Burleigh, a hugely experienced correspondent and no mean judge of fighting men, was once again in the field on behalf of the *Daily Telegraph*. Of the men who fought at Spion Kop he wrote:

> Through it all our soldiers behaved like heroes, with a courage and a dash that none could surpass . . . Glory and honour to them, who only needed leaders and direction! All that flesh and blood could do, and more, they accomplished.[1]

In his book *The Natal Campaign* Bennet Burleigh recounts an incident which took place during the fighting on Ntabmnyama. He got the story from a Catholic padre called Father Matthew. Approaching an Irish private swathed in bloodied bandages, the priest enquired 'Where were you shot, my man?' 'I was shot in the head' came the reply. 'It took my eye out, carried it into my mouth, and I spat it out with three teeth. But we gave it to them Boers this time and I am content.' Father Matthew told Burleigh that the soldier 'did not seem to mind much'. Stories of this sort are legion. That the men in the ranks were possessed of tremendous resilience and formidable fighting spirit represents the safest of assumptions. It seems certain, therefore, that where disaster occurred, 'Tommy' had generally been let down in some way by his superiors.

Before briefly reviewing the mistakes made in the course of these campaigns, it is only fair to observe that high command in war is one of the most testing and stressful activities known to man. One of its most difficult facets is that the commander must live with the knowledge that his decisions will inevitably cost the lives of men who have placed their trust in him. The best he can do for them is to try and minimize the extent of the army's loss. Even then the onerous demands of good generalship might require that he pursue one of his more costly options in the conviction that it offers the prospect of a more decisive outcome. Sometimes it can be the case in war that a hundred lives lost today will preserve a thousand lives tomorrow. Redvers Buller for one found that kind of responsibility difficult to live with. Inevitably it is a whole lot easier for historians to pick out a general's mistakes with the benefit of hindsight, than it was for the general himself to realise in the heat of the moment that he was making them. To draw in passing on some of the language used to describe the successor generation of British generals in prominent mid-twentieth-century histories of the Great War, it is important to recognize that the officers who feature in these pages were not 'butchers' or 'bunglers' or 'donkeys', but mere men, possessed of a random selection of the vulnerabilities and failings implicit in the human condition. Importantly they were also loyal servants of their nation, were trying their best to do their duty and in most cases showed little or no regard for their own safety. That said, where they failed and men lost their lives unnecessarily, it is only right that sometimes harsh truths are laid bare in the history books. The causes of British military disaster in Queen Victoria's reign, while they often overlap and combine, can fairly readily be grouped by categories. The first and most obvious is personal failure on the part of the commander, which in turn can be divided into failures of competence and failures of character.

Personal Failings of the Commander

Outright Military Incompetence In the majority of military scenarios a wide array of tactical options will present themselves. Some will offer a strong prospect of success, some a reasonable prospect, some can be argued either way and, at the other end of the spectrum, some options will be indifferent, some will be gambles and some will be identifiable as outright acts of madness. There is some excuse for gambling if a general finds himself on the back foot, provided always that he has done everything he can to tip the odds in his favour – for example by incorporating surprise as a principal feature of a plan of attack. Even then he must live with the knowledge that aiming for surprise and actually achieving it are two entirely different things.

If, in studying a campaign, one takes special care to discard the benefit of hindsight, and yet the commander's major decisions still appear inexplicable or illogical, the chances are that outright military incompetence is in play – that the general in question has been over-promoted, has no intuitive grasp of the art of war and quite simply is not up to the task in hand. Why for example did Sir Redvers Buller feel moved to try his luck against Louis Botha's centre when, from the very first, his soldierly instincts whispered that the position around Colenso was impregnable? 'I had to have a play at Colenso, but I did not think I could get in.' What a remarkable admission. And why after completing a successful night approach march specifically designed to achieve surprise, did Sir Charles Warren squander his advantage by dithering so long in the vicinity of Trichardt's Drift? In such glaring cases the question of military incompetence must inevitably come into play. Is the commander so badly out of his depth that muddle-headed thinking has taken over? The arguments to be made around the performances of Buller and Warren at Colenso and Ntabmnyama respectively would of their own accord be sufficiently compelling to warrant charges of military incompetence, but the subsequent fiasco at Spion Kop puts the issue so far beyond doubt that no credible defence of their reputations is possible. It is clear that neither Buller nor Warren had the requisite talent to handle a military force as large as the South Natal Field Force. Nor did they have the single-mindedness, originality or ingenuity required to unpick a layered defensive position step by step.

And yet it can still also be true that Buller was one of the best colonels of his generation. It can be argued that he was unfortunate in being the man left holding the parcel when the music stopped and modern warfare was born, but it is difficult to gainsay his admission to the Secretary of State for War, on first appointment to the South African command, that he was not the man for the job. It is clear that the skill sets required at various levels of command are distinctly different, and that widely lauded success in intermediate ranks can breed great personal failings such as conceit, stubbornness and a reluctance either to seek or accept advice at more senior levels.

Failings of Character It seems perverse that Val Baker led his Egyptian soldiers and policemen to one of the most notable disasters of the era without his competence ever being called into question. As the Officer Commanding the 10th Hussars, Baker had been regarded as one of the leading cavalry theorists of his day. His brother cavalrymen took particular care to listen to his latest thoughts and, when in doubt, actively sought his opinion. Setting his unfortunate 'indiscretion' to one side, he was able to make the transition to the next level of command with ease and by the time of El Teb enjoyed a track record to prove it. In the Russo-Turkish War he performed highly creditably against a sophisticated European enemy in the most trying of circumstances. Yet at Suakin he succumbed to a self-evidently foolish decision in electing to advance into the interior. Why did he do it? Because a troubled conscience told him he must act to save a few hundred hapless *fellaheen* besieged at Tokar, no matter what the odds? Or were there perhaps more sinister motives in play? Did he perchance gamble, not to restore an adverse operational situation, but rather to redeem his name and rehabilitate himself in the service of the Crown? Sir Evelyn Baring, no mean judge of character, was sure that Baker's decision was shaped by selfish motives. We have seen how a similarly selfish desire for redemption led Sir George Colley to defy governmental intent in mounting the ill-fated Majuba operation. Selflessness is one of the most important personal qualities of the successful commander. All too commonly, however, its absence proves no real bar to the attainment of high rank.

Poor Campaign Planning

Planning a campaign entails identifying the steps, measures and activities necessary to attain a considered sequence of intermediate goals which will combine to generate victory. To be credible a campaign plan must be adequately resourced. In all of the cases we have examined, resources were an issue: Buller had too few cavalry regiments; Stewart insufficient camels; Burrows was badly outgunned. Well intentioned willingness to 'have a go' is a common a refrain in British military affairs, but it is an attitude of mind that can all too readily slide over the dividing line into the realms of arrogance and folly. Sir George Colley for example dashed an outnumbered force of fewer than 1,500 men against Piet Joubert's defences in a hopelessly ill-conceived offensive movement, when a far more measured approach would have been to await the arrival of the 'Indian Column' before making an attempt on Laing's Nek. Instead he set too much store by the notion that the fall of any of the besieged garrisons would represent a serious blow to British 'prestige'. Whilst this might arguably have been true of the fall of Pretoria, the capital was in no danger whatsoever, be it from artillery bombardment, assault or starvation. It did not follow that the minor garrisons were anything like as important in a wider strategic context. The correct approach would have been to weigh the consequences of the surrender of one or two of them against the far worse consequences of the wholesale defeat of the Natal Field Force. Far better that Laing's Nek and Ingogo had never happened, at the price, say, of the fall of Potchefstroom – an insignificant garrison in an irrelevant place – than that the only British field force be defeated in an overly precipitate offensive.

The worst that could happen as a consequence of a wholly prudent delay was that Lieutenant Colonel Richard Winsloe would be obliged to surrender his command into benign captivity. Potchefstroom was not another Lucknow, the Boers were not merciless killers and, in any case, Winsloe held out until 20 March (Laing's Nek was fought on 28 January and the Indian Column came up in the last week of February). Even then Winsloe had to be tricked by Cronje into surrendering.[2] Instead of the fleeting embarrassment which might have attended the fall of one or more of the garrisons, Colley's disastrous defeat in the field really did do lasting damage to British prestige. Not only did it lose the Transvaal in 1881, it also gave the Boers reason to believe that they might one day be able to eject the British from the Cape. Thus not only did it impel a foolish and futile challenge for regional hegemony, it was also instrumental in shaping the unhappy history of twentieth-century South Africa.

Like Colley, William Hicks also failed to plan his campaign so as to maximize his prospects of success. The desert wastes of Kordofan were already in Muhammad Ahmad's hands and in any case were of no value or relevance to the

Egyptian colonial regime in the Sudan. There was no necessity whatsoever for Hicks to advance on a wing and prayer into a waterless furnace. Above all else it takes time to turn around a poorly trained and motivated army. In mounting the Kordofan expedition when he did, he presented the military advantage to the Mahdi on a platter. He should instead have waited at Khartoum, protected by a score of well-armed river steamers, improving the city's defences and getting his troops in order. One of the principal problems a rebel leader faces is maintaining the momentum of his insurrection. The Mahdi would have to emerge from the desert sooner or later, or face the failure of his jihad through apathy, and that would be the point at which to seek a decisive engagement – on ground of Hicks's own choosing.

If the collapse of Colley's campaign plan had the most far-reaching implications for the British Empire, the failure of Wolseley's plan for the relief of Khartoum was perhaps the most surprising. He was, after all, supposed to be better than that. Although to his eternal discredit Wolseley succeeded in shifting the military blame onto the shoulders of the hapless Sir Charles Wilson, we have seen how his insistence on the Nile route ahead of Suakin–Berber fell some 4–6 weeks short of achieving the aim. Nor does Gladstone's vacillation provide an all-encompassing excuse – it was just one more factor for a prudent commander to plan around. That the final scheme of manoeuvre made no allowance for Sir Herbert Stewart throwing his troops into the city in any numbers demonstrates that Wolseley's principal object was not the relief of Khartoum by any means, but the relief of Khartoum to the greater glory of Garnet Wolseley. Failings of character, then, can influence the conduct of a campaign, just as much as they can influence the conduct of a battle. At so great a distance from the campaign, nobody can ever know for sure that Suakin–Berber would have worked; but the Nile route assuredly did not, precisely as the Royal Navy, GOC Cairo and the *Sirdar* had predicted.

Tactical Misjudgement on the Day

The penultimate cause of disaster, and perhaps the most forgivable, is the straightforward tactical misjudgement on the day. Everybody, we know, makes mistakes, generals no less than anybody else. In the case of George Burrows at Maiwand, it can be argued that he was compelled to deploy forward of the Mahmudabad Ravine in order to support Blackwood's battery in bringing fire to bear on the hard-marching Afghan columns. Had he not done so the RHA could have been driven off or menaced by the enemy's irregular horse, leaving Ayub Khan free to continue his bypassing movement for Kandahar. Burrows tactical misjudgement came after the enemy had committed himself to turn and give battle, by which time he had gained a much clearer impression of Ayub

Khan's great strength. The obvious numerical disparity in the two forces should have told him that sooner or later his open flanks would be subjected to intolerable pressure. In failing to seize the narrow window of opportunity to withdraw to a tenable defensive position, before he became decisively engaged, Burrows automatically ceded a winning advantage to the enemy.

Sometimes the intimate conduct of the close battle can pass beyond the control of the general officer commanding. Whilst it is probably true that Sir George Colley's decision to mount the attack on Laing's Nek in broad daylight doomed it to failure from the outset, Colonel Deane and Major Brownlow both played less than helpful supporting roles. We have seen that Deane misdirected the 58th Regiment against a steep spur when, if Brownlow is to be believed, the attack should have fallen upon a saddle further to the right. It should not be forgotten, however, that the 58th had a perfectly capable battalion commander in Major Hingeston, who was dislodged at the last gasp on Colley's say-so. We have seen that Colley's campaign plan embodied making unnecessary haste with insufficient resources. Because so many of the British failures at the acute tactical level can also be traced back to him, it is painfully apparent that he would have been as poor a battalion commander, a post he had never held, as he was a major-general. Meanwhile, in choosing to launch a mounted charge on Commandant Engelbrecht's position, Brownlow made a decision which was at best imprudent and at worst foolhardy. We have seen the disastrous effect of many other tactical misjudgements – Hart's right turn into the loop at Colenso; Fred Burnaby's wheel from the rear face of the square at Abu Klea; Woodgate's failure to secure Aloe Knoll and so on. These though were spur of the moment failures, some of which could be redeemed as at Abu Klea, and some, such as the entrapment of the Irish Brigade, which could not. In war tactical misjudgements are inevitable. Even the 'great captains' of military history are susceptible to them – military history offers no better example than the supremely talented Lee's ill-fated decision to assault Meade's centre on the third day at Gettysburg.[3]

Systemic Failure

We have examined many striking examples of personal failure between 1879 and 1900, or little more than two decades. A question mark hangs, therefore, over the extent to which the failures of the late Victorian Army were institutional. That British military affairs were over-centralized, over regulated, and administered by narrow-minded bureaucrats may be taken as read. We observed in Chapter 1 how each of the principal fighting arms adapted to the age of the breechloader at variable rates and with varying degrees of success. The cavalry remained fixated on shock and mass for far too long and were inclined to look down their noses at the American-pioneered skills of systematic reconnaissance, raiding and screening. In South Africa, where they were confronted with an enemy who could shoot, the cavalry proved incapable of scouting enemy defensive positions to the satisfaction of their commanders. In the infantry the standard of shooting was generally poor throughout the period. Too much reliance was placed on massed volley fire, while insufficient time and attention was devoted to individual marksmanship – though to be fair history records a remarkable instance of a musketry instructor bowling a lone Zulu over with a Martini at a range of 1,300 yards. It is said that in the aftermath of Majuba a cabal of 58th Regiment officers pledged that they would never be out-shot again. Sure enough the regiment quickly became renowned for the standard of its musketry and began scooping the Army's shooting prizes. After the Anglo-Boer War and the final demise of volley fire, the average standard improved across the board with dire consequences for the German divisions of 1914. Attention to marksmanship was one of the most beneficial of the timely string of lessons to emerge from the South African War.

We also noted that very little attention was given to the professional development of the officer corps. The majority of officers serving on the staff were untrained for the role. Against the less sophisticated tribal enemies of the era, modern military professionalism after the fashion of the German General Staff seemed barely to matter. As long as regimental officers had a basic grasp of drill and musketry, led from the front and showed themselves to be without fear, they could continue drawing their pay with a clear conscience. When at a dinner held in the aftermath of the Egyptian campaign the Duke of Connaught proposed a toast to the newly knighted Colonel Ashburnham, 'Old Bristles' rose from the table and responded:

> I am very much obliged for the kind way his Royal Highness has proposed the toast of my health. I have been in the Rifles over 30 years, and owe everything to the Regiment. I never wore a red coat. I was never on the Staff. I hate the Staff, damn them![4]

With this not entirely unreasonable sentiment, Sir Cromer slumped back into his seat.

Amongst the many things killed by the Boers between 1899 and 1902 was the 'cult of the amateur'. That purchase was both iniquitous and generally harmful goes without saying, but promotion from colonel to major general by strict seniority continued long after Cardwell had dispensed with the buying and selling of regimental vacancies. Most of the officers commanding brigades in 1899 were doing so on the basis of length of service alone – in more enlightened times a good proportion of them would have retired as majors or lieutenant colonels. In his *Times History of the War in South Africa*, Leo Amery wrote that the war had:

> ...revealed the fact that many of our generals, who had risen simply by seniority, were nothing more than rather aged regimental officers, with brains and willpower atrophied by a long life spent in unmilitary routine and in the unintelligent execution of orders, incapable alike of devising a plan or of carrying it into execution. Others, again, had won cheap reputations by partaking in some successful and popular little expedition, or had risen to high positions by the writing of incisive minutes, or by personal and social influences. There must always be failures when an army, which has long enjoyed immunity from serious conflict, is suddenly brought to the test of a great war, and it must also be remembered that the new conditions that our generals were called upon to face in South Africa made that test of the very severest. Still it is certain that the proportion of failures would have been far less had there been any proper system by which capable officers could have been selected and trained for high command.

The twentieth century was nigh by the time Wolseley, as C-in-C, was able to persuade Parliament to dispense once and for all with promotion on the basis of seniority alone.

It is a military truism that soldiers cannot be expected to do well in war, what they have not been trained to do in peace. We have seen how military developments rendered conventional notions of parade-ground training largely irrelevant. Yet still the late Victorian Army remained obsessed with inspections, pipe clay, spit and polish. Probably the greatest failing of the chain of command was that it never really came to terms with collective training in peacetime. The typical infantry battalion deployed for a three-week period of field training in the summer, devoted about 20 miscellaneous days in the year to route marching, and fired an annual allocation of 200 rounds a man on the ranges. For the most part they practised on fixed targets at known ranges. Given the rapid pace of change, the equivalent of two months' serious military training a year was not nearly enough. Ultimately the upper echelons of the military chain of command can bear only part of the blame, as such deficiencies can only be addressed if government is concerned enough to embrace and resource the need for change. Inevitably the worst failings were to be found at formation level. In essence brigades and divisions formed up only in wartime and had no choice but to learn all-arms co-operation on the job. By virtue of the string of campaigns it waged on the North-West Frontier in the 1890s, the Indian Army was more tactically adept than the home Army. It is interesting to reflect on how the Boer War might have gone had it been fought a decade later, by which time lessons from India would have been much more widely assimilated.

Although the British performance in the first six months of the war was broadly unsatisfactory, it cannot be allowed that the Germans, the French or any other major military power would have fared any better – a key point in evaluating the competence and efficiency of the high Victorian Army. Ultimately there were few significant variations in the tactical and organizational practices of the nations. Whilst the continental armies were capable of concentrating mass on a scale that Wolseley and other reformers could only dream of, the European conscript soldier was clearly no better trained and was certainly far less adaptable than the British regular. Importantly we sometimes forget that early failure in South Africa was by no means all-encompassing; Elandslaagte, for example, represented a very neat operation of war. Remove Buller from the equation as a mis-selection for high command, and the chances are that Colenso and Spion Kop would have had no equivalent, and that the war would have had an altogether different complexion. It is clear that the small wars of empire inculcated an unrivalled aptitude for improvization in the British and Indian Armies. As a result supply, transport and medical matters generally worked well in the Ladysmith and Kimberley campaigns, notwithstanding a daunting array of adverse logistic factors. Leo Amery put it succinctly when he wrote, 'France or Germany could no more have sent an army to Pretoria than Lord Roberts could have marched to Paris or Berlin'.

If the small wars waged by Queen Victoria's Army demonstrated that tribal enemies could generally be over-matched by concentrated firepower, resolve and naked courage, the defeat of the digging, dispersed, invisible Boers would demand an unprecedented degree of military sophistication. Describing the period 17–23 January 1900, when Warren was fighting around Ntabmnyama, John Atkins of the *Manchester Guardian* encapsulated something of the way in which the face of battle had changed:

> It would be unprofitable and tedious to describe all the details of a six days' battle which was visible only on one side. On all those days in varying degrees the hills crashed with guns and rattled with musketry. At a little distance you might have supposed that the resonant noises came from some haunted mountain; for the hills looked sleepy and peaceful and deserted, and there seemed to be no reason for all those strange sounds – the bark of field guns, the crackle of musketry, the rapping of Vickers-Maxims and the tat- tat- tat- tat- tat- tat of Maxims.[5]

In the late 1980s military theorists would coin the phrase 'the less dense battlefield'. In fact they were merely describing the continuation of a tactical trend which originated in turn-of-the-century South Africa.

Even with the Boer capitals in British hands, this most resourceful of enemies would shift the goalposts once more and invent an entirely new style of warfare to test the mettle of the British Army even further. It is one of the saddest aspects of Southern Africa's all too unhappy history that the last 'gentleman's war' turned ugly in the process. By the time the last of the commandos had been run to ground, the Victorian Army had gone forever.

Conclusion

It may have been an uphill struggle and it may have required an unprecedented effort, but in the end the British Empire emerged victorious from its long conflict with the Boers. Cetshwayo may have celebrated a magnificent victory over Lord Chelmsford in the Isandlwana campaign, but Rorke's Drift was held, the Zulu regiments shattered and Ulundi duly razed to the ground. Ayub Khan might have defeated George Burrows, but would prove no match for Fred Roberts. Muhammad Ahmad may have gazed upon the Governor-General's decapitated head, but Gordon would not be the last Royal Engineer to fly the Egyptian flag over Khartoum.

In *Into the Jaws of Death* we have examined the Victorian Army in defeat, have probed its fault lines and have encountered some of its less talented or less fortunate commanders. But for all that, defeat and incompetence were not the norm. For every George Colley there was a John Nicholson and a Henry Havelock, for every Buller, a Roberts and a Kitchener, for every Maiwand a string of Tel-el-Kebirs. If the list of defeats is at least statistically significant, and the list of military incompetents no less so, a glance at the chronology at the front of the book will reveal just how impressive is the countervailing list of victories. From Ashantiland to Abyssinia, from Peking to the Punjab, and from Cairo to the Cape, the Victorian Army achieved some truly remarkable successes against the odds. That sufficient reverses occurred to provide material for a book of this sort was a function of such factors as imperial overstretch, the undoubted resourcefulness of Queen Victoria's enemies, distance and forbidding terrain, poor generalship and, to an extent, the law of averages – fight enough battles and there are sure to be a few mishaps along the way. At the same time, it is clear that the front-line components of the Army, in particular its peerless array of fighting regiments, were handicapped by a number of serious systemic failings which could and should have been addressed in Whitehall rather earlier than they were. Mercifully, the gradual eradication of these deficiencies between the Crimean War and the Great War, a process brought to a head by Louis Botha and his comrades, would serve to ready the British Army for the herculean challenges it would face in the twentieth century. No longer to be regarded as a vigorous field sport for gentlemen, war had transmuted into a science. In next to no time it would be industrialized.

And for the old world order, the consequences would prove terminal.

NOTES

Preface (pages 15–23)

1. Quoted in Capt. H. B. Latham, 'E/B RHA at Maiwand', *Journal of the Royal Artillery*, 1928.
2. The nickname 'Tommy' dates back to 1829, when the notional service details of a fictitious Private Thomas Atkins appeared on a sample proforma issued across the Army. Later in the century Kipling's poetry would play a prominent role in popularizing the sobriquet, until at length it became a commonplace expression even in civil society. 'Tommy' has now faded from everyday use, to be replaced in the popular vernacular by the much uglier and, in the author's view, somewhat pejorative 'squaddie'.

Prologue (pages 35–41)

1. For an anthology of Henderson's writing see, *The Science of War: A Collection of Essays and Lectures 1891–1903*, ed. Capt. Neill Malcolm.
2. Now held by the Royal Regiment of Wales Museum, Brecon. It is possible that other unidentified soldiers were found alongside Shaw but the three privates mentioned are the only ones Bassage names.
3. I have allowed for an arbitrary 50 Black African civilians on top of the traditionally accepted military losses.

Chapter 1: The Victorian Army in an Age of Transition (pages 42–68)

1. A unit's establishment regulates the number of officers and soldiers the taxpayer is prepared to pay for. The wartime establishment is an expression of the number of officers and men a regiment needs to fight effectively in accordance with the tactical practice of the day. By operating a system of smaller peacetime establishments, the War Office (and successor ministries since) was able to save tax money at the expense of military efficiency.
2. J. W. Wightman, 'One of the "Six Hundred" in the Balaclava Charge', *Nineteenth Century*, May 1892.
3. See Edward Spiers, *The Late Victorian Army*, p. 61, for a breakdown by corps as of 1899.
4. Sir John Fortescue, *A History of the British Army*, Vol. XIII, pp. 537–8.
5. This last figure included: 19,267 cavalrymen (31 regiments); 150,376 infantrymen

(9 battalions of Foot Guards and 148 line or rifle battalions); 40,152 gunners (organized into 21 batteries of horse artillery, 94 of field artillery, 10 of mountain guns, and 99 companies of garrison artillery); 8,100 sappers; and around 8,000 men in the various service corps. Of the overall total some 74,467 men were stationed in India, including 9 regiments of cavalry and 52 battalions of infantry.

6. Fortescue, *History of the British Army*, Vol. XIII, p. 526.
7. Spiers, *The Late Victorian Army*, pp. 3–24.
8. See John Sweetman, *War and Administration: the Significance of the Crimean War for the British Army*.
9. Renamed more straightforwardly as the 'Commander-in-Chief' from 1887.
10. Spiers, *The Late Victorian Army*, p. 7.
11. Over 500 instances.
12. See Spiers, *The Late Victorian Army*, pp. 90–2, for detail of the Penzance recommendations.
13. It was not an entirely new idea – the Duke of York had proposed just such a scheme at the beginning of the century.
14. The name for the Scots Guards 1831–77.
15. The 21st would later be re-roled as a lancer regiment, in which guise it would make its famous charge at Omdurman.
16. Spiers, *The Late Victorian Army*.
17. Correlli Barnett, *Britain and her Army 1509–1970*.
18. *Field Exercise & Evolutions of Infantry 1877*, Part 3, S 42.7, pp. 217–18
19. The post had only recently changed in nature. Prior to the abolition of purchase the adjutant had been intimately concerned in drill and training, when it had been commonplace for an ex-sergeant-major to hold the post.
20. See Spiers, *The Late Victorian Army*, pp. 109–12 for the organization and syllabus of the Staff College.

Chapter 2: 'Wounded and Left on Afghanistan's Plains' (pages 69–146)

1. FM Lord Roberts VC, *Forty-One Years in India*, p. 383.
2. Lytton's poetry was published under the pseudonym Owen Meredith.
3. See QMG's Office, Army HQ India, *The Second Afghan War*, Part 1, pp. 252–3. The date of Stolietoff's departure was probably 14 June. He is believed to have reached Kabul on 10 August.
4. *Ibid.*, pp. 263–7, for Lytton's directive to Chamberlain.
5. *Ibid.*, p. 261.
6. Roberts, *Forty-One Years*, p. 345.
7. QMG's Confidential Report, Part 1, pp. 281–2.
8. Roberts, *Forty-One Years*, p. 346.
9. QMG's Confidential Report, Part 1, p. 255.
10. Roberts, *Forty-One Years*, p. 381.
11. Jemadar equates to lieutenant and subadar to captain. The subadar-major was the senior Indian officer in a battalion and would be a highly respected figure. Even so it was the practice that the most junior British lieutenant took precedence over any Indian officer.
12. QMG's Confidential Report, Part 2, p. 279.
13. *Ibid.*, pp. 281–5, for the risaldar-major's eyewitness account
14. Roberts, *Forty-One Years*, pp. 384–5.
15. See Roberts, *Forty-One Years*, for the British adoption of Abdur Rahman.
16. Intelligence Branch, Army HQ India, *Second Afghan War*, p. 482.
17. A Bombay cavalry regiment at full strength consisted of 3 squadrons each of 2 troops. There were 8 European officers, consisting of the commandant, 3 squadron

commanders, a subaltern for each of the squadrons and a surgeon. The Indian officers consisted of a *risaldar-major*, 2 *risaldars*, 3 *ressaidars* and 6 *jemadars*. There were 66 NCOs made up of a *kote duffadar* per troop (the equivalent of a troop sergeant-major) 30 *duffadars* or sergeants and 30 *naiks* or corporals. Finally there were 6 trumpeters and 400 sowars.

18. Sydney H. Shadbolt, *The Afghan Campaign of 1878–80*, pp. 94–5.
19. Burrows to the Assistant Adjutant-General, Kandahar Field Force, 30 August 1880.
20. Capt. Mayne, *Intelligence Branch Narrative Account.*
21. Col. Leigh Maxwell, *My God Maiwand*, pp. 102–3.
22. Lt. Col. Galbraith, Maj. Oliver, Surg.-Maj. Preston, Capts. Beresford-Peirse, Cullen, Garratt, McMath and Roberts, Lt. & Adjt. Rayner, Lts. Chute & Lynch, 2nd Lts. Barr, Olivey, Lonergan and Honywood. In addition to the 15 officers with the main body of the battalion, Major Ready was the field officer of the day, Capt. Harris was serving on Burrows's staff as DAAG, Capt. Quarry and 2nd Lt. Bray were guarding the baggage with G Company, Lt. Faunce was commanding a division of the smoothbore battery and 2nd Lt. Melliss was in charge of the regimental transport. Counting Dr Preston the 66th had 21 officers in the field in all.
23. Col. Anderson, Lt. Col. Griffiths, Capt. Grant, Surgeon Dane, Lt. & Adjt. Hinde, Lts. Aslett and Whittuck. Lt. Whitby commanding the baggage company was the eighth officer in the field.
24. Col. Mainwaring, Maj. Iredell, Capt. Harrison, Capt. & Adjt. (H. F.) Smith, Surgeon Kirtikar, Lts. Cole and Justice. 2nd Lt. Salmon commanding the baggage company was the eighth officer in the field.
25. Capt. Slade, Lts. Fowle, Jones and Faunce.
26. Maj. Currie, Capt. Mayne, Surgeon Street, Lt. & Adjt. Owen, Lts. Geoghegan and Reid.
27. Col. Malcolmson, Maj. Gordon, Lt. & Adjt. (E. V. P.) Monteith, Lt. Smith, Lt. (A. M.) Monteith.
28. Maj. Blackwood, Lts. Maclaine, Fowell and Osborne.
29. Capt. Quarry, 2nd Lts. Bray and Melliss.
30. See Marquess of Anglesey, *History of the British Cavalry*, Vol. III, pp. 425–6.
31. Capt. Mosely Mayne, *A Personal Account of the Battle of Maiwand*, 6 November 1880, from the handwritten original in the possession of the Mayne family.
32. Many contemporary British sources refer to the village as Mundabad.
33. Note that Mayne's manuscript *Personal Account* demonstrates that the *Official History* is incorrect in stating (p. 501) that he commanded his regiment's '1st Squadron'.
34. *Official History*, pp. 477–8.
35. A distance established during Col. Leigh Maxwell's visit to the battlefield in the 1970s. As we shall see it was overestimated in a number of participant accounts at 500 yards and more.
36. In full Capt. William John de la Poer Beresford-Peirse.
37. There is no primary source which definitively pins down how the battalion was formed and which officers were serving in which companies. The order of battle and deployment presented here has not to my knowledge ever been published before, and is based on a series of passing references in the Intelligence Branch Narrative Accounts, Army HQ, Simla 1881 and Lt. M. L. O'Donel's account, held by the Royal Gloucestershire, Berkshire and Wiltshire (RGBW) Regiment Museum, Salisbury, coupled of course with processes of elimination and deduction.
    Lt. Lonergan's narrative account tells us that he was in C Company which was second from the right, with B Company to its right. Unfortunately Lonergan does not name his company commander. Lt. Lynch's narrative tells us that he was in D Company,

which was deployed as the centre of five and was commanded by Capt. McMath. Quarry, we know, commanded G Company with the baggage, with Mr Bray to assist and Mr Melliss joining later. This means that F and H Companies were on the left of the firing line. Beresford-Peirse is independently corroborated as commanding the left-flank company, and says in his own narrative account that he was OC H Company. All this serves to confirm that the companies were deployed in their lettered sequence 'by the right': hence B, C, D, F, H. Lt. O'Donel's reconstruction written in Kandahar on 13 September 1880 is not in itself a primary source but is clearly based on his personal conversations with survivors. It recounts that the company 'thrown back firing to the right' was Cullen's company. Assuming, logically, that this must be the right-flank company, then by cross-referring to Lonergan we can deduce that Cullen commanded B Company. This leaves Garratt and Roberts to be assigned. O'Donel tells us that the companies on the right, naming B and C, were under Cullen and Roberts. If Cullen is commanding B, then Roberts is Lonergan's company commander in C Company. Garratt then must have been commanding the only company left – F Company.

38. Quoted in Ian Knight, *Marching to the Drums*, p. 134.
39. *Ibid.*, p. 134.
40. F. L. Petre, *The Royal Berkshire Regiment.*
41. Lt. Lynch, *Intelligence Branch Narrative Account.*
42. Lt. O'Donel's Account, RGBW Museum, Salisbury.
43. Lt. Lonergan, *Intelligence Branch Narrative Account.*
44. O'Donel, *op. cit.*
45. Maxwell, *My God Maiwand*, p. 132.
46. O'Donel, *op. cit.*
47. *Official History*, pp. 512–13.
48. *Ibid.*, p. 511.
49. *Ibid.*, p. 511.
50. Quoted in Maxwell, *My God Maiwand*, p. 143.
51. Mayne, *Personal Account.*
52. Quoted in Knight, *Marching to the Drums*, p. 134.
53. O'Donel, *op. cit.*
54. *Ibid.*
55. Maxwell, *My God Maiwand*, p. 159.
56. *Ibid.*, p. 158.
57. Lt. Geoghegan, *Intelligence Branch Narrative Account.*
58. In line the eight companies of a battalion are covered off sequentially from No. 1 (A) Company on the right flank, through to No. 8 (H) Company on the left. When the order to form square is given, the battalion forms four ranks from two, ordinarily a quick and easy change effected by the odd-numbered men in the front rank taking one pace forward, followed by a sidestep to the right, while their rear-rank counterparts take one pace back and a sidestep. Nos. 4 and 5 Companies close up the resultant intervals by dressing to the right, but in essence stand fast as the front face. Nos. 2 and 3 Coys about turn and then begin right wheeling through 90 degrees. When they have completed the pivot, they halt and again about turn so as to face outwards as the square's right face. Nos. 6 and 7 Companies execute a mirror image of the evolutions performed by Nos. 2 and 3 Companies, substituting a left wheel for a right wheel, to become the left face. The rear face is occupied by the two flank companies, Nos. 1 and 8, who with the furthest distance to cover, will double round to the rear of the formation under the direction of their company officers. With a certain amount of jostling back and forth and some shouting from the sergeants, the battalion is ready to 'receive cavalry'.

59. *Official History*, p. 516.
60. Beresford-Peirse, *Intelligence Branch Narrative Account*.
61. Quoted in Knight, *Marching to the Drums*, p. 139.
62. Maj. Hogg, *Intelligence Branch Narrative Account*.
63. Quoted in Knight, *Marching to the Drums*, p. 139.
64. *Official History*, p. 517.
65. Mayne, *Personal Account*.
66. O'Donel, *op. cit.*
67. *Official History*, p. 515.
68. O'Donel, *op. cit.*
69. Shadbolt, *The Afghan Campaign*, pp. 136–7.
70. Maxwell, *My God Maiwand*, p. 169.
71. According to Lt. Lynch (*Intelligence Branch Narrative Account*), the water in the ditch was two feet deep.
72. Shadbolt, *The Afghan Campaign*, p. 89.
73. O'Donel, *op. cit.*
74. *Ibid.*
75. *Ibid.*
76. *Ibid.*
77. Later in the day, some way down the line of the retreat, Lynch would be transferred to a *doolie* by 2nd Lt. Melliss.
78. O'Donel, *op. cit.*
79. *Official History*, p. 520.
80. Shadbolt, *The Afghan Campaign*, p. 111, quoting General Primrose's official report.
81. Collis's account quoted in Knight, *Marching to the Drums*, p. 140
82. Capt. Slade, *Intelligence Branch Narrative Account*.
83. *Official History*, p. 527.
84. Burrows to the Assistant Adjutant-General, Kandahar Field Force, 30 August 1880.

Chapter 3: 'Floreat Etona' (pages 147–88)

1. See John Nixon, *The Complete Story of the Transvaal*, pp. 63–78.
2. Not a reference to his stature but to his character: *slim* is an Afrikaans word meaning cunning or canny.
3. The Boer population of the Transvaal in 1880 was about 40,000 souls. On that basis a universal call-out of medically fit males between 16 and 60 would have produced around 7,000 men. In addition the *uitlander* population was about 5,000 strong, mostly but by no means universally British. Some of the *uitlanders* had bought farms but about two-thirds of them lived in the towns and were in business or trade. This marked division between town and country, Boer and Briton, agriculture and business, modernity and tradition would continue over the next two decades and would be one of the underlying causes of the Boer War.
4. See Charles Norris-Newman, *With the Boers in the Transvaal*, pp. 123–4 for de Beer's statement.
5. Anstruther refers to de Beer as 'the interpreter' because after the battle he translated for Frans Joubert.
6. Lady Bellairs, *The Transvaal War 1880–81*, p. 84. Though published in his wife's name, it is obvious that this is the work of Colonel Bellairs himself.
7. Departmental rank equating to lieutenant.
8. See Norris-Newman, *With the Boers*, pp. 121–2.
9. *Ibid.*, pp. 126–8 for Capt. Lambart's eyewitness account of the Elliott murder.
10. Brownlow's report put it at 6.00 a.m.

11. Colley's official despatch of 1 February 1881.
12. 1st KDG Record of Service: Maj. & Bvt. Lt. Col. W. V. Brownlow, *A Short Account of the Part Taken in the Boer War of 1881 by the Depot Troop, 1st King's Dragoon Guards.*
13. See Norris-Newman, *With the Boers*, p. 343.
14. Personal accounts by Madden and Venables appear in Norris-Newman. However, he has accidentally transposed them; what he suggests is Venables's account is in fact Madden's and vice versa.
15. Colley to Childers, 12 February 1881.
16. Company officers were: C Company – Capt. Smith, 2nd Lts. O'Connell, Howard-Vyse, Thistlethwayte; G Company – Lt McGrigor, 2nd Lt. Haworth; H Company – Capt. Thurlow, Lt. Baker, 2nd Lt Pixley; I Company – Lt Garrett, 2nd Lt. Beaumont; K Company – Lt Ryder, 2nd Lt. Marling. P. S. Marling would win the VC at Tamai three years later and subsequently fought with MICR in the Nile expedition.
17. Not to be confused with Lt. Ian Hamilton.
18. Colley to Childers, 12 February 1881.
19. See Norris-Newman for Carter's accounts of Ingogo and Majuba.
20. The remark was not literally true but reflected Parsons's reading of the situation at the time.
21. He subsequently died of his wounds.
22. Brownlow, *op. cit.*
23. Colley to Childers, 12 February 1881.
24. As a result of the officer casualties sustained at Laing's Nek, Hornby had returned to his regiment from his duties with Brownlow's mounted squadron. It is possible, given Brownlow's fury over the performance of his second troop, that there was bad feeling between them.
25. Colley to Childers, 12 February 1881.
26. Oficers killed were Lts. Garrett and O'Connell; wounded 2nd Lts. Haworth, Pixley and Thistlethwayte; missing were the adjutant and 7 men drowned and 1 man captured.
27. Figures cited by Norris-Newman, though his annex listing Boer casualties by name shows only 9 killed and 6 wounded.

Chapter 4: Hill of Doves (pages 189–218)

1. Henderson, *The Science of War*, p. 411.
2. Relayed to London from Pietermaritzburg in Deputy Governor of Natal to Secretary of State for the Colonies, 19 February 1881.
3. Secretary of State for the Colonies to Deputy Governor of Natal (for onwards relay to Colley), 19 February 1881.
4. FM Sir Evelyn Wood VC, *From Midshipman to Field Marshal.*
5. Colley to Kruger, 21 February 1881.
6. Hamilton gives 9.30 p.m.
7. Thurlow himself and Lts. Charles Pigott and Howard Vyse. Pigott will reappear in Chapter 6, serving with the Gordon Relief Expedition as a captain.
8. Gen. Sir Ian Hamilton, *Listening for the Drums*, p. 134.
9. Hamilton's memory fails him here; his left rested on the naval brigade; the 58th were on his right.
10. A commissary was the departmental equivalent of a major.
11. Hamilton, *Listening for the Drums*, p. 134.
12. Account of Surgeon Edward Mahon RN, see Norris-Newman, *With the Boers*, p. 291.
13. Hamilton, *Listening for the Drums*, pp. 134–5.
14. *Ibid.*, p. 135.

15. John Cameron, 'The Fight on Majuba Hill', *Illustrated London News*, 24 April 1881.
16. Hamilton, *Listening for the Drums*, p. 137.
17. *Ibid.*, p. 137.
18. Quoted in Butler, *The Life of Sir George Pomeroy-Colley*, p. 367.
18. Sub-Lt. Augustus Scott, see Norris-Newman, *With the Boers*, p. 291.
19. *Ibid.*, p. 215.
20. *Ibid.*, p. 215.
21. Sir Evelyn Wood VC, *British Battles on Land and Sea*, Vol. II, p. 843.
22. Hamilton, *Listening for the Drums*, p. 144.
23. Joseph Lehmann, *The First Boer War*, p. 250.
24. Lt. Col. Stewart. Maj. Fraser was also captured but escaped.
25. Cdr. Romilly died at Mount Prospect on 2 March.
26. Capt. Anton and Lt. Miller were attached to the 58th for the operation.
27. Surg. Landon and Surg.-Maj. Cornish both died of their wounds.
28. Wood, *From Midshipman to Field Marshal*, Vol. II, p. 112.
29. Hamilton, *Listening for the Drums*, p. 130.

Chapter 5: White Pashas (pages 219–59)

1. O'Donovan to Sir John Robinson, quoted in F. Lauriston Bullard, *Famous War Correspondents*, p. 231.
2. On 26 June 1879.
3. For the vessels of the flotilla, their captains, tonnage and armament see Charles Royle, *The Egyptian Campaigns 1882–1899*, pp. 65–8 and Beresford, *The Memoirs of Admiral Lord Charles Beresford*, Vol. I, pp. 186–7.
4. Ashburnham would receive a knighthood after Tel-el-Kebir.
5. With only four sub-units in a battalion, Egyptian infantry companies were often around 200 strong.
6. Col. H. E. Colvile, *History of the Sudan Campaign*, Part 1, p. 7.
7. Also today rendered as 'Baqqarah'.
8. Today rendered as 'al-Ubayyid'.
9. *Fellaheen* was how Egyptian conscript infantry, recruited from the peasant or *fellah* class, were referred to.
10. Hicks had begun his service in the HEIC Bombay Fusiliers. He was now late of the Bombay Staff Corps indicating service on the staff or with native regiments.
11. Bennet Burleigh, *Desert Warfare: Being the Chronicle of the Eastern Soudan Campaign*.
12. Or *Farik* in the Egyptian service.
13. Colvile, *History of the Sudan Campaign*, Part 1, pp. 13–14.
14. One British colonel (Farquhar); one German major (Baron Alfred von Seckendorff); three British majors (Warner, Massey and Evans); two Austrian captains (Herlth and Mattiaga); and one British lieutenant (Morris Brody or Brady, formerly a sergeant-major in the RHA. The surgeons were Douloglu (a Greek) and Rosenberg (British). They are listed in their Egyptian ranks which, certainly in the case of the British officers, are mostly one or two grades senior to their former British Army ranks.
15. Thomas Archer, *The War in Egypt and the Soudan*, Vol. II, pp. 242–3.
16. Quoted in Fergus Nicol, *The Sword of the Prophet*, p. 151.
17. There is a possibility that the battle was fought on 4 November.
18. Also rendered as 'Shaykan'.
19. Colvile, *History of the Sudan Campaign*, Part 1, p. 18.
20. Earl of Cromer (formerly Sir Evelyn Baring), *Modern Egypt*, Vol. I, Part 3, p. 397.
21. *Ibid.*, pp. 399–400.
22. *Ibid.*, p. 400.

23. *Ibid.*, p. 398.
24. *Ibid.*, p. 401.
25. *Ibid.*, p. 404.
26. For biographies of Burnaby see Michael Alexander, *The True Blue* and Thomas White, *The Life of Colonel Fred Burnaby*.
27. More properly rendered today as Rahman Mansur az Zubayr.
28. For comprehensive coverage of the Zubeir issue see Cromer's *Modern Egypt*.
29. Colvile, *History of the Sudan Campaign*, Part 1, p. 19.
30. See Alexander, *True Blue*, pp. 155–8 for Burnaby's account of the battle.
31. Archer, *The War in Egypt and the Soudan*, Vol. II, p. 261.
32. Approximate casualties by unit were: European police 2 & 35; mounted gendarmerie 24; Turkish *bashi-bazouk* cavalry 6; Turkish infantry 16 & 352; Senhit Sudanese battalion 10 & 268; Massowah Sudanese battalion 13 & 234; Alexandria gendarmerie battalion 15 & 380; Cairo gendarmerie battalion 16 & 280; Zubeir's irregulars 17 & 414; Egyptian artillery 8 & 101; headquarters staff 12 & 30. Archer, Vol. II, p. 263. These figures add to 109 and 2,124; the totals of 112 and 2,250 given in the text are from Baker's report.
33. Cromer, *Modern Egypt*, Vol. I, Part 3, p. 404.
34. *Ibid.*, p. 405.
35. Wood to Wolseley, 28 January 1884, quoted in Wood's *Winnowed Memories*.
36. Sir Reginald Wingate (who was present), *Wingate of the Sudan*, London, 1955. Wood makes no mention of the incident in *From Midshipman to Field Marshal*, but in a letter to Wolseley dated 28 January 1884 wrote, 'He [Gordon] made himself excessively pleasant, and I think was happy here, except for an hour or two, when he wanted to call ______ [insert 'Zubeir'] Pasha out.'
37. Stewart to Cromer, 13 February 1884, quoted in *Modern Egypt*, Vol. I, Part 3, p. 469.
38. By some accounts Khartoum's population had dwindled to around 14,000 by the time of its fall. It appears to have been a commonplace occurrence for people to leave the defences and throw themselves on the mercy of the Mahdi.
39. Rendered as 'Fort Bourre' in Gordon's Journal.
40. According to Gordon's Journal, by 30 October the garrison of the North Fort had been reinforced to 1,300 including a strong contingent of Shaigiya irregulars.
41. Gordon's Journal.
42. See Maj. Gen. Henry Brackenbury, *The River Column*, pp. 224–34 for comprehensive coverage of the *Abbas* disaster. See also Colvile, *Official History*, Vol I, pp. 97–101.
43. Gordan's Journal shows that *Safieh* and *Mansoura* arrived back at Khartoum on 22 September with a loss of 3 killed and 4 wounded.
44. Gordon's Journal.
45. See Colvile, *History of the Sudan Campaign*, Part 1, pp. 27–43 for the debate over the choice of route, including reports by Vice Admiral Lord John Hay, C-in-C Mediterranean, and a joint report by McNeill, Buller and Butler. See also Commander Hammill's Report on the Nile Route in Colvile, Appendix O, pp. 141–72.
46. *Ibid.*, pp. 61–7.
47. *Ibid.*, see 'Report on Canadian Voyageurs', Part 1, Appendix 4, pp. 185–8.

Chapter 6: Desert Column (pages 260–326)

1. See Count Gleichen, *With the Camel Corps up the Nile*, Appendix 1, pp. 309–13, for organization of the Camel Corps.
2. Amongst Poe's subalterns was one Lt. Charles Townshend, later of Chitral Fort and Kut-al-Amara fame.
3. See Anglesey, *History of the British Cavalry*, Vol. 3, pp. 344–6 for further detail.

4. Interestingly Beresford's services had also been pressed upon Wolseley by the Prince of Wales. Unlike Stanley Clarke, he was able to win the general's confidence.
5. A veteran of Tel-el-Kebir.
6. Gleichen, *With the Camel Corps*, pp. 6–7.
7. The RMLI company did not receive an issue of the brown leather waistbelt, pouch and bandolier sported by their comrades and paraded instead in the conventional infantry pattern white waistbelt and ammunition pouches, as did the Royal Sussex. It is not altogether clear whether the Sussex received an issue of riding breeches and puttees in time for their new role as camel-borne troops. On balance it would seem unlikely.
8. Knight, *Marching to the Drums*, p. 221.
9. Referred to as the Yataghan bayonet.
10. Gleichen quotes the record time achieved in rehearsal as 1 minute 20 seconds; *With the Camel Corps*, p. 57.
11. *Ibid.*, p. 64.
12. *Ibid.*, p. 106.
13. *Ibid.*, p. 24.
14. *Ibid.*, p. 38.
15. Col. Sir Percival Marling VC, *Rifleman and Hussar*, journal for 2 January.
16. Colvile, *History of the Sudan Campaign*, Part 2, p. 5.
17. See Gleichen's sketch in *With the Camel Corps*.
18. Journal Entry for 7 January 1885, quoted in Adrian Preston, *In Relief of Gordon*, p. 108.
19. See Colvile, *History of the Sudan Campaign*, Part 2, pp. 6–10, for the full text of Wolseley's orders to Stewart, Wilson and Beresford respectively.
20. Maj. Dickson (Royals), Lt. Stuart Wortley (KRRC) and a third officer to be nominated at Metemmeh.
21. Col. Sir Charles Wilson, *From Korti to Khartum*, Appendix V, pp. 300–3.
22. Sir Redvers Buller, serving as Wolseley's Chief of Staff, had proposed appointing Burnaby to command the cavalry with General Earle's River Column but had been overruled.
23. Gleichen, *With the Camel Corps*, p. 188.
24. Beresford, *Memoirs*, Vol. I, p. 258.
25. Gleichen, *With the Camel Corps*, p. 124.
26. Bennet Burleigh's account, quoted verbatim in Anon., *The English in Egypt*.
27. Each of the companies was about 60 strong.
28. Burleigh, quoted in *The English in Egypt*, p. 420.
29. *Ibid.*, p. 419
30. Though Burleigh gives 7.35 a.m.
31. John Edward Leveson Jervis, the 4th Viscount St Vincent, 16th Lancers, had seen extensive service in Africa. He was a veteran of the Zulu War, the Transvaal Rebellion and the Egyptian campaign. He had been at both Ulundi and Tel-el-Kebir and had been twice mentioned in despatches. The family seat was at Norton Disney near Newark.
32. Gleichen, *With the Camel Corps*, p. 126.
33. Dawson's account, 'The Desert March', first published in the *Quarterly Review*, 1886, also found in Thomas Archer's *The War in Egypt and the Soudan*, Vol. IV, pp. 27–9.
34. Marling, *Rifleman and Hussar*, journal for 17 January 1885.
35. See Wilson's sketch in *From Korti to Khartum*, p. 27.
36. Sudanese shields tended to be manufactured from crocodile, rhino or elephant hide. Although such items were not carried at Abu Klea, they were popular with the Beja.
37. Dawson, *The Desert March*.
38. Marling, *Rifleman to Hussar*, journal for 17 January 1885.

39. Gleichen specifically identifies the man as a member of KRRC.
40. Lt. Col. Hon. Reginald Talbot, 'The Battle of Abu Klea', *Nineteenth Century*, January 1886.
41. Knight, *Marching to the Drums*, p. 224.
42. Not to be confused with Maj. Hon. G. H. Gough of MICR.
43. Talbot, 'The Battle of Abu Klea'. As the officer commanding HCR he is an authoritative source.
44. Beresford, *Memoirs*, Vol. I, p. 263.
45. Talbot, 'The Battle of Abu Klea'.
46. Burleigh, quoted in *The English in Egypt*, pp. 424–5.
47. Not to be confused with Capt. Charles Berkeley 'Bloody-Minded' Pigott of MICR.
48. Wilson, *From Korti to Khartum*, pp. 28–9.
49. Burleigh, quoted in *The English in Egypt*, p. 425.
50. Major Hon. Ralph Legge Pomeroy, *History of the 5th Dragoon Guards*.
51. Carmichael's wife had died in childbirth only a short time before. The orphaned infant was awarded a state annuity of £20 following Abu Klea.
52. Beresford, *Memoirs*, Vol. I, p. 265.
53. Royle, *The Egyptian Campaigns*, p. 345.
54. Quoted in Knight, *Marching to the Drums*, p. 226.
55. Col. F. G. Burnaby (HQ Staff/Blues); Maj. W. A. Gough (HCR/Royals); Maj. W. H. Atherton (HCR/5th DG); Maj. L. M. Carmichael (HCR/5th L); Capt. J. W. W. Darley (HCR/4th DG); Lt. R. Wolfe (HCR/Royal Scots Greys); Lt. C. W. A. Law (HCR/4th DG); Cdr. A. Pigott and Lt. R. E. De Lisle RN (Naval Bde).
56. Maj. Hon. G. H. Gough (MICR/14th H) severely; Maj. J. B. B. Dickson (Intelligence Staff/Royals) severely; Capt. Lord St Vincent (HCR/16th L) mortally; Capt. Lord Airlie (Brigade-Major/10th H) slightly; Surg. J. Magill (GCR/AMD) severely; Lt. J. D. Guthrie (RA) mortally; Lt. R. J. Beech (HCR/2nd LG) slightly; Lt. H. Costello (HCR/5th L) slightly; Lt. Lyall (RA) dangerously.
57. See Wright, *The Life of Colonel Fred Burnaby*, pp. 298–306.
58. The incident is recounted in Wilson's *From Korti to Khartum*, but the officer is not named. It is possibly Beresford, who describes a similar incident in his memoirs.
59. Marling, in a letter to his father, cited in James Grant, *Recent British Battles on Land and Sea*.
60. Colvile, *History of the Sudan Campaign*, p. 23.
61. Frederic Villiers, *Peaceful Personalities and Warriors Bold*, pp. 184–5.
62. Wilson, *From Korti to Khartum*, p. 64.
63. Later the Earl of Dundonald. See Chapter 7.
64. Wilson, *From Korti to Khartum*, p. 68.
65. Burleigh, quoted in *The English in Egypt*, p. 431.
66. Wilson, *From Korti to Khartum*, p. 76–7.
67. Somerset was the third son of the 8th Duke of Beaufort. In 1889, whilst employed as the head of the Prince of Wales's stables, Somerset was forced to flee to the continent after being implicated in a notorious rent-boy scandal known as the Cleveland Street affair.
68. Marling, *Rifleman and Hussar*, journal for 20 January 1885.
69. *Ibid.*, Vol II, p. 282.
70. Wilson, *From Korti to Khartum*, p. 167.
71. See Wilson, *From Korti to Khartum*, p. 132–3, for a description of the steamers' 'turrets' and other defences.
72. See Beresford's *Memoirs* Vol. II, pp. 295–305 for the most important participant account.

Chapter 7: 'Sold by a Damned Gunner' (pages 327–65)

1. See Elizabeth Longford, *Jameson's Raid: The Prelude to the Boer* War, for detailed analysis of Chamberlain's role.
2. In the presidential election of 1893 Joubert polled 7,246 votes to Kruger's 7,911.
3. Julian Symons, *Buller's Campaign*, p. 92.
4. For Hely-Hutchinson's account of the meeting with White see Leo Amery's *Times History of the War in South Africa*, Vol. II, pp. 128–9. The tiny size of the electorate is noteworthy.
5. For the official account of Talana Hill and the subsequent retreat see Maj. Gen. Sir Frederick Maurice, *History of the War in South Africa 1899–1902*, Vol. I, pp. 123–50. See also Amery, *Times History*, Vol. II, pp. 141–74.
6. See Maurice, Vol. I, pp. 157–71, and Amery, *Times History*, Vol. II, pp. 175–211 and 332–6.
7. Rhodes was not long back from the Sudan. He had been wounded early in the day at Omdurman.
8. See Maurice, Vol. I, pp. 270–2 and Amery, *Times History*, Vol. II, pp. 314–16.
9. See *London to Ladysmith* for Churchill's personal account of his adventures.
10. See Amery's *Times History*, Vol. II, Ch 7 pp. 265–98 for the decision to split the 1st Army Corps. See also Maurice, Vol. I, p. 200, for the text of Buller's 4 November notification to London of his intention to do so.
11. See Maurice, Vol. I, pp. 214–15 for detailed composition of Methuen's force.
12. *Ibid.*, pp. 218–27.
13. *Ibid.*, pp. 229–42.
14. *Ibid.*, pp. 243–60.
15. Sir George Douglas, *The Life of Major General Wauchope*.
16. An ailing Joubert died in Pretoria on 27 March 1900.
17. Zuid Afrikaanische Republiek Politie – the Transvaal Police.
18. Maurice, Vol. I, pp. 285–303.
19. *Ibid.*, pp. 316–29.
20. He would be succeeded by 'Fighting Mac' whose career had continued to flourish since Majuba.
21. Maurice, Vol. I, p. 339.
22. At the time of the Nile campaign he had yet to succeed to his later title and was known as Lord Cochrane.
23. See Leo Amery, *Times History*, Vol. II, pp. 436–7. The order was physically signed on Clery's behalf by his Assistant Adjutant-General, Colonel Bruce Hamilton – the late Sir George Colley's brother-in-law.
24. The battalion had originally been with Symons at Dundee but had been withdrawn south of the Tugela before the siege of Ladysmith tightened.
25. Boy Dunn was singled out by the Army as one of the heroes of Colenso and on being invalided home was presented to the Queen at Osborne House. She gave him an inscribed silver bugle to replace the one he lost when he was wounded.
26. A brigade-division, commanded by a lieutenant colonel RA, was in effect a composite artillery regiment consisting of three otherwise independent batteries, each of six guns, commanded by majors.
27. Some sources say 700 yards.
28. Bennet Burleigh, *The Natal Campaign*, p. 219.
29. Maurice, Vol. I, p. 361.
30. Amery, Vol. II, p. 451.
31. In 1880 Hamilton had been Primrose's ADC at Kandahar.
32. Maurice, Vol. I, p. 366.

33. *Ibid.*, p. 374.
34. Amery, Vol. II, pp. 456–7.
35. Quoted in Thomas Pakenham, *The Boer War*, p. 240.

Chapter 8: 'That Complete Shambles' (pages 366–94)

1. Maurice, Vol. I, p. 377.
2. See Amery, Vol. II, pp. 459–64 for scathing criticism of Buller on the subject of cipher No. 87.
3. Maurice, Vol. I, p. 379.
4. Buller to Warren, 15 January 1900.
5. See Maurice, Vol. II, Appendix 9 (C), p. 632.
6. Buller to Lansdowne, 30 January 1900.
7. For 'Force Orders by Sir C. Warren, 22 January 1900', see Maurice, Vol. II, Appendix 9 (L) p. 635.
8. Woodgate had commanded the 1st Battalion.
9. For 'Brigade Orders by Maj. Gen. Woodgate, 23 January 1900', see Maurice, Vol. II, Appendix 9 (O), pp. 637–8.
10. For 'Attack Orders by Maj. Gen. Coke, Commanding Right Attack, 23 January 1900', see Maurice, Vol. II, Appendix 9 (N), p. 637.
11. Churchill, *London to Ladysmith.*
12. A damning admission by a signals officer. Regulations required that all signals be written by an officer before being handed to a signaller for transmission.
13. Maurice, Vol. II, Appendix 10 (B), p. 639.
14. A week after the battle Crofton wrote to his brigade headquarters, 'I beg most strongly to protest against the message reputed to me from Spion Kop on the 24th, stating "All is lost". Such a message was never sent by me, nor did it ever enter my thoughts to send such a message, as the circumstances did not call for it.'
15. Maurice, Vol. II, Appendix 10 (C), p. 639.
16. *Ibid.*, p. 388.
17. *Ibid.*, p. 394.
18. *Ibid.*, pp. 394–5.
19. Churchill, *London to Ladysmith.*
20. Maurice, Vol. II, Appendix 10 (E), p. 640.
21. *Ibid.*, Appendix 10 (J), p. 642. Churchill had by now acquired a volunteer commission in the South African Light Horse.
22. Churchill, *London to Ladysmith.*
23. Extracted from Maurice, Vol. II, Appendix 2, p. 597.
24. Buller to Lansdowne, 30 January 1900.
25. John Atkins, *The Relief of Ladysmith*, p. 237.

Epilogue: School of Hard Knocks (pages 395–405)

1. Burleigh, *The Natal Campaign*, p. 333.
2. See Ian Beckett, *Rain of Lead*, for a comprehensive modern account of the siege of Potchefstroom.
3. It is interesting that Lee was Wolseley's hero. Whilst serving in Canada, Wolseley had visited the Confederate Army in the autumn of 1862, not long after Antietam, and interviewed both Lee and Jackson. He went on to write extensively about the American Civil War.
4. Col. Leigh Maxwell, *The Ashanti Ring*, p. 236.
5. Atkins, *The Relief of Ladysmith*, p. 225.

Bibliography

Alexander, Michael, *The True Blue: The Life and Adventures of Colonel Fred Burnaby*, London, 1957

Allen, Bernard, *Gordon and the Sudan*, London, 1931

Anon., *The English in Egypt*, London & New York, nd

Amery, L. S. *The Times History of the War in South Africa 1899–1902*, Vols. II & III, London, 1902, 1905

Anglesey, Marquess of, *A History of the British Cavalry 1816–1919*, Vols. II–IV, London, 1975, 1982, 1986

Archer, Thomas, *The War in Egypt and the Soudan* (4 vols.), London, 1887

Arthur, Sir George (ed.), *The Letters of Lord and Lady Wolseley 1870–1911*, London, 1923

Asher, Michael, *Khartoum: The Ultimate Imperial Adventure*, London, 2005

Atkins, John, *The Relief of Ladysmith*, London, 1900

Baker, Anne, *A Question of Honour: The Life of Lieutenant General Valentine Baker Pasha*, London, 1996

Barnett, Correlli, *Britain and her Army 1509–1970: A Military, Political and Social History*, London, 1970

Barthorp, Michael, *Afghan Wars and the North-West Frontier 1839–1947*, London, 1982

———, *War on the Nile: Britain, Egypt and the Sudan 1882–1898*, Poole, 1984

Beckett, Ian F. W., *The Victorians at War*, London, 2003

Beckett, Ian H. W., *Rain of Lead: The Siege and Surrender of the British at Potchefstroom*, London, 2001

Bellairs, Lady (ed.), *The Transvaal War 1880–81*, London, 1885 [It is clear that this book was actually written by Colonel William Bellairs.]

Beresford, Lord Charles, *The Memoirs of Admiral Lord Charles Beresford*, London, 1914

Bond, Brian, *The Victorian Army and the Staff College, 1854–1914*, London, 1972

Brackenbury, Maj. Gen. Henry, CB, *The River Column*, London, 1885

Brownlow, Maj. & Bvt. Lt. Col. W. V., *A Short Account of the Part Taken in the Boer War of 1881 by the Depot Troop, 1st King's Dragoon Guards*, Canterbury, 1882

Bullard, F. Lauriston, *Famous War Correspondents*, London, 1914

Burleigh, Bennet, *Desert Warfare: Being the Chronicle of the Eastern Soudan Campaign*, London, 1884

———, *The Natal Campaign*, London, 1900

Butler, Lt. Gen. Sir William, *The Life of Sir George Pomeroy-Colley*, London, 1899

Cameron, John, 'The Fight on Majuba Hill', *Illustrated London News*, 24 April 1881

Childs, Lewis, *Ladysmith: Colenso, Spion Kop, Hlangwane, Tugela*, London, 1998

———, *Ladysmith: The Siege*, London, 1998

Chisholm, Ruari, *Ladysmith*, South Africa, 1979

Churchill, Winston, *London to Ladysmith & Ian Hamilton's March*, London, 1900

Colvile, Col. H. E., *History of the Sudan Campaign* (3 vols.), compiled in the Intelligence Division of the War Office, London, 1889

Creswicke, Louis, *South Africa and the Transvaal War*, Edinburgh, 1900

Cromer, Earl of, *Modern Egypt* (2 vols.) London, 1908

Douglas, Sir George, Bart., *The Life of Major General Wauchope*, London, 1904.

Dunlop, Col. J. K., *The Development of the British Army 1899–1914*, London, 1938

Duxbury, George, *David and Goliath: The First War of Independence 1880–1881*, SA Museum of Military History, 1981

———, 'The Battle of Bronkhorstspruit', *SA Military History Journal*, Vol. 5, No. 2, December 1980

———, 'The Battle of Laingsnek', *SA Military History Journal*, Vol. 5, No. 2, December 1980

———, 'The Battle of Schuinshoogte', *SA Military History Journal*, Vol. 5, No. 2, December 1980

———, 'The Battle of Majuba', *SA Military History Journal*, Vol. 5, No. 2, December 1980

Farwell, Byron, *Queen Victoria's Little Wars*, London, 1973

———, *The Great Boer War*, London, 1977

———, *For Queen and Country: A Social History of the Victorian and Edwardian Army*, London, 1981

Ferguson, Niall, *Empire: How Britain made the Modern World*, London, 2003

Fortescue, Hon. J. W., *A History of the British Army*, Vols. XII & XIII, London, 1927, 1930

German General Staff, *The War in South Africa*, translated by Col. W. H. H. Waters, London, 1904

Gleichen, Count, *With the Camel Corps up the Nile*, London, 1888

Gordon, M. A., *Letters of General C. G. Gordon to his Sister*, London, 1888

Grant, James, *Recent British Battles on Land and Sea*, London, 1900

Gurney, Lt. Col. Russell, *History of the Northamptonshire Regiment 1742–1934*, Aldershot, 1935

Hall, Darrell, *Halt! Action Front! With Colonel Long at Colenso*, South Africa, 1999

Hallows, Ian S., *Regiments and Corps of the British Army*, London, 1991

Hamilton, Gen. Sir Ian, *Listening for the Drums*, London, 1944

Hanna, Col. H. B., *The Second Afghan War 1878–79–80: Its Causes, Its Conduct, and Its Consequences* (3 vols.), London, 1904

Hare, Maj. Gen. Sir Steuart, *The Annals of the King's Royal Rifle Corps*, London, 1929

Headlam, Cecil (ed.), *The Milner Papers*, London, 1931

Henderson, Col. G. F. R. (ed. Capt. Neill Malcolm), *The Science of War: A Collection of Essays and Lectures 1891–1903*, London, 1908

Hensman, Howard, *The Afghan War of 1879–80*, London, 1882

Hillegas, Howard C., *With the Boer Forces*, London, 1900

Intelligence Branch, Army Headquarters India, *Reports and Narratives of officers who were engaged at the battle of Maiwand*, Simla, 1881

———, *The Second Afghan War 1878–80: Official Account*, London, 1908; this is the public version of the Indian Army's original confidential 2-volume report – see below under 'Quartermaster-General's Office'

James, David, *Lord Roberts*, London, 1954

James, Lawrence, *The Savage Wars: British Campaigns in Africa 1870–1920*, London, 1985

Knight, Ian, *Marching to the Drums*, London, 1999

Kochanski, Halik, *Sir Garnet Wolseley: Victorian Hero*, London, 1999

Kruger, Rayne, *Goodbye Dolly Grey: The Story of the Boer War*, London, 1959

Laband, John, *The Transvaal Rebellion: The First Boer War 1880–1881*, Harlow, 2005

Latham, Capt. H. B., 'E/B RHA at Maiwand', *Journal of the Royal Artillery*, 1928

Lehmann, Joseph, *The First Boer War*, London, 1972

Longford, Elizabeth, *Jameson's Raid: The Prelude to the Boer War*, London, 1960

MacMichael, H. A., *The Tribes of Northern and Central Kordofan*, Cambridge, 1912

Marling, Col. Sir Percival, VC, *Rifleman and Hussar*, London, 1931

Marlowe, John, *Mission to Khartum: The Apotheosis of General Gordon*, London, 1969

Mason, Philip, *A Matter of Honour: An Account of the Indian Army its Officers and Men*, London, 1974

Maurice, Maj. Gen. Sir J. F., *History of the War in South Africa 1899–1902*, London, 1906–1910

———, *Military History of the Campaign of 1882 in Egypt*, War Office, 1887

Maurice, Maj. Gen. Sir J. F. & Sir George Arthur, *The Life of Lord Wolseley*, London, 1924

Maxwell, Col. Leigh, *My God Maiwand! Operations of the South Afghanistan Field Force 1878–80*, London, 1979

———, *The Ashanti Ring: Sir Garnet Wolseley's Campaigns 1870–1882*, London, 1985

Menepes, Mortimer & Dorothy, *War Impressions*, London, 1901

Miller, Stephen M., *Lord Methuen and the British Army: Failure and Redemption in South Africa*, London, 1999

Myatt, Frederick, *The British Infantry 1660–1945: The Evolution of a Fighting Force*, Poole, 1983

Nicoll, Fergus, *The Sword of the Prophet*, Stroud, 2004

Nixon, John, *The Complete Story of the Transvaal*, London, 1885

Norris-Newman, Charles, *With the Boers in the Transvaal and Orange Free State in 1880–81*, London, 1882

Pakenham, Thomas, *The Boer War*, London, 1979

Petre, F. Loraine, *The Royal Berkshire Regiment*, Reading, 1925

Pomeroy, Maj. Hon. Ralph Legge, *History of the 5th Dragoon Guards*, London, 1924

Powell, Geoffrey, *Buller: A Scapegoat – A Life of General Sir Redvers Buller* VC, London, 1994

Preston, Adrian (ed.), *In Relief of Gordon: Lord Wolseley's Campaign Journal of the Khartoum Relief Expedition 1884–1885*, London, 1967

Quartermaster-General's Office, Army Headquarters India, *The Second Afghan War, Compiled and collated by and under the orders of Maj. Gen. Sir C. M. MacGregor*, confidential report in 2 vols., Simla, 1885

Rait, Robert S., *The Life of Field Marshal Sir Frederick Paul Haines*, London, 1911

Ransford, Oliver, *The Battle of Majuba Hill: The First Boer War*, London, 1967

———, *The Battle of Spion Kop*, London, 1969

Reitz, Col. Deneys, *Commando*, London, 1929

Roberts, FM Lord, VC, *Forty-One Years in India*, London, 1905

Robson, Brian, 'Maiwand, 27th July 1880', *Journal of the Society for Army Historical Research*, 1973

———, *The Road to Kabul: The Second Afghan War 1878–1881*, London, 1986

———, *Fuzzy Wuzzy: The Campaigns in the Eastern Sudan 1884–85*, Tunbridge Wells, 1993

Royle, Charles, *The Egyptian Campaigns 1882–1899*, London, 1900

Shadbolt, Sydney H., *The Afghan Campaigns of 1878–1880 compiled from Official and Private Sources*, London, 1882.

Slatin Pasha, Col. Sir Rudolf, *Fire and Sword in the Sudan*, London, 1896

Soboleff, Maj. Gen. L. N., *The Anglo-Afghan Struggle* (3 vols.), St Petersburg, 1880–2; translated from the original Russian by Maj. W. E. Gowan and published in Calcutta, 1885

Spiers, Edward M, *The Late Victorian Army 1868–1902*, Manchester, 1992

Strawson, John, *Gentlemen in Khaki: The British Army 1890–1990*, London, 1989

Sweetman, John, *War and Administration: The Significance of the Crimean War for the British Army*, Edinburgh, 1984

Symons, Julian, *Buller's Campaign*, London, 1963

———, *England's Pride: The Story of the Gordon Relief Expedition*, London, 1963

Talbot, Col. Hon. Reginald, 'The Battle of Abu Klea', *Nineteenth Century*, London, January 1886

Thompson, Brian, *Imperial Vanities*, London, 2001

Trench, Charles Chenevix, *Charley Gordon: An Eminent Victorian Reassessed*, London, 1978

Villiers, Frederic, *Peaceful Personalities and Warriors Bold*, London, 1907

Waller, John H., *Gordon of Khartoum*, New York, 1988

Watson, Col. Sir Charles M., *The Life of Major General Sir Charles Wilson*, London, 1909

Welsh, Frank, *A History of South Africa*, London, 1998

Wightman, J. W., 'One of the "Six Hundred" in the Balaclava Charge', *Nineteenth Century*, May 1892

Wilson, Col. Sir Charles, *From Korti to Khartum*, London, 1886

Wolseley, FM Viscount, *The Story of a Soldier's Life*, London, 1903

Wood, FM Sir Evelyn, VC, *From Midshipman to Field Marshal*, London, 1906

———, *British Battles on Land and Sea* (2 vols.), London, 1915

———, *Winnowed Memories*, London, 1918

Wright, Thomas, *The Life of Colonel Fred Burnaby*, London, 1908

Wylly, Col. H. C., CB, *A Short History of the Cameronians (Scottish Rifles)*, Aldershot, 1939

Glossary

ADC: aide-de-camp

AG: Adjutant-General

AHC: Army Hospital Corps; the corps provided medical orderlies and the departmental officers (not doctors) set over them

AMD: Army Medical Department; the corps to which the Army's doctors belonged, prior to the merger of the AHC and AMD into the RAMC

amir: From the Arabic 'emir' but used in Afghanistan to mean 'great prince'

ansar: Islamic term meaning 'helpers' – the followers of the Mahdi (and originally the Prophet Muhammad)

ASC: Army Service Corps

bashi-bazouk: irregular mercenary cavalryman in the employ of the Ottoman Empire or khedival Egypt; they could be of Middle Eastern, Turkish Asiatic or Balkan origin

bhisti: Indian camp follower employed to carry water to the troops

burgher: citizen of the Boer republics with full political rights

cacolet: a pair of counter-balancing seats suspended on the flanks of a baggage camel

commando: Boer citizen unit

DAAG: Deputy Assistant Adjutant General; a staff appointment concerned with personnel and logistic matters; a DAAG is not a general officer

donga: watercourse, typically dry for most of the year; the equivalent of a *nullah* in India, or a *wadi* or a *khor* in Egypt and the Sudan

doolie: (Indian Army) a stretcher covered against the sun, typically carried on the shoulders of four camp followers

drift: river ford

firman: proclamation

ghazi: Islamic fanatic

GOC: general officer commanding

havildar: Indian Army equivalent of a sergeant

havildar-major: Indian Army equivalent of a sergeant-major

HEIC: Honourable East India Company

impi: Zulu army

jemadar: Indian Army equivalent of a lieutenant

jezail: long barrelled flintlock locally produced on the North-West Frontier

jibbeh: Mahdist uniform – a long, loose Arab shirt with three-quarter-length sleeves, white in colour and decorated with square patches of coloured cloth

KDG: King's Dragoon Guards

khor: desert watercourse, dry for most of the year

kloof: densely wooded, steep-sided cleft or valley (South Africa)

kop, koppie, kopje: (Afrikaans) hill or hillock

KRRC: King's Royal Rifle Corps

long-twelve: nickname given to Royal Navy 12-pounder guns mounted on land carriages

lunger: nickname for the 1876 Pattern bayonet

MI: Mounted Infantry

mullah: adopted into English usage from the Urdu word for an Islamic cleric

nek: (Afrikaans) a saddle or pass

NMP: Natal Mounted Police

nuggar: open river-boat on the Nile

OR: other rank

pasha: Ottoman officer or official of senior rank or standing; the term originated with the seventeenth-century Turkish word *pasa*

QF: quick-firer

QMG: Quartermaster-General

RA: Royal Artillery

RAMC: Royal Army Medical Corps

RBL: rifled breech-loader

RE: Royal Engineers

RHA: Royal Horse Artillery

RML: rifled muzzle-loader

RMLI: Royal Marine Light Infantry

RMO: regimental medical officer

risaldar: Indian cavalry subaltern

risaldar-major: the senior Indian officer in a cavalry regiment

rooinek: (Afrikaans) derogatory expression applied to British soldiers and roughly translated as 'red-neck' – a reference to pale-skinned Europeans burning in the sun

RSF: Royal Scots Fusiliers

sangar: (Indian Army) rough stone breastwork erected to provide cover from fire

schanz: (Afrikaans) equivalent of a *sangar*

sepoy: Indian Army infantryman

sirdar: from the Persian *sardar* or leader; in Egypt the term was applied to the C-in-C of the Army

sowar: Indian Army cavalryman

spruit: (Afrikaans) stream

subadar: Indian Army equivalent of a captain, who in the absence of a British officer would command a company

subadar-major: the senior Indian officer in an infantry battalion, equating to a British major

tarboosh: traditional Egyptian military headgear, often erroneously referred to as a *fez*

tulwar: curved Indian sword

veldt: (Afrikaans) the field, prairie or countryside

veldtkornet: (Afrikaans) literally 'field cornet'; although this was the most junior officer rank within the Boer commando system, it equated more readily to a British company commander or captain than to a lieutenant; a veldtkornet's command was divided into a number of 'corporalships', the equivalent of a section

Volksraad: the Transvaal's parliament

voorlooper: (Afrikaans) literally 'one who goes ahead'; an assistant to a wagon driver, usually a black African, who walked at the head of the trek-oxen to set direction

wali: governor (Afghanistan)

wing: a half-battalion of infantry consisting of four companies under the command of a major

zareba: thorn-bush perimeter fence around a camp or defensive position

ZARP: (Afrikaans) Zuid Afrikaansche-Republiek-Politie; the Transvaal's uniformed police service

INDEX